PALMERSTON

'THE PEOPLE'S DARLING'

JAMES CHAMBERS

ISBN-10: 1-909609-05-6
ISBN-13: 978-1-909609-05-1

For Josephine

$\mathcal{C}$ONTENTS

$\mathcal{I}$LLUSTRATIONS

The author and publishers would like to thank the following for permission to reproduce illustrations: Plates 1, 18, 27 and 31, Mary Evans Picture Library; 3, 8 and 9, National Portrait Gallery, London; 5, The Royal Collection © 2004, Her Majesty Queen Elizabeth II; 6 and 20, Lord Romsey; 7, © Tate, London 2003; 10, 15 and 29, Hulton Archive; 11 and 34, Archivo Iconografico, S.A./CORBIS; 12, Rex Features; 13, Trustees of the British Museum; 16, Michael Nicholson/CORBIS; 17, popperfoto.com; 21, The Royal Archives © 2004, Her Majesty Queen Elizabeth II; 22, Victoria and Albert Museum, London/Bridgeman Art Library, London; 23 and 28, Bettman/CORBIS; 24, Private Collection/ Bridgeman Art Library, London; 25, Bibliothèque Nationale, Paris/ Bridgeman Art Library, London; 30, The Illustrated London News Picture Library; 32, Museo del Risorgimento, Roma/Scala, Florence; 33, Punch Cartoon Library; 35, Sean Sexton Collection/CORBIS.

$\mathcal{P}$REFACE

Palmerston's political career was almost the longest in British history. It was also, without doubt, the most entertaining, and it was probably the most influential internationally.

In attempting to embrace all that in one volume and at the same time reassess the man, I am glad to acknowledge that I have been guided by some of the most eminent scholars who have examined him already in print, particularly Herbert Bell, Kenneth Bourne, David Brown, Muriel Chamberlain, Jasper Ridley, Donald Southgate, David Steele and Sir Charles Webster.

I am very grateful to Her Majesty Queen Elizabeth II for graciously granting her permission to quote from manuscripts in the Royal Archive at Windsor. In addition I would like to thank the Trustees of the Broadlands Archive, the British Library and the National Archives for allowing me to quote from some of the documents in their care, the Reader and Head of Special Collections in the University of Southampton Library, Chris Woolgar, for his assistance, the General Committee of the Royal Literary Fund for the support that made completion possible, the staff of the London Library for their courteous patience, my wife for her encouragement, Grant McIntyre for his confidence and Caro Westmore, Lizzie

Dipple, Matthew Taylor and Douglas Matthews for all their help with obtaining illustrations, preparing the text and creating an immaculate index.

James Chambers
London, 2004

1. IN THE SHADOW OF THE HILL

By the time he went to school at Harrow in 1795, at the age of ten, Harry Temple, heir to the second Viscount Palmerston, was already cheerfully self-possessed. He spoke French and Italian confidently. Unlike most of his schoolfellows he had travelled widely in Europe; and unlike any of them, he had lived on the edge of great events and enjoyed much more than his fair share of adventure.

The cause of all this precocious worldliness was Harry's father, the second viscount, who was almost a caricature of an eighteenth-century nobleman. He was charming and handsome, with a slight and apparently attractive stammer. He studied the arts, science and literature with the same shallow enthusiasm that he had applied as a bachelor to his pursuit of actresses and dancers; and he held seats in Parliament for forty years without ever achieving more than minor ministerial offices at the Admiralty and the Treasury.

He was descended, he claimed, from Lady Godiva, and more demonstrably from William Temple, the gallant Warwickshire gentleman who held the dying Sir Philip Sidney in his arms at the Battle of Zutphen. Thirteen years after the battle, in 1599, William Temple went to Ireland, in the train of the earl of Essex, and stayed on to become Master of Trinity College, Dublin. In the course of the next two generations his family provided the crown with a Master of the Rolls in Ireland and a Speaker of the Irish House of Commons, acquiring substantial estates in the process; and in 1723 one of his great-grandsons, an obedient Whig back-bencher in the English House of Commons, was rewarded with a peerage and took his title from the village of Palmerston on the family estates near Dublin.

When the first viscount died, in 1757, he was succeeded by his orphaned grandson. At the age of only eighteen, the second viscount inherited two large English houses: Temple Grove, which his great-grandfather had bought at East Sheen, near London, and Broadlands, a Jacobean pile in Hampshire, which his grandfather had bought shortly after marrying the daughter of a governor of the Bank of England. In addition he inherited annual incomes of £3,000 in share dividends and £11,000 in rents, about a quarter of which came from a few flourishing agricultural estates in England and the rest from 10,000 sad, stone-strewn acres in Sligo, where the indigent tenants had not yet recovered from being more than decimated in the year of his birth by the worst famine Ireland has ever suffered.

For the rest of his days the second viscount indulged himself. He travelled widely and often in Europe, following itineraries planned for him by the historian Edward Gibbon. On the best advice he bought pictures and statues, mostly by dead or well-established artists. He commissioned Sir Joshua Reynolds to paint him, although he sat for him so seldom that, when Reynolds went at last to his grave in 1792, with Palmerston as a pall-bearer, the portrait was still unfinished. He engaged the great landscape gardener Capability Brown and his brilliant architect son-in-law Henry Holland to remodel the house and grounds at Broadlands in accordance with the current fashions for Neo-classical buildings and 'natural' vistas. He bought a big telescope and began a correspondence with the King's astronomer, Sir William Herschel. He was elected to Dr Johnson's Literary Club, although not at the first attempt; and he wrote poetry so banal and florid that it is difficult to believe even a snob of Johnson's ornate tastes would have praised it, which he did, if the author had not been a peer.

The second Lord Palmerston's notoriously hectic night life halted briefly after 1767, when he married his first wife, Frances Poole, who was somewhat older and calmer than he was. Two years later, however, she died giving birth to a stillborn child. After an appropriate period of genuine mourning Lord Palmerston returned to his former ways. When he was in London, most of his evenings were spent with cultured or dissipated gentlemen in the clubs, coffee houses and fashionable taverns of St James's, and most of his nights were spent with actresses, dancers and Mary Anne Campbell of Pimlico.

Yet for all his pretension and self-indulgence, the eager and engaging Anglo-Irish peer was capable of forging and maintaining friendships with clever, serious and eminent men. Among these were the President of the Royal Society, Sir Joseph Banks, the multi-talented American scientist Benjamin Rumford and several members of the Literary Club, including not only Gibbon and Reynolds but also the actor David Garrick and the slightly disreputable politician and playwright Richard Brinsley Sheridan.

Through Gibbon, Palmerston was introduced to another leading man of letters, the brilliant but garrulous Dr Samuel Parr. Like Sheridan, Parr had been at Harrow and had gone back to teach there after leaving Cambridge. When the headmaster died suddenly in 1771, Parr had been expected to succeed him. But the school governors, Whigs though they were, had been alarmed by Parr's open support for the aspirations of the increasingly disruptive American colonists. Instead they played safe and appointed Benjamin Heath, who was then an undermaster at Eton. Furious at the rejection of one of their own and at being treated as 'an appendix to Eton', the boys of Harrow resorted to rioting. After several days of merry vandalism, the governors managed to restore order, but only through the temporary closure of the school and the draconian expulsion of all the ringleaders, among them eleven-year-old Viscount Wellesley, who was sent to complete his education at Eton, to which he was followed in due course by his brother Arthur, later Duke of Wellington.

Although he took no part in the rebellion, Parr resigned discreetly when it was over. After an unsuccessful attempt to set up a school of his own, he became a curate at Hatton in Warwickshire, where he wrote pamphlets and earned a reputation as 'the Whig Dr Johnson'. It was there that Palmerston renewed his acquaintance with the capricious Benjamin Mee, a Director of the Royal Exchange and a governor of the Bank of England, who had been an unlikely friend of the cultured Dr Parr ever since they were at Harrow together. Mee's father and Palmerston's maternal grandfather had been business associates in the City of London. As a young man, Palmerston had met the Mee family a few times and had left a lasting impression on Benjamin's sister Mary. When Mary, now twenty-eight, met the 43-year-old viscount again, in her brother's house in Gloucestershire, her infatuation was reborn.

Many, many years later, it was widely believed and recorded that the second viscount and Mary Mee had met in Dublin. According to the story, Palmerston was making one of his rare and brief visits to his Irish estates when he was thrown from his horse in a Dublin street and carried unconscious into a house rented by Mary's father. By the time she had nursed him back to health, it was said, he had fallen in love with her. In truth, however, Mary never went to Dublin and her father was dead before she met Palmerston again. The only element that the myth had in common with the true story of their courtship was that there really was an accident involving horses.

At the end of the eighteenth century, for the first time, English gentlemen developed a passion for fast vehicles. Between 1750 and 1770 the number of English miles covered by well-maintained turnpikes was trebled, and the times for most major journeys by stage-coach were halved. Young 'bucks' bet fortunes on the outcome of races along the new roads, and special carriages were built for the purpose, in which comfort and capacity were sacrificed for speed. One of the most popular of these was the phaeton, which was usually drawn by a pair of horses and was little more than a light frame with large wheels at each corner and a little bench scat for the driver and one passenger perched high on thin springs above it. Palmerston took Mary and her elder sister Sarah for a drive in one, squeezing both of them onto the seat beside him. Since he approached his driving as enthusiastically as he approached every other fashionable activity, and with the same limited level of aptitude, he soon drove too fast at a corner and turned the tall vehicle over. In the fall Mary dislocated her elbow. Although she made light of the incident, her penitent driver was so overcome with guilt and humiliation that he doubled his efforts in pursuit of a cause that had never really been in doubt. On 7 January 1783 Miss Mary Mee and Henry, second Viscount Palmerston, were married fashionably in Bath.

Like her husband's mother and both his grandmothers, the new Lady Palmerston came from a family that derived its income only from commerce, rather than the more genteel ownership of land. Yet, like them, she moved easily into her new role. She was friendly, generous and almost too obliging; and although there were a few who found her vulgar, she was generally popular and widely regarded as a beauty. After their first meeting, Sheridan's wife, Eliza, another acknowledged beauty, described her as 'a pleasing unaffected woman who, tho' she *did* squeeze thru' the City Gates into a Viscountess, wears her blushing honours without shaking them at you every moment'.

Lady Palmerston added her own circle of friends to her husband's already extensive and eclectic guest list. Among these, two of the most regular new visitors to Broadlands were her closest friend, Harriet Amyand, and her sister Anna Maria, both of whom married successful diplomats with slightly *risqué* reputations. Anna Maria married Sir Gilbert Elliot, who was to be made Baron Minto in 1798 and Earl of Minto in 1813; and Harriet, less happily, married Sir James Harris, who was to be made Baron Malmesbury in 1788 and Earl of Malmesbury in 1800. As time passed, the two men learned to share their wives' affection for Lady Palmerston, and they both became lifelong and supportive friends to her husband and her children.

If it had been up to her, Lady Palmerston would probably have pre-ferred to limit her social life to house parties, dinners and trips to the theatre with safe old friends such as these, but she was too much in love with her husband to risk losing him by depriving him of the life he had enjoyed for so long. Instead she became his companion in it. She joined him among the fops and big-wigged 'macaronies' in the airless candlelight of the gaming tables. She gave an endless series of dinners, routs and assemblies, naïvely issuing her invitations to anyone and everyone. As time passed, the growing proportion of 'women of equivocal character' among her guests provoked Lord Glenbervie, a dour Scottish lawyer with a new Irish peerage, to dub her 'a great protectress of the class of demi-reps'. 'I never saw any two people make such toil of pleasure, as both he and she', wrote Sir Gilbert Elliot to his wife. 'She seems com-pletely worn down by her raking, but is always eager for the next labour.'

Most of Lady Palmerston's assemblies were held in what Elliot called the 'prodigious great magnificent old-fashioned house' in East Sheen, which was conveniently close to London and large enough to accommodate any amount of 'junketing'. But most of her dinners in the early years of her marriage were given in the terraced house her husband rented in Westminster, close to the House of Commons, in the street now known as Queen Anne's Gate. For any MP, even a dilettante one, it was essential to have some sort of base in central London; and for any aspiring hostess it was equally essential to have a house. If she wanted to invite members of 'the ton', the cream of society, to dinner, a meal that was then eaten in the afternoon, she needed a place from which they could easily go on in sedan chairs or carriages to their inevitable London engagements afterwards; if she wanted to receive casual calls from busy statesmen such as Sheridan and Charles James Fox, she needed somewhere central and appropriate in which to be at home to them; and there were times when she just needed somewhere to change. In the course of one day, for example, Lady Palmerston spent the morning in East Sheen, came up to the London house to be hostess at a dinner, went on from that to a private assembly and from there to the public pleasures of Ranelagh Gardens in Chelsea, and then came back to the London house at one o'clock in the morning to change into a costume and accompany her husband to a masquerade at the Opera House.

In the middle of October 1784 the Palmerstons went up from Broadlands to spend a few days in the London house, not for any social reason this time, since Lady Palmerston was heavily pregnant, but because her husband had promised Reynolds one of his rare sittings for the famously unfinished portrait; and wherever Lord Palmerston went, whenever possible, Lady Palmerston went too. It was therefore in the bustle of the little London house and not, as expected, in the tranquillity of Broadlands that, on 20 October, Lady Palmerston gave birth to an heir.

So Henry John Temple was born, fortuitously but appropriately, in the heartland of English politics, in the late evening of the 'Age of Enlightenment', at a time when 'society' was still self-indulgent and small, and when the principal source of almost all wealth was still land. But he was also born in the early morning of a new age. His world was on the brink of changes more radical than any it had seen for centuries, and the seeds of those changes, and the conflicts that accompanied them, had already been sown.

In the year when Harry Temple was born, James Watt, who was already manufacturing several types of steam engine, applied for a patent that described a steam locomotive. The Revd Edmund Cartwright visited the water-driven spinning mill of Richard Arkwright in Nottingham and was inspired by what he saw to adapt one of Watt's engines and create a power-driven loom. And Henry Cort introduced the 'puddling and rolling' process, enabling the British coke-fed foundries to begin mass production of the purest and cheapest iron in Europe. Crafts and trades were turning into industries. The course was set that was soon to turn Great Britain into the richest nation on earth.

At the beginning of the year, in Constantinople, the Turkish government accepted that it could not for the moment resist the armies of Catherine the Great and formally assented to the Russian annexation of a Black Sea peninsula that very few people in Britain had ever heard of: the Crimea. In April, at the new Theatre Français in Paris, Beaumarchais's lampoon of the decadent aristocracy *The Marriage of Figaro* opened to rapturous acclaim from the citizens and furious denunciations from King Louis XVI and the more prescient of his courtiers. In August, in London, the newly elected government of the younger Pitt passed the India Act, which took the first step towards direct rule over an eastern empire by establishing a Board of Control to supervise the political activities of the East India Company. On the very day of Harry's birth, again in Paris, a young cadet called Napoleon Bonaparte underwent his first day of training at the splendid Ecole Militaire. And in Brussels on that day, as on almost every day in the second half of 1784, fifteen-year-old Arthur Wesley, who had been forced to leave Eton early by his widowed mother's lack of funds, and who was not yet ready to go on to the French military academy at Angers, devoted his morning to violin practice and whiled away the afternoon on a hired horse in the Forest of Soignes, which he reached by riding out on the road that runs through the village of Waterloo and down towards Genappe and Quatre Bras, between the farms of Hougoumont and La Haye Sainte.

Meanwhile, among the fashionable few in London, life went on as it had always done. Charles James Fox took up with Mrs Armistead. The Prince of Wales contracted a secret marriage with Mrs Fitzherbert and committed extravagant sums to Henry Holland's plans for Carlton House and his Pavilion in Brighton. The Palmerstons christened Harry, fashionably, at St Margaret's, Westminster, and celebrated his first birthday with a huge ball for all their friends, neighbours and tenants at the assembly rooms in Winchester, near the Broadlands estate.

In the course of the next five years, with minimal interruption to her social life, Lady Palmerston gave birth to four more children: Frances, who was born in February 1786, William, who was born in January 1788, Mary, was was born almost exactly a year later, and Elizabeth, who was born at the end of March 1790. Characteristically, Lord Palmerston had all of them inoculated against smallpox by Baron Dimsdale, the leading practitioner of the new procedure.

Introduced from Turkey by Lady Mary Wortley Montagu, whose husband had been ambassador there, inoculation was the only certain protection against a disease that was the principal cause of premature death throughout the eighteenth century, and which left many of its survivors hideously scarred. But the procedure was not without risk, since it only induced immunity by infecting the patient with a mild dose of the disease itself. It was not nearly as safe as the vaccination procedure which Edward Jenner was then developing in Gloucestershire. Mary died from it, and the frightening fever that it brought on in Harry left Lady Palmerston with a lifelong anxiety about his health and Harry himself with recurring eruptions of painful bright red blisters on his face and inflammation of the eyes, both of which continued for several years. His French governess, Thérèse Mercier, who was engaged shortly after his fourth birthday, found that in her first two years with him there were often times when he could not see well enough to read. By the time he was five, however, he was at least looking less frail. In writing to his wife, Elliot reported that 'even Harry, who used to look so washy, has got quite stout, with a fine high colour', and he added that he was now 'a vastly pretty boy'.

Lady Palmerston's devotion to her husband's social life did not distract her from those duties that were closer to her true nature. She was an attentive and ambitious mother, and she created a calm and merry home for her children at Broadlands. Harry had everything that he needed to prepare him for the diplomatic career which his father had already planned for both his sons. He had Mademoiselle Mercier to teach him French. He had his father to show him the world: when he was still only four, his parents took him with them when they spent six weeks touring and buying pictures in the Netherlands and the Rhineland. And he had his mother to teach him manners and letter-writing, a craft he practised with prolific zeal.

On his seventh Christmas Day Harry copied the customs of 'society' by writing a letter addressed to 'Viscountess Palmerston in her dressing room up stairs, Broadlands', in which he formally accepted her invitation 'to goble up mince-pyes or whatever else there is for dinner'. But 'society' itself was kept at a distance, in East Sheen and Westminster. The only ladies and gentlemen of the great world whom Harry met were the neighbours who came to dine, such as Thomas Pelham, the future Earl of Chichester, or friends who came to stay, such as the Malmesburys, the Elliots, the Sheridans and Mrs Campbell of Pimlico, whom Lady Palmerston invited to come down from time to time with her son Henry.

At Broadlands, Lady Palmerston was a mother and a lady of the manor; in East Sheen she was a patroness of the arts and of artists; in Westminster she was a political hostess. But as she grew more confident she also became more ambitious. She was no longer satisfied with the house in Westminster. She wanted one of the newer and larger London houses, which had double front doors, broad halls and 'circuits' of interconnecting rooms around the stairwells. If a house had double doors and a broad hall, the chairmen could carry guests inside, instead of depositing them on the muddy pavement. More importantly, if a house had a 'circuit', a hostess could entertain larger numbers and have different activities in different rooms: dancing in one, cards in another, supper in a third. Predictably, her husband needed little persuading. In 1792 he surrendered the lease on his house in Westminster and bought a new lease on a larger one in Hanover Square, north of Piccadilly.

While the new house was being decorated and made ready for occupation, Lord Palmerston decided to take his family on a Grand Tour to

Italy. Several of the leading members of the 'ton' were out there already, including Lady Bessborough, and so too were some of Palmerston's Broadlands neighbours: the Pelhams, the Sheffields and the bibulous, ill-tempered Sir Godfrey Webster with his bored, beautiful wife, Elizabeth, who at twenty was less than half his age. These neighbours had gone out via Paris and Lausanne, where they visited Edward Gibbon, who had been living there for the last eight years; and Palmerston intended to go by the same route.

It was not a prudent decision. In the last decade of the eighteenth century, when many of the attractions of European civilization were dimmed by the shadow of revolution, the custom of touring was not nearly as popular as it had once been. Since the storming of the Bastille by the Paris mob on 14 July 1789, the French capital was no longer the first stop on every itinerary; and in the year since Palmerston's neighbours had managed to pass through it safely, conditions in the city had gone from bad to worse. The 'moderates' had been replaced by radical leaders from 'the left' of the assembly. France was at war with Austria and Prussia. The royal family was under house arrest in the Palace of the Tuileries.

Lord Palmerston was not oblivious or indifferent to what was happening in France. Although the Whig opposition, to which he still nominally belonged, had so far supported the revolution, and although his friend Elliot was a lifelong friend and admirer of the 'moderate' leader Mirabeau, Palmerston had been more influenced by the Tory detractors and had expressed surprisingly prophetic misgivings about what might happen next. In 1791 Fox had sent him to Paris as part of a goodwill mission from the opposition to the revolutionary government, but the experience had done nothing to change his opinion. Instead he had come back with a head full of horror stories about what the peasants were doing to their landlords, and from that moment on he had voted with the Tories. Nevertheless, his desire to follow in the footsteps of his fashionable friends, coupled perhaps with his curiosity, was stronger than any anxiety about the safety of his family. In the fateful summer of 1792 he loaded four carriages onto a ship, crossed the Channel and set out for Paris with his wife, their children, their governors and the necessary nucleus of their servants.

They arrived on 1 August. The atmosphere in the hot city was dense with anger, anticipation and fear. Units of the new National Guard from Marseilles, which were among the most militant in the revolutionary army, had set up camp in the Champs-Elysées. But Lord Palmerston behaved as though nothing was amiss. He took his wife to the palace, where, in accordance with protocol, they were presented to the king and queen by the wife of the British ambassador. In the course of the audience, however, Lady Palmerston talked to a young officer who told her that, in his opinion, the Marseillais were preparing to storm the palace and that, if they did, the units of the National Guard that had been stationed there to defend the king would simply run away or join them. By the time she left the palace Lady Palmerston was convinced that it would be better to see Paris on some other occasion.

At his wife's instigation Lord Palmerston applied for the necessary travel passes at once. On 6 August he collected them from the Hôtel de Ville, and the following morning his party set out for Switzerland. Beyond the Bastille, in the Faubourg Saint-Antoine, they halted at a makeshift barricade. A guard looked into the leading carriage, which contained only Harry and his parents. After inspecting their passes, he stood back and waved them through. The carriage went on for a while, south-eastwards through the suburban streets, and then the coachman and the footman and their passengers realized the other three carriages were not following.

The onlookers at the barricade had decided that the younger children and their obviously aristocratic entourage ought to be interrogated by the local revolutionary committee. Despite the presence of a French governess, the terrified victims were not giving a very convincing account of themselves. In the end they were released only through the intercession of the sympathetic commander of the Saint-Antoine militia, a rich brewer called Antoine Joseph Santerre, who had made his fortune selling expensive English-style ale. By evening the younger children and their escort were reunited with their parents, who had been waiting anxiously less than three miles away at Charenton.

The Palmerstons and their party continued their journey. On 10 August, as they were approaching Lyons, the Marseillais and the Paris militiamen, including Santerre's, attacked the Palace of the Tuileries. As expected, the defending National Guardsmen fled and the mercenary Swiss Guards, who stood their ground, were all slaughtered. The king and his family were led away to prison, the National Assembly proclaimed a republic, and Santerre was appointed commander of the Paris National Guard.

The Palmerstons heard the news in Lyons and hurried on towards Switzerland, halting nervously from time to time as they found their path blocked by contingents of the National Guard marching north to join the army on the Prussian border. In the welcome tranquillity of Lausanne, they visited Gibbon, who had long since finished the last volume of *The Decline and Fall of the Roman Empire* and was happy to spend time with old friends in his beautiful garden. Then they turned south, working their way slowly from city to city towards Naples. For the next twenty-one months, while France suffered the bloodbath of 'the Terror', and while the leaders of the revolution guillotined the king, the aristocracy, the queen and then each other, the Palmerstons travelled up and down Italy visiting the Classical and Renaissance sites and dining and dancing with fashionable friends as they might have done in England.

They spent the winter in Naples with the other English tourists, left in the spring to travel north as far as Switzerland, came back for another winter, and then set out again in the spring of 1794 to make their way slowly homewards. For Harry the winters in Naples and the prearranged summer gatherings in other cities were his first real glimpse of the life his parents led in East Sheen and Westminster.

In Naples 'society' centred on the royal court and the home of the scholarly British Ambassador, Sir William Hamilton, who had recently intrigued everyone by marrying Emma Lyon, the pretty, uncouth daughter of a Cheshire blacksmith, who had until then made her way in the world as a model, mistress and erotic dancer. Most of the leading English personalities in this tight-knit little community were the fashionable tourists whom Lord Palmerston had hoped to find there, but during the second winter they were joined by a group of boisterous young men who had recently come down from Oxford. One of these was Lord Holland, the nephew of Charles James Fox. Holland fell in love at first sight with Lady

Webster. Before long they were lovers. Three years later, after they had returned to England and after Lady Webster had borne Lord Holland a son, her husband divorced her and the lovers were married.

At their last gathering with the other tourists, which was in Florence, shortly before they left Italy, the Palmerstons had an unexpected meeting with Sir Gilbert Elliot, the husband of Lady Palmerston's friend Anna Maria. By then revolutionary France was formally at war with Great Britain. In August 1793 the royalist citizens of Toulon had opened their vital Mediterranean harbour to a British fleet. Elliot had been sent out to take charge as Commissioner. But in December, amid wanton bloodshed, the town and harbour had been retaken by republican troops commanded for the first time by Napoleon Bonaparte. After a precarious escape, in which at one point he was shipwrecked, Elliot landed in Italy and joined his friends in Florence. The adventure did nothing to subdue him, however. One evening he was taken home from the theatre in Lady Webster's carriage. As he often did on such occasions, he pressed his attentions on his companion. Anyone who had been in Italy for longer than he had would have known that Sir Godfrey's pretty lady had eyes for nobody but Holland, but Elliot ignored her protests and continued his advances. In the end she was forced to halt her carriage, climb out and walk. It was an embarrassing indignity which was eventually forgiven, but never forgotten, by the woman who was soon to become the famously imperious Lady Holland.

When he was not at his lessons, visiting ruins or being displayed to his parents' friends, Harry Temple found time for a life of his own, particularly in Bologna, where he developed a passion for the local sausages, met Lady Bessborough's youngest son, seven-year-old Willie Ponsonby, and made friends with a boy of his own age, Francis Hare, whose historian father, a friend of Fox, was living there at the time. But from Harry's point of view the most important meeting of the whole tour was one that took place soon after their first arrival in Naples, between his governess, Thérèse Mercier, and an Italian scholar called Gaetano Ravizotti. Attracted as much by the Company of 'Mademoiselle Thérèse' as by Lord Palmerston's offer of employment, 'Signor Gaetano' agreed to tutor Harry in Italian and later in

Spanish. By the time Elliot met up with them all in Florence, in May 1794, he was able to report to his wife that his young hero was already speaking French and Italian well.

When the Palmerstons returned to England, Ravizotti went with them. Apart from continuing to tutor their children, he published poems, translations and an Italian grammar, which he dedicated to Harry. For many years he and his Thérèse, whom he married at last in 1800, were much loved and respected members of the Broadlands household; and to them alone must go the credit for making the future Foreign Secretary fluent in the languages of so many of his allies and adversaries.

The Palmerstons went home via Austria, Hanover and Holland, where they visited Lady Palmerston's brother. 'Uncle Ben' had suffered a few reverses in business. Before setting out on the tour Lord Palmerston had found him a job as a commissary supplying the army which was about to be sent to reinforce the fragile Dutch Republic, in case, as suspected, the militant French revolutionary 'rabble' attempted an invasion. Since then, the French had indeed invaded – with soldiers, not rabble – and the British were now opposing them, with 'the Grand Old Duke of York' in command of the army and the furiously frustrated Colonel Arthur Wesley in command of the 33rd.

After spending a month in Holland, during which they saw the notoriously ill-supplied British army do little other than fall back, the Palmerstons set sail for Harwich. They landed on 2 October and soon afterwards learned that two of their companions on the tour had died unexpectedly. The first, Lady Sheffield, had died after her return to England the previous year. On hearing the news, the second, Edward Gibbon, had hurried home to comfort his friend her husband. But he had died in London, after undergoing a series of emergency operations on his swollen testicles, and he had been buried close to Lord Sheffield's house in Sussex, beneath an epitaph composed by his friend Samuel Parr.

Less than three weeks after his return Harry celebrated his tenth birthday. It was time to send him to school; and there could be no other choice but Harrow. It had always been 'Uncle Ben's' choice. In the ten years since their friend Dr Joseph Drury had succeeded his brother-in-law Heath as headmaster, it had been Parr's and Sheridan's choice as well.

Furthermore, a factor that was as important as any in the Palmerston household, it was the choice of fashion.

Lord Palmerston wrote to Dr Drury. On Drury's advice he agreed that Harry should board in Dr Bromley's house, and Lady Palmerston then corresponded with Mrs Bromley, the sister of Mrs Drury, learning the types and quantity of clothing that she would need to provide and insisting anxiously that a thick nightshirt should be added to the list. Meanwhile, in equally important academic preparation, Signor Gaetano gave Harry introductory lessons in the only two languages that he would study at the school, Latin and Greek.

On 25 May 1795 Harry climbed into a carriage with his parents in Hanover Square and set out for Harrow on the Hill. He had travelled through France during one of the most dramatic and significant weeks in the whole history of Europe. He had been shown the glorious relics of Imperial Rome and the Italian Renaissance. He had seen the English aristocracy at play. He had seen the equally unimpressive camps and lines of a beleagured British army. And now he was off to receive an English education under the direction of the great Dr Drury.

Drury was the first and one of the best of the great headmasters who reformed the English public schools. Under his enlightened and liberal leadership Harrow rose to an eminence that it has never quite equalled since. For the only time in its history it was larger than Eton. The American Minister in London, Rufus King, had sent his sons there because, he said, it was the only school in which no special privileges were attached to rank. Yet at the same time it was so fashionable that it contained a greater proportion of aristocratic pupils than any other school before or since.

During two decades coinciding almost exactly with the Tory government of the younger Pitt, Drury taught the Whig values that had been traditional at Harrow since the Glorious Revolution. Unlike his predecessors, however, he also applied them. He abolished beating for all but the most junior boys and he delegated much of the responsibility for running the school to the senior ones. But his success and his reputation stemmed not so much from his regime as from the patient optimism with which he motivated even the dullest of his charges, and above all from his boundless passion for discovering, developing and promoting talent.

Drury's pupils rose and shone in almost every art and profession, many of them beyond their natural ability; and they shone the brightest of all in politics. During the first half of the nineteenth century there was hardly a Cabinet that did not contain at least two of them; and almost as often as not there was another in the chair. In a record that has never even been equalled, Joseph Drury was personally responsible for the education of no fewer than five Prime Ministers. As an assistant master he tutored Spencer Perceval, and as headmaster he taught Goderich, Peel, Aberdeen and Palmerston.

Drury's memory has since been overshadowed by the reputations of sterner men, but during his lifetime he was the most respected member of his profession; and unusually for a successful schoolmaster, he was as popular with his pupils as he was at the dinner tables of their parents. The most famous of his writers, Lord Byron, described him as the best and worthiest friend he ever had, and the last of his Prime Ministers, Lord Palmerston, said that even his rebukes were so charming that they were almost an incentive to transgress.

It was at Harrow, therefore, that the seeds of Palmerston's political career were sown, not only because it exposed him to the influence of Dr Drury but also because it introduced him to so many of the leading players in his story. Inevitably at the end of the eighteenth century, many of those who sat opposite or beside him on the benches of the Old Fourth Form Room were equally privileged young gentlemen who would soon be sitting in similar positions in the House of Commons; and not surprisingly perhaps, given the extraordinary influence of Dr Drury, a disproportionately large number of them would one day be his colleagues at the Cabinet table. But there were many boys in the school who had been born with even greater advantages and expectations than Harry Temple; and among these there were two future colleagues – Charles Spencer, Viscount Althorp, and John Ponsonby, Viscount Duncannon – with whom he also sat down daily at the breakfast table in Dr Bromley's house.

Althorp and Duncannon were cousins. Althorp's father, Earl Spencer, had two famously beautiful sisters, one of whom was Duncannon's mother,

Harriet, Countess of Bessborough. The other was Georgiana, Duchess of Devonshire. Since the Bessboroughs were entirely preoccupied by their separate, selfish pleasures, and by the countess's melodramatic illnesses, Duncannon and his two brothers, who were also in Dr Bromley's house, spent their holidays with their lisping sister Lady Caroline in the inattentive care of their Aunt Georgiana. At Chatsworth, the duke's great house in Derbyshire, and at Devonshire House in London, they lived as part of an extended family that included the duke's mistress, Lady Elizabeth Foster, and the son she had borne him, Augustus Clifford, who followed the Ponsonbys to Dr Bromley's in 1796.

The gauche Althorp, who was similarly neglected, spent most of his holidays in Northamptonshire, at the great house that bore his name, with nobody but servants for company. But from time to time, when he was summoned to London to be civilized, he was able to walk round the corner from Spencer House to join his cousins in the house that was both the hub of fashion and the principal rendezvous of the Whig opposition. Here the young people of the household mingled freely with the princes, statesmen, painters and writers who came by day to call on the duchess and by night to attend her assemblies.

This exalted world was not unknown to Harry Temple. Although he had not been introduced to many of them, he knew that his mother's regular guests included most of the statemen and artists who also called on the duchess. But Lady Palmerston's patronage was of little consequence. Her invitations were less sought after than those of the duchess, and her gatherings were less lavish and reputedly less decorous. Fine though they were, her husband's two country houses were modest beside Chatsworth and Althorp; and his new London house, in Hanover Square, was humble compared with the great houses of Spencer and Devonshire.

The young men with whom Harry Temple lived most closely at Harrow came from families that were richer, more fashionable and much more influential than his own. But the even greater gulf between them was the one that Jane Austen described as 'the distinction of rank'. Duncannon and Althorp, who already had courtesy viscountcies, were also heirs to English earldoms. Like several other young men in Dr Bromley's house, they would one day be entitled to seats in the House of

Lords. Harry was only the heir to an Irish viscountcy, an empty honour that carried with it no such privilege. His father's title was merely one of the many 'potato peerages' that the Whigs had distributed in return for very little during the first half of the century. Such things might not matter at Drury's Harrow, but they still mattered everywhere else, and Harry Temple was well aware of it. For all his cheerful self-confidence, he was also cautiously reserved and noticeably eager to please.

Harry started in the third form with, among others, Viscount Haddo, heir to the earldom of Aberdeen. After a year they were promoted to the fourth form, where the two future Prime Ministers were joined by a third, Frederick Robinson, who was to hold the office as Viscount Goderich. As Harry progressed through the school, he fulfilled all his parents' hopes for him. He earned the approval of Dr Bromley, who described him as 'a most charming boy' and 'very quick at his books'. He earned the respect of Dr Drury, who made him a monitor. He was popular; and he was happy. In his first letter to his parents he wrote, 'I like the Scool [sic] very much.'

In the many letters home that followed, his preoccupations were typical of his age: a request for a cricket bat, thanks for cakes and reports on important events, such as the purchase of a half-share in a ferret, its subsequent sad loss and a meeting with a man who had a nest of hedgehogs. 'If I had known where to have put it, I should certainly have bought one to keep Fanny's guinea-pig company.' His more adult correspondence was on the whole reserved for his contemporaries.

In 1798 he received a pompous letter from Bologna, in which his friend Francis Hare hoped that he took no part in 'those vices which are common to a public school, such as I suppose Harrow, as swearing and getting drunk.' After asking him to give a kiss to his sisters, Hare wrote, 'I still persist in my opinion of never marrying, and I suppose you think the same, as you must have read as well as myself of the many faults and vices of women.' And he began his last paragraph with, 'Perhaps I at Bologna may have learnt more Greek than you, and that you at Harrow may know best how to fight with your fist.'

Harry wrote back with better grammar and just a touch of irony. He assumed humbly that Hare must have made more progress in the classics than he had and then outlined his curriculum. 'I am now doing Caesar, Terence, Ovid, Horner, Greek Testament, and a collection of Greek epigrams, and after the Easter holidays, which are now drawing near, I shall begin Virgil, Horace and some more.' Then he went on to deal more straightforwardly with his friend's moralizing and prejudices. 'I am perfectly of your opinion concerning drinking and swearing, which, though fashionable at present, I think extremely ungentleman-like.' But at the end, almost as an afterthought, he added prophetically, 'I cannot agree with you about marriage, though I should be by no means precipitate about my choice.'

Once a statesman has stood for a while in the centre of the political stage, he is usually credited with a few epic but previously unrecorded schoolboy exploits. The third Viscount Palmerston was no exception. When he and Aberdeen were arguing across the Cabinet table, it was said that at Harrow they had once engaged in a marathon pillow fight, from which Harry Temple had eventually emerged victorious. Perhaps they did, although it is unlikely, since they were in different houses. But there is one source for those days which is more credible than most. Just as 'no man is a hero to his valet', so no monitor can have been a hero to his 'fag', the junior boy who waited on him, ran his errands and answered to his every whim. Yet Harry Temple's fag, Augustus Clifford, remembered him as 'merciful and indulgent'. A lifetime later, when he was living in retirement in Ryde, Rear-Admiral Sir Augustus Clifford, Usher of the Black Rod, wrote to Prime Minister Palmerston's first biographer, Sir Henry Bulwer. 'Temple', he wrote, 'was reckoned the best-tempered and most plucky boy in the school, as well as a young man of great promise.'

What Clifford saw as even temper, however, was only one facet of Harry Temple's extraordinary reserve and self-control. As a schoolboy and a student he was always cautiously reluctant to reveal or com-mit himself. It was as though he was only willing to run the risk of other people's judgement when he knew and accepted all the terms on which he was to be judged. He was diligent in his work, where he knew he would be marked on his scholarship. He took part eagerly in Drury's speeches, where the level of applause would depend on his memory and his delivery. He was enthusiastic in games, particularly cricket, where his performance could be measured precisely by the score sheet – although, sadly, in this case the measure has been lost. (All the records of the earliest school matches, including the ones in which Harry Temple played for Harrow against Eton and Westminster, were destroyed by a fire in the pavilion at Lord's.) He could give as good as he got in a fight. But in everyday life, among the fashionable contemporaries whom Dr Bromley described affectionately as 'young men of wit and pleasure', he held back, almost reticently. He never took sides or expressed an unorthodox opinion; and it was impossible to provoke him. Soon after he arrived at Harrow, Haddo locked him in a dark storeroom and stood outside with a few friends, waiting to hear sobbing or pleading or rage. But all they heard was the merry chanting of a collect for evensong, 'Lighten our darkness, we beseech thee, oh, Lord.'

As an example of 'pluck', Clifford wrote, 'I can remember well Temple fighting "behind school" a great boy called Salisbury, twice his size, and he would not give in, but was brought home with black eyes and a bloody nose, and Mother Bromley taking care of him.' Salisbury, who later became a clergyman, cannot really have been twice Harry's size, since Harry was not small and they were in the same form. But it is probable that the story is substantially true. Harry mentioned such a fight in a letter to his mother. Writing in 1798, shortly after his brother had joined him at Harrow, he reported that they were both 'well in health, tho' not in beauty, Willy's lip being rather swelled by a lick with a ball, and my two blue eyes being exchanged for two black ones in consequence of a battle'.

It may have been a mistake to tell Lady Palmerston about the injuries. She was always so anxious about Harry's health that she was in the habit of appearing at Harrow unannounced almost every time she was informed of the slightest set-back. She even managed to influence the usually unruffled Mrs Bromley. On one occasion 'Mother Bromley' became quite agitated when she heard that Harry had risked a fever by cooling off after a game of cricket with a swim in the 'Duck Puddle'. On another she actually had the temerity to rebuke Lady Palmerston for endangering his health by sending him the rich plum cakes on which he was gorging himself.

Harry spent most of his holidays at Broadlands, riding, shooting and learning modern languages with Mademoiselle Thérèse and Signor Gaetano. In the summer of 1799, however, he went on a riding trip with his father along the south coast from Broadlands to Brighton. After attending a ball at the newly fashionable resort they went up to London, where Harry and his brother were taken to Westminster and introduced to William Pitt, to whom their father had now formally transferred his allegiance.

When Christmas came that year, Harry spent the whole crowded holiday in Hanover Square. Here he saw a great deal of the Malmesburys and the Elliots (now Lord and Lady Minto), renewed his acquaintance with some of the ladies and gentlemen whom he had first met in Italy and was introduced for the first time to other fashionable friends who until then had only been names to him. He was taken to see the King and Queen and wrote afterwards that the Queen looked like a housemaid. He went regularly to the theatre, and even trod the boards himself, playing a small part in a masque performed in front of the new Princess of Wales.

The Prince's secret marriage to the Roman Catholic Mrs Fitzherbert might have been valid in the eyes of God and the papacy, but it was not valid under English law: the Prince had contravened the recent Marriage Act by marrying without the King's permission. It had therefore been deemed legitimate for Lord Palmerston's diplomat friend Lord Malmesbury to negotiate a more suitable marriage with Princess Caroline of Brunswick. Unfortunately the Princess was not in the habit of washing or changing her underwear very often. When Malmesbury brought her to England and introduced her, the Prince courteously embraced her and then withdrew hurriedly. 'Harris, I am not well,' he said, 'pray get me a glass of brandy.' Nevertheless, the Prince still managed to do his duty. The couple were married on 8 April 1795, and nine months to the day later the Princess gave birth to the ill-fated Princess Charlotte. But by then, inevitably, the parents were already leading separate lives. In the years that followed, the Prince returned to his earlier bride and left it to others to keep his awkward Princess amused. The masque in which

Harry performed, *Cupid's Cure*, had been written for her entertainment by Lord Palmerston's other diplomat friend, Lord Minto.

Harry played the part of a mute in the masque. Throughout his schooldays his experience of speaking in front of an audience was limited to his subsequent performances on speech days at Harrow, but he appeared at these more often than any of his contemporaries. On 8 May 1800 he recited a piece from Tacitus. On 5 June he recited a piece from Cicero. Then, unusually, he recited again on 3 July, when another boy dropped out; and also unusually, at his father's request, he recited in English. After Drury's favourite, the angular, earnest, dignified Lord Haddo, had delivered Dido's lament at the departure of her lover from Virgil's *Aeneid*, handsome, light-hearted and slightly untidy Harry Temple declaimed 'The Bard', by Thomas Gray. Although now forgotten, the poem was very popular at the time, and it may be that Lord Palmerston was still enough of a radical Whig at heart to appreciate the parallel between its disparaging depiction of Edward I's ruthless oppression of the Welsh and George III's less successful intransigence with his North American colonists.

At the end of that summer term Lord Palmerston took Harry away from Harrow. Harry was third head of the school by then. If he had stayed on, he would undoubtedly have had the distinction of being head of it. But his father believed that young men should not remain at school beyond their sixteenth birthday, and he also believed that, having supposedly mastered the Classics, Harry had already acquired everything that Harrow had to offer.

To be fair to Dr Drury, Harry had acquired a bit more than that. In the first place, he had learned a lot from exercising the heady authority of a monitor in what he described himself as 'a nation in miniature'. 'A boy who puts himself at the head of his associates', he said, 'would most likely equally distinguish himself at the head of an army or a council.' In performing his monitor's duties with almost jaunty nonchalance, he had revealed how easily he accepted responsibility; and he had impressed both tutors and contemporaries alike by his rare lack of self-importance. In addition, through his eager efforts to please in the form room, he had developed an indefatigable capacity for painstaking preparation and attention to detail – a disconcertingly unexpected attribute that was to prove a powerful ally in the years to come. Through memorizing and rehearsing his speeches with Drury he had learned to address an audience expressively and with a certain amount of confidence, at least when he had prepared his text. And like almost every poet and statesman who came under Drury's influence, he had picked up something of the headmaster's impetuous, quixotic idealism.

2. A WANT OF SPIRITS

In preparation for the career that he had planned for him in the diplomatic corps, the second Viscount Palmerston wanted his heir to complete his education at Cambridge. It was, perhaps surprisingly, the university from which he himself had graduated, although as a nobleman he would have received his degree automatically, *de jure natalis*, without actually having to sit any of the examinations. But before Harry went to Cambridge, for which he was not yet old enough, his father wanted him to go to Edinburgh.

Like Harrow School, Edinburgh University was then at its zenith. In the wake of such giants as the philosopher David Hume and the political economist Adam Smith the leading Scottish universities were among the most prominent intellectual centres in Europe. At Edinburgh and Glasgow young men could study subjects and ideas that were not even discussed at Oxford or Cambridge. Unfortunately, since the French Revolution, the Scottish universities had lost some of their popularity among the Tories. The party of William Pitt, who had once told Adam Smith 'we are all your scholars', now regarded his progressive ideas as dangerously radical. But it was still highly fashionable for Whigs to send their sons to Edinburgh, which may be more evidence that Lord Palmerston was still at heart a Whig, as well as a follower of fashion.

Since his death the theories of Adam Smith had been presented at Edinburgh in a series of lectures by his friend Dugald Stewart, the much respected Professor of Moral Philosophy; and by happy chance Professor Stewart was now supplementing his modest Scottish stipend by accommodating a few well-bred young lodgers in the large new house that he rented from the Marquess of Lothian in the square then known as St

Andrew's. Arrangements were made that Harry should be one of them. On 11 September 1800, Harry and his parents, accompanied by their American friend Rumford, set off slowly northwards, visiting friends for a few days here and there as they went. They arrived in Edinburgh a month later; and for another month, while Harry settled in with the genial professor and his family, the Palmerstons and Rumford stayed on to keep an eye on him and admire 'the Athens of the North'.

Throughout the second half of the eighteenth century the people of Edinburgh had been embellishing their city not only with magnificent new civic and university buildings but also, in response to a suggestion first put forward by Lord Minto's father, with an ambitious 'New Town' development, which had dignified, stone-clad, classical houses laid out on a grid pattern between St Andrew's and Charlotte Square. The scheme had been so successful that a second stage was now being planned, even before the first was finished. There were still many houses to be built or completed in the smaller side streets on the original grid; and throughout Harry's stay in Edinburgh the elegant squares and the parallel thoroughfares between them echoed daily with the clatter of construction close by.

Several of Stewart's lodgers went on to become statesmen. One of these, Lord Henry Petty, a future Marquess of Lansdowne, had only just left and was now at Cambridge. But when Harry arrived the only other lodger was the alarmingly eccentric Lord Ashburton, who, according to Harry, looked like a hippopotamus. It was not until after the start of Harry's second year that they were joined by a third lodger, and another prospective Foreign Secretary, John Ward, the future Earl of Dudley, who had already taken a degree at Oxford.

By then, however, there were plenty of people at Edinburgh-whom Harry had known before. Some of his contemporaries from Harrow had arrived, and so had several of his acquaintances from London, including the Mintos' eldest son, Gilbert, for whom the doting parents had rented an entire house. But Harry hardly had a chance to be lonely, even in his first few months of freedom. The professor and his wife, who was a well-known songwriter, had seen to it that he received a steady flow of suitable invitations; and they were generous hosts themselves, introducing him at dinner to their own extremely varied circle of friends and acquaintances. On one occasion Harry dined at their table with the African explorer Mungo Park, and on several others he dined with the Irish novelist Maria Edgeworth and her very Irish father, the politician, educationalist and inventor Richard Edgeworth, who had recently spoken in favour of the Act of Union in the Irish parliament and then voted against it, and who had once been inspired to devise a simple telegraph system by his pressing need to know the results of the races at Newmarket as soon as possible after they had been run.

Harry's free hours in the daytime were as busy as his evenings. He took Scottish dancing lessons. In the absence of any opportunity to play cricket, he learned to play golf. When he developed dizzy spells and headaches after cantering round and round in small circles twice a week in a riding school, he gave up for a while and took drawing lessons, which he continued when he returned to riding. When the first summer came, he found time for fencing, an art that, surprisingly, he does not seem to have tried at Harrow, where he could have taken lessons from the incomparable Harry Angelo. And he spent so much time shooting rabbits with local landowners that he bought himself a terrier which he kept in Stewart's attic, where Ashburton had already installed a variety of pets.

As expected, his academic programme was equally varied. He began by attending Stewart's lectures on moral philosophy and others on 'universal history' and algebra; and in the next two years he went on to botany, chemistry, geometry and Stewart's convincing presentations of Adam Smith's doctrines on political economy, most of which — such as the advantages of free trade and the value of universal education — became thereafter the substance of Harry's own opinions on the subject. Outside the university curriculum he continued his Latin and Greek with a private tutor and took lessons in handwriting and double-entry bookkeeping. For a while he even studied German, but he did not progress with it as easily as he had with the Romance languages. When his tutor, a Benedictine monk, left Edinburgh, he did not look for another.

Dugald Stewart professed himself delighted with Harry, not only as a student but also as a guest. 'His abilities are excellent, his temper most amiable and his industry unremitting. Indeed I don't know any young man of whom I am disposed to think more highly, or who unites in one greater degree all the qualities to be wished for at his age.' Mrs Stewart agreed, describing him as 'the idol of the whole family'. It may be that there were a few of his contemporaries who were not so enthusiastic, but the only one who committed himself to writing was equally impressed. In a letter to his mother, who was a friend of Lady Palmerston, Francis Cholmeley described Harry as 'proof that it is possible to unite the manners of a perfect gentleman with the utmost attention to science', implying a little snobbishly that the study of science might be tainted with the same indignity as trade. And as always Lord Minto was an ardent admirer. After one of his many visits to his son, he wrote extravagantly to Lady Palmerston. 'Diligence, capacity, total freedom from vice of every sort, gentle and kind disposition, cheerfulness, pleasantness, and perfect sweetness, are the catalogue of properties by which we may advertise him if he should be lost.'

It was left to Lady Minto to make the only perceptive report. 'He is charming,' she wrote, 'having no fault or failing, unless it be a want of the spirits belonging to his age.' Harry was still sheltering in his shell of reserve. Everyone agreed that he was clever and charming but in truth, as yet, nobody really knew him. He was occasionally high-spirited in the warm safety of the Stewart household: he once sprained his ankle jumping over the sofa. But elsewhere he was cautious, still unwilling to show his feelings or express an opinion, still careful not to risk being judged.

Edinburgh University had several debating societies, the most famous of which was the Speculative Society. All Harry's ambitious contemporaries were members, but Harry never went near it. There can surely be little doubt that, if he had done so, he would at least have acquitted himself honourably. He had the proven ability to prepare his case thoroughly; in studying philosophy with Stewart he had learned how to present it lucidly and simply; and he had earlier learned from Drury how to put it across confidently. He was an eager participant in the genteel, informal debates on uncontroversial subjects, such as the existence of ghosts, which Stewart occasionally organized at home for his sons and lodgers; and he had even expressed his frustration at their courteously inconclusive endings. But he showed no inclination to take part in any other debates. Of all the many eminent statesmen and jurists who attended Edinburgh University at the turn of the eighteenth and nineteenth centuries, the only one who did not join the Speculative Society, let alone take part in any of its debates, was Harry Temple.

At the end of March 1802 Lord Palmerston developed what he thought was a cold and a sore throat. A fortnight later his condition had deteriorated so much that Harry was summoned from Edinburgh. Gilbert Elliot accompanied him on the long journey south. On 19 April, as instructed, they stopped at a house that Gilbert's parents owned just north of London in Barnet. Here they were met by a manservant who apparently knew neither of them by sight. Thinking that Gilbert was Harry, the man took him straight upstairs to Lord Minto and then rejoined Harry in the hall, where he expressed his sympathy for the young gentleman whose father had died three days earlier. The well-meant effort to break the news gently had ended in clumsy and painful embarrassment. Shaken and miserable, Harry went on to Hanover Square to comfort his heart-broken mother.

Under the terms of the second Viscount Palmerston's will, Thomas Pelham and Lord Malmesbury were appointed to act as the third viscount's guardians until he came of age. At only seventeen Harry was even younger than his father had been when he inherited the title. But he was not as rich. His houses were more splendid, and they contained many more works of art, but the portfolio of shares was less valuable, there was a £10,000 mortgage on the estate at Broadlands and for the time being at least the income from land was greatly diminished. Since the Irish rebellion of 1798 very few rents had been forthcoming from Sligo. Furthermore, the late Lord Palmerston had been generous as well as extravagant. It was now revealed that Harry's Uncle Ben had been in financial difficulties more than once. On the first occasion his father had lent him at least £2,000, but since Uncle Ben had died destitute in Holland there was now no hope of recovering it. Above all, unlike his father, the new Lord Palmerston was not sole heir. The will made large settlements of £20,000 each on the other three children, together with annual allowances of £500 for their education. And in addition there was an allowance of £300 a year for Mrs Campbell of Pimlico and a legacy of £10,000 for her son, who was now a curate in Antigua. Harry wrote to him personally to break the news and began the letter, 'My dear Brother'.

Once all these dispositions had been deducted from the estate, there was barely enough income left to service the mortgage on Broadlands and provide for Harry and his mother. It was decided therefore to make a considerable reduction in overheads and a modest increase in income by letting the houses in East Sheen and Hanover Square, the former to Lord Castlereagh, the latter to Lord Minto. Once this had been done, Lady Palmerston was secure at Broadlands and there was £1,000 a year for Harry. It would not be enough to keep him at Cambridge in the style of his more fashionable contemporaries, but it would be enough to enable him to live as a young man of his rank might be expected to live.

After the funeral the new Lord Palmerston spent a day looking round Cambridge and then returned to Edinburgh to complete his courses. Lord Minto, who saw him there early in June, wrote to his wife to tell her that he was still dejected and echoed her own earlier comment: 'he has too little spring for his age'. Harry's distraught mother had been dissuaded from following and setting up house for him with his sisters, but she came up to Edinburgh from time to time to visit Harry and his fellow lodgers and brought his elder sister Fanny with her. John Ward recalled the visits later with a cruel lack of charity. 'I detested that woman', he told Lady Glenbervie. 'She was so fawning and mean. There was no sort of bassesse she was not guilty of in order to get that monster Ashburton to marry her ugly daughter.' Fortunately Fanny did rather better than the 'monster', although she waited a long time for it. In 1820 she married a captain in the navy, William Bowles, who ended his career as an admiral.

Harry Palmerston completed his courses at Edinburgh in May 1803. After a tour of the Highlands he set out southwards in a mail coach, which he shared with a retired colonel who had commanded Cherokee irregulars during the American War of Independence. As always, the coach made one of its halts in Doncaster to change horses. Doncaster had grown rich on horses. It had been a staging post for as long as there had been a Great North Road and carriages. Its famous race course was home to England's oldest Classic race, the St Leger; and the crowds that it attracted justified the cost of the unusually large and splendid 'Great Room' in the Mansion House, which was used for extremely profitable assemblies during race weeks. But in the course of Harry Palmerston's short lifetime, like many other towns and cities in the north and midlands, Doncaster had found additional and more lucrative sources of wealth. It lay at the heart of the south Yorkshire coal fields. It had become a centre for the sale and transport of coal and iron, and it now boasted its own foundry, from which, as the mail coach came in, the usual heavy cloud of smoke drifted across the clear summer sky.

There was, however, another, less usual cloud of smoke in the sky above Doncaster on that day. It came from the Rendlestone beacon, warning the militia and the townsfolk that the French had landed. While Harry Palmerston had been at Harrow and Edinburgh, Great Britain and most of Europe had been at war. In the years since his family came home from Holland, followed soon after by a shamefaced British army, French soldiers had advanced irresistibly into the Rhineland, Switzerland and Italy. Elsewhere in the world British soldiers had seen some success, particularly in Egypt and India, where the army of the East India Company was now commanded by a young major-general who had changed his surname from Wesley to the more aristocratic-sounding Wellesley, which was one of the family titles. And at sea, everywhere, the French had been thwarted consistently in battle after battle by the British navy. But in Europe, now led by Napoleon Bonaparte, the armies of France reigned supreme.

In March 1802, in recognition of the uneasy stalemate, the British and French had signed the Treaty of Amiens, which Sheridan had described as 'a peace which all men are glad of but no man can be proud of'. But neither side had made much effort to fulfil the terms of the treaty, and by the end of the following May they were at war again. Napoleon was now assembling barges in Boulogne and preparing for an invasion; and the British were building a network of warning beacons and hurridly assembling new regiments of militia.

So far the war, like the Industrial Revolution, had intruded very little on Harry Palmerston's life. He had been aware of it. At Harrow he had won a prize for a piece of Latin verse celebrating Nelson's victory at the Battle of the Nile. He had heard his parents and their friends talking anxiously about it. Yet, despite their anxiety, the world he lived in remained very much the same as ever. Indeed, to a great extent, it was the war that had kept it the same. Revulsion at the bloody revolution in France, and at the equally bloody fighting that followed it, had induced a passionate resistance to change among the British people and the majority in their Parliament. For the time being Pitt had been forced to abandon the domestic reforms on which he had set his heart.

Furthermore, the war had so far had very little financial effect on the lives of the aristocracy. The value of their stocks and shares had fallen, owing mostly to their own lack of confidence; and they were now required to pay a supposedly temporary income tax. But the additional tax was a small burden for landed families who lived on agricultural rents. Despite the loss of some European markets, Britain's agricultural and industrial economies were still expanding. Rents and profits were rising rapidly. In the towns in particular, new wealth was widespread among manufacturers, merchants and the growing number of professionals who served them, creating a huge demand for all kinds of goods and justifying Napoleon's description of the English as 'a nation of shopkeepers'. Most of the money that paid for the army, the navy and the subsidies to allies was being raised either through loans, which, it was confidently predicted, could be repaid easily in the prosperous and peaceful future, or through taxes on a wide variety of so-called luxuries – from horses and hats to ribbons and candles – which spread the burden tolerably thinly throughout the large new bourgeoisie. So far the cost of defending Doncaster against the cause of the burning beacon had been met mostly through the efforts of the men who fed the furnace in the foundry.

But it now seemed clear that the worst of the war was yet to come. While some intrepid citizens joined the militias and learned how to fend off the French with muskets, others, terrified by the long white rows of tents that could be seen on a clear day across the Channel beside Boulogne, shut up their houses on the south and east coasts and moved their families inland. The first beacons had been built in a flurry of frantic apprehension; and when one of them began to burn, conditions in Doncaster were reduced to little short of chaos. All business came to a halt. There were no ostlers at the inn to change the horses on the mail coach. A court martial that was sitting at the time broke up, and the officers climbed to the top of the church steeple in a vain attempt to discover which direction the French were supposed to be coming from.

Eventually, however, somebody established that the alarm was false. Doncaster was restored to normal. The ostlers returned to work; the coachman consented to continue; and Harry Palmerston went on southwards to discuss his future with Lord Malmesbury.

Inevitably, the late Lord Palmerston had wanted his son to go to one of the large, academically eminent and fashionable colleges at Cambridge – St John's or Trinity – rather than the one he had attended himself, Clare. For a long time St John's had been the most popular with the aristocracy and the most successful academically, but in the last twenty years Trinity had equalled it in the former and overtaken it in the latter. Lord Malmesbury, who had been at Merton College, Oxford, favoured St John's, the college with the oldest reputation, and so did Harry's old housemaster at Harrow, Dr Bromley, who had been at St John's himself. But before she accepted their choice Lady Palmerston rather naïvely consulted two Harrow friends with more recent experience of the colleges, both of whom, by coincidence, were future prime ministers. One was the attorney-general, Spencer Perceval, who had come down from Trinity in 1781; the other was young Frederick Robinson, who, like another future Prime Minister, Haddo, was one of the many Harrovians currently at St John's. As might have been expected, each one recommended his own college. So the opinions of Malmesbury and Bromley prevailed, and fortunately Harry agreed with them, partly because there were more Harrovians at St John's than at Trinity, and partly because, during his visit in the previous year, he had discovered that the authorities at St John's were much more likely to let him keep a horse.

Knowing that Harry's studies would not be as closely supervised at Cambridge as they had been at Edinburgh, Dr Bromley persuaded his mother and his guardians to engage Dr Edmund Outram as a private tutor. Outram had been a master at Harrow before Harry went there, and afterwards he had been a fellow of St John's until, as a result of his recent marriage, the ancient rules of the college had required him to resign his fellowship. On 22 October 1803, two days after Harry's nineteenth birthday, the kindly Dr Bromley took him up to Cambridge, introduced him to Outram and saw him settled into St John's. While a horse was installed in the college stables, young Viscount Palmerston and his manservant George were installed in a large set of rooms which had been completely redecorated and fitted with one of the smokeless fireplaces which had recently been invented by Rumford.

Lord Palmerston intended to enjoy himself at Cambridge. But he did not intend to be as idle as he could have been. He was genuinely frustrated by the statute passed in the reign of Queen Elizabeth which prohibited noblemen from demeaning themselves in the hazard of examinations and gave them a degree automatically after two years. He insisted on taking all the biannual college examinations; he prepared for them thoroughly with Outram; and his results were rated in the first class every time.

Cambridge was admittedly less challenging intellectually than Edinburgh had been. But, even so, it was difficult to be diligent and do well when the courses in such subjects as mathematics, morality, law and divinity were much more superficial, and the lecturers much less impressive. Harry Palmerston had not been at Cambridge two months before he was writing to Lord Malmesbury:

> The Cambridge men appear to be satisfied with what they know, and devote their whole time to teach others what they themselves have acquired, while the Scottish dedicate only a certain portion of their time to instruction, and are in the meantime constantly corresponding with all the Savants on the Continent, they keep pace with all the discoveries, many of which are either unknown, or disregarded by the Cambridge Professors.

But Cambridge provided Harry Palmerston with something that Harrow and Edinburgh had not. It gave him his first close friends: Edward

Clive, grandson of the great Governor of Bengal; George Shee, the son of an Irish baronet; and Laurence Sulivan, the grandson of a chairman of the East India Company, who had been one of Dugald Stewart's lodgers before Harry. With these three Harry founded a little club which met to drink, in moderation, every Saturday evening. In their company, and in the atmosphere of Cambridge, he came just a little bit out of his shell. He even joined a debating society. It was called the Speculative, after the famous one in Edinburgh, but it was very small and did not require its members to argue impromptu. At the weekly meetings one member read an essay and then the others commented on it. Meanwhile, outside the university Harry Palmerston began to develop a very active social life, visiting the local gentry and aristocracy to ride, shoot, dine and dance with their daughters.

By now Lady Palmerston had returned to dancing as well. But her junketing was a little frantic, and Lord Minto was again getting worried by the 'toadies' and 'abigails' with whom she was keeping company. Perhaps she was trying to hide her grief – she never really recovered from the death of her husband – or perhaps she was putting on a brave face because she already knew how ill she was. In May 1804 Lady Palmerston was diagnosed as having cancer of the womb. She shared the secret with only a few of her friends, making them promise not to tell her children and persuading Lord Malmesbury to give Harry an extra £300 from the family funds so that he and his friend Laurence Sulivan could spend the summer vacation travelling in Wales.

With her sister for company Lady Palmerston retired to Broadlands and continued to keep up appearances for the sake of her daughters. It was quiet at Broadlands now. Harry was in Cambridge, his younger brother Willy was in Edinburgh, and Signor Gaetano and Mademoiselle Thérèse had just left to set up a small school for young ladies in Kensington, for which Lady Palmerston had persuaded her son and his guardian to provide the initial working capital. Within months, however, Gaetano was writing a little shabbily to his former pupil asking for more. On Malmesbury's advice, Harry settled an annuity on the couple, which he continued to pay for the rest of their lives, even after they moved to Paris in 1817.

When Harry next saw his mother, after his return from Wales, she was in a wheelchair. But she was still making light of her condition and urging her children to dance and enjoy themselves. She survived to see one more family Christmas at Broadlands and died in January 1805, at the age of only fifty.

Her elder son was devastated. A little older now, he was more composed than he had been when his father died. But the forgivably sentimental letters to his friends reveal the extent of his grief, just as his letters to his mother reveal how close he had been to her. There were times when it almost looked as though young Harry Temple was somewhat embarrassed by his parents. If he was, it may have contributed to his reserve. But there can be no doubt that he loved them; and they, despite all their follies, did what they saw as best for their children and created for them, in the secure oasis of Broadlands, the warm, simple, merry family life that was denied to so many of their noble contemporaries.

When Lord Palmerston returned to Cambridge and the new social life that he had made for himself, Lords Minto and Malmesbury began to worry about his reputation with the ladies. In their time both men had earned reputations of their own. But they were concerned by the extent of the reputation which young Palmerston had earned already. Everywhere he went there were stories about his flirtations – in Cambridge, London, Hampshire. By his own admission there had even been a redhead in Wales.

Looking at the portraits of the third Viscount Palmerston as a young man, it is easy to see that he was attractive to women. They all show an intense, amused, inquisitive expression, a studied untidiness in the hair and the simple, elegant outfit of the early dandies. But there was also something about his demeanour and personality that made men recognize him as a leader, someone 'capable of distinguishing himself at the head of an army or a council'. When he arrived at Cambridge, like many young men in the prevailing emergency, he joined the university volunteers, the Rangers, and quickly rose to the rank of captain. Since he was a nobleman, it was perhaps not unusual that he was promoted so quickly, although there were plenty who were not. But of all the captains in the battalion Harry Palmerston was the one who was given what was regarded as the élite job, command of the light company, the one command that required its captain to operate alone on his own initiative out in front of the battle line. And in the same way there was something about him which made those who taught him recognize him as a potential statesman. When William Pitt died, creating a vacancy in one of the Cambridge University seats in the House of Commons, Dr Outram and the fellows of St John's suggested that Palmerston should stand as the Tory candidate to replace him.

Three months earlier, on 21 October 1805, Lord Nelson had destroyed the French and Spanish fleets at Trafalgar. Without a navy to support him Napoleon could no longer risk an invasion of Britain. But the relief and the rejoicing had been short-lived. The emperor had marched his army east and on 2 December had inflicted a crushing defeat on Britain's Austrian and Russian allies at Austerlitz. Pitt's death, it was said, had been caused by the news. When he heard it, the exhausted Prime Minister, who was already terminally ill, went into a rapid decline and died on 23 January.

Dr Outram and the fellows of St John's made their suggestion when it was known that Pitt was dying. Lord Palmerston had not yet shown any inclination towards politics, or indeed towards any particular party, but he was flattered by the suggestion. After discussing it with Lord Malmesbury, who, like his father, was a Whig turned Pittite Tory, he agreed without any further thought to put himself forward.

On the night of Pitt's death Palmerston was at a ball in London. When Malmesbury gave him the news next day, he went straight back to Cambridge and was accepted as the Tory candidate. Since he had come of age in the previous October, he was now old enough to stand, but since he had not bothered to take his degree, he was not yet eligible to do so. Fortunately, however, his nobleman's degree was only a formality, and by the afternoon of 27 January he was ready to start canvassing.

His election was not a foregone conclusion. The Tories were out of favour. In the continuing emergency the King had agreed to a 'Ministry of all the Talents'. Radical Whigs were back in power. The distribution of offices around the Cabinet table read like the *placement* for a dinner at Devonshire House. Lord Grenville was to be Prime Minister, young Lord Henry Petty was to be Chancellor of the Exchequer, the Duchess's brother Earl Spencer was to be Home Secretary, her lover Lord Grey was to be First Lord of the Admiralty, her friend Fox was to be Foreign Secretary and her friend Sheridan was to be Treasurer of the navy. With that much power behind him, the Radical Whig candidate was likely to be the favourite, and the man they had chosen was the Chancellor of the Exchequer, Henry Petty.

Although he was already MP for a safe family seat in Wiltshire, Petty was happy to exchange it for a more enjoyable and influential university seat. But there was one ray of hope for the Tories in the fact that the Whigs were split. The traditional Whigs had put up a candidate of their own: none other than Lord Althorp, one of Palmerston's companions from Dr Bromley's house at Harrow. Like Petty, Althorp had been at Trinity while Palmerston was at Edinburgh, and he too was already an MP. As soon as his father, Earl Spencer, took office as Home Secretary, he was given a post at the Treasury, which technically made him one of Petty's junior ministers.

Since every Cambridge MA was entitled to vote, Laurence Sulivan canvassed in London at the Inns of Court, while Palmerston canvassed in Cambridge, where, at least between Palmerston and Althorp, the campaign was conducted in the best of spirits. It was as though two of Drury's boys were still playing at politics; and as they played, another one of Drury's boys was watching and laughing. Lord Byron, who had gone to Harrow the term after Palmerston left, was now at Trinity. Perhaps Byron felt that clever but still gauche little Althorp was too insignificant to bother about; or perhaps he felt that, as a Whig, a Harrovian and a Trinity man, Althorp was the candidate to be supported. Either way, he reserved his very accurate fire for the other two candidates.

> Then would I view each rival wight,
> Petty and Palmerston survey,
> Who canvass there, with all their might,
> Against the next elective day.
> One on his power and place depends,
> The other on – the Lord knows what!
> Each to some eloquence pretends,
> But neither will convince by that.

Byron's criticism of Palmerston was well judged. The novice campaigned in generalities. He had not worked out what the main issues ought to be, and he had therefore failed to tell anyone where he stood on them. Petty, on the other hand, had recognized that among graduates the abolition of slavery was bound to be a major issue, and it was one on which he had been a very active campaigner. He had held meetings for the leader of the anti-slavery movement, William Wilberforce, at the London house of his half-brother the Marquess of Lansdowne and he believed that he could rely on his influential support. But at some point someone in the Radical Whig camp remembered that Wilberforce was a Pittite Tory and that he had also been at St John's. If the current Tory candidate at St John's were to come out in favour of abolition, Wilberforce might shift his support. Before the young Tory could recognize the opportunity, the Radical Whigs struck.

Henry Brougham, a Scottish advocate who had been at Edinburgh with Palmerston, sent a letter to the editor of the *Christian Observer*, the leading abolitionist newspaper, in which he described Palmerston as 'a young man who only left college a month ago and is devoid of all qualifications for the place'. 'The family', he wrote, 'are enemies to abolition in a degree that scarcely ever was exceeded. I presume that he is so himself.'

It was true that the second Viscount Palmerston had spoken against immediate abolition in a debate of 1791 and had proposed instead a gradual programme of reform. But even if this was enough to justify calling him the 'enemy' of abolition, it was hardly honourable to 'presume' that his son held similar views; and in the light of the third viscount's subsequent record on the subject it is unlikely that he ever gave such an impression. Sadly, however, it was not until the night before the election that the President of Queens' College, Isaac Milner, who was a friend of Wilberforce, decided to confront the artless young candidate and ask him directly if he was an abolitionist. Palmerston convinced him that he was and in so doing won over his vote, but by then the harm had been done. Wilberforce was actively supporting Petty. In the election next day Petty won with 331 votes. Althorp got 145 and Palmerston 128.

'It was an honour to have been supported at all,' wrote Palmerston, 'and I was well satisfied with my fight.' He had come last, 'where a young man circumstanced as I was could alone expect to stand', but the experience had been enough to convince him that he wanted more. While he waited for the next opportunity, he rented a house in Pall Mall, continued his active social life and fulfilled his new role as head of the family. He saw his elder sister Fanny presented at court. In August he went up to Edinburgh to collect Willy and took him to say goodbye to Lord Minto, who had been appointed Governor-General of India. In the following month his whole family spent a fortnight staying with Edward Clive in Shropshire.

Meanwhile Lord Malmesbury was looking for a pocket borough, and by October he had found one. It was the double seat of Horsham in Sussex, where his own son Viscount Fitzharris had been elected as one of the members two years earlier. The other seat was now available. But on 13 September, shortly after moving the abolition of slavery, Charles James Fox died. The government survived long enough to take the first step by outlawing the slave trade and then, after clashing with the King over Catholic emancipation, it collapsed. Instead of standing in a by election, Palmerston found himself standing with Fitzharris in a general election.

The rest of the story was a disastrous farce. The seats were thought to be in the gift of Viscountess Irwin, to whose agents Palmerston and Fitzharris paid £1,500, with a promise of another £3,500 if they were elected. But the neighbouring Duke of Norfolk claimed that the pocket borough was his and put up candidates of his own. The duke's influence bought more votes and his candidates were elected. When the election was appealed to the House of Commons, the House found in favour of the duke. Palmerston and Fitzharris had lost £1,500 each and Fitzharris had lost his seat as well.

Palmerston regretted that he had not had another try at Cambridge. But the result of the general election was not completely negative. The Tories were elected by a narrow majority and the Duke of Portland, an old friend of Malmesbury's, kissed hands with the King as Prime Minister. Malmesbury approached Portland on Palmerston's behalf, and the 'dull, dumb duke' agreed to make the young viscount a junior Lord of the Admiralty. The old-fashioned patronage that had failed to find him a seat had made him a minister of the crown. The job involved little more than turning up occasionally to sign his name, but it made it more important that he should find himself a seat. And the opportunity was not long in coming. Recognizing that he could not govern effectively with so small a majority in the Commons, the Duke of Portland called another general election.

This time Palmerston was determined to stand again for Cambridge, but Malmesbury was fairly sure that he would not get elected. The Whig candidates for the two university seats were Lord Euston, who was so popular that he was bound to come top, and Lord Henry Petty, who had made himself so unpopular with his recent budget that he was bound to come bottom. Of the two Tory candidates, the other, Sir Vicary Gibbs, was the one most likely to get government support and therefore win the other seat by coming second.

Malmesbury advised his former ward to have a pocket borough standing by in case of failure; and once again he had found such a seat. Deaf old Malmesbury was so preoccupied with other things that he always got the name of the constituency wrong, usually referring to it as Newton, and naturally Palmerston was influenced by the mistake and referred to it as Newton himself, even in later life. In fact the seat was Newport on the Isle of Wight, a seat that had once been represented by Palmerston's father. It was definitely in the gift of Sir Leonard Holmes, whose only stipulation was that the member should never visit his constituency, even during an election. All that Palmerston had to do was deposit £4,000 at Drummond's bank. If he won in Cambridge, he could have the money back. If he lost, the money would pass to Holmes and he could have 'Newton'. Palmerston agreed, deposited the money and hurried off to Cambridge.

In a general election at the university, where two seats were at stake, each eligible elector had two votes. But university men could not be expected to vote entirely on party lines. Sometimes they voted for what they saw as the two best men; and sometimes they just 'plumped' and cast only one vote for one candidate. On the night before the election Palmerston and Gibbs agreed that as much as possible they would each ask their supporters to cast their second vote for the other. Next day, however, an agitated 'Vinegar Gibbs' came up to Palmerston in the Senate House, where the election was being held, and told him that he had heard that Palmerston's supporters were just plumping for him and not casting a second vote.

Palmerston strode furiously towards the entrance. At the bar, where the remaining MAs were lining up to cast their votes, he found Dr Outram, who was acting as one of his agents. Outram confirmed that Palmerston's supporters were plumping. They had been taking a count of the people coming out. Euston was well ahead and Gibbs was second. The only way to get Palmerston elected was to plump. 'I said this would not do', wrote Palmerston later. 'I was bound in honour.' He turned to his remaining supporters and insisted that if they had the slightest regard for him they must cast their second vote for Gibbs. It cost him the election – by an excruciatingly narrow margin. Euston came top with 324 votes. Gibbs was second with 313, Palmerston third with 310 and Petty last with 265.

Next day the deposit was removed from Drummond's and on the following day Palmerston received a note from Malmesbury informing him that he had been elected for a seat which on this occasion he called 'Winton'. It was, to say the least, an anticlimax. A proper campaign had been fought honourably – and lost because it had been fought honourably. Instead, an easy seat had been found through the same corrupt, old-fashioned patronage that had found a junior ministry. But at least the long career had started. The orphaned Irish peer, who had been destined for the diplomatic corps, had drifted into politics. He had been born among Whigs, brought up among Whigs and, until he went to Cambridge, educated among Whigs. But now, in May 1807, at the age of only twenty-two, he was about to take a seat in Parliament as the Tory representative of a constituency to which he had never been, and of which he could not even remember the name.

3. LORD CUPID

On 27 August 1807 a fleet of over forty British ships, commanded by Admiral Sir James Gambier, landed 27,000 troops on the coast of Denmark, a country with which Great Britain was not then at war. Led by Lieutenant-General Lord Cathcart, with General Sir Arthur Wellesley in command of the reserves, the soldiers set out overland to invest Copenhagen; and while they advanced, the admiral sailed on with sixteen ships of the line and stationed them across the mouth of the city's long, narrow harbour, where the entire Danish fleet was lying peacefully at anchor. Once the soldiers were in position, the admiral sent in an envoy inviting Denmark to make an alliance with Great Britain and virtually demanding the surrender of its fleet. When the invitation and the demand were refused, he signalled to his captains to open fire.

After three days of ceaseless bombardment, which caused many more casualties among civilians than among seamen or soldiers, the garrison commandant called for an amnesty and reluctantly accepted that the only way to save the burning capital was to sacrifice the helpless fleet. The Danish crews were put ashore. Seamen and marines rowed in from the blockading fleet to replace them. Every Danish ship that was still seaworthy was towed out of the harbour; and as soon as the besieging British soldiers had been returned to their transports, the two fleets set sail for England.

For neither the first time nor the last, a British government had sought to protect its island with a pre-emptive strike against an ostensibly friendly fleet. The justification for the attack lay in the treaty that Napoleon and the defeated rulers of Russia and Prussia had signed seven weeks earlier at Tilsit, in northern Prussia. Napoleon and Tsar Alexander had first met ceremoniously on 25 July on a splendid tented raft in the middle of the River Niemen, which divided Russia from conquered Prussia. They talked for over half an hour, while the rain-soaked King of Prussia waited on the south bank to join them; and in the course of the days that followed, Napoleon charmed the young Tsar into abandoning his Prussian ally. Under the terms of the treaty that the three signed on 7 July, Prussia's wings were clipped by the creation of the kingdom of Westphalia, which was given to Napoleon's brother Jerome, and the Duchy of Warsaw, which was given to his puppet the King of Saxony.

But there were also secret terms to the treaty; and within only a fortnight of its signing the new British Foreign Secretary, George Canning, had put enough evidence in front of the Cabinet to convince it that, under these terms, Tsar Alexander, who resented what he saw as Britain's failure to support him sufficiently or soon enough, had made an alliance with his former enemy. The Tsar had agreed to join in the so-called 'Continental Blockade', which Napoleon had set up to stifle British trade. As so many other countries had done or been forced to do already, Russia would now close all its ports to British shipping and would combine with France in forcing the remaining uncommitted countries – Sweden, Denmark, Norway and Portugal – to do the same. Once this had been achieved, the barrier would stretch right round Europe from the Baltic to the Adriatic. Worse still, Alexander had also agreed that, if the Danes refused to put their fleet at Napoleon's disposal, Russia would stand aside and do nothing while he seized it; and worst of all, according to separate intelligence, French troops were already massing on the Danish border.

Since the destruction of the French and Spanish fleets at Trafalgar, the Danish fleet, which included seventeen ships of the line, was the second largest in the world – after the British one. If Napoleon were to get his hands on it, everything that had been achieved at Trafalgar would be lost. The French would have a new fleet and England would again be under threat of invasion. In these circumstances, Canning argued, the only immediate option was to offer the Danes an alliance and ask them to move their fleet to England. If they refused, there would be no choice but to get to their fleet before Napoleon.

The Cabinet agreed with him. On 18 July the staff of the Admiralty and its lords, including Lord Palmerston, were suddenly thrown into unaccustomed fluster by a secret instruction to make a large fleet ready for immediate service in northern waters. On 19 July the Prime Minister formally advised the King to command the execution of Canning's plan. On 20 July the Minister for War and the Colonies, Lord Castlereagh, invited the King's second son, the Duke of York, who was Commander-in-Chief, to muster the necessary troops.

There is still no certainty as to how Canning found out so much so soon. On coming to office he had inherited an unusually effective and well-established network of secret agents in the Low Countries and around the Baltic, one of whom was none other than 'Brother James' Robertson, the Benedictine monk who had been Palmerston's German tutor in Edinburgh. In the years that followed the attack on Copenhagen the most popular theory was that the controller of this network, another Scot called Colin Mackenzie, had concealed himself on the raft during the meeting between Napoleon and the Tsar. But this fanciful theory does not stand up to scrutiny. Both banks of the river were heavily guarded; the raft itself was surrounded by boats full of soldiers; and even if Mackenzie had managed to get through all the guards, the only place in which he would have been able to conceal himself on the raft would have been in the water beneath its planks. Furthermore, although he did come to London, presumably to report on what had happened at Tilsit, he did not arrive until 23 July, by which time the expedition to Copenhagen was already being prepared.

More plausibly, Canning's opponents argued that he had merely been guessing. But his knowledge of the treaty was much too comprehensive to be guesswork. Not only did he warn his own Cabinet about the impending danger in Denmark, but he also sent Arthur Paget to Constantinople to warn the government there that France and Russia had agreed to combine in expelling the Turks from all their territories in Europe. When the Tsar's copy of the treaty was published in 1891, it revealed that Canning had been correct in every detail.

The most probable sources of the information were Canning's own contacts. Canning had formed a close friendship with the Russian

Ambassador in London, Semen Romanovich Vorontzov, who was an ardent opponent of any compromise with Bonaparte, and who, in a letter dated 14 July, before the expedition was ordered, told his son Michael that he was 'disquieted' by the news that the Tsar was about to make peace with 'that monster'. In his communications with the many anti-Bonapartists in the Russian court and army Vorontzov sometimes used the same courier as Canning used to communicate with his ambassador in Russia and even with the Tsar, a British colonel called Sir Robert Wilson. This popular, dashing but, in Wellesley's words, 'very slippery' cavalry officer had fought with the Russians and Prussians in the recent campaign. He was in Tilsit with the Russian army during the negotiations; and his constant companion, Vorontzov's son Michael, was one of the officers who accompanied the Tsar on the raft.

It seems likely therefore that Canning discovered the terms of the Treaty of Tilsit through the Vorontzovs and Wilson. And if he needed corroboration, he may have found it with the Count d'Antraigues, one of the many French royalist exiles living in London. D'Antraigues, who was a known Russian agent, sometimes sold information to the British. Immediately after the attack on Copenhagen, however, he was dismissed from the Russian secret service; and shortly after that, for no apparent reason, Canning arranged for him to receive a pension.

Whatever the sources, they were clearly reliable enough to be convincing and valuable enough to be worth protecting. But the opposition and even some supporters of the government regarded the Cabinet's reaction to their information as unprincipled and inexcusable. There could be no justification for an action that dishonoured Britain in the eyes of the civilized world. Palmerston's old friend Sheridan declared that the government was trying to compete with Bonaparte in knavery; and his guardian and mentor Lord Malmesbury, who had been acting as a special adviser to the Prime Minister and the Foreign Secretary, resigned in disgust.

For Palmerston, however, there were no principles involved. In his view Canning had merely come up with the only practical solution in an emergency. Indeed, he was so sure that the Copenhagen raid was justified that he chose it as the subject of his maiden speech. On 3 February

1808, when the opposition 'moved for papers', calling on the Foreign Secretary to disclose all the evidence that had induced the Cabinet to sanction the attack, Palmerston was one of those who rose after Canning to oppose the motion on behalf of the government. As he wrote to his sister Elizabeth afterwards, 'It was impossible to talk any very egregious nonsense upon so good a cause.'

He began by asserting that the only dishonour lay in acceding to the motion, since this would betray and endanger the sources of the information and discourage others from trusting the British government with intelligence in the future. He then went on to argue, as Canning had done, that Napoleon's intentions were obvious and that the Danes had neither the will nor the strength to resist him. And when William Windham, Castlereagh's predecessor as Minister for War, interrupted him to point out that, even so, the government's action had violated the law of nations, he answered, 'In the case before the House the law of nature is stronger even than the law of nations. It is to the law of self-preservation that England appeals for the justification of her proceedings.'

Canning's three-hour opening for the government was more than enough to defeat the motion on its own. Nevertheless, Palmerston's half-hour in support was on the whole well received and was contrasted favourably with the pompous, ill-judged attack that another novice, Robert 'Orator' Milnes, launched against the naïvety of the opposition. Although Lady Holland reported enigmatically that the speech 'was not attended either with the bad or good qualities of a young beginner', the Leader of the House told the King that the new Lord of the Admiralty had spoken well, and Sir Vicary Gibbs wrote in similar terms to the President of St John's. In retrospect, however, the real significance of the speech lay in its foretaste of the Palmerston to come, rather than in its contribution to the debate.

At the heart of the argument there was a protective pragmatism, which at the time echoed Canning but which would one day be the essence of Palmerston's own foreign policy; and in his delivery of it, as Lady Holland had hinted, Palmerston revealed all the strengths and weaknesses that were to mark and mar his oratory throughout his career. When he stuck to his well-prepared text, his performance would not have disappointed Dr Drury. But when he added to it or argued with a heckler, he hesitated, stretching out his arms in silence and clasping impatiently at thin air, as though the words he wanted could be found there. He did not, like so many contemporaries and successors, make do with stuttered approximations. Instead, he kept his audience waiting until precisely the right words were within his grasp. As a result, Palmerston's speeches often read better than they sounded; and there were times, even at the end of his life, when the House of Commons listened because of what he had to say rather than the way in which he said it.

By the time this debate took place, the raid on Copenhagen had already driven the Danes into an alliance with the French, and Napoleon, who had been denied the chance to enforce his blockade effectively by sea, had decided to impose it as thoroughly as possible by land instead. In November he had sent an army across Spain to invade England's oldest ally, Portugal. But his own Spanish allies had also refused to take part in the blockade of England. In the course of the following March and April, therefore, Napoleon occupied Spain as well, deposing its king and enthroning his own brother Joseph in his place. Again Canning persuaded the British government to intervene. Thirteen thousand soldiers were sent as soon as possible to Portugal – and this time Sheridan approved. It was, he said, 'a bold stroke for the rescue of the world'.

Throughout all this Lord Palmerston made no further contribution to the debates in Parliament, and when the House rose in the autumn he went off to Ireland with his brother Willy, who had just come down from Cambridge, to visit the largest and least productive of his estates. What he saw in Sligo cannot have been what he expected. This was the sad, neglected Ireland described in the novels of Maria Edgeworth. As in the rest of the island, most of the land was leased to 'middlemen', who made their living by subletting it in smaller plots; and, as on most of the west coast, the plots were so tiny and infertile that the wretched 'under-tenants' could barely pay the excessive 'profit-rents', let alone feed their families.

Like most of the other absentee landlords, generations of Temples had been content to take what they could and leave things as they were. But the third Viscount Palmerston was not like other absentee landlords.

To this recent student of political economy the plight of his tenants was a challenge; and he rose to it with unsentimental sympathy.

Only six days after he first saw his estate, on 12 September, he wrote to his sister Elizabeth outlining his long-term plans for improvement.

I find there is a great deal, I may almost say, everything, to be done, and it will be absolutely necessary for me to repeat my visit next summer, and probably make it annual for some time ... The present objects which I must in the first instance set about, are to put the parish church in a state of repair, so as to make it fit for service; to establish schools, to make roads, and to get rid of the middlemen in some cases where it can be accomplished. After that, as opportunities occur, I mean to endeavour to introduce a Scotch farmer, to teach the people how to improve their land; to establish a little manufacturing village in the centrical part of the estate, where there are great advantages of water and stone; and to build a pier and make a little port near a village that stands on a point of land projecting into Donegal Bay, and called Mullaghmore.

At the end of the letter Palmerston turned away from family business to express his delight at the 'admirable news' that had reached the west of Ireland from Portugal. At the beginning of the previous month Canning's 13,000 British troops, who had set sail from Cork, had landed in Mondego Bay. Before their commanding generals had joined them, a subordinate commander, Sir Arthur Wellesley, had beaten off a French attack at Vimiero, and the French had withdrawn from Lisbon. 'What will the croakers say now', wrote Palmerston. 'They have not a twig left to perch on.'

By the end of the month Palmerston was back in the house that he now rented in Lower Brook Street. The new house was big enough to make a home for his brother, who was about to start reading for the bar, as well as to provide rooms for his sisters when they came up to London; and its drawing-room and dining-room were spacious enough to accommodate the large supper parties that he was giving with increasing regularity. Lord Palmerston's social life was already a mirror of that of his parents. Brother Willy wrote to sister Lilly outlining a programme that was every bit as exhausting as his mother's: Tuesday, the opera and a ball at Lady Castlereagh's; Wednesday, Vauxhall Gardens and another ball;

Thursday, the theatre and a ball at Lady Shaftesbury's; Friday, Vauxhall again; and so on. And the gossips were already implying that his more intimate life, although a little more refined, was every bit as active as his youthful father's had been.

At this stage there was very little hard evidence to support the gossip. At the age of almost twenty-four the third Viscount Palmerston was still protected by an impenetrable, diffident shell. Many of the women who met him during his first few years in London mistook his reserve for pompous indifference; and the press nicknamed him 'Lord Cupid' on account of his boyish good looks rather than as a result of any romantic reputation. Nevertheless, ever since he had been at Cambridge, aristocratic matchmakers had been recommending him to their sisters and nieces for his promise and 'gentlemanlike' qualities, and the gossips had continued to predict impending marriages with a succession of eligible ladies, even though the ladies had almost always refuted them by announcing their engagement to someone else soon afterwards.

If Lord Palmerston did indeed conduct any illicit liaisons during his time at the Admiralty, he did so with great discretion. But he stayed so late nightly at balls and at his clubs that he left himself very little time for it anyway. He was a member of all the fashionable clubs, including the oldest and most aristocratic, White's, and the most exclusive, the dandy club Watier's, where the food was the best, the play was for the highest stakes and the permanent president was 'the observed of all observers', Beau Brummell. Most enviable of all, in the eyes of early nineteenth-century London, he had a subscription to the Wednesday night balls at Almack's.

Held throughout the season in the assembly rooms that had been established in 1765 in King Street, St James's, by a Scotsman called William Macall, these peerless gatherings were presided over by a small group of ruthless patronesses. They were not expensive or elaborate events: the only drinks served were tea and lemonade, and the only food available was bread and butter, biscuits or cake. But they were deliciously, cruelly exclusive. Nobody who had any aspirations to 'ton' issued or accepted invitations for Wednesdays, for fear of revealing that they were not going to Almack's. A subscription, it was said, was harder to come by than a peerage. Wealth and breeding were not enough. What mattered most was a sufficient combination of what the infallible patronesses regarded as beauty, wit, charm, talent and style. Once they had been accepted, subscribers were allowed to invite guests, but even the names of these had to be submitted well in advance for the approval of the patronesses; and when this had been given, the guests had to collect their 'vouchers of admission' in person and undergo further scrutiny.

At the end of 1808 these socially omnipotent goddesses included Viscountess Castlereagh, whose patronage was essential to any aspiring young Tory, the beautiful Countess of Jersey, whose name, like so many, had been linked with Palmerston's before her recent marriage, and the pretty, warm-hearted and mischievously witty Countess Cowper. Lady Cowper was the only surviving daughter of the first Viscount Melbourne. Like Palmerston's, her father's title was only a 'potato peerage', but his family, the Lambs, were not as distinguished as the Temples had been. The fortune he was now dissipating at the gaming tables had only been founded by his barrister grandfather, and his title had only been acquired through the lobbying of his formidable wife.

Handsome, shrewd and disarmingly down-to-earth, Lady Melbourne was the adviser and confidante of several society ladies, including the Spencer sisters, to whom she preached a precise but liberal eighteenth-century morality. In her view, for example, a man had a right to be sure that the heir to his estate and, if he had one, his title, carried his own blood in his veins. It was therefore a woman's duty to remain faithful to her husband until she had borne him an heir. After that, if he failed to keep her happy, there was no shame in seeking solace elsewhere.

It was a rule to which Lady Melbourne herself adhered strictly. Her first child, Peniston, was undoubtedly her husband's. The next two, however, William and Frederick, were with almost equal certainty the sons of the Earl of Egremont, a notoriously promiscuous patron of the arts, who filled his fine house at Petworth with as many mistresses as masterpieces, and who, it was said, had acquired his place in Lady Melbourne's affections by pensioning off her previous lover, Lord Coleraine. On the basis of an ill-concealed liaison and an extraordinary physical and facial likeness, her fourth child, revealingly christened George, was probably the son of the Prince of Wales. For the fathering of her fifth, Emily, she seems to have returned to Lord Egremont. But nobody was quite sure who fathered the last one. Lady Melbourne's second daughter, Harriet, died in early childhood, before any of the characteristics of several candidates could become convincingly apparent.

Unfortunately the fates did not respect Lady Melbourne's philosophy. At the end of January 1805, 35-year-old Peniston died unmarried, leaving Lord Egremont's son William as heir to her husband's title. Lady Melbourne's conscience did not seem too troubled by the loss, however, and her family emerged indecorously early from its mourning. As early as the beginning of the following June, William married the extrovert Lady Caroline Ponsonby; and in July eighteen-year-old Emily married a worthy but dull and often drunk neighbour, 27-year-old Earl Cowper.

Following her mother's example, Lady Cowper remained faithful to her neglectful husband until at last, in June 1806, she bore him an heir. After that she immersed herself more and more in a conspicuously vivacious social life, often winning hearts and occasionally sharing beds, most notably with Lord Henry Petty.

Palmerston had met the Lamb family quite often when he was a child. When he began to live in London he inevitably renewed his acquaintance with William, just as he renewed his friendship with the Ponsonby brothers, who had been his companions at Harrow. Society was still small. In the little world of St James's and Mayfair, young men such as the Temples, the Lambs and the Ponsonbys met regularly in their clubs as well as in drawing-rooms and in the inner sanctum, Almack's, to which all of them were subscribers. It was hardly surprising, therefore, that in August 1805 – soon after Lady Caroline Ponsonby married William Lamb, and shortly before her eldest brother, Lord Duncannon, married Lady Jersey's sister – Palmerston was invited to stay with the Lambs at Brocket Hall, the large Neo-classical brick house in Hertfordshire that had been built for their grandfather by James Paine.

In the course of the next year Lamb and Duncannon joined Palmerston in Parliament, although on the other side of the House. But in those days political differences were less of a threat to friendships than rivalries within the same party. Palmerston continued to visit Brocket. In

November 1808, shortly after his return from Ireland, he went there for a while to hunt. It was a large house party. Apart from William and Lady Caroline, the assembled members of the Lamb family included George and his new wife, another Caroline, who was the illegitimate daughter of the Duke of Devonshire and the sister of Palmerston's Harrow fag, Augustus Clifford; and although they were neighbours, Lady Cowper and her husband were there as well. By then the Cowpers had moved in to spend almost two years at Brocket while the earl's house, Panshanger, was being remodelled for him, with a Greek interior and a Gothic exterior, by William Atkinson. And at Brocket Hall, perhaps on this visit, perhaps later, but certainly before March 1810, when she became pregnant for the second time, Lady Cowper and Lord Palmerston became lovers. It was hardly an exclusive love for either of them, but their 'attachment' was deeper than in any of their other relationships and lasted for the rest of their lives.

Beyond the safe, romantic world of Broadlands, Brocket and Almack's, 1809 began badly and then got worse. In January the British army in Spain retreated to Corunna on the north-west coast with an overwhelming French force in close pursuit. On the day before the exhausted survivors were taken off the beach by the Royal Navy, their commander, Sir John Moore, was killed directing the rearguard action that saved them. In London the Cabinet's capacity to cope with the crisis was diminished by long-standing animosities and mistrust, particularly between the two Ulstermen Canning and Castlereagh.

Both men were unpopular with the British public. But Castlereagh did not care. The remote and haughty heir to the first Marquess of Londonderry regarded it as 'ungentlemanlikc' to be popular. For passionately ambitious George Canning, on the other hand, elusive public support would have been more valuable. Many of his colleagues openly despised his vulgar opportunism and what they saw as his humble origins. His father, the disinherited wastrel son of a landed family in Derry, had died when George was only one year old; and his actress mother, to whom he was devoted, had provided for her children by returning to the stage and forming a few lucrative liaisons with admirers. It was the sympathetic generosity of his banker uncle that enabled him to go to Eton and Christ Church, and it was marriage to an heiress that brought him the wealth that compensated for his lack of connections. In drawing-rooms Canning was charming and witty, but in the Cabinet, in Parliament and in print he relieved and revealed his resentment in bitter, sneering criticisms. Always eager to dissociate himself from collective responsibility for failures in policy, and convinced that Castlereagh was unfit to be Minister for War, he made the most of it when Castlereagh honourably but unnecessarily accepted the blame for the collapse of Sir John Moore's expedition.

On 28 July it looked for a moment as though 1809 was going to get better. Now led by Wellesley – something for which Castlereagh had argued from the outset – the British army in Spain held off a French army over twice its size at the bloody Battle of Talavera. Wellesley was rewarded for his welcome victory with ennoblement as Viscount Wellington. But the euphoria was short-lived. Abandoned by his Spanish allies, who had been little more than spectators at the battle, and cut off by the French force which Marshal Soult managed to put between his rear and his base, Wellington was forced to make a circuitous retreat back into Portugal.

The wasted victory was another gift for Canning, who had by now persuaded the Prime Minister to get rid of Castlereagh. But his criticisms soon switched to the better opportunities offered by a fiasco closer to home. On the day when the Battle of Talavera began, a British fleet set out to land 40,000 men on the swampy island of Walcheren, on the coast of Holland. The objective was to offer belated support to the Austrians by opening up a second front, seizing the docks at Antwerp and then persuading the Dutch to rise against Napoleon. But the landing was slow, the French were waiting, the British commanders quarrelled and, by the time the exercise was abandoned, almost half their men were dead or disabled with malarial fever and dysentery.

While Canning was launching a further invidious attack on the blameless Castlereagh, the 71-year-old Duke of Portland announced that he was no longer well enough to continue as Prime Minister, and in bemoaning the things that he had left undone inadvertently revealed that Canning had persuaded him to ask for Castlereagh's resignation.

Realizing that he now appeared to have acted dishonourably by continuing to serve with a colleague in whom he had lost confidence, Canning attempted to save his reputation with an immediate resignation. Then Castlereagh resigned as well and sent Canning a long letter in which he accused him of plotting behind his back and challenged him to a duel. Canning said he would rather fight than read the letter. So on 21 September, at a time when isolated Britain was precariously committed to a war with the mightiest European emperor since the Caesars, the two ablest men in the Cabinet, the Foreign Secretary and the Secretary of State for War and the Colonies, fought a duel with pistols at ten paces on Putney Heath.

Their first shots missed. With the second, Canning took off one of Castlereagh's buttons and Castlereagh grazed Canning's left thigh. Soon afterwards the Prime Minister died in a fit. The government, or what was left of it, collapsed; and the man who was invited to pick up the pieces was Dr Drury's first Prime Minister: tiny, uxorious, evangelical Spencer Perceval.

Perceval's first problem was that there was now a shortage of men with experience as well as ability. For the time being Canning and Castlereagh were unacceptable, and most of their recent colleagues were no longer prepared to work with each other. The only ministers who were willing to stay on were stiff, reactionary Lord Eldon, who continued as Lord Chancellor, and steady but unimaginative Lord Liverpool, a friend of Canning since their days at Christ Church, who moved from the Home Office to replace Castlereagh as Secretary of State for War and the Colonies. Fortunately Wellington's eldest brother, Marquess Wellesley, who was a former Governor-General of India and recent ambassador in Madrid, agreed to accept the Foreign Office. But for most other ministries, large and small, Perceval found himself issuing invitations to so many untried novices that the wags in Westminster began to suggest he was building a 'babyhouse'.

One of these novices, 24-year-old Viscount Palmerston, had spent the long summer recess at a safe distance from the bickering government – reviewing the progress of his many schemes in Sligo, training with the South-West Hampshire Militia, of which the Lord-Lieutenant of the county, Lord Malmesbury, had appointed him Colonel, and shooting with the Lambs at Brocket. He had completed his vacation with a few days' sailing and was resting at Broadlands when he received a summons from the Prime Minister.

At 11 a.m. on 16 October Palmerston called on Perceval at 10 Downing Street and was invited to become Chancellor of the Exchequer. He was flattered, but also reluctant. Perceval, who had been Chancellor in the previous government, tried to reassure him by saying that he would continue to carry some of the burden. When that seemed to fail, he suggested that Palmerston could become a Lord of the Treasury and then, when he felt that he had mastered the business, he could come into the Cabinet and take on the Exchequer, which would be kept vacant for him. Finally, when Palmerston still seemed uncertain, Perceval told him that, if he could not accept the Exchequer, it might be possible to offer him the junior post of Minister at War instead.

After pleading successfully for two days in which to think it over, Palmerston left Downing Street and wrote at once to Lord Malmesbury.

Of course one's vanity and ambition would lead to accept that brilliant offer first proposed; but it is throwing for a great stake, and where much is to be gained, very much also may be lost. I have always thought it unfortunate for any one, and particularly a young man, to be put above his proper level, as he only rises to fall the lower. Now, I am quite without knowledge of finance, and never but once spoke in the House. The approaching session will be one of infinite difficulty. Perceval says that the state of the finances of this country, as calculated to carry on the war, is very embarrassing; and from what has lately happened in public affairs, from the number of speakers in opposition, and the few debaters on our side of the question, the warfare of the House of Commons will certainly be for us very severe. I don't know on which of the two points I should feel most alarmed. By fagging and assistance I might get on in the office, but fear I never should be able to act my part properly in the House. A good deal of debating must of course devolve upon the person holding the Chancellorship of the Exchequer; all persons not born with the talents of Pitt or Fox must make many bad speeches at first if they speak a great deal on many subjects, as they cannot be masters of all, and a bad speech, though tolerated in any person not in a responsible situation, would make a Chancellor of the Exchequer exceedingly ridiculous, particularly if his friends could not set off against his bad oratory a great knowledge and capacity for business; and I should be apprehensive that instead of materially assisting Perceval, I should only bring disgrace and ridicule upon him and myself.

Palmerston rejected Perceval's second offer for the same reasons and then went on to say that he was strongly inclined to be Secretary at War, even though Perceval had not mentioned whether or not it was to be accompanied by a seat in the Cabinet. 'We may probably not remain in long enough to retrieve any blunders made at the outset,' he wrote, 'and the ground of the War Office is, I think, quite high enough for me to leave off upon.'

Malmesbury was no longer obliged to divide his advice and influence between his former ward and his son. Although he had succeeded in getting his son appointed under-secretary to Canning, Fitzharris had soon become disillusioned by what he saw as the duplicity of politics. Shortly after the raid on Copenhagen, he had resigned his post, retired from politics and accepted a less demanding appointment as Governor of the Isle of Wight. The disappointment made Malmesbury all the more delighted by the opportunities that were now being offered to Palmerston and he answered his letter enthusiastically, agreeing with everything that Palmerston had said. 'I am strongly inclined to recommend you to take the Secretaryship at War (with the Cabinet). It is a very reputable situation, which, without bringing you too forward at once, will, if you hold it a short time, infallibly lead you to the higher posts in the Cabinet.'

A few days later, however, Malmesbury received a letter telling him that Palmerston had accepted the Secretaryship but had turned down a seat in the Cabinet. It was unusual for the Secretary at War to have a seat in the Cabinet, and Palmerston felt that, if he accepted, people 'would perhaps only wonder how I got there'.

Palmerston was still diffident, but it is clear from these letters that his refusal of the Exchequer was due to cautious common sense rather than any lack of ambition. He was aware of his own shortcomings and, like everyone else, he could see the pitfalls. Even at the best of times the Exchequer was an office in which a young novice could easily make himself unpopular, as Lord Henry Petty had recently demonstrated. Eventually, when the office had been turned down by everyone else to whom it had been offered, Perceval was left with no choice but to retain it and serve simultaneously as Chancellor and Prime Minister.

The War Office was 'high enough'. If Palmerston failed, or if the government fell, little would be lost. If he made a success of it, and if the government survived, he could expect promotion to a 'higher post' within 'a short time'. But Malmesbury's last assertion was their first false assumption. If Palmerston had even been able to guess how long he might now have to wait for a seat in the Cabinet, let alone how long he might have to serve at the same desk in the War Office, he might well have played for a 'higher stake'.

The now extinct office of Secretary at War had evolved from the role of the secretary to King Charles I's military council during his war with Parliament. After the death of the Duke of Albemarle in 1670, the Secretary at War began to take over some of the duties of the Commander-in-Chief, and by the end of the seventeenth century he had replaced him as the servant through whom the crown exercised its prerogative of command. In 1782 the power of the Secretary was further increased with responsibility for pay and expenditure on supplies. But since then the job had been modified and reduced to an indefinable miscellany of less important duties. In 1793 the honour of conveying the King's commands was restored to the Commander-in-Chief; and the following year responsibility for military policy was given to a newly created Cabinet minister, the Secretary of State for War and the Colonies, who exercised his authority from the Colonial Office.

By the end of the eighteenth century the man in charge of the War Office, the Secretary at War, had become in essence the government's auditor. On behalf of the Commander-in-Chief and the Secretary of State for War and the Colonies, he was responsible for presenting the annual army estimates to Parliament; and on behalf of Parliament he was responsible for ensuring that the resulting expenditure was made in accordance with its directions.

Beyond this, a leftover from his former power, the Secretary at War was also burdened with the difficult role of an intermediary spokesman. It was he, and not the more senior Secretary of State for War and the Colonies, who represented the Commander-in-Chief in Parliament; and in military matters he was also responsible for presenting Parliament's policies to the people.

It was in the former capacity that Palmerston sometimes found himself charged with the distasteful duty of defending flogging, a barbaric punishment first inflicted on British soldiers on the orders of William of Orange and allowed to continue with horrifying frequency long after it had been abandoned by most other European armies. But when he was not bound by duty he was not always so ready to uphold established practice or toe the Tory party line. Within two years of taking office he wrote a defiantly liberal definition of his role for the Prime Minister.

> The Secretary at War seems, indeed, to be the officer who stands peculiarly between the people and the Army to protect the former from the latter; to prevent their public revenue from being drained by any unauthorized increase of military establishment, and their persons and property from being injured by any possible misconduct of the soldiery; and upon him would Parliament and the country justly fix the responsibility for any neglect of this part of his duty.

The principal duty of the Secretary at War was, however, the annual presentation of the army estimates in Parliament. After Palmerston's first presentation, in May 1810, Lady Minto reported his performance to her husband in India. 'He will never boast of shining talents, or great views, but he is painstaking & gentlemanlike to the greatest degree, & will always swim where greater talents might sink.' Painstaking was right. Palmerston performed his duties with a conscientious attention to detail that would not have surprised those who taught him but which came as a revelation to those who had only met him in society. With a war on, the House of Commons gave him an easier ride than it was later to do in peacetime, but with over a dozen departments to deal with, the preparation of figures and the supervision of expenditure were formidable tasks.

Foremost among these departments was that of the Commander-in-Chief, who was responsible for the management of all regular cavalry and infantry regiments. Yet, although his duties included providing them with clothing, they did not include supplying them with arms and equipment, feeding them, transporting them, paying them or taking care of them when they were sick or wounded. All these were the responsibilities of separate offices, the first of which, the Board of Ordnance, was also responsible for the management of all artillery and engineers, and only the last of which, the Army Medical Board, was directly answerable to the Secretary at War. Beyond these, the other pieces in the puzzle included the militia, which was run by the Home Office, and the volunteer regiments, each of which was virtually an independent club.

This confusion was perfect camouflage for corruption and incompetence – and the War Office was notorious for both. Employees assigned profitable contracts to friends or even to themselves, and there was at least one who only turned up to draw his salary and passed on a small portion of it to the woman who actually did his work for him. When Palmerston took office there were around 40,000 regimental accounts in arrears, some of them dating back as far as the end of the American War of Independence in 1783. By then, however, as Commander-in-Chief, the Duke of York had started to make a few changes. Convinced that the King's commission was an honour to be earned and not a privilege to be purchased, he had established a college for training officers and, knowing that he could not yet abolish the sale of commissions completely, he had set limits on the rate of promotion and transferred supervision of the system from the Secretary at War to himself. Having thus reduced still further the authority of the Secretary at War, he then added to his workload by instituting a thorough programme of reform and reorganization. But the programme had hardly begun before new accusations of corruption were being aimed at the highest level of the military hierarchy, at the very man who had instituted the reforms and on the very subject that was dearest to his heart.

On 27 January 1809, in the House of Commons, Lieutenant-Colonel Gwyllym Lloyd Wardle MP alleged that the Duke of York's recent mistress, Mary Anne Clarke, had accepted bribes from ambitious officers and then persuaded her lover to secure their promotion. His Royal Highness was summoned to answer the charge before the bar of the House, where he denied all knowledge of the bribes. Although the captivating and apparently contrite Mrs Clarke pleaded guilty and claimed before the House that the Duke had been her accomplice, the relevant colonels and civil servants testified over and over again that, in those cases where her clients had indeed received subsequent promotion, no undue inflence had been exerted by anyone. Eventually, after a hearing that lasted seven weeks, the majority of the House found that Mrs Clarke had been acting on her own, defrauding a seemingly endless supply of gullible and not entirely honourable officers. The Duke was acquitted. But since the Whigs, who composed over forty per cent of the House, had voted against him, he felt honour-bound to resign. When Palmerston took office as Secretary at War, the Commander-in-Chief was not the reforming Royal Duke but the 74-year-old author of the army's drill books, General Sir David Dundas.

It was in his dealings with Dundas that Palmerston at last revealed some of his less restrained characteristics. In Parliament, in public and even in private the new Secretary at War was still much closer to the unassuming student he had been in Edinburgh than he was to the flippant, high-handed Foreign Secretary he was to become. Lady Malmesbury was still convinced that his diffidence was hindering his capacity to debate. She conceded that he was successful when he had time to prepare. 'But where opinions are to be given & effect to be produced by spontaneous eloquence I doubt it. He is reserved & so very cautious, so singularly so for a young man, so afraid of committing himself even in common life & conversation with his most intimate friends, that it will throw a coldness & want of effect on such speeches of his.' But when he found himself in disagreement with the Commander-in-Chief, the new Secretary at War was mischievously resolute.

The discord between them began when Dundas asked Palmerston to sign a warrant appointing his father-in-law, General De Lancey, who was fourteen years his junior, as commissioner in charge of Chelsea Hospital. After consulting the general's record and discovering that the last time he had been in charge of public money he had been found guilty of putting too much of it into his own pocket, Palmerston referred the matter to the Prime Minister and the Prime Minister forbade the appointment.

Having lost round one, Dundas conceded round two. When Palmerston issued instructions preventing generals from drawing any further allowances for aides-de-camp who did not in fact exist, Dundas agreed that the dishonourable custom should be ended immediately, although he argued that the order should have come from him and not from the Secretary at War. Round three, however, was the one that grew into the longest and bitterest battle.

In 1810 Parliament passed an act requiring the tradesmen who supplied uniforms to the army to submit their bills directly to the War Office, where the costs could then be recovered in 'stoppages' from each man's pay. The purpose was to prevent another abuse, whereby the colonels of regiments had previously applied for clothing allowances which were calculated on the basis of their regiments being at full strength. Since this was seldom, if ever, the case, the colonels were able to buy uniforms for such men as they had mustered and then share what was left of the allowance with the supplier. When Palmerston issued a directive in pursuance of the new act, Dundas protested at his impertinence and demanded that the act be repealed. When the Prime Minister supported Palmerston, Dundas escalated the argument to a constitutional level by demanding a ruling as to whether the Commander-in-Chief was subordinate to the Secretary at War or the Secretary at War to the Commander-in-Chief.

Palmerston's immediate response was to swamp everyone with paperwork. After subjecting Dundas to the opening volleys of a learned and lengthy correspondence – a kind to which he was clearly unaccustomed – he warned the Prime Minister that Dundas was 'a little irritable and hasty in transacting business' and then sent him a 30,000-word memorandum, in which he recounted the history of his office and argued convincingly for its independence. While Perceval deliberated, the discord continued, even, sadly, after May 1811, when the entirely exonerated Duke of York was reinstated as Commander-in-Chief. At the beginning of the previous year the newspapers had revealed that, since well before the hearing in the House of Commons, the Whig Colonel Wardle had been keeping Mrs Clarke as his mistress, in a style that he could ill afford, and that he had cajoled her into making her confession and implicating the innocent duke in her swindles.

Reformer though he was, the duke was as eager as anyone to preserve the independence and, if possible, superiority of his office; and Palmerston was in no way deterred by the eminence of his new adversary. The Prime Minister was still required to make a ruling. For a while Perceval consulted others and the buck passed backwards and forwards between the Prime Minister, the Lord Chancellor and the Prince of Wales, who, as a result of the King's mental illness, was now acting on his behalf as Regent. Eventually, however, when nobody else was prepared to make a decision, Perceval ruled that the Secretary at War was not subordinate to the Commander-in-Chief. But he also recommended that he should consult him wherever appropriate and that, if the two disagreed, they should refer their disagreement to the Prime Minister and the Secretary of State for War and the Colonies. The compromise pleased nobody, least of all the Duke of York, and the most petty of all contemporary conflicts continued intermittently for years. Long after the guns in Europe had fallen silent and Napoleon had taken up residence in his last home on St Helena, the Commander-in-Chief was still letting off the occasional indignant salvo from Horse Guards and the Secretary at War was still sniping back merrily from the moral high ground in the War Office.

It was not long before Palmerston was equally unpopular with his own staff at the War Office. Where once almost all promotions had been earned through seniority, and where most replacements had been found among friends and relations, Palmerston made it clear that from now on all appointments would be made on the basis of merit alone. Unfortunately, however, the only capable men that he knew were also his friends. Most prominent among these were his Cambridge companions Laurence Sulivan and George Shee. When he took office he persuaded

Sulivan to abandon the Bar and become his private secretary. At the end of 1810 he appointed Shee to succeed the retiring Agent-General for Volunteers, and soon afterwards he promoted Sulivan to Junior Superintendent of Accounts.

In December 1811, as had long been expected, the now well-set-up Laurence Sulivan married Palmerston's sister Elizabeth at St George's, Hanover Square, in a ceremony performed by Lord Malmesbury's second son, the Revd the Hon. Alfred Harris. As always, Lady Minto dipped her pen in acid before reporting the event to her husband. 'I think Sulivan is in love with Harry, & as he cannot marry him takes Lilly.' Like Lady Malmesbury, she was a little disappointed that Lilly had not done better, although they both agreed that the groom was more likely to be marrying her for her modest dowry than her looks. In reality they were wrong. It was a love match. Lilly Sulivan died in 1837 at the age of only forty-six; and when her brother received the news in a note from her husband, the ink was blotched with tears.

The clerks at the War Office sneered at what they saw as their Secretary's hypocrisy, but they were roused to even greater indignation by his energy and the demands he made of them. They were affronted by the haughty memoranda reminding them that when he issued instructions he expected them to be carried out, they grumbled at their continually increasing workload and they resented his unpredictable, interfering punctiliousness. On one occasion, when a shipment of overcoats was one short, he even became personally involved in the dispatch of a single coat to Portugal. But this selective attention to detail was only his way of monitoring and ensuring the efficiency of his office. After all, there was a war on.

Far away in the Iberian peninsula, Wellington was performing one of the most formidable logistical feats in the history of the British army. He was advancing across Spain without being able to live off the land. The retreating French could plunder the Spaniards, but the British, who were their allies, could not. Until he conceived the master stroke of sending the navy to seize San Sebastian ahead of him and ordering his soldiers to fight their way through to their next shipment of provisions and ammunition, he had to rely on a long supply line stretching back almost 500 miles into Portugal. The chain of command that fed that line began on Palmerston's desk in the War Office, and while he drove his staff to keep it effective, he also drove them to redeem their earlier omissions. Within eight years of his taking office a Select Committee of the House of Commons found that the 40,000 accounts in arrears had been reduced to an 'inconsiderable' residue.

Palmerston was as energetic outside the the War Office as within it. In March 1811, when the death of the Duke of Grafton raised his son Euston to the House of Lords and created a parliamentary vacancy at Cambridge, Palmerston resigned as member for Newport and stood for the seat he had always wanted. Two years earlier the strongest possible opponent had been removed from the race when Henry Petty, who was by then leader of the opposition, had unexpectedly succeeded his half-brother as Marquess of Lansdowne. Despite his support for Catholic emancipation, an unpopular cause in Cambridge, Palmerston defeated his opponent, John Smyth, with a comfortable majority of over a hundred.

Two months later he moved house. He had raised a little extra capital with an increased mortgage on Broadlands and the sale of Temple Grove in 1808, after the Castlereaghs moved out; and in May he bought a lease on a house off Park Lane at 12 Stanhope Gate (then known as Stanhope Street). Two years later he moved again, buying the lease on number 9 and selling the lease on number 12 to his new parliamentary friend Robert Peel, the heir to England's largest cotton and calico fortune, who had arrived at Harrow the term after Palmerston left. In these houses he continued his frequent supper parties, and both here and in his many clubs he earned a new reputation as an enthusiastic, skilful and exasperatingly lucky billiards player.

Palmerston also found time to join with Canning, Sheridan and other less active statesmen and men of letters in establishing a new dining club, a society for the improvement of the English language, which met in each member's house in turn. By this time Sheridan was penniless. He had lost everything when his uninsured Theatre Royal in Drury Lane had burned down in 1809. On the very morning of the day when he was due to be host at the first dinner of the new society, bailiffs appeared at his lodgings to take away his furniture. But 'Sherry' had lost none of his Irish charm, at least when he was sober. When Palmerston, Canning and the other guests arrived, the furniture was still in place and the bailiffs had agreed to stay on and act as waiters. Many years later the essayist Abraham Hayward asked Palmerston if the society had in fact done anything to improve the English language. 'Not, certainly, at that dinner,' said Palmerston, 'for Sheridan got drunk, and a good many words of doubtful propriety were employed.'

Throughout the war with Napoleon the Secretary at War continued to appear regularly at the Wednesday night assemblies at Almack's, where several observers remarked on how often he was seen in the company of the popular Countess Lieven, the wife of the new Russian Ambassador, who arrived in London in 1812 and was invited soon afterwards to become a patroness. In later life, when her husband's promotion had made her a princess, 'Madame de Lieven' claimed that she and Palmerston had been lovers, but at one time or another she made the same claim about almost every eminent man in Europe, and in the many instances when it was true there was usually a large body of corroborating evidence.

More often than not Palmerston was seen in the company of the countess because her new intimate and fellow patroness Lady Cowper was there as well. Palmerston was always noticably attentive to Lady Cowper, and to her two younger children. When her first daughter was born in November 1810 and given her own name, Emily, there were few in their immediate circle who did not believe that Palmerston was the father; and when her second son was born in December 1811 and christened William, a Temple name, nobody doubted it.

Palmerston hunted and shot as often as he could, not only at Broadlands but also with friends; and on the many occasions when he stayed at Brocket, Lady Cowper usually came over with her children from Panshanger. Palmerston believed that 'every other abstinence will not make up for abstinence from exercise', but it was his passion for shooting that nearly cut short his career.

Even by the traditionalist standards of the time the game laws at the beginning of the nineteenth century were an anachronism. Passed in the mid-seventeenth century, and designed to protect game from being exterminated by the over-use of the latest fowling-pieces, these laws limited the right to shoot to the owners of large estates and their eldest sons. The result was that by the end of the eighteenth century poaching was not just the petty crime of a few starving farm labourers; it was a widespread, well-organized and highly lucrative black market. Almost all the plentiful game that found its way onto the tables of innkeepers, smallholders and rich but landless professionals and industrialists had been obtained illegally. To stem the flow large landowners resorted to desperate measures, and the worst of these were spring-guns, which were concealed in undergrowth and went off when their victims trod on a spring or nudged a wire. Since the spring-guns were often forgotten and their locations seldom recorded, they were as much a menace to landowners as to poachers. One day in 1810, while shooting on a friend's estate in Essex with William and Lady Caroline Lamb, Palmerston nudged a wire. Fortunately, as often happened when black powder was left to lie in the dew, the gun failed to fire. But Palmerston was shaken and for a while thereafter was noticeably nervous when he walked through undergrowth.

The Prime Minister was not so lucky. On 11 May 1812, while walking into the House of Commons, Spencer Perceval was killed by a single shot from the pistol of a Liverpool agent called John Bellingham. The assassin, who was hanged for it, had lost his wits after being bankrupted in the recession caused by Napoleon's blockade.

Despite the recession and the other deprivations of war, Perceval had been a popular Prime Minister. He had been straightforward with his colleagues; he had always been admirably composed in the Commons and in the still bickering Cabinet; and yet he had been wily and ruthless when he needed to be. Two months before his assassination, when Wellesley had resigned, ostensibly in protest at the plotting of his colleagues but probably in the hope of creating a crisis and making his own bid for the premiership, Perceval had made no effort to dissuade him and instead had calmly grasped the opportunity to replace him with a better man and brought back Castlereagh.

In June 1812, after others, including Wellesley, had failed to form a government, the compromise candidate, the Secretary of State for War and the Colonies, Lord Liverpool, kissed hands with the Prince Regent and took over. Liverpool did not make many changes. While Eldon and

Castlereagh continued as Lord Chancellor and Foreign Secretary, a few other Cabinet ministers moved from one office to another and Nicholas Vansittart, another of Liverpool's friends from Christ Church, courageously agreed to take on the Exchequer. One of the few who joined the Cabinet for the first time was Frederick Robinson, Palmerston's form-mate at Harrow, who soon afterwards left the Admiralty to become Vice-President of the Board of Trade. For Palmerston, however, the only office that Liverpool could offer was Chief Secretary for Ireland. For his own replacement as Secretary of State for War and the Colonies he had chosen another old friend, Lord Bathurst.

In some ways the offer of Secretary for Ireland was a promotion, although it was not accompanied by a seat in the Cabinet, but in a world at war it seemed like a sideline. Palmerston turned it down on the grounds of 'particular circumstances and considerations', and the office was given instead to Robert Peel. Since Peel rose rapidly, it is easy to imagine Palmerston looking back in later life and regretting the refusal, just as he may have regretted refusing the Exchequer. But in reality, this time it would have made no difference. For Palmerston at least, Liverpool also saw Ireland as a sideline.

Palmerston deserved better. He was now acknowledged to be a conscientious and effective Secretary at War. He had earned the right to promotion, and the few obvious excuses for withholding it were hardly substantial enough to be taken seriously. During the last three years, as he grew in confidence with experience and success, he had also shed his diffident shell and developed an increasingly jaunty manner. Just as the young ladies at Almack's had once mistaken his diffidence for pomposity, so now Lords Eldon and Bathurst, who had more influence than most over Liverpool, mistook the new jaunty manner for an inappropriate lack of ministerial *gravitas*. Palmerston may also have raised a few eyebrows by poking fun at some of his colleagues in the articles and verses that he wrote for a Tory newspaper, *The Courier*, most of which were 'radical' enough to be republished a few years later by John Murray in *The New Whig Guide*. But the new manner did nothing to invalidate his achievements at the War Office, and it would have been childish to regard his tame contributions to *The Courier* as some sort of sedition, particularly when similar contributions were being made by men with impeccable Tory credentials such as Robert Peel and the Irish literary critic John Wilson Croker.

In other circumstances a more significant reason for keeping Palmerston out of the Cabinet might have been his support for Catholic emancipation, to which Liverpool was strongly opposed. As always, Palmerston's opinions were practical rather than ideological. When the subject was eventually debated in the House in 1813, he simply argued that it was a waste of human resources to reject the services of able men on no better ground than their religion. 'If it had unfortunately happened,' he said, 'that by the circumstances of birth and education, a Nelson, a Wellington, a Burke, a Fox or a Pitt had belonged to this class of the community, of what honour and of what glory might not the page of British history have been deprived?' But Palmerston was not alone. Several leading Tories agreed with him, including Castlereagh. Liverpool would never have been able to form a competent government if support for this cause had been a bar to membership. In assembling his Cabinet he conceded that Catholic emancipation would always be an open question, on which ministers would be free to vote in accordance with their consciences.

The real reason why Palmerston was denied a seat in the Cabinet was less obvious and more personal. Liverpool was wary of him. Having served until recently as Secretary of State for War, Liverpool was the one man in his Cabinet with personal experience of working with Palmerston. He had more than once been called upon to mediate between the impudent young Secretary and the exasperated Commander-in-Chief. He was aware of the capacity for criticism and contempt that lay close to the surface beneath the charm; and he was beginning to suspect that Palmerston was too much of an individualist to be a tractable ally in Cabinet. He may even have offered Ireland in the hope of pleasing the Duke of York, and through him the Prince Regent, by moving Palmerston away from the War Office.

So Palmerston stayed at his old desk and served on loyally. The only occasion on which he spoke in the House about anything other than military matters was in the debate on Catholic emancipation. Time passed. In 1814 the fighting in Europe ended and the last remnants of Napoleon's blockade were lifted. Travel and transport were again as easy as they had been at the beginning of the century. Lord Minto, who had held off Napoleon's influence in India and extended Britain's in the process, came home and died soon afterwards. Willy Temple, who had always wanted a career in the diplomatic corps, left to join the British legation in Stockholm and spent most of the rest of his life living abroad and drinking.

In March 1815 Frederick Robinson introduced the 'corn law'. Designed to protect British farmers from being undercut by cheap European grain, the new law prohibited the import of corn until the price on the home market had risen to 80s. a quarter. Since the home price had already been inflated by the long blockade, the immediate result was a riot, in which Robinson's London house was attacked. By then, however, Napoleon had escaped from exile on Elba. Europe was at war again.

On 21 June Palmerston rose in the House to attempt yet another defence of flogging. This time the attack came from Henry Bennet, who called the practice a national disgrace and cited an incident in the Peninsula in which sixty-three men in the Prince of Wales' own regiment, the 10th Hussars, had been sentenced to 14,000 lashes between them. If the lashes were evenly divided, they were within the recently set limit of 300 per man. All that Palmerston could do was to divert the Tory majority from the Whigs' righteous indignation by telling them that the compassionate Commander-in-Chief had now ruled that, where a sentence had been suspended by a colonel or a medical officer, it could only be resumed in the gravest cases.

Ironically, that very evening a dusty chaise and four raced into London from Broadstairs carrying a naval officer, Captain James White of HMS *Peruvian*, an army staff officer, Major the Hon. Henry Percy of the 14th Light Dragoons, two French Eagles, those of the 45th and 105th Regiments, and a despatch from Wellington to the Prince Regent reporting that, three days earlier, on the sloping farmlands of Hougoumont and La Haye Sainte, at a horrifying cost in allied lives, Napoleon had been conclusively defeated. This time the war really was over.

In the course of the next month Palmerston made three proposals which, unusually, were accepted with enthusiasm by the Duke of York and the Prime Minister. The first was that, in estimating the increases in a soldier's pay or pension, his presence on that terrible day should count as an additional two years' service. The second was that, in commemoration of the victory, the pensions paid to officers in respect of wounds should be raised each time the officer was promoted and not, as before, remain at the amount due to the rank that he held when he was wounded. And the third was simply that the men who had fought in the battle should thereafter be entered on the payrolls of their regiments as 'Waterloo men'.

In August, when Parliament rose, Palmerston went off to occupied Paris to congratulate Wellington and visit the allied armies. He had played his part in their victory. Surely now he had earned his right to preferment. The Prime Minister and some of the 'old guard' might still have reservations, but he had won the support and respect of many others on both sides of the House, and many outside it as well. He had even been singled out for success by the man whose opinion was valued above all others in London society, Beau Brummell.

One evening Palmerston went on from a ball at Lady Castlereagh's to a small gathering at the house of London's leading courtesan, Harriette Wilson, where the elegant Mr Brummell, who had once been a captain in the Prince Regent's precious 'China Tenth', was one of the company. Brummell's father had been private secretary to the Prime Minister and had sent his sons to Eton and Oxford, but it was an essential part of the dandy's self-mocking nihilism to pretend that he had been nothing but a servant. In the course of one of the snobbish conversations common in such a house, Miss Wilson, the daughter of a shopkeeper, teased Brummell knowingly by announcing that she was in favour of 'cutting all the grocers and valets who intrude themselves into good society'. The famous answer, which is seldom quoted in full, was made just as Palmerston entered the room. 'My father was a very superior valet and kept his place all his life,' said Beau Brummell, 'and that is more than Palmerston will do.'

4. $\mathcal{L}$ORD PUMICESTONE

In the summer of 1816, almost exactly a year after the Battle of Waterloo, Henry Brougham seduced George Lamb's wife, Caroline. 'Caro George', as she was known in the family, was not the first Caroline to make a cuckold of a Lamb. By then all London had been shocked and delighted in equal measure by the vaunting, spectacular liaison between capricious Lady Caroline – 'Caro William' – and Lord Byron. But most members of the family were much more cross about 'Caro George's' affair with Brougham. The blind admiration which they shared with almost everyone for the romantic author of *Childe Harold* was more than matched by their amused contempt for eager, animated Brougham, whose features had once been described by Lady Cowper as 'a fright'. And anyway, spoilt, wilful 'Caro William' could take care of herself; quiet and impressionable 'Caro George' could not. When 'Caro George' left England to keep an assignation with her lover in Geneva, Lady Cowper quickly persuaded her husband to take her on a tour of Switzerland and set out with the declared intention of finding 'Caro George' and bringing her home.

At the end of August, when he heard that the Cowpers had gone, Lord Palmerston was overwhelmed with jealousy and decided to follow them. There was no immediately obvious reason for his passion. The last few months had certainly been trying, tiring and depressing. In the spring, when he presented his first post-war army estimates, the opposition had no longer felt constrained to give them an easy passage and several members, particularly Henry Brougham, had made him argue over every penny. At the beginning of July he had been one of the hundreds of fashionable but genuinely melancholy mourners who had followed Sheridan's coffin from Drury Lane to Westminster Abbey. But so far Lady Cowper had contributed very little to his troubles. His only known rival for her affections had been her husband, who, surprisingly but in almost everyone's opinion undoubtedly, was the father of the boy she had borne at the beginning of June.

Perhaps Palmerston suspected that Lady Cowper's marriage was mending and was afraid that it might recover completely among the lakes and mountains, or perhaps, knowing her as he did, he was afraid she might find a more exciting lover on her travels. But it is also possible that his jealousy and fear were induced by a guilty conscience. What he was already doing to Lady Cowper could also be done to him. For the last two years he had been conducting an affair with 'Mrs' Emma Murray, a one-time actress who, it was said, was the daughter of an innkeeper in Hereford. In January 1816 she had borne a son, Henry John Temple Murray, and soon afterwards Palmerston had burdened himself with another lease and set her up at 122 Piccadilly.

With the long war over at last, almost everyone who could afford it was touring in Europe. At the end of August Lady Malmesbury and Palmerston's sister Fanny were in Paris, where he had earlier arranged to meet them and travel on with them to Geneva. When he was a few days overdue, however, they received a message telling them that he had changed his plans and was already on his way to Geneva via Lyons. Setting out on their own, the two ladies now became the last starters in a comical, disjointed relay race. When they reached Lyons, they found that Palmerston had already passed through. But when they reached Geneva, they learned from Lady Minto, who had taken a villa there, that he had not yet arrived.

Fanny and Lady Malmesbury never did manage to catch up with Palmerston. After waiting in vain for a few days in Geneva, they returned to England, where Lady Malmesbury eventually received a letter from Lady Minto saying that, shortly after their departure, she had seen Palmerston and Lady Cowper being very attentive to each other at an assembly.

On his way to Geneva, Palmerston had somehow found out that Brougham and 'Caro George' had gone on to Italy. Assuming that the

Cowpers were in pursuit, he had turned south himself. It was only after he had at last caught up with the runaway lovers in Milan that he discovered they were not being followed at all. Lady Cowper had found so many friends in Geneva that she had abandoned her mission and stayed on to enjoy herself.

In October, after spending only three happy days in Geneva, Palmerston returned reassured to his desk at the War Office, while Lady Cowper went south with her husband and friends to spend the rest of the winter in Italy. Two months later the runaway lovers parted in Rome and came home separately; and at the beginning of the summer the Cowpers came back, followed very shortly afterwards by large, loud, overdressed and ceremonious Antonio, Marchese di San Giuliano.

More of a Scaramouche than a marquess, Lady Cowper's latest conquest was known simply as 'Count' Giuliano. It was said that he had been orphaned in the first year of his life, when his father shot his mother and then fled to north Africa, and it was also said that he was no longer able to return to his native Naples because he had worked for the French during their recent occupation of it. If the mysterious count had not already become Lady Cowper's lover in Italy, he lost no time in doing so after his arrival in England.

Over the next four years the prettiest patroness of Almack's divided most but not all of her affections between Giuliano and Palmerston. There were tensions between rivals in public and heated arguments between lovers in private. From one Wednesday night assembly to the next all the ton waited eagerly to see which lover was in favour. Friends and relations took sides. In April 1818, as she lay on her deathbed, Lady Melbourne pleaded with her daughter to stay faithful, not to her husband but to the worthiest of her lovers, Palmerston. On 18 May, still saddened by her mother's death and still shaken by an attempt to assassinate Palmerston, which had taken place only two days later, Lady Cowper miscarried somebody's son. Palmerston recorded the event briefly in his diary. 'Premature confinement at 6 this morning at Brighton. Figlio Morto.' If he had not used Italian regularly as a shorthand, its use on this occasion might have been more significant.

Like Perceval's successful assassin, Palmerston's assailant was a madman, David Davies. He had once been commissioned into the 62nd Foot, the Wiltshire Regiment, but he was too unstable to hold his lieutenancy for long. In 1816, when the regiment retired him on half-pay after only two years' service, he began to write to Palmerston complaining about his treatment and demanding an interview. Soon afterwards he was admitted to an army hospital, where he managed to perform a successful amputation of his own penis. After that Palmerston arranged for his family to take him away and commit him to an institution. But the letters continued; the lunatic escaped; and on 8 April 1818 he went to the War Office with a pistol that he had bought from a pawnbroker and waited at the bottom of the stairs leading up to Palmerston's office.

When Palmerston rushed in, jaunty as ever, Davies stepped out, put the pistol to his back and fired. Fortunately, Palmerston was in the habit of leaping up the stairs. He was already turning the first corner when Davies pulled the trigger. Instead of the hole that would surely have killed him, his only wounds were a burn from the blast and a bruise from the ball as it passed through his coat. Believing that he had succeeded, the grinning assassin made no effort to avoid capture and was led away shouting triumphantly, 'I have killed him'. Despite what had happened, Palmerston felt so sorry for him that when he heard there were no funds for his defence he sent money to the prison chaplain and paid for it himself. But the outcome of the trial was hardly in doubt. Davies was much too mad to hang and was sentenced instead to be detained securely in Bedlam during His Majesty's pleasure.

Palmerston was back at his desk three days after the attack. But the responsibilities of his office were not as demanding as they had been during the war, and the Prime Minister had not yet seen fit to find him any other responsibilities. He had time for a busy social life, time for sport, time for improvement schemes in Ireland and time for Broadlands. The beloved estate in Hampshire was his one tranquil refuge from society and politics. The sums that he spent in Ireland were investments: by improving the conditions of his tenants, he also increased their productivity and therefore his own income. But the money that he spent at Broadlands, mostly on horses, game and the gardens, was spent purely for pleasure. It was from Broadlands that he began his long, enthusiastic association with the turf. His first filly, Mignonette, ran unplaced in her first race at nearby Winchester in 1815, in colours that by happy coincidence were later to be the colours of the Irish Republic: green shirt, white breeches and orange cap.

Palmerston was also a generous patron of local charities in Hampshire – he founded and maintained a school for the poor and made large dona-tions to several churches, although he rarely attended any of them – and by the standards of the time he was a good landlord and employer. He was slow to evict anyone who was late with a rent; he provided houses and pensions for retired servants; and he was so preoccupied with other interests that it was a long time before he noticed that his kitchen staff were allowing local tradesmen to overcharge him in return for a share of the added profit. Many of the residents of Romsey told stories of his kindness and his concern for the sick, but there were also a couple of episodes on the estate from which his opponents and critics were able to spin less creditable stories.

The first concerned the death of a dog. One day when he was out shooting with his gamekeeper, Palmerston jumped over a hedge into the garden of a local brickmaker and surprised his sleeping bulldog, which sprang at him. Palmerston leaped back across the hedge, but the dog followed him. When he turned on the other side and saw the guard dog snarling at him with its paws on top of the hedge, he raised his gun and shot it.

Under the game laws a landlord with shooting rights was entitled to follow his quarry onto another man's land, and it was reasonable for Palmerston to believe that the dog, which was after all a bulldog not a spaniel, was about to attack him. But his Radical Whig opponents made the most of the brickmaker's sad little daughter, who nursed her 'pet' for several days in vain, and they represented Palmerston's actions as the typical thoughtless arrogance of a Tory landlord.

The second, more serious episode, involved the conviction of a local poacher. The young poacher, Charles Smith, was on Palmerston's land one evening with his brother-in-law when one of their shots attracted the attention of seventeen-year-old Robert Snelgrove, whom Palmerston had just engaged as an assistant gamekeeper. Soon afterwards, as the two poachers stepped out of a copse in the moonlight, they came face to face with Snelgrove. Snelgrove seized Smith's brother-in-law, but, while the two were struggling, Smith took careful aim at Snelgrove's thigh and fired, causing a wound that left him limping for the rest of his mercifully long life. Leaving the bleeding boy to crawl home, the two poachers made good their escape, and soon afterwards Smith left the district. It was not until many months later that he was apprehended in Southampton, where he had joined a well-known gang of professional poachers.

At Smith's trial in Winchester the prosecution did not suggest that the shooting was attempted murder. Nevertheless, under Lord Ellenborough's act, which was one of the many harsh laws passed by successive governments in a vain attempt to suppress poaching, the judge had a discretion to impose the death penalty on a poacher who wounded a gamekeeper with malicious intent. When the jury convicted Smith, the circuit judge exercised his discretion and sentenced him to death.

The news of the sentence came as a shock to Smith's former neighbours around Broadlands, most of whom regarded him as no more than an amiable rogue. They approached the Mayor of Romsey and through him petitioned Palmerston for help. Palmerston wrote to the circuit judge, who was now in Salisbury, diplomatically acknowledging the justice of the sentence but asking very respectfully if it might not be possible in the circumstances to commute it to transportation for life. When that failed, he wrote in similar terms to the Home Secretary. When that also failed, Smith was duly hanged.

Palmerston had done as much as he could. As he pointed out in a long letter to the Mayor, the presumption that the verdict of a jury and the sentence of a judge could be overturned through 'private Influence' alone was one of the 'great abuses' that had been 'provided against by the Bill of Rights'. But the Radical Whigs, who were campaigning to repeal the game laws and all the oppressive criminal acts that enforced them, attacked him for not doing more. They questioned his sincerity in Parliament, suggesting that his appeals had only been cynical gestures, and once again they represented him to the public at large as just another effete, callous nobleman who valued his right to kill a few birds higher than a human life.

Similarly, but with a bit more justification, the Radical Whigs attacked him regularly in Parliament for continuing to defend the practice of flogging in the army; and to add to his discomfort their number now included several soldiers, among whom one of the most prominent was the devious and headstrong Sir Robert Wilson, Canning's former agent on the Baltic, whose chequered career had since brought him to the rank of Major-General and a seat in Parliament representing Southwark. In this case, however, Palmerston had no choice. Within the War Office he made several unsuccessful attempts to have the maximum number of lashes reduced and limit the punishment to habitual offenders, but before the House of Commons it was his duty as Secretary at War to defend the policies of the Commander-in-Chief – although in doing so his summaries of all the arguments in favour of flogging and against it were usually so dull and even-handed that it is easy to agree with one of the government's military supporters, Quartermaster-General Sir Henry Hardinge, who described Palmerston's defence with some fury as 'lax'.

In other debates there was never any doubt about Palmerston's affection and respect for men whom he extolled at every opportunity. After watching a review of allied armies in France he compared the British with the Prussians and Russians in his journal. 'The foreign troops look like figures cut out of card, ours like a collection of living men ... In short, one marks a character of individual energy about our people which one does not see in theirs.'

Palmerston's efforts to improve the conditions of these 'people' brought him into conflict with Parliament and sections of the army every bit as often as his half-hearted commitment to corporal punishment. On one occasion, when he proposed the provision of support and facilities for Sir William Adams, the Prince Regent's oculist, he was opposed and obstructed by every medical officer in the army as well as every MP they could persuade to listen to them, including the Prime Minister.

Adams claimed to have developed a surgical procedure for curing Egyptian ophthalmia, an infectious disease that had become widespread among British soldiers during the recent war and which had left many of them blinded by the growths that it produced on the inside of their eyelids. But the army doctors argued that the civilian and undeniably self-important Sir William was a charlatan and that Palmerston had been duped by him. This, however, was one of the occasions when Palmerston and the Duke of York worked together. With the help of the Prince Regent they enabled Adams to demonstrate his procedure successfully on a group of volunteer pensioners from Chelsea Hospital. Armed with this evidence, Palmerston at last convinced a sceptical House of Commons to give Adams the funds to train a team of surgeons and put them to work, and as always his argument was practical. He pointed out that Adams was not working for any remuneration, and that the modest cost would soon lead to a huge saving, partly because it would prevent the disease from spreading from the army into the rest of the community, and partly because every patient cured was one less disability pension. Eventually, in July 1821, when Adams and his surgeons had completed their task, Palmerston had less trouble in persuading Parliament to vote him a gratuity of £4,000.

In peace as in war, the Secretary at War spoke seldom in Parliament on matters that did not concern his own office. During the half-dozen repressive years that followed the Battle of Waterloo, at least in the House of Commons, Palmerston sat back in loyal but increasingly scornful silence while the government struggled to cure the ailing economy and quell the widespread unrest that resulted.

After the war the recession induced by the blockade developed into a full-scale slump, which affected almost everyone. Those who suffered least were the largest landowners, who lived off rents and were protected by the corn law. Those who suffered most were manufacturers and the men who once worked for them. Exports to allies declined and the government discontinued its huge annual orders for ammunition, guns, uniforms and supplies. Customers were scarce, jobs were few, wages were low and the price of bread was disproportionately high. In the first few months after Napoleon's downfall the new industrialists and their workforce were united in their indignation. But the middle classes were mollified in 1816, when Brougham led the assault on income tax and succeeded in winning its abolition by the narrow margin of 238 votes to 231.

The result was not quite as Brougham and the Whigs had hoped, however. The government made up for the loss of revenue by imposing duty on such everyday goods as tea, sugar, soap, paper, candles, beer and tobacco, which, for the poor at least, turned necessities and simple pleasures into inaccessible luxuries. Since most of this new tax was used to pay political salaries or interest to fundholders for the national debt, it was said by the Radicals that the 'tax-paying poor' were supporting the 'tax-eating rich'.

Nevertheless, when Lord Liverpool called a general election in 1818, his Tories were returned with an undiminished majority; and he knew for several reasons that they would be. The opposition was divided. A better than usual harvest and a slight upturn in trade had misled many into thinking that the economy was on the mend. The enfranchised few – rich rural freeholders and burghers – were more than willing to give another term to the party that had introduced the corn law and agreed to abolish income tax; and the angry, hungry, underpaid or unemployed bulk of the population did not have the vote.

With no effective voices in Parliament, the poor found them instead in populist orators and pamphleteers such as Henry Hunt and William Cobbett. 'Orator' Hunt, the conceited and frenetic son of a rich Wiltshire farmer, took great delight in stirring up his audiences with invective and slogans. Before the election, when one of his meetings in London led to rioting and looting, the anxious government responded with the 'Gagging Acts', forbidding all public meetings without a licence from a magistrate, increasing the prison sentences for sedition and suspending the Habeas Corpus Act, which enabled it to imprison agitators without charging them. Although the government felt confident enough to restore Habeas Corpus after the election, the economy did not improve. The good harvest was followed by a bad one and the textile industry slumped lower than ever. On 16 August 1819 a crowd of around 60,000, many of them weavers and their families, assembled at St Peter's Fields, Manchester, to hear Hunt demand higher wages, repeal of the corn law and 'universal suffrage – or nothing'. Fearing another riot, the local magistrates called out the yeomanry and ordered them to arrest Hunt and disperse the crowd, which they did with such incompetent enthusiasm that they killed nine men and two women and injured another 400.

The volunteer yeomanry regiments were mostly composed of Tory landowners and farmers. Unlike the regular cavalry regiments, some of which had handled similar situations more effectively and less brutally, they came under the control of the Home Office, not the War Office, which was why the apprehensive Home Secretary had been able to have them standing by. But the horrified nation did not differentiate between uniforms. The grateful respect that the army had enjoyed since the defeat of Napoleon was destroyed in an instant; and as they did at every other opportunity, the Radical propagandists made the most of the dreadful image of British soldiers swinging their sabres at British subjects. Within days 'the Manchester massacre' at St Peter's Fields had become 'the Battle of Peterloo'.

Subscriptions were raised throughout England for the families of victims. The Lord Mayor and Common Council of the City of London condemned the Manchester authorities for their 'unprovoked and intemperate conduct'. In Parliament the indignant opposition argued that the only way to prevent further disorder was to extend the franchise and give the discontents a voice. But Liverpool and his Cabinet insisted that the Radical movement was a conspiracy to undermine the constitution. Instead of compromising, they attempted to suppress the movement with the notorious 'Six Acts', some of which, in their hurridly drafted provisions, revealed the extent of the government's anxiety. One forbade unauthorized military training. Another prohibited public meetings of more than fifty people. Another put all pamphlets beyond the pockets of the literate poor by subjecting them to the tax of 4d. per copy which had already been imposed on newspapers.

In opposing the acts Lord Holland warned that the prohibition of public meetings would only lead to 'secret cabals and conspiracies', and within a matter of months he was proved right. In February 1820 one of the many informers whom the Home Secretary, Lord Sidmouth, had planted among the Radicals warned him that a group was planning to assassinate the entire Cabinet while it was dining with Lord Harrowby. The conspirators were surprised and arrested by Bow Street Runners as they assembled in a stable in Cato Street; and after the swift trial for which the Six Acts provided, five of them were hanged and the other five were transported for life to Australia.

If the 'Cato Street Conspiracy' had succeeded, it would probably have been the only event that could have created a seat in the Cabinet for Palmerston. Two years before the election Liverpool had strengthened his Cabinet considerably by persuading Canning to return to it as President of the India Board, and immediately after it he had increased the military representation by bringing in the Duke of Wellington as Master-General of the Ordnance. But there was still no promotion for the Secretary at War; and it has to be admitted that by now Palmerston was hardly behaving in a way that was likely to lead to it.

The relationship between Palmerston and the Duke of York had not improved. Both men attempted to make it more amicable. Now and then the duke invited Palmerston to dine with him in London; and Palmerston occasionally invited the duke to stay with him at Broadlands. When they agreed, they also worked well together, as they did in the elimination of Egyptian ophthalmia. There were even times when Palmerston was a staunch and energetic ally. He fought long and hard for the funding that saved the duke's Academy for Officers from closing and moved it from High Wycombe to larger and more permanent quarters at Sandhurst. But the duke was still being reduced to regular fits of impotent rage because Palmerston persisted in issuing what the duke regarded as military instructions without his authority.

There were many occasions when the duke had very little justification for his rage, such as when Palmerston instituted checks to prevent his officers from claiming fodder allowances for horses that did not exist. Nevertheless, when Palmerston sent direct instructions to commanding officers, it was at best tactless not to consult the Commander-in-Chief first, particularly after the previous Prime Minister had asked him to do so. Each time he did it, the duke sent him a haughty letter demanding to know why he had not been asked to authorize the instructions; and each time Palmerston simply passed the letter on to the embarrassed Prime Minister, who was again obliged to mediate and restore some semblance of harmony between them.

Eventually the duke became so furious that he actually attempted to sever all direct connections between the army and the War Office. At the beginning of 1823, after the responsibility for managing barracks had been transferred from the War Office to the Board of Ordnance, Palmerston, quite reasonably, sent a circular to all the commanders of overseas bases asking them to lay off all the War Office clerks who were no longer needed. When he received the usual notification of the circular, the duke lost all sense of proportion and ordered all commanding officers to ignore all future instructions from the War Office unless they were sent to them from the Horse Guards. As usual, the Prime Minister was called upon to arbitrate and in the end, after a more than usual degree of grovelling, he managed to calm the duke down and persuaded him to withdraw his order.

Although it was not known at the time, however, the man who did most to keep the peace between the War Office and the Horse Guards was not the Prime Minister but the Commander-in-Chief's military secretary, Sir Herbert Taylor. Many years later Sir Herbert admitted that some of Palmerston's letters and memoranda were so offensive that he never showed them to the duke.

Palmerston made no secret of his contempt for the Duke of York. When passing on one of the duke's protests to the Prime Minister, he attached a heavily ironic covering letter, in which he pretended to excuse 'the general tone of the duke's letter' by saying, 'I always impute any roughness of expression in his official letters to the want of epistolary dexterity on the part of those who frame them for him, rather than any disposition on his part to take an undue advantage of his personal Rank'. On another occasion he wrote to Peel after the two had successfully cut down the cost of maintaining garrisons in Ireland. 'The Irish Government have behaved very handsomely to us about reductions; for which however the D. of York does not thank them.' But the duke was by no means Palmerston's only victim. He was equally scathing in his correspondence about several senior members of the government.

In one letter, written to his brother from Ireland, he mocked them all simultaneously for their opposition to Catholic emancipation, and at the same time expressed his bewilderment at how anyone he respected could agree with them.

> I can forgive old women like the Chancellor, spoonies like Liverpool, ignoramuses like Westmorland, old stumped-up Tories like Bathurst; but how such a man as Peel, liberal, enlightened, and fresh minded, should find himself running in such a pack is hardly intelligible. I think he must in his heart regret those early pledges and youthful prejudices which have committed him to opinions so different from the comprehensive and statesman-like views which he takes of public affairs ... It is strange that in this enlightened age and enlightened country people should be still debating whether it is wise to convert four or five millions of men from enemies to friends, and whether it is safe to give peace to Ireland.

Palmerston had become exasperated by the mediocrity of most of his senior colleagues and frustrated by his own lack of preferment; and by now his busy but complicated private life was equally unfulfilling and baffling. In 1820 Lady Cowper had borne him another child, christened Frances Elizabeth after his sisters, but she was still sharing her affections, not only with Count Giuliano but also with two much younger lovers, first the witty little Earl of Clanwilliam, who was Castlereagh's private secretary at the Foreign Office, and now a tall, dark and famously handsome officer in the Life Guards, Lord Francis Conyngham, whose mother was the new King's latest mistress. On many, if not most, of his evenings in London, Palmerston had no choice but to seek solace elsewhere, usually with Emma Murray at their house in Piccadilly or with beautiful Eliza Blackburn, whose busy barrister husband had been at Harrow and St John's with him.

Palmerston was thwarted in the two aspects of his life that mattered most to him, and his impatience and resentment were evident everywhere, not just in the comparative privacy of his correspondence.

Within half a dozen years of the victory at Waterloo, 'Lord Cupid' had earned himself a new nickname – 'Lord Pumicestone'. In the conduct of daily business at the War Office his jauntiness had evolved into reckless, disparaging flippancy. At Almack's his famous charm was all too often replaced by an acerbic 'put-down' or a 'cut'. In the House of Commons there was usually a bitter edge to his banter in debate; and the antipathy that this aroused among the members of the opposition came to a head in February 1822, when Parliament debated the fate of Sir Robert Wilson MP, whose conduct at the funeral of Queen Caroline had cost him his commission.

Caroline of Brunswick had always been an embarrassment to her husband. Ever since they set up separate households, after the birth of their daughter Princess Charlotte in 1796, her way of life had been even less edifying than his. But it was the Princess of Wales who had retained the sympathy of the public at large. In 1806, when the Prince rashly invited a committee of the Privy Council to investigate her morals, she wrote a long letter in her defence to the King and then leaked it to the press, ensuring that only her side of the story was common knowledge. After she went to live abroad, in 1814, there were endless, entertaining reports and rumours about her scandalous indiscretions. She had made love in a coach and danced half-naked with her servants. While crossing the Mediterranean on a hot summer's night, she had slept openly with a lover in a tent on deck and later shared a bath with him in her cabin. But the reports and rumours only circulated at court and in 'society'. To the British people she remained the wronged and rejected wife of an increasingly unpopular prince; and in November 1817 their misplaced sympathy and ignorant affection were heightened when Princess Charlotte, who had married Prince Leopold of Saxe-Coburg only seventeen months earlier, died giving birth to a stillborn son. 'It really was', wrote Brougham, 'as though every household throughout Great Britain had lost a favourite child.'

In 1820, after the death of King George III, Princess Caroline decided to return to England and take her place beside her husband on the throne. Fat, fifty-two and foolishly dressed in clothes that were far too young for her, she landed at Dover on 5 June and was cheered all the way to London by well-organized Radical mobs. But King George IV was determined that she should not be his Queen. He ordered his government to get rid of her somehow and threatened to dismiss it if it did not. Only Canning had the sense to see that the government could not possibly emerge from such an episode with dignity. After resigning again from the Cabinet, he took his family to Italy to avoid what he hoped would not be a revolution.

Since the King could not divorce the Queen in one of his own law courts, the government set out to achieve the same end with an Act of Parliament. But when the bill nearly failed in the Lords, Liverpool abandoned it rather than risk a defeat in the Commons. As the news spread, huge crowds assembled in the streets chanting 'God save the Queen'. Her Majesty's popularity had never been higher. It plunged suddenly in the following year, when she made an undignified and unsuccessful attempt to defy the King's orders and force her way into Westminster Abbey to attend his coronation. But a swelling current of sentimentality lifted it again less than three weeks later, when she died of cancer from which she had clearly been suffering for some time.

The King, who was by then on his way to Ireland for his first state visit, saw no reason to turn back and left all the arrangements to his government. Fortunately the Queen had asked to be buried in her native Brunswick, so there was no need for a service or an interment, both of which would have presented the most revolutionary Radicals with perfect opportunities for rabble-rousing and rioting. All that was required was to transport the coffin with appropriate ceremony to Harwich, where a frigate was waiting. Unfortunately, however, the direct road to Harwich from the Queen's house in Hammersmith lay through the City of London, where the Lord Mayor and Common Council, who were as radical as their mob, had declared their intention to meet the cortège and pay their respects at Temple Bar.

Without the benefit of any practical advice from the Duke of Wellington, who was in Paris at the time, and who said afterwards that he would simply have kept order by lining the route with soldiers, the government decided to avoid the city altogether and send the cortège round the north of it. On the appointed day, 14 August, the procession set out through Kensington, escorted by only a squadron each from the Life Guards and the Royal Horse Guards. When it was prevented by barricades from turning north up Kensington Church Street, Canning's former agent, Major-General Sir Robert Wilson, who was provocatively riding at the rear with Brougham and several other Whig and Radical MPs, rode forward, warned the two captains in command that they were likely to meet barricades all the way and suggested that it would be better to ignore their orders and lead the cortège through the City. But the captains continued on their appointed route, forced their way through a mob with the flats of their sword blades, and reached the northern end of Park Lane, where their entrance to the Edgware Road was also blocked by an even bigger barricade and a much uglier mob.

While the Horse Guards remained around the hearse, the Life Guards attempted to dismantle the barricade, bombarded all the while with stones and pieces of torn-up railings. After several of them had been unhorsed, they drew their pistols; and regrettably not quite all of them fired in the air. A carpenter fell dead and a bricklayer fell mortally wounded. Hearing the shots, Wilson cantered forward again and demanded to know who had given the order to fire. On learning from the troopers, who knew who he was, that there had been no such order, he implicitly assumed command and shamed them into putting up their pistols by yelling that it was disgraceful for men who had earned honour at Waterloo to lose it by firing on an unarmed crowd.

With the crowd calmed and the cavalry restored to order, Wilson returned to the rear and played no further part in the proceedings. The cortège went round the barricade through side-streets, but it met so many further barricades that eventually it was forced to go through the City, where it was greeted by the waiting Lord Mayor and cheered all the way as though it was a victory parade.

Embarrassed and humiliated, the government turned on Wilson as an obvious scapegoat, and the Duke of York was easily persuaded to dismiss him from the army for what was represented as unjustified interference. Six months later, supported by his Whig colleagues, Wilson moved for papers, demanding a public review of the reasons for his dismissal. As the Commander-in-Chief's spokesman in the House, it was Palmerston's duty to lead for the government.

When the opposition opened by suggesting that the Tories were victimizing a political opponent, Palmerston derided them. There were several troublesome senior officers on the Whig benches, most notably General Sir Ronald Ferguson, who was one of Wilson's most forceful supporters. If the government had wanted to have any of them dismissed, it would have attempted it long before now. As for the suggestion that the charges against Wilson were groundless, there could be no doubt that, technically at least, he was at fault. He had probably prevented further bloodshed and perhaps even a riot, although his own long-winded justification made it sound as though he had prevented another Peterloo, but at the bottom of Kensington Church Street he had attempted to persuade junior officers to disobey orders, and at the top of Park Lane he had usurped their authority. 'It was an act of great military insubordination to address troops under such circumstances at all', said Palmerston. 'But the language in which, by the honourable gentleman's own admission, he addressed them, highly aggravated the character of his military offence.'

Palmerston's case was irrefutable. The government was vindicated by an overwhelming 199 votes to 97. But it was not so much the case as the way in which Palmerston presented it that aroused the indignation of the opposition. His tone was disdainful throughout. He was petty. He ignored parliamentary custom and simply referred to the former soldier as 'the honourable gentleman', rather than 'the honourable and gallant gentleman'; and each time he did it the opposition booed him. According to Brougham, his 'vile, unfeeling & dull attempts at sneer' were received with 'disgust by every part of the House'. Other Whigs described his performance as 'abominable' and 'miserable'; even a Tory colleague, William Wilberforce, called it 'ungenerous'.

Palmerston knew he had not behaved well. Three years later, when the opportunity arose, he implicitly acknowledged it. The opposition was as usual objecting to the size and cost of the army, and Joseph Hume, a former military surgeon, had just suggested that the garrison of Gibraltar could be reduced to 4,000 men. Before Palmerston could answer, Wilson came to the rescue, declaring that, if anyone thought that, 'he had never looked at it with the eye of a soldier or the knowledge of an engineer'. When Palmerston rose again, he began by expressing his gratitude to 'the honourable and gallant member'.

Yet the debate on Wilson's dismissal was only the most notorious example of 'Lord Pumicestone's' objectionable manner. Despite the occasional indication of regret, the 'sneering' continued and even increased, as much outside Parliament as within it; and although many remarked on it, there is no evidence that anyone attempted to restrain it. The ladies at Almack's seem to have found the haughty 'Lord Pumicestone' as attractive as they had once found the charming 'Lord Cupid'; and his male friends, few of whom were close and almost all of whom were Whigs, had little incentive to curb a course of action that was doing more damage to the government than to the opposition. The death of Lord Malmesbury in 1820 had not only deprived him of the last patron with enough influence among powerful Tories to promote his political ambitions; it had also removed the only friend with enough influence over Palmerston himself to persuade him that the greatest barrier to his advancement was nothing more than his own behaviour. Politically at least, embittered 'Lord Pumicestone' was isolating himself.

Five years after the Wilson debate, in 1827, the Duke of Wellington's close companion Harriet Arbuthnot wrote, 'Lord Palmerston is always quarrelling with everybody.' By then, however, his private and public lives had sunk to such a low ebb that his frustration had given way to despair. In 1824 both Lady Cowper and Lord Palmerston had lost a lover: Count Giuliano had gone back to Italy and Mrs Blackburn had accompanied her husband to Mauritius, where he had been appointed Chief Justice. But Lady Cowper was the one who had filled the gap effectively and abundantly. At the end of 1826, a few months before Mrs Arbuthnot remarked on Palmerston's quarrelling, she had gone to Paris, where she had enjoyed a lively liaison with a secretary at the British Embassy, Major John 'Beauty' Caradoc, and had come home in time for Christmas, accompanied by Earl Grosvenor's youngest son, Robert, who was fourteen years her junior. Then, adding a new dimension to Palmerston's discomfort, she had not been in the least perturbed and had shared none of his parental anxieties when Robert Grosvenor abandoned her and embarked on a long flirtation with their daughter Minny, who was now a pretty and wilful sixteen-year-old.

According to Mrs Arbuthnot, Palmerston attempted a fresh start and made two unsuccessful proposals of marriage to her cousin the eccentric and supercilious Lady Georgiana Fane, whose much more beautiful half-sisters were the Viscountess Duncannon and the Countess of Jersey. But it seems more likely that Palmerston conducted his very public affair with Lady Georgiana in order to make someone else jealous. Even Mrs Arbuthnot had to admit that, after the second supposed refusal, Lady Georgiana was the one who looked miserable. Lady Jersey, who was more put out by the relationship than anyone, claimed that she was the one with whom Palmerston was really in love; and Lady Cowper, who was more put out than she pretended, insisted that it was Lady Georgiana who was pursuing Palmerston and asserted as nonchalantly as she could manage that 'if she was handsomer she would have a better chance'.

Still thwarted in love, Palmerston could no longer find consolation in a commercial relationship. He was still paying the rent on 122 Piccadilly and still paying an allowance to the occupant, but Mrs Murray had begun to entertain other noblemen there as well. In the last few years she had given birth to twins and a son, none of whom was Palmerston's. His private life had become painfully empty; and his public life, if anything, was worse. Another Cabinet reshuffle and another general election had convinced him, if he still needed convincing, that he would never have a seat in any Cabinet as long as Liverpool remained Prime Minister.

The Cabinet reshuffle was caused by another death. On 12 August 1822 the new Marquess of Londonderry, who was still known to most men by his courtesy title, Castlereagh, committed suicide at his house in Kent. He had been a very great Foreign Secretary, although at the time few in Britain would have acknowledged the fact. One of those few was an ardent adversary, Henry Brougham, who conceded reluctantly that he had more talent than the rest of the Tory Cabinet combined. But it was the monarchs and statesmen of Europe who had seen him at his best. The Chancellor of Austria, Prince Metternich, who had never been an easy ally, spoke for all of them when he described Castlereagh as 'absolutely straight, a stranger to all prejudice'.

Since the defeat of Napoleon, Castlereagh's sole objective had been to confine France within its pre-revolutionary borders and to ensure that it stayed there by maintaining the powerful Quadruple Alliance between Britain, Russia, Prussia and Austria. So far he had succeeded. But the job had never been easy. The radical and liberal majority among his countrymen were not convinced that it was either right or safe to entrust their security to an alliance with 'despots'; and his reactionary allies, led by Russia, were determined from the outset to create a coalition of all the Christian kings, each pledged to defend the 'absolute monarchies' of the others against any further liberal or nationalist revolutions. For the British, whose 'constitutional monarchy' was the result of revolutions, the Tsar's proposal was out of the question. As Castlereagh put it, 'The House of Hanover could not well maintain the principles upon which the House of Stuart forfeited the throne.' When the Tsar's 'Holy Alliance' was formed, therefore, the one European monarch who failed to sign up to it was King George III, who, to the relief of his government, had been left indisposed by mental illness.

Despite the repressive aspirations of his allies, Castlereagh never doubted that the peace of Europe depended on their continued co-operation. The last seven years of his life were consumed by his constant struggle to keep the Quadruple Alliance credible and in check; and for the last two of those years his patience and subtlety were tested to breaking point. In 1820 and 1821 the revolutions that the Tsar had feared broke out in Spain, Portugal and Italy. When the Tsar proposed that the Four Powers should intervene jointly in Spain to restore the deposed King Ferdinand VII to his throne, Castlereagh's was the only forceful but courteous voice in opposition. The Quadruple Alliance had been established to contain France; it was 'never intended as a union for the government of the world or for the superintendence of the internal affairs of other states'.

Castlereagh's veto was enough to prevent joint action in Spain, but it was not enough to prevent Metternich from acting independently elsewhere. In order to protect Austria's Italian possessions from any revolutionary contagion, he sent soldiers south to crush the revolts in

Naples and Piedmont. It was a dangerous precident, as Castlereagh was quick to point out to him. The Greeks had by then risen in rebellion against their Turkish conquerors. If, as was likely, the Tsar were now to follow Metternich's example and intervene independently in Greece, the Russians could establish themselves permanently in Constantinople, a prospect that was in neither of their interests.

With Metternich's convinced but unrepentant support, Castlereagh sent a flattering letter to the Tsar, reminding him that he had always been the strongest proponent of combined action and successfully persuading him to stay his hand at least until the allies met for the next of their many congresses, which was due to take place in Verona in October 1822. But Castlereagh did not live long enough to attend the congress. His long diplomatic balancing act had left him exhausted. Behind his still cold and imperious façade he had become neurotic and a little paranoid; and, at least in his private life, his judgement was failing.

On fine evenings Castlereagh often walked home from the House of Commons or the Foreign Office to his London house on the corner of King Street and St James's Square. On the way, like many of his colleagues, he sometimes succumbed to the spurious charms of the prostitutes who hung around at the bottom of the Haymarket in the flattering glow of the new gas lamps. On one such evening in 1819 he was approached by a woman who led him to a room in a nearby house. The woman undressed with her back to him and then turned, revealing that 'she' was not a woman but a boy. Seconds later the door burst open and two men rushed in, informing Castlereagh that they knew who he was, accusing him of sodomy and demanding money in return for their silence. In panic Castlereagh gave them all the money he was carrying and fled. But the two had learned who he was by following him home from a previous encounter. In the months and years that followed they returned frequently for further payments and loitered menacingly in St James's Square until they got them.

The pressure increased in 1822, when the worn-out Castlereagh was least able to cope with it. At the end of July he received two letters from a man calling himself Jennings. The first threatened to reveal that he had been visiting prostitutes, the second threatened to expose what

Mrs Arbuthnot later described as 'a crime not to be named'. At the time that particular crime was the principal subject of society gossip. Only two weeks earlier the Bishop of Clogher, a neighbour of Castlereagh in Northern Ireland, had been apprehended *in flagrante delicto* with a guardsman behind the White Hart in Westminster. Terrified by the bishop's disgrace, Castlereagh panicked again.

The proud Foreign Secretary who had seldom deigned to consult anyone was suddenly consulting everyone. He consulted the Lord Chancellor, the Attorney-General, the Duke of Wellington, Mrs Arbuthnot, whose husband was the government Chief Whip, and his friend Lord Clanwilliam, who was now Under-Secretary at the Foreign Office. He even consulted the bewildered King. Everyone accepted that he had been set up, and most of them advised him to report the blackmailers and make a clean breast of it. But Castlereagh could not agree. He was convinced that he was the victim of a huge conspiracy. When his wife and his doctor took him away to rest at his house in Kent, he began to believe that they were plotting against him as well.

Fearing the worst, Lady Castlereagh hid the key to her husband's pistol case. But she did not take the precaution of making sure that he always had a servant in attendance. Left alone for a moment, he found a penknife, hacked through an artery in his neck and bled to death slowly in his doctor's arms.

The unexpected loss of Castlereagh enabled Liverpool to accelerate his efforts to make his Cabinet younger and more liberal. At the beginning of the year, on the resignation of Lord Sidmouth, he had appointed Robert Peel to succeed him as Home Secretary. Now, to replace Castlereagh as Foreign Secretary and Leader of the House of Commons, he appointed an overjoyed George Canning, who had by then given up all hope of political promotion and was on the point of accepting the Governor-Generalship of India. At the beginning of the following year Canning's friend and supporter William Huskisson became President of the Board of Trade and another of Dr Drury's boys, Frederick Robinson, became Chancellor of the Exchequer.

Yet again, there was no place for Palmerston. Instead, Liverpool was still trying to tempt him into the sidelines. Before he began the reorganization of his Cabinet, he had offered to give him an English peerage if he would leave the War Office to become Commissioner of Woods and Forests, 'with the expectation of being appointed to the Post Office or some other more agreeable situation, when the opportunity may offer'. For a man who had learned to love the House of Commons the House of Lords was hardly sufficient compensation for such an obvious and humiliating demotion. Palmerston had found no difficulty in refusing. When the reorganization of the Cabinet was complete, however, Liverpool came back with a much more attractive offer and presented Palmerston with the opportunity to become Governor-General of India. But even this glittering prize was not enough to tempt Palmerston away from the War Office. It had been a long time since life in Westminster had seemed so attractive. He now had friends in the Cabinet, and Canning was back at the Foreign Office.

Palmerston was not blind to Canning's shortcomings. In a letter to Laurence Sulivan he suggested that Liverpool was going to find him a much less reliable and disinterested Leader of the House than 'Londonderry' had been. In his view Peel, despite his lack of experience, would have been much better. 'No man who has seen him do his work can doubt that in discretion, in personal following, in high-mindedness he is superior to Canning.' Nevertheless, Palmerston had always enjoyed Canning's company. He admired his oratory and he shared his patriotic pragmatism. Indeed he may even have learned it from him. The last time Palmerston had spoken on foreign affairs in the House of Commons, it had been in support of Canning, back in 1808; and the next time he did so, it was again in support of Canning.

Canning sent Wellington and Clanwilliam to the congress in Verona. When Russia, Austria and Prussia agreed to support a French royalist invasion of Spain, he instructed them to protest and withdraw. But he knew that there was nothing practical he could do to halt the huge French army which was already assembled to the north of the Pyrenees. The last time a little British army had fought against the French in Spain, one of the main reasons for its success had been the fact that the bulk of the French army was fighting in eastern Europe. This time the entire French army was concentrated on Spain, and the eastern European powers were behind it.

On 7 April 1823 the French army entered Spain and restored the worthless and vindictive King Ferdinand to his throne. On 30 April Canning defended the government's declared neutrality against a Radical attack in the House of Commons; and Palmerston supported him, speaking with fresh authority and unusual eloquence. As always, he wrapped Britain's best interests in a convincing cloak of high-minded integrity. There was nothing to be gained and a lot to be lost by risking intervention in Spain, and it was better to let the world know that Britain would stand by and do nothing than to make empty threats and hold out false hope to the Spanish Liberals. 'To have talked of war and to have meant neutrality, to have threatened an army and to have retreated behind a state paper, to have brandished the sword of defiance in the hour of deliberation and to have ended with a penful of protests in the day of battle would have been the conduct of a cowardly bully.'

Although the opposition's motion of censure was defeated, the government's indifference to the crisis in Spain was not repeated elsewhere. Canning was not so reticent where the odds were less weighted against him or where British interests were at stake. As Wellington put it, 'There are some people who like to fish in troubled waters, and Mr C. is one of them.' When France and Spain threatened to overstretch their resources and assist the Portuguese army in its attempt to overthrow the new democratic constitution and replace the liberal king with his reactionary younger son, Canning revealed his readiness to support the king by sending a fleet to Lisbon. Fearing that the restored Spanish monarchy might attempt to recover its newly independent American colonies, with whom Britain had already built up a hugely profitable trade, he offered them help and recognition. He even discussed joint action on their behalf with the President of the United States, James Monroe, who, on the advice of his Secretary of State, John Quincy Adams, had already recognized their independence. But at the end of 1823, to Canning's disappointed indignation, Monroe acted independently and, in a warning that was directed as much at Britain as at anyone, asserted 'that the American continents, by the free and independent condition which they have assumed and maintain, are henceforth not to be considered as subjects for future colonization by any European powers'.

The United States were no more capable of providing effective military support in South America than the British had been capable of providing it in Spain. But there was another element in this equation which made the Monroe Doctrine enforceable. Spain was separated from her former western colonies by the Atlantic Ocean, and the Atlantic Ocean was dominated by the British navy, the largest in the world, which had recently been enlarged still further at Canning's instigation. One by one the Spanish-American republics fought off the mother country's attempts to recover them, and one by one Great Britain recognized their independence: Colombia, Mexico and Argentina in 1814, and Chile, Bolivia and Peru in 1825. Although British ships had assisted some of them in their struggle, Canning, characteristically, claimed considerably more of the credit than was due to him. In an astonishing boast that was to become almost as famous as the Monroe Doctrine, he told the House of Commons, without a hint of irony, 'I called the New World into existence to redress the balance of the old.'

Palmerston's active support for the government's more aggressive and self-centred foreign policy did nothing to improve his relationship with the Prime Minister. On the contrary, having failed to push him into the sidelines, Liverpool now decided to get rid of him altogether; and he chose to do so by defeating him in the general election of June 1826.

At first sight Palmerston had every reason to be confident about the forthcoming election. In 1818 and two years later, in the general election necessitated by the death of the King, he had been returned unopposed, partly because his previous Whig opponent, Smyth, had obtained the other Cambridge seat when Sir Vicary Gibbs became a judge in 1812. In 1822 he was given slight cause for concern when the by-election called after Smyth's death was won by a Tory, William John Bankes, who was strongly opposed to Catholic emancipation. Anti-Catholic feeling in the university was clearly on the increase, but Palmerston felt that it would be enough not to remind people of his opinions and stay silent on the subject. In the course of the next three years he never spoke in the House of Commons on Catholic emancipation, even during the acrimonious debate of May 1825. In December of that year, however, in time for an unusually long campaign, the government announced two additional Tory candidates for Cambridge University in the general election.

As intended, both candidates were formidable threats to the sitting members. Not only were they Trinity men and strongly anti-Catholic; they were ministers of the crown as well. One was the Irish Secretary, Henry Goulburn, and the other was the Attorney-General, John Copley, the son of the American portrait painter John Singleton Copley. If the Tories had put up only one such candidate, it might have been thought that the intention was to get rid of Bankes, who was also out of favour for cloping with the Countess of Buckinghamshire. But with two such candidates it was clear the target was Palmerston.

Several members of the Cabinet, including Canning, were shame-faced and tight-lipped on the subject of the Cambridge election. Others, particularly those who had borne the brunt of Palmerston's sneers, were openly opposed to him. While acknowledging that Catholic emanci-pation was still, of course, an open question, they suggested to their Cambridge friends that it would be better for the government if both the university members were 'Protestants'. Although not himself a member of the Cabinet, one of the busiest, and most inappropriate, canvassers on behalf of the new Cambridge candidates was the Duke of York, whose personal animosity towards Palmerston was by now even stronger than his political opposition to Catholic emancipation. But the most influential was the Lord Chancellor, 'old woman' Eldon, not so much among his own profession as among the clergy, who still made up the large majority of Cambridge graduates. Most Church of England clergymen were anti-Catholic anyway; and when they knew Eldon's preference, an unusually large number of them expressed their willingness to travel to Cambridge and vote accordingly, if only because there was always the hope that they might be rewarded with one of the many lucrative livings in the Lord Chancellor's gift. With the votes of the 'rural reverends' in their pockets, the new Tory candidates had nothing to fear from Palmerston's liberal lawyers.

In the Cabinet, Palmerston's only real friends were Wellington, who openly condemned his colleagues' dishonourable conduct, and the supremely self-confident Robert Peel, who even reproached the Duke of

York at a dinner party for abandoning the tradition of royal neutrality. On the back-benches of the Tory party, where most of the members were at least as right-wing as Lord Eldon, the proportion that supported him was not much better. But the Tory party had never been Palmerston's natural habitat. He had only joined the Tories on a youthful impulse in answer to a flattering invitation; and with experience and the passage of time both he and they had come to realize how little they actually had in common. Most of the men with whom he dined and hunted were Whigs. Most of the women with whom he spent his evenings were the wives and daughters of Whigs. Palmerston had more friends on the opposition benches than he had on the government's; and it was the opposition that now rallied round him. Even Brougham supported him. In the general election of June 1826 the Whigs did not put up even one candidate for the Cambridge University seat. Instead they instructed their supporters to vote for Palmerston.

From Trinity the witty, Whig professor of geology, Adam Sedgwick, brought the drama down to earth in a letter.

> I am now in the Committee room of a Johnian, a Tory, and a King's Minister; and I am going to give him a plumper. My motives are that he is our old Member, and a distinguished Member, and that I hate the other candidates ... Bankes is a fool, and was brought in last time by a set of old women ... Copley is a clever fellow, but is not sincere, at least when I pass him I am sure I smell a rat. Goulburn is the idol of the Saints, a prime favourite of Simeon's, and a subscriber to missionary societies. Moreover he squints.

Shortly before the election Palmerston wrote to the Prime Minister informing him that he intended to resign as Secretary at War if he lost his seat. He also wrote to his brother in Berlin: 'Liverpool has acted as he always does to a friend in personal questions – shabbily, timidly, and ill.' When the votes were counted on 15 June, the members elected for the University of Cambridge were Copley with 772 votes and Palmerston with 631 – 123 ahead of Bankes. The Whigs had saved the day. But the result was a relief rather than a triumph, and it was a relief tinged with bitterness. Many years later Palmerston looked back on that election and wrote, 'This was the first decided step towards a breach between me and the Tories, and they were the aggressors.'

Amid the bitterness there was also disillusion. In the quiet days that followed the long campaign Palmerston had time to reflect. On 17 July he wrote again to his brother. After reporting the result of the election, and before passing on the important news that three of his horses had won at Bath, he gave his assessment of the party and the government, and in so doing revealed just how far he was now out of step with both of them.

> In truth the real opposition of the present day sit behind the Treasury Bench; and it is by the stupid old Tory party, who bawl out the memory and praises of Pitt while they are opposing all the measures and principles which he held most important; it is by these that the progress of the Government in every improvement which they are attempting is thwarted and impeded. On the Catholic question; on the principles of commerce; on the corn laws; on the settlement of the currency; on the laws regulating the trade in money; on colonial slavery; on the game laws, which are intimately connected with the moral habits of the people: on all these questions, and everything like them, the Government find support from the Whigs and resistance from their self-denominated friends.

Nevertheless he had not yet given up on his party completely. There were about 150 new members in Parliament and 'the young squires are more liberal than the old ones'. 'The next session', he wrote, 'will be interesting.'

Lord Palmerston was three months away from his forty-second birthday when he wrote that letter. Half-way through his life he had fulfilled very little of the promise that so many had seen in him as a student and a young dandy at Almack's. He was still one of the leading figures in London society. Yet, although at one time or another the gossips had associated his name with most of its most beautiful women, and although he was by now the father of at least four children, he had never been married. 'Lord Cupid' still lived alone. Four days before his twenty-fifth birthday he had been offered a seat in the Cabinet. Since then, however, while several of his contemporaries had progressed from one ministry to another and had eventually taken up such seats, Palmerston had held only one ministry and had never again been invited to join them. Now, in what could have been the most humiliating disappointment of all, he had almost lost his seat in Parliament to a member of his own party. After almost twenty years in the House of Commons the best that could be said for him was that he had survived.

5. THE SORCERER'S APPRENTICE

During 1827 the confused and increasingly discordant course of British politics was diverted more than once by further interference from the Angel of Death. In January the Duke of York died. In February Lord Liverpool suffered a stroke, which left him paralysed and semi-conscious for the remaining two years of his life; two months later, accepting at last that he was not going to recover, the King reluctantly invited Canning to replace him.

From Palmerston's point of view Liverpool had been pedestrian and ineffectual, as well as a barrier to his own advancement. Yet for almost fifteen years, while the gulf grew wider and wider between the 'ultras' on the right of the Tories and the Pittites and Canningites on the left, Liverpool had kept their party in office. By caution, conciliation and compromise he had maintained a sufficient semblance of harmony to enable his government to govern; and there can be no better indicator of his success than Canning's failure when he tried to do the same.

The moment Canning kissed hands with the King the harmony evaporated. No fewer than seven of Liverpool's ministers resigned and refused to play any part in the new government. One of them, not surprisingly, was the most 'ultra' of the 'ultras', Lord Eldon, but they also included Wellington, who was alarmed by Canning's adventurous foreign policy, and the new Home Secretary, Robert Peel, who, in resigning, abandoned the huge programme of reform that had long been close to his heart.

Among other changes Peel had already improved the prisons, halved the number of crimes punishable by death and set up two commisions: one to examine the merits and injustices of transporting convicts, the other to consider the creation of a Metropolitan Police Force for London. Like Palmerston, Peel was instinctively a progressive Pittite. Unlike Palmerston, however, he had made promises to the men who had supported him in the course of his career – the English landed gentry, the Protestant ascendancy in Ireland, the clergy in his new Oxford University constituency – and so far he was more inclined to stay constant to his commitments than to his conscience. Although Catholic emancipation was still an open question, he was not prepared to betray his supporters by serving a Prime Minister who was one of its most ardent advocates.

Canning had no choice but to turn to the Whigs, whose ideas, at least on home affairs, were anyway closer to his own. But the opportunity to join a coalition also divided the Whigs. The leader of the party in the House of Lords, Earl Grey (one of the many who still regarded Canning as an arrogant upstart), refused to support him, as did two of the most radical members of the House of Commons, Lord John Russell and Lord Althorp, one of Palmerston's mess-mates at Harrow. Nevertheless there were several equally eminent Whigs who were more than ready to serve in Canning's Cabinet. Edward Stanley, the future Earl of Derby, became Under-Secretary for the Colonies; Lady Cowper's brother William Lamb became Irish Secretary; and Palmerston's first opponent at Cambridge, Henry Petty, Earl of Lansdowne, joined them, at first without portfolio and then in July as Home Secretary.

Brilliant lawyer though he was, Brougham had promoted the coalition with such passion in the House of Commons that he was now thought to be a little too emotional to make a dignified and reliable minister. Instead Canning gave the Lord Chancellorship to the Tory Attorney-General, John Copley, who took the title Lord Lyndhurst.

Another new Tory peer was Palmerston's old form-mate Frederick Robinson, who was created Lord Goderich and appointed Leader of the House of Lords. At his own request, Goderich also resigned as Chancellor of the Exchequer and took on the less demanding duties of Secretary of State for War and the Colonies. To replace him Canning offered the Exchequer to Palmerston, and this time Palmerston accepted without hesitation.

In those days a government minister in the House of Commons was required to resign his seat and stand for re-election each time he was appointed to a new office. But it was hardly easy for Palmerston to take time off in the middle of a busy parliamentary session and fight what might be a difficult by-election in Cambridge. Apart from all the additional work involved in preparing for a new office and helping to establish a fragile new government, the burden of duty in his current office had never been heavier. After the death of the Duke of York, the Secretary at War had automatically taken over as temporary Commander-in-Chief. Although Wellington had been appointed to succeed the duke at the end of January, his recent resignation from all his offices had meant that Palmerston was again in charge of both the War Office and Horse Guards. Canning therefore agreed that Palmerston could come into the Cabinet immediately as Secretary at War and postpone his by-election until the end of the session. Meanwhile Canning would act as Chancellor as well as Prime Minister.

It was a generous concession on Canning's part. Like several recent Prime Ministers, he was willing, indeed eager, to take charge of a second ministry, but what he wanted was to keep his precious Foreign Office, not take on the Exchequer. Since it was bound to be unacceptable for the Prime Minister to hold three offices, even at this delicate moment, Canning had to appoint the sarcastic and increasingly eccentric John Ward, Viscount Dudley, one of Dugald Stewart's old pupils, to act under his close direction as temporary Foreign Secretary.

Before the session was over, however, Canning was obliged to inform Palmerston that he was no longer in a position to offer him the Exchequer. Palmerston was already well aware that the King was strongly opposed to any promotion for his brother's impudent tormentor, and the King was undoubtedly the most powerful influence on Canning, but there was opposition, or at least scepticism, elsewhere as well. When the proposed appointment was announced, *The Times*, which was then said to be deeply influenced by Brougham, described it as 'ridiculous' and blamed the news for a fall in government securities. With the unluckiest of timing Palmerston's financial affairs had recently aroused a certain amount of curiosity in Westminster, and one of his projects had even been the subject of critical debate in the House of Commons.

For a long time Palmerston had been living beyond his means. He was a regular recipient of writs from tradesmen, only half of whom were paid before a court had delivered judgement in their favour. But this in itself was neither unusual nor disgraceful. For most of the nineteenth century, as in all of the eighteenth, it was accepted that gentlemen kept their tradesmen waiting for as long as possible before settling their accounts. It is also likely that in many instances Palmerston was unaware of what was happening. In London, where most of the writs originated and where many related to the establishment of Mrs Murray in Piccadilly, his domestic affairs were managed for him by a firm of solicitors, Oddie, Lumley and Forster.

The cost of maintaining Emma Murray's establishment was also the only expense Palmerston made any serious attempt to reduce. At the beginning of 1827 he cut her allowance from £300 a year to £200. He was to cut it again to £100 and then £50 at the beginning of the following year, when she married one Edmund Mills, but he allowed the happy couple to live at 122 Piccadilly, on which he continued to pay the rent, and in the years that followed Emma was to cost him a great deal more as Mrs Mills than she had ever cost as Mrs Murray.

Within a year Edmund Mills was in prison for debt, and he was not released until Emma had been compelled to pay off his creditors by selling a little country house which had apparently been given to her by one of her other lovers. Soon afterwards, when the couple decided to rent another country house, Emma somehow persuaded Palmerston to let the lease be put in his name, so that the house would not be lost if Edmund got into trouble again. By the end of 1831, inevitably, Mills was back in debtors' prison and Palmerston had been held liable for the arrears of all the rent and rates.

For some reason, perhaps because he was afraid of what they might do or say if he did not, Palmerston continued to help. He sub-let 122 Piccadilly and from then until the end of 1835, when he sold the lease, he allowed Emma to use the income to pay off her husband's debts. After Edmund abandoned Emma, Palmerston continued to send her money until at last she went to live abroad, and at the same time he supported Henry, the son whom she had borne him in 1816. He sent Henry to school and then to Sandhurst; and when Henry decided not to complete the course at the military academy, he found him jobs, first in the Audit Office and finally in the Consular Service.

Rather than make any serious reduction in his expenditure, Palmerston hoped to cover his cost of living by increasing his income, but by 1827, when Canning offered him the Exchequer, few of his investments had as yet borne fruit. He was still borrowing heavily to complete the huge programme of improvements on his estates in Ireland, which now included a harbour at Mullaghmore. He had also borrowed to enlarge and improve a lime works which his father had bought in Yorkshire, and although the works had tripled in value, their greatly increased profits had not yet recovered the cost of the improvements. He had speculated on the stock market, but he had bought most of his shares early in 1825, at the end of a long boom, when the prices were at their highest, and he had watched their prices tumble almost immediately afterwards in the sudden nervous slump that wiped many millions off the value of all shares, broke over fifty small banks and for a while even threatened to break the Bank of England.

The loss of confidence in the stock market also caused a temporary set-back in the development of the Welsh Slate Company. Palmerston had set up the company at the beginning of 1825 and sold shares in it in order to raise the capital to develop a quarry that he had inherited in Caernarvon. When the value of the shares then fell with the rest of the market, Palmerston behaved impeccably and bought them back from any of the investors who had lost their nerve. At the time it added considerably to his debts, but in the long run he was rewarded for his unneccessary conscientiousness, since he had increased his personal holding in a company that was eventually very profitable.

It was, however, his association with the Devon and Cornwall Mining Company that raised eyebrows in Westminster. In 1825, like many other peers and MPs, Palmerston bought shares in the company from its secretary, the member for Sudbury, John Wilks. Unfortunately Palmerston also accepted an invitation to join the board. When the value of the shares subsequently fell further than most, some of the shareholders began to ask questions and on 9 April 1827, the day before Canning offered Palmerston the Exchequer, they brought a petition before the House of Commons alleging that the original directors had acted fraudulently. They had apparently issued a false prospectus and pushed up the value of the shares on the stock market by buying them with company funds; and Wilks had made a fortune by selling the company its mining leases at a hugely inflated price before he had even bought them for much less from the original owner.

Palmerston opened the debate by informing the House that he had nothing to fear from any investigation. He had not been a director at the time of the fraud and as a subsequent investor he was now just another of its victims. He said the same thing when the matter was debated again a month later, shortly before Canning withdrew the offer of the Exchequer. But by then the chairman of the company, Peter Moore MP, was already in prison, and Wilks had been exposed as the mastermind behind several other frauds as well as this one. Although Palmerston was completely exonerated of any wrongdoing, he had been so anxious for a quick profit that he had temporarily tainted his reputation by allowing himself to be associated rather too closely with a group of clearly shady characters; and he could not, and did not, claim that he had no suspicions about them. As early as September 1825 he wrote to his brother-in-law Laurence Sulivan, who was also a director, describing Wilks as 'a bit of a rogue' and adding, 'at the same time he is a clever fellow & as long as his interest goes hand in hand with ours will probably do well by us'.

The combination of the King's displeasure and the disapproval of the House of Commons was too much for Canning. The Exchequer was no longer available to Palmerston. In an attempt to compensate him Canning offered two other appointments, which, since they would have taken him away from Westminster, may well have been suggested by the King. The first was Governor of Jamaica, at which Palmerston 'laughed heartily'. The second was Governor-General of India, which he refused again. After so long a wait, a seat in the Cabinet was compensation enough, and that at least had not been withdrawn. Lord Pumicestone's public demeanour was already noticably more genial. He now took part in the discussion and formation of government policies, and he had access to Cabinet papers on foreign affairs, in which, under Canning's direction, the British navy remained a major instrument of policy.

In 1826 Canning had sent another fleet to Lisbon, this time accompanied by an army, to prevent a further French threat of interference in the continuing family struggle for the Portuguese throne. So far he had not interfered in Greece, even though the cause of Greek liberation had earned widespread support in Britain, particularly after Lord Byron had gone to fight for it and died of marsh fever at Missolonghi in 1824. But by 1826 the situation in the eastern Mediterranean had altered dramatically. In the first place the Ottoman Sultan had called for help from his nominal vassal the Viceroy of Egypt, Mehemet Ali, who had sent him his navy. The Aegean and Ionian seas were now dominated by a large Turko-Egyptian fleet commanded by the Viceroy's adopted son Ibrahim Pasha. Supplied and protected by this fleet, the Turkish army was brutally recovering all the land that had been lost to the Greeks over the last five years. Secondly, and more ominously, at the end of 1825 the Russian Tsar Alexander had died suddenly and had been succeeded by his bellicose and more energetic brother Nicholas.

Fearing that Nicholas was about to interfere unilaterally in his own interest between the Greeks and the Turks, Canning purported to share his anxieties and persuaded him that Britain and Russia should act together as mediators. When the Prussians and Austrians were appalled by their plan and refused to have anything to do with it, they turned to France, where the cause of Greek liberty was as popular as it was in Britain. Having threatened the French on one front as Foreign Secretary, Canning now offered them an alliance on another as Prime Minister. In July 1827, in accordance with the terms of the Treaty of London, Britain, Russia and France demanded that the Turks and Greeks should stop fighting and accept their representatives as mediators; and to back up their demands and keep the peace, they sent a combined fleet to the eastern Mediterranean under the command of Vice-Admiral Sir Edward Codrington, a former pupil of Dr Drury and a veteran of Trafalgar.

Like many more recent commanders of peacekeeping forces, Codrington was baffled by the ambiguity of his orders. The allies had simply declared the intention of putting an end to the fighting 'without, however, taking any part in the hostilities'. When the Greeks agreed to an armistice and the Turks did not, Codrington asked for more specific instructions, only to be fobbed off with further diplomatic double-talk. The more he tried to fulfil his mission and halt the horrifying bloodshed, the more his own actions crept closer to hostilities.

Eventually, on 20 October 1827, Codrington led twenty-six allied ships, including a dozen ships of the line, into the Bay of Navarino, where the sixty-five Turkish and Egyptian ships, including seven ships of the line, were lying at anchor. Ostensibly his purpose was to impose an armistice on Ibrahim Pasha and, if possible, escort his ships to their home ports in Constantinople and Alexandria. When a British boat was sent to instruct one of the Turkish ships to shift her station, because her guns were covering the entrance to the bay, the Turkish sailors opened up on it with muskets, claiming afterwards that they thought it contained a boarding party. A British ship responded with cannon shot. Within minutes the fire-fight had developed into a general engagement, in which the allies more than made up for their smaller number with the greater size of many of their ships and the superior quality of their guns and gunners. Four hours later the allies had lost 650 men, and several British ships had been so badly damaged that they had to be sent home for a refit. But the Turks and Egyptians had lost over 4,000 men, and the bay was cluttered with the drifting debris of one ship of the line, fifteen frigates and almost thirty other ships.

The Battle of Navarino filled the final paragraph in one volume of world history and the first paragraph in the preface to another. It was the last great battle fought between wooden-hulled sailing ships of the line. By the time the fleets met, French gunners had already conducted several successful experiments with exploding shells that could shatter the thickest timbers, and English shipwrights were putting the final touches to the first three vessels in the Royal Navy to be driven in all weathers by steam engines and paddle wheels. Navarino, which Metternich saw as 'a dreadful catastrophe', was also the most devastating naval defeat that the Ottoman Empire had suffered since Lepanto in 1571. Admiral Codrington, who was very nearly charged with exceeding his authority by a subsequent board of inquiry, had brought Greece within grasp of independence. Once the Greek nationalists had achieved their goal, the other Turkish dominions in the Balkans were bound to follow their example.

But Greek independence was not as close as it could have been. The embarrassed allies did nothing to exploit their inadvertent victory, partly because they had different objectives and partly because the one man who might have shown them how to make the most of the opportunity was no longer among them. The Angel of Death had struck again in Westminster.

Canning had caught rheumatic fever at the Duke of York's funeral in January, and never fully recovered. For the next six awkward months he kept himself going with daily doses of laudanum. When he caught a cold at the end of July, the continuing struggle to create a viable government and keep up the momentum of his foreign policy had left him so exhausted and dejected that his system was unable to cope. Barely a month after the signing of the Treaty of London, to the undisguised relief of Prince Metternich, the British buried the Prime Minister whom Castlereagh's great admirer described bitterly as 'the malevolent meteor hurled by an angry providence upon Europe'.

In the slightly desperate hope that he might be able to hang on to his fragile coalition Cabinet, the King decided that the new Lord Goderich was the man most likely to be acceptable to everyone and invited him to take over; and to the surprise of everyone, whether they found him acceptable or not, Goderich was not daunted by the responsibility. Unlike Canning, however, he did not feel that he could take on the burden of the Exchequer as well. Instead, he offered it to Palmerston. But as soon as he had done so, the King made it very clear to him that he would much rather see the Exchequer in the safe hands of a successful financier, such as John Herries.

Yet again the offer of the Exchequer was withdrawn, and yet again Palmerston accepted his disappointment graciously, even though this time he had another option. He knew that the Whig ministers were willing to support him, if only because they were opposed to the 'ultra' Tory Herries. There was therefore a good chance that a majority of the

Cabinet could be persuaded to insist that Goderich should defy the King and keep Palmerston at the Exchequer. But Palmerston also knew that, if he split the Cabinet and then failed, some of his Whig colleagues would feel honour-bound to resign. And if that were to happen, as he wrote to his brother:

> One of two things must follow: either a mixed Government would be made by Goderich of some of his present colleagues and the Tories, or the whole Cabinet would march, and the Tories come in bodily. The last, it is obvious, would be most unfortunate in every possible way, and would produce the worst consequences on our foreign relations and domestic policy, including commerce and Ireland. The first event would bring back a Government just like Liverpool's, consisting of men differing on all great questions, and perpetually on the verge of a quarrel.

But a magnanimous reluctance to risk leaving the nation at the mercy of an impotent or reactionary government cannot have been Palmerston's only consideration. There was clearly a more selfish motive for his restraint as well. Like most of Goderich's friends, Palmerston was now convinced that the Prime Minister did not have 'that firmness and energy necessary for his situation'. The man who had been Dr Drury's favourite at Harrow was unquestionably clever, cultured and charming; and he had been an effective and imaginative Chancellor of the Exchequer. But he had none of Canning's intuition. He was hesitant and academic in his approach to problems, examining them slowly from every angle before making a decision; and his deep grief at the recent death of a daughter had brought on a new and embarrassing inability to control his emotions. Since such a man was unlikely to last for long in the current climate, it was probably better for Palmerston to bide his time rather than be associated too closely with a failure. Besides, he still had a seat in the Cabinet, and since taking on responsibility for Horse Guards as well as the War Office, he had been enjoying his present job more than ever.

Within days of becoming temporary Commander-in-Chief, Palmerston wrote to remind the Adjutant-General that all orders must be submitted for his approval before being issued. It was the first of many such letters, all of which must have been signed with the well-known mischievous smile, and few of which can have been meant to be taken too seriously by men who had lived through the long duel between Horse Guards and the War Office.

The same mischievous smile was also seen and shared more publicly when Palmerston was invited to review the Coldstream Guards. Wearing the only uniform to which he was entitled, the temporary Commander-in-Chief took the salute from the soldiers of that great regiment arrayed more elaborately than any of them in the pretentious full dress of a mere colonel of militia.

Much more seriously and significantly, when troops were posted from the West Indies to west Africa, Palmerston arranged to commission some of them and create the first black officers in the British army. This extraordinarily radical move cannot have come as much of a surprise to most MPs. Just over a year earlier, on behalf of his Cambridge constituents, Palmerston had brought a petition before the House of Commons calling for the education and gradual emancipation of all the slaves who still existed in the West Indies. Yet, despite this, there were many abolitionists on the opposition benches who still purported to suspect the sincerity of his commitment to their cause.

Since the abolition of the trade in slaves in 1807, the Tory government had done little to abolish the institution itself. As a member of that government, Palmerston did not feel that it was appropriate for him to play a prominent public role beside Brougham in the activities of the Anti-Slavery Society, but he had been very active in encouraging others to establish a branch of the society in Hampshire and he regularly provided it with more generous funding than he could afford.

In 1823 Palmerston was one of the majority in the House of Commons who voted in support of Brougham's motion calling on the government to declare itself in favour of gradual emancipation and the eventual abolition of slavery. Tragically, however, when the news of this resolution reached the West Indies, the slaves in Demerara thought that it meant they were already free. Some of them refused to work and resisted when the planters tried to force them, killing three white overseers in the process. Over 150 executions later, Brougham brought another motion before the House of Commons, deploring the brutality with which the colonial authorities had suppressed the so-called rebellion and demanding, as Palmerston was later to ask less peremptorily, that immediate provisions be made for the education of West Indian slaves, with a view to giving them all their freedom as soon as possible. This time Palmerston was one of the majority that voted against the motion.

It was their resentment at this supposed betrayal that led Brougham and the other radical Whig abolitionists to question Palmerston's sincerity; and their charge was revived and supported by one twentieth-century biographer, who suggested that Palmerston revealed himself in his true colours when he turned down the governorship of Jamaica by telling Canning that he 'preferred England and the War Office to Jamaica and the negroes'.

But Palmerston only disagreed with the Whigs on one point: their condemnation of the conduct of the colonial authorities. Like many other abolitionists on the Tory benches, he could not condone what he saw as lawless violence, no matter how much he sympathized with its perpetrators. If Brougham and his colleagues had divided their motion, he would undoubtedly have voted with them on the other points, as his previous support and his own subsequent motion clearly demonstrated.

As for the way in which he dismissed the governorship of Jamaica, the remark was at worst no more than the flippant snobbery of a fashionable nineteenth-century gentleman. Palmerston's committment to the freedom of all the people whom even the Anti-Slavery Society's pamphlets called 'negroes' as often as 'Africans' was a matter of principle and perhaps even idealism, but it was not sentimental. He was equally committed to Catholic emancipation and the education of his tenants, but that did not mean that he would happily have swapped Hampshire and the hunting field for Sligo and the Irish.

Palmerston's attitude was no different from that of any other patrician supporter of the Anti-Slavery Society. In the edition of *The*

Times for 22 June 1815, which contained the first report of the Battle of Waterloo, as well as a report of the parliamentary debate in which Palmerston defended the practice of flogging in the army, there was an advertisement for the anniversary dinner of the African and Asiatic Society in the Freemasons' Tavern. At the very bottom, after announcing that the dinner was to be attended by the society's president, William Wilberforce MP, and after listing the places where tickets could be purchased, the advertisement added that 'about a hundred Africans and Asiatics are expected to dine in an adjoining room'.

The best evidence of Palmerston's attitude, so far at least, lay in the very fact that he was prepared to put his principles into practice as soon as the opportunity arose, and in the letter that he wrote to the Cabinet justifying his action as an 'arrangement' that in his view would 'tend to raise in their own and the public estimation that class of men in the West Indies from which these individuals are selected'.

Very few West Indians were actually commissioned. Soon after Goderich became Prime Minister, Wellington returned to Horse Guards and at once put a stop to what Palmerston's successor at the War Office, Sir Henry Hardinge, described as his 'radical liberal proceedings'.

The difference of opinion over the propriety of appointing 'officers of colour' did nothing to damage a friendship that had been growing steadily since 1817, when the grateful nation gave Wellington the park and house at Stratfield Saye in Hampshire and he and Palmerston began to shoot regularly on each other's estates. But the friendship was not yet so strong that it could emerge unscathed from even a brief exposure to the old rivalry between Horse Guards and the War Office. Wellington was as eager as any Commander-in-Chief to maintain the independence of his office; and Palmerston was as determined as ever to ensure that the elected government exercised a proper control. Palmerston protested every time financial instructions were issued from Horse Guards without his approval. Wellington complained that Palmerston was making cuts in costs and manpower without proper consultation. The new friendship faded amid the continuous hiss of petty bickering; and it could not have done so at a worse time for Wellington. He was about to need all the political friends he could find.

Goderich's government was doomed from the moment he failed to defy the King and accepted Herries in Palmerston's place as Chancellor of the Exchequer; and according to the new Secretary of State for War and the Colonies, William Huskisson, who was the leader of the remaining Canningites, it was all Palmerston's fault. 'Huskisson blamed me for not having stood out', wrote Palmerston later. 'He said if I had insisted upon the fulfilment of Goderich's promise, that promise would not have been retracted, especially as it was spontaneously made, and Herries would not have been thrown like a live shell into the Cabinet to explode and blow us all up.'

When Herries picked a quarrel with Huskisson, over 'literally nothing more than who should be proposed as chairman of a finance commit-tee', Goderich had neither the subtlety to conciliate nor the strength to back one and sack the other. On 8 January 1828, less than six months after taking office, he went to Windsor, broke down 'blubbering' as he told the King that he did not know what to do, and then wiped away his copious tears with the handkerchief that his disconcerted monarch had drawn from his sleeve and handed to him. Having accepted, and perhaps induced, Goderich's resignation, the King sent for Wellington and invited him to form a government.

Despite Wellington's feigned reluctance, the invitation was one for which he had been hoping and preparing ever since Goderich was appointed. His only genuine reluctance came when he was required to pass on command of the army to his old friend and comrade in arms 'Daddy' Hill. The High Tory duke had actually hoped that he might be allowed to combine the roles of Prime Minister and Commander-in-Chief but, as Palmerston pointed out to the Cabinet, in England unpopular laws sometimes led to public disorder, and it would be embarrassing if the soldiers sent to quell it were ever to be ordered out by the very man whose actions had caused it in the first place.

Unexpectedly, however, Wellington did not attempt to create an entirely Tory government. He built a backbone of Tories, which included Peel as Home Secretary and Leader of the House of Commons, Palmerston's unsuccessful opponent at Cambridge, Henry Goulburn, as Chancellor of the Exchequer, and the Earl of Aberdeen, who as

Haddo had been in Palmerston's form at Harrow, as Chancellor of the Duchy of Lancaster. But after that he invited Huskisson and all the Canningites to join them. The Canningites had only two conditions: that Catholic emancipation must remain an open question and that Dudley must remain at the Foreign Office, where he could continue Canning's policies. Wellington accepted, although he insisted that the more reliably Tory Aberdeen must be recognized as Dudley's assistant and heir. When the Canningites agreed, the rest of them were also reappointed to their ministries: Palmerston to the War Office, Charles Grant to the Board of Trade and Huskisson to the Colonial Office. Even William Lamb stayed on as Irish Secretary. But the other Whigs departed, contemptuously denouncing the Canningites as traitors, just as the 'ultras' had similarly denounced them for allying themselves with the Whigs nine months earler.

Palmerston was sorry to see the Whigs go, although he rejected their criticism. In a letter to his brother, who was now chargé d'affaires in St Petersburg, he wrote, 'I very sincerely regret their loss, as I like them much better than the Tories, and agree with them much more; but still we, the Canningites, if we may be so termed, did not join their Government, but they came and joined ours.' At the same time he was optimistic about the new alignment. 'All this, instead of a pig-tail Tory Government, shows the great strides which public opinion has made in the last few years. Such a Government as Liverpool's even cannot now be established.' But he was wrong. With the best of intentions Wellington had done what Palmerston had dreaded in an earlier letter and recreated precisely that: 'a Government just like Liverpool's, consisting of men differing on all great questions, and perpetually on the verge of a quarrel'. And the one who differed most often and most openly with Wellington was none other than Palmerston himself.

Their deepest and bitterest division was over Greece. Knowing that it was far too late to halt the liberation of Greece completely, Wellington wanted to limit it to nothing more than Morea, the Peloponnesian peninsula south of Athens and the Gulf of Corinth. Furthermore he was inclined to accede to the Turkish demand that the Greeks should pay compensation for all the property they had seized, and he was strongly opposed to the Russian proposal that the signatories of the Treaty of London should send troops to support the Greek rebels. But Wellington was not so much pro-Turk as anti-Russian, an attitude that, in Palmerston's opinion, owed more to the influence of Mrs Arbuthnot and Lady Jersey, both of whom loathed Princess Lieven, than to any political reasoning. Through his brother and the Princess, Palmerston hinted indiscreetly to the government in St Petersburg that Wellington faced opposition within his own government and urged it to be patient.

But before the differences on any great issue could come to a head, the Cabinet broke up over a little one. On 19 May 1828 the government introduced a bill to disenfranchise the corrupt rural constituencies of Penryn and East Retford, neither of which had more than a hundred voters. When the bill had been discussed in Cabinet, the Tories had wanted to give both the vacant seats that this created to the neighbouring rural constituencies, and the Canningites had wanted to transfer them to the new and as yet unrepresented manufacturing towns of Manchester and Birmingham. Eventually they had compromised: Penryn was to go to the neighbouring constituency and East Retford was to go to Birmingham. But during the debate a Tory back-bencher, Nicholson Calvert, moved an amendment that also gave East Retford to its neighbouring rural constituency, and all the Tory Cabinet ministers supported it.

Palmerston was furious and felt betrayed. He was convinced that it was no longer acceptable to have populous places unrepresented 'whilst a green mound of earth returned two members', and yet, as usual, he preferred gradual change to radical reorganization. As he told Parliament shortly afterwards, 'To extend the franchise to large towns, on such occasions as the one in question, was the only mode by which the House could avoid the adoption, at some time or other, of a general plan of reform.' When Huskisson dithered, Palmerston insisted that he must do as he did and vote against his Tory colleagues and the amendment.

During the following afternoon Palmerston received a note asking him to come round at once to the Colonial Office. When he got there he found Huskisson dithering again, and again blaming Palmerston for his problem. After the debate, distressed by the fact that he had been persuaded to vote against a government of which he was a member,

Huskisson had written to Wellington offering his resignation. Although he now regretted the resignation, he had since then received a letter from Wellington accepting it.

Palmerston went straight to the House of Lords. For half an hour he and the duke paced up and down the long gallery together, Palmerston pleading, Wellington adamant. Although the duke was unaware of Palmerston's diplomatic disloyalty, he was already exasperated with the Canningites and still smarting because their recent vote in Cabinet had prevented him from raising the duty on imported corn. The opportunity to be rid of their leader, and perhaps some of the others as well, was not something to be thrown away. Huskisson had resigned and that was all there was to it. As the duke famously wrote to him later, 'It is no mistake, it can be no mistake, and shall be no mistake.'

During the next few days Huskisson continued to exchange letters with the duke, pleading with him to believe that he had not intended to resign. The following Sunday some of the Canningites and Whigs, whom Palmerston was already describing in his journal as Liberals, attended a dinner given by Sir Thomas Farquhar in St James's Street. After the dinner, Palmerston, Lamb and Dudley called on Huskisson at his house in Downing Street, where they learned that Wellington had appointed his successor. There was no more to be done. As the three middle-aged dandies strolled away along Whitehall, with their carriages following them, they discussed their own obligations. With Huskisson gone, they were honour-bound to follow. 'In or out?' said Dudley as they passed the sentries outside Horse Guards. 'Out', said Palmerston. 'Out', said Lamb. Within a week all three had resigned and Grant had followed their example.

'Damn 'em; let them go', said Wellington. The old soldier was relieved to be rid of his mutineers. Since they had stood in his way on almost everything, he was now convinced that he could survive and achieve more without them. But the resignations were to have many far-reaching consequences, one of which arose simply through the appointment of successors. In appointing Vesey Fitzgerald to replace Grant at the Board of Trade, Wellington inadvertently lit a time bomb. In the by-election that this necessitated in Fitzgerald's seat, County Clare, the Irish electors threw him out and returned a supposedly ineligible Roman Catholic, Daniel O'Connell.

For the first time in over twenty years in Parliament, Palmerston was out of office. Rather than discourage him, however, the experience served only to increase his energy and at last draw him all the way out of his shell, revealing that he had a more resolute ambition than anyone had suspected.

In the autumn, as usual, he went to Ireland, but this time he did not go only to review the progress of his schemes in Sligo. He watched, questioned and listened; and he had several long meetings with the apprehensive Lord-Lieutenant, the Marquess of Anglesey. The whole nation was enveloped in an aura of anger and anticipation. Through the oratory of Daniel O'Connell and the efficiency of his Catholic Association the people and clergy of Ireland had been mobilized into a mass movement demanding civil rights for Roman Catholics. Ireland was still at peace, but only because O'Connell still believed that he could achieve his ends by peaceful means. When he went back to England after two months, Palmerston was convinced that the time had come for the government in Westminster to make its choice 'between the pen and the sword'.

At the beginning of 1829 Palmerston went to Paris for three weeks to meet as many statesmen and diplomats as he could find and prepare himself for an onslaught on the government's foreign policy in the forthcoming parliamentary session. He discussed Greece with the Russian Ambassador, the Corsican-born Count Pozzo di Borgo. He had a long, slightly subversive talk with the great Talleyrand, who had been eminent in every French government since the revolution but was now out of favour with the autocratic King Charles X. He met the Finance Minister, Casimir Perier, and one of Napoleon's oldest supporters, the Corsican Count Sebastiani; and in renewing his acquaintance with the Emperor's aide-de-camp, Count Flahaut, he built the basis of a long-lasting friendship, even though the count had been the most ardent of Lady Cowper's many unsuccessful admirers during his long exile in London, and even though, according to some, his English countess was soon to succumb discreetly to Palmerston's advances. On the ship that brought him home from Calais, one of his fellow passengers was

Byron's friend Hobhouse, who wrote soon afterwards, 'He is a frondeur now and talked the Liberal just as well and as freely as if he had played that part all his life.'

By the time Palmerston returned, Robert Peel had undergone a Pauline conversion over Catholic emancipation and had persuaded Wellington that it was the only alternative to civil war in Ireland. 'I am one of those who have probably passed a longer period of my life engaged in war than most men,' said Wellington, 'and I must say this: that if I could avoid by any sacrifice whatever even one month of civil war in the country to which I am attached, I would sacrifice my life in order to do it.' Reluctantly he agreed that an Act for the Relief of His Majesty's Roman Catholic Subjects must at last be brought before Parliament. As a result, when Palmerston rose in the House of Commons to speak for the first time from the opposition benches, he spoke, not against the government, but in support of it.

In his speech of 18 March 1829 Palmerston spoke the same sense as he had spoken before on Catholic emancipation, but with more emotion.

> If I wished to convince any impartial Englishman of the policy of repealing these laws, I should bid him repair to the south of Ireland; to mix with the Catholic gentry; to converse with the Catholic peasantry ... to see what a fierce and unsocial spirit bad laws engender; and how impossible it is to degrade a people without at the same time demoralizing them too.

There were also times, however, when he diluted his argument with over-emotional embellishment. The well-chosen quotation from Shakespeare's *Romeo and Juliet* – 'They jest at scars who never felt a wound' – would have had more impact if the long paragraph that led up to it had not begun:

> Can one believe one's ears when one hears respectable men talk so lightly, nay, almost so wishfully, of civil war; do they reflect what a countless multitude of ills those three short syllables contain? It is easy to denounce against a nation this

awful doom; but when Heaven shall once have opened the windows of its wrath, when the foundations of social order shall once have been broken up, when the deluge of civil war shall once have burst upon the land, where is the man who shall presume to set limits to its fury, or foretell the extent of devastation?

It would have been enough to chide the gentlemen of England, as he then did, for talking of civil war 'as if it were some holiday pastime'. Nevertheless this was not the Palmerston that Parliament had heard before, and the speech was greeted generously by its audience. It was 'excellent and very well listened to'; it 'astonished everybody'; it was 'an imitation of Canning, and not a bad one'.

For Wellington and Peel the aftermath was less satisfying. Their bill became law, Catholics were emancipated and the 'ultra' Tories never forgave them. The clerical majority among the electors at Oxford removed Peel from his seat and forced him to seek another at Westbury; and Wellington found himself fighting a duel.

Lord Winchilsea declared that Wellington intended to introduce popery into every department of the state. When he refused to apologize, Wellington challenged him. They met on 21 March in Battersea Fields, where both pistols had to be loaded by the doctor, John Hume, because Winchilsea's second, Lord Falmouth, was shaking too much and Wellington's second, Sir Henry Hardinge, had lost his left hand at Waterloo. After the drama of the loading, the duel itself was an anticlimax. Wellington fired to the side and Winchilsea fired into the air. When Winchilsea then apologized, Wellington bade everyone good morning, rode away and, after calling to give a full report of the meeting to Mrs Arbuthnot, returned to his desk in Downing Street to study a draft of Peel's Metropolitan Police Bill.

Ten weeks after the duel Palmerston launched his attack on the government's foreign policy. Not long before midnight on 1 June he stood up in a half-empty House of Commons to support Sir James Mackintosh's motion of censure on the present relationship between Great Britain and Portugal.

In Palmerston's opinion Canning's conduct towards Portugal had been entirely honourable and liberal. In 1823 he had sent a fleet to support the constitutional monarch, John VI, and deter the other Great Powers from helping his absolutist younger son, Miguel, to oust him. After King John's death, when his elder son and heir, Pedro, abdicated in favour of his seven-year-old daughter Maria Gloria, Canning had sent an army and another fleet to deter a second attempt at a coup. Since Canning's death, however, with the naïve approval of the British government, Miguel had been appointed regent and it had been agreed that, when his niece came of age, he would marry her.

'Was it fitting', asked Palmerston, 'that the King of England should be made a stalking horse under whose cover this royal poacher should creep upon his unsuspecting prey?' As anyone could have predicted, Maria was now in exile, the democratic Portuguese government had been replaced by a puppet parliament and the 'faithless usurper' Miguel had been proclaimed king. While British troops and ships continued to withdraw in accordance with a broken contract, the representatives of Wellington's government did nothing but make empty protests. 'Buonaparte in the plenitude of his power never treated the humble representatives of a petty German principality with more contemptuous disregard than that which our remonstrances have met with at the hands of Don Miguel.'

Although he had risen to support a criticism of the government's dealings with Portugal, Palmerston broadened his fire to take in Wellington's proposals elsewhere, deriding 'the notion of establishing a Greece which should contain neither Athens, nor Thebes, nor Marathon, nor Salamis, nor Plataea, nor Thermopylae, nor Missolonghi; which should exclude from its boundaries all the most inspiring records of national achievements, whether in ancient or in modern times'.

There were superfluous passages in the speech which were as embarrassingly sentimental as anything in the speech on Catholic emancipation. The King kissing Donna Maria when she came to visit him in London was described as 'a recognition in which the inborn nobleness of royal nature contrived to infuse into the dry forms of State ceremonial something almost partaking of the charm and the spirit of chivalrous protection'.

But there were also several slightly clumsy 'purple passages' which were soon to be seen as the essence of Palmerston's own foreign policy. Most famous of all, and most often quoted, was his dismissal of the government's claim that its inactivity in Portugal was a principled refusal to interfere in the internal affairs of another nation.

> If by interference is meant interference by force of arms, such interference, the Government are right in saying, general principles and our own practice forbade us to exert. But if by interference is meant intermeddling, and intermeddling in every way, and to every extent, short of actual military force; then I must affirm that there is nothing in such interference which the laws of nations may not in certain cases permit.

Taken overall, the carefully constructed and well-rehearsed speech was a pale imitation of Canning and no more. It was not great oratory. It lacked Canning's easy cadence. It contained none of the perceptive maxims that decorated the speeches of the elder Pitt. The long-winded passages had none of the idealistic profundity that so often exonerated the verbosity of Burke. But in 1829 there were no Cannings or Pitts or Burkes in the British Houses of Parliament. Although the House was half empty, the speech had the impact that Palmerston had hoped for and intended. Although it did not influence government policy, it influenced opinions in Westminster and beyond, not least because Palmerston had done something that nobody had done before and which every statesman with any sense was soon to do for ever after. He had created copies of the speech before he made it and distributed them to the press. 'It was', said his friend Charles Greville in his diary, 'the event of the week.'

After the speech Palmerston rested on his laurels for a while. Like the other Canningites, he had not joined the Whigs; and without a party there was little more he could do to promote himself. In the course of the summer, when it became known that the Canningite Palmerston, the Tory Goderich and the Whig Lamb were regularly travelling down together to meet with Huskisson at his house in Sussex, many observers deduced that they were planning to form a new party. And after July, when

Lamb succeeded to the peerage which, through his mother's continuing influence on the King, had been elevated from 'the potato patch' to the English viscountcy of Melbourne in Derby, some wags suggested that the new party should be known as the 'Party of the Three Viscounts'.

It was clear now that Palmerston was preparing to make foreign affairs his speciality and take on the mantle of Canning. At the end of the year he went back to Paris to play the student. He took a room in the attic of the Hôtel de Rivoli. He conducted several reckless affairs, including one with the beautiful Emily Rumbold, who had recently married the King of Prussia's banker, Baron de Delmar, for his money. He attended the public lectures on history and current affairs that were being given by some of the Sorbonne's leading professors, among them the historian François Guizot. By the time he came home he was sufficiently well informed to predict that, if King Charles X did not dilute his anachronistic absolutism, it might lead to 'a change of name in the inhabitants of the Tuileries, and the Duke of Orleans might be invited to step over the way from the Palais Royal'.

Before leaving for Paris and his dalliance with other ladies, however, Palmerston found time for a holiday with a few friends and their families at the Royal Sussex Hotel in Tunbridge Wells, where he and Lady Cowper managed many evening assignations and solitary walks together, despite the inhibiting presence of her husband and the prying eyes of Princess Lieven. It may be, however, that they found it easy to slip away unnoticed because all eyes were on another couple: their vivacious daughter Minny and the earnest but gregarious evangelical philanthropist Anthony Ashley Cooper, Lord Ashley. As a boy at Harrow, Ashley had watched a group of drunken pall-bearers stagger up the hill with a crude coffin on their shoulders and break into blasphemies when they dropped it outside the churchyard, and he had decided there and then to devote his life to improving the conditions of 'the poor and friendless'. He was now, like so many social reformers, a Tory MP; and at twenty-eight, ten years older than Minny, he was desperate to be married. Having recently met Minny in London, he followed her down to Tunbridge Wells and paid court to her throughout the holiday. By the end of it he had proposed to her, and after teasing him cruelly for a while she accepted. But it was not a match about which many, except perhaps Palmerston, felt much enthusiasm. Lady Cowper's family was anxious because Ashley had no money, and Mrs Arbuthnot expressed her concern at such a highly principled young man marrying into 'one of the most profligate families in the Kingdom'.

Minny and Lord Ashley were married the following June at St George's, Hanover Square. A few days later King George IV died and was succeeded by his brother William IV. Soon afterwards, just as Palmerston predicted, King Charles X lost his throne. He had recklessly appointed a reactionary Cabinet, dissolved the Liberal Chamber of Deputies and imposed censorship on the press. In response, revolutionaries took to the streets of Paris. They overwhelmed the inadequate and dispirited garrison, drove the King into exile in England and replaced him on the throne with his distant cousin the Duke of Orleans, who took the name Louis-Philippe. As the news spread, the spirit of revolution spread with it. Almost immediately Belgian nationalists rose in armed rebellion against the Dutch king who had been imposed on them by the Treaty of Vienna in 1815.

Palmerston was overjoyed. He wrote to Charles Grant, 'How admirably the French have done it. Who that remembers the excesses and outrages and horrors and insanity of 1792 and '93 could have expected to see, in so short a time, a nation of maniacs and assassins converted into heroes and philosophers?' He wrote to Sulivan, 'We shall drink to the cause of Liberalism all over the world. The reign of Metternich is over and the days of the Duke's policy might be measured by algebra, if not by arithmetic.'

The days of the duke's policy were indeed numbered. In the election that followed the death of King George, which was held during an agricultural slump and accompanied by widespread and sometimes violent demonstrations against corn laws, tithes and low wages, the Tories were returned without a working majority. Wellington needed at least some of the Canningites, and he sent Palmerston's old friend Clive to invite him to join his Cabinet. Although Palmerston was not prepared to say yes unless all the Canningites came with him, he did not immediately say no. But before he could do so the Canningites were left leaderless.

Huskisson attended the opening of the Manchester to Liverpool Railway. On seeing Wellington, he hurried over obsequiously to greet him. As he stepped across the track he heard a noise, turned to see the famous locomotive the *Dart* bearing down on him, dithered for the last time in his life and died beneath its wheels.

In October Wellington invited Palmerston to Apsley House and renewed his offer in person, but by now Palmerston had broadened his terms. He was no longer prepared to join the Cabinet unless it was a real coalition and included not only all the Canningites but also the Whig leader Earl Grey and his deputy Lord Lansdowne; and this, as he must have known, was much more than Wellington could concede.

Wellington tried to explain Palmerston's obstinacy by saying that it was personal. 'I stood in his way when he attempted and all but succeeded in subordinating the office of Commander-in-Chief to that of Secretary at War,' he said, 'and he never forgave me.' But in reality Palmerston and Wellington held opposing views on everything that mattered, as the Irish Secretary of the Admiralty, John Wilson Croker, realized when he called on Palmerston on 6 November to make Wellington's offer yet again.

'Are you resolved, or are you not, to vote for Parliamentary Reform?' said Croker. 'I am', said Palmerston. 'Well then,' said Croker, 'there is no use talking to you any more on this subject. You and I, I am grieved to see, shall never again sit on the same bench together.'

On 15 November Palmerston, the other Canningites and the resentful anti-Catholic 'ultras' joined with the Whigs to defeat the government in a vote on the civil list. Rather than face a certain defeat on something more serious, such as reform, Wellington resigned, and King William IV invited Earl Grey to form a government.

Grey was the fifth Prime Minister to consider Palmerston for the Exchequer. But before he could make the offer, he was persuaded to consider him for another post. In turning down the Foreign Office, his first choice, Lansdowne, suggested that Palmerston was the best man for the job; and Holland, who may also have been offered it, agreed with him. So on 22 November 1830 Palmerston became Foreign Secretary, an appointment that was greeted with such enthusiasm in St Petersburg that Princess Lieven, who counted 67-year-old Grey among her current lovers, claimed that it was all her doing.

Grey's Cabinet was a broad but mostly liberal coalition. After pushing hard for it, Brougham was Lord Chancellor, Althorp was Chancellor of the Exchequer, Melbourne Home Secretary, Goderich Secretary for War and the Colonies, Lansdowne President of the Council, Holland Chancellor of the Duchy of Lancaster and Grant President of the Board of Control. Most of them were men with whom Palmerston had been dining regularly for years, in some cases since childhood. At last he had the job he wanted; and at last, for the most part, he was among friends.

6. PROTOCOL CALMERSTON

With his appointment to the Foreign Office at the age of forty-six, Lord Palmerston strode into the centre of the political stage as impatiently as an eager understudy who had been kept waiting too long in the wings. He was by now so familiar with that stage that he was neither impressed nor daunted by it. He had seen so many bad performances that he was convinced he could do better; and in his own role he had seen just enough good ones to have learned how it ought to be played. The last traces of his youthful reticence had been eroded long ago by experience. He was now so sure of himself that he was jauntily contemptuous of criticism and disdainfully exasperated by any disagreement.

He was also lucky. He took over his role at a time when there was much that could be made of it. The totalitarian shadow of the Holy Alliance was beginning to shrink. All over central Europe the seeds of nationalism and revolution, which had been dormant beneath that shadow since the Congress of Vienna, were pushing up their shoots at last and reaching out westward for the sustenance of 'Liberal' sunlight. In almost every city the emerging middle classes were demanding the right to influence their own government. For a Foreign Secretary who had declared his support for 'Liberalism' and had openly acknowledged that he was not averse to 'intermeddling' there were plenty of opportunities.

Yet, for all his confidence, the latest leading player was still a novice – something the men who had been sent by the other Great Powers to play opposite him were not. As the new Ambassador of France, King Louis-Philippe and his Foreign Minister, Sebastiani, had appointed none other than 76-year-old Prince Talleyrand, whose only living rival in reputation and achievement was the Austrian Chancellor, Prince Metternich.

The Prussian Ambassador, another recent arrival, was 38-year-old Baron Heinrich von Bülow, the rising star of Prussia's diplomatic corps. Bülow came from a family that was accustomed to standing centre-stage on battlefields, at court and even in the arts. There were many in the capitals of Europe who expected him to be his country's next foreign secretary.

By contrast, the other representatives of Great Powers were long-standing leaders of London society. The Russian Ambassador, Prince Lieven, had come to the Court of St James as long ago as 1812, and the Austrian, the extravagant Prince Esterhazy, had followed only three years later. Since then these two had seen so much that they were now at least as knowledgeable about the ways and workings of British politics as most members of the new Whig Cabinet. Although Palmerston had known both men well since their arrival, he had so far known them only as companions on the hunting field, at the dinner table and on the dance floor at Almack's, where both their wives, like Lady Cowper, were patronesses.

A week after he became Foreign Secretary, Palmerston dined at the Austrian Ambassador's residence with Esterhazy and Talleyrand. As they moved from the drawing-room to the dining-room, the two ambassadors stood back to let Palmerston walk ahead of them. But Palmerston refused to take precedence in such distinguished company; and when each of the others followed his example and also refused to walk ahead, all three walked arm in arm through the tall double doors together. Palmerston could match such men in charm, and he could probably have bettered them in gratuitous discourtesy, but beside their wealth of experience in statecraft and diplomacy his own obvious lack of it seemed all the more feeble.

No leading player ever needed a director more than Palmerston did in his first years at the Foreign Office. And here too he was lucky. The three ministers who had appointed him, recommended him and stood back to make way for him – Grey, Holland and Lansdowne – had done so in part because the ideals to which he was now attached by instinct and emotion were the traditional Whig principles to which they had long been committed by conviction. Unlike most other ministers, who were almost exclusively preoccupied with reform and other home affairs, these three were sufficiently concerned with foreign policy to want to contribute to it. Although they knew Palmerston too well to dictate to him or challenge him too often in Cabinet, they devoted as much time as seemed necessary to tactful assistance in the formulation of his policies and active support in their execution; and when it looked as though their ebullient protégé was about to take one risk too many, Grey exercised his prerogative as Prime Minister by writing to the relevant ambassadors with more restrained instructions, and Holland, as he admitted to his diary, did the same thing unofficially and discreetly. For as long as Grey was Prime Minister, Palmerston's policies were at least moderated by the subtle influence of an old-fashioned, francophile, Whig triumvirate.

Nevertheless, although initially there were other minds at work in the creation of the policies, the style in which they were promoted and conducted was always and entirely Palmerston's. The duties of his ministry brought no interruption to his famously hectic social life. Instead they became the essence of it. His London house in Stanhope Street was no longer quite large enough to fulfil all his needs, and Broadlands was too far away to be useful. Indeed, since it took a full day to reach the Hampshire estate in a carriage, he seldom had time to go there himself. But Palmerston had willing friends whose splendid houses were ideal settings for the glittering assemblies that smoothed the course of international negotiations. Diplomats were soon meeting regularly at Lord Holland's huge mansion in Kensington and at Panshanger in Hertfordshire, where within no more than a couple of months Lady Cowper was complaining that 'there was no going into any room without disturbing a conference'.

Within the Foreign Office itself Palmerston was soon as unpopular among the well-bred clerks as he had been among their less fashionable colleagues at the War Office. Foreign Office clerks had been accustomed to spending their weekends on their fathers' estates and devoting only a small proportion of their weekdays to their duties. They arrived late and left early. When they were not lounging at their desks, engaged in the undemanding business of copying despatches, they gathered round the windows waving and signalling with mirrors to the young seamstresses in the dressmaker's across the street. By the time they left each evening, the atmosphere in the entire building was thick with the smoke and stench of cigars, which were the latest craze among young men of fashion, not least because they were so deplored by their elders, whose fastidious dandy generation regarded snuff as the only inoffensive form of tobacco.

With the arrival of Palmerston, however, all that was swept away. Smoking, signalling and all other forms of horseplay were halted immediately. Without any increase in their salaries, the clerks found themselves working long hours and late, often for seven days a week; and since their new master's own working habits were, as always, diligent but disorganized, his unpredictable demands disrupted what was left of their social lives. If their despatches were not copied in black ink, and in a neat, large, legible hand, they were sent back to be copied again, often accompanied by a scathing sneer. 'Has the writer of this letter lost the use of his right hand? If not, why does he make all his letters slope backwards like the raking masts on an American schooner?'

It was probably no comfort to the clerks to know that British representatives abroad were subjected to the same demands and indignities. After several consuls had been warned that 'indecipherable' despatches would be returned for recopying, the haughty threat was actually carried out on at least one occasion, even though the possibly significant report came from the southern tip of the Ottoman Empire and had taken over three months to reach London. And it was probably no comfort to either consuls or clerks to know that the scorn they suffered was as nothing compared with the invective in some of the despatches the Foreign Secretary sent to even the most senior ambassadors, or with the flippant comments that were occasionally added in his own neat hand in the margin. The intemperate language that sometimes emanated from Palmerston's Foreign Office was a match for anything that he had sent out from the War Office, only now it was aimed, not at soldiers, but at men who were accustomed to the courteous formalities of diplomacy.

There were even times when Palmerston addressed foreign ambassadors in language that was worthy of 'Lord Pumicestone' at his worst. Those who knew him well enough accepted that it was only his manner. But to those who did not, his passionate commitment to his policies made a difference of opinion look like personal animosity. Talleyrand, who was to suffer more than most from Palmerston's 'passion', wrote in his memoirs that it was the one all-tainting flaw in a man whom he otherwise described generously as 'certainly one of the most able, if not the most able, of the men of affairs whom I have met in all my official career'. And the always condescending Esterhazy, who acknowledged that Palmerston was the only Whig who was 'practical and well informed about foreign affairs', was nevertheless affronted by his 'insouciance'.

It was not, however, Palmerston's style that most offended the Foreign Office clerks. Nor even was it his campaign to improve the quality of their paperwork. The most offensive and painful innovation, the one that kept clerks at their desks on Sundays, was the huge increase in the quantity of their paperwork. The Foreign Secretary's greater interest and involvement in what was happening in Europe led to the drafting of many more protocols for conferences; and it also necessitated much more frequent correspondence between the Foreign Office and British embassies. On taking up new postings abroad, ambassadors and ministers were sent minutely detailed instructions, which were altered thereafter as often as neccessary; and the reports that they sent back received equally long replies, a few of which ended with criticisms of their English, complaints if the writing was illegible and rebukes when the paper smelt of tobacco.

By the end of Palmerston's first four years in office, during which he had produced no fewer than seventy-eight protocols on the subject of Belgium alone, he had earned yet another nickname: 'Protocol Palmerston'. But there was nobody in the Foreign Office, neither clerk nor under-secretary, who bore a greater share of the added burden than he did. Rather than dictate, Palmerston wrote the first drafts of almost all important documents himself; and he sat late at his desk writing memoranda, and even articles, outlining his policies for the Whig and independent newspapers, such as *The Observer*, the *Morning Chronicle* and *The Globe*.

Palmerston was so slow in answering letters and so often late for appointments that his opponents were soon accusing him of laziness. But the real reason was the unfortunate combination of a painstaking attention to detail with a complete inability to manage his time. Palmerston wrote and said nothing until he was sure that he was fully briefed. Despatches and visitors were dealt with in order of arrival, rather than in order of importance or rank; and if they took longer than expected, the next in line was obliged to wait. A few of the younger diplomats managed to save time and disappointment by calling on Palmerston unexpectedly when he was at home in Stanhope Street. But the many who were bound by the traditional formalities knew that, even for men as eminent as Talleyrand, an appointment with the Foreign Secretary usually began with an hour or more in a Foreign Office ante-room; and society hostesses soon learned to accept that the price of inviting Lord Palmerston to dinner was the certainty that he would not arrive until after the soup had been served.

It is possible, however, that Palmerston's unpunctuality was not always genuine and that some of it may have been part of the studied nonchalant style. If it was important enough, he could be on time. For example, he was hardly ever late when he was due to speak in the House of Commons, although in this case it would not have made much differ ence if he had been. During his first four years in office the important debates on foreign policy took place in the House of Lords between the Prime Minister and the Leader of the Opposition, between Grey and Wellington. Although the members of the House of Commons were passionately interested in every aspect of reform, they had very little interest in anything else. When Palmerston spoke on foreign policy, he spoke in a House that seldom had more than twenty people in it. And here, yet again, he was lucky. He had little time to rehearse, and it showed. He often spoke from notes rather than a full text, and as a result the stuttering and hesitations and grasping for words were worse than ever. In most cases the polished versions of the speeches that subsequently appeared in newspapers or in T. C. Hansard's journals were written afterwards, not before. Even if the House had only been half-full, as it was when Palmerston made his impressive speech on Portugal and Greece, the reputation earned by 'the event of the week' would soon have been lost. Those who, like Talleyrand, admired his 'great facility of speech in Parliament' had only read the speeches. They had not been there to hear them.

As for the policies propounded in those speeches, according to the often repeated paradox that first appeared in the *Morning Herald* in 1853, Palmerston was a Liberal abroad and a Tory at home. But these apparent contradictions were simply two sides of the same attitude. Palmerston had an enthusiastic, Panglossian faith in the merits of the British constitution. It was not perfect. It had recently needed a nudge in the direction of Catholic emancipation; and it still needed a little bit of not too radical electoral reform. But it was the best possible, and he wanted everyone else to have one like it.

This was not due to any crusading idealism, however. The motive was purely practical. As before, sincere idealism was simply the cloak in which Palmerston camouflaged more selfish objectives. It was clearly in the best interest of an expanding industrial Britain to avoid the costly distractions of war and ensure that the European market place was peaceful and, if possible, prosperous. In the recent past Castlereagh had managed to maintain the peace by cynically fostering an unassailable alliance of absolute monarchies, but those days were over. The forces of nationalism and revolution had now grown too strong. The best way to keep Europe at peace in the future would be to make sure that it was predominantly composed of independent, democratic nation-states, preferably constitutional monarchies, in which the newly enfranchised middle classes would be much more interested in promoting their own prosperity than in supporting the territorial ambitions of kings and emperors. For the most part, therefore, it was in Britain's best interest to support the men who were attempting to create such states. But the only constant in Palmerston's policy was the pursuit of Britain's best interest. Where there was nothing to be gained, or where there was too much at risk, Liberal Britain was unlikely to be helpful. As it turned out, most of the nationalists and moderate revolutionaries who reached out to Palmerston for practical support received nothing more than encouragement.

No refusal was more regretted than the one he was forced to make to Poland. By the Treaty of Vienna in 1815 the often partitioned Poland had been partitioned yet again. The west went to Prussia, Austria retained Galicia, Cracow became a free city, and the remainder, the largest part, became a satellite grand duchy ruled over by the Russian Tsar. In the very week when Palmerston became Foreign Secretary, the Poles rose in rebellion against the oppressive new Tsar Nicholas. While the Russian army advanced on Warsaw in a wave of atrocities, Metternich, through Esterhazy, warned that, under the terms of the Treaty of Vienna, Britain had no right to interfere. At the same time the French, through Talleyrand, suggested that Britain and France should offer to mediate and even proposed that the two great Liberal democracies should send their huge combined fleets to the Baltic and support the Polish revolutionaries with money and arms. But Palmerston and Grey argued that the Tsar's support was so vital elsewhere, particularly in Greece, that it would be folly to antagonize him. An offer to mediate would lead only to a humiliating rebuttal; and if they tried to do anything more, France and Britain would find themselves at war with Russia, Prussia and Austria. Nevertheless, as Palmerston admitted privately to his ambassador in Paris, 'One cannot help wishing the Poles heartily success; and one should be glad to help them in any way consistent with our good faith towards Russia.'

Warsaw fell. In breach of the Treaty of Vienna, and in defiance of protests from France and Britain, the Polish Grand Duchy became part of Russia. Hundreds of thousands of Poles were deported in misery to Siberia. Refugees streamed westward across the borders. When most of those who were passing through Austria were imprisoned, Palmerston made it plain to Metternich that his conduct was 'repugnant to the common feelings of mankind'. But he hid his passion and was almost as 'cold' with the leader of the Polish revolution, Prince Adam Czartoryski, who escaped from Warsaw in disguise and arrived in London soon afterwards. Although Palmerston assured the prince that, like all Englishmen, he wished him well, he also pointed out that he had been reckless to gamble so much on the hope of support from the Liberal democracies, who had no 'direct interest' in interfering and who were not in a practical position to do anything useful anyway. 'We cannot send an army to Poland', he said, 'and the burning of the Russian fleet would be about as effectual as the burning of Moscow.'

Many of the activists among the Polish refugees combined with revolutionaries in other countries. In April 1833 a group joined forces with students from Heidelberg and Göttingen and attempted to start a new German revolution by seizing the guardhouse in Frankfurt. By then, however, the tide of German revolution was on the ebb and Palmerston and Metternich had grown tired of exchanging rhetoric, at least on the subject of Germany.

Inspired by the French revolution of 1830, several small states in the German Confederation – another creation of the Treaty of Vienna – had forced their rulers to grant them constitutions. But in 1832, led of course by Metternich, Austria and Prussia had forced the Diet of the Confederation to pass Six Acts, which, among other provisions, had given its princes the right to overrule their elected assemblies and abolished the freedom of the press. On 2 August, in a House of Commons containing only ten other members, Palmerston deplored the Six Acts and defended Britain's right to interfere if she chose. Immediately afterwards he wrote to Lady Cowper's brother Frederick, who was Ambassador in Vienna, knowing that Metternich's agents would read the letter. 'It is strange that Metternich cannot be content with despotic authority over thirty millions of well behaved Austrians ... but why on Earth must he set all the rest of the world by the ears, to gratify his priggish vanity?'

Then he drafted a blunt despatch protesting to the President of the Diet. But William IV would not allow it to be sent. As King of Hanover, one of the states in the Confederation, he had already approved the Six Acts: he could not now, as King of England, oppose them. Palmerston was infuriated. If England and Hanover were to act in concert, it ought to be England that led. Eventually the King agreed to let Grey moderate Palmerston's language and send additional copies of the despatch to the courts of Prussia and Austria. Yet, moderated though it may have been, the despatch still warned that, if the Diet tried to enforce the Six Acts with the support of Austrian and Prussian soldiers, 'it might produce a general convulsion in Europe'; and that was still enough to offend. The Prussians refused to receive the despatch and Metternich fired back furiously, instructing his ambassador to inform Palmerston that the Diet was acting within its rights and to suggest to him, 'in a friendly manner', that he was wasting his 'precious time'. In addition, since Metternich was beginning to understand the way Palmerston worked, he instructed his ambassador to warn the Foreign Secretary that, if he passed on his despatch for publication to a newspaper, the Austrians would also publish their despatches and conduct the entire argument in publc.

Palmerston never had any intention of publishing the moderated despatch. Instead he took the polished version of his last speech, which had been prepared for publication in *Hansard*, arranged for someone to translate it into German, the one important European language that he did not speak fluently himself, and then had 200,000 copies printed and distributed in the German states.

Palmerston's warnings had no effect on Metternich. Both knew that Britain and Austria were not about to go to war over the constitutions of a few small German states, even when one of them was Hanover. But at least Palmerston had the satisfaction of knowing that he had seriously irritated the Austrian Chancellor and that the citizens of the German states were aware of Britain's moral support; and the speech of 2 August survived to become yet another oft-quoted exposition of his supposedly radical, 'intermeddling' foreign policy.

> The independence of constitutional states, whether they are powerful like France or the United States, or of less relative political importance such as the minor states of Germany, never can be a matter of indifference to the British Parliament, or, I should hope, to the British public. Constitutional states I consider to be the natural allies of this country; and whoever may be in office conducting the affairs of Great Britain, I am persuaded that no English ministry will perform its duty if it be inattentive to the interests of such states.

The dust had barely settled when the Poles and German students took over the Frankfurt guardhouse. Metternich, who was forewarned, let it happen and then used it as an excuse to occupy Frankfurt with Austrian and Prussian troops, quashing the little revolution in the process. This time Palmerston had to be circumspect. Britain had recently signed a trade agreement with Frankfurt, and he did not want to see a vengeful Austria force Frankfurt to repudiate the agreement and join the German Customs Union, which would have required it to impose duty on British goods. Nevertheless, after allowing the occupation to continue for over a year, he did at last sent a despatch pointing out that it contravened the terms of the Treaty of Vienna and insisting that as a signatory of the treaty Britain had a duty to protest. Predictably the Austrians and Prussians were furious. To save the trade agreement, haughty Palmerston was obliged to send a second despatch reiterating the first in conciliatory language. 'It was far from the intention of His Majesty's Government to give anything like an unfriendly character to the expression of that communication.' But the harm had been done. When his Minister in Frankfurt warned him that Metternich might still force the city to repudiate the treaty and impose a complete ban on British goods, Palmerston accepted that it was better to pay duty than not to export at all. The treaty was annulled and, with Palmerston's agreement, Frankfurt joined the German Customs Union.

Similar events took place in Switzerland, where a group of Polish nationalists joined forces with some Italian radicals, stole a boat, crossed Lake Geneva to the Sardinian province of Savoy and set out to attack a Sardinian army post. Nothing came of it. On the way their leaders fell to quarrelling and the little army, hardly a hundred strong, disintegrated before it reached its objective. But Metternich milked the situation for all it was worth. He convinced Sardinia and the German Confederation that Switzerland had become a haven for revolutionaries; he persuaded them to demand that the Swiss expel all Poles and any Germans who were Liberals or Italians who were Radicals; and in menacing support of their demand, he massed an Austrian army on the Swiss border.

True to form, Palmerston gave both Switzerland and Austria the benefit of his opinion. He suggested to the Swiss that it would be unjust to expel anyone other than those who were known to have taken part in conspiracies or breaches of the peace; and he reminded Metternich that Austria was one of the nations that had recognized and guaranteed Switzerland's neutrality in the all-pervading Treaty of Vienna.

This time, however, beyond the promotion of natural justice and the association of Britain with the highest ideals, Palmerston had a more practical motive. In his view it was in Britain's best interest that the Swiss should keep as many Poles as possible. For a while he had been alarmed by the large numbers of Polish refugees who were being given asylum in France. If the flow continued at the same rate, it was only a matter of time before the overflow arrived in England, and if the Swiss expelled their Poles, they might well arrive in thousands, destitute and unable to support themselves. But an irrefutable moral argument was not as influential as an army and a border closed to trade. The Swiss expelled the Poles; some came to England, in hundreds rather than thousands; and the idealistic majority on the Whig back-benches compelled a reluctant Cabinet to provide for them out of public funds.

In Italy, Palmerston was more active, but here again his objective – Britain's best interest – was to prevent a European war rather than promote constitutional government. Within his first few months at the Foreign Office new revolutions had broken out in Parma, Modena and the eastern Papal States: Romagna, the Marches and Umbria. In France, where exiles had planned most of the revolutions, support was widespread, although the government was not prepared to provide the military assistance for which the revolutionary leaders had been hoping. As Casimir Perier, who had just taken over as President of the Council, put it, 'the blood of Frenchmen belongs only to France'. In introspective Britain the revolutions in Italy were the only overseas events outside Belgium that had much influence on public and parliamentary opinion – and in this case the opinion was entirely united. The traditional Tories, who had opposed Catholic emancipation, were happy to support anyone who was trying to overthrow a papal government; and the reforming Whigs were eager to support anyone who was trying to establish a constitutional government. In Austria, however, the government was as nervous as before. Once again Metternich sent his emperor's armies south and restored the old order not only in the client states of Parma and Modena, where the rulers were virtually Austrian puppets, but also in the Papal States.

Palmerston was afraid that, if the Austrians stayed too long in the Papal States, the French might be tempted to abandon their neutral stance and intervene, using support for the radical revolutionaries as an excuse to make territorial gains at Austria's expense. He warned Austria that a permanent settlement could not be secured through 'the temporary application of external force'; and he warned France 'that it would not be worth her while to risk involving all Europe in war for the sake of protecting the revolutionists in Romagna'. At first it looked as though he had been unfair to the French. France and Austria actually got together and set up a conference in Rome to advise the Papacy on reform. When they invited Palmerston to send a representative, he accepted eagerly, although, as the Foreign Secretary of a kingdom that had not had formal diplomatic relations with the Vatican since the Reformation, he insisted that his representative could only act as an unofficial adviser.

Knowing that the ultra-conservative new Pope, Gregory XVI, was unlikely to accept anything close to a constitutional government, Palmerston instructed his first representative, Sir Brook Taylor, to advise that 'the Pope should grant to his subjects such improvements in their Institutions and in the Form and administration of their government, as may remove the main part of those practical grievances which they have hitherto suffered'. But even this was far too much for the Pope, and a bit too much for the Austrians. Eventually, in order to let the Italians know that he was doing his best for them, Palmerston arranged for the publication of all the correspondence between the British and Austrian representatives at the conference. Provoked by this first experience of Palmerston's methods, Metternich furiously accused him of being more of a threat to stability than the French. 'The exposure of the British cabinet's views unquestionably constitutes an incitement to revolt for the people of the Roman states.'

Perhaps Metternich was right. Frustrated by the Pope's intransigence, the people of Romagna rose again in rebellion. The Austrian army, which had only recently left, returned and occupied the city of Bologna. This time, however, the French sent a fleet and landed an 'army of observation' in the papal port of Ancona, 130 miles to the south. During the Franco-Austrian stand-off, the restored rulers of the other states indulged in unrestrained repression and retribution. In the other Papal States in particular, under the direction of Cardinal Bernetti, mass executions were conducted on a scale that amounted to massacre. In order to avoid being associated in any way with what was happening, Palmerston ordered his second representative, Sir George Seymour, to return to England. On 19 April 1833 he wrote to his brother: 'The affairs of Italy seem to be in a miserable state ... The cardinals are supposed to be in their sound senses, and it is lamentable to see what the sound sense of a cardinal amounts to.'

Like the Germans, the Italians had learned from Palmerston's publications that Britain was at least with them in spirit. The Foreign Secretary was becoming better known abroad than he was at home. He had done nothing to promote constitutional government in Italy; and since the posturing armies of Austria and France had the sense not to call each other's bluff, it is arguable that his practical part in the preservation of peace was small. But the story was far from over. In its death throes the latest Italian revolution had produced the first great hero of Italian nationalism, Giuseppe Mazzini. From the safety of Marseilles, Mazzini established a new movement, Young Italy, dedicated to the creation of a united democratic nation. From this sprang other movements, Young Europe, and then Young Germany, Young Poland and Young Switzerland. The greatest era of revolutions had yet to come.

It was in Belgium that Britain's best interests and the cause of constitutional government coincided most closely; and it was in Belgium that Palmerston earned his reputation as a statesman. The Belgian revolution had destroyed one of the most important provisions of the Treaty of Vienna. In order to create a strong barrier to any further French expansion northwards, Castlereagh, Metternich and the representatives of the other allied Powers had compelled Talleyrand to accept that Belgium, which had been seized from Austria by revolutionary France in 1792, must now be combined with Holland to make one United Kingdom of the Netherlands under the rule of the House of Orange; and they had arranged for a line of formidable fortresses to be built along its southern border under the direction of the Duke of Wellington. But the arranged marriage had been doomed from the outset. Although the Roman Catholic and predominantly French-speaking Belgians outnumbered the Protestant Dutch by almost three-quarters, they only had equal representation in the lower chamber of the States-General.

Most of their senior civil servants were Dutch; cases in their courts were conducted in the Dutch language; and they were required to contribute in taxes to the Dutch national debt. Inspired by the revolution in France, the Belgians rose, drove out the Dutch, elected a Congress, which voted to establish a constitutional monarchy, and successfully spilled their revolution across the border into Luxembourg, which, although a member of the German Confederation, was ruled by the Dutch King, just as another member, Hanover, was ruled by the King of England.

The Belgian revolution was the one that came closest to causing a war. When the Dutch King William appealed for help, the Russians prepared an army of 60,000 men and the Prussians conducted manoeuvres on their western border. But the Russian army was then diverted by the revolution in Poland. Prussia and Austria would not fight without Russia. For the time being the fragile French government preferred to exploit the situation through the diplomatic prowess of Talleyrand rather than the use of force. And for as long as the French army stayed at home, the British were prepared to adopt a policy of 'non-intervention'.

By the time Palmerston took over from Aberdeen, all the interested parties had assembled in London for a conference on Belgium, but so far all they had achieved had been to persuade the Dutch and Belgians to agree to an armistice. Esterhazy, Lieven and Bülow were supporting the absolutist King of Holland and insisting that the Treaty of Vienna must be observed and that the United Kingdom of the Netherlands must be reinstated. If it had been at all practicable, this would also have the easiest solution for Palmerston, since it 'would have been the most advantageous to the general interests of Europe'. He was wary of the French, and a 'barrier state' was still the best way of containing them. But he was also realistic enough to recognize that the Belgian revolution was irreversible. Although he was arguing everywhere else that the Treaty of Vienna must be observed, he argued in this case that the treaty had been overtaken by events; and in this at least he had an ally in the great man whom he was soon to be calling 'Old Tally'. On the election of the Whigs, Talleyrand had written to his government in Paris. 'England is the country with which France should cultivate the most friendly relations ... The Powers still believe in the divine right of kings; France and England alone no longer subscribe to that doctrine ... Let both declare loudly that they are resolved to maintain peace, and their voices will not be raised in vain.'

Throughout Palmerston's first month in office Talleyrand supported him in his efforts to persuade the representatives of 'the Powers' that, short of war, they had no choice but to accept the partition of Holland and Belgium and recognize Belgium as an independent state. Five days before Christmas 1830 the conference agreed formally. After that, however, when Palmerston proposed the creation of a new barrier state by uniting Belgium with Luxembourg, Talleyrand opposed him and instead proposed a series of territorial redistributions, the most outrageous of which was that Luxembourg should be ceded to France.

Palmerston's proposal was that the conference should call on the Dutch King to cede Luxembourg to Belgium, and as compensation persuade the Belgians to accept the Dutch King's eldest son, the Prince of Orange, as their constitutional monarch. Once he had been convinced that even Luxembourg was not enough to make Belgians accept a Dutchman as their king, he withdrew it and agreed that it would probably be sufficient for Europe's security if the conference guaranteed Belgium's neutrality. But in the course of the next month Talleyrand fought for his own proposals 'like a dragon', and in the end Palmerston only 'brought him to terms by the same means by which juries become unanimous – by starving. Between nine and ten at night he agreed to what we proposed, being, I have no doubt, secretly delighted to have got the neutrality of Belgium established.' On 20 January 1831 the conference recognized the neutrality of Belgium and agreed that Luxembourg should remain part of the German Confederation under the rule of the King of Holland. A week later it agreed the financial provisions for the separation of the two nations.

Although the disappointed Dutch accepted their loss and agreed to the provisions of the conference, the now overconfident Belgians did not. They argued, with some justification, that they had been assigned too large a share of the divided debts, and they refused to be parted from Luxembourg. On 3 February, in the hope of earning a powerful democratic ally, they elected Louis-Philippe's son the Duke of Nemours as their king. But Palmerston had seen it coming. Using a well-established diplomatic device that allowed one nation to be frank with another without subjecting it to the embarrassment of a formally recorded threat, he wrote to his ambassador in Paris, Lord Granville, on the day before the election and asked the French embassy to deliver the letter, knowing that it would be opened and read before delivery. 'We are reluctant even to think of war,' he wrote, 'but if ever we are to make another effort, this is a legitimate occasion, and we find that we could not submit to the placing of the Duc de Nemours on the throne of Belgium without danger to the safety and a sacrifice of the honour of the country.' On the morning of 4 February, the day after the election, the letter was delivered to the British embassy in Paris. Late that afternoon the French government informed the British ambassador that the King had refused to let his son accept the throne of Belgium.

As to who should be offered the throne instead, Palmerston and Talleyrand agreed again. The only candidate who was acceptably neutral was Prince Leopold of Saxe-Coburg, although what seemed neutral to Palmerston and Talleyrand was not quite as neutral to everyone else. The dashing Prince Leopold had been married to King George IV's only child, merry Princess Charlotte, whose tragic death in childbirth in 1817 had broken England's heart; and now, after a short and miserable second marriage to a German actress who looked like her, he was engaged to be married to King Louis-Philippe's daughter Princess Louise. If he had affections for any countries more than others, they were likely to be England and France. Palmerston had known him since the days when they both went to Almack's as often as anyone. He knew him to be shrewd; and by now the other members of the conference knew him to be shrewd as well: he had recently refused the invitation to sit on the precarious new throne of Greece.

Unfortunately from Palmerston's point of view, the shrewdness was stronger than the affection or the gratitude. Once the conference had accepted the Anglo-French candidate and the Belgians had been persuaded to elect him, Leopold refused to accept the throne until he knew the exact boundaries of his new kingdom, and he made it plain that he would not accept unless those boundaries encompassed all the lands that were claimed by his potential subjects, including Luxembourg. Fearing that, without Leopold, Belgium might become a republic and a hotbed for radical revolution on the other side of a narrow channel, Palmerston played for time under the guise of attempting to agree. Eventually, on 26 June, he presented yet another protocol to the conference proposing that the decisions made in January should be altered. The debts of Holland and Belgium should be divided in fairer proportions, and the future of Luxembourg should be made the subject of further negotiations between Belgium, Holland and the German Confederation. The conference agreed. For Leopold it was enough. A few days later he left London to become King of the Belgians.

Now it was Holland's turn to say no. The Dutch King let it be known that he would accept no changes to the provisions that the conference had made at the end of January, and that he would consider himself at war with any prince who ascended the throne of Belgium on any other terms. Since Leopold already fell within this description, he repudiated the armistice and on 2 August sent his army into Belgium. The ill-equipped Belgian army was routed at Louvain. Within a week of his arrival the first King of the Belgians was a fugitive in his new kingdom. He appealed for help. The conference asked Britain and France to provide it. Although the assigned squadron of the British navy, commanded by Codrington, was delayed by contrary winds, the French army, which was suspiciously well prepared, marched at once, led by the experienced and accomplished Marshal Gerard, who had made his name at Austerlitz, and who had campaigned in Belgium before. Only ten days after the Dutch army crossed the new Belgian border, it was crossing it again, in the opposite direction.

For the time being King Leopold and his throne had been saved. But the aftermath was almost as embarrassing for Palmerston as it was for the King of Holland. The French army did not leave Belgium. In the half-empty but highly indignant House of Commons, Palmerston's assertion that France and Britain had been acting in concert at the request of the conference was met with jeers from the opposition benches. The Tories had always sympathized with the Dutch; and it seemed to the more melodramatic among them that the British blood spilled at Waterloo had been wasted.

The more Palmerston pushed Talleyrand, the more Talleyrand insisted that the French could not leave without gaining something from their intervention – perhaps the demolition of the border fortresses. After all, if Belgium was going to be neutral, there was no longer any need to defend her. But Palmerston was adamant that the demolition of the fortresses was none of France's business, even though he had been secretly discussing that very possibility with Bülow and Esterhazy's first secretary, Baron Philipp von Neumann. As he wrote to his minister in Belgium, 'You might as well consult a housebreaker which of the bars & bolts of your doors & windows you might most safely dispense with.'

Eventually, in desperation, Palmerston turned to a tactic that had worked before. He wrote several letters to Granville in Paris and had them forwarded by the French embassy. The gist of them all was contained in one sentence in the letter of 17 August. 'One thing is certain – the French must go out of Belgium, or we have a general war, and a war in a given number of days.' A fortnight later the French army began to break camp, and on 15 September the last contingent in Belgium, which had remained at Leopold's request for his protection, received its orders to withdraw.

The humbled Belgians were no longer in a position to make demands. They owed their survival to France. With the Russian army in possession of Warsaw and almost free from its preoccupation with Poland, they might not be so lucky next time. Over the next month Palmerston made the representatives at the conference work 'like dray horses'. On 14 October they agreed new terms of separation. The German Confederation and King William of Holland could keep Luxembourg; the debts of the two nations were to be more evenly divided; and as a result of the most intense negotiations, in which Palmerston astonished even those who knew him with his command of the relevant navigation laws, he had persuaded the conference to make one more concession to the Belgians. To provide access between Antwerp and the North Sea, they were to have navigation rights through Holland along the Scheldt.

Not everyone was satisfied. The Dutch King still felt that he had given up too much, the Belgians felt that they had received too little, and the French complained that they had not gained anything. But the conference ignored the Dutch King, Leopold persuaded the Belgians to accept the terms by threatening to abdicate if they did not, and Palmerston temporarily calmed the French by promising that some of the hated fortresses would be demolished as soon as possible. On 15 November 1831, Britain, France, Austria, Prussia and Russia incorporated the terms in a formal treaty with Belgium, recognizing her as an independent, neutral nation with Leopold as her king. 'The Dutch King may sulk if he will,' wrote Palmerston on the following morning, 'but he can no longer endanger the peace of Europe.'

The story was not ended. The treaty had yet to be ratified. But it looked as though the worst was over. Whatever his critics had to say, Palmerston alone had held the conference together and brought it to a satisfactory conclusion. Some of the Cabinet, even the Prime Minister, had sometimes been alarmed by his belligerence. In so far as they took any notice, the Whig back-benches and the Radical press had reproached him when he appeared to be supporting the Dutch. The Tories and *The Times* had ridiculed him when he appeared to be supporting the Belgians or, worse, the French. But the novice had pulled it off. Although he had worked as closely as he could with Talleyrand, his prime objective had been to contain the French. In a dangerous combination of bluff and brinkmanship he had prevented a war, consolidated a liberal revolution and created a new constitutional kingdom.

He was exhausted. On 15 October, the day after the final terms had been agreed, he had spent the entire day in bed. While presiding over the conference on Belgium, he had been 'intermeddling' almost everywhere else in Europe as well; and now, just as the Belgian treaty brought a welcome reduction in his burden, the one domestic issue that required the attention of even the Foreign Secretary – reform – was coming to a head.

The preparation of the first Reform Bill had been the work of Lord Durham, the Prime Minister's son-in-law, but the honour of presenting it in the House of Commons fell to tiny Lord John

Russell. Like the rest of the Cabinet, Palmerston supported him. Although he would have been content with less drastic measures, he regarded the changes as a just and necessary realignment between parliamentary seats and centres of population. As he explained to the House of Commons, they only extended the franchise; they did not change the type of people who were likely to be elected. 'Property, rank and respectability would still maintain the same influence in representation.'

When Russell presented the bill on 31 March 1831, it was carried by only one vote. When it was subsequently defeated at the committee stage, Grey asked the King to dissolve Parliament and went to the country for one of the most enthusiastic general elections in British history. The Whigs were returned with a majority of over a hundred. They won seats that had been Tory for generations. But they also lost some; and one of these was Cambridge. The university, which was as opposed to reform as it had been to Catholic emancipation, took its revenge and elected two Tories, Henry Goulburn and William Peel, the brother of Sir Robert, who, like Palmerston, had been at Harrow and St John's. Palmerston came bottom of the poll and in an immediate and deeply ironic by-election was returned instead for Bletchingley in Surrey, one of the rotten boroughs the bill sought to eliminate.

At the end of June, Russell's second Reform Bill was carried in the Commons by a large majority. In October, however, the House of Lords rejected it by a majority of forty-one. Palmerston pressed for compromise, but the modified bill that passed through the Commons in March 1832 was again rejected by the Lords in May. In the Cabinet, Palmerston proposed that the only solution was to create enough new peers to carry the bill in the Lords. Although the King had just rewarded him for his efforts with the Order of the Bath, he refused to consider the suggestion, and the government was left with no choice but to resign.

For nine days Wellington attempted to cajole his Tories into forming a government that would be prepared to compromise and carry out just enough electoral reform to satisfy the demands of the nation. But there was a run on the Bank of England; there were riots in almost every city; in London the mob threw stones at the duke and broke the windows of his house; and Peel refused to join the government, declaring that it would be hypocrisy for a Tory to have anything to do with reform. Grey returned. The King agreed to create new peers if neccessary, and the threat was enough to sway the Lords. On 7 June, amid widespread rejoicing, the Reform Bill received royal assent. The House of Commons still contained 658 seats, but 143 had been abolished and replaced with 65 new seats in counties, 65 in boroughs, 8 in Scotland and 5 in Ireland.

To the embittered Tories support for the Reform Bill was the worst of turncoat Palmerston's treacheries. When they taunted him in the debate for deserting the principles of Canning, he countered them by quoting his mentor. 'They who resist improvement because it is innovation may find themselves compelled to accept innovation when it has ceased to be improvement.' Outside the House, however, their disdain for his desertion and his 'radical' foreign policy found more effective expression in one of the many witty verses written by the member for St Germans, Winthrop Mackworth Praed:

> There was a time when I could sit
> By Londonderry's side,
> And laugh with Peel at Canning's wit,
> And hint to Hume he lied;
> Henceforth I run a different race,
> Another soil I plough,
> And though I still have pay and place,
> I'm not a Tory now.
> I've put away my ancient awe
> For mitre and for crown;
> I've lost my fancy for the law
> Which keeps sedition down;
> I think that patriots have a right
> To make a little row;
> A town on fire's a pretty sight:
> I'm not a Tory now ...

Parliamentary reform eliminated Palmerston's rotten borough at Bletchingley. In the election that followed its passing, he was returned for the constituency that contained his estate at Broadlands, South Hampshire, where his nomination was seconded by his friend and neighbour William Nightingale, a very rich, old-fashioned gentleman whose twelve-year-old daughter had been christened Florence, after the Italian city in which she was born.

After the election, which, despite the reform of the franchise, brought no substantial increase in the Whig majority, the general programme of reform continued. But the next step brought no benefit to the electors of Britain. On the contrary, it burdened them with the additional £20 million in taxes that the government needed in order to pay compensation to the planters in the dominions whose slaves had been freed by it.

On taking office as Foreign Secretary, Palmerston had assigned one of his clerks exclusively to matters concerning the abolition of slavery and the slave trade. Since then he had concluded an anti-slave-trade treaty with France, which authorized the navies of each nation to stop and search the merchant ships of the other. But French shipowners were simply avoiding search by instructing their captains to hoist Spanish flags when they sighted British warships. The treaty would not be effective until similar treaties had been signed with other nations. And it was the same with the Abolition Act which the reforming Parliament passed in 1833. To ensure that the plantation owners would still be able to harvest their crops, and to enable the emancipated slaves to support themselves, the act provided that for the next few years the former slaves would undergo a form of apprenticeship. But the apprentices were soon to be subjected to duress and punishment as harsh as any they had suffered as slaves. Conditions in the West Indies had improved only in name; and the slave trade between other nations was flourishing. There was still a long way to go.

The Abolition Act was soon followed by the most famous of the Factory Acts, which limited the working hours of children and appointed inspectors to enforce the limitations. The act produced some strange divisions, in the Cabinet as much as in the parties. Melbourne was against it; Palmerston supported it. But then one of the driving forces behind

the act was Lord Ashley, towards whom Palmerston was already showing all the supportive pride of a doting father-in-law.

Lady Cowper, who was less impressed by their daughter's worthy
husband, attended the wedding of her eldest son and then left for
France with her own ailing husband. Lady Jersey, who had planned
to go with them, decided at the last moment to stay on for a while in
London, where she was seen often enough in Palmerston's company
for the gossips to suggest they were having an affair. When she did at
last leave for France, Princess Lieven sent a mischievous note ahead
of her to Lady Cowper. 'Lady Jersey is leaving tomorrow and will be
joining you. Her good understanding with Lord Palmerston is causing
quite a stir.'

Palmerston on the other hand was flattered by the rumour and
delighted that it distracted attention from the truth. The woman with
whom the fifty-year-old Foreign Secretary was really spending such time
as he could spare, and with whom he was having his last great fling, was
Laura Maria Petre, the 21-year-old, beautiful but neglected new wife of
a 42-year-old fool who cared about nothing but horses.

But the hours available for Mrs Petre and Lady Jersey were never all
that many. Palmerston's first few years at the Foreign Office were hectic,
tiring and sometimes, by the standards of his earlier life, somewhat lonely.
The pace never slackened. By the time the Reform Bill had been settled,
Belgium was in crisis again; and this time Palmerston was under greater
pressure both at home and abroad. The new House of Commons was
much more inclined to support radical revolutionaries; and 'the Powers',
who since the Reform Bill saw Britain as a dangerous Liberal, were ready
to oppose her everywhere on principle.

The treaty of separation between Belgium and Holland had been ratified by Belgium, France and Great Britain soon after it had been signed
by all but one of the representatives at the conference. A few months
later it was ratified by the Russians – after Palmerston had guaranteed
that they would continue to receive interest on the loan they had made
during the Napoleonic Wars to the now non-existent Kingdom of the
Netherlands. Once Russia had ratified, Austria and Prussia followed
her example. But the King of Holland still refused to have anything to

do with it; and he also refused to open the Scheldt to Belgian ships, or to withdraw the garrison that he had left in Antwerp when his army withdrew from the rest of Belgium. In desperation, working alone, Palmerston drew up another compromise, famously known as 'Le Thème de Lord Palmerston', which was greeted by an astonished conference as a masterpiece of manipulative, detailed diplomacy. But it was received with contempt by the Dutch King.

Talleyrand and Palmerston lost patience and agreed that the time had come to use force. While the horrified 'Powers' withdrew from the conference – although without offering any assistance to the Dutch – Palmerston persuaded a divided Cabinet to trust the French again and make an alliance. At the end of 1832 a British and French fleet blockaded the Scheldt and a French army bombarded Antwerp. The citadel surrendered on 23 December. Soon afterwards, contrary to the expectations of half the British Cabinet, the French army went home. Treaty or no treaty, independent, neutral Belgium was a reality.

Yet, despite the continuing blockade and the consequences for Dutch commerce, the Dutch King remained 'evasive and unreasonable'. It was not until 19 April 1839, over six years later, that all the parties, including Holland, formally recognized the reality in the treaty that was to become tragically world-famous in 1914, when the belligerent German Kaiser dismissed it as 'a scrap of paper'. In a letter to Madame Flahaut, who always maintained an affectionate interest in the activities of the British Foreign Secretary, Talleyrand looked back on the long, exasperating but in the end successful conference and wrote, 'Among all of us, it is Palmerston who is the true statesman.'

The other incomplete independence struggle that Palmerston inherited was in Greece. By the time he took office, the Russians had at last acted on their own and brought the Turks to terms by force. By the Treaty of Adrianople the reluctant Turks had agreed to recognize a semi-independent Greece with reduced boundaries; and in addition they had ceeded teritories in the Caucasus and the Balkans to Russia. In the hope of restoring the original boundaries to a totally independent constitutional monarchy, Palmerston sent Stratford Canning, a cousin of his mentor, to negotiate in Constantinople.

Canning could not have hoped for an easier ride. As a reward for sending his ships and soldiers to support the Sultan against the Greeks, the independent Viceroy of Egypt, Mehemet Ali, had recently demanded that he be made Viceroy of Syria as well. When the Sultan refused, he had decided to take it anyway. As a result, while Canning and Sultan Mahmud II were negotiating, the murderous army of Mehemet Ali, commanded again by Ibrahim Pasha, was advancing victoriously out of Egypt from Gaza to Jaffa and on through Jerusalem to Acre, Damascus and Aleppo. In the hope that the British would help him to save his rapidly diminishing empire, the Sultan readily accepted an independent Greece with the boundaries that had originally been agreed in London; and after Prince John of Saxony and Prince Leopold of Saxe-Coburg had refused to take on the precarious throne, the eager Prince Otto of Bavaria was crowned King of the Hellenes.

While Ibrahim Pasha continued to advance, Stratford Canning wrote to London warning Palmerston that the Ottoman Empire was on the verge of collapse. If the British did not send help, the Russians would send it, making more territorial gains in the process. The threat changed Palmerston's mind about Turkey. Until then he would not have been sorry 'to see the Turk kicked out of Europe, & compelled to go and sit cross-legged, smoke his pipe, chew his opium, & cut off heads on the Asiatic side of the Bosphorous'. Now he was anxious to help and send a fleet. The Ottoman Empire lay across the overland routes between Britain and India. If that empire were to fall under the influence of the Tsar, north-western India would be left exposed to the open jaws of the Russian bear; and if Mehemet Ali were to conquer it, the equally dangerous influence would be French instead of Russian. The French regarded Mehemet Ali as an ally: for some time French administrators and engineers had been helping him to consolidate his independence and bring Egypt into the nineteenth century. But Palmerston pleaded in vain to the Cabinet that 'the mistress of India cannot permit France to be the mistress directly or indirectly of the route to the Indian dominions'. His colleagues refused to risk antagonizing the French, with whom they were acting as allies elsewhere, and they argued with some justification that the British navy was already overstretched with other commitments, one of which was the joint operation with the French navy in blockading the Scheldt.

'A drowning man clings to a serpent', said Sultan Mahmud. With his capital threatened, he turned as a last resort to the Russians, whose army was waiting on the border. Ibrahim Pasha was halted; Mehemet Ali was recognized as ruler of Syria, in return for no more than nominal allegiance; and on 8 June 1833, by the Treaty of Unkiar Skelessi, grateful Turkey gave Russian warships exclusive rights of passage through the Sea of Marmara, between the Black Sea and the Aegean, and agreed to consult Russia on all matters of foreign policy. The former made the Black Sea 'a Russian Lake', and the latter, as Palmerston put it, turned the Russian Ambassador into the 'chief Cabinet Minister of the Sultan'. A few years later, bemoaning Britain's failure to help in a letter to Lord Holland, he wrote, 'No British Cabinet at any period of the History of England ever made so great a mistake in regard to foreign affairs.'

The Treaty of Unkiar Skelessi was by far the worst set-back in Palmerston's early years at the Foreign Office, but he matched it with a triumph at the other end of the Mediterranean. When he took office, the Portuguese were still in the throes of a nasty civil war. By the end of 1833 the Spaniards were fighting one as well, following exactly the same plot. Both of them were melodramas, in which Absolutist 'wicked uncles' were attempting to wrest the ancient thrones from supposedly Liberal infant queens.

In Portugal, at the end of 1830, the supporters of the rightful queen, Donna Maria, were almost beaten, and her uncle, 'the usurper', Dom Miguel, controlled nearly all the kingdom. But the following year her father, Dom Pedro, who had been deposed by revolutionaries from the imperial throne of Brazil, returned to restore his daughter to the throne which he had earlier relinquished in her favour. In July 1832, with the help of British and French 'volunteers', he made a successful landing and captured the city of Oporto.

Soon afterwards Palmerston sent Stratford Canning to ask the King of Spain to help in the restoration of the rightful Portuguese Queen. But the wretched King Ferdinand VII, whose views, in so far as he had any, were Absolutist anyway, was much too frightened to defy 'the Powers', who he knew were supporting Miguel with money and arms. It was all that Canning could do to persuade him not to help Miguel. Nevertheless, as Palmerston wrote to his brother, it was still 'anybody's race'. Without any overt support Pedro's success continued. At the beginning of July 1833 his ships, mostly fitted out in French or English ports, sailed out of Oporto commanded by one Carlos Ponza, an alias for the flamboyantly eccentric Captain Charles Napier RN, who had fought as both soldier and sailor in the Napoleonic Wars and had returned to active service after losing his inherited fortune running a steamboat company on the Seine. Three hundred miles to the south, Napier met and annihilated Miguel's fleet off Cape St Vincent. By the end of the month he had taken Lisbon, and Donna Maria had been crowned Queen of Portugal.

Two months later civil war broke out in Spain. When King Ferdinand died, leaving the throne to his three-year-old daughter Isabella, his younger brother Carlos claimed it, supported by the Basque separatists and, like Miguel, by the church and by the three 'Powers', whose representatives had recently been assembled by Metternich at Munchengratz, where they had promised their united support to all totalitarian princes.

In the long run Palmerston could see that the days of the absolute rulers were numbered. As he wrote to his brother:

> The Triumph of Maria, and the accession of Isabella, will be important events in Europe, and will give great strength to the Liberal party. England, France, Belgium, Portugal and Spain, looked upon merely as a mass of opinion, form a powerful body in Europe; and Greece, further on, is rising into a state upon similar principles.

But in the short run, it was clear that clandestine opposition to the pretenders was no longer going to be enough. What was needed was an 'alliance among the constitutional states of the West which will serve as a powerful counterpoise to the Holy Alliance of the East'.

The easiest task was getting the idea accepted in Spain and Portugal. To the supporters of the young queens, a commitment to constitutional government was a small price to pay for their survival, and it was almost as easy in England. 'I carried it through the Cabinet by a coup de main taking them by surprise and not leaving them time to make objections.' Talleyrand took longer, if only because he wanted it to be his idea. But eventually, on 22 April 1834, Britain, France, Spain and Portugal signed the treaty that created the Quadruple Alliance, pledged to compel the two pretenders to withdraw from the peninsula.

'I should like to see Metternich's face when he reads our treaty', wrote Palmerston in another letter to his brother. There was nothing practical that 'the Powers' could do. France was the only country that had a border with the peninsula, and the British navy controlled its coasts. In the face of such a threat the pretenders surrendered. Miguel went to Genoa, and Carlos to London. For the time being the Iberian queens were safe. Palmerston had a right to be proud. 'The treaty was a capital hit, and all my own doing.'

By the time the news of the Quadruple Alliance had raised blood pressures in Vienna, Berlin and St Petersburg, the Russian court was already in a fury over a much more trivial matter. At the end of October 1832 Palmerston had appointed Stratford Canning as the next Ambassador to St Petersburg and had announced the appointment in the *London Gazette*. Palmerston believed that a nation had the right to choose anyone it wanted as its representative at a foreign court, and he maintained that principle throughout his career. On several occasions he accepted ambassadors whom he knew to be enemies of Britain. But the Tsar, in keeping with tradition, maintained that the host nation had the right to say no; and he refused to receive the man who had worked so hard against his interests in Constantinople. Canning, he claimed, had once insulted him, even though everybody knew that the two had never met.

Since Princess Lieven boasted regularly to St Petersburg about her influence with Grey and Palmerston, the Tsar instructed her to change their minds. She pleaded with Grey, who was still her lover. She claimed that Palmerston had once promised to her that Canning would never go to St Petersburg – a claim Palmerston dismissed as 'a fib'. She suggested that Grey's son-in-law Durham would make a much better ambassador. She knew that Durham wanted the job, if only because he wanted Palmerston's and saw it as a stepping-stone; and she knew that he was acceptable to St Petersburg, if only because the impression that he had made on a recent visit had led them to believe he would be easy to handle. On his way home Durham had visited several capitals in an attempt to promote himself; and from Vienna, Frederick Lamb had written to warn Palmerston about what was happening. But Palmerston was not worried. 'I am not afraid of him,' he wrote back, 'he has no influence in the Cabinet except upon Grey, being by all the rest most especially disliked.'

It was partly in the hope of a compromise that Palmerston had sent Canning to Spain. If he liked it enough, he might be persuaded to accept the Madrid embassy, and then someone else could be appointed to St Petersburg. But Canning insisted that it was a matter of honour that he should retain the St Petersburg appointment; and to Palmerston it was a matter of honour that he should continue to support him. He suggested another compromise: Canning could go to St Petersburg for a few months and then be withdrawn. But even this the Tsar refused. In that case, said Palmerston, there would be no ambassador in St Petersburg and the British would have to make do with a chargé d'affaires. In diplomatic terms this meant that the Russians had to return the insult, withdrawing their own ambassador and leaving only a chargé d'affaires in London. Princess Lieven had become the victim of her own strategem.

For twenty years Almack's and London society had been all that ever mattered to Princess Lieven. The woman who only a few weeks earlier had been saying that the British 'needed taking down a peg' was now begging for a reprieve. She wept to Grey. She turned for help to Lady Cowper, who had recently returned from France. It was from Lady Cowper's house, Panshanger, that she wrote to the Foreign Secretary: 'Remember, my Lord, you are about to destroy and overturn my whole existence.' But there was nothing that could now be done.

The Lievens left London in May 1834, to be replaced by Pozzo di Borgo, whom Palmerston had met in Paris. Almost everyone was glad to see them go. It was probably the only subject on which the King and *The Times* ever agreed. And yet, although Talleyrand later suggested that the Foreign Secretary had engineered the whole thing, Palmerston seemed genuinely to regret their passing. In the honest intimacy of a letter to his brother, he wrote, 'I am very sorry on private grounds to lose old friends and agreeable members of society, but on public grounds I do not know that their loss will be great.'

The next to leave the scene was the Prime Minister. In July, old, tired, exasperated by Russell's continuous arguements over Ireland, and convinced that he had taken reform as far as was possible, Grey tendered his resignation to the King. To the fury of Brougham, the King invited Melbourne to replace him, believing him to be the least likely to lead his government any further to the left. Melbourne accepted and took office as nonchalantly as if he had been asked to deal a hand at whist. He made no changes in his Cabinet. Palmerston remained at the Foreign Office and Althorp at the Exchequer, and Duncannon was appointed as his own replacement at the Home Office. The three who once sat together round the breakfast table in Dr Bromley's house at Harrow now sat round the Cabinet table, and the man who sat at the head of the table was brother-in-law to one of them and brother to the long-standing mistress of another.

The following month Talleyrand retired. After the farewell dinner that Palmerston gave in his honour, his niece complained that their fellow guests had not been distinguished enough. And then, in October, as if to emphasize the passing of an era, the old Palace of Westminster caught fire. Most of the makeshift buildings which had grown up over the past 300 years to provide inadequate accommodation for both Lords and Commons were left in ashes.

A month later Earl Spencer died. His heir, Althorp, who was Leader of the House of Commons, was promoted to the House of Lords. It was excuse enough for the nervous King to exercise the royal prerogative for what was to be the last time in British history and get rid of his Radical government, despite its huge majority. He summoned Melbourne to Brighton and told him that, without a Leader of the House of Commons, the government must resign. Melbourne made several suggestions for replacements, but the King would have none of them. He had already written a letter inviting Wellington to take over. Melbourne withdrew, climbed into his carriage and drove back to London, accepting his dismissal as impassively as he had accepted his appointment.

On the evening of 14 November, as he was making his way home from a dinner at Holland House, Palmerston called on Melbourne, who had returned a few hours earlier, and learned that they were out of office. He was one of the very few ministers who did not learn of it from the newspapers the next day. Brougham had called earlier; and although he had been asked to keep it to himself, he had gone straight from Melbourne's house to his old friends at *The Times*. 'We are all out', wrote Palmerston to his brother. 'Turned out neck and crop.'

When despatches went out from the Foreign Office to spread the news across the world, Palmerston wrote one of his notes at the top of the one that was destined for Vienna. 'Take this, without loss of time, to Prince Metternich. I am certain that he will never have been more delighted in his life than when he reads it, and that I shall never have been so popular with him as on my departure from office.'

7. BARBARIANS
AND BUNTING

When Sir Robert Peel became Prime Minister for the first time, he received the King's invitation while he was on holiday with his family in Italy. In compelling Melbourne to resign, William IV had hoped to replace him with Wellington. But the canny duke declined the offer and insisted that, in the wake of reform, and with the Radicals so strong and disruptive, it was essential to have the Prime Minister in the Commons. In his view Peel was the only man for the job. Nevertheless, at the King's request, he agreed to hold the reins until Peel came back, and he set about his task with his usual, blunt, oblivious efficiency, taking over not only as Prime Minister but also as Foreign Secretary, Home Secretary and Secretary of State for War and the Colonies. As Earl Grey put it in a naively confidential letter to his recently departed mistress Princess Lieven, 'His Highness the Dictator is concentrating in himself all the power of the State, in a manner neither constitutional nor legal.'

Peel had inherited his father's baronetcy and millions in 1830. On receiving the King's invitation, he returned to England as rapidly as only a rich man could. Hauled by a frequently changing succession of the fastest horses his fortune could hire, he covered the 800 miles from Rome to Calais in five days. By the middle of December 1834 he had formed his government, with Wellington in Palmerston's place at the Foreign Office. Without a majority, however, he could not govern, and in January he went to the country in the hope of winning one.

While candidates canvassed in the constituencies, huge teams of craftsmen laboured hurriedly from dawn to dusk to provide the accommodation they would need when they reassembled. Apart from the eighteenth-century law courts and Westminster Hall, which had been mercifully saved by a sudden change of wind, the only parts of the Palace of Westminster still standing after the fire in October had been the walls of the House of Lords and the once glorious Painted Chamber. Under the direction of Sir Robert Smirke, the architect of the British Museum, the craftsmen were now re-roofing and restoring these shells, so that the Lords could be promoted to occupy the Painted Chamber, which had been the private apartment of medieval monarchs, and the Commons could rise to replace them in what till then had been the House of Lords.

Soon after their return from the hustings the members of the House of Commons moved into the fresh, simple chamber that was to be their temporary home for the next twelve years. There were a few new faces among them. The Tories had made gains, including one spectacular success in the seat of the former Foreign Secretary, South Hampshire, where their mediocre candidates had achieved a narrow victory by concentrating their generous canvassing on the new voters in the coastal towns. But they were still outnumbered and in April, after several exasperating but inevitable defeats, Peel resigned. With some embarrassment, the thwarted King invited Melbourne to return.

Melbourne's position was not as strong as it had been before. His reduced majority now depended on the support of Daniel O'Connell and the Irish members. In the hope of earning their vote as often as possible, he entered into what became known as the 'Lichfield House Compact' with O'Connell. In return for O'Connell's support, or at least a reduction in his agitation for repeal of the Act of Union, Melbourne agreed to embark on a programme of reform in Ireland, which included the abolition of the iniquitous system whereby Roman Catholic farmers paid tithes to support the established Protestant Church. In addition, as evidence of his commitment to the programme, he made one major change in his Cabinet. He appointed Duncannon Lord Privy Seal and replaced him at the Home Office with Lord John Russell, whose angry advocacy of the Irish cause had hastened Grey's resignation and had been the main reason for his own dismissal in November.

The other major change that Melbourne nearly made was at the Foreign Office, although only for the sake of the quiet life which meant so much to him, rather than out of any personal animosity. The extent to which Palmerston had alienated Austria, Prussia and Russia had spread serious alarm among many of the traditional Whigs, including Lansdowne and even hospitable Holland, who managed to separate his growing aversion to Palmerston's policies from the pleasure that he still took in his company. They pressed Melbourne to make a change; and they were supported by Esterhazy and Bülow, who assured him that relations with Austria and Prussia would be improved by Palmerston's removal. In Vienna, ever since Melbourne first became Prime Minister, Metternich had been imploring his brother the British Ambassador to persuade him that it would be in his best interests to replace his Foreign Secretary; and in Paris, ever since his return from London, Talleyrand had been insisting to his government that Palmerston was untrustworthy. Despite his respect for his occasional ally as a statesman, Talleyrand had been humiliated by him too often to like him. Allowing personal animosity to influence policy – a weakness he once identified as Palmerston's one all-pervading flaw – he suggested that, if Palmerston returned to the Foreign Office, the French should refuse to be represented in London by an ambassador.

But Palmerston, as usual, called what he hoped was their bluff. He refused to accept any other ministry or any office outside the Cabinet. It was to be the Foreign Office or nothing; and Melbourne could not risk offering him nothing. Even Holland allowed himself to be convinced that the removal of Palmerston from the Foreign Office so soon after Talleyrand's departure might suggest in Europe that Metternich had succeeded in demolishing the Anglo-French allance; and his removal from the government altogether was likely to suggest that the government was rejecting his policies, which might not be enough to turn opponents into allies but would certainly turn allies into suspicious opponents, and would lose the government the vital support of the Radicals in the Commons.

So Palmerston survived. On 26 April he returned to the Foreign Office. Now all he had to do was get back into the House of Commons. For the next month, while he searched and negotiated frantically for a seat, his unconstitutional lack of one was defended stoutly in the Commons by the new Leader of the House, Russell, whose recent marriage to a widow had already induced his colleagues to change his nickname from 'Little Johnny' to 'the Widow's Mite'. Eventually, towards the end of May, after receiving a payment of £2,000 from Palmerston, a charming but impecunious barrister called James Kennedy resigned as one of the members for Tiverton in Devon. Palmerston stood as his replacement. On 1 June he was elected unopposed for the seat that he was to represent for the rest of his life; and not long afterwards Kennedy was appointed to a salaried position on a commission investigating the illegal slave trade in the Caribbean.

Palmerston found the Foreign Office much as he had left it. There had hardly been time for Wellington to make any changes in his policies, but there had been time to make one change in the composition of the diplomatic corps. The recent appointment of George Shee as Ambassador to Prussia had been cancelled. Palmerston's old friend from Cambridge had followed him from the War Office to the Foreign Office, where he took on the duties of Political Under Secretary after the first choice, Lord Ashley, had turned them down. Shee was loyal, industrious and comparatively shrewd. He had been particularly useful to Palmerston as the first civil servant to act as a regular intermediary between his minister and the press. But he did not have the ability or experience, or indeed, what was then equally important, the social standing, to justify his appointment to one of the four most important embassies in the world. It is possible that the appointment would not have been made if Grey had still been Prime Minister. Certainly Wellington regarded it as inappropriate; and Palmerston took the hint. On his return to the Foreign Office, he did not renew it. Instead Shee was sent to Stuttgart as Consul, a level from which he never rose. Nine years later he was dismissed by a Tory government for an indiscretion that only the most senior statesman could presume to commit with impunity: he had married his mistress.

For a while afterwards Palmerston was careful not to make any appointment that could be open to misinterpretation, even when it was only an insignificant sinecure of the kind Wellington might have endorsed. During the first few months after his return to office he resisted all pressure to find a comfortable consulate for Beau Brummell. Brummell had been living in France since 1816, when he left England in a hurry to avoid his creditors. In June 1830, only three months after the death of the relentlessly embittered George IV, William IV and his first Prime Minister, Wellington, had generously arranged Brummell's appointment as British Consul in Caen, a post that carried a small but much needed salary. Two years later, however, when Wellington was out of office and Palmerston was Foreign Secretary, Brummell wrote to Palmerston asking if he could be moved to a more active and perhaps more lucrative consulate. Since this was at a time when Palmerston was attempting to make his ministry more efficient and economical, he wrote back asking if there was actually any need for a British Consul in Caen. When Brummell answered honestly that there was not, Palmerston abolished the post, although he paid Brummell a small sum in compensation and indicated that he might consider transferring him to another consulate if a suitable one became available. Since then no such consulate had been found; and now, when Brummell's position was pitiable and his friends were pressing for charity, there was no hope of one. The model to whom Melbourne and Palmerston owed so much of their style was condemned to spend his last five years in a French debtors' prison and a mad house.

Under the old 'beau' Melbourne the old 'buck' Palmerston was on his own at the Foreign Office. As with most of his ministers, Melbourne simply gave him a job and left him to get on with it. He no longer had Grey to guide him, or Lansdowne and Holland to restrain him; and his recent narrow escape from the censure of the traditional Whigs had done nothing to tame him. On the contrary, if anything it had made him bolder, and it had driven him closer to O'Connell and the Radicals, whose Liberal colours he now flew prominently over every argument, if only as a flag of convenience. His manner became even more haughty and at the same time more carelessly light-hearted. The few Tories and traditional Whigs who bothered to attend debates on foreign policy began to complain that he treated the House of Commons with contempt. His halting delivery was seen as a sign of casual indifference rather than nervousness or ineptitude; and since his ill-prepared speeches contrasted starkly with his lucid letters, despatches and protocols, there was plenty of evidence to support the case. To *The Times* — which was not without motive, since it had just shifted its support from Brougham to Peel and was engaged in a fierce circulation war with Palmerston's most ardent supporter, the *Morning Chronicle* — he was insufferable. 'What an offensive union is that of a dull understanding and an unfeeling heart!' wrote one leader writer with a pomposity worthy of Palmerston at his worst. 'Add to this the self-satisfied airs of a flippant dandy, and you have the most nauseous specimen of humanity — a sort of compound which justifies Swift in his disgusting exhibition of the Yahoos.'

Although there had been no actual changes in foreign policy during the dandy's brief absence, not everything was quite as it seemed. Disparaged by Talleyrand as worthless, and without Palmerston to sustain it, the Quadruple Alliance was no longer 'a capital hit'. Since the recent death of the Portuguese Queen's father, the French had been conducting an intensive diplomatic campaign aimed at persuading her government that they needed no friend but France. In May, while Palmerston was looking for a seat in Parliament, the Portuguese Foreign Minister was in Paris negotiating a marriage between Queen Maria and the Duke of Nemours.

Fortunately the Portuguese Foreign Minister went home to Lisbon via London. When he arrived in England, Palmerston discovered that one of the members of his party was the Count Lavradio, with whom he had spent many evenings during his days as a mature student in Paris. Palmerston went to work on Lavradio. For centuries England and Portugal had been united by a profitable alliance in which each had treated the other as an equal. But the British government could not be expected to continue that alliance if the Portuguese Queen contracted a marriage that would inevitably transfer her nation's principal loyalty to France. There was no need for any heavy-handed reminder that it was only twenty-five years since a British army drove the domineering French across the Portuguese border into Spain. An implication that Portugal was about to exchange a partner for a patron was enough. Lavradio saw the point and convinced his minister.

The marriage negotiations were halted. In the following February, at Palmerston's suggestion, Queen Maria was married by proxy to Prince Ferdinand of Saxe-Coburg, a nephew of King Leopold of the Belgians. In March, on his way to Lisbon, Ferdinand visited the British royal family at Windsor with his father and brother. Six weeks later, this time at the suggestion of King Leopold, his eldest brother, the dissolute Duke Ernest, who was the head of the Saxe-Coburg family, came to London and went to Kensington Palace to visit their sister the widowed Duchess of Kent, and to introduce his sons Ernest and Albert to their cousin Victoria, the seventeen-year-old heir to the throne of England.

While Palmerston was restoring Britain's ancient alliance with Portugal, the Spanish corner of the Quadruple Alliance was disintegrating in another ferocious civil war. In May 1834 the exiled Spanish pretender Don Carlos had come to London, rented a house that once belonged to George Canning and opened negotiations with Wellington, ostensibly in the hope of getting support from the Tories. A few weeks later, however, he had cancelled all his engagements and announced that he was not well enough to leave his bed. By the time someone discovered that the supposedly sick man in the bed was a servant, Carlos was half-way back to Spain. Palmerston wrote reassuringly to his ambassador in Madrid: 'He will not land like Murat with half a dozen followers, nor march like Bonaparte from a sea-port to the capital.' But this time he was wrong. Carlos landed in San Sebastian and used the Basque guerrillas in the mountains to create the nucleus of a new army.

The Spanish Queen Mother, Christina, who was acting as regent for her daughter Isabella, called for help from her allies; and the other members of the Quadruple Alliance responded with varying levels of reluctance. The Portuguese closed Spain's southern border and sent 8,000 men; the French closed the northern border; and the British and French navies blockaded the ports that were held by the 'Carlistas'. If the blockade had been as effective as it could have been, Carlos would have been starved of supplies, arms, ammunition and money, and the war would have been over in weeks. But Palmerston could not persuade the British government to defy international law and allow the navy to fire on ships flying neutral colours. Since the French were not prepared to take such provocative action alone, ships from Holland and Italy continued to sail in past the allied fleets to supply the 'Carlistas', and the terrible fighting escalated.

The war might also have been ended quickly if the French and the British had done what they originally agreed to do and sent their armies into Spain in sufficient strength. But the two nations were much too wary of each other to act in unison – even at sea their fleets were operating separately – and each was as reluctant as the other to commit an army unilaterally. At Westminster, however, despite this reluctance, there was a widespread but unfounded suspicion that the French were planning to invade. Since the prospect of another French invasion of Spain was equally abhorrent to both sides of the House, Palmerston set out to forestall it by persuading the French to accept a more modest plan, which at least allowed each nation to make a gesture towards the obligations of their alliance.

As their part of the bargain the French cheerfully agreed to lend the Spanish government several thousand men from what was already known as *le plus beau Corps de France*, which Louis-Philippe had founded in 1830 and filled with revolutionary refugees from Poland and Germany: the Foreign Legion. Meanwhile, for his part, Palmerston persuaded the British government to amend the Foreign Enlistment Acts, so that a 10,000-strong British Legion, composed mostly of destitute Irishmen, could be sent out to serve in the Spanish Queen's army under the command of an extrovert Radical MP, Colonel George de Lacy Evans, a veteran of Waterloo, who had previously served in Spain with Wellington and had been wounded twice at the Battle of New Orleans.

As time passed, the news from Spain turned stomachs in England. Both sides shot prisoners. Since the Church supported the 'Carlistas', the 'Isabelinos' sometimes slaughtered priests and monks. When a 'Carlista' general shot a particularly large number of prisoners as well as several provincial mayors, the 'Isabelinos' shot his wife; and in response the general shot many more prisoners and the wives of four leading government supporters. When the legions arrived, Carlos decreed that all foreigners who were captured while fighting for the government were to be shot; and his supporters carried out the order thoroughly and with relish.

The indignation in Westminster increased the interest in foreign policy and rose to a noisy climax in a four-day debate that began on 17 April 1837. The Tories, who for the most part supported Carlos, attacked Palmerston for subjecting Spain to 'the ravages of foreign mercenaries' and for allowing British subjects to take part in atrocities. On his own side of the House, the Radicals attacked him for not sending the British army to support Isabella, and the traditional Whigs, who would have preferred not to be involved at all, sat in unsupportive silence.

Fortunately, for the first time in a long time, Palmerston had prepared his speech. For three hours either side of midnight on 19 April he outlined and defended all his policies since he first took office, constantly playing to the Radicals and occasionally illustrating his arguments with inappropriate references to history. From the creation of Belgium to the forming of the Quadruple Alliance, his overriding objective had been the promotion of constitutional government, and this, he told them, was the cause that he now supported in Spain. 'It is there and upon that contracted scene that is to be decided by issue of battle that great contest between opposing and conflicting principles of government – arbitrary government on the one hand and constitutional government on the other – which is going on all over Europe.' By the time he sat down he had won over the Radicals, and with their support his policy in Spain was vindicated by a majority of thirty-six votes.

In reality, however, the 'great contest' in Spain was dissolving into less creditable contests. The 'Isabelinos' had divided into 'Moderados' and 'Progresistas'. When the Queen Regent Christina dismissed her Prime Minister and attempted to install a more conservative 'Moderado' government, the 'Progresistas' staged a coup and forced her to accept a more radical one instead.

The 'Progresistas', who looked to Palmerston for support, were on the whole more fortunate than the 'Moderados', who looked to France. Frightened and manipulated by Metternich, King Louis-Philippe had begun to believe that the security of his throne and the future of his dynasty depended on the acceptance of 'the Powers'. In an attempt to appease them he allowed them to send supplies to Carlos through France, secretly instructing his border guards to look the other way as they passed, and he did all that he could to ensure that his nominal opposition to Carlos was in no way decisive. There were times when his Foreign Legion was suspiciously slow in coming to the assistance of the 'Moderados'.

The British Legion was, if anything, even less effective, although only because a lack of pay had left it mutinously disaffected. But the 'Progresistas' were able to rely on regular supplies from England and on at least one occasion, when they were attacking a town on the coast, they were assisted by a landing party from a British frigate which just happened to be carrying an exceptionally enormous detachment of marines.

As often happens in ugly civil wars, the fighting was ended by treachery. A British agent, Lord Edmund Hay, arranged a secret meeting between the government commander, General Baldomero Espartero, and a 'Carlista' general, Rafael Maroto. In return for an amnesty and a promise that after the war he and his men would be accepted into the government army, Maroto agreed to seize the unsuspecting Don Carlos and hand him over to Espartero. Carlos, who was good at escaping, got away before the handover and went to France; and as soon as the French had sent him on to more welcoming Austria, they found themselves playing hosts to the Regent Christina, who thought it best to leave Spain after the failure of a 'Moderado' coup. Espartero became both Regent and radical Prime Minister; peace was restored to Spain, at least for a while; and for want of anyone else to reward, the relieved British government recommended that the barely deserving Colonel George de Lacy Evans MP be given a knighthood.

One of the few ridiculous episodes in an otherwise relentlessly cruel war occurred in 1837, when de Lacy Evans abandoned his command for a few weeks and went home to defend his Westminster seat in the general election that followed the death of the King. William IV died on 20 June 1837 after a few weeks of obviously terminal illness. During those weeks Princess Victoria turned for advice to her favourite uncle

Leopold, who sent over his personal physician and confidential adviser, Baron Stockmar, to guide her. But within weeks of her accession Queen Victoria had put her trust in additional advisers of her own.

The 'most truly honest, straightforward and noble-minded' Lord Melbourne, her 'Primus', whom she admitted to her journal she regarded as a father figure, became, uniquely, the Queen's private secretary as well as her Prime Minister. He taught her and guided her on almost every subject, and she recorded his 'dashing opinions' indiscriminately. Matters of state and good advice, such as 'try to do no good, and then you won't get into any scrapes', were accorded the same innocent respect as mere whimsy, such as 'people who talk much of railroads and bridges are generally Liberals'. Only the tutorials on foreign affairs and diplomatic protocol were left to the 'good friend' of Uncle Leopold, 'clever' and 'amusing' Lord Palmerston, who explained the creation of Belgium 'in such a very clear, plain and agreeable manner, as to put me quite au fait of the whole thing'.

Melbourne and Palmerston were besotted with the young Queen. They attended on her as frequently as they could, often when there was no official need for it, and they were regularly seen riding with her at Windsor. Indeed, so devoted was their attention that it was soon raising eyebrows. Some Tories saw it as ominous. Aberdeen, another of Princess Lieven's indiscreet correspondents, told her that the relationship between the Queen and her Prime Minister reminded him of the young Edward VI and Protector Somerset. But to London society in general it was simply unseemly and perhaps even unsafe for their young Queen to spend so much time with these two ageing remnants of Regency dandies. A famous cartoon, published within four months of the Queen's accession, showed Palmerston playing chess with her, as he often did, and Melbourne looking over her shoulder. The caption beneath read simply, 'The Queen in Danger'. As Peel put it, 'She may not know their character – but they must know their own.'

Both men had reputations that stretched back to their days as a beau and a buck. Apart from Palmerston's well-known and long-standing affection for Lady Cowper, several of his other liaisons had been sufficiently obvious for people to suspect, correctly, that there must have been many more. But the resulting reputation, although far from respectable, was in essence no more than a matter of gossip. It was Melbourne's less colourful reputation which came closer to what his hypocritical contemporaries regarded as disgraceful. As yet his predeliction for spanking was known only to the willing victims, and his patience with his late, psychotic wife, Lady Caroline, had earned him a certain amount of sympathy. But his relationships, innocent or otherwise, outside his disastrous marriage had led to his being brought before three separate courts.

The first two legal actions arose as a result of a long, indiscreet relationship with Lady Branden, which began in Dublin, in the days when Melbourne was living there, without his wife, as Chief Secretary for Ireland. When Lord Branden, a clergyman, discovered some of Melbourne's letters to his wife, several of which contained references to whipping, he brought an action for criminal conversation against Melbourne in the Court of King's Bench, claiming damages for adultery, and sued for divorce in the ecclesiastical court, citing Melbourne as co-respondent. To the astonishment of everyone, both actions failed for sudden lack of evidence. But long after all the parties were dead, surviving documents revealed that, just before the proceedings began, Lord Branden received a payment of £2,000 from Lord Melbourne.

The third action, also for 'crim. con.', was brought in the Court of Common Pleas as a result of Melbourne's close friendship with the Hon. Mrs Norton, the granddaughter of Richard Brinsley Sheridan. Once again the action failed for lack of evidence, and in this case it seems likely from their letters that the relationship, although foolhardy, was indeed innocent. Nevertheless, as with Palmerston, Melbourne's bank account revealed many payments to several ladies besides Elizabeth Branden and Caroline Norton. Reviewing his depleted estate after his death, one of his executors, Brougham, remarked, 'What a sad pillage! Women of Course.'

To the Queen, however, Melbourne was always 'truly excellent and moral'. It was her image of Palmerston that was to alter; and although it was eventually to alter in many more significant ways, the first change came with the loss of any illusions she may have had about his morals.

All that is known about the incident is that on a winter's night in 1839, when Palmerston was staying with the Queen at Windsor Castle, he crept into the bedchamber of one of the ladies-in-waiting, Mrs Brand, locking one door behind him and then blocking the other with a piece of furniture. When Mrs Brand woke to find the Foreign Secretary advancing on her in the dark, she leaped out of bed and called for help, which caused the Foreign Secretary to leave as quietly and quickly as he had entered. Next day she complained to Melbourne. Fearing that a scandal might bring down the government and even damage the reputation of the Queen, Melbourne did all that he could to placate her and hush the matter up. He insisted furiously that Palmerston must write an apology to Mrs Brand, which he did, and which Mrs Brand accepted. But she had already talked enough for the news to reach the ears of the Queen, and Melbourne, as embarrassed as he was angry, found himself placating the indignant Queen as well, assuring her that Palmerston had never forced his attentions where they were not welcome, and using his fortunately considerable inflence to persuade her that it would be best to take no further action.

Not all of Palmerston's biographers have recorded this incident, and only a few have recorded the explanation suggested later by Prince Albert's secretary, George Anson: that Palmerston had made an assignation with some other lady and had entered Mrs Brand's chamber by mistake. In the absence of anything from Palmerston himself, this remains the only recorded explanation, and it is particularly plausible because the labyrinthine corridors of Windsor Castle were notorious. With little help from limited lighting and the resentfully underpaid servants, guests frequently failed to find their way to their rooms at night. But what nobody has pointed out in this context is that one of the guests in the castle was Lady Cowper. Surely the most likely explanation is that the lady whom Palmerston had intended to visit, and whose reputation he was protecting with his silence, was Lady Cowper, especially since, by now, the two were engaged to be married.

Earl Cowper died on 21 June 1837, two days after the King. As soon as was seemly, Palmerston proposed to his widow, but it was over two years before she gave him an answer. Surprisingly for a woman who had spent her entire adult life defying convention, she was more concerned about how it would look than whether it would work. She consulted everyone so many times that some of those who had originally opposed the idea changed their advice in the hope of putting an end to the tedious questioning. Her children were always against the marriage, but Melbourne was one of those who eventually came round to it, although he continued to worry about Palmerston's finances, sharing his anxiety indiscreetly with the Queen, and he reminded his sister that the price of the marriage would be a considerable demotion in the still significant social hierarchy. Once Lady Cowper was married to Lord Palmerston, the widow of an English earl would become no more than the wife of a commonplace and seatless Irish viscount.

While the consultations were in progress, Palmerston became increasingly agitated and jealous. The longer he waited, the more he believed that he had rivals. When the Queen and her court went to Brighton, he was unable to restrain himself from writing to Lady Cowper, who was also there, suggesting that she had another suitor among the courtiers. But it was clear from the tone of the letter that she wrote to reassure him that the answer to his proposal was eventually going to be yes. 'There is not another person in the world of whom I would ever think for one moment in that light.' When the news of the engagement at last became public, one of those who had always been in favour of it, Lady Holland, wrote, 'It will be the union of the best tempered persons in the world. Never did I see a man more in love and devoted.'

The negotiations which culminated in an engagement between the Prime Minister's sister and the Foreign Secretary coincided exactly with those that led to the engagement of the Queen. At first Melbourne was perplexed by the problem of finding a consort. He disliked the idea of an Englishman because this would inevitably exalt his entire family above the rest of the nation; and he disliked the idea of a foreigner because on the whole Her Majesty's subjects were not fond of foreigners. But it is a truth universally acknowledged that, where a Queen of England is in want of a husband, there is usually an uncle in the background with a nephew to promote; and it soon became clear that this was indeed the only worthwhile candidate.

According to a rumour that has reappeared regularly ever since, Melbourne came round to accepting King Leopold's nephew Prince Albert only after he had been told that the Prince's father was the brilliant court chamberlain at Coburg, Baron von Meyern, and that therefore his veins contained none of the bad blood that had produced his elder brother, who was as dissolute as the duke. But there were other male members of Prince Albert's family who were far from dissolute – King Leopold, for example – and his mother's many intimate and uninhibited letters to her friend Augusta von Studnitz reveal that, neglected though she was, her only lover was Baron Alexander von Hanstein, whom she met three years after Prince Albert was born, and whom she married two years later, when the duke divorced her. In reality Melbourne favoured the Prince because he was clearly the best man for the job and because, equally clearly, he was the man whom the Queen had set her heart on. The long delay before the announcement of an engagement was due, not to Melbourne, but to the Queen, who was as mischievously reluctant to commit herself as Lady Cowper. It was not until the autumn of 1839, when Prince Albert came over for another visit, that she at last got round to proposing to him.

Broadlands, the once dilapidated estate in Hampshire which the extravagant second Viscount Palmerston transformed into this 'modern' Neo-classical house surrounded by a fashionably 'picturesque' park

The Hon. Harry Temple and his youngest sister, Lizzie, painted in
Munich on their way home from Italy in 1794

Thomas Heaphy's portrait of the dandy student was the first for
which Palmerston sat after succeeding his father as third Viscount

Spencer Perceval, who was shot by a deranged bankrupt, is the only
British Prime Minister to have been assassinated

Almack's, where the ladies first nicknamed young Palmerston 'Lord
Cupid', was the most fashionable and exclusive nightclub in the world

Painted by Sir Thomas Lawrence when she was only seventeen, the Hon. Emily Lamb, the future Lady Palmerston, was already a vivacious and confident beauty

Lawrence's unfinished portrait of Princess Lieven, 'the Sibyl of diplomacy', who was the mistress of several statesmen and the confidante of many others

Prince Leopold of Saxe-Coburg with his first wife, Princess Charlotte, whose early death was described by Wellington as a serious national misfortune

Queen Victoria's first Prime Minister and unlikely mentor, '
dear Lord Melbourne'

The diminutive, abrasive and resolutely radical Lord John Russell was
Palmerston's most mercurial colleague

One of the greatest if least principled statesmen of his era, Prince Talleyrand was as skilful at survival as at diplomacy

Louis-Philippe Egalité, the able but corrupt 'Citizen King' of France

The exposure of a young queen to the influence of men with the reputations of Melbourne and Palmerston was the object of much cheerful innuendo

In John Doyle's famous lithograph *The Last Rose of Summer*, Palmerston sits alone in heroic, nonchalant opposition to the government

After more than ten gruelling years at the Foreign Office, Palmerston
still looked closer to forty than to sixty

Dour, scholarly, cultured and cautious, the fourth Earl of Aberdeen
was the Tory antithesis to Palmerston

Louis-Philippe's chief minister, François Guizot, was as much an
academician as a statesman

More fop than dandy, the young, opportunistic novelist Benjamin
Disraeli was the Tory party's only able orator in the House of Commons

The brilliant, reactionary Prince Metternich was Europe's leading
enemy of all constitutional reform

At the age of fifty-three the powerful Lady Palmerston, wife of the
Foreign Secretary and sister of the Prime Minister, was still one of the
most beautiful women in London

While he was waiting for his Queen and his sister to make up their minds, Lord Melbourne and his government went out of office for almost a week. At the beginning of 1839 the plantation owners on Jamaica, who were notoriously the cruellest in the West Indies, rose in a bitter rebellion and attempted to turn back the clock. The abolition of slavery had reduced their sugar exports by twenty per cent, and the recent cancellation of the apprenticeship system had raised their costs. As part of the successful suppression of the rebellion, the government introduced a bill that suspended the Jamaican constitution and put the island under the direct rule of the Governor. To the Tories it was too harsh, and to the Radicals it was not enough. The bill was passed in the House of Commons by 304 votes to 299, a majority of only five. Arguing that this made the government too weak to continue, Melbourne, who never enjoyed being Prime Minister anyway, persuaded his Cabinet to resign.

The Queen wept at the news. When Sir Robert Peel came to see her, his awkward formality was a painful contrast to Melbourne's confident warmth. At the end of the interview Peel implied clumsily that, with the change of government, Her Majesty would be asked to give up those of her ladies-in-waiting who were the daughters, sisters or wives of recent Whig ministers. When the anxious Queen told him that she saw no reason why she should be required to do any such thing, Peel explained that, if she did not remove the Whig influence from her household, the Tories would not feel able to form a government. Clutching gratefully at the straw, the Queen then refused to part with a single lady, neither maid of honour nor lady of the bedchamber. Even when the formidable Duke of Wellington came to reason with her, she remained adamant. Baffled by their own inflexibility, the Tories could do nothing but resign in protest; and the delighted young Queen, who was growing in confidence daily, invited 'dear Lord Melbourne' to dine with her and form another government.

Apart from the 'Bedchamber Crisis', Lord Melbourne was also diverted during his wait by rising prices, the growth of trade unionism, huge Chartist demonstrations in favour of universal male suffrage, a French rebellion in Canada and the relentless opposition of the House of Lords to all his attempts at reform in Ireland, all of which were dealt with as dispassionately as ever. The only events that he admitted to losing any sleep over were the limitless activities of his friend the Foreign Secretary. The suspense of waiting for a decision from Lady Cowper had done nothing to diminish Palmerston's energy. He was 'intermeddling' as busily as ever, so busily that apparently he was still unable to control his unpunctuality. When Queen Victoria gave her first state banquet, her Foreign Secretary did not arrive until after Her Majesty and all her guests had been seated.

Just as peace and constitutional governments were settling precariously at the western end of the Mediterranean – despite the shortcomings of the Quadruple Alliance – the disintegration of peace at the eastern end was presenting Palmerston with the opportunity *to* reverse the set-backs suffered as a result of the Treaty of Unkiar Skelessi.

At the beginning of 1839, when the Syrians rose in rebellion against the oppressive rule of Mehemet Ali, the sick, old Ottoman Sultan, Mahmud II, decided to take advantage of the chaos and end his reign in a blaze of glory. For the last three years his army had been training and reorganizing under the direction of a modest but ingenious Prussian officer called Helmut von Moltke. Confident that his men were now a match for Ibrahim Pasha, the Sultan sent them east into Syria, while his ships sailed south to prevent Mehemet Ali's fleet from supporting his army.

For Palmerston no possible outcome could be of any advantage to Britain. A victory for either side would put the puppet of a potential enemy in control of all the roads to India. Furthermore, if the Russians joined in on the side of the Sultan and the French on the side of Mehemet Ali, direct hostilities between the two could easily escalate into a general European war; and worst of all, now that Louis-Philippe had begun to woo the totalitarian Powers, there was a chance that France and Russia might get together and divide the Middle East between them.

At first Palmerston continued to act as the ally of France. Since the most immediate threat was intervention by the Russians, he readily agreed to the French suggestion that British and French fleets should be sent to the Dardanelles to deter them. But at the same time he invited not only France but also Russia, Austria and Prussia to a conference to discuss the future of 'the Levant'. If the five nations could be persuaded to act in unison, it might just be possible to impose a peace, and perhaps even return the northern and southern roads eastward to the influence of separate powers.

When the representatives of the five nations met, not in London as Palmerston had intended but, at Metternich's insistence, in Vienna, the principal proposal before them was Palmerston's.

Mehemet Ali has too much, not to wish for more; and the Sultan has lost too much, to be able to sit down contented with his loss ... The only arrangement, therefore, which could appear to Her Majesty's Government to be calculated to secure peace for the future, would be the evacuation of Syria by Mehemet Ali, and the withdrawal of his authorities civil and military, into Egypt. By such means, the Desert would be interposed between the two parties; and the chances of conflict between them would be almost entirely prevented. But Mehemet Ali would justly require some counterbalancing advantage, in return for such a concession on his part; and Her Majesty's Government conceive, that this might be given him by making the Pashalic of Egypt hereditary in his family.

All the envoys, even the Frenchman, agreed that the plan was worth recommending to their governments. But before Europe's five most powerful nations could impose their will on the internal affairs of the Ottoman Empire, news came that events had overtaken them. On 24 June the Ottoman army had been routed by Ibrahim Pasha at Nezib; while the galloper carrying the report of the defeat was still on his way to Constantinople, the Sultan died, leaving his empire to an eighteen-year-old boy; and as as a result of some generous bribery among its senior officers, the Turkish fleet had sailed into the harbour at Alexandria with its colours struck and defected to Mehemet Ali. In the space of three weeks, it was said, the Turks had lost their army, their Sultan and their navy. Without waiting for ratification from their governments, all the envoys in Vienna adopted a new proposal and allowed Metternich to send an immediate note on their behalf to Constantinople haughtily instructing the young Sultan and his viziers to do nothing and allow the European Powers to negotiate a settlement. It arrived only just in time. A few hours later a messenger was due to set sail for Alexandria recognizing Mehemet Ali as Viceroy of Syria.

Palmerston never made any secret of his contempt for the Egyptian Pasha. 'I hate Mehemet Ali, whom I consider as nothing better than an ignorant barbarian', he wrote in a letter to Granville, the Ambassador in Paris. 'He is as great a tyrant and oppressor as ever made a people wretched.' He was still convinced that, quite apart from any gain for Britain, there was 'no possibility of a permanent settlement without making Mehemet withdraw into his original shell of Egypt'. Now that the tyrant was victorious with the Ottoman Empire at his feet, however, it was clear that it was going to take force to move him; and judging by the many enthusiastic articles that were suddenly appearing in the French press, it was now equally clear that, if force was to be used, France would no longer be willing to play any part in it.

Yet Palmerston had good reason to expect that France would not use force to support Mehemet Ali if anyone else tried to remove him. Talleyrand's successor as Ambassador in London was another distinguished acquaintance from his days in Paris, the recent Foreign Minister, Sebastiani. In private Sebastiani admitted that, like everyone else, most French ministers wanted to see Mehemet Ali withdraw from Syria. But their government was too fragile to defy the widespread and passionate public opinion that had been whipped up in his favour by the French press. Mehemet Ali had been making good use of the profits from the expanding Egyptian economy and his huge trade in Sudanese slaves. Not only had he bought most of the senior officers in the Turkish navy; he had bought most of the relevant French journalists as well.

There was no way in which Palmerston was going to be able to persuade the British government to act alone. Even if he had done so, the action would have been more than likely to fail, not least because it would have aroused unanimous, but for the most part disingenuous, opposition in the rest of Europe. Without the French therefore, he had no choice but to draw closer to 'the Powers'. Since he was opposing them and thwarting them everywhere else, however, this could well have been a daunting prospect; and to make the prospect even worse, he had recently been preparing a show of strength in Afghanistan, which was designed to deter the eastern ambitions of Russia, 'the Power' whose help he needed most.

Much of the paranoia in Parliament and elsewhere about the Russian threat to India originated in a pamphlet published in 1829 by none other than Colonel George de Lacy Evans, in which he argued that the mobility of the Cossacks was such that the Russians could take Kabul before anyone in India knew they were coming, and could then advance south through the Khyber Pass before a sufficient force had been assembled to oppose them. Although the leading expert on the area, Sir Alexander Burnes, had since argued that an attack would take much longer, the paranoia prevailed. In 1837, when the conqueror of Kabul, Dost Muhammad, joined the Persian Shah in a fortunately unsuccessful attack on the independent city of Herat, many in London believed that Russian agents in Persia had put him up to it. Ignoring the contrary advice in a recent report submitted by Burnes, and indeed concealing from Parliament the passages in which he suggested that Dost Muhammad was interested in making an allance with the British, Palmerston and Melbourne decided to make a pre-emptive strike into Afghanistan. As a result, at the very moment when the assembled envoys in Vienna were considering Palmerston's proposals for Syria, a British army was marching across the North-West Frontier of India to seize Kabul, depose Dost Muhammad and replace him with the much less popular pretender Shah Shuja.

But the Tsar and his advisers were as pragmatic as Palmerston. Despite Louis-Philippe's recent overtures, he was still regarded in St Petersburg as a dangerous revolutionary. The opportunity to lure Britain away from him and turn the gap between the Liberal Powers into a gulf – to succeed where Metternich had failed – was far too good to be missed; and there was the added chance of an amusing irony if the British navy, which had prevented the Russians from assisting Turkey in the first place, could now be used to do the job for them. As evidence of his good intentions and his readiness to consider joint action against Mehemet Ali, the Tsar recalled his agents from Persia, sent his son, the Tsarevich Alexander, on a goodwill visit to London, where Palmerston gave a banquet for him at the Foreign Office, and soon afterwards sent a special envoy, Baron Ernst Philip de Brunnow, to discuss Palmerston's proposals for the Levant.

Palmerston knew that, if he was to obtain sufficient support for armed intervention, he had to win the approval of two men: not only Brunnow but also the man who had Metternich's ear, Baron Philipp von Neumann, the pompous chargé d'affaires at the Austrian Embassy, whom Palmerston was in the habit of describing as 'Baron Cocksure'. Not for the first time, Neumann had been left in charge of his embassy because Esterhazy, like Bülow, had become accustomed to taking regular long leaves in order to recover from his furious frustration with Palmerston. To give himself as much time as possible undisturbed with Brunnow and Neumann, Palmerston invited them to spend Christmas with him at Broadlands. It would have been a generous invitation at any time, but for the Christmas of 1839 it was exceptional. Palmerston was on honeymoon.

Lord Palmerston and Lady Cowper were married very quietly in St George's, Hanover Square, on 16 December. A few days earlier the Queen, whose own wedding was due to take place the following February, wrote with the news to Prince Albert.

> Palmerston is to be married within the next few days to Lady Cowper ... They are, both of them, above fifty, and I think that they are quite right so to act, because Palmerston, since the death of his sisters, is quite alone in the world, and Lady C. is a very clever woman, and much attached to him; still I feel sure it will make you smile.

There were many who smiled, and just as many more who muttered, but none could deny that the marriage was a mighty alliance, in politics as much as in society. In the past Lady Cowper had been able to support the Foreign Secretary only informally, and even then only when she was not distracted by the desires of other lovers or the demands of her marriage. Now that she was Lady Palmerston, the mistress of his household and the hostess at his table, she brought a new and permanent dimension to all his diplomacy.

When Lady Palmerston died, thirty years later, several of her family and friends praised the perception of her warm obituary in the *Morning Chronicle*.

> To place her husband and keep him in what she thought his proper position; to make people see him as she saw him; to bring lukewarm friends, carping rivals or exasperated enemies within the genial atmosphere of his conversation; to tone down opposition and conciliate support – this was henceforth the fixed purpose and master passion of her life... The services of the great lady to the great statesman extended far beyond the creation of a salon. What superficial drawers mistook for indiscretion was eminently useful to him. She always understood full well what she was telling, to whom she was telling it, when and where it should be repeated, and whether the repetition would do harm or good. Instead of the secret that was betrayed, it was the feeler that was put forth; and no one ever knew from or through Lady Palmerston what Lord Palmerston did not wish to be known.

The Christmas party of 1839 was the new Lady Palmerston's first house party at Broadlands. On the morning of Christmas Eve, Neumann went shooting while Palmerston and Brunnow discussed his proposal. In the afternoon, while Brunnow went shooting, Palmerston discussed the same proposal with Neumann. On Christmas Day all three discussed it. By the time they dined they had agreed. Russia, Austria and Great Britain would continue to demand that Mehemet Ali must abandon Syria, and they would warn him formally that, if he did not, they would remove him by force.

Confident that the European Powers would never do more than issue empty threats, and that the young Sultan and his viziers would eventually capitulate, Mehemet Ali had ordered Ibrahim Pasha not to advance across Turkey after his victory at Nezib. It was this pause which had given

Palmerston plenty of time in which to prepare his ultimatum, but by the end of January 1840 it was becoming clear that, if the ultimatum was ever going to be more than the empty threat that the Pasha expected, plenty of time was what he needed most. When the Russian and Austrian couriers returned from their distant capitals with their governments' endorsements of the Broadlands agreement, their superiors in London were still waiting for Palmerston to persuade his own government to endorse it.

After the Christmas party at Broadlands the Palmerstons went to see the New Year in with the Tankervilles at Watton in Hertfordshire. The French Lady Tankerville, who was one of Lady Palmerston's closest friends, was the sister-in-law of Sebastiani. Knowing who Palmerston's guests had been at Christmas, Sebastiani turned up uninvited at Watton. Throughout their stay Palmerston teased him and refused to reveal anything. Only when they all returned to London did he show Sebastiani the agreement that he had signed with Brunnow and Neumann. As he then explained to his two new allies, he did so in the hope that France might still be persuaded to join them, at least in demanding Mehemet Ali's withdrawal from Syria. But the revelation only provoked the French government into protesting that a new 'Grand Alliance' was being formed against France; and as the irritated Brunnow predicted, Sebastiani appealed to the old-fashioned, francophile Whigs and begged them to oppose Palmerston's plan.

For the next six months Palmerston faced as much opposition in England as in France; and he met it all with an infuriating but convincing air of jovial confidence. When *The Times* attacked him, he fed enough information to the *Morning Chronicle* to counter the attacks. So great was the opposition within his own party that many of these attacks were said to be the work of fellow Cabinet ministers but, although some certainly were, most were fuelled by a plausible fanatic, a former Foreign Office clerk called David Urquhart, who had been recalled from the embassy in Constantinople in 1837 because of his embarrassingly passionate hostility to Russia. Urquhart addressed meetings and published pamphlets, in which he described the Foreign Secretary as 'the Minister for Russia'; and he wrote to Melbourne accusing Palmerston of treason and circulated copies of his letter to the entire Cabinet.

When the angry Radicals in the Commons reminded Palmerston that the Russians were the cruel oppressors of Poland, he replied calmly that in this instance 'it was impossible for any government to have acted with more honour and good faith'. When some in the Cabinet warned that an alliance with the northern Powers against Mehemet Ali was bound to lead to war with France, he continued to insist that the French would not fight; and when others argued that even a war with the victorious Egyptian army would claim too high a price in British blood, he countered with evidence that the Egyptian army was far from as formidable as it seemed. For the last three years a Polish revolutionary refugee, Colonel Chrzanowski, had been acting as Palmerston's agent in the Middle East. According to Chrzanowski, the Egyptian army in Syria was corrupt, ill disciplined and no match for a properly equipped European force. The Battle of Nezib had been won partly because the Ottoman army was not yet fully equipped, let alone fully trained, and partly because a large number of its units defected to Ibrahim Pasha before the fighting started.

When spring came, it looked for a moment as though Palmerston was going to be able to win over the French before he had convinced the Whigs. A change of government in France brought a change of ambassador in London. The Corsican soldier Sebastiani was replaced by yet another acquaintance from Palmerston's days in Paris, the charming, intellectual, anglophile François Guizot. But behind Guizot the new chief minister was the obstinate nationalist Louis Thiers, who was convinced that it was not in France's interest to restore Syria to the Sultan; and at the beginning of the summer Guizot was joined by his new mistress, Princess Lieven, which put him permanently under the influence of an antagonistic attitude to Lord Palmerston, and which brought an end to the intimate, flirtatious dinners at which Lady Palmerston tried to persuade him to have one more go at his government. Even when Metternich introduced a compromise and suggested that Mehemet Ali might be allowed to keep Syria during his lifetime, the French turned it down, although not before they had incensed everyone by saying that they would like to consult Mehemet Ali first.

The negotiations with Guizot were conducted in an atmosphere of the utmost courtesy. Despite their disagreement over Syria, Palmerston complimented the French by inviting them to mediate in Naples, where, on his orders, British ships were blockading the port in order to force the King to revoke a sulphur monopoly which denied trade to British subjects. Although he was his ally over Syria, Metternich was appalled by Palmerston's high-handed action in Naples. He accused him of encouraging the Neopolitans to rebel against their autocratic King. If that happened, he claimed, Austria would be bound to support the King, and if the French then intervened in spurious defence of democracy, the whole petty quarrel could escalate into a European war. His indignation was multiplied when Palmerston invited France and not Austria to mediate; and it was multiplied again when the French persuaded the King of Naples to relent. It seemed that the Liberal constitutional monarchies could disagree on one subject and still confound the Absolutist 'Powers' on another. But the courtesy came to a sudden end when Palmerston received a despatch from the embassy in Constantinople warning him that, while all this was going on, the French were negotiating secretly with the Sultan to let Mehemet Ali keep Syria.

The need for action was now more urgent; and now all that stood in the way of action was the British Cabinet. Palmerston wrote to Melbourne on 5 July threatening to resign if the Cabinet did not endorse his agreement with Brunnow and Neumann. Britain's best interest lay in maintaining a united and independent Ottoman Empire. The fact that it was weak only added to the advantage. Without intervention by the allies that empire would be divided 'into two separate and independent states, whereof one will be the dependency of France, and the other a satellite of Russia; and in both of which our political influence will be annulled'. Palmerston had been overruled in 1833, when he offered his colleagues the opportunity to prevent this from happening in the first place. He would not now accept responsibility if they refused the chance to reverse the mistake.

When they learned that Palmerston had threatened to resign if his agreement was not endorsed, Holland, Russell and Clarendon, the Lord Privy Seal, threatened to resign if it was. Poor, harrassed, peace-loving Melbourne knew that any resignation would lead to the fall of the fragile government. He pleaded with Holland and the others to reconsider, using not Palmerston's argument but a less contentious one of his own. The Queen, who was already terrified at Palmerston's audacity, was even more terrified at the prospect of losing her Whig government. It would hardly be the conduct of gentlemen to present her with such a crisis when she was about to give birth to her first child. Reluctantly they agreed, although only on condition that they could send their own memoranda to the Queen recording their reservations.

On 15 July Palmerston and the ambassadors of Austria, Russia, Prussia and Turkey signed a convention in which they instructed their consuls in Alexandria to demand that Mehemet Ali should return the Turkish fleet to the Sultan and withdraw his forces from Syria and Crete. If he withdrew within twenty days, the allies would advise the Sultan to recognize his family as hereditary Pashas of Egypt. If he withdrew within ten days, they would in addition advise that he be allowed to retain the Syrian fortress of Acre and the surrounding land for life. If he did not comply with the demands, the Sultan would be advised to replace him as Viceroy of Egypt.

Mehemet Ali rejected the demands contemptuously, describing them as a declaration of war. When the time limit elapsed, the Sultan formally but ineffectively appointed another Viceroy, and Palmerston ordered the British Mediterranean fleet to sail east. Of all his gambles this was the greatest. Many believed that he had brought Britain to the brink of war with France. To Metternich, who conceded that he had taken the right side 'for the first time in his career as a Whig', he was nevertheless 'acting like those gamblers who try to break the bank'. His career was at stake. In the event of complete success, he could at least expect to be vindicated; but in the event of even the slightest failure he, and he alone, would bear the blame. Yet from the moment he was committed to action, the pressure began to ease. First Lord Holland died, which meant that the dinner table at Holland House no longer provided the French embassy with direct access to the secrets of the British Cabinet. Then anxious Melbourne tried one of Palmerston's tricks and wrote a letter to King Leopold, hoping that he would show it to his father-in-law, King Louis-Philippe. The letter confided that, if the French maintained their intransigent support for Mehemet Ali and continued the suspicious expansion of their navy, a war with Britain would be inevitable. When he saw the letter, the cautious King of France dismissed Thiers, recalled Guizot and installed him as Foreign Minister and effectively leader of his government.

Meanwhile news of military and naval success had started to arrive from the eastern Mediterranean. While Ibrahim Pasha's army was being distracted by another Syrian rebellion, to which Palmerston was supplying arms, a British squadron was seizing the Syrian ports, and the remainder of the British fleet, accompanied by an Austrian flotilla, was keeping Mehemet Ali's ships at bay in Alexandria and nervously watching the horizon for the French.

The commander of this squadron, who insisted that all his officers were immaculate in regulation uniforms and yet dressed himself in one so elaborate that it was more suited to a pantomime than a quarterdeck, was 'Mad Charlie' Napier, the man who destroyed Dom Miguel's fleet off Cape St Vincent. On 16 September, after a brief bombardment, Napier landed British and Turkish troops to take Beirut. On 26 September he took Sidon. On 3 November he took the mighty fortress of Acre, which had once fallen to Richard the Lionheart but which more recently had defied all the efforts of Napoleon.

The Egyptian position was now untenable. With the allies in command of the ports, the army in Syria was cut off from its supplies. Its only road home was overland, across 300 dangerous miles of desert. Napier had completed his task. But the victor of Cape St Vincent, who was corresponding privately with Palmerston, had decided to continue on what seemed to be his own initiative. He sailed to Alexandria, where he persuaded Mehemet Ali to surrender the Turkish fleet and abandon Syria in return for the hereditary Pashlik of Egypt, something he had no official authority to bestow, and then courteously sailed his ships back to Syria and brought Ibrahim Pasha's army home in them.

Palmerston, who had just written 'Napier for ever' in a letter to the Paris embassy, was happy to overlook the apparent presumption. On 13 February 1841, on the advice of the allies, the Sultan appointed Mehemet Ali hereditary Viceroy of Egypt. On 13 July France joined the allies in signing the Straits Convention, which made the Treaty of Unkiar Skelessi obsolete and excluded the warships of all foreign nations, including Russia, from the Bosporus, the Sea of Marmara and the Dardanelles while Turkey was at peace. Guizot had earlier asked that the allies issue a statement acknowledging that it was in response to a request from France that they had advised the Sultan to let Mehemet Ali remain in Egypt. But even though the humble request was supported by King Leopold and Queen Victoria, Palmerston was adamant that nothing must be done to save France's face. After suffering so much from the French and their allies in his own Cabinet, he was in no mood to be magnanimous, even in his hour of triumph. But in the long run it was a mistake. He had made an enemy.

Britain's prestige was now higher than it had been since the victory at Waterloo. In Europe at least, Palmerston was famous. But at home his opponents and even his colleagues were more relieved than exalted by his triumph. Although the danger of war with France had been by far their greatest anxiety, it had not been their only one. While 'intermeddling' in Iberia and calling France's bluff in the Levant, Palmerston had also taken Britain to war with China and brought her to the brink of war with the United States. It would not have been a good moment in which to fight the French as well.

The war with China became known as the Opium War. Opium was still legal in most of the world, where the tincture, laudanum, was one of the most widely used medicines. In China, however, the use of opium in pipes had become such a debilitating national weakness that growing it, dealing in it and smoking it had all been made crimes punishable by death. But the law was very seldom enforced, and the demand remained so great that by the mid-1830s over half the tea exported to Britain was being paid for by British merchants with opium, which they bought cheap in Calcutta. When their ships were off Canton, the only-port in which the barbarian British were allowed to trade, they hove to just outside Chinese territorial waters and carried their forbidden cargoes ashore by night in boats, under the noses of the well-bribed Chinese coastguards.

In 1836 the Emperor sent one of his leading Mandarins, Lin Tse-hsu, to take charge and make a serious attempt to suppress the smuggling in Canton. But even though he received every possible assistance from the British Superintendent, Captain Charles Elliot RN, a nephew of the late Lord Minto, Lin's efforts had very little effect. Eventually, at the beginning of 1839, after a group of British merchants had attempted to prevent the public strangling of a Chinese smuggler, Lin confined all the British merchants, over 200 of them, under house arrest in their factories — the buildings that contained their homes as well as their warehouses. Barring all access and surrounding the factories with thousands of soldiers, he refused to let any food supplies pass through his lines until the merchants who traded in opium agreed to hand over not only all the stock in the factories but also all the cargo on their ships.

When Elliot came in from his frigate to find out what was happening, he too was locked up in the factories. After many days of starvation he promised the opium merchants that the British government would compensate them for their loss and persuaded them to do as Lin demanded. The Chinese soldiers removed the opium from the factories; and the crews of Chinese war junks boarded the British ships and poured all their opium into the sea, which was effectively an act of piracy, since no payment was made and the ships were lying in international waters, where opium was a legal cargo.

Before Elliot could receive any instructions from the other side of the world, events entirely unconnected with the opium trade led to the first shots of the war. In July a Chinese man was killed in a brawl with a group of drunken sailors from one of the two British warships in Canton harbour. When the murderer could not be identified, Lin insisted that, in accordance with Chinese custom, one man from the crew should be selected at random to pay the penalty and serve as a warning to the others. On 3 November, after Elliot had refused to surrender anyone, Lin sent out twenty-nine war junks to surround the ships and seize a victim. But the British ships responded to their demands with broadsides, blowing four junks out of the water immediately and causing the others to beat a hasty retreat.

By then news of the earlier 'outrage' had reached London, and Palmerston had persuaded the Cabinet that what looked like a small crisis was actually an ideal opportunity to increase Britain's access to a market that already accounted for almost seventeen per cent of all her international trade. On 20 February 1840 he wrote to the Emperor of China. He acknowledged that the Chinese had the right to seize smuggled opium, but he protested at the seizure of legal cargo in international waters, at the ill treatment of Her Majesty's representative and at the imprisonment of so many of her innocent subjects. In compensation, he demanded that the Chinese government pay the cost of all the opium that had been seized or destroyed, that several islands, including Hong Kong, should be ceded to Great Britain, to provide secure harbours for her ships, and that, in addition to Canton, British merchants should be allowed to trade with China through Shanghai, Ningpo, Foochow and Amoy. Finally, while expressing the hope that the Emperor and his government would 'see the equity of the foregoing demands', he warned that sixteen troop ships and warships had been ordered east to enforce them.

On 7 April 1840 the Tories called for papers and moved a vote of censure on the government's policy in China. The tone of their attack was predictably high-minded; and the most righteous and impassioned speech came from the devout young William Ewart Gladstone. Gladstone attacked Palmerston for protecting an 'infamous contraband traffic' and slightly misrepresented the facts by arguing that the denial of provisions to British merchants was a justifiable method of making them leave. But he then destroyed his case completely by adding, 'and then of course they poisoned the wells'. Nobody had ever suggested that the Chinese had gone that far. An embarrassed Gladstone was compelled to correct himself, and when Palmerston spoke at the end of the debate, two days later, he was still able to raise a few laughs at the expense of Gladstone's over-enthusiasm.

By then, however, Cabinet colleagues had ably defended the government's policy with speeches so emotional and patriotic that they could have been written for them by Palmerston. The new Secretary at War, Thomas Babington Macaulay, now better remembered as a historian than as a politician, asserted that the government was only defending the rights of British merchants, which was no more than the duty of 'a country which had made the farthest ends of the earth ring with the fame of her exploits in redressing the wrongs of her children', and he reminded the House of Oliver Cromwell's great vow to 'make the name of Englishman as respected as ever had been the name of Roman citizen'.

When Palmerston rose, all that was left for him to do was to point out that the war had nothing to do with opium. Could any man opposite, he asked, 'say that he honestly believed the motive of the Chinese Government to have been the promotion of moral habits?' 'Why', he asked, 'did they not prohibit the growth of the poppy in their own country?' And then he gave the answer. 'This was an exportation of bullion question.' The demand for opium in China was so great that, in addition to the opium that was being bought from the British with tea, huge quantities were also being bought from them with silver dollars. Although there were still plenty of British merchants who paid for their tea with silver dollars and not with opium, the amount of silver coming into China was nothing like as large as the amount that was leaving. The Emperor's campaign against opium smuggling was in reality an attempt to protect his silver reserves. Palmerston sat down amid cheers and aplause, but the Tory motion was only defeated by a majority of nine: 271 votes to 262.

The war between Great Britain and a third of the human race was never likely to be as 'close run' as the debate about it. The ill-led, disorganized and almost medieval Chinese navy and army failed so calamitously in conventional action against broadsides and musket volleys that they resorted instead to a series of imaginative but hopelessly unrealistic schemes. On one occasion they planned to set fire to British ships by putting monkeys on board with fireworks tied to their tails. On another they persuaded the Emperor to ban the export of rhubarb, so that the famously constipated British would be rendered prostrate and powerless for lack of it. But Elliot, who commanded the British forces, did have one formidable enemy: malaria. Two months after he took the island of Chusan a quarter of the men he had landed on it were dead and half the survivors were unfit for service. In August 1840, while he still had the strength to be a convincing threat, he made peace with the Chinese commander, who agreed to pay 6 million silver dollars in compensation for the lost opium and to cede the island of Hong Kong to Great Britain.

But the British government refused to ratify the treaty. The money and 'a barren Island with hardly a House upon it' were not enough. Seven months later Elliot received a letter from Palmerston informing him with regret that he was to be replaced by Sir Henry Pottinger, the political agent in Sind, who was under strict instructions to enforce all Britain's demands. No sooner had the crisis in the Middle East been settled than the fighting in the Far East had started again.

The causes of conflict with the United States were several and in one case a great deal more righteous. The oldest, which had been conducted on and off with varying degrees of acrimony since the end of the War of Independence, was a dispute over the position of parts of the border between the United States and Canada. In 1828 the King of Holland had been invited to arbitrate. By the time he reached a decision, however, in 1831, Palmerston and his allies were well on the way to divesting him of Belgium, and it was perhaps not surprising therefore that his decision was slightly weighted in favour of the United States. Nevertheless it was Palmerston who accepted the decision and the United States Senate that rejected it. Since then the dispute had continued, and the resulting resentment along the border had led to further confrontation.

In 1837, during a rebellion of French Canadians in Montreal, Ebenezer Greely, who was conducting a census near by in the state of Maine, strayed across the disputed border into what the Canadians claimed was New Brunswick and was arrested. Although Palmerston approved of the arrest, the Governor of New Brunswick freed Greely as a gesture of gratitude because the people of Maine had done nothing to support the rebels in Montreal, unlike some of their compatriots in the state of New York, who were actively supporting a group of rebels from Toronto.

After the outbreak of the rebellion in Montreal, William Lyon Mackenzie, a former republican Mayor of Toronto, had attempted to take over his city. When his rebellion failed, he had withdrawn with 900 followers to Navy Island in the Niagara river, where he survived on the food and ammunition that was sent out to him from the New York river-bank in a little steamer, the *Caroline*. So successful was this operation that Mackenzie's resistance remained unbroken until 29 December, when an audacious contingent of Canadian militia invaded the United

States and burned the *Caroline* while she lay in dock, killing an American citizen, Amos Durfee, in the process.

Three years later a vainglorious Canadian called Alexander McLeod visited New York State, got drunk in a tavern and infuriated the other customers with truthless boasts about his exploits as a militiaman on the night of the raid. By the time he was sober again he was in Lockport gaol, charged with the murder of Amos Durfee. When Palmerston heard the news he wrote to the British Minister in Washington instructing him to demand the immediate release of McLeod, to remind the United States Government that no individual could be held answerable for an act of state and to warn it that 'McLeod's execution would produce war, war immediate and frightful in its character, because it would be a war of retaliation and vengeance'.

The Federal government believed the threat and was inclined to comply with Palmerston's demand. But the indignant state government of New York insisted that McLeod must be tried for murder. With the help of America's finest attorneys, all of whom were paid for by the Federal government, McLeod proved beyond doubt that he had not been on the raid; and when the prejudiced jury failed to agree, he was acquitted and smuggled back into Canada before a lynch mob could get to him.

Even by his own standards, Palmerston's attitude towards the United States in border disputes and the McLeod affair was caustic and aggressive; and this was due only in part to his belief that 'with such cunning fellows as these Yankees, it never answers to give way'. For the most part it was due to an overflow of passion from another dispute, in which Palmerston was sincerely and profoundly aggrieved by the conduct of the United States. By 1841 the United States were all that stood between Palmerston and total triumph in the only cause that he ever allowed to take precedence over patriotism. As he reported to the House of Commons in May, he was close to crowning a long campaign with a treaty between the Five Powers. 'If we succeed,' he said, 'we shall have enlisted in this league against slave-trade every state in Christendom which has a flag that sails on the ocean, with the single exception of the United States of North America.'

Since he first took office as Foreign Secretary, Palmerston had been quietly but steadily building up the number of flags whose protection was denied to the 'diabolical Slave Trade'. After concluding the treaty that gave the British and the French the right to search each other's ships, he had concluded similar treaties with Holland, Denmark, Sweden and Spain. But Britain still led the crusade; and as Palmerston told Parliament, this moral responsibility was one that she alone would have to carry for some time to come. 'If ever by the assault of overpowering enemies, or by the errors of her misguided sons, England should fall ... I do not know any nation that is now ready in this respect to supply our place.' Only the British navy, in the form of the West Africa squadron, was actively and continuously engaged in stopping and searching the ships of other nations. Where the British captains found human cargoes, they were liberating them and landing them on the free soil of Sierra Leone; and when, in keeping with a small but proud tradition, they went a little further on their own initiative, Palmerston was more than ready to support them.

In 1840 Captain Joseph Denman, whose father was the Radical Lord Chief Justice and a passionate opponent of the slave trade, learned that a few British sailors from the West Indies had been kidnapped and were now being held with other prisoners in a Spanish trading station on the estuary of the Gallinas river, where they were awaiting illegal shipment to Cuba. With three sixteen-gun brigs, *Wanderer, Saracen* and *Rolla*, Denman sailed into the estuary, drove the terrified Spanish traders up river with a few threatening cannon shots and then put parties ashore to rescue their prisoners. Four slave barracoons were burned to the ground; and when the 841 men and women who had been held in them were safely on their way to Sierra Leone, the local ruler and his son were compelled to sign a treaty, whereby they were to receive an annual payment in return for cessation of their terrible trade.

Palmerston was overjoyed. 'Taking a wasp's nest', he said 'is more effective than catching the wasps one by one.' Before Captain Denman could be sued for damages by the Spanish traders or disciplined for exceeding his authority by the Royal Navy, Palmerston wrote to the Admiralty, accepting full responsibility for what had happened and recommending that Denman should be promoted and that other captains should be encouraged to follow his example. During the next few months, while six more captains released slaves and destroyed over a dozen barracoons on either side of Sierra Leone, Denman negotiated more suppressive treaties with the African rulers of the coastal kingdoms.

By then Palmerston was well advanced with his own negotiations for a five-Power anti-slave-trade treaty with the rulers of France, Prussia, Russia and Austria. When he started, little more than a year earlier, the only nations still unwilling to consider a mutual right of search had been Portugal, Brazil and the United States. All three had passed laws proscribing the slave trade; the United States even had the occasional frigate cruising off west Africa. But Portugal and Brazil were restrained by the influence of the many within their armed forces and political establishments who were still earning fortunes from illegal trading; and the United States were suspicious. During Britain's blockade of Napoleonic Europe, neutral American merchantmen had been regularly stopped and searched by British cruisers, and America's consequent indignation had been one of the pretexts for the war of 1812.

To a man such as Palmerston, Portugal and Brazil were not a problem. In August 1839 he introduced a bill in the House of Commons which gave the Royal Navy the authority to stop any ship flying the Portuguese flag. The bill was opposed in the House of Lords by the Duke of Wellington, who argued with considerable justification that Britain might just as well declare war on her ancient ally. But the bill became law anyway; and after casually informing the Portuguese minister in London that he could declare war if he pleased, Palmerston made arrangements to increase the number of ships in the West Africa squadron to thirteen and instructed their captains to treat Brazilian ships as though they were Portuguese.

It was not so easy, however, with the United States, which, with France and Russia, was one of the only three nations that Palmerston had once described as capable of challenging Britain's supremacy at sea. While he negotiated with the Powers, he built up the diplomatic pressure on the Americans, putting his case as bluntly as he dared: if they were not prepared to enforce their own laws effectively, even though they had more than enough ships for the task, it was not unreasonable to ask them to let others do it for them.

By the summer of 1841 he had agreed mutual rights of search with the newly independent Republic of Texas, which he, unlike the French and Americans, had refused to recognize until it abolished slavery. By then also the Five Powers Treaty had been signed and ratified by all but the French, who were only procrastinating because vengeful Guizot, who was convinced that the Whig government was about to fall, wanted to make Palmerston watch his successor take the credit for completing his most precious project. But the United States were still deaf to all his badgering, even though all he was asking for now was a 'right of visit'. When the captain of a merchantman hoisted the Stars and Stripes, either a British officer should be allowed to go on board and check that his papers matched his flag, or else the captain of the merchantman should be required to bring his papers across to the British warship.

On 27 August Palmerston repeated his demand impatiently in a note to the American minister in London, emphasizing that Her Majesty's Government could not accept 'that a merchantman can exempt herself from search by merely hoisting a piece of bunting with the United States' emblems and colours upon it'. As he must have expected, and perhaps even hoped, the Americans were furious, protesting perversely that he had referred to 'Old Glory' as 'a piece of bunting'. But it no longer mattered what they said. Guizot had been right: 27 August 1841 was the last day of Palmerston's second term at the Foreign Office.

In domestic affairs, which were what mattered most to the electorate, the reforming Whig government had actually run out of steam by the time Melbourne took over as Prime Minister. There was no way in which events at home could be said to have kept pace with Palmerston's 'radical' and alarming intermeddling abroad. Grey had been right to resign when he did. Under Melbourne's mellow leadership the government had merely been managing the reforms it had already made, earning more blame than praise as the unforeseen flaws began to emerge and its own inadequacies became increasingly apparent. In the wake of the well-intentioned Poor Law Amendment Act of 1834, it had grown progressively more and more unpopular as each grim new workhouse rose to replace the more humane but cripplingly more expensive system of providing poor relief from parish funds. In the election of 1837, the year in which Charles Dickens aroused the nation's conscience with *Oliver Twist*, the Tory squires, who had mostly administered the old system of poor relief, dangerously diminished the Whig majority by campaigning principally on their opposition to the hated act. Since then, Palmerston's policy in China had survived their censure by only nine votes, and his defiance of the French in the Middle East had been possible only because the enthusiastic Francophobe Tories who supported him outnumbered the Radicals in his own party, who did not.

In the last two years, ever since Queen Victoria postponed reluctant Melbourne's retirement by refusing to part with any of her 'Ladies', the government had lost what was left of the nation's respect through its inability to cope with a recession. In his budget for May 1841 the new Chancellor of the Exchequer, the banker Sir Francis Baring, attempted to reduce the cost of food and stimulate internal trade by lowering the tariffs on imported corn, Canadian timber and sugar from countries outside the British dominions. The Tories and the Radicals leaped to the attack. Reducing the tariff on sugar was making a concession to the Brazilian slave owners.

By a cruel irony, it was Palmerston who was called on to answer for the government. He mocked the Tories' hypocritical inconsistency. They were happy to decry the trade in slave-produced sugar from Brazil, but they had never said a word about the slave-produced cotton imported from their friends in the southern United States – a jibe that may have brought a slight blush to the faces of men such as Peel and Gladstone, whose huge fortunes were founded on cotton. 'The party opposite', he said,

> stand upon principle against interest. The principle they stand upon is the principle of humanity; the interest they oppose is that of 25,000,000 of people who inhabit these islands ... True it is there are millions of suffering negroes abroad; true also is that we have millions of suffering fellow-countrymen at home.

Why should our humanity bestow itself exclusively on the former, instead of giving a share of its attention to the latter?

As for the suggestion

> that the free-labour sugar of the West Indies cannot compete with the slave-labour sugar of the Brazils; now what is this but declaring to the Brazilians and the Spaniards, that we have been telling them untruths all this while as to the comparative cheapness of free labour ... Let us convince them that we do believe free labour to be, as it unquestionably is, cheaper than slave labour. Let us do so by admitting their slave-labour sugar into competition with free-labour sugar in our market.

It was the best that could be done in the circumstances, but it was not enough. Although Palmerston questioned the Tories' sincerity and suggested that they were prostituting the principles of humanity and justice to serve the party purpose, the Radicals on the left of his own party were too idealistic to compromise, and the landowners on the right of it, who feared that their incomes were under threat, joined them in voting with the opposition. The government was defeated by thirty-six votes, 317 to 281.

For a while Melbourne dithered. He could resign and let Peel form a government, or he could do as Palmerston suggested, call a general election and hope to earn a larger majority at the hustings. Eventually, after Peel's motion of censure for his failure to resign had been carried by a majority of one, he went to the country.

In the June general election, campaigning again on their opposition to the poor law, the Tories won a majority of almost a hundred. Returned unopposed for Tiverton, Palmerston went back to his ministerial desk to make ready for his successor. In those days a government remained in office until defeated in a motion in the new Parliament; and when that happened, on 28 August, the day after Palmerston wrote his abrupt note to the American minister, Melbourne's Whig government duly resigned.

With the exception of a few months at the beginning of 1835 and a week in 1839, Palmerston had been Foreign Secretary for almost eleven years. In that time he had set himself so many tasks that inevitably a few were still uncompleted; and among the many that seemed completed there were a few that were still to have repercussions, sometimes as a result of nothing more than the suspicions and resentments felt by men who had been bested by him. In France the humiliated Louis-Philippe and Guizot were powerless to do more than thwart him in the ratification of the Five-Power Anti-Slave-Trade Treaty. But in Russia the frustrated Tsar Nicholas began to plan a new policy. He had gained nothing from maintaining the integrity of the Turkish Empire. Perhaps he could gain more from its partition. He had been persuaded to do nothing to prevent foreign warships from entering the Black Sea in wartime. Perhaps he should prepare for their arrival. He began to build a huge fortified naval base in the Crimea at Sevastopol. 'Sooner or later', said the Baron de Barante, who was French Ambassador in St Petersburg, 'this will be the cause of a European war.'

Palmerston's critics, then and ever after, concentrated on the caustic, domineering style that at one time or another antagonized almost every diplomat and statesman in Europe; and in so doing they usually ignored or overlooked his achievements. His means were often unattractive, but there was no denying the quality and quantity of his ends. In northern Europe he had created the constitutional monarchy of Belgium, which has survived ever since. He had brought peace to the Middle East; he had saved the Turkish Empire from Russia and the road to India from France; and he had established a virtually independent Egypt under a dynasty that was to survive until the abdication of King Farouk in 1952. He had saved Spain and Portugal from Absolutism and planted the fragile seeds of constitutional democracy in their fiercely infertile soil. He had taken more practical and constructive steps towards the destruction of the slave trade than any other statesman. To the people of Britain he was not yet the hero that he was soon to become; but if he had died in 1841, he might have died a hero to history.

After many frustrating years at the War Office, watching Canning and sneering at others, Dr Drury's eager idealist and Professor Stewart's bashful scholar had turned into a cynical, impatient opportunist. But as such he had already achieved more than any of them would have dreamed possible.

8. *T*HE LAST ROSE
OF SUMMER

Lord Melbourne missed his regular audiences with Queen Victoria as much as she did. For several months after his resignation in 1841 they exchanged two or three letters a week, and their correspondence might have continued for longer if Prince Albert had not intervened.

The Prince began by asking an embarrassed George Anson to call on Melbourne and read him the withering memorandum they had received from Stockmar, in which the baron pointed out that the exchange of letters on matters of state between the Queen and her former Prime Minister was constitutionally irresponsible, as well as politically disconcerting for his successor. When this only provoked an uncharacteristically ill-tempered 'God eternally damn it', Stockmar was invited to speak to Melbourne personally, which he did with devastating candour. He informed Melbourne that Mrs Norton, with whom he was again on intimate terms, was boasting about her knowledge of the letters at every Mayfair dinner table. He warned him that Peel had threatened to resign if he discovered that the Queen was consulting anyone other than himself; and he left him in no doubt that, if the letters continued, it would be necessary to inform the Queen that he had betrayed her confidence with Mrs Norton. At last Melbourne recognized the impropriety of the correspondence and quickly but tactfully reduced it to an occasional and harmless exchange of news.

The *ingénue* Queen had felt confident and comfortable in the company of warm and witty Melbourne. But her consort had much more in common with high-minded, hard-working Peel; and it was through Prince Albert's patient persuasion that she came to accept the most liberal of her Tory Prime Ministers and to respect him even more than she had respected the most conservative of her Whig ones. Within two years she was writing to her uncle King Leopold, describing Peel as 'undoubtedly a great statesman, a man who thinks but little of party and never of himself'.

Although hardly as clever as Peel, Prince Albert was almost as well educated and at least as cultured. He was a capable composer and such a genuinely talented musician that when connoisseurs praised him, as many did, they were not just flattering a prince. He was a knowledge-able collector of Early Renaissance painting; he was eagerly fascinated by every aspect of contemporary design and technology; and since his arrival in Britain, unfortunately for Palmerston, he had developed a keen interest in foreign policy. But at the outset he was as much of a political novice as the Queen. His first formal experience of working with politicians came in 1841, shortly after the formation of the Tory government, when Peel invited him to be chairman of the new Royal Commission on the Fine Arts, which was set up soon after work began on the huge new Houses of Parliament.

The suitably imposing replacement for the rambling old Palace of Westminster was being built to designs by Charles Barry, who had made his name as the leading exponent of the neo-Renaissance style, and young Augustus Pugin, who was about to make his name as the leading exponent of the uniquely British Gothic Revival; and the purpose of the royal commission, which included all the leading statesmen from both sides of both Houses, was to appoint and instruct the craftsmen and artists who would provide the new palace with apropriate furnishings, sculpture, paintings and, at the insistence of Prince Albert, frescoes.

At first the members of the commission were condescendingly amused by the solemn young Prince's methodical and apparently unaesthetic approach to the job. But they were soon surprised and impressed by his taste, knowledge and unassuming common sense. He was so discreet and industrious that they found it easy to understand why Peel had accepted him so readily as the Queen's new private secretary, although it was not so easy to approve of the extent to which the Prime Minister was also consulting the foreign Prince separately on what he described rather pompously in one of his letters as 'the legislative measures in contemplation of Her Majesty's servants'.

Back in the alarming weeks of November 1840, when the birth of the Queen's first child temporarily prevented her from holding her regular audiences with her Prime Minister, Melbourne had not deigned to share the burdens of state with anyone else in the royal household. Exactly a year later, during the less dramatic days that preceeded and followed the birth of the Queen's second child, Peel sent Prince Albert nightly reports, not just on the debates in the House of Commons but on the discussions in Cabinet as well.

Yet for all his curiosity and useful common sense, the Prince was not as quick to learn about politics and politicians as they were to learn about him. He was openly surprised when Melbourne appointed Russell to lead the opposition in the House of Commons. He had expected the job to go to Palmerston, whom, until then, he had always described as the Queen's 'second' minister. But he had not understood the significance of Russell's previous office or recognized the extent of his influence. Having been Leader of the House under the Whig government, Russell was more appropriately qualified; and as the third son of the Duke of Bedford, he could rely on far more support among the other great Whig families than could the ebullient Irish viscount, whose strongest claim to powerful connections came only from his recent marriage to the outgoing Prime Minister's sister.

The surprise may not have been a disappointment, however. By then the Queen and her family had lost a little of the grateful and unquestioning respect that they had initially felt for her first Foreign Secretary. In November 1840, just as it was becoming clear that the great gamble in the Middle East was about to pay off, an exasperated King Leopold had written at length to Prince Albert criticizing the Foreign Secretary's dangerously intemperate bluffing and describing the man to whom he owed his throne as 'Palmerston, rex and autocrat'. Soon afterwards, having returned to her royal duties after the birth of her first child, the Queen had begun to suspect that the 'autocrat' was conducting some of his foreign policy behind her back. By the end of the following May she was so sure of it that she wrote to him. 'The Queen fears that there must be some mistake about sending the despatches, as she has not received one box for the last five days … She has also perceived once or twice that they [the Foreign Office clerks] have sent to her drafts to approve when the originals have already been sent away.' Unconvinced by Palmerston's apology for what he tried to pass off as the negligence of his staff, the Queen had then written to Melbourne, repeating the suspicion that she was only being shown some despatches after they had been sent and adding the fear that those which were 'rough in language' were not being shown to her at all. Before the matter could be resolved, however, the Queen was writing again to both Melbourne and Palmerston regretting the loss of their 'valuable services'.

By the time Melbourne's government fell, Palmerston's star had begun to decline in the eyes of his once enthusiastic sovereign. But, by contrast, it was soon in the ascendant in the eyes of her subjects. While the French were wooing the new government and attempting to reverse their recent humiliation, the British people became more aware of the clearly admirable fellow who had inflicted it; and in the course of the next five years, by far the longest period that he ever spent in opposition or out of office, Palmerston learned how to cultivate their approval and make the most of their support. He made them laugh. No longer restrained by any obligation to maintain ministerial gravity, he became the government's most scornful and entertaining critic, not only on the floor of the House of Commons but also in frequent characteristic but unattributed leaders in the *Morning Chronicle*, which now belonged to his friend Sir John Easthope, the MP for Leicester, for whom he had recently secured a baronetcy.

In the summer of 1842, like several of his colleagues and many Whigs before him, Russell lost all interest in impotent opposition politics. Thereafter, until the next opportunity for office emerged, he seldom appeared in Parliament. In November, Melbourne was incapacitated by a stroke. For all practical purposes, although not in name, Palmerston became leader of the opposition. It was no coincidence that this was the year in which the satirist John Doyle published his lithograph of the still fit and youthful dandy sitting all alone on a long front bench and entitled it simply 'The Last Rose of Summer'.

Beyond the bounds of party politics, Palmerston adopted any cause that took his fancy – he once spoke in support of Prince Albert's attempt to suppress duelling in the army – and his taunting critical forays ranged with equal whimsy across every aspect of the government's activities. He derided the Tories for their lack of original policies and mocked them for 'living off our leavings … like a band of men who have made a forcible entrance into a dwelling, and who sit down and carouse upon the provisions they found in the larder'. But, for the most part, his assaults were only penetrating and sustained when their targets were topics close to his heart, or when they dealt with matters on which his years in office had armed him with impregnable expertise.

One such subject was the state of the nation's defences, which had been declining steadily since the days when War Office clerks shuddered at the sound of Palmerston's footsteps in the corridors. Selecting what seemed like the easiest target, he opened his campaign with a direct attack on the senior commanders in what was left of the army, denouncing their archaic attitudes and general incompetence. And for anyone who wanted to make such a case in 1842, there was no better body of supporting evidence than the horrifying and humiliating fate of the expedition that he and Melbourne had sent to Kabul in 1838.

At the outset the expedition had been successful. The city of Kabul had been occupied and the ruler, Dost Muhammad, imprisoned. But within two years his popular and energetic son Akbar Khan had raised an army large enough to challenge the invaders. After sacking the British Residency and killing everybody in it, including the Resident, Sir Alexander Burnes, Akbar Khan pinned down the British forces in their absurdly ill-sited encampment by placing thousands of marksmen behind the rocks in the hills directly above it. Cut off from their supplies, which, unbelievably, were situated in a separate camp a quarter of a mile away, the British soon sued for terms. In return for the promise of safe conduct they agreed to hand over all their artillery and evacuate Afghanistan.

On 6 January 1842 over 4,000 demoralized soldiers set out eastwards into the snow-clad mountains, accompanied and impeded by 12,000 wives, children, servants, merchants, tradesmen, musicians, dancers, jugglers and prostitutes. They were doomed from the outset. Their commander, Major-General William Elphinstone, who had recently been brought out of retirement and had not seen action since Waterloo, was so crippled by gout, arthritis and a fresh bullet wound in a buttock that he had to be carried in a litter; and he was soon so distracted by dysentery that he could barely concentrate, let alone make a decision. Their clothing and equipment were pathetically inadequate for the rigours of the infamous Afghan winter. Ahead of them the fiercest and hardiest of the eastern tribesmen, the Ghilzyes, were already gathering eagerly on either side of the frozen Jagdulluck Pass; and Akbar Khan, who watched as they went, had no intention of keeping any promise to protect them.

On 13 January, after a journey of less than a 100 miles, Surgeon-Major William Brydon stumbled down the last hill on a lame mare and rolled off her into the arms of a patrol from the British garrison at Jalalabad. Shortly afterwards, Major Lisant of the 37th Native Infantry arrived with barely half a platoon of sepoys and two or three merchants. Behind them, the naked corpses of almost all their companions were lying in piles by the sides of the pass, the victims of exposure, ambush and treachery. The only other survivors were nine officers' wives, eight of their children and two of their wounded husbands, all of whom were now hostages in the hands of Akbar Khan.

Before he could attack this disgracefully easy target, however, Palmerston found himself on the defensive. First he had to exonerate the Whigs for having sent an army to Kabul in the first place, a measure he represented, with just a hint of irony, as an attempt to civilize the Afghans rather than as a manoeuvre to check the Russians. Then, more precariously, he had to defend his own reputation against the charge that he had originally justified the expedition by suppressing the dissenting passages in Burnes's report; and in this he was fortunately supported by the government, which refused to publish the full report on the grounds that it would not be in the public interest. It was only when he had emerged from these diversions, almost unscathed and apparently undaunted, that he was able to take up his own offensive.

Palmerston portrayed the bungled occupation of Kabul and the conse-quent catastrophic withdrawal as ominous examples of the long-neglected army's general ineptitude. It was an argument that found immediate favour with the disillusioned and indignant British public, but it found none in Parliament, even among his handful of colleagues on the opposition benches. The Whigs were as sure as anyone else that responsibility for the tragic fiasco lay entirely with the original commander, General Sir Willoughby Cotton, his successor, the recently deceased Major-General Elphinstone, and perhaps the Indian Governor-General, Lord Auckland, who appointed them; and since both commanders had been appointed while the Whigs were still in office, there was no political capital to be made from their failure.

Britain's prestige had undoubtedly suffered; but with the culprits so conclusively identified and condemned, almost everyone in the the press and Parliament was eager to be convinced that the disaster was at worst an unlucky military aberration. In better hands, they said, it would not have happened. There was no real reason for concern. The successors to the victors of Waterloo were still the steadiest soldiers in the world; and while Britannia ruled the waves, her people were safe in their impregnable island. But Palmerston was equally eager to convince them they were wrong. This had not been one of those occasions when he was just trying to embarrass the government. To him the disaster was a distant symptom of a widespread infection, and in the course of the next three years he returned to his theme as often as he could. If the complacent Tories could not be persuaded to spend more on defence, they might soon be faced with a far worse disaster 4,000 miles closer to home, in the southern counties of England.

King Louis-Philippe had increased the strength of his standing army to 340,000 men, twice the size of the British army. On top of that he had a million men in his citizens' militia, the National Guard, which effectively meant that all his regular soldiers were available for service abroad. Worse still, he was expanding his navy. The consoling tenet that Britannia ruled the waves was beginning to look more like a dangerous heresy. While Queen Victoria's shipyards lay almost idle, and while her ships, which were still mostly wooden-hulled sailing ships, were spread out across the world in defence of her empire, Louis-Philippe was building large ironclad steamships and stationing most of them in the English Channel. While Guizot was making friendly overtures to the new British government, several of his ministerial colleagues were boasting that France would soon be strong enough to invade England any time she chose.

Palmerston pleaded in vain with the government to increase the naval estimates and hire 'the most scientific men' to assist in the design of modern warships. In 1844 his hopes were briefly raised when Lord Ellenborough, who had succeeded Auckland as Governor-General of India, was recalled and appointed First Lord of the Admiralty. In a letter to his brother he wrote, 'I am glad of Ellenborough's appointment; it will be doubly advantageous. First, it will give us an efficient navy; and, secondly, it will render the Government unpopular.' But his optimism was misplaced on both counts. Peel was not willing to risk the unpopularity of additional expenditure.

On 13 June 1845, in a long speech to the House of Commons, Palmerston outlined all his fears and all his proposals to allay them. 'The Channel is no longer a barrier', he said. 'Steam navigation has rendered that which was before impassable by a military force nothing more than a river passable by a steam bridge.' Troop ships and their escorts were no longer at the mercy of the wind and the weather. Britain needed a modern navy, a large militia and extensive new fortifications all around her principal ports. Until all these were in place, the French could launch a surprise attack and land enough men on the beaches in one night to seize the ports from the rear, destroy their docks and arsenals and then march unopposed on London.

The speech sowed the seeds of anxiety among the British public, and within Parliament it won the support of many on both sides of both Houses, including men whose experience should have made them more influential than they were – in the Commons a colourful new member, Admiral Sir Charles Napier, who had been promoted and knighted for his services in the eastern Mediterranean; and in the Lords none other than the Duke of Wellington. After the debate the duke wrote to Peel 'begging' and 'intreating' him to take notice of 'this great and important subject, compared with which all other interests of the country are mere trifles'. To him, Palmerston's 'bridge' was more 'a multitude of bridges';

and as for the suggestion that the ports could be taken from the rear, 'this hypothesis', he wrote, 'is not the representation of an impossibility, or even extravagant, considering what I have seen done myself'.

By then, however, unprecedented 'cordial' relations had developed between the British and French Foreign Ministers, and indeed between their royal families. Even the most bellicose of Guizot's colleagues had given up boasting about the strength of their army. Despite the continuing expansion of the French navy, it was now difficult for Peel and most of his ministers to imagine any disagreement that could not be settled by diplomacy; and they were supported in this optimistic prejudice by the apparent evidence of recent events.

Prompted perhaps by Britain's thwartingly nimble annexation of New Zealand, a French admiral, on his own initiative, had annexed Tahiti and expelled a group of Protestant British missionaries, including the Revd George Pritchard, who, until shortly before, had been the accredited British Consul on the island. To the embarrassment of both governments, the indignant British public had demanded the restoration of independence to Tahiti and retribution for the affront to Her Majesty's representative, and the French public had made it plain that its government would fall if it gave in to British demands. Judging by the headlines in the newspapers on both sides of the Channel, the two countries were on the verge of war; and if Palmerston had still been in office, that impression would probably have been allowed to continue, at least until a few British frigates had altered the balance of power in Tahitian waters. But Guizot had soon come up with a compromise which was enough to save everyone's face and which a grateful Peel had been only too ready to accept. The French had recognized Tahiti only as 'a protectorate', and King Louis-Philippe had paid Mr Pritchard a generous compensation of £1,000 out of his own pocket.

Knowing nevertheless that the British public did not share his new trust of the French, Peel countered Palmerston's proposals with the one argument that was guaranteed to diminish public support: expense. At £787 million the national debt was already far too high to justify the cost of all of them. All that he could manage for the time being were a few cosmetic fortifications and an additional £1 million on the next navy estimates, far from enough to prevent Palmerston and Wellington from continuing their cross-party lobbying.

A much less popular cause, but one that Palmerston promoted just the same, was the improvement of conditions in Ireland. He had no sympathy with Daniel O'Connell's noisy campaign for repeal of the 1801 Act of Union, which had been renewed soon after the Tories took office. Like Russell, who was passionate about the plight of Ireland, Palmerston dismissed 'Home Rule' as no more than an idealistic focus for Ireland's many more material grievances, and he concentrated his energies instead on denouncing the causes of the grievances.

The worst of these – one that had been highlighted eloquently in several novels by Palmerston's old acquaintance Maria Edgeworth – was still the iniquitous system of land tenure. Outside the Protestant counties of Ulster tenants had virtually no rights at all. If a landlord wanted to combine several smallholdings in one larger, economically more viable unit, he could evict the necessary tenants at will, even if they were up-to-date with their rents. If a farmer was successful, his landlord could turn him out and let the land that he had improved to someone else at a higher rent. There were even times when tenants were evicted for no other reason than that the landlord wanted to replace a Roman Catholic with a Protestant.

In the wake of a huge rise in population, the resulting thousands of innocent homeless had no hope of finding work or shelter. They were left, as Palmerston put it, 'to perish by the road side, or to eke out a miserable and lingering existence as squatters on the fringe of a bog, or in the outskirts of some neighbouring town'. But, for all his righteous indignation, he stopped short of demanding that this wrong should be righted by legislation. 'To do so', he told the House of Commons, 'would be to establish a principle of confiscation – to interfere with the rights of property, the foundation of all human society.' He was, after all, an Irish landlord himself. As he wrote frankly in a letter to Henry Petty, Marquess of Lansdowne, his opponent at Cambridge and his friend ever since, 'I, for one, have no particular fancy for being compelled to buy back my estate from time to time from my tenants.'

With unusual – or perhaps unconvincing – naïvety, Palmerston apparently hoped that something charitable could be done to alleviate the suffering of the evicted, and that the offending majority of absentee landlords could be shamed into mending their ways by the example of the minority, of which he was one, and by the weight of public disapproval. He was contented therefore when Peel set up a commission under the Earl of Devon to consider the system of land tenure in Ireland. Although he continued to deplore the suffering of the homeless, he did not, like Russell, propose reforms, and he made no protest when Parliament consistently failed to discuss any of the commission's recommendations.

Palmerston was not always opposed to legislating for the Irish, however. He supported the bill that enabled Roman Catholics to sit on juries, and he supported anything aimed at improving their standards of education. When Peel introduced a bill to raise the government's grant to the Roman Catholic College at Maynooth, which educated young men for the priesthood, Palmerston went out on a limb and spoke enthusiastically in its favour.

Palmerston had even less respect for the Catholic Church than he had for most others. In a letter to Russell he once described it as 'a bad political institution, unfavourable to morals, to industry, and to liberty'. Nevertheless he recognized that it was the only source of education and moral guidance acceptable to the vast majority of Irishmen. He had been one of the first of the very few Anglo-Irish landlords to set aside plots for the support of the priests who ministered to their tenants. In another letter to Russell he wrote with undeniable conviction: 'To raise and improve the condition of the Catholic clergy is an object which all rational men must concur in thinking desirable.'

But this was not a popular opinion in mid-nineteenth-century England. The recent runaway success of the high-church Oxford Movement had made the Anglican establishment more than usually suspicious of Rome; and since it was now clear that Catholic emancipation was far from enough to satisfy the demands of the Irish, most Englishmen had lost all patience with Ireland and Catholicism. Although Peel was only proposing to raise a long-standing grant to a level that would enable the run-down college to restore its buildings and operate effectively, his bill aroused a nationwide storm of indignant, bigoted opposition, uniting Anglicans, Baptists, Free Churchmen and other strange bedfellows in a common cause. The response was out of all proportion to the proposal, even within Parliament, where it created the crack that was soon to grow into a yawning rift between progressive Peel and his party. Almost half the Tory back-benchers voted against the bill, and Gladstone resigned from the Cabinet in protest. All that saved it from defeat was the united support of O'Connell's Catholic Nationalists and Palmerston's proudly secular Radicals.

Ironically, it was a different cross-bench combination that saved Peel's proposal to establish colleges in Belfast, Cork and Galway and create a Queen's University of Ireland, which was to include no religious instruction in the curriculum and have no affiliation to any church. This time it was O'Connell's Catholics and the Evangelical Tories who opposed the 'Godless Colleges', and it was Palmerston's Whigs and the 'liberal' Tories, including Gladstone, who outvoted them.

Despite their fundamental disagreement on Home Rule, Palmerston and O'Connell were often allies in liberal causes. The big Irishman was as forceful as anyone in his condemnation of slavery, for example. But in the course of Peel's government Palmerston became increasingly disdainful of him. He disliked his heavily caustic antagonism to Peel, which was as much personal as political, and which originated on a distant day when Peel, then Secretary for Ireland, had challenged O'Connell to a duel — an assignation that had only been prevented by the resourceful Mrs O'Connell, who had arranged for her husband to be arrested and bound over to keep the peace. When the Tories contrived O'Connell's conviction and imprisonment on a trumped-up charge, Palmerston's voice was conspicuously silent in the angry debate that followed.

O'Connell knew that he could never extend his parliamentary support beyond his forty-five Irish Catholic Nationalists, so many of whom were his sons or married to his daughters that they were collectively known as his 'household brigade'. He therefore returned to what he did best and made passionate speeches to huge gatherings in Ireland. On 7 October 1843, alarmed by the success of earlier meetings, the Lord-Lieutenant prohibited the one that was due to be held next day at Clontarf, the site of a great Irish victory over the invading Vikings. On receipt of the order O'Connell, who had always been emphatically opposed to violence, insisted that it must be obeyed and persuaded the thousands of loyal supporters who had already assembled to return peacefully to their homes. Despite this, on government instructions, he was arrested, tried, convicted, fined and imprisoned for conspiracy.

Fortunately for the reputation of the Tories, the conviction was quashed on appeal a year later by the House of Lords; and fortunately for England, the consequences of the shameful injustice were not as disruptive as they might have been. For the barely three years of life that were left to him O'Connell was no longer a threat. Emerging from prison with his health broken, he declined steadily into a deep, remorseful, Celtic melancholy. The direction of the Home Rule movement passed to the leaders of the 'Young Ireland' party, who were far from opposed to the use of violence, but who were too busy arguing with each other to be effective; and while they were still squabbling, Nature turned on Ireland and oppressed her with suffering much more terrible than anything a human enemy could have planned for her.

The conditions in Ireland and the state of the nation's defences were subjects on which Palmerston had not been able to spend much time as Foreign Secretary. Once he was free from the burdens of office, however, the many daily hours that had been devoted to his duties could be devoted instead to cherished causes such as these, as well as to the more general business of making a merry nuisance of himself to the government. But, in opposition as in office, the bulk of his time and energy was still expended on foreign policy, often in exasperated lamentation, and sometimes in sincere fury, at the mess that his successor was making of his 'leavings'.

Like Wellington, Peel gave the Foreign Office to Aberdeen, a man about whom Palmerston had no illusions. The two men had known each other well for all but the first few years of their lives. As Lord Haddo, Aberdeen had been Harry Temple's contemporary at Harrow, and he had still been at St John's, having succeeded to his earldom, when Harry, now Viscount Palmerston, arrived there from Edinburgh. In the last years of the Napoleonic Wars, while Palmerston was at the War Office,

Aberdeen had been a special envoy in Vienna, where he had acquired an immutable awe of the 'Great Powers' and laid the foundations of a lifelong friendship with Metternich. He and Palmerston had served very briefly together in Wellington's Cabinet; and it had been Aberdeen who, as Foreign Secretary, had borne the brunt when Palmerston left the government and, in 'imitation of Canning', launched his celebrated attacks on its policies in Portugal and Greece.

In the course of the last twenty years Aberdeen's natural reserve had evolved into what now looked like cold, unapproachable pride; but the haughty demeanour was only the mask with which a shy man tried to hide indomitable sorrow. During those years he had stood beside the new graves of two wives, four daughters and a son. His only surviving heirs were the sons of the second marriage, which had been as miserable as the first had been happy.

President of the Royal Society of Antiquaries and a Trustee of the British Museum, Aberdeen was at heart an ascetic scholar; and like so many scholarly men – such as Goderich – he could see all sides of an argument, although in his case the gift inclined him to compromise rather than indecision. It was his declared ambition to achieve more by harmonious give-and-take than Palmerston had managed with stubborn bluster; and it was Palmerston's declared fear that he might indeed try to do just that and reverse everything that had been gained so far in the process. When Aberdeen's expected appointment was announced, Palmerston had shared his anxiety with Melbourne, and Melbourne, inevitably, had passed it on in one of his indiscreet letters to the Queen.

The 'leavings' that were least affected by Aberdeen's approach were in China. In 1842 and 1843 the 'Opium War' was brought to an end by the treaties of Nanking and the Bogue, which were concluded on terms close to those proposed by Palmerston. Although the compensation paid to merchants for their lost opium was less than Palmerston had demanded, the island of Hong Kong was ceded to Great Britain, British merchants were granted access to the major ports, and the settlement on the whole was enough to earn Palmerston's approval when it was debated in the Commons.

His response to the agreement with the United States was very different, however. Determined to put an end to the increasingly bitter disputes that Palmerston had left outstanding, Aberdeen had sent the banker Alexander Baring to negotiate with the American Secretary of State, Daniel Webster. A fellow Trustee of the British Museum and the Tory uncle of Francis Baring, the recent Whig Chancellor of the Exchequer, Alexander Baring had served as President of the Board of Trade and had been created Baron Ashburton in 1835. He had widespread business interests in America and he was well known and well liked in Washington, where his father-in-law was a senator. With hardly a hint of discord he and the Secretary of State concluded an agreement in August 1842 which was to be known by their names, the Webster-Ashburton Treaty, and which settled what had been the two most acrimonious disputes between their nations: the position of the eastern border between the United States and Canada, and the British insistence that their navies should have a mutual right of search in the Atlantic.

On what was regarded as the most important point, the eastern border, it was agreed that the boundary between the United States and Canada should run through Lakes Superior, Huron, Erie and Ontario, and that to the east of the lakes, as far as Canadian New Brunswick, the disputed high land south of the St Lawrence river, which the Dutch King had assigned to Canada in his 1831 arbitration, was to be divided equally between Canada and the state of Maine.

News of the treaty, which reached London while Parliament was in recession, was widely welcomed by both Whigs and Tories; and it was therefore all the more surprising when a series of vitriolic articles appeared in the *Morning Chronicle* attacking it. Although the articles were unattributed, and although, at first, Palmerston disclaimed them, their intemperate language was so obviously his that several leading Whigs, including his Harrow mess-mate Spencer, prevailed on Russell to rebuke and, if possible, restrain him. But the reply to Russell's letter was unrepentant and defiant.

All that I claim for myself is freedom of action according to the best judgement I can form of the interests of my country;

and that freedom I shall always exercise as long as it may please heaven to continue to grant me my faculties, whether Radicals or old Whigs are pleased or displeased with the line I may think it my duty to take.

True to his resolve, on 21 March 1843, after Parliament had reassembled, Palmerston spoke on the treaty for three and a half hours, damning every article in turn, often with criticisms that were much too far-fetched to be convincing. At one point he even went so far as to suggest that allowing the Americans to keep the part of Michigan that reaches north between the lakes on the west flank of Ontario was simply granting them 'additional means of threatening us in case of new differences, or of attacking us in the event of war'. The whole treaty, he said, was nothing more than 'capitulation'; and he concluded his tirade with what was seen by many as a most improper attack on the integrity and suitability of the negotiator. Few could deny that Ashburton had an inappropriately close 'private connexion with the other party'. Indeed it was because of this that Aberdeen had at first expressed reservations about sending him. But the House was embarrassed when Palmerston described him as 'the most unfit person that could have been selected for so important a mission'.

In his response to Russell's rebuke Palmerston had made it clear that he would not be restrained and that he was prepared to launch a lone attack in Parliament if necessary, although he had also expressed the hope that his arguments might 'influence the minds of fair and impartial men'. But his party was in no mood to support him, and he did indeed attack alone. To Radicals and old Whigs alike, improved relations with the United States were worth a few sacrifices.

One of the very few Whigs who had any sympathy at all with Palmerston was Russell, who was cynical enough to suggest that the only people likely to gain from the treaty were 'Baring and Co. and the land sharks of Maine'. But even he was disconcerted by the abusive tone, which he felt was as damaging to the party as to Palmerston. Like the other Whigs, he sat in silence amid Tory jeers and took no advantage of the opportunity when Peel, in a totally unjustified attempt to blame

Palmerston for everything, actually admitted that the treaty was not all that it might have been. 'I must condemn the conduct of the noble Lord opposite in having weakly conceded so much as to have rendered such a compromise necessary.'

There was obviously an element of personal bitterness in Palmerston's unusually virulent attack. Everyone in Parliament could remember Ashburton's relentless criticism of his policies in the eastern Mediterranean, even after they had been successful. But there was much more to it than that. The real cause of Palmerston's sincere indignation – which was even more passionate in his private correspondence – was the price that had been paid for a settlement on the border. Under the other terms of the treaty the British had withdrawn their demand for a mutual right of search. Instead it had been agreed that the United States Navy would maintain a squadron with a power of at least eighty guns off the west coast of Africa, in order to search suspicious ships flying the American flag, and that wherever possible American and British warships would operate in pairs.

Although most of the ships in West African squadrons were fast little ten-gun brigs, the minimum of eighty guns would not have been enough for the job even if the American squadron had been kept up to strength, which it very seldom was; and, as might have been expected, the two wary navies never hunted in couples. In failing to sanction the sought-after 'right' which the Royal Navy had till then been exercising unofficially anyway, the Webster-Ashburton Treaty had effectively drawn its teeth and considerably reduced the threat to the slave trade. No longer would British warships sail into New York harbour to return the captured American slavers that they had towed back empty from the coast of Africa after taking off their human cargoes, as *Buzzard, Harlequin, Dolphin* and several others had done during Palmerston's last days at the Foreign Office. Furthermore, British captains would no longer sail up African rivers and destroy the Portuguese and Spanish baracoons knowing that they had the Foreign Secretary's protection: a cautious memorandum submitted to Peel's Cabinet by the Attorney-General had advised rather obviously that the practice was probably unlawful.

223

And all this had been achieved by a 'half Yankee' whose family owed much of its fortune to slaves, and who was himself a director of a company that was still acting as one of the bankers to the trade. Ashburton's father-in-law, Senator William Bingham, had built the foundations of his great wealth in the West Indies in the days when their economy was still based on slavery. Like Kleinwort and a few other London bankers, Baring & Co. was still deriving considerable profits from the Cuban slave-tended sugar trade. Worst of all, while Ashburton was negotiating with Webster, several of the leading Portuguese slave traders in the Caribbean were continuing to use cheques drawn on Baring & Co. to supply their ships and buy the goods which they then bartered for their human cargoes.

There is no reason to believe that Peel was not telling the truth when he told the House, 'I approve of this treaty'. But he was at least deceiving himself when he added, 'I recognize the eminent services of the distinguished individual who has negotiated and brought it to a satisfactory conclusion.'

Discouraging though it was, however, the squandering of Palmerston's leavings in America was as nothing compared with the fate of his leavings in France. Where Britain's new concord with the United States was merely offensive to Palmerston personally and crippling to his campaign against the slave trade, the new 'cordial' relations with France were humiliating for the former and almost lethal to the latter.

As intended, Guizot waited vengefully until Palmerston was out of office and then, in December 1841, signed the Five-Power Treaty on behalf of France. But he never ratified it; and early in 1842, urged on by the Americans, he cancelled the mutual right of search, which had been negotiated by Palmerston, and later replaced it with an impotently limited 'right to visit'. Although, like the Americans, the French then stationed their own squadron off the Slave Coast, and although that squadron was sometimes as large as the British one, it was there as a presence rather than a deterrent. In the course of its first six months on station, after October 1842, it visited only twenty-five ships – barely one a week – and all but two of them were British.

Powerless in opposition to do anything else, Palmerston could only plead. He wrote to Guizot pointing out the consequences of his politics and imploring him to reconsider, but the plea was dismissed as peremptorily as Guizot's last plea had been dismissed by Palmerston. He spoke passionately against the slave trade in Parliament on 16 July 1844 and again on 8 July 1845. The first speech, another of over three hours, was so moving in its accounts of the terrifying raids and the cruel conditions in the holds of the ships that it was later published as a pamphlet by the Anti-Slavery Society. But neither his descriptions of the suffering nor his accusations of complicity had any effect on the government. Behind a high-principled façade, the French and the Americans had ruined his strategy for stifling the slave trade; and he blamed Aberdeen for letting them do it.

Aberdeen and Guizot had much in common. Under the eager influence of Princess Lieven, the dour, aristocratic antiquarian and the austere but worldly bourgeois historian developed what, to Aberdeen at least, was a scholarly friendship. At the same time, under the equally energetic influence of King Leopold, a friendship developed between the British and French royal families. In September 1843, when the British royal couple crossed the Channel in their new yacht, *Victoria and Albert*, to spend five days as the guests of King Louis-Philippe and Queen Amélie at Château d'Eu in Normandy, Aberdeen and Guizot accompanied their sovereigns. It was the first official visit of a reigning British monarch to France since 1520, when Henry VIII met Francis I on the 'Field of Cloth of Gold'. This time, however, the meeting was a much greater diplomatic success, particularly for the French.

Still fearful of Russia and Austria, whose absolutist ministers mistrusted her precarious and supposedly liberal government, and whose proud emperors regarded her 'Citizen King' as an upstart, France needed the support of the only secure and powerful constitutional monarchy much more than Great Britain needed France. Yet, under Guizot's careful guidance, it was France who dominated the relationship. In every instance, just as in the awkward confrontation over Tahiti, Guizot led and Aberdeen followed, anxiously grateful for anything that seemed to strengthen the peace between them, and credulously oblivious to any hidden agendas. When the French chargé d'affaires in London coined a phrase for the rapprochement, impressionable Aberdeen seized upon it and repeated it everywhere as if it were his own. The new harmony between Great Britain and France was not simply a matter of mutual self-interest, it was a sincere understanding: an *entente cordiale*.

Although, for the time being, Palmerston was also unaware of any hidden agendas, he was nevertheless far from happy with the *entente*. There was, he wrote in a letter to Russell, 'a general disposition on the part of the Government to sacrifice in every direction abroad the future and permanent interests of the country in order to procure relief from momentary embarrassments'. Incredibly, it looked as though the Tories had become as Francophile as the old Whigs. They were acquiescing while Guizot wiped away the humiliations of the recent past. Palmerston's worst fears were coming true. If the concessions continued, it was only a matter of time before France replaced Britain as leader of liberal Europe.

Even the Queen had become part of the process, despite being aware of Palmerston's warnings. Ever since her visit to Normandy, which had been kept suspiciously secret till she sailed, she and her husband had been almost evangelical in their open affection for the 'admirable and truly amiable' French royal family. So far, this enthusiasm had failed to influence her subjects, who, like most of the press, still clung stubbornly to their traditional prejudices, but at court and in Parliament it was beginning to look as though the only people who still mistrusted the French were Palmerston and Wellington.

Palmerston's exasperation was as evident in private as anywhere. Writing from Broadlands to her mother, the young Countess Cowper described the mood of her mother-in-law's new husband. 'He abuses everything and everybody connected with the Tories. Thinks Lord Ashburton a rascal, Sir R. P. ditto: Lord Aberdeen ditto: ditto.' But for the most part the abuse was more genial than caustic. Real rage was usually reserved for those who were indifferent or contributed to the survival of the slave trade. Palmerston was undoubtedly frustrated by being in opposition, but he did not resent it. Provided it did not last too long, he was content to enjoy himself and make the most of every opportunity it presented. As he wrote to his brother soon after the government resigned,

'I should much like to have two good years' holiday, if holiday it is for those who have to attend Parliament regularly. But indeed that is an amusement, and not a labour, for those who are out of office.'

When Parliament was not sitting, a man out of office had time for travel. In October 1841, at the end of the Whig government's last session, and at the beginning of one of the worst winters on record, Lord and Lady Palmerston set out on a long overdue trip to inspect some of his properties in the west. They took the packet-boat across the grey Irish Sea to Dublin. From there, shivering beneath thick rugs in a cold, swaying coach, they struggled on through a snowstorm to Sligo, where Lady Palmerston was introduced to some of the 900 tenants on the now thriving estate and shown the new roads and the almost completed harbour. On the way home they paused briefly at the slate quarry in northern Wales and then lumbered on southwards, with their horses still stumbling as they hauled the heavy coach through snow as thick as any they had met in Ireland.

Sadly, however, for the next two years all further plans for travel had to be set aside. After Lord Melbourne's stroke the Palmerstons devoted large parts of each parliamentary recess to keeping him company at Brocket or entertaining him at Broadlands. It was not until August 1844 that they set out again, this time for the continent.

They started in Belgium, where they dined twice with King Leopold, and then crossed into Prussia to take the waters at Wiesbaden, where they found 'an English colony', which included Palmerston's old friend Lansdowne. After delaying for a fortnight longer than intended, owing to the 'bad effects of the Wiesbaden waters', they went to Dresden, where they dined with King Frederick William IV and his Foreign Minister, Bülow. Palmerston was impressed, not only by the King – 'a man of great acquirements, much natural talent, and enlightened views' – but also by everything that he saw and learned in his kingdom. He made copious notes, and he made them with such conspicuous diligence that some of those who saw him reported his activities. When one such report reached Paris, the British Ambassador, Lord Cowley, who was Wellington's youngest brother, wrote to warn Aberdeen that he suspected Palmerston was amassing evidence 'to prove the advantages which would result from the abrogation of the Corn Laws'. But in reality his purpose was more general, and his conclusions more prescient. As he wrote to his brother, 'Prussia is taking the lead in German civilization; and as Austria has gone to sleep, and will be long before she wakes, Prussia has a fine career open to her for many years to come.'

From Dresden the Palmerstons went north to Berlin, then back south through Saxony, where they dined with the King, and on into the Austrian Empire, to Prague. At the outset they had planned that their itinerary would include visits to Vienna, where they hoped to meet Metternich, and then Paris; but the delay in Wiesbaden had denied them the time. From Prague they went straight home, in less time than it had taken them to get from Wiesbaden to Dresden. In the entire tour that six-day ride from Wiesbaden had been the only journey that they made by coach. Every other leg of the tour, including the one from Dover to London, had been made much faster and in the comparatively greater comfort of a train.

In Europe, as in Britain, the sudden explosion of 'railway mania' was well under way. In the course of the next three years the number of British miles covered by track would multiply to over 9,000, and would include two lines through Wales to the Dublin packet ports at Fishguard and Holyhead; and among the 2,000 miles already completed and in use there were 77 running through Hampshire from London to Southampton. Broadlands was now only three or four hours away from Westminster, no longer too far for a front-bench spokesman, or even a Foreign Secretary, to spend a weekend there when Parliament was in session, and close enough at any time for him to return in an emergency if he received a summons on the new electric telegraph.

The convenience of the railways combined with the spare time afforded by opposition enabled Palmerston to make the most of Broadlands and use it as a base for all the sports he had not been able to enjoy since he took over at the Foreign Office. There was plenty of time now for hunting and shooting, and time to make regular visits to his trainer's yard twelve miles away, near Stockbridge – a much discussed custom that soon became one of the sights of Hampshire, since he galloped the whole way there and back with his unbuttoned frock coat billowing behind him. There was even time to watch his horses run occasionally, although the apex of his racing career came just after he left office, when one of his mares, Iliona, won the Cesarewitch.

Between them the Palmerstons also set about the systematic reorganization of the Broadlands gardens. They read all the latest books on trees, shrubs, flowers and design, then issued instructions to the new head gardener with the assumed authority of experts, and gave guided tours to their many guests, reviewing their progress and outlining the next stages in what they regarded as a 'scientific' programme.

With the new Lady Palmerston as its mistress, Broadlands became more than ever the setting for memorable house parties. But it was in London that she established herself as the great political hostess that everyone knew she was going to be. Soon after their marriage the Palmerstons rented a large and splendid new house in St James's designed by John Nash: 5 Carlton House Terrace. Here, throughout each parliamentary session, they held regular weekend receptions which soon became known as their 'Saturday Reviews'. Invitations were as coveted and cherished as tickets to Almack's had been back in the heyday of the patronesses and the dandies. Among the other hostesses the adventurous Lady Palmerston was soon envied for her ability to mix incongruous guests successfully at her now much larger dinner table – a talent she did not always exercise without a modicum of mischief. On one occasion the company included the two protagonists from the drama in the eastern Mediterranean: Ibrahim Pasha and Sir Charles Napier. When the evening was over, one of the other guests, Palmerston's old friend Gilbert Elliot, now second Earl of Minto, confided that he was not sure which of the two had drunk the most or which was 'the greater blackguard'.

Like Broadlands, the London house was the scene of frequent and often spontaneous family gatherings, a way of life that Palmerston had not known for over thirty years, and one that he treasured all the more in consequence. During the parliamentary sessions the two members of the family who were seen at Carlton House Terrace most often were Lady Palmerston's daughters, both of whom she came close to admitting were the children of her second husband. Like Minny, who was married to Lord Ashley, Fanny, who was ten years younger, had recently married another Tory MP, Lord Jocelyn. A cheerful sportsman with more interest in the militia than politics, Jocelyn had much in common with the lighter and more obvious side of Palmerston's personality, but he was no rival for devout and solemn Ashley, who was already closer to Palmerston than almost anyone in Parliament, let alone anyone in the family.

There was so much in Palmerston and in Ashley that the other might have deplored or mocked. Yet instead, to universal amazement, the obviously sincere affection and respect that the two men felt for each other had grown steadily with the passage of time. Somehow, the obsessive and puritanical young Tory reformer had taught the genial and probably agnostic Whig statesman to take an interest in domestic affairs; and in so doing he had revealed a radical vein in what had seemed till then to be flawless conservative bedrock. While the Whigs were still in office, the two had not always seen eye to eye on foreign policy, but even here Ashley had occasionally managed to influence the minister. In 1840, while a British fleet was sailing east across the Mediterranean, it had been at Ashley's instigation that Palmerston attempted in vain to persuade the Turks to let Jewish immigrants settle in Palestine after it had been restored to them. The influence was by no means all one way, however. Peel, who found Ashley too temperamental to be tolerable as a colleague in Cabinet, despite their shared education at Harrow and Christ Church, was nevertheless so convinced that Palmerston was about to turn him into a Whig that he tried to ensure his continued loyalty by offering him the honour of a position in the royal household, an offer that Ashley disdainfully declined.

Palmerston supported all Ashley's efforts to improve working conditions in factories and mines. When Ashley introduced a bill prohibiting mine owners from assigning any jobs under ground to females or boys under the age of ten, Palmerston spoke from the opposition front bench in its favour, arguing with his usual practicality that the morals of the labouring classes would never improve until boys were given the opportunity of a basic education before they went to work. But the arguments that won over both Houses most effectively and turned Ashley's bill into the 1842 Coal Mines Act were the illustrations in the recently issued report of the Royal Commission on Children's Employment. Some depicted women hauling heavy trucks on all fours with the chains of the harness stretched tight between their legs. Others showed half-naked boys and girls clinging to each other as they were lowered precariously down the narrow shafts. The illustrations were so graphic and piteous – and so obviously effective – that the desperate mine owners in the House of Lords threatened to have Ashley prosecuted for publishing obscenities.

Having released Palmerston's latent social conscience, Ashley was soon to see it running ahead of him. Ashley's brand of philanthropy was traditional, aristocratic patronage. He believed that it was his Christian duty to take care of the working man and do what he knew was best for his family. He did not believe that the working man had the right, or even the ability, to make any decisions about such matters himself. Universal suffrage and all the other demands of the Chartists were as much anathema to Ashley as the Oxford Movement; and in essence Palmerston's attitude to Chartism was identical. Until the summer of 1842, on the many occasions when Radical members had risen on Palmerston's side of the house to protest at the injustices being meted out by magistrates to Chartist campaigners, he, like Ashley, had sat in silence and voted against any action being taken on their behalf. After the passing of the Coal Mines Act, however, Palmerston's attitude changed.

A magistrate near Wolverhampton had improperly warned that if any Chartists came within his jurisdiction he would order their arrest on sight. In defiance of this, or perhaps in ignorance of it, a group of Chartists held a meeting near by in Sedgley. As soon as the first speaker started to address the crowd, a policeman pushed him off his makeshift rostrum and arrested him. On the uncorroborated evidence of the policeman the eight Chartists were charged with unlawful assembly; and the speaker countered with a civil suit for assault against the policeman. In court, however, both cases were heard by the magistrate who had issued the unconstitutional threat. The policeman was acquitted and the Chartists were all sentenced to short terms in prison.

In the House of Commons the Radical Thomas Duncombe, another of Drury's pupils, demanded that the Home Secretary, Sir James Graham, should overturn the decision. When he sat down, Palmerston rose, not to oppose but to support him. No matter what anyone thought of their views, Chartists were entitled to the same justice as any other Englishmen; and they had the same rights, including freedom of speech. Duncombe's motion had no hope of succeeding. From the outset it had been clear that a majority of the House would oppose any attempt to interfere with the decision of a court. But a warning shot had been fired just the same. The province of the Home Secretary was no longer exempt from Palmerston's curiosity and censure.

After the success of the Coal Mines Act, Ashley continued to campaign as a leader of what was known as the 'Short Time Movement'. In February 1844, with the support of Russell, Palmerston and many others on the opposition benches, he moved an amendment to Clause 8 of a new Factory Bill. The clause prohibited mill owners from employing women and boys under the age of eighteen for more than twelve hours in any one day; and Ashley proposed that this limit should be further reduced to ten hours. His amendment failed, but only by a margin of seven votes, and only because five of his confused supporters, who had just voted 'no' to twelve hours, voted 'no' again instead of 'yes'. It was unlikely to fail at a second reading, and since the twelve-hour limit was fundamental to the bill, the Tories withdrew it entirely.

Ashley's opponents included not only the Tory representatives of the mill owners but also some of the Radicals who saw it as their duty to represent their workforce. The men in the mills could work only when there were women and boys supporting them. Without that support their own hours would also be cut, which would mean a reduction in their wages as well as a reduction in profits for their employers. Even Peel, whose father had been the first man ever to propose a reduction in working hours, was convinced that a limit of twelve was enough. With a twelve-hour limit, it would be possible to work the women and boys in shifts; and in theory at least, a mill could still be kept running round the clock.

At the end of March the Home Secretary, Graham, brought in a new bill which again imposed only a twelve-hour limit. Again Ashley and his supporters proposed ten hours. But this time Graham rallied all the Tories by threatening to resign if the bill was not carried. The twelve-hour limit became law. As might have been expected, the women and boys were worked in shifts. As a result, sickness and suffering increased dramatically among the exhausted male workforce, which was required to work longer hours than ever. Eventually, in 1847, under a Whig government, and in response to a proposal not from Ashley but from a Radical mill owner, John Fielden, the limit was reduced to ten and a half hours.

One of Ashley's trade union supporters, Philip Grant, afterwards wrote a *History of Factory Legislation*, in which he gave a famous account of a surprise visit that he and a colleague called Haworth apparently made on Lord Palmerston to win his support for their cause. Arriving at the house in 'Carlton Gardens' at 'getting on for two o'clock', the two men found a carriage waiting outside, but were told by the footman that 'His Lordship' was not at home. Not believing him, they pressed their case; and while they argued they were overheard by Palmerston, who was at that moment making an unlikely journey across the hall 'from his dressing-room to the dining-room'. After finding out who they were from the footman, Palmerston allowed them to be admitted and took them into the dining-room.

Many noisy minutes later Lady Palmerston, who was waiting impatiently to be taken for a drive, went into the dining-room to discover the cause of the commotion and found her husband and a footman, who had been summoned for the purpose, pushing large chairs on castors up and down the room. Under the direction of their experienced instructors they were imitating the process of 'spinning' and 'piercing'. When they paused, 'a little fatigued', Haworth showed Palmerston the injured hands and knees that he had acquired through years of labour in a factory. 'The illustration given had deeply impressed his Lordship's mind', wrote Grant. Palmerston professed himself convinced that Ashley was right when he claimed that children in factories walked or trotted twenty-five or thirty miles a day, and he promised that, if Ashley corroborated everything else they had told him, they could rely on his support. It was a promise, wrote Grant, 'which that great man ever afterwards kept'.

The charming story is in many ways typical of Palmerston, but it also smacks heavily of poetic licence. In the first place Grant wrote that the house that he visited was in Carlton Gardens, an address to which the Palmerstons did not move from Carlton House Terrace until 1847.

It is just possible therefore that Grant was remembering a visit made in 1847, just before the reading of the successful bill, but in that case it is unlikely that Palmerston would have mentioned Ashley, since Ashley was no longer directly involved. Either way, Grant had no justification in claiming that it was he who converted Palmerston. If the visit was made in 1844, the conversion had already been completed by Ashley; and in addition, if the visit was made in 1847, it was by then a matter of record that Palmerston was voting in favour of 'Short Time'.

Later in 1844 the Palmerstons made their tour of the continent, and in the following autumn they returned to Ireland. This time they travelled all the way to the port at Holyhead by train; and this time the weather, although cold, was bright enough for Lady Palmerston to enjoy a few picnics overlooking Sligo Bay. Before they set out, Palmerston wrote to his brother.

> On the way back I shall visit our slate quarry, which is going on well. We are gradually paying off our heavy debt, and in two years from this time I hope we shall be thinking of some sort of dividend. Our summer by the almanack has been autumn by the feelings; no hot weather; August resembling October, but the crops have ripened all the same ... In some places in England the potatoes have been blighted, but in Ireland they have been abundant and good.

He was wrong. Nearly half the Irish potato crop had been destroyed by an unknown fungus. And it was worse elsewhere. Holland had lost two-thirds of its potato crop and Belgium had lost over three-quarters. In the wake of a cold, wet summer, almost every country in Europe was facing some kind of agricultural disaster. In several, including England, the corn crops had failed. In an average year it might have been possible to send England's surplus cereal to Ireland, where half the 8 million inhabitants depended entirely on the potato for survival, but in the autumn of 1845 there was not even enough in England to feed the English. Without an additional supply of inexpensive corn, the price of bread was bound to rise beyond the reach of the working man.

To Peel and several of his Cabinet colleagues the answer was simple and obvious. The time had come to suspend the duties on imported corn. But there were still plenty in his party whose wealth was entirely derived from land, and who stood to gain from any shortage. To them 'Protectionism' was fundamental to the traditional Tory ethos. By the time the Palmerstons returned from Ireland, a little wiser than they had been before they left, Peel's Cabinet was hopelessly divided between pragmatic common sense and self-interest masquerading as principle.

Ironically, it was easier for Peel to help Ireland than to help England. While his ministers continued to argue over repeal of the corn laws in England, they agreed nevertheless to the secret importation of American maize into Ireland, a move that enabled him to claim later that no man in Ireland had died of famine during his administration. Towards the end of November, with the Cabinet still deadlocked and a growing majority of the public clamouring for repeal, Russell took advantage of Peel's predicament. He wrote an open letter from Edinburgh to his constituents in the City of London, in which he blamed the corn laws for almost all the ills in society and committed the Whigs to their repeal. Ironically again, the letter assured Peel that he was now in a position to do what he knew was right, but only with the support of the opposition and without the support of a substantial number in his own party and his Cabinet. It was a humiliation he preferred to avoid. On 5 December he went to Buckingham Palace and resigned.

On 11 December the Queen invited Russell to form a government. But the Whigs, despite their near-unity on repeal of the corn laws, were as bitterly divided as the Tories on a different issue: Palmerston. There were many in the House, including many potential ministers, who believed that Palmerston's return to the Foreign Office would mean the destruction of what had become known as the *entente cordiale*. The humiliation of Guizot's government in the Middle East had been only the worst example of what they saw as chronic Francophobia. In the election of 1841 Palmerston had made a passionate speech to his constituents condemning the disgraceful brutality of the French army in North Africa and comparing it with the conduct of the British in India, which he described as so scrupulously just and so widely appreciated that 'our officers ride about unarmed and alone among the wildest tribes of the wilderness'. Despite the growing entente, he had continually argued for the improvement of defences against a possible invasion and criticized France's failure to commit herself to the effective suppression of the slave trade. He had accused Aberdeen of disregarding Britain's best interests in order to keep Guizot in office, and he had developed a friendship with Guizot's bitter rival Louis Thiers, who had visited him in London as recently as October, shortly after his return from Ireland.

In the light of all this, the traditional Francophile Whigs urged Russell to offer Palmerston any office other than Foreign Secretary, or perhaps no office at all; and they were supported in their pleadings by none other than the Queen. Nobody had done more than Queen Victoria to foster the *entente cordiale*. Since her first meeting with Louis-Philippe at Château d'Eu, the friendship between their families had flourished. In October 1844 she had invited the French King to Windsor, where she had installed him as a Knight of the Garter. In the following September the two royal families and their Foreign Ministers had assembled again at Château d'Eu. She valued what had been achieved and she feared for its loss. To her, Palmerston's return to the Foreign Office was bound to mean a return to brinkmanship and the threat of war.

To Russell, however, Palmerston was essential. Russell was daunted by the prospect of forming a government at so critical a moment, and by the effect that the stress might have on his shy, sick, second wife, who was the daughter of Palmerston's friend Minto. He was not prepared to accept the responsibility without the support of all the ablest men in his party, and he argued his case so convincingly that within days he had persuaded the Queen and all but one of the leading Whigs to accept Palmerston as Foreign Secretary. Unfortunately, however, the odd man out was Earl Grey, the son of the recent Prime Minister, and one of the other able men without whom Russell was not prepared to accept office. Grey was impervious to all persuasion and remained adamant that he would not serve in any Cabinet in which the bellicose Palmerston was Foreign Secretary. Knowing that Palmerston was equally adamant that he would not accept any other office, Russell accepted defeat and resigned.

By Christmas, Peel and the Tories were back in office. The bitterly thwarted Whigs blamed Grey; the apprehensive people of England blamed Russell; and the mood of the nation was caught precisely by a cartoon that appeared in *Punch* on 3 January 1846. It showed the diminutive Russell standing like a page before the little Queen, who, although seated, was looking him straight in the face and telling him, 'I'm afraid you're not strong enough for the place, John.'

When Parliament reassembled in January, the Tory protectionists turned on Peel. In the House of Lords several dukes made it plain that members of the lower House who sat for constituencies that they controlled need not expect to be re-elected if they supported him. In the House of Commons new Tories and 'Old Guard' alike launched a fierce attack on him, the new men led by a landless upstart, Benjamin Disraeli, and the 'Old Guard' by Lord George Bentinck, who had hardly ever spoken before and admitted he knew more about horses than politics.

But Peel was too rich and too principled to care about the consequences of doing right. He introduced a bill reducing the duty on all imported wheat, oats and barley to a nominal one shilling a quarter, and he fought for it doggedly debate after debate. One outcome was inevitable: sooner or later, win or lose, the protectionists were bound to bring him down. The Whigs were waiting for their second chance; and this time they knew that Grey would not thwart them. Their furious censure had left him so chastened that he was was unlikely to risk political oblivion by opposing Palmerston again. It was only a matter of time before Palmerston was restored to his old office; and in the light of Russell's recent failure, and particularly in the light of a letter Lady Palmerston had received from her brother Frederick, he may even have dared to hope for something more.

Frederick Lamb, the elder of Melbourne's surviving brothers, had been created Lord Beauvale in 1839 and had recently retired from the diplomatic corps after serving for ten years as British Ambassador in Vienna. In January 1846 he dined with the Queen and Prince Albert at Windsor, accompanied by his new Prussian wife, who was arrestingly pretty, painfully shy and thirty-five years younger than he was. They talked about Palmerston and the French, about Guizot and about Thiers, who, according to Beauvale, regarded Palmerston as 'the first statesman of this age'. They talked about little Johnny Russell's indecisive collapse. The Queen expressed her amusement at the cartoon in *Punch*. And they talked about the possibility of Peel's resignation. In the long letter that he wrote afterwards to his sister, Beauvale reported that there was 'every disposition, if the case shld occur, to send to some other Person than Johnny', and he added that in that event it was 'impossible to stand better than P.'.

Whatever his hopes or expectations, Palmerston decided to show his critics that he could get on as well with the French as anyone. He had been planning a visit to France anyway; and as soon as Parliament rose for the Easter recess, he set out with Lady Palmerston for Paris.

In an exhausting, incessant round of dinners and assemblies they were received by every hostess who mattered in the city and met all the leading statesmen, diplomats and literary lions. They dined with the King, with Thiers and with Guizot and Princess Lieven. Palmerston was ebulliently charming to everyone and did all that he could, as Lady Palmerston put it, to 'set to rest for ever all such absurd reports as Lord Grey put about'.

But the visit was not the triumphant success that Palmerston's supporters professed it to be. The claim that 'ce terrible Lord Palmerston' had become 'ce cher Lord Palmerston' was more fanciful than factual. The humourless Victor Hugo, then at the height of his fame, thought Palmerston too vulgar, more suited to the pages of fiction than history. Lord Lansdowne, who was also present when they met, was much more Hugo's idea of what an English nobleman ought to be. Princess Lieven, who was still too bitter to be a reliable witness, described him in a letter to Aberdeen as looking like 'an old dandy of second-rate society'. The King admitted that he only received him because it would have been counter-productive to snub him. As for Guizot, in the part of Princess Lieven's letter which was less seasoned with spite and more seriously objective, she told Aberdeen:

> M. Guizot has not altered his opinion concerning him. He believes that Lord Palmerston will be circumspect, that he will

restrain himself a little, and that he will perhaps even pretend to sentiments different from those which he has professed so far; but he is convinced that the former man will reappear ... and more than ever prays to God to be spared from him.

On the afternoon of 25 June 1846, with the support of the precariously united Whig peers, Peel's bill for repeal of the corn laws survived its third reading in the House of Lords and became in consequence an Act of Parliament. Two hours later, in the House of Commons, Bentinck, Disraeli and the vindictive majority among the protectionist Tories allied themselves with the ambitious Whig Radicals and the habitually distructive Irish Nationalists, in what Wellington famously described as 'a blackguard combination'. Their objective was simply to defeat the government on whatever bill it placed before them next; and it so happened that it was a bill designed to limit the distribution and possession of arms in Ireland. This precautionary measure had met with little opposition on its first reading, but this time an amendment resulted in its defeat by seventy-three votes. On 29 June the Prime Minister resigned.

Peel never led another government. Four years later he died in agony after being thrown and trampled on by his horse. He was the ablest of Drury's Prime Ministers, and the only one who Drury himself predicted would one day hold the office. By the time he died the Tories had begun to realize what they had done to themselves by defeating him. To the Tory press he was the greatest statesman of his age. To Gladstone he was the greatest man he had ever known. And he was not much less to Wellington. 'I never knew a man', said the Duke, 'in whose truth and justice I had a more lively confidence, or in whom I saw a more invariable desire to promote the public service.'

On 30 June the Queen summoned Russell, not Palmerston, and invited him to form a government. This time Grey said nothing and was rewarded with the Colonial Office. Palmerston was Foreign Secretary again.

9. SLEEPING ON A BARREL OF GUNPOWDER

When Lord Palmerston returned to the Foreign Office in 1846, the opportunities for 'intermeddling' were at least as many and varied as they had been when he first went there in 1830. All over Europe the forces of liberalism and reaction were squaring up to each other again. This time, however, the liberal and nationalist demands had an angry, urgent edge to them. The bourgeois idealists were now supported by the mass of the workers and the peasants. The fall in the value of foreign securities, which had been attributed by many cynics to the news of Palmerston's return to office, had in reality been caused by a European industrial slump. Two years of blighted potatoes in Ireland and the horrifying famine that followed were only the worst and most westerly symptoms of the crop failures and consequent shortages that were afflicting almost every country on the continent. The revolutionary leaders had found the force of numbers among the hungry unemployed in city slums and wasted farms.

Yet Palmerston was almost the only statesman in Europe who could see that the continent was about to explode. 'We are all sleeping on a barrel of gunpowder', he wrote. If the British government could not induce the absolutist monarchs to make a few concessions to democracy, and persuade the nationalists and other reformers to settle for a little less than total freedom, revolutions were inevitable. As soon as the first revolution broke out, one of the Great Powers would be bound to intervene to exploit the embarrassment of another. The result would be European war. And as soon as all the Great Powers were distracted by a war, the other revolutionaries would rise in their rear and take advantage of their distraction. The case for 'intermeddling' had never been stronger.

In 1846, however, there were so many long fuses burning at equal pace towards Palmerston's barrel that nobody could be certain which one was going to get there first. From his own point of view the favourite was the one that led out of Italy; and since the conclave in the Vatican had just elected a liberal pope, Pius IX, Italy was also the best place in which to start pressing for progress and compromise. On 30 July Palmerston wrote from the Foreign Office to Russell.

Italy is the weak part of Europe, and the next war that breaks out in Europe will probably arise out of Italian affairs. The government of the Papal States is intolerably bad … Leave things as they are, and you leave France the power of disturbing the peace of Europe whenever she chooses. Two or three millions of francs, properly applied, will organize an insurrection at any time, and the ascendancy of the Liberal party at Paris, whenever it may happen, either by the result of an election or by the death of the king, will soon be followed by an outbreak in Italy. That is the point to which the French Liberals look; they know that if they tried to get back to the Rhine they would have against them all Germany united, Russia and more or less England; but in supporting an insurrection in Italy against Papal misgovernment, they would stand in a very different position. England would probably take no part against them; Prussia would not stir a foot; Russia would not be very active, and, perhaps, secretly not displeased, at anything that might humble and weaken Austria. But Austria would interfere, and could scarcely help doing so, even though not very efficiently backed by Russia; France and Austria would then fight each other in Italy, and France would have all the Italians on her side. But the war, begun in Italy, would probably spread to Germany, and at all events, we can have no wish to see Austria broken down and France aggrandised, and the military vanity and love of conquest of the French revived and strengthened by success. If these things should happen, and they may not be so distant as many suppose, people will naturally ask what the Whig Government of 1846 was about

241

and why they did not take advantage of the liberal inclinations of the new Pope to encourage and induce him to make reforms, which, if then made, might have prevented such events.

Russell had declared himself in favour of an energetic foreign policy, and he was almost as passionate about the future of Italy as he was about injustices in Ireland, but the letter, convincing though it was, provoked no immediate reaction. Palmerston's arguments and opinions were clearly not as instantly persuasive as they had been when he was last Foreign Secretary; and he was already well aware that this time he was not going to be left to run his office like an independent autocrat. Where previously he had only been answerable to the insouciant Melbourne, he was now subjected to the scrutiny of disorganized but officious Russell. The Queen, whom he remembered as naïve and trusting, was now an inquisitive, wilful and confident mother of five. And beside her, in the role of mentor, Melbourne had been replaced by Prince Albert, who had come to expect the same levels of briefing and consultation as any Cabinet minister, who conducted his own correspondence on matters of state with several European monarchs, and who did not seem to understand that royal restraint and political neutrality are essential elements in a democratic constitutional monarchy. If Palmerston was planning to intermeddle on his own initiative again, he was going to have to be a lot more subtle and circumspect than last time.

Although Russell had persuaded the Queen and Prince Albert to set aside their misgivings about Palmerston, they had not been persuaded to forsake them. They were still convinced that it would not be long before he began to destroy their precious *entente cordiale*. But as it turned out it was the French who made the first destructive move. It happened during what Palmerston regarded as the uncontroversial continuation of one of Aberdeen's 'leavings', and it concerned the marriages of the fifteen-year-old Queen Isabella of Spain and her fourteen-year-old sister the Infanta Luisa.

Aberdeen, Guizot and their two sovereigns had discussed the marriages and reached agreement during their meetings at Château d'Eu. Unfortunately, however, nothing had been recorded in writing and everybody subsequently seemed to have a slightly different recollection of what had actually been agreed. According to Aberdeen, they had decided that the only appropriate candidates for the hand of the Queen were her ugly cousins Francisco, Duke of Cadiz, and his brother Enrique, Duke of Seville. Once the Queen had married one of these and borne an heir to the Spanish throne, it was further agreed that the British would have no objection if the French sought the hand of the Infanta Luisa for King Louis-Philippe's son the Duke of Montpensier.

This was acceptable to Aberdeen. It had never been in Britain's interest to see the thrones of France and Spain united; and this was particularly so now that France had conquered most of north-west Africa. A Franco-Spanish alliance would have put a pincer grip on the whole western Mediterranean. But once the Spanish succession was secure elsewhere, there could be no objection to an insignificant marriage between a French prince and a Spanish princess.

It was not quite so acceptable to the Spanish Queen Mother, Christina, however. During her brief exile in France, with the help of Guizot's government, Christina had planned another 'Moderado' coup; and this time the coup had been successful, partly because, to Palmerston's vociferous disgust, Aberdeen had done nothing to support the 'Progresista' regent, General Espartero. Christina was now back in Madrid and in control of a government that was much closer to absolutist than moderate. To Christina, Enrique was not suitable for either of her daughters because he was a radical 'Progresista'; and Francisco, although a reactionary absolutist, which made him politically acceptable, was profoundly decadent, effeminate and, as Guizot well knew, unable, or at least disinclined, to sire any children. The most suitable candidate in Christina's eyes was Prince Leopold of Saxe-Coburg.

But this was entirely unacceptable to Guizot. Although Leopold's sister was married to one of Louis-Philippe's sons, the Duke of Nemours, it was not in the best interests of France that the King Consort of Spain should be the brother of the King Consort of Portugal, the cousin of both the Queen of England and her husband and the nephew of the King of the Belgians. It was, however, in France's best interest to exploit the suggestion, even though Aberdeen had said and done nothing to support it. On 27 February 1846, when it was obvious that the Tory government was about to fall, the chargé d'affaires at the French embassy in London visited Aberdeen and read him a memorandum from Guizot in which he warned that, if the marriage of the Spanish Queen or her sister to Prince Leopold seemed probable or imminent, the French would regard themselves as freed from all promises and at liberty to seek the hand of either sister for the Duke of Montpensier. Since he had no intention of supporting such a match, and since he had not even been given a copy of the memorandum, Aberdeen took little notice of it. But in reality there was, and always had been, a hidden agenda. This was the beginning of Guizot's attempt to obtain the Spanish throne, as he put it, *par un détour.*

When, during the changeover at the Foreign Office, Aberdeen briefed Palmerston on all current business, he said very little about the Spanish marriages and did not even mention the threatening memorandum. In consequence, two weeks later, on 19 July Palmerston wrote an almost routine despatch to the British Ambassador in Madrid, his friend Henry Bulwer, the brother of the novelist. 'I have not at present any Instructions to give you in addition to those which you have received from my Predecessor in Office. The British Government is not prepared to give any active support to the pretensions of any of the Princes who are now candidates for the Queen of Spain's hand, and does not feel itself called upon to make any objection to any of them.' Then, after pointing out that, as long as there was no threat to the balance of power in Europe, it was none of Britain's business who married the Queen of Spain, he went on to express his 'deep regret and concern' at the 'violence and Arbitrary Power' that passed for government in her unhappy kingdom.

Next day the chargé d'affaires at the French embassy visited Palmerston at the Foreign Office and among other things inquired about the new government's policy on the Spanish marriages. Without any qualms Palmerston showed him the despatch and allowed him to make a copy. It was an unusually trusting thing to do, but he had no reason to be suspicious, and he had recently received a visit from Minto, who, in response to entreaties from Russell, had impressed on him the importance of being as friendly and open as possible with the French.

Guizot and Louis-Philippe could hardly believe their luck. Their usually canny opponent had just played the worst stroke of his career; and they stepped in without scruple to exploit every opportunity that the unexpected error presented. It was not that they did not already know the contents of the despatch to Bulwer – one of Princess Lieven's admiring agents had made a copy as it passed through Paris. But Palmerston's candour had enabled them to address the issues openly. Since he had placed Prince Leopold first in his list of candidates, they insisted that this meant Leopold was his first choice, and they disingenuously ignored everything else to the contrary in the despatch. In consequence of this, they declared that they no longer regarded themselves as bound by any of the promises that they made at Château d'Eu. And they sent a copy of the scathing despatch to Queen Christina and her ministers, destroying at a stroke all chance of a marriage between her eldest daughter and Prince Leopold, and any hope of good relations between the Spanish government and the Whigs.

Early in September the royal yacht, carrying the Palmerstons among Her Majesty's guests, sailed from the Isle of Wight to the Channel Isles and back round the toe of Cornwall to Penzance, where boxes of state papers were rowed out in a boat for the Queen and her ministers. Among Palmerston's there was a report of a notice in the French government's *Journal des Débats* announcing that the marriages of the Queen of Spain to the Duke of Cadiz and the Infanta of Spain to the Duke of Montpensier would take place at the end of October.

Palmerston protested to both the French and Spanish courts and attempted to enlist the support of Metternich; but it was all in vain. The marriages took place, even earlier than announced. On 10 October, her sixteenth birthday, the Queen of Spain was led sobbing to the altar beside her repulsive cousin; and a quarter of an hour later her sister was married to Montpensier.

Somehow Guizot found the gall to claim that he had kept his side of the bargain. The French Prince did not marry the Infanta until after the Spanish Queen had been married; and neither Guizot nor his King could remember making any promise about waiting until the Queen had borne an heir. But the Queen's miserable marriage did not turn out quite as the French court had hoped or expected. Over the years she gave birth to several children, although, to the dismay of puritan Prince Albert, there were a few good, handsome reasons in the ranks of her guards for concluding that her husband was never the father.

Louis-Philippe and Guizot had persuaded each other that Queen Victoria did not trust Palmerston and that Russell intended to keep him on a tight rein. But if they hoped that their little coup might destroy his credibility and persuade them to get rid of him, they were about to be disappointed. All that they did was to earn him the sympathy of those who till then had been wary of him. The Tories were as outraged as the government at what even Aberdeen had to admit was a 'breach of engagement'. To a disillusioned Queen Victoria the conduct of the king she had taken for a friend was 'beyond all belief shameful, and so shabbily dishonest'. As for Palmerston, Russell spoke for everyone when he wrote to the French chargé d'affaires, 'In my opinion he has conducted himself with the greatest moderation and calm reflection throughout this painful transaction.' Great Britain was united in its censure. The only reputations that the French King and his minister had damaged were their own. Thiers accused them of destroying the entente cordiale and, in so far as they dared, the hardly free French press denounced the dishonesty and dynastic ambitions of the man who had once been called 'Citizen King'.

The new antipathy towards France encouraged Palmerston to return to some of his old themes and attitudes. He urged Russell to improve Britain's defences, proposing the creation of a central arsenal and again advocating expansion of the militia, which in his view could only be effective if it consisted of at least 100,000 men in Great Britain and another 40,000 in Ireland. When the Treasury pointed out that all this would require a staggering seventy per cent rise in income tax – from seven pence in the pound to a shilling – he suggested that it could be paid for with loans rather than taxes. But, just as before, his arguments only induced a few improvements in coastal defences, despite the sympathy of the Queen, which he had earned through an exchange of memoranda with Prince Albert, and despite the continuing support of Wellington, who prepared a long and very detailed memorandum of his own and sent it to Sir John Burgoyne, the inspector-general of fortifications.

When Guizot suggested that Britain and France should join in sending a protest at the Austrian annexation of Cracow, Palmerston felt confident enough to snub him again and told him curtly that Britain had already sent one. The annexation of this last nominally free part of Poland had followed a nationalist revolution in the pastoral province of Galicia, which was already ruled by Austria. In this exceptional case, however, the far from radical nationalists were mostly aristocrats and lesser landowners; and in consequence the cunning Metternich had been able to exploit the more immediate grievances of the majority and reduce their rebellion to a shambles by arming their hungry and resentful peasantry, which had left him with more than enough spare soldiers to suppress sympathetic Cracow. He had then invited Russia and Prussia, which ruled the other Polish provinces, to send representatives to the Austrian court, where he persuaded them to endorse the annexation, even though it was clearly in breach of the terms of the Treaty of Vienna.

As Palmerston had pointed out before, Poland was too inaccessible for Britain to make any credible threat of interference. While most of the British press published passionate pieces in support of free Cracow, and while, in response, Prince Albert induced *The Times* to expose their prejudices in what he regarded as a more balanced article, Palmerston could do nothing but make no secret of his sympathies. In his despatches he described the annexation as 'wicked and foolish' and suggested that the three absolutist northern Powers were trying to outdo Louis-Philippe at treaty-breaking. In his speech at the Lord Mayor's banquet he attacked the Austrians so vehemently that the group of grateful refugees who had formed the Polish Historical Society presented him with a medal. But his formal complaints to the offending Powers were much more restrained – so much so that the Russian Foreign Minister, Count Nesselrode, confessed that they surpassed all his expectations, although he appears to have suspected a subtle reason for the restraint. 'Palmerston's protest is as moderate as it can be, and Cracow has not re-established the *entente cordiale.*'

Deprived of its alliance with Great Britain, Guizot's fragile government had no choice but to ingratiate itself with the disdainful absolutists. But there were still bound to be times when the interests of Great Britain and France coincided; and as if to reassure the French that co-operation on these occasions would not be out of the question, Palmerston sometimes surprised them by condescending to grant his support on some less vital issue, such as their blockade of the River Plate.

The blockade had been set up by the French fleet eight years earlier, after the Argentinian dictator Juan Manuel de Rosas had refused to pay any more interest on French loans and had confiscated the property of French merchants in Buenos Aires. At the time Palmerston, who was still in office, had refused to help, if only because Rosas had not interfered with any British merchants. Later, while in opposition, he had maintained the same line and denounced the gullible Tories for accepting a French invitation to intervene in the civil war across the estuary in Uruguay. By then the war seemed to be in its final stages. The oppressive 'Blancos', who were heavily supported and effectively controlled by Rosas, had overrun most of the country and bottled up the remnants of their democratic opponents, the 'Colorados', in Montevideo. If the defenders of the city had not included a formidable legion of exiled Italian freedom fighters, it would probably have fallen already. Nevertheless, in keeping with the spirit of entente, Aberdeen had rather recklessly agreed to assist in the relief of Montevideo.

When Palmerston returned to office, therefore, everyone expected him to cancel Aberdeen's instructions. But instead he confirmed them. The task force sailed for the south Atlantic. It was an almost whimsical change of heart, which the famously arrogant Rosas was at first inclined to dismiss as typical Palmerston bluff. But when he learned that British redcoats had landed and joined forces with the redshirts of Giuseppe Garibaldi, he had a sudden change of heart of his own. Before the defenders of Montevideo could take the offensive, he compensated the dispossessed French merchants, paid the interest on his debts and withdrew his support for the 'Blancos' – a lethal betrayal that eventually led to his downfall.

The relationship between Britain and France had returned to what it was when Palmerston last reigned at the Foreign Office. Although the two nations could still work together, the *entente cordiale* had been destroyed, not by Palmerston but by the deceitful diplomacy of Louis-Philippe and Guizot. But the unexpected concord they had engendered between Palmerston and his monarch did not extend into other aspects of British foreign policy, as the farcical response to events in Portugal was about to demonstrate.

To the disappointment of the meddling liberal statesman who had put Maria II on her throne, although perhaps not to his surprise, the Queen of Portugal had turned out to be as absolutist as any other Iberian monarch; and she was supported and even encouraged in her attitudes by her husband King Ferdinand and his 'tutor' Dr Dietz, who had followed him from Coburg and who played the same role in his life as the more judicious Baron Stockmar played in Prince Albert's. When a general election returned a large Radical majority to her parliament, the Cortes, Queen Maria suspended the democratic constitution, dissolved the Cortes and installed the ruthless Marshal Saldanha as dictator. In response, the Radicals seized Oporto, established a rival government, which they called the Junta, and published leaflets in which they threatened to follow the examples of earlier revolutionaries and decapitate their monarch. While the kingdom tumbled towards civil war, and while mobs and soldiers on both sides vied with each other in brutality and treachery, Queen Maria turned to the Quadruple Alliance for support.

In England, the Queen and her Foreign Secretary agreed that they must help. But they disagreed on how and whom to help. Although Queen Victoria admitted to her journal that Queen Maria was 'as foolish as ever', she was nevertheless inclined to be guided by her Ambassador in Portugal, Lord Howard de Walden, who had always been an enthusiastic supporter of Queen Maria and her advisers, and who advocated sending British ships and soldiers to assist in suppressing the revolt. Besides, Maria was an anointed queen, a factor that meant a great deal to Queen Victoria and Prince Albert; furthermore, she was married to their cousin. Unfortunately, however, de Walden retired soon after the revolt began and was on his way back to England before any help could be offered. In his place, British interests in Portugal were being represented by the legation secretary, Henry Southern, who was inclined to believe that, despite its unattractive shortcomings, the Junta was the party with right on its side; and Lord Palmerston was regretfully inclined to agree with him. For the time being, the only action the Foreign Secretary was prepared to take was to send a few ships to Lisbon with instructions to do nothing but lie in the Tagus and rescue Queen Maria if her life was in danger.

Both the Queen and Prince Albert wrote to Palmerston deploring the pro-Junta articles in the *Morning Chronicle*, which they knew full well originated in the Foreign Office, and making it plain that they had 'no good opinion' of Southern, who was, 'as Lord Palmerston must well know, an ultra Progresista and a most violent party man'. When Palmerston replied with mere bland reassurances, they took matters into their own hands and sent one of the Prince's equerries, Colonel Wylde, to act as their representative at the Portuguese court and to advise Queen Maria to make a few concessions before it was too late.

Presented with this high-handed and entirely unconstitutional *fait accompli*, Russell meekly acknowledged Wylde as a representative of the British government, which Palmerston, not unreasonably, interpreted as entitling him to send Wylde instructions of his own. He wrote to the colonel charging him to visit the Junta, convince them that they could not win a civil war and promise them that, if they renewed their allegiance to Queen Maria, the British government would do all that it could to persuade their Queen to grant an amnesty, dismiss her reactionary ministers, restore the constitution and recall the Cortes.

The result was a rebuke from Prince Albert. 'I return the copy of your letter to Colonel Wylde, which you have sent me. We could not help being very much disappointed with it.' Queen Maria had turned to an old friend for help, but now she believed that 'England wished well to the cause of the Rebels', and 'the language of the *Morning Chronicle* and the bearing of Mr Southern amply justify such an impression ... What is the bearing of your letter ... That the Queen is to understand that she must immediately return to constitutional government... else we would not meddle in the affair?'

The answer was yes, but instead Palmerston made more bland reassurances and returned to his old habits, only to discover that Queen Victoria already knew him too well to be deceived for long.

The Queen has several times asked Lord Palmerston through Lord John Russell and personally, to see that the drafts to our foreign Ministers are not despatched previous to their being submitted to the Queen; notwithstanding this is still done, – as for instance to-day with regard to the drafts for Lisbon. The Queen therefore once more repeats her desire that Lord Palmerston should prevent recurrence of this practice.

Palmerston apologized, pleaded that the last Lisbon despatches had only been sent before the Queen saw them in order to catch the afternoon packet, and then went on to point out at greater length that haste was essential if the Portuguese sovereign was to be saved from 'the desperate condition' to which she had been 'reduced by the wrong-headedness, the prejudices, the folly and dishonesty of a set of advisers by whom she has been surrounded'. There was no need to say more about the advisers. In an earlier letter to Russell, which he knew had been shown to the Queen, he had described them as 'a pedantic and bigoted tutor, a furious political Portuguese Fanatic, a newspaper editor, a vulgar man suddenly raised to power and full of low resentments and a gambling, drinking, unscrupulous Priest'.

In reality Palmerston was now hopelessly handicapped; and the hapless Colonel Wylde was too confused by conflicting instructions to be effective. At one point, in desparation, he resorted to Palmerstonian tactics and wrote a letter to Prince Albert which ended, 'I have therefore ventured to take the liberty of enclosing my letter to Lord Palmerston to your Royal Highness trusting that your Royal Highness will be pleased to consider it as addressed to yourself and not forward it if you think I have taken a mistaken view of the matter in communicating its contents to his Lordship.'

The only certainty was that nothing was going to be achieved this way. The field was wide open for the Spanish to step in and support an absolutist, or for the French to offer help to Queen Maria and become the mentors that they had always wanted to be in Portugal. In exasperation therefore, and in the hope of pre-empting any unilateral intervention by either of them, Palmerston invited their representatives in London to a meeting and persuaded them that, as the other three members of the Quadruple Alliance, it was their duty to offer themselves as joint mediators in the internal quarrel of the fourth. Knowing that France and Spain were well disposed towards her, Queen Maria agreed to accept their mediation. But the proposals for which Palmerston won their approval were a little less than she had hoped for, and very close to those which he had made earlier through Colonel Wylde. In essence, they were that the Junta should disband its army and itself and instruct all its supporters to swear allegiance to the Queen, and that in return the Queen should grant them all an amnesty, recall the Cortes and restore constitutional government, freedom of speech and the independence of the judiciary.

By now, however, Queen Maria was in no position to argue. With her soldiers unpaid and her crown jewels on the point of being pawned, she had little choice but to give in to what Prince Albert described as 'the knife at her throat'. She accepted the terms proposed by her allies. It was the members of the Junta who did not. The radicals in Oporto demanded in addition that the Queen should dismiss her absolutist advisers and guarantee free elections. But if they were gambling on Palmerston's liberal sympathy, they were mistaken. He knew that he had taken France and Spain as far as they would go. To maintain their alliance, and to stay in control, he could only agree that the time had come to use force. In the spring of 1847, while British ships blockaded the bay at Oporto, an Anglo-Spanish army advanced overland against the city. The Junta surrendered; and both sides in Portugal, with equal reluctance, accepted the allies' original proposals.

It was probably the best that could have been done in the circumstances. Spain had been prevented from upholding an absolutist government; France had been prevented from gaining influence in Iberia and at the same time had been kept happy by being allowed to play an apparently equal part in imposing a solution; and Palmerston could claim, as he did, that he had secured the Portuguese crown without oppressing the Portuguese people. But he was attacked for it ferociously from both sides of both Houses of Parliament. The Tories denounced him for not supporting the Portuguese sovereign; the Radicals in his own party reproached him for not supporting an elected government; and everyone criticized him for meddling in other people's business.

As he had done so often before, Palmerston presented his pragmatism as principle. On 5 July 1847 he told the House of Commons:

> Our duty – our vocation – is not to enslave, but to set free; and I may say, without any vain-glorious boast, or without great offence to anyone, that we stand at the head of moral, social, and political civilization. Our task is to lead the way and direct the march of other nations. I do not think we ought to goad on the unwilling, or force forward the reluctant; but when we see people battling against difficulties and struggling against obstacles in the pursuit of their rights, we may be permitted to encourage them with our sympathy ... and even, if occasion require, to lend them a helping hand.

But this hardly unassuming oratory was not in itself enough. Russell confided to the Queen that he thought his government was about to fall. What saved them was the disorganization of their opponents, some of whom weakened the attack on Palmerston by breaking away indignantly to question the role of Colonel Wylde, who, they said with some justification, appeared to have been acting as the representative of the House of Coburg rather than of Great Britain.

Outside the Cabinet the only words of approval came unexpectedly from Prince Albert, who conceded that this was the first time a foreign power had 'intervened in the internal affairs in Portugal in favour of the crown'. It was a truth that Palmerston would probably have preferred not to emphasize. In doing just that, his Quadruple Alliance had behaved in a manner more characteristic of Metternich's Holy Alliance. Indeed, if Metternich had not been heavily preoccupied in Switzerland and Italy, he would certainly have made the most of the irony.

In 1845 the seven predominantly Roman Catholic cantons of Switzerland had seceded from the increasingly radical federation and, under the influence of the Jesuits, had established their own conservative league, the Sonderbund. In the summer of 1846, after Radicals had gained control of all the other twelve cantons, the Federal Diet in Berne voted to disband the Sonderbund, reform the complicated constitution that had been imposed on it by the Treaty of Vienna, and expel all Jesuits from Switzerland. But the Sonderbund refused to accept the rulings of a government it no longer recognized. Just as the civil war in Portugal was drawing to a close, Radicals and Catholic Conservatives were drawing up the battle lines for another one in Switzerland.

To Metternich a Radical influence on the flank of Austria's Italian satellites was not a comfortable prospect. He had never before supported a rebellion against an established government, but this time the rebels were the reactionaries. In Austria's best interests Metternich supported the Sonderbund; and with a more characteristic but equal variance from the policies he was applying elsewhere, Palmerston cheerfully supported the legitimate majority government in the country that, even in the darkest moments, he always called and spelled 'Swizzerland'. The Powers, he said, had no right to interfere in the internal affairs of an independent nation. If the democratically elected government chose to alter its constitution, it was nobody's business but its own.

The Radicals in the Swiss Diet were grateful and a little surprised to discover that the only European statesman who supported them was one who also supported Queen Maria of Portugal. But moral support and diplomatic ingenuity were as much as Palmerston could offer. Switzerland was as inaccessable to the British navy as Cracow. While Palmerston stood and spoke alone, Metternich surrounded Switzerland with allies. To the south, the support of the Italian principalities of Piedmont and Savoy was, to say the least, a little tentative. Indeed, it might not have been offered at all if their ruler, King Carlo Alberto of Sardinia, had not been so worried by Austrian activities elsewhere in Italy. But the nervous King of Prussia, who, although a Protestant, felt much more threatened by radicals than by Roman Catholics, joined in as readily as Austria's satellites in the neighbouring German Confederation. And Guizot, allowing his common sense to be overruled by his fear of the absolutist Powers, and by his continuing rancour at Palmerston's disdain, reversed his government's previous policies and obsequiously offered his support.

When Metternich suggested that Austria and France should invade Switzerland, however, Guizot politely declined. The Liberal majority in France was fully in sympathy with the Swiss Federal Diet, and it was that same Liberal majority which had once put Louis-Philippe on the throne and since then lost faith in him. If French soldiers were to be ordered east to overthrow the legitimate government in Berne, it was almost a certainty that their own government and their King would be overthrown before they got there. Instead Guizot made a preposterous proposal. Austria would invade Switzerland to support the Sonderbund. In response, France would send an army apparently to support the Federal Diet. And then, before any fighting had started, France and Austria would save Europe from war by negotiating a peace that, in the spirit of compromise, recognized the independence of the Sonderbund. But this was not the sort of suggestion that a man of Metternich's experience was going to accept from a man with Guizot's reputation. He too declined politely; and he advised his Emperor that, while Austrian troops were engaged in Italy, it would not be wise to divide his strength and commit others on their own in Switzerland.

As Palmerston predicted, the Italian fuse had come closest to the barrel. Ever since the Franco-Austrian stand-off and the failed insurrections of the early 1830s, the nationalist hero Guiseppe Mazzini had been living in exile, plotting the creation of a united, Christian, socialist Italy, inspiring other nationalists throughout the continent and dreaming of the day when they would all join together in founding a federation of European states. But the regular raids and risings organized under his direction by the bourgeois radicals in his 'Young Italy' movement had failed consistently in the face of popular apathy. It was the election of Pope Pius IX that changed the attitude of the Italian masses. His reforms whetted their appetites.

Pope Pius admitted the laity to the civil administration of his domains, establishing a council of state and a municipal government in Rome. He allowed a degree of freedom to the press; he granted an amnesty to political prisoners; and he drew up plans for the creation of a Civil Guard and even a network of railways. In response, right across northern Italy, delighted but impatient demonstrators took to the streets demanding more, most dramatically and violently in Parma and Modena. In

Piedmont, King Carlo Alberto attempted to appease them with similar concessions. But the riots drew the opposite reaction from Austria. In the papal city of Ferrara, where the Austrians had retained the right to keep a garrison in the citadel, the garrison marched out with fixed bayonets and took over the entire city. When reinforcements reached them, commanded by the ancient but ruthless Marshal Josef Radetzky, they made ready to march on and occupy Parma and Modena.

Through the Roman Catholic Earl of Shrewsbury, the Pope appealed to Palmerston for moral support. It was a request that was unlikely to be refused. Now that Palmerston's predictions were coming true, cautious Russell was more than ready to indulge his romantic passion and sanction some serious meddling.

Although Palmerston had never lost his boyhood love for Italy, it was Russell who shared Mazzini's dream of creating a united nation out of what Metternich contemptuously described as 'a geographical expression'. During the previous Tory government, when the exiled Mazzini came to live in London for a while, a disenchanted civil servant had revealed that the Home Secretary, Sir James Graham, had instructed agents to read the Italian nationalist's letters in the Post Office, and had then passed on any useful contents to the appropriate governments. The result had been the thwarting of a rebellion in Naples and the suppression of a mutiny in the Austrian navy. When Russell and most of his opposition colleagues indignantly but unsuccessfully moved a vote of censure on the government for what they saw as an unjustified violation of individual liberty, Palmerston had stayed away from the debate.

On that particular occasion Palmerston had chosen to regard the exile's activities as an abuse of Britain's hospitality. When it came to considering the current emergency in Italy, however, he was a little more consistent. To him, the principal objective was practical rather than idealistic. Britain's business was not to support a noble cause but to promote enough constitutional reform to satisfy the Italian democrats and prevent the unrest rising to a level that might further force the heavy hand of Austria or tempt the French to intervene.

Thus, though they approached the problem from different premises, Palmerston and Russell agreed that a British diplomatic mission to the papacy might, as before, raise morale among the democrats and strengthen the Pope's resolve to continue his programme of reforms. Since they were about to hold a general election, however, there was little point in embarking on a major diplomatic initiative until they were sure that they were going to be in office long enough to complete it.

Meanwhile Palmerston made the most of the opportunity to mock Metternich. Claiming that the unrest in Italy threatened the long-standing stability imposed on Europe by the Treaty of Vienna, the Austrian Chancellor had called on all the signatories to the treaty to support his firm military response. In his answer Palmerston pointed out merrily that it would be easier to accept Metternich's sincerity if he had not just broken the treaty himself by annexing Cracow, and he suggested that the real threat to the stability of Europe lay in denying constitutional government to the Italians.

With Metternich distracted by Italy, Palmerston played for time over Switzerland. Since the Treaty of Vienna was still the gospel to which all European statesmen turned for justification of anything and everything, and since it was, of course, this treaty that had imposed their clumsy constitution on the Swiss, he proposed that the Powers who signed the treaty should meet in Berne to discuss a peaceful settlement. Knowing that Palmerston was alone in his support for the new Swiss government, even Metternich agreed. But when Guizot wrote on behalf of the Powers to inform the Diet in Berne of their intention, Palmerston objected to the wording of his letter and then dawdled over the drafting of a replacement. Then he added to the delay by suggesting that some less fundamental issues could be settled before the Powers met; and without betraying the slightest hint that he saw himself as saying anything contentious, he proposed that everyone should endorse the Diet's expulsion of the Jesuits and persuade the Diet to pay them compensation for the buildings they had been forced to abandon.

So the summer of 1847 passed unprofitably for the absolutist Powers. Palmerston probably never intended to let his congress meet. If it had, the other Powers would certainly have found in favour of the Sonderbund. But the delay bought him the time to deal with his own domestic and political distractions. At the end of 1846 the landlord of 5 Carlton House

Terrace had decided to get married and terminate the lease, so that he could live in the house himself. Loath to leave London's most fashionable terrace, the Palmerstons had therefore moved a couple of hundred yards along it, into one of the houses in its new extension, 4 Carlton Gardens, which Lady Palmerston was still decorating. If her husband had not been required to contest an election in Tiverton, it would have been a perfect excuse for spending more time at Broadlands.

The Whigs were not a majority in the House of Commons. Russell had only been able to form a government because the Tories were bitterly divided between the Peelites, who were in favour of repealing the corn laws, and the protectionists, led now by Disraeli, who were not. It was only because the Peelites had been willing to support him on other issues that Russell had survived until now; and his hope was that an election fought principally on free trade might give him a majority.

In Tiverton, however, free trade was not the principal issue. For the sake of the publicity that it was bound to bring them, the Chartists sent their leading spokesman on foreign affairs, Julian Harney, a friend of Karl Marx and Friedrich Engels and editor of the *Northern Star*, to stand against Palmerston. It was a stunt that backfired on them badly. Harney was defeated by charm from the outset. By his own admission he arrived on polling day not knowing what Palmerston looked like and was astonished to discover that the opponent beside him on the hustings was the gentleman who had been so courteous and friendly to him at the preliminary luncheon in the guildhall.

Harney spoke first. After associating Palmerston with what he presented as a long line of Whig failures in home affairs, he led his audience in detail through his opponent's career at the Foreign Office, somehow finding reasons for criticizing every aspect of his policies and dismissing him as a mere pupil of Canning and an enemy of liberty. In reply, Palmerston entertained the predominantly Chartist audience for over three hours, dismissing every criticism with a joke, and providing every episode in his foreign policy with a jovial, down-to-earth justification. If, for example, the people of Syria had really welcomed the rule of Mehemet Ali, as Mr Harney had suggested, how was it that they 'kicked him out neck and crop' as soon as the British sent a few hundred marines and said, 'Go it my boys ... here we are to back you'? For a man who had been 'charged with disturbing the peace of Europe by giving encouragement to every revolutionary, anarchical set of men', it was 'somewhat amusing to hear charges the very reverse' made by his present opponent.

The speech was a triumph. Delivered simply, as if in conversation between equals, and with a cleverly contrived appearance of artlessness, it contained none of the hesitation and inadvertent pomposity that so often marred his speeches in the House. It was reported in all the London and most of the provincial newspapers, often verbatim, and in all but *The Times* with admiration. So widespread was the interest in it that it was published separately soon afterwards as a pamphlet. But the laughing audience at Tiverton, although clearly as amused as the rest of the British public, was not nearly so impressed. When they were asked to vote on a show of hands, it looked as though Palmerston had been defeated. Knowing, however, that most of the Chartists in the audience had no right to vote in Tiverton, Palmerston called for a proper ballot; and Harney, who had indeed brought most of them with him, withdrew his candidature, in what he said was a protest against an election in which most men were still not entitled to vote.

Overall the general election was less of a triumph. The Tories returned 335 members, the Whigs only 330, among them the usual handful of uncontrollable Radicals and a solid block of Irish Nationalists. But the Tories were still too bitterly divided to work together, and on most matters the Peelites were still willing to vote with the Whigs. So the Queen invited Russell to form another government, and Palmerston returned to office.

One of the new members was Palmerston's fanatical and unworthy old adversary David Urquhart, who had been dismissed from the embassy in Constantinople in 1837. Almost immediately Urquhart began to prepare his latest attack; and six months later he introduced a motion demanding Palmerston's impeachment for treason. Beginning with the charge that he was a Russian agent while he was at the War Office, Urquhart and his only articulate supporter, an eccentric Radical Catholic convert called Thomas Anstey, followed Harney's example and worked their way through Palmerston's career, amassing another twenty-two equally absurd charges.

In reply, as at Tiverton, Palmerston gave an amiable answer to each charge in turn, only this time using the language he felt was more suitable to the House. At the end, in summary, he told the House:

> I hold that the real policy of England – apart from questions which involve her own particular interests, political or commercial – is to be the champion of justice and right; pursuing that course with moderation and prudence, not becoming the Quixote of the world, but giving the weight of her moral sanction and support wherever she thinks that justice is, and wherever she thinks that wrong had been done ... We have no eternal allies, and we have no perpetual enemies ... If I might be allowed to express in one sentence the principle which I think ought to guide an English minister, I would adopt the expression of Canning, and say that with every British minister the interests of England ought to be the shibboleth of his policy.

The speech was reported and received as widely and well as the speech in Tiverton, only this time even the audience was impressed. Urquhart had completed what Harney had started. Between them they had given an accelerated boost to the popularity Palmerston had begun to earn in opposition. In their inept attempts to discredit him they had aroused a sporting interest in foreign affairs among the voters, and they had presented Palmerston with a platform on which to portray himself as the embodiment of all the qualities the English most admired in themselves, and as the champion of all the generous ideals they thought ought to matter most to them: fair play, standing up to tyrants, defending the underdog.

Palmerston returned to the Foreign Office with the growing support of a new ally. During the next few years, while Europe stumbled from crisis to crisis, and while Court and Cabinet carped and cringed at the Foreign Secretary's alarming audacity, public opinion never wavered in its approval and affection for him, even during the eighteen months when he was obliged to operate without the unquestioning support of a major newspaper.

Shortly after Urquhart's attack Palmerston's friend Easthope sold the *Morning Chronicle* to a consortium of Tories. Since they were Peelites, they often recorded their approval of Palmerston's policies, but their support was neither constant nor certain, and they no longer provided him with a perpetually available outlet for his own opinions. The only newspaper that supported him consistently was the politically insignificant *Globe;* while *The Times*, as always, inveighed against him, partly because regular attacks on Palmerston had become the most entertaining feature of its long circulation war with the *Chronicle*, and partly because its series of editors all shared Aberdeen's admiration for autocrats. It was not until 1850, when another friend, Peter Borthwick, became editor of the *Morning Post*, that Palmerston found another unquestioning supporter and mouthpiece. In the meantime the man in the street was more influenced by what Palmerston himself had to say than by any editorial comment on it.

Since the formation of Russell's Whig government in 1846, Palmerston had been its most prominent member. Next to Wellington he was the best-known statesman in the kingdom; and now he was by far the best liked. From 1847 onwards his popularity became an increasingly significant factor in British politics. While the Queen's displeasure with him hardened at an almost commensurate rate, poor 'little Johnny Russell' was caught between them, unable to pander or stand up entirely to either of them, for fear of losing the support of the other, and with it his office.

Surprisingly, the Queen's doubts about the next initiative in foreign policy, the mission to the Papacy, were much less severe than Prince Albert's. After the election Russell and Palmerston had decided that the ideal envoy was the father-in-law of the former and an old friend of the latter, Gilbert Elliot, second Earl of Minto; and at the end of August Palmerston had written to the Queen outlining the expanded 'Objects' of his mission.

First, Minto was to go to Switzerland, 'to ascertain the real views and intentions of the present rulers of the Confederation and to expect them to abstain from all violent acts and from any extreme measures which could afford either to Austria or to France any pretext for interference by force of arms'. Then, 'at Turin', he was 'to encourage the Sardinian Government to draw closer their relations, political and commercial, with Great Britain; but to abstain from any unnecessary rupture either with Austria or with France', and to support the Pope in all his reforms. 'At Florence', he was 'to give similar advice'. And 'at Rome' he was 'to encourage the Pope to advance steadily and gradually in reforming the numerous abuses which exist in the government of his states,' and 'to endeavour to obtain from the Pope the exertion of his spiritual authority over the Catholic priesthood of Ireland to abstain from repeal agitation and to urge them not to embarrass but rather to assist your Majesty's Government'.

After a certain amount of reassurance the Queen agreed to permit Minto's mission, provided he did not set out until Palmerston had written explaining his purpose to the Austrian and French governments. But Prince Albert remained adamant that the mission could only be seen as hostile to Austria, which he regarded as an 'old and natural ally', and that 'the diplomatic support given to the Pope will give additional strength to the prevalent accusation against us that we are, for selfish purposes, trying to disseminate disorder and anarchy in all other states under the name of liberty'.

In September, however, the Queen gave her Foreign Secretary another opportunity to convert the Prince. Out of what by then can only have been her well-developed sense of duty she invited the Palmerstons to stay with the royal family at Ardverikie, the Marquess of Abercorn's remote fishing lodge on the southern shore of Lough Laggan. Every day, amid the cold, wet splendour of the Grampians, and every evening, beside large log fires, amid huge and equally splendid highland frescos by Landseer, Palmerston listened with patient, flattering intensity to the Prince's views on every aspect of European affairs. By the time they all returned to London, Prince Albert had been so assuaged by the extent to which Palmerston apparently agreed with him that he had at least acquiesced in Minto's mission.

Back in Westminster the criticisms were rather more pithy and dismissive than the Prince's. Sending an agent, as Disraeli put it, 'to teach politics in the country where Machiavelli was born', was hardly likely to be a fruitful enterprise. 'To found in Italy a Whig party, a sort of Brooks's club at Florence' was idealism worthy of Fox at his most impractical. Besides, with mobs on the streets and armies on the march, it was too late to have any influence. Yet, despite the obvious justification for some of Disraeli's cynicism, the mission, which was not without its own Machiavellian undertones, turned out to be a little more successful than he expected.

In October, while Metternich was diverted not only by events in Italy but also by the demands of Nationalists in Hungary and Liberals in Austria itself, while Prussia and the German states were diverted by the noisy aspirations of Radicals who could not yet see any difference between Nationalism and Liberalism, while the King of France and his ministers were diverted by a frightening campaign for electoral reform, which united every party from Monarchists to Radicals, and while Queen Victoria and Prince Albert, now deeply in love with Scotland, were excitedly diverted by plans to purchase Balmoral, to which Aberdeen had just inherited the lease, Lord Minto set out for Switzerland.

On 10 November, soon after Minto left for Italy, General Guillaume Dufour, commander of the Swiss federal army, invaded Fribourg, the most westerly of the Sonderbund cantons. On 23 November, at Gislikon, he routed the Sonderbund army. By 5 December the Swiss Civil War was over. Of the 179,000 men who took part, most of whom were ill armed and untrained, only 128 had been killed. The Sonderbund was abolished; the Diet at Berne drew up plans for the revision of its constitution; and the Jesuits accepted that it was time to leave Switzerland.

The absolutist monarchs and their obedient press were outraged by what they saw as Palmerston's treachery. But the Foreign Secretary denied any responsibility for what had happened in Switzerland. The plan that he submitted to the Queen, his written instructions to Minto, even the despatch he sent to the Swiss government at the end of October, had all made it clear that he was opposed to solving the problem by fighting. The only evidence to the contrary was the rumour that the British representative in Berne, Robert Peel, the son of the last Tory Prime Minister, had told the Swiss government to 'finish quickly'. If he did, it was good advice. The federal forces could only succeed while their absolutist enemies were still busy elsewhere.

Whatever the truth, Palmerston got the blame from the Conservatives and the credit from the Liberals. When the disconcerted Metternich and Guizot suggested that Palmerston's proposed conference should still take place, he rejected the suggestion with a shrug and a smile; and he instructed Peel not to join in if the representatives of the other Powers in Berne chose to meet anyway. Now that the Swiss had solved their own problems, there was nothing for anyone else to discuss.

In Italy, Minto was welcomed everywhere by enthusiastic crowds. Every time they called for a speech, he began with, 'Viva l'indipendenza italiana'. Before long it looked as though he was about to accomplish a great deal more than had been intended, and that his triumph was going to be as much of an embarrassment to Palmerston as to Disraeli. By the time he began to talk to the Italian governments about continuing the liberalization of their constitutions, their deluded citizens were already convinced that the British were prepared to support them in the expulsion of the Austrians; and within a few days of his reaching Rome he had surprised even himself by persuading the Pope to curb the agitations of his Irish priesthood.

The Catholic clergy of Ireland had only been provoked into political activity by their dismay at the suffering of their starving parishioners, and by their anger at an apparently indifferent government's inadequate response to it. The partial failure of the potato crop in 1845 had been followed by its total destruction in 1846. Although the recent harvest of 1847 had been good, the labourers were by now so few and so feeble that only half the fields had been planted. After three years so little had been done that Ireland was still starving.

But the undoubtedly inadequate response to this continuing catastrophe was due not so much to indifference as to inexperience and ideology. By yet another of history's cruel ironies Russell, who had always fought so fervently to improve the lot of the Irish, had gone on to lead the government that failed them so fatally in the famine. Where Peel and the Tories had imported corn and set up a series of depots to distribute it, the doctrinaire Whigs had made no concessions to the emergency, innocently believing that a free-market economy could be relied on to solve the problem on its own. As a result, some of the rare Irish corn was actually being exported, to be bought by foreign merchants who were prepared to pay more for it than the Irish could afford. The Whigs' only attempt to provide the destitute rural unemployed with enough income to pay rent and feed their families was to continue Peel's programme of public works, on such projects as new roads; but with prices heavily inflated by the free market, the weekly wages were hardly enough to buy food for the labourer, let alone his wife and children. Many thousands of families were soon homeless as well as hungry. By 1847 the government had replaced public works with straightforward soup kitchens; and since this was still not nearly enough, it was preparing to provide the Irish with their own version of the grim, forbidding workhouses.

Beset by all this, hundreds of thousands accepted that their only option was to emigrate. Several charities were set up to help with the cost of their passage, and a few Irish landlords, including Palmerston, contributed directly. But deep grudges and pitiless swindlers were now so numerous that even the best of intentions foundered on misunderstandings and treachery. In instructing his agents to organize the transport of 2,000 of his tenants in nine ships to Canada, Palmerston at first arranged for them all to be given hot rum punch when they went on board. But the famine coincided with the height of the Irish temperance movement; priests accused Palmerston of encouraging drunkenness, and the rum punch was replaced with coffee and biscuits. He also made provision for every family to receive a cash payment of up to £5 on arrival, but the money never found its way as far as Canada. Some of the Foreign Secretary's agents and captains allowed his tenants to reach their destination in such an exceptionally wretched condition that one of the legislative councillors of Lower Canada – a crown appointee, not an elected representative of the colonists – reported indignantly to the Colonial Secretary that they had been transported tight-packed like slaves, delivered destitute on the docks and then abandoned half-naked to beg in the snow.

In the fifteen years that followed the outbreak of the famine, 2 million men, women and children emigrated from Ireland. Of the 6.5

million who remained, another 1 million died, not so much from hunger as from the diseases that their wasted bodies were no longer fit enough to fight. The birth-rate fell; empty villages crumbled; everywhere but in Ulster the first symptoms of an industrial revolution vanished. Despite the decline in a dependent population, the Irish economy continued to decline for decades after the famine; and the scar that was left on the Irish consciousness was to last for ever.

As the representatives of the only institution that the Irish tenants trusted, the Catholic clergy began by offering succour to the victims and support to those who sought to right the wrongs. But when Minto reported that they were using churches for political meetings and that some were suspected of condoning or even encouraging the murder of the most callous landlords, the Pope instructed his Irish bishops to prevent the use of churches for 'secular concerns' and reminded them that it was the business of God's ministers to 'abhor blood and vengeance'.

Obedience to the Pope's instructions was satisfyingly immediate but disappointingly brief. Within a year 'Young Ireland' had risen in armed rebellion, with several Protestants among its leaders and a large proportion of the Catholic clergy in support; and this time instructions from Rome were replaced by the more conclusive arguments of redcoats, muskets, transportation and the hangman.

With regard to the most important 'object' of Minto's mission, he and Palmerston later claimed that he had helped to establish constitutional governments in several Italian states. In the light of subsequent events it is almost certain that this would have happened anyway, and in most cases it was hardly a long-standing achievement. But Minto did at least nudge a few states in that direction; and while he and Palmerston were slightly diverted by his first efforts, Austria, Prussia and France did exactly as Palmerston suspected they might and demanded that the Swiss government should hold an international conference to discuss its own future. When the demand was refused, they began to plan a joint invasion. But before they could put their plan into effect, the first of many more fuses suddenly caught light.

On 3 January 1848 the Austrian garrison was called out to suppress a riot in Milan. Nine days later the Sicilians rose in rebellion, demanding separation from the Kingdom of Naples and the restoration of their former constitution. By the time the only Neapolitan soldiers left on the island were the garrison of Messina, King Ferdinand seemed ready to make concessions. Then on 27 January the people of Naples decided that they too wanted a constitution and rose in rebellion against him as well. Too weak to win, the King negotiated. On 10 February he proposed a constitution based on the one introduced by Louis-Philippe in France in 1830, with a monarchy and two legislative chambers. When this was not enough to satisfy his radical revolutionaries, he invited Minto to come down from Rome and mediate.

By then King Ferdinand's misfortune was having more effect than Minto on the consideration of similar constitutions in Piedmont, Tuscany and the Papal States. Alarmed by the widespread unrest, the Austrians had again sent armies south to protect their interests and maintain the status quo. It was the one response that was likely to make matters worse and lead to everything that Palmerston feared most when he wrote to Russell on his return to office.

On 11 February Palmerston sent a despatch to the British Ambassador in Vienna instructing him to warn Metternich.

> If he remains quiet, and does not meddle with matters beyond the Austrian frontiers, peace will be maintained, and all these Italian changes will be effected with as little disturbance as is consistent with the nature of things. If he takes upon himself the task of regulating by force of arms the internal affairs of the Italian States, there will infallibly be war.

He was still certain 'that in defence of Constitutional liberty in Italy the French nation would rush to arms'; and he was equally certain that, if they did, their success was in nobody's interest but theirs.

> We set too great a value upon the maintenance of Austria as the pivot of the balance of power in Europe to be able to see without the deepest concern any course of action begun by her Government

which would produce fatal consequences to her, and which would place us probably, against our will, in the adverse scale.

There was, however, one element in Palmerston's fearful hypothesis that had not yet come to pass. In his letter to Russell he had predicted that the event that would turn Italian insurrections into war would be 'the ascendancy of the Liberal party at Paris'. On 24 February it happened. While Minto was helping the Bourbon King of Naples to remain on his throne, the Bourbon-Orleans King of France stepped down from his.

The French had run out of patience. After many years of growing prosperity their still predominantly agricultural economy was in crisis. The peasants and urban workers were angered and frightened by the government's failure to cope with the continuing rises in prices and unemployment, which, as in most other European countries, had been set off by successive crop failures. The middle classes, who had put Louis-Philippe on his throne in the first place, were disappointed by his increasingly conservative and unsuccessful foreign policy, embittered by a financial slump caused by over-speculation on railway shares, and enraged by his government's refusal to lower the tax qualification for voting, which effectively limited the franchise to the 200,000 richest men in France. Guizot was dismissed, but it was not enough. Crowds continued to assemble in the streets of Paris in defiance of the government's bans on public meetings. On the evening of 23 February regular troops fired on a crowd of demonstrators outside the Foreign Ministry. In the course of the night barricades were erected in the eastern part of the city, manned mostly by tradesmen and National Guards, and armed mobs marched on the centre, unopposed by the municipal police.

Next day, while Guizot went into hiding, the 75-year-old King abdicated and left the city with his family in several carriages. They were escorted as far as St Cloud by a troop of cavalry under the command of General Dumas. When the cavalry turned back, the carriages separated and disappeared in different directions. Behind them a few hundred from one of the mobs broke into the Palace of the Tuileries, drank themselves delirious in the cellar and then wandered onto the upper floors, where they smashed the furniture, burned the throne and relieved their bursting bladders on the royal bed.

On 28 February, acting on instructions from Palmerston and on information provided by the Dumas family, the British Vice-Consul in Le Havre found the late King and Queen of France hiding from revolutionary agents in a house in Honfleur. After reassuring them that Princess Clementine and the Duke of Nemours were already safe in England, he escorted them to Le Havre, where they were seen safely on board the express steam packet, the Queen travelling with the appropriate clothes and papers as Madame Lebrun, and the ugly King, shorn of his side-whiskers and wearing a pair of thick spectacles, as an English gentleman, Mr William Smith. On 3 March, the day when Guizot arrived in London after escaping through Belgium, they registered as a married couple at the Bridge Hotel, Newhaven. The Queen was now Mrs Smith, but their alias does not seem to have deceived anyone in Sussex. That evening they were welcomed with speeches in French and Latin by the pupils of the Free Grammar School in Lewes. Next day they set out for their new home, Claremont Park in Surrey. The former seat of Clive of India, which Jane Austen described as 'a house that seems never to have prospered', Claremont had been bought by the government for Princess Charlotte and Prince Leopold, and had been assigned for life to Leopold after the tragic death of the Princess in child-birth.

In Paris a small group of extreme Radicals, most of them bourgeois, declared a republic and formed a provisional government, with the poet Alphonse Marie de Lamartine as its President. In Vienna, Metternich collapsed into an armchair when Anselm de Rothschild broke the news to him. In London, Palmerston reviled the new French government as 'eight or nine men who are the mere subordinates of 40, or 50,000 of the scum of the faubourgs of Paris'. But he accepted that they were all that stood between France and chaos; and despite Queen Victoria's reservations, he urged the governments of Russia, Prussia and Austria not to interfere and to do as he did and recognize them. As he put it in his despatch to St Petersburg, 'The only hope for the maintenance of internal tranquillity, and for the permanent restoration of order in

France, lies in the continuance, for the present at least, of M. Lamartine and his Colleagues in Power.'

It was a policy that earned dividends in France. When Irish Nationalists sent a deputation asking for support, the grateful Lamartine turned them away. But for the most part Palmerston's energy was wasted. Within weeks the only Power capable of interfering was Russia, which was too far away to act independently. The others had problems of their own. In March the 'barrel of gunpowder' exploded.

All over Europe the example of the latest French revolution inspired Radicals to press their demands and terrified the more prudent rulers into making concessions. On 3 March, the day when Guizot and Louis-Philippe reached England, Louis Kossuth persuaded the members of the Hungarian Diet to call on Austria to grant them their own independent administration. On 4 March King Carlo Alberto granted a constitutional charter to Sardinia, Piedmont and Savoy. Within a fortnight the Papal States had been granted the same. On 5 March Liberal scholars met at Heidelberg and proposed that all Germany should be represented in one national assembly. For the rest of the month the people of Baden, Saxony and most of the smaller German states took to the streets demanding their own versions of liberal constitutions and a united Germany. On 18 March a revolution broke out in Berlin. Next day, when most of the Prussian cities were in the hands of revolutionaries, King Frederick William withdrew his troops and agreed to summon a national assembly and discuss the creation of a constitution. In Bavaria, on the day after that, in response to riots that were as much in protest at the arrogance of his mistress, Lola Montez, as in demand for a constitution, extravagant King Ludwig conceded the latter and then abdicated in favour of his son Maximilian.

Meanwhile, in the very heart of Absolutism, the Austrians themselves demanded a constitution. On 13 March, to the total surprise of Metternich and his secret police, who had seen nothing coming, huge crowds surged through the streets of Vienna. As they passed the Hofburg they cheered their Emperor, but when they reached the Chancellery in the Ballhausplatz their mood turned ugly. Metternich resigned. During the next few days revolutions against Austrian rule broke out not only in

Hungary but also in Bohemia, Croatia and Illyria. On 18 March Milan drove out its Austrian garrison. Four days later Lombardy did the same and Venice announced that it was again a republic. Next day King Carlo Alberto declared war on Austria. Then Tuscany, Parma and Modena followed his example and placed themselves under the leadership of the Sardinian King.

The tremors of revolution were felt as far away as Spain. On 16 March, when he saw them approaching, Palmerston wrote to Bulwer instructing him to recommend 'the adoption of a legal and constitutional course of government in Spain' and warning that recent events in France 'ought to teach the Spanish Court and Government how great is the danger of an attempt to govern a country in a manner at variance with the feelings and opinions of the nation'. But his unwelcome advice had no more effect than a similar attempt to stay Austria's heavy hand in Lombardy. The only difference this time was that the Spanish government and army were strong enough and cruel enough to withstand an attack. When Bulwer showed Palmerston's despatch to the Spanish Foreign Minister, it was simply handed back to him. When the revolution came, on 26 March, it was suppressed with sickening brutality. In the weeks that followed, Bulwer was accused of assisting in a plot to assassinate the Spanish Prime Minister and then given forty-eight hours to leave the country. To Palmerston the only appropriate response to the insult was to blockade Seville and threaten to seize Cuba if the Spanish Prime Minister was not dismissed, but in the Year of Revolutions the Whig Cabinet did not have the nerve to agree to such a Palmerstonian solution, and the national insult was not entirely unwelcome to Russell, who had asked Palmerston not to send his offensive despatch in the first place.

Amid the turmoil to the north, sick, deaf and 75-year-old Metternich escaped as ignominiously as the King of France. After his resignation soldiers were sent to guard the front of the Chancellery. With the angry crowd still gathered in the Ballhausplatz, the Metternichs slipped away through the gate at the back of their garden and went to a friend's house, where they later ordered a cab to take them out of Vienna. When the cab driver recognized his passengers, however, he refused to take them, and another friend climbed up and took over in his seat. Halting sometimes to hide and sometimes simply to rest a while for the sake of his health, Metternich moved slowly westward across Europe. After he had spent a week in Feldsberg, the nervous mayor insisted that he move on; and the Bishop of Olmutz refused even to let the party travel across his diocese. It was not until 20 April that the Metternichs at last reached London and registered in the Brunswick Hotel, Hanover Square.

In London and the home counties the 'Year of Revolutions' was also the year of the eminent exiles. Now posing as Herr and Frau von Meyer, Prince Metternich, his proud Princess and her parrots left their hotel after a fortnight and moved into 44 Eaton Square. A few months later they moved to the Old Palace, Richmond Green, and from there, eventually, to Brighton. One of their neighbours in Richmond was Princess Lieven, who divided her time between a house in Richmond large enough to hold grand receptions and a house in Pelham Crescent, South Kensington, where Guizot had reverted to his old profession and was writing a *History of the English Republic and Cromwell*, a sequel to his *History of the English Revolution*, which he had written before his political career began.

Living at Claremont as the guests of King Leopold, the destitute Louis-Philippe and his family survived on a small allowance paid to them by Palmerston, with Queen Victoria's approval, out of the unaccountable Foreign Office funds normally reserved for secret operations. Since they were told only that the money came from an anonymous supporter, the kindness did nothing to inhibit their unjustified resentment. They blamed Palmerston more than anyone for their misfortune, and they felt no compunction about saying as much when they first visited Queen Victoria and Prince Albert at Windsor.

Metternich was worse. Like Guizot and Princess Lieven, he accepted Palmerston's hospitality, both formally at the Foreign Office and privately at Carlton Gardens. But he could never quite conceal his animosity towards their courteous but slightly condescending host, who always made a much better job of disguising his own understandable satisfaction at the downfall of his adversaries. The once great Metternich was much more comfortable reminiscing and pontificating to an awe-struck Disraeli. Misled by the predominantly Tory press into believing that

Palmerston did not represent the bulk of British public opinion, he was ready to tell anyone who would listen that the man was nothing but 'a red republican'.

With Aberdeen as their ally, the exiles from Paris and Vienna soon seemed to have more influence at Court than the government. Prince Albert, who was deeply alarmed by events in Europe and desperate for sympathetic advice, wrote in a forgetful passion to the Swedish-born Baron Stockmar, who was in Coburg, begging him to come back soon, if not for the sake of the royal family then at least for love of his German fatherland. Meanwhile the Queen left her Foreign Secretary in no doubt as to her displeasure at her Ambassador's interference in Spanish party politics, her concern at her government's apparent opposition to Austria and her bewilderment as to how Carlo Alberto of Sardinia, who was after all a king, could have turned into a revolutionary. As the weeks went by their correspondence degenerated into a series of almost trivial bickering matches, in which Palmerston did not always come off best.

When Palmerston sent the Queen a draft of a despatch protesting at one of the worst of the Austrian army's atrocities in Italy, she wrote back, 'The Queen returns this draft to Lord Palmerston which she thinks had better not be sent. It is already well known that we sympathize with the Italians against the Austrians ... These accounts are sure to be much exaggerated.' In his reply Palmerston assured the Queen that there was 'every reason to believe the account to be correct'; but it was not enough for her. She rejected his explanation – 'it must be extremely difficult at a distance and from ex parte statements to decide upon acts committed during a war' – and then went on to reprove his 'partiality'. 'The Queen does not recollect our having protested on account of the cold-blooded murder of the Governor of Venice or any other acts of treachery on the part of the Italians.'

The offending despatch was never sent. It did not become one of the 28,000 unsolicited lectures, encouragements, protests, cries for help and howls of impotent indignation sent or received by the Foreign Office during 1848, which made Palmerston equally a hero and a villain from the toe of Italy to the tundra. In later years the painter and humorist

Edward Lear used to tell a story of how, while walking in southern Italy at the time, he was stopped by a drunken Neapolitan gendarme, who arrested him when he saw the Foreign Secretary's name on his passport and marched him away proclaiming loudly that he had captured the arch-enemy, until his sober colleagues convinced him that he was wrong and persuaded him to release his prisoner. The novelist Ivan Turgenev recorded a meeting in the depth of the Russian countryside with an illiterate old peasant who had heard of Palmerston and asked if he was still alive. Everywhere in Austria and throughout all the principalities of the 'German Fatherland' there was a couplet popular among opponents of reform:

> Hat der Teufel einen Sohn
> So ist er sicher Palmerston.

In England the Foreign Secretary's Radical admirers were delighted with it and promoted their own translation:

> If the Devil has a son
> His name is surely Palmerston.

Most European Liberals and even some Republicans saw Palmerston as a supporter, although only a few of them went so far as to credit him with playing a part in their success. Among those who were now struggling to reverse that success, however, the blame was almost unanimous. But the charge that 'the Devil's son' had promoted revolutions was only the bitter recrimination of those who had rejected and resented his advice. He had simply predicted revolutions. What he had promoted was the constitutional reform that he believed would avert those revolutions and prevent the continental war which he had also predicted would follow in their wake. In that he had failed. When the revolutions came, and when governments met them with repression, he had repeated his case and attempted to restrain them before they made matters worse. And in that he had failed as well. The job now was to prevent the war.

10. THE BOTTLE HOLDER

Britain could not live through the 'Year of Revolutions' without displaying its own inimitable symptoms of the public disorder that had brought change and chaos to the rest of Europe. As in France there had been crop failures, shortages and rising prices. As in France there had been 'railway mania' and a subsequent slump on the stock market. And as in France there was a well-supported organization, in this case the Chartist movement, campaigning for electoral reform. So when, as in France, the campaigners announced that they intended to defy a government ban and hold a huge public meeting on 10 April 1848, there were many who feared that, as in France, the meeting might develop into something worse.

The Chartist leader, and the organizer of the meeting, was a charming Irish Radical, Feargus O'Connor, who was MP for Nottingham and proprietor of the *Northern Star*, which Julian Harney edited. O'Connor claimed to have over 5,706,000 signatures on a petition demanding the Chartists' traditional 'Six Points', which included universal male suffrage; and his plan was to assemble 500,000 of the signatories at Kennington Park, which was then a twenty-acre common, and lead them over Westminster Bridge to deliver the petition to Parliament. But, although O'Connor was himself passionately opposed to any kind of violence, there were many among his followers who were known to disagree, and there were even some who wanted to carry arms on 10 April. In the opinion of the government, his huge meeting was bound to be a threat to public order and could even be a cover for a full-scale revolution. After all, Chartist meetings had degenerated into riots in the past; and someone had recently frightened Queen Victoria by smashing the street lamps outside Buckingham Palace and shouting 'Vive la république!'.

A few days before the demonstration the Queen, who had just given birth to Princess Louise, took the advice of Russell and Wellington and moved down to Osborne, the new Italianate villa on the Isle of Wight which Prince Albert had designed with the help of Thomas Cubitt, the builder of Eaton Square. Meanwhile the 79-year-old duke, who was still Commander-in-Chief, methodically and unobtrusively prepared the capital to withstand a revolution. The lights burned late every night at his London home, Apsley House, where a steady stream of visitors called on him with helpful suggestions; and it was said afterwards that when the suggestions were any good they were usually met with 'Done already'. Nine thousand regular soldiers were brought into the city and concealed at strategic points. Over 170,000 special constables were sworn in, among them the earliest surviving royal exile from France, Prince Louis Napoleon. The Chelsea Pensioners were briefed and put on stand-by to defend Battersea, on the left flank of the demonstrators. Many of the nobility and gentry brought up gamekeepers, gardeners and farm-hands from their country estates to reinforce the indoor servants who already garrisoned their London houses.

On the morning of 10 April Lady Palmerston visited and inspected the Foreign Office, where the clerks, translators, librarians and secretaries, commanded by her husband, had blocked the windows with books and stood at their posts behind them incongruously armed with naval cutlasses, infantry hangers and muskets. Around noon she left the front lines and rode in her carriage through pouring rain along Piccadilly and up Park Lane to call on her daughter Lady Ashley in Upper Brook Street. In the early afternoon she sent a footman back to the Foreign Office to inform its commander that she awaited his orders. But when the footman returned with orders to stay where she was, she climbed into her carriage again, rode back towards the battle lines and sent another message to the Foreign Office informing her husband that he would find her waiting for him at home.

Lady Palmerston was never in danger. Instead of the boasted 500,000, only 30,000 demonstrators assembled on Kennington Common. Shortly after noon, when their bedraggled column reached the south side of Westminster Bridge, the Commissioner of Police for the metropolis, another Irishman, came over to meet them and informed O'Connor that there were cavalry, infantry and four hidden batteries of artillery waiting to prevent them from crossing. O'Connor turned to his followers and persuaded them to disperse peacefully. Instead of delivering the huge piles of paper containing their precious petition themselves, they lifted them off their farm carts and sent them on to Parliament in three hackney cabs. Despite its bulk, however, even the petition was a disappointment. There were only 1,975,496 signatures on it, less than a third of the figure claimed, and many of them were fake, most obviously 'Mr Punch', 'Victoria Rex' and 'the Duke of Wellington'.

The Chartist movement never really recovered from the ridicule that followed. There were a few violent incidents outside London, but they were easily quelled, and others were soon deterred by the prison sentences and transportations meeted out to the ringleaders. The only subsequent Chartist gathering that came close to the demonstration of 10 April 1848 in size was the funeral of Feargus O'Connor in 1851. Like so many of the most attractive Irish Radicals, he had spent his last years in a state of hopeless insanity.

The day after the demonstration the defenders of the Foreign Office and their commander returned to the more customary and more hazardous business of coping with the consequences of real revolutions elsewhere. It was a delicate task made all the more difficult by the fact that the Court and the Foreign Secretary seemed to hold opposing opinions on almost every significant issue. While the Queen's sympathies lay wholeheartedly with the Austrian Emperor and the established government of his empire, Palmerston appeared to be in sympathy with the insurgents who were fighting to be rid of them in Italy and Hungary, and even with the constitutional reformers within Austria itself. While Prince Albert dreamed of establishing liberal constitutional governments in all the German principalities and uniting them under the leadership of Prussia, Palmerston, who had predicted such a possibility during his last continental tour, now regarded the whole idea with an air of what the Duke of Argyll described in his memoirs as 'ridiculing disbelief'. In so far as he expressed any serious opinion on the subject at all, Palmerston was opposed to German unity, if only because it would act as an enlargement of the commercial union, the Zollverein, which was imposing prohibitive import duties on British goods. Since Germany was probably the only subject on which the Prince was better informed than Palmerston, and since it was also the one area in which, like Palmerston, the Prince was prepared to support the cause of constitutional reform, he was incensed to discover that he had been misled in Scotland and that the Foreign Secretary had no real regard for his opinions.

There was already some justification for Palmerston's attitude towards a united Germany, however. When a German national assembly met for the first time in Frankfurt on 18 May 1848, there was so little unity among the delegates that they could not even agree on what a united Germany ought to be. Some thought a republic, others an empire. In the course of their first sessions, when they were supposed to be creating a constitution, most of their time was devoted to admirable but ineffectual debates on human rights and the obligation of the state to guarantee them. Although they created an executive, its only powers were those which the individual states conceded to it. Since this meant that it was difficult to get agreement on any domestic policies, which the state governments tended to regard as usurping their authority, the only effective early decision was made, unfortunately, in the field of expansionist foreign policy. In the spring of 1848, ignoring the indignant warnings of King Frederick William, the assembly agreed to send some of his Prussian soldiers to invade the Grand Duchy of Schleswig-Holstein, on the neck of the Danish peninsula.

The predominantly Danish state of Schleswig and the predominantly German state of Holstein had been combined in one grand duchy since the fifteenth century; and the kings of Denmark had been their hereditary grand dukes since 1721. Like many German states, however, Holstein was subject to the Salic Law, which prohibited any title from being inherited by, or even through, a woman. It was this law which had prevented Queen Victoria from inheriting the Electorate of Hanover when she succeeded her uncle on the throne of England; and the late King Christian VIII of Denmark had attempted to avoid a similar loss by decreeing that Schleswig-Holstein was to be incorporated totally within his kingdom, so that when, as was almost certain, his son and heir Frederick died childless, all his families lands and titles could be inherited through the female line. Three years later, however, when revolutions in the rest of Europe inspired the resentful Germans in Holstein to attempt a rebellion of their own, the new King Frederick VII had sent in Danish troops to restore order. It was in response to this that the German national assembly had dispatched Prussian soldiers to drive out the Danes and had invited Schleswig-Holstein to send delegates to Frankfurt and to join the German republic or empire or whatever their federation was eventually going to be.

Inevitably Prince Albert and consequently Queen Victoria were eager supporters of the German national assembly, which, among its many other virtues, had been wise enough to choose Queen Victoria's half-brother Prince Charles of Leiningen to lead it. Since this assembly aspired to be liberal and democratic, the royal couple began by hoping that, on this subject at least, the man they had started to call 'Pilgerstein' would agree with them; and they were almost petulantly baffled when the supposed champion of liberalism and democracy appeared to be supporting the arbitrary aggression of an autocrat instead. They were not alone in misjudging by appearances: for the first time in a long time Princess Lieven, who saw things from a very different perspective, actually expressed her approval of what Palmerston seemed to be doing. But she at least should have known him better. As usual, pragmatic Palmerston was simply taking the line most likely to prevent a little local conflict from escalating into a major war.

The Danish army was certainly no match for the might of Prussia, but the Danish navy was still one of the strongest in the world, and the Tsar of Russia had declared his support for a king whom he regarded as a fellow absolutist. With a Danish fleet dominating the Baltic and threatening to cripple Prussian trade, and with a huge Russian army on the eastern flank, King Frederick William might soon discover that the assembly in Frankfurt had committed him to a great deal more than it anticipated.

To Palmerston the only way to avoid this now was somehow to persuade the Prussians to withdraw and then persuade the King of Denmark to restore Schleswig-Holstein as far as possible to its former independence. The fact that in attempting to do this he appeared to be opposing the Prussians and was closer to the Danish point of view did not mean that he was intentionally supporting it. Indeed the Danish King's point of view could hardly have been described as absolutist since the vast majority of his subjects agreed with it, including the many liberal democrats who were campaigning for a constitution. Liberalism and Nationalism were as synonymous in Denmark as they were in Germany. Within a year of the Prussian invasion, after King Frederick had granted a constitution based on the British model, the new Danish government confirmed its enthusiasm for his policy by issuing an ultimatum to the Prussians and repudiating the armistice that Palmerston had negotiated.

In October 1848, after both belligerents had originally agreed to the armistice, Palmerston had invited all the interested parties to a conference in London, at which he proposed that Schleswig should become part of Denmark and that Holstein should join the German federation while remaining nominally under the rule of the Danish King, despite the provisions of 'the Law Salic'. It was after the Danes had rejected this proposal that their representative at the conference handed their ultimatum to Palmerston and asked him to pass it on to the Prussian representative, the famously devout and scholarly Baron von Bunsen. Overworked and somewhat distracted by the part he was playing in every other European conflict, Palmerston stuffed the piece of paper in his pocket and forgot about it for a couple of days. When the Danes then repudiated the armistice and started fighting again, the Tories, who supported the Danes, and the Radical Whigs, who supported the Germans, combined gleefully in the House of Commons to blame Palmerston for the renewal of a conflict which, they said, both parties had been trying to avoid. But, as Palmerston pointed out, his acknowledged oversight was irrelevant. The new Danish government did not yet seem to understand the proper diplomatic procedures. If the Danes wanted to present an ultimatum to the Prussians, it should have been presented to the Prussian Foreign Minister by their envoy in Berlin. Palmerston was not their representative and Bunsen did not have the authority to accept an ultimatum, let alone answer it.

Peace was restored when Austria threatened to invade Prussia on behalf of Denmark, and Britain and Russia threatened, insincerely, to abandon the Danes if they were not a bit more flexible. At Palmerston's suggestion one of the terms of the peace was that, until a permanent settlement was made, Schleswig was to be administered by a triumvirate of governors, one each from the contestants, Denmark and Prussia, and one from an independant nation, Great Britain. Eventually, again at Palmerston's proposal, all the parties represented in London, Austria, France, Great Britain, Prussia, Russia, Sweden and Norway, signed a protocol which recognized that the King of Denmark was also Grand Duke of the separate Duchy of Schleswig-Holstein and that Prince Christian of Glucksburg was heir to both, despite the provisions of Salic Law and despite the fact that under that law there were nineteen other princes and noblemen who had a better claim to the Grand Duchy. In due course, in 1852, the protocol was ratified as the Treaty of London.

The negotiations that culminated in the signing of the London protocol were one of Palmerston's unqualified successes. But Queen Victoria and Prince Albert never came round to seeing them that way. From start to finish they questioned and protested at every step.

Sometimes, with the help of Prince Albert, the Queen subjected her Foreign Secretary to a general history lesson and a moral lecture, along the lines of:

> The union of Schleswig with Holstein is not an ideal one, but complete as to constitution, finance, customs, jurisprudence, Church, universities, Poor Law, settlement, debts etc. etc. and is not established by the Kings Dukes but has existed for centuries. To defend Holstein against the attack made by Denmark upon this union, Germany joined the war ... Lord Palmerston cannot be more anxious for a speedy termination of the Danish

war than the Queen is, but she thinks that the mediation will not effect this, as long as the mediating power merely watches to see which of the two parties is in the greatest difficulties for the moment, and urges it to give way.

But Palmerston had learned enough about the history and constitution of the Grand Duchy to convince the other delegates at the conference that he had mastered them, and each time, not always hiding his irritation, he answered with just enough to dismiss the criticism. 'The former history of Denmark and the two Duchies seems to be so confused and to be so full of irregular transactions, that some events may be quoted in support of almost any pretension.'

Sometimes the Queen's reproach was more specific. She objected, for example, when one of the the mediating team, Colonel Hodges, was appointed to act as the British representative among the three temporary governors of Schleswig. She did not, she told Palmerston, 'think the choice a very good one, considering the strong partiality Colonel H. has shown throughout the war, against Schleswig and for Denmark'. When Palmerston refused to cancel the appointment and replied that he was 'not aware that the people of Schleswig entertain any prejudice against Colonel Hodges', she wrote back in pure huff.

The Queen has to acknowledge Lord Palmerston's letter of yesterday. She did not expect that her objections to Colonel Hodges' appointment would alter Lord Palmerston's opinion on the subject, but she mentioned them as she has the satisfaction to recollect that she always has done, whenever she saw that a mistake was going to be made, as she thinks Colonel Hodges' appointment will be.

Even after all had gone well and the protocol had been signed, she could not bring herself to do anything but condemn it as 'repugnant to all feelings of justice and morality'.

Yet the stubborn friction over Schleswig-Holstein was nothing compared with the resentful royal antagonism aroused by so many other subjects. If Palmerston had only been more patient in the presentation of his policies and more diplomatic when he found it necessary to deceive, he might have managed to continue his European scheming without too much royal interference and opposition. Although the lecture on government to the Spanish court was not the only impetuous lapse in judgement, his policies were usually well reasoned and based on a shrewd assessment of the protagonists. But, when he bothered at all, he presented them to the Court as if he was presenting them to the Cabinet, and when it looked as though reason had not prevailed, he became all too easily exasperated.

The best advice he ever received on the subject came from Lady Palmerston, who knew the Queen as well as anyone and warned him that she did not have the intellectual capacity to respond to reason. 'You always think you can convince people by Arguments,' she wrote,

and she has not reflection or sense to feel the force of them... I should treat what she says more lightly & courteously, and not enter into argument with her, but lead her on gently, by letting her believe you have both the same opinions in fact & the same wishes, but take sometimes different ways of carrying them out.

But somehow, sadly, it was not advice that her husband was ever able to follow. When what he saw as reason failed, he resorted, as elsewhere, to a brusque assertiveness which was only distinguished from the way in which he then pursued his policies by an added air of scornful impatience. Eventually it was not so much what he said and did as the way in which he said and did it that turned Queen Victoria from a wincing, uncomprehending critic into an obstinate opponent.

The only explanation, and the only excuse, for this obdurate and persistent misjudgement was that, at the age of sixty-four, 'Protocol Palmerston' was working himself even harder than before. As usual, he was gambling, but this time the game was larger and more desperate, and it was changing so fast and so often that it would have been futile to spend time explaining or deliberating over every necessary alteration in tactics. Palmerston had witnessed a revolution as a child. His first experience of political office had been dominated in the early years by the terrible European war that followed. Nobody but Wellington knew better than he that he was playing for the highest stakes. Perhaps it was hardly surprising therefore that, in a man too old to change his ways, the stresses and strains only served to magnify the characteristics that had long ago earned him the nickname 'Lord Pumicestone'.

As the 'Year of Revolutions' progressed, no story unfolded as it looked as though it might, or as anyone had predicted it would. The only initial judgement that still seemed justified when the year was drawing to a close was Palmerston's doubt about the tenacity of the Italians. It turned out that the Pope was at best too timid to stay committed to reform in the face of armed opposition or that at worst he had been insincere from the outset. Although the romantic Carlo Alberto was almost recklessly courageous, he did not have the diplomatic skill to control his disputatious allies, and their combined cause suffered in consequence. The King of Naples was exposed as a sadistic and treacherous opportunist. And to the north of the Alps the Hungarians became so optimistically over-ambitious that they threw away their initial gains. It might have been different if the French had intervened, at least in Italy, but for most of the year they were so preoccupied by their own social and political discord that they were powerless to fulfil any of their threats, which also enabled the Austrians to surprise everyone with an unimagined level of resilience and resourcefulness. Lord Palmerston may have had right and reason on his side, but Queen Victoria had fate and fortune on hers.

By the end of April Carlo Alberto had defeated the Austrians at the battles of Goito and Pastrengo, and the people of Rome had persuaded the Pope to send an army to support him. Despite appearances and the Queen's perception, Palmerston still believed in 'the importance of maintaining the Austrian Empire as united and as strong as possible', but with Marshal Radetzky in full retreat he accepted without regret that it had lost its hold on northern Italy. As he told King Leopold, 'Her rule was hateful to the Italians, and has long been maintained only by the expenditure of money and an exertion of military effort which left Austria less able to maintain her interests elsewhere. Italy was to her the heel of Achilles, and not the shield of Ajax. The Alps are her natural barrier and her best defence.' Palmerston's objective now was 'to see the whole of Northern Italy united into one kingdom'. This, he believed, 'would be most conducive to the peace of Europe, by interposing between France and Austria a neutral state strong enough to make itself respected'.

In Vienna, Metternich's successor, Count Ficquelmont, had come to a similar conclusion about Austria's future south of the Alps, and he sent Baron Hummelauer to London to invite Palmerston to mediate between Austria and the north Italian states. Throughout May they discussed terms. By the end of the month Palmerston had pushed Hummelauer far enough to accept that Lombardy should be given complete independence and that, if Venice was to remain within the Austrian Empire, it should at least be granted self-government. For a moment it looked as though a settlement might be possible. But the terms were still not enough for the British Cabinet. Urged on by Russell, who allowed his idealistic passion for Italian independence to cloud his understanding of Palmerston's larger European objectives, the Cabinet insisted that Austria should grant complete independence to at least some of the Venetian territory as well. Since it was beyond his authority to agree to this, Hummelauer returned to Vienna for instructions, taking with him Queen Victoria's sincere wishes for the welfare of the Imperial family and for the well-being of the Austrian Empire.

By then, however, it was too late. Austria was no longer in a mood to make drastic concessions. Events in Italy had overtaken the negotiations. On 29 April, the day before Carlo Alberto's second victory at Pastrengo, the Pope had announced that he no longer wished to make war on another Catholic nation and had sent orders recalling the Roman army. In the weeks that followed, it had looked as though his cautious breach of faith had been a signal for a general falling out between all the north Italian states and between all the already arguing factions within each of them. Under cover of the confusion, and with the Roman army no longer threatening their lines of communications, the Austrians had sent an army south to reinforce Radetzky. By the time Count Hummelauer was back in Vienna, the 82-year-old Austrian marshal was again on the offensive in Italy.

Palmerston guessed rightly that Carlo Alberto would now turn for help to France, and he knew for sure that the French army was already eager to support him, no matter what the squabbling politicians in Paris said. In consequence, in the hope of pre-empting the use of force, he tried a trick that had worked before and proposed that Great Britain and France should offer to act as joint mediators. It might not come to anything, but, as he admitted in a despatch to the British Ambassador in Paris, Lord Normanby, supporting the King of Sardinia was not as important as stopping the French from doing it.

To Queen Victoria, however, there was no merit in the proposal that her kingdom should join with a republic in mediating between a legitimate emperor and a revolution. After informing Palmerston that he had overestimated the French and that, in her view, it was 'out of the question for a French Republic to take a part in any other arrange-ment except that of driving the Austrians out of Italy', she wrote equally directly to Russell. 'The Queen is afraid that Lord Palmerston has a scheme of establishing a Kingdom of Upper Italy reaching from one sea to the other and that it is for that scheme that all considerations of ancient alliance with Austria, of the peace of Europe, the regard for treaties, etc., etc. are to be sacrificed.'

It was a shrewd enough assessment of Palmerston's long-term objec-tive. But it missed the point. The Queen and Prince Albert, who probably drafted her letter, had allowed their imperial prejudices to cloud their understanding of what Palmerston was trying to do – and meanwhile the need to do it was becoming ever more urgent. On 27 July, the very day when Queen Victoria wrote that letter to Russell, Radetzky com-pleted the four-day rout of Carlo Alberto's diminished army in a series of battles around Custoza.

It looked as though the time for talking was over. Surely the only way in which the French could help now was by force. Indeed it was reported in Paris that many enthusiastic Republican officers had packed their kit and were already on their way to the Italian border. Yet, despite the new strength of Austria's military position in Italy, the Imperial government in Vienna was still as insecure as its Republican counterpart in Paris. Both Austria and France were willing to talk, if talking could get them what they wanted. On 9 August the Austrian and Sardinian armies concluded an armistice, and in the sceptical respite that followed the confident British mediator made no concessions and proposed terms similar to those he had suggested earlier to Hummelauer. As he wrote to the Ambassador in Vienna, 'The real fact is that the Austrians have no business in Italy at all.'

As the summer weeks went by, everybody played for time. Palmerston pressed for the acceptance of his terms without any modification. The French placated their Republican officers and their supporters by publicly threatening to intervene if Palmerston's terms were not accepted, although some said that at the same time they were reassuring the Austrians by secretly signalling that they did not really mean it. The Austrians listened to everything and agreed to nothing. And throughout it all Queen Victoria continued to misunderstand what was happening.

On 11 August she wrote to Russell to express her indignation at Palmerston's intransigence, which she ascribed to what she saw as his 'vindictiveness', and she added, 'the Queen must say she is afraid that she will have no peace of mind and there will be no end of troubles as long as Lord Palmerston is at the head of the Foreign Office'. A fortnight later, when she was sure that his conduct was now enough to convince even the Prime Minister that he was not acting as an honest broker, she wrote to Russell again.

> Now that Charles Albert hears of the mediation and expects of it better things than he bargained for, Lord Palmerston advises that the armistice should not be considered as a political one but merely as a military one. Is this mediating between belligerents? Or merely trying to obtain advantage for a client? What is the meaning of a basis for an armistice if this is not political? The armistice would otherwise only consist in an agreement to suspend hostilities and exchange prisoners. – All this is very unfortunate.'

The Queen was not alone in her attitude. All the articles on the subject in *The Times* and the now Peelite *Chronicle* were strongly in support of the Austrians. Convinced by these and by opinions in his own small circle, Metternich wrote to tell friends in Vienna that Palmerston's policies did not represent British public opinion; and his new disciple Disraeli derided the prospect of Her Majesty's Government acting in concert with treacherous Jacobins. But Palmerston had so far succeeded in his objective. Everyone was still talking. The French had not yet intervened against the Austrians in northern Italy. Europe was not yet at war; and Palmerston had bought a little more time in which to deal with all the repercussions of revolutions elsewhere.

The outcome of the long battle at Custoza had influenced events in southern Italy as well as in the north, and the situation down there was now every bit as dangerous. Frustrated by King Ferdinand's continuing refusal to grant them complete independence from Naples, the Sicilian revolutionaries had offered their throne to Carlo Alberto's second son, the Duke of Genoa. After the defeat of his father's army, however, the duke was disinclined to undertake what now looked like a risky adventure. On the other hand, the victory for the Austrians had enabled King Ferdinand to recall the army which he had sent north to help them. Abandoning any further pretence at negotiations, he had sent the army to reassert his authority over Sicily instead. If it looked as though his soldiers were going to be successful, the Sicilians would undoubtedly turn to the nearest powerful republic for support; and if it looked as though they were likely to fail, it was equally certain that King Ferdinand would call for help from his absolutist allies. There was now just as much chance that France and Austria would lead Europe into a war over Sicily as over Lombardy.

Again Palmerston invited the French to join him in mediation, even though Minto's efforts had already foundered; and again the French were happy to let diplomacy delay the need for more active intervention. This time, however, the prospect of more talking did nothing to halt or even limit hostilities. The King of Naples continued his campaign, and he did so with such unremitting brutality that it eclipsed even the Austrians, and with such extravagant use of artillery that it was soon to earn him the nickname 'Bomba'. But his relentless slaughter and devastation did not earn him the early victory that he expected. The Sicilians fought bravely and often effectively – someone was supplying them with arms.

As the 'Year of Revolutions' drew to a close, curtains came down on the capitals of Europe as if on the first acts of a series of spectacular melodramas. In Rome the discontent that followed the Pope's betrayal of the nationalists culminated in the assassination of his moderate Prime Minister, Count Pellegrino Rossi. Nine days later Pius IX revealed his true personal and political colours by running away to take refuge under the protection of the reactionary King of Naples. The Eternal City, the Vatican and the Papal States were left to keep Christmas in a state of violent anarchy.

In Berlin, King Frederick William lost patience with Liberalism. On 5 December he dissolved the Prussian Parliament and introduced a much more conservative constitution with a very limited bourgeois franchise. Having extricated himself from the embarrassment in Schleswig-Holstein, he felt no need to do more about the German national assembly than be wary of it. But at the end of the year the delegates in Frankfurt announced that they had reached agreement over a constitution and that Germany was to be an empire. Shortly afterwards they invited Frederick William to be their emperor. By now, however, the pious King of Prussia was a convinced conservative: he was only prepared to accept such an offer if it came from the rulers of the German states and not just from the representatives of their subjects, and he refused to approve the constitution, which, despite its imperial title, was otherwise much too liberal. Without Prussian support the empire was doomed. Most of the German states recalled their delegates there and then, and one by one the more resolute remainder lost heart and followed their example. Within months the German national assembly had disintegrated.

In Vienna, after a newly confident government had sent an army to force Hungary back into the empire, radicals rose in rebellion and murdered the Minister of War. The court and most of the members of the Assembly fled to Olmutz. But the army came back. At the end of October the rebels surrendered and many of the radical leaders were shot. By the end of November a new, reactionary government had been installed, led by Prince Felix Schwarzenberg; and at the beginning of December the Emperor Ferdinand, whom Palmerston had described as 'next thing to an idiot', abdicated in favour of his eighteen-year-old nephew Franz Joseph.

Archdukes were sent to present the news of the young Emperor's accession to every court in Europe but one. Schwarzenberg did not feel inclined to pay such a compliment to the court that allowed itself to be represented by a man who was 'a little too much inclined to consider himself the arbiter of the destinies of Europe' and 'the devoted protector of the Emperor's rebellious subjects'. Infuriated, Queen Victoria snubbed her Foreign Secretary by sending his predecessor, Aberdeen, to let it be known at the Austrian Embassy that she took no personal offence at the slight and was indeed in sympathy with it. But the Foreign Secretary himself was not in the least put out. As if to make sure that there was no misunderstanding as to his attitude, the uncompromising new Austrian Chancellor had passed on a copy of his inimical instructions to the British Embassy in Vienna. When Palmerston saw it, he merely compared the contents to 'the outpourings of an enraged woman of the town when arrested by a policeman in the act of picking a pocket'.

In Paris, in November, the government at last completed the drafting of a new republican constitution. By then, however, most Frenchmen were exasperated and frightened by continuous social instability and regularly rising taxes. The assembly had been reduced to impotence by the destructive opposition of the extreme Radical minority; and the destitute Paris mobs, who had originally supported those Radicals, had become so furiously disillusioned by their failure to find work for them that they had more than once taken to the streets. On the last occasion, at the end of June, troops and National Guards had been brought in by train. The boulevards and avenues of the city centre had been left stained and strewn with blood, bodies and broken barricades. It was little wonder therefore that, in the by-elections that followed, all the departments that took part returned moderate or conservative deputies, among them none other than Prince Louis Napoleon, who stood *in absentia*, from London.

When the French went to the polls again in December, this time to elect a president of the new republic, the prince was one of the candidates. There were several others, including Lamartine, but in the circumstances none of them stood a chance. To a nation desperate for stability, the surname Bonaparte was reassurance enough. From Republicans to traditional Royalists, 5.5 million of them elected the nephew of the Emperor Napoleon, giving him a fifty per cent majority over the combined votes of all his opponents. Few of them knew that he was a devious, ambitious, awkward, ineffectual little man; but none of them would have cared if they had known. As Victor Hugo put it, they had elected an idea.

In London, less dramatically, the little world of 'Society' and statecraft came one step closer to the end of an era. Some of the last letters dated 1848 from Palmerston to Queen Victoria were written at the bedside of 'one who was not more distinguished by his brilliant talents, his warm affections, and his first-rate understanding, than by those sentiments of attachment to your Majesty which rendered him the most devoted subject who ever had the honour to serve a sovereign'. The second Lord Melbourne died on 26 November and was succeeded by his brother Frederick.

To the many who still cared about such things, Melbourne was the embodiment of an age that was almost gone. To them he was bound to be remembered as the last real Regency dandy ever to lead a government. None of them at the time would have believed it if they had been told there was going to be another. A few of his kind were still around, of course. In the Cabinet there were Lansdowne and Palmerston, who had been called 'Cupid' for his looks long before there was any reason to add other connotations. In the House of Lords there was the stiff, grey figure of the man who was to be known to posterity as 'the Iron Duke' but who had been known simply to the men he commanded as 'the beau'. Some of the lesser 'exquisites' had survived as well. Little Captain Gronow was now living in Paris, married to a dancer and teaching the French the essence of *l'Esprit Dandy*. Big-haired 'Poodle' Byng was still sitting at every dinner-table that would have him, regaling the company with doubtful anecdotes about how much merrier and better for it the world of fashion used to be; and he was still enough of a would-be Lothario for Lady Palmerston to refuse to ride alone in her carriage with him. But he was right: times were changing. Excitable, over-dressed, curly-headed 'butterflies' such as D'Orsay and Disraeli were what passed for dandies now. Most statesmen now hid their true feelings behind a mask of self-conscious dignity, not self-deprecation and disdain. The world no longer had any use for men who bore their burdens lightly and could act on their own if the need arose. Travel and communications were now so fast that, even in an emergency, a minister could be expected to consult with his colleagues before formulating a policy – a lesson Palmerston had already learned, and which he was to learn again before the new year was a month old.

In January 1849 a sensational article appeared in *The Times* claiming that during the previous November the Foreign Office had sanctioned the supply of artillery pieces from the Royal Arsenal at Woolwich to the nationalist insurgents in Sicily. It was true. The editor of *The Times*, the famous John Thadeus Delane, who was passionately devoted to hunting, had learned the story while riding to hounds with Tom Hood, the casually indiscreet manufacturer of the guns. At Court and in Parliament, at home and abroad, Palmerston's opponents were delighted. Surely there could be no doubt now that he was encouraging and supporting revolutions. Having instructed his representative to accept the role of mediator in a contest between revolutionaries and a monarch, he had disregarded the essential neutrality of the role and, without consulting any of his colleagues, had allowed cannon to be removed from the British army's own arsenal and supplied to the revolutionaries.

The true story was not quite as bad as the bare outline made it seem. When the provisional government of Sicily approached Hood in September, he had just made a huge delivery to the British army and had no guns in stock. But he knew that many of the guns in the royal arsenal had not yet been assigned and that it would be a while before they were needed. He therefore asked the War Office if he could use these to fulfil the export order and then make up the shortfall with subsequent production. The War Office asked the Foreign Office, and Palmerston agreed. The story was still more than enough, however, to enable Grey to persuade the Cabinet that, if only to prevent a vote of censure from the opposition, Palmerston must write to apologize to the King of Naples and give a full explanation to the House of Commons.

Since the guns had been delivered several months ago, and since King Ferdinand had not yet bothered to complain, Palmerston at first saw no need for an apology, which encouraged Grey and the royal couple to hope that he was about to give them grounds for demanding his dismissal. But he eventually disappointed them by writing an appropriate letter to King Ferdinand and infuriated them with an explanation that made light of what had happened and reduced the House of Commons to laughter and applause.

When Russell went to Buckingham Palace to discuss the embarrassing episode with the Queen, she informed him that 'she did not see how Lord Palmerston could retain his office after this'. But, as Prince Albert recorded in his memorandum of the meeting, Russell remained loyal to his colleague, pointing out that 'the Government had approved of the whole foreign policy', and that 'both he and Lord Lansdowne felt very strongly that, after the many most unjust attacks made from all sides upon Lord Palmerston', it would be 'cowardly' to 'throw him over' now. So for the time being the Queen could only 'beg' Lord John 'to remember in what a painful position she was placed by having in one of the most important places as her adviser a man in whom she could not place the slightest confidence'.

Back in Sicily the revolutionaries showed no signs of appreciating how much Palmerston had risked for them, or indeed of realizing how much they needed him. They were still adamant that they would accept nothing less than complete independence from Naples. They refused every compromise that the French and British mediators put to them, even rejecting Palmerston's innocuous proposal that they might maintain a merely nominal connection by accepting a junior member of King Ferdinand's family as an honorary viceroy. But as the weeks went by, their position became more and more precarious. In the long run a few British guns were not going to be a match for King 'Bomba's' many batteries.

By the end of January the French had withdrawn their services as mediators. Their new government was soliciting the support of the clergy; and now that the Pope had come out as a reactionary, the

Prince-President's advisors felt that it might be wiser not to look as though they were opposing his allies. With the weight of French support withdrawn from Palmerston's proposals, and still confident that he could rely on the Austrians if he needed them, King Ferdinand was as intransigent as the Sicilians. In April, Palmerston lost patience and instructed Minto to withdraw from mediation as well. No longer inhibited by the menacing presence of British and French fleets, which had earlier intervened to restrain his barbarity, King 'Bomba' decided to demonstrate what enough guns and bayonets could really do. The beautiful city of Palermo was reduced to a crumbling, blood-soaked shambles. The few revolutionary fighters who survived the immediate slaughter were rounded up and eliminated by firing squads. The dungeons were crammed with democrats. By the end of May, King Ferdinand was so sure that the revolution was over that he cancelled the democratic constitution that he had granted to the citizens of Naples.

Although Palmerston's mediations had failed, he had succeeded again in his main objective. In southern Italy, as in the north, he had prevented the French and the Austrians from starting a war. By the time he withdrew from mediation, however, it looked as though the Franco-Austrian confrontation was going to take place in central Italy instead.

On 5 February, Rome was proclaimed a republic, with a triumvirate, which included Mazzini, at the head of its government. The Pope called for help, and the most powerful Roman Catholic kingdoms – Austria, Spain and Naples – announced their determination to support him. The French assembly also voted funds for an army, but its objective was identified a little ambiguously as upholding Roman liberties against the threat of suppression by Austria, which could just as easily have meant defending the Pope and his liberal constitution as fighting for the survival of the Roman Republic. While the French army, 9,000 strong, assembled in the naval base at Toulon, and while a Spanish fleet sailed for Naples, Radetzky marched his Austrian army south towards Rome. Within a fortnight he had occupied Ferrara.

Having already failed to persuade Mazzini to make some constitutional compromise with the Pope, Palmerston pleaded with the Catholic Powers 'that every endeavour should be made to bring about a settlement between the Pope and his subjects by negotiation and moral influence before resorting to the employment of force'. But he pleaded in vain. The worldly dominance of central Italy was a much more attractive prospect than the spiritual satisfaction of serving the papacy or the empty glory of defending a democracy.

Radetzky marched on southwards, apparently racing to reach Rome before the French army landed. In his wake, his ill-equipped and ill-disciplined brigades of military police, many of them armed with cut-down sabres which had first been issued to the armies of Napoleon, strove enthusiastically to surpass the despicable levels of atrocity for which they were already infamous. Urged on by their commander, Baron von Haynau, who took a special delight in the public flogging of aristocratic women, they raped, pillaged and hanged indiscriminately. A wave of revulsion and indignation swept through what was left of democratic Italy. In response to the demands of his subjects and surviving allies, Carlo Alberto renounced his armistice. Ignoring Palmerston's pleas and warnings, he mustered the Sardinian army and gallantly declared his support for the Roman Republic.

Radetzky turned back. On 21 March he routed the Sardinian army conclusively at Novara. Carlo Alberto abdicated in favour of his eldest son, Victor Emmanuel, and went into exile in Portugal, where he died of a broken heart shortly afterwards.

The news of the battle reached London on a day when Queen Victoria was holding a drawing-room reception at Buckingham Palace. When the Queen congratulated the Austrian Ambassador and wished his country well, everyone present, except Palmerston, followed her example. The Queen was furious. Two days later Charles Greville, the clerk to the Privy Council, wrote in his diary, 'I do not think anything Palmerston has done has excited so great a sensation, and exposed him to so much animadversion.' By then Greville knew that Palmerston had already instructed the Ambassador in Vienna, Lord Ponsonby, to do all that he could to persuade the Austrians not to impose ruinous peace terms on Victor Emmanuel, which induced him to add, 'the impolicy of this unmistakeable display of animus is the more striking, because we are now (through Ponsonby) entreating the Austrian Government to show moderation, and not to exact large contributions'.

Clearly Palmerston knew from the outset that a suppliant tone was unlikely to have much effect on Austria. Indeed his despatches to Austria were so threatening and reproachful that even Russell dared to wonder whether his 'meddling' was being any help to the Italians. What neither Russell nor the Queen nor Greville nor anybody knew at the time, however, was that Palmerston was also negotiating with the French. He had discussed the problem with the French Ambassador, Admiral Cecille, who had then informed the French Foreign Minister, Edouard Drouyn de Lhuys, that Britain would support any threat his government chose to issue in order to persuade the Austrians to moderate their demands on the new King of Sardinia.

The Queen became aware of what was happening only when, in the normal course of events, she saw a despatch from Paris to London. Furious again, she wrote to Palmerston.

> The Queen finds reference to Lord Palmerston's conference with Admiral Cecilie on the terms of peace between Austria and Sardinia in Lord Normanby's Despatch No. 213, according to which M. Drouyn de L'Huys expressed himself 'much satisfied with Lord Palmerston's assurance of the moral support of England in case of neccessity, etc.' As Lord Palmerston has not reported anything concerning his communication with Admiral Cecilie, to the Queen, she must now ask him to supply her want of information on this point.

Palmerston replied with an outline of his attempt 'to rescue from such oppressive terms an ancient ally whose political independence is an important element in the balance of power in Europe'. He then pleaded that, although the Cabinet had authorized him to prepare an instruction to that effect for the Ambassador in Vienna, which implied that Her Majesty would have learned what was happening when she saw it, he was 'so pressed with urgent matters' that he had 'not yet had time to do so'.

It was a far from satisfactory explanation. Prince Albert joined in the fury. If the Queen's continuous commands were not in themselves enough to compel obedience from her Foreign Secretary, the Prime Minister would have to accept the responsibility as well. Prince Albert wrote to Russell demanding that in future, before being despatched, all Foreign Office drafts must be sent first to the Prime Minister and then passed on by him to the Queen, together with his own written comments. Russell concurred and conveyed the Prince's demand to Palmerston. It was a vote of no confidence which might have induced a resignation from many other members of the Cabinet, and even, perhaps, from the deceptively confident young Palmerston in his first few years at the War Office. Since then, however, obdurate old 'Pumicestone' had grown much too thick a skin for that. Tersely informing Russell that he would give instructions accordingly, he returned to the 'urgent matters' in hand.

By the time Austria and Sardinia signed a treaty, the Austrians had been persuaded to reduce their demands for reparation to a level that was at least bearable, and they had agreed that Victor Emmanuel could retain his father's liberal constitution. Loath to let Palmerston take any part of the credit, Schwarzenberg claimed that it had all been due to the entreaties of the French; and the cynical but probably realistic French claimed to be convinced that Palmerston would never have stayed with them if they had been forced to fulfil their threat to use force. But King Victor Emmanuel and his Prime Minister, the Marchese d'Azeglio, acknowledged that they owed most to the influence of Palmerston; and it was a debt the young King never forgot.

On 25 April the French fleet from Toulon arrived in Italy at last, landing its army on the west coast at Civitavecchia, little more than forty miles to the north of Rome. The French had persuaded the citizens to let them come ashore by assuring them that they had come to defend the Roman Republic against the Austrians. But the commander whom Prince Louis Napoleon had chosen for the army was the devoutly Catholic and conservative royalist Nicolas Oudinot, whose famous father had been one of his uncles most devoted marshals; and most of the officers who had been selected to serve him were men of 'the old school' with similar views. The Prince-President was now confident that support for the Republicans in his assembly was diminishing; and he was still eager to win the approval of the influential clergy. He had never intended to rescue the Roman Republic, although he did at least hope that a Pope who had been restored by the French would be susceptible to French influence and retain his new constitution.

By the time the French army was within sight of Rome, it was obvious to everyone that it had come to seize the city, not save it. The Republic was ready for it. Dug in ahead of it, around the Porto San Pancrazio, an almost equal force was waiting, led by a romantic idealist in a red shirt who had recently returned from exile, and who just happened to be a brilliant commander of irregulars. On 30 April Giuseppe Garibaldi defeated the French outside the walls of Rome and forced them to withdraw.

While Mazzini concluded an armistice with Oudinot, Garibaldi turned his attentions to other enemies. To the north-east of him, beyond the Apennine mountains, Radetzky's Austrian army was marching south again; and to the south-west a Neapolitan and Spanish army was closing on him from Naples. In the course of the next month Garibaldi routed and scattered the Neapolitan and Spanish forces. But the month of May also saw a general election in France, in which two-thirds of the deputies returned to the assembly were members of the 'Party of Order'. The Radical Republican minority was now so small that there was no longer any need to waste time placating it or even deceiving it. Reinforcements were sent to Civitavecchia. As soon as they arrived, on 1 June, Oudinot renounced the armistice and returned to the offensive.

Garibaldi fell back to defend Rome against the besieging French; and meanwhile, beyond the mountains, Radetzky kept coming. Palmerston watched with growing apprehension. It was difficult to believe that the French and the Austrians were not about to fight over the spoils. But then, on 12 June, to the astonishment of many and to the profound relief of Palmerston, the Austrians reached Ancona and announced that they intended to advance no further.

With the field to themselves, and with overwhelming force, the French broke in and became masters of Rome at the beginning of July. When they invited the Pope to return, however, he declined to do so until they guaranteed that all his old temporal powers would be restored to him. Despite Palmerston's warning that he would never be reconciled with his subjects unless he confirmed their constitution, and despite even his French benefactors' demands that he should do so, he refused to run the risk of democracy again. Eventually the French relented. For the next twenty years the frightened and irresolute Pius IX, who was soon to include among his achievements the proclamation of papal infallibility, owed his authority beyond the Vatican entirely to the support of a strong French garrison.

The Consuls of Great Britain, the United States, Switzerland, Bavaria and of course Sardinia cheated the firing squads by issuing 3,500 passports to leading Republicans – although the British Consul found it necessary to reassure Palmerston that the 500 he had issued had been only to men of respectable families. Mazzini fled to Switzerland and Garibaldi, eventually, to New York, after an epic escape through the mountains to Ravenna, in which he and his followers eluded the 86,000-strong armies of Austria, France, Naples and the Papacy.

While the Absolutist Powers looked on, one new republic had been destroyed by another. By now there were several who suspected that all along the French and the Austrians had been operating in accordance with a secret agreement, and there must have been some who were beginning to suspect that Louis Napoleon was harbouring a few old-fashioned dynastic ambitions. But there was also a more simple and practical explanation for why the Austrians halted when they did. Quite apart from the need for more men than ever to retain control in northern Italy, they were fighting in Hungary again and they needed every man they could muster for that.

When Franz Joseph replaced his uncle on the Austrian throne, the Hungarians, who had not been consulted, refused to recognize him. Delighted by the excuse to renew hostilities, the Austrians invaded again, and within two months they had repressed resistance, reclaimed Hungary for the empire and imposed a new oppressive constitution. But the oppression united the Hungarians with the minority Slav and Romanian inhabitants, who had previously supported the Austrians. Led by Louis Kossuth and Arthur Gorgei, and supported by Polish revolutionaries commanded by Joseph Bern, they drove the Austrians out of Hungary. And then, like the Austrians, they went too far and declared Hungary a republic, with Kossuth as President. Horrified at the prospect of a republic on his doorstep, the Tsar was only too happy to help when the Austrians appealed to him. In June he invaded Hungary with an army of the size only Russia could raise.

On 13 August the last Hungarian army surrendered at Vilagos. While Kossuth and the other leaders escaped into Turkey, the Austrian soldiers, now commanded by Haynau, indulged the pre-delictions for which he and the worst of them had become infamous in Italy. In a private letter to Ponsonby, which neither the Queen nor his colleagues had a right to see, Palmerston asked him to make sure that the Austrians were aware of the effect their actions were having on 'the public opinion of England' and allowed himself a revealing release for some of his own impotent fury at what even the Russians had described as 'wholesale butcheries'. 'The Austrians are really the greatest brutes that ever called themselves by the undeserved name of civilized men. Their atrocities in Galicia, in Italy, in Hungary, in Transylvania are only to be equalled by the proceedings of the negro race in Africa and Haiti.'

Yet Palmerston could not allow British foreign policy to be influenced by his contempt for the Austrians or his personal sympathy for the Hungarians. As he told the House of Commons, the Austrian Empire was essential to the balance of power in Europe, 'a barrier against encroachment on the one side, and against invasion on the other'. It was alarming, therefore, when the integrity of that empire was preserved only by the intervention of the power against whom it was supposed to be a barrier.

Nevertheless the escape of the revolutionary leaders did at least present Palmerston with an opportunity to make a contribution, if not to their cause, then at least to their welfare, and to issue an obvious warning to the Russians. After the Hungarian and Polish leaders had crossed the border into Turkey, the Russians and Austrians demanded their extradition and threatened to declare war if they were not handed over. But the British Ambassador in Constantinople at the time was none other than Sir Stratford Canning, a man after Palmerston's heart. Knowing that there was no time to wait for instructions, Canning acted on his own initiative. He persuaded the Turks to defy the Austrians and Russians, promising that if it came to war the British would support them. To show them that he meant what he said, he persuaded the British commander in the Mediterranean, Admiral Sir William Parker, to obey his unsupported order and move his fleet from Malta to the mouth of the Dardanelles; and he persuaded the French Ambassador to exceed his own authority and issue a similarly effective order to the French fleet.

Palmerston was delighted. He was so justifiably confident in the support of his Cabinet colleagues that, before even consulting them, he wrote privately to Normanby in Paris and asked him to start winning the equally certain approval of the French. When all had been agreed, a despatch was sent to Canning, officially instructing him to do everything he had done already, and reminding him not to let any French or British ships enter the Dardanelles themselves, which would be in breach of the 1841 convention.

The despatch was entrusted to a royal messenger called Townley, who famously covered the distance from London to Constantinople on horseback in only twenty-four days; and while Townley rode, Palmerston made no secret of what was happening. With characteristic flippancy he informed the Russian envoy Baron de Brunnow that the British fleet had been ordered to the Dardanelles to strengthen the resolve of the Turks, 'just as one holds a bottle of salts to the nose of a lady who has been frightened'.

He also set about strengthening public opinion, which was already enthusiastically behind him. He had access to the press again. His friend Peter Borthwick had just become editor of the *Morning Post;* and he wrote to him suggesting that 'there can be no objection to the publication' of stories about Austrians flogging young ladies, using slow strangulation as a method of execution and imprisoning Kossuth's 72-year-old mother. 'And you might', he added, 'make such observations as may suggest themselves upon this unmanly war waged against Hungarian women and children by those Austrians who were unable to stand up against the Hungarian men until they had called to their assistance an army of 150,000 Russians.'

The threats worked. The demands for extradition were withdrawn. On a smaller scale it was another unqualified success. But there was more to it than simply securing the liberty of a few revolutionary refugees. The Russians, who had already moved an ominously large army into Romania on the pretext of quelling another revolution, had been left in no doubt that the British would fight if it came to it; and if they needed it, they had also been reminded that the British were always ready to uphold the independence of Turkey and protect their overland routes to India. 'Certainly I hate Palmerston as much as Prince Schwarzenberg can hate him', wrote the Russian Foreign Minister, Count Nesselrode, to his special envoy in Berlin. 'But Palmerston is not eternal, and a war with England would be the worst of all wars. God preserve us from that!'

11. $\mathcal{C}$IVIS ROMANUS SUM

Palmerston's success in keeping Kossuth and the other leaders of his defeated revolution at liberty was, on the face of it, blamelessly compassionate. But it was no more impressive to Queen Victoria than any of his other achievements. 'What business have we', she wrote to Russell, 'to interfere with the Polish and Hungarian refugees in Turkey?'

When Russell passed the question on, Palmerston replied only two days later with a full account and analysis of the Hungarian rebellion; and since he knew that his answer would be shown to the Queen, he sprinkled it with mischievous comments. 'The Hungarian leaders may certainly be called revolutionists', he wrote, 'but they are revolutionists in the same sense as the men to whose measures and acts at the close of the seventeenth century it is owing that the present Royal Family of England, happily for the nation, are seated on the throne of these realms.'

By now Queen Victoria and Prince Albert had persuaded Russell to discuss ways of moving Palmerston, at least to another office. They were far from enthusiastic, however, when he made the not entirely selfless suggestion that, if he, Russell, were to be moved to the House of Lords, and if his father-in-law, Minto, were to be given the Foreign Office, Palmerston could probably be induced to accept the Home Office, combined with leadership of the House of Commons. The Prince had reservations about Minto's intellectual ability, and he felt that it would be 'a dangerous experiment' to give the leadership of the House of Commons to 'a man of expediency, of easy temper, no very high standard of honour and not a grain of moral feeling'. But Russell knew that it would be fatal for his government if he gave in to them. This was not the moment to offer Palmerston anything less than what he had already.

Palmerston's popularity with Her Majesty's subjects had become a powerful political force. The suggestion that he and his policies did not have the backing of the British public, which Metternich passed on to his friends in Austria, came only from the pages of *The Times* and from the exclusive little London milieu of Tories and old-fashioned Whigs. To this self-styled 'mass of educated public opinion', he might be nothing but a dangerous 'firebrand'. But to the cynical Radicals he was a more influential advocate than any they could find among themselves, to the Liberals of Europe he was an inspiring if practically ineffective ally, and to the real mass of all the British public, educated or not, he was the unlikely but entertaining hero whose opinions were theirs as soon as they heard them. They were probably not too sure what he was doing, but they liked the way he did it and they were pugnaciously proud to be represented by a man who seemed to be defying tyrants.

In England the middle of the nineteenth century was a moment of prosperity and hope. Free trade and good harvests had brought an end to 'the hungry years'. Factory Acts and other reforms had alleviated at least a fraction of the misery in the foundries, mines and mills. The Industrial Revolution had begun to bear abundant fruit. In the year of revolutions Britain's annual national production of iron, which eighty years earlier had been less than that of France, surpassed the production of every other country in the world put together. Half the world's cotton came from England, and two-thirds of the world's coal. Prince Albert was planning a Great Exhibition to show off what only 'the Workshop of the World' could do. For better or worse this was a time when Britain was still 'absent-mindedly' accumulating and developing the colonies and dominions that were soon to constitute the largest empire the world has ever known, and she was doing it as yet unchallenged by the other European powers, who were still too preoccupied by their own domestic difficulties.

What is less often remembered, however, is that this was also a moment when, for better or worse, the increasingly powerful, uniquely stable and morally overconfident United Kingdom dominated the international affairs of Europe; and it did so through the slightly incongruous medium of jaunty and apparently reckless Palmerston. No other peacetime British statesman has exercised so much influence over the history of so many other nations; and for many of those nations, as well as for Britain, it was only peacetime because he kept it that way. The revolutions at the close of the eighteenth century culminated in a devastating war. The revolutions in the middle of the nineteenth century did not, not least because the long shadow of Palmerston lay between so many of the potential belligerents.

But the style that cowed and infuriated so many of Palmerston's opponents, and which so many of his detractors mistook for substance, was as much of a handicap as an advantage. It made enemies where none were necessary; and one of its weaknesses was bluster. Bluster has no sense of proportion. Although Palmerston was always deceptively measured in determining his dramatic response to great issues, he could sometimes be hasty and heavy-handed in seizing an easy solution to a little one. When he sent a British fleet to defy two overbearing empires in the name of a few revolutionary refugees, he was seen as the champion of Liberalism and the enemy of all despots. In the light of so much popular acclaim it was not easy for his opponents to censure him. But they had no such difficulty when he then used the same fleet to impose his own will on an irritating little kingdom. That made him look like a bully. It was a blunder that set hearts beating with hope on the thrones of every kingdom but Denmark and Sardinia.

Palmerston's patience with the kingdom of Greece had been diminishing steadily for some years. Bavarian King Otto was a disappointment. He made no effort to introduce any kind of representative government. Even after a revolution had forced him to grant a constitution, he still took no notice of his parliament and appointed all his ministers himself. He was ostentatious and extravagant; and he never made any repayments on the large loan that Rothschilds had granted to his government when he was given the throne. Since the guarantors of Greek independence – Britain, France and Russia – were also guarantors of the loan, they had been paying the annual interest ever since. Yet, although Britain, through Palmerston, complained and regularly pressed King Otto to contribute at least towards some of the interest, the others had more important objectives than the repayment of the Rothschilds. The French were busy intriguing with the corrupt little group that passed for a parliamentary opposition; and the Tsar of Russia was eagerly encouraging King Otto to remain as Absolutist as he could.

Eventually Palmerston became so exasperated with the Greek government that he was ready to oppose it in almost every local dispute, and to support any individual who had even the slightest claim against it. His support for British subjects who were in trouble with foreign governments had always been as scrupulous as was practically possible; and he was quick to admonish any consular officer who did not provide them with all 'such assistance as might appear expedient and proper'. But when the supposedly offending government was Greek, he seemed so eager to support a claim that he hardly paused to consider its validity.

The first of these claims was made by the Scottish historian George Finlay, who accompanied Byron during the Greek war of independence. In 1830, when the fighting was almost over, Finlay bought a fine estate near Athens, for which he paid a pittance to a rapidly departing Turk; and since then he had been living on it, writing his seven-volume *History of Greece*. In 1836, however, under the provisions of a new law, King Otto appropriated part of the estate in order to create a large garden for the new palace which he had begun to build near by. Although the law provided that no compensation need be paid, Finlay insisted that he should be compensated anyway and claimed that the piece of land, which had cost him around £10, was now worth £1,500. The British Embassy and the Foreign Office took up his case, and Palmerston inherited it when he returned to office in 1846. He wrote his first demand soon afterwards, and the following year the Greek government offered to pay a fixed but much smaller sum to everyone who had been dispossessed in the building of the palace. All the Greeks who had lost land accepted it, but Finlay continued to demand his full £1,500, plus an unreasonable interest of fifteen per cent for every year since the land was taken, which effectively raised his claim to £3,750. So Palmerston simply went on pressing without questioning the claim, although he was no more successful on behalf of Finlay than he was on behalf of the more justified Rothschilds; and as time passed he added others to his list of lost causes.

The next claimant, and a much more worthy one, was an Ionian blacksmith who was arrested for robbery with violence in the Greek port of Patras in July 1846. He refused to confess, even after the Greek police had flogged him, twisted a piece of rope round his scrotum and jumped up and down on his chest; and in the absence of any evidence he was eventually released without charge. But the blacksmith was a British subject. Corfu, Cephalonia and the other Ionian islands had been ceded to Great Britain by the Russians in 1815; and along with cricket, brass bands and ginger beer, the protection of Her Majesty's Government was one of the few benefits of British rule that her reluctant subjects on the islands appreciated.

Palmerston had already insisted that a British consular observer be present to ensure a fair trial when a few Ionians were charged with felony in a Turkish court in Constantinople; and he had recently protested, although without much effect, when two Ionians were imprisoned without trial by the Russian army in Romania. It was therefore as a matter of course that he took up the blacksmith's case and energetically demanded that he be paid compensation, although it can hardly have been a disappointment to have another cause with which to torment King Otto's government.

The Greek government refused to pay anything to the blacksmith. The police in Patras insisted that they had not tortured him, and their story had been corroborated by several witnesses, including more than one doctor. But the doctors admitted to the British Consul in the port that the police had blackmailed them into committing perjury. As with Finlay, Palmerston kept pressing. He demanded £20 compensation, not only for the blacksmith but also for each of two other Ionians, who were flogged soon afterwards; then, with far less justification, he demanded the same sum for each of a group of fishermen whose boats had been stolen by bandits near the Albanian border, alleging on the basis of no more than rumour and instinct that the bandits had been put up to it by the local Greek governor.

Another claimant, and by far the least worthy, was a Jew called David Pacifico, whose house in Athens was ransacked and burned down at Easter 1847. It was the Athenian custom at Easter to burn Judas Iscariot in effigy, but this year Anselm de Rothschild had come to Athens to discuss a delicate business matter, and, in order to avoid any possible offence to an exasperated creditor, the King and his government had issued an order prohibiting any burning of effigies. During the celebrations, however, a large mob, emboldened by wine and egged on by the fourteen-year-old son of the Minister for War, decided to torment a real Jew instead. Since it was rumoured that Pacifico had persuaded the government to issue the ban in the first place, he was selected as the victim.

On the face of it Pacifico deserved nothing but sympathy, but he claimed afterwards that the value of his ruined house, together with all the fine furniture, art treasures and magnificent jewellery that he said had been stolen or destroyed in the outrage, came to an unbelievable total of £5,000. On top of that, he also claimed that the fire had burned a number of documents that were essential evidence in a case he was currently conducting, and that in consequence he would no longer be able to substantiate an otherwise irrefutable claim for over £26,000 against the Portuguese government. He soon discovered, however, that he would not be able to recover damages through the courts. Quite apart from the fact that none of the Athenian lawyers was prepared to risk representing him in a case in which one of the defendants was the son of the Minister for War, there was hardly a man among them who did not regard his claim as certainly excessive, probably fanciful and quite possibly fraudulent.

Since Pacifico had been born in Gibraltar, however, and since he had used this to obtain a British passport, he had a right to turn for help to the British government. It subsequently transpired that Pacifico, like his claim, was not all that he made himself out to be. His parents came from Spain, which may have been why he called himself 'Don Pacifico', and he had indeed been born in Gibraltar. But he had been brought up in Portugal and had become a naturalized Portuguese subject – a fact that he had omitted to mention when he obtained a passport from the British Embassy shortly after his arrival in Athens. In 1839 he had been appointed Portuguese Consul-General in Athens, but he had been dismissed a few years later for submitting a few obviously forged letters in support of a very large claim for expenses.

As yet unaware of all this, or at least unconcerned by it, Palmerston cheerfully added Pacifico's misfortune to his list of the Greek government's petty iniquities. He instructed the British attaché in Athens to demand that the government must settle Pacifico's claim in full, that it must pay an additional £500 in compensation for the fear and indignity suffered by his wife and children, who were manhandled in the attack, and that it must institute criminal proceedings against the perpetrators. But the Greek government replied reasonably enough that it was not its business to satisfy claims that should properly be made through the courts, and less reasonably that it could not now prosecute anyone because Pacifico had made his complaint to the British legation and not to the Greek police.

By May 1847 Palmerston had become so scornfully impatient that he wrote not only to the government of Greece but also to the government of Bavaria, where Otto's father was king, warning them that, if Finlay, Pacifico and the Ionians were not now compensated in full, he would have to use force to obtain satisfaction. He then sent a despatch to Munich, in which he revealed the real reason for his disdain in dangerously undiplomatic language, and instructed the Ambassador to read it to the Bavarian Prime Minister. He described the Greek Prime Minister as 'destitute of the acquirements, the knowledge or the parliamentary faculties which are necessary for a Constitutional Minister'; and he expressed his disappointment that 'a son of the wise and enlightened Sovereign of Constitutional Bavaria' should have acquired 'a fixed aversion to Constitutional Government'. 'Greece', he wrote, 'was not detached from Turkey and erected into a separate and independent state, merely for the personal Benefit and Advantage of a Younger Prince of the house of Bavaria.'

But when the threats and insults proved ineffective, Palmerston did not renew them, let alone make ready to use force. The following year, the 'Year of Revolutions', at the very moment when the British High Commissioner was preparing to endow the Ionian islands with constitutional government, the islanders rose in rebellion and demanded union with Greece. While the British garrisons on the islands were reinforced, additional ships were sent to patrol the straits between the islands and the mainland, which by chance gave rise to yet another cause for complaint. When a boat from HMS *Fantome* put in to Patras to take on water, the police arrested the midshipman in command and held him overnight. Palmerston demanded an apology. When the police refused, insisting that they did not at first know that the young man was an officer because he was not in uniform, and that he then lied about which ship he was off, Palmerston, as usual, continued to press, adding indignantly that they had compounded the offence by accusing a British officer of lying. But at a time when flogging Ionians had become the principal British weapon in the suppression of their rebellion, it would have been a little too obviously hypocritical to threaten force, let alone use it, in support of a separate series of demands which included compensation for flogged Ionians.

Towards the end of 1849, however, when the Ionians had been pacified and the emperors of Austria and Russia had withdrawn their demands for the extradition of revolutionaries from Turkey, there was a British fleet lying idle off the mouth of the Dardanelles. The temptation was too much for the weary Foreign Secretary. All too often his own demands had been frustrated because he had no practical way of bringing the forces at his disposal to bear. But this time the ships which had so successfully discouraged two great empires were near by and free to be used again to coerce one little kingdom. Without any further thought Palmerston matched his imperious words with deeds that were just as heavy-handed.

On 30 November he wrote to Admiral Parker instructing him to take the fleet to the harbour of Athens at Piraeus and await further orders from the new British Minister, Thomas Wyse, another charming, cultured Irish Radical, who happened also to be the long-estranged brother-in-law of Louis Napoleon. Three days later he wrote to Wyse instructing him to renew the demands for full compensation and interest on behalf of Finlay, Pacifico and the Ionians, and for an apology on behalf of the midshipman from *Fantome*. If the Greeks refused, he was to obtain payment in any way he saw fit, perhaps by landing marines and seizing Greek government property.

On 15 January 1850 Parker dropped anchor off Piraeus with fifteen ships of the line. Next day Wyse delivered a letter to the Greek Foreign

Minister demanding full payment within twenty-four hours. The Foreign Minister asked for more time and suggested that they should invite a third party to arbitrate, but Wyse refused, and twenty-four hours later Parker seized a Greek warship. When even this produced no result, Wyse ordered Parker to blockade Piraeus and prevent any Greek ships from entering or leaving. By the end of the month, with still no effect, they had blockaded every Greek port and added several merchantmen to their tally of ships.

The Greek people and the opposition in their powerless parliament were delighted to see somebody standing up to King Otto, but everyone else was furious: the Queen, Prince Albert, the Tories, most of the Whigs, the governments of all other nations, the vociferous diplomatic representatives of those nations at the courts in London and in Athens, and of course *The Times*, which accused Palmerston of arousing 'the indignation of the civilized world'. As the co-guarantors of Greek debts, the French and the Russians professed themselves to be particularly incensed by his attempts to play debt collector on his own, although in this case he could at least argue that he was only collecting debts owed to British subjects. But in the face of so much general opposition he had no choice but to give in to the wishes of his indignant and apprehensive Cabinet. He agreed to accept French mediation and negotiate with the Greek Ambassador; and he wrote to Wyse instructing him to suspend the blockades and enter into similar negotiations. So while Drouyn de Lhuys, who was now the French Ambassador in London, was mediating between the Greek Ambassador and the British Foreign Secretary, identical but separate negotiations were taking place in Athens, with the French envoy there, Baron Gros, mediating between the British envoy and the Greek Foreign Minister.

On 19 April Palmerston and the two ambassadors in London reached an agreement. The midshipman was to receive an apology, Finlay and the Ionians were to be paid all that was claimed for them, Pacifico was to get £8,500 for his house and possessions, and the claim for his lost documents was to be referred to three arbitrators, one from each country, who would meet in Lisbon and examine what was left of the evidence. Drouyn de Lhuys wrote at once to Gros, who could not have been more relieved. He had become so exasperated with Wyse's intransigence that he had given up acting as mediator, and the despatch arrived just as Wyse was about to reimpose the blockades. But Palmerston had not sent a despatch to Wyse, and it was several days before he did. In the absence of any instructions Wyse refused to change his orders and the ports were closed again to Greek shipping.

After only two days of blockade, however, the Greeks, who till then had been so resolute in their refusals, suddenly agreed to everything that Wyse had demanded. The midshipman would receive his apology, Finlay and the Ionians would be paid in full, Pacifico would be paid £6,400 for the loss of his house and possessions – rather less than Palmerston had obtained – and until the true value of his frustrated claim against the Portuguese government could be assessed, £5,000 worth of securities would be deposited with Wyse. When Palmerston's despatch arrived at last, there was no need to make any changes: one of Palmerston's specific instructions was that any agreement that had already been reached in Athens should take precedence over the agreement in London. Wyse might have been a bit more cautious and courteous in enforcing it, however, if he had known that the Greeks' unexpected capitulation had been made only on the advice of the Russians, who persuaded them that it would be better for both of them if they let it look as though the British navy had bullied them into submission.

Louis Napoleon felt betrayed. He was convinced that he had been the victim of an intentional deception. His was the only government that had tried to help, but its impartial and well-intentioned mediation in London had only been used as a cover to distract attention while Palmerston imposed his will in Athens; and to add insult to injury, the agent of Palmerston's treachery had been the wretched Irishman who abandoned his sister. It was to no avail that Palmerston pointed out that the terms agreed in Athens were better for Greece than those that had been agreed in London. The French recalled their Ambassador to the Court of St James. The Russians threatened to do the same. Queen Victoria was convinced that her Foreign Secretary had brought Britain to the brink of war. When the Tories asked why the French Ambassador had gone home, Palmerston told them that he had gone to be the personal medium of communication between the two governments, adding misleading the House of Commons to their growing list of charges against him.

On 17 June the House of Lords debated a motion to censure the injustice and severity of the government's negotiations with Greece. It was proposed by Lord Stanley and forcefully supported by Aberdeen and Brougham, all of whom, it was said, had been put up to it in the first place by Guizot and Princess Lieven and had been further encouraged by a few intentionally indiscreet courtiers, who had let it be known that they had the approval of the Queen. By 169 votes to 132, a majority that, although little more than twelve per cent, was described by *The Times* as 'overwhelming', their Lordships decided that Finlay's demands were outrageous, that all the Ionians were clearly thieves and that the unfortunate midshipman, who may well have lied about his ship, had not suffered enough in any event to warrant a government apology. As for Pacifico, it was shameful that a British government should be so overbearing on behalf of such an obvious rogue.

On 19 June Palmerston gave in on the one term of the Athens agreement that was harsher than the terms agreed in London. He informed the French that the securities on deposit with Wyse would be returned to the Greek government and that Pacifico's claim would be referred, as agreed, to three arbitrators in Lisbon – a concession that eventually resulted in his being awarded a mere £150 for the alleged loss of his documents. Next day Disraeli asked in the House of Commons if the government intended to resign. But Russell's notoriously fragile resolve had been stiffened by his resentment of what he saw as shabby tactics. The Tories had defeated the government only on home ground in the House of Lords, and then only on the very narrow issue of Palmerston's questionable conduct towards Greece. The result might be very different if a larger issue were to be debated in the House of Commons, where Palmerston could rely on the enthusiasm of the Radicals and the self-interested, if grudging, support of other Whigs, and where the government could hope for at least a few votes from the Peelites, many of whom feared that its fall might bring in a protectionist administration, and some of whom even suspected that Palmerston had enough protectionist sympathies to cross the house if that happened.

Before the Tories launched their attack, Russell would have done anything to be rid of Palmerston if he thought he could do it without loss of office. He had just rejected Palmerston's conscientious offer of resignation and politely refused another demand for his dismissal from the Queen, but only because he was afraid that the departure of the most popular, and most populist, member of his government would lead to its defeat in the Commons at the hands of the Radicals and then to a trouncing in the country at the hands of the electorate. Now, however, when the Tories were trying to use Palmerston's blunder to bring down the government with him, Russell was determined that the government must stand with him instead. In answer to Disraeli he told the House that he would ask it for a vote of confidence and stand or fall by the result.

The well-planned debate began five days later, on 24 June, when the 'independent' Radical and founder member of the Reform Club John Roebuck QC proposed 'that the principles on which the foreign policy of of Her Majesty's Government have been regulated have been such as were calculated to maintain the honour and dignity of this country'. After Roebuck had delivered his own invective against what Palmerston later described as 'the petulant and factious and foolish vote of the House of Lords', a few Tories attacked and a few Whigs defended, and then, at a quarter to ten the following evening, Palmerston rose. Lady Palmerston, who sat in the Ladies' Gallery throughout the debate, recorded afterwards that he was on his feet for four hours and fifty minutes. Drawn from over 2,000 volumes of Foreign Office papers, it was one of the best of his few great speeches.

Palmerston began by condemning the Tories for attempting to seize 'the citadel of office' by trivializing the issues, mocking the victims and misrepresenting the principles on which government policy was based. 'The resolution of the House of Lords', he said,

> involves the future as well as the past ... The country is told that British subjects in foreign lands are entitled to nothing but the protection of the laws and the tribunals of the land in which they happen to reside. The country is told that British subjects abroad must not look to their own country for protection ...

Now I deny that proposition, and I say it is a doctrine on which
no British Minister ever yet has acted, and on which the people
of England never will suffer any British Minister to act.

From his general statement of principle Palmerston moved straight
to a particular examination of his negotiations on behalf of Pacifico and
the other claimants in Greece. He made no attempt to ignore them or
hide them behind the huge sweep of foreign policy that he was about to
make. Instead he made them the first example of his principle. Where
Roebuck had already quoted Shakespeare to condemn the anti-Semitism
that had coloured some of the criticisms in the House of Lords – 'Hath
not a Jew eyes?' – Palmerston added his own scorn for any reference
to Pacifico's character. 'The rights of a man depend on the merits of a
particular case; and it is an abuse of argument to say that you are not to
give redress to a man because in some former transaction he may have
done something which is questionable.'

After following with an attack on the iniquities of the Greek government he moved on to a long examination of his entire foreign policy,
starting in Portugal and working his way round through 'the sunny plains
of Castille', 'the gay vineyards of France', 'the mountains of Switzerland',
over 'the rugged Alps' to 'the smiling plains of Lombardy' and then on
down to Sicily and across to Turkey. He dismissed the overall criticisms
of his opponents with the resignation of a martyr. 'It has always been the
fate of advocates of temperate reform and of constitutional improvement
to be run at as the fomenters of revolution.' And when the charges were
fanciful, such as the suggestion that it was his personal animosity that
had led to the downfall of Guizot and Louis-Philippe, he demolished
them with light-hearted mockery. 'What will the French nation say when
they hear this? They are a high-minded and high-spirited nation, full of
a sense of their own dignity and honour – what will they say when they
hear it stated that it was in the power of a British Minister to overthrow
their Government and their Monarchy?'

In conclusion he returned to general principles. So far, although
obviously well rehearsed, his speech had been read from notes. But from
here on it had been learned by heart.

I do not complain of the conduct of those who have made these matters the means of attack upon Her Majesty's Ministers ... It is a noble thing to be allowed to guide the policy and to influence the destiny of such a country; and if ever it was an object of honourable ambition, more than ever must it be so at the moment at which I am speaking ... While in almost every country of Europe the conflict of civil war has deluged the land with blood, from the Atlantic to the Black Sea, from the Baltic to the Mediterranean, this country has presented a spectacle honourable to the people of England, and worthy of the admiration of mankind. We have shown that liberty is compatible with order; that individual freedom is reconcilable with obedience to the law ... I contend that we have not in our foreign policy done anything to forfeit the confidence of the country. We may not, perhaps, in this matter or in that, have acted precisely up to the opinions of one person or of another; and hard indeed it is, as we all know by our individual and private experience, to find any number of men agreeing entirely in any matter on which they may not be equally possessed of the details of the facts ... But, making allowances for those differences of opinion which may fairly and honourably arise among those who concur in general views, I maintain that the principles which can be traced through all our foreign transactions, as the guiding rule and directing spirit of our proceedings, are such as deserve approbation.

And then he challenged the house to vote on the motion, to decide

whether the principles on which the foreign policy of Her Majesty's Government has been conducted, and the sense of duty which has led us to think ourselves bound to afford protection to our fellow subjects abroad, are proper and fitting guides for those who are charged with the government of England; and whether, as the Roman, in days of old, held himself free from indignity, when he could say 'Civis romanus sum'; so also a British subject, in whatever land he may be, shall feel confident that the watchful eye and the strong arm of England will protect him against injustice and wrong.

When Palmerston sat down, the House, which according to Lady Palmerston had been 'attentive and breathless' throughout, erupted in long, enthusiastic cheering. Eventually the debate continued, others had their say; and when at last the House divided, the motion was carried by 310 votes to 264, a majority of forty-six.

Two days later, in a letter to Normanby, Palmerston wrote, 'I scarcely ever remember a debate which, as a display of intellect, oratory, and high and dignified feeling, was more honourable to the House of Commons.' He described Russell's speech as 'admirable and first-rate' and he paid equal and generous tribute to some of the opposition. 'Gladstone's was also a first-rate performance, and Peel and Disraeli both spoke with great judgement and talent with reference to their respective positions.' But Peel had already paid generous tribute to Palmerston. It was his last appearance in the House of Commons: he was to suffer the fatal fall from his horse next day on Constitution Hill. Like so many, he had come to carp, and carp he did, pointing out a little pettily that the return of securities to the Greek government was being claimed by the French as a diplomatic triumph. But, like so many, he stayed to cheer. The last words the great Tory statesman ever said to the House of Commons were, 'We are all proud of the man who delivered that most able and temperate speech.'

But the speech was only a personal triumph for Palmerston. It did not influence the vote. No matter how many hearts he had moved, he had not won many minds, or at least not in the House of Commons. The government's majority, which at eight per cent was proportionately a third less than the majority by which it had been defeated in the Lords, was exactly what Russell had gambled it would be. As Palmerston admitted to Normanby, 'We had about the majority which we had reckoned upon; our calculation fluctuated between forty and fifty.'

It was only in the days that followed that the full extent of Palmerston's achievement became evident. As usual he circulated copies of his speech, and every leading newspaper, including *The Times*, printed it in full. The tone of their accompanying editorial made little difference; Palmerston's words were all that mattered to their readers. Now the British public knew more about what he stood for, and they liked it. For some time they had accepted and admired the image he presented to them. They saw him as the epitome of a British ideal, the sportsman-like champion of freedom and fair play for the underdog. Now they saw him as their own champion as well: and they were to see him as that for the rest of his life.

A dinner was held in his honour at the Reform Club; and there was another at the House of Commons, at which a hundred Radicals presented Lady Palmerston with a hurridly completed work by John Partridge, Queen Victoria's favourite portrait painter, depicting her husband standing beside his cluttered French desk with a bust of Canning in the shadows behind him. Several MPs who had voted against him expressed the fear that it would cost them their seats. One of his opponents, Grey, acknowledged that they had made him 'the most popular man in England'; and a tragic coincidence had also made him by far the most influential statesman. Peel's death had removed his only possible rival. There were great elder statesmen, such as Wellington, in Westminster, and there were rising stars such as Gladstone and Disraeli, but on both front benches in either House there was now nobody who could match the people's champion. Palmerston was actually underestimating his position when he boasted to his brother, 'Instead of expelling and overthrowing me with disgrace, as they intended and hoped to do, they have rendered me for the present the most popular Minister that for a very long course of time has held my office.'

Lord Clarendon, who was then Lord-Lieutenant of Ireland and was eager to exchange jobs with Palmerston, found his 'physical and mental power almost incredible in a man of his age', and reflected the view of almost everyone when he predicted that his speech would 'place him on a pinnacle of popularity at home, whatever it may do abroad, and completely settle the question about which I never had a doubt, that no change at the F.O. is possible, and that Lord John must either go on with him or go out with him'. It was a bitter truth which only Queen Victoria and Prince Albert seemed unable to accept. According to her ladies-in-waiting, the Queen almost wept with fury at the news of Palmerston's success; and Prince Albert wrote in despair to his brother Duke Ernest, 'You and all Europe certainly feel with us in the unhappy combinations of circumstances that granted our immoral one for foreign affairs such a triumph in the Commons.'

Ten days after the debate Prince Albert sent a memorandum to Russell, emphasizing that 'the Queen has no more confidence in Lord P. than she had before' and imploring him to take over 'the management of the Foreign Department' himself. But, in a flash of uncharacteristically shrewd political perception, he added that, since 'the lamentable death of Sir R. Peel', it was vital that Russell remain in the Commons. Russell did not agree. He would consent to take over from Palmerston, and thereby risk the downfall of his administration, only if he could watch what happened next from the safety of the House of Lords.

The response was a summons to Buckingham Palace. On 11 July, at the end of a long meeting, in which neither side gave an inch, Prince Albert 'took the opportunity of seeing Lord John alone' and swore him to secrecy on a discussion that has failed to remain secret only because the Prince included a record of it in his memorandum of the meeting. He confided to Russell that he and the Queen were afraid that, if Palmerston were left alone to dominate the Commons, he might one day become Prime Minister; and he then resorted to a tactic that descredited nobody so much as himself. He recounted the story of the night when Mrs Brand awoke to find Palmerston in her bedchamber. 'How could the Queen consent to take a man as her chief adviser and confidential counsellor in all matters of State, religion, society, Court, etc. etc ... who while a guest under her roof at Windsor Castle had committed a brutal attack upon one of her ladies?'

According to Prince Albert, 'Lord John said that it was very bad and made it absolutely necessary to take care to protect the Queen from Lord P.'s being thrust upon her as Prime Minister.' But he was still not moved to take any immediate action. That evening he wrote to the Prince. 'I have not altered my opinion that the retirement of Lord

Palmerston from the ministry would make it impossible for me to hold my present position.'

The Queen did not give up. Two weeks later she sent Russell a passionate and paranoid diatribe. She reproached her government for agreeing to get rid of Lord Palmerston 'each time that we were in a difficulty' and then doing nothing 'as soon as these difficulties were got over'; she insisted that there was 'no chance of Lord Palmerston reforming himself in his sixty-seventh year'; and as an example of his inclination to expose his country to danger 'without reference to his colleagues or sovereign', she warned that in her opinion he was at that moment 'secretly planning an armed Russian intervention in Schleswig'.

After that the relationship between the Court and the Prime Minister deteriorated so much that both parties were relieved when Russell's brother the Duke of Bedford, who was regarded as a friend by the Queen and Prince Albert, attempted to mediate. His only achievement was to convince the royal couple that his brother could not get rid of Palmerston without losing office himself, but this did at least induce them to change tactics. They modified a memorandum that Stockmar had drawn up a few months earlier and sent it to Russell, asking him to show it to Palmerston. In essence the memorandum asserted that the Queen had the undeniable right to approve all a minister's policies and despatches in advance, and warned that in future, if any despatches were sent out without her approval, or altered after her approval, she would exercise 'her Constitutional right of dismissing that Minister'.

If the Queen hoped that her humiliating demands would induce Palmerston to resign, she was to be disappointed. After vindicating himself so triumphantly in the Commons, he did not believe that anyone would see any justification for it. Besides, as he wrote later in a letter to Lansdowne, with what may have looked like humbug, to have resigned in response to an ultimatum from the Queen would have been to reveal that she had involved herself in politics and thereby expose her to public criticism. Instead he asked Russell to provide him with two more clerks, so that he could make copies of his despatches more quickly for the Queen, and he wrote to Prince Albert asking for a an interview.

They met on 14 August. According to the Prince's inevitable record of the meeting, Palmerston pleaded 'with tears in his eyes'. He deeply regretted that he had offended the Queen. If he had ever failed to inform her of everything that was being done and said, it was only because he had been delayed from doing so by the size and quantity of his responsibilities, and by his need to deal with them as quickly as possible. The meeting was interrupted before the sympathetic Prince could say everything that he wanted to say in reply, but in the weeks that followed it did indeed look as though the 'old dog' – who was coming to the end of his sixty-fifth year, not his sixty-seventh – was capable of learning 'new tricks'. At the beginning of September the Prince reported to Russell that Palmerston was conscientiously sending all despatches to the Queen and attentively explaining everything that he was doing. But then, in the same month, the obnoxious General Haynau, who was known even in Austria as 'General Hyena', came to London on a private visit.

The first expedition on Haynau's itinerary was a trip to Southwark to inspect the splendid modern riverside brewery of Barclay, Perkins & Co., which had become a popular attraction with visitors to London. As it turned out, however, it was also his only expedition. The Austrian government later suggested that the misfortune that befell him there had probably been organized by an Austrian exile, Dr Trencke, who had once been the editor of a Liberal newspaper in Vienna and who was now working as a clerk in the brewery. But, as Palmerston pointed out, Haynau was so universally despised, and so easily identified by his huge blond moustaches, that what happened would almost certainly have happened anyway.

As soon as the draymen in the brewery saw Haynau, they yelled 'Down with the Austrian Butcher', leaped on him, beat him with brooms, tore his coat, threw him to the ground and then used his famous moustaches as handles with which to haul him through the gutter. He was only saved from more or worse because he and his companions managed to scramble into a nearby tavern, from which they were eventually rescued by the river police.

On receiving a report of the incident, the Queen told Palmerston that in her view 'it would be proper if a draft were written to the Austrian government expressive of the deep regret of this government at the brutal outrage on one of the Emperor's distinguished generals and subjects'. Palmerston agreed and drafted an appropriate despatch, although he ended it with a paragraph in which he pointed out bluntly that a man with Haynau's reputation should have had more sense than to expose himself to British public opinion. He knew that Metternich had warned Haynau that something like this was bound to happen if he came to England, and that on his arrival, the Austrian envoy in London, Baron Koller, had advised him to cut off his moustaches; and he was rightly convinced in consequence that nobody had much sympathy for the general. When Schwarzenberg responded to his despatch by instructing Koller to demand that the draymen be prosecuted, Pamerston confidently assured his colleagues that he was only making the minimum necessary gesture to uphold the dignity of the Austrian army; and Koller, whom Palmerston found 'very reasonable', was easily persuaded that a prosecution would be counter-productive, 'because the defence of the accused would necessarily be a minute recapitulation of all the barbarities committed by Haynau in Italy and Hungary, and that would be more injurious to him and to Austria than any verdict obtained against the draymen could be satisfactory'.

The incident was insignificant, and most people agreed that it was no more than the general deserved. When Palmerston very properly reported his communications with Koller to the Home Secretary, Sir George Grey, he made no secret of his own flippant feelings on the subject. His only criticism was that 'the draymen were wrong in the particular course they adopted. Instead of striking him, which, however, by Koller's account, they did not do much, they ought to have tossed him in a blanket, rolled him in the kennel, and then sent him home in a cab, paying his fare to the hotel.'

Unfortunately, however, the royal family had left for Balmoral just after the Queen instructed Palmerston to write to the Austrian government. It was the end of the month before she saw her copy of the despatch, long after it had been sent; and when she saw the last paragraph she was as furious as she had ever been. Despite the fact that the Austrians had responded, she demanded that Palmerston send another despatch with the 'very objectionable' closing paragraph deleted. In reply, Palmerston told Russell that such a despatch would have to be signed by another Foreign Secretary; and he then wrote a long explanatory memorandum for the Queen, in which he insisted that 'the people of this country are remarkable for their hospitable reception of foreigners' and 'assured' her that the 'feelings of just and honourable indignation' that were demonstrated in this case were not 'confined to England'. It was only on second thoughts that he decided the incident was too trivial to merit a resignation and agreed to sent another, royally approved despatch. But the little lull in the long battle was over. As the Queen told her Prime Minister at his next audience, the episode clearly demonstrated that Palmerston had not changed his ways, although she was at least pleased to see that the Prime Minister was now able to control him.

In the course of the winter, despite Palmerston's resentful opposition, the Queen managed to persuade Russell to replace some of the ambassadors and other envoys whose attitudes were too close to Palmerston's; and in February fate handed her what looked like her next chance to be rid of him. When the Pope announced that, for the first time since the reign of Mary Tudor, he intended to appoint an Archbishop of Westminster and a hierarchy of Roman Catholic bishops throughout England, Russell climbed onto the bandwagon of anti-Catholic hysteria, published an open letter denouncing 'Papal aggression' and introduced a meaningless Ecclesiastical Titles Act, which prohibited the Roman Catholic bishops from using territorial titles that were the same as any of the Anglican dioceses. In retribution the Irish and other Radicals voted with the Tories and defeated the government on its next budget. Russell resigned, but it was impossible to find a coalition to replace him. Nobody was prepared to defy the Queen by including Palmerston in his Cabinet, and yet everyone agreed that the House of Commons, let alone the country, would be unmanageable without him.

After only ten days Russell was back in office – and so were the rest of his Cabinet, including Palmerston. Russell had persuaded the Queen that it would look as though she had intervened personally if Palmerston were to be omitted without reason, and he had promised her that he would dismiss him in a reshuffle during the Easter recess. But Easter came and went, Palmerston stayed at the Foreign Office and Russell continued to plead that, much as he would like to do so, he could not govern without him.

The summer went by warily but without incident, and the royal pique was diverted for a while by the Queen's happy satisfaction at the success of Prince Albert's Great Exhibition in Crystal Palace in Hyde Park. It was an enterprise about which Palmerston appears to have had reservations. Like everyone else he congratulated the Queen on the achievement, but in a letter to Normanby he wrote, 'the building itself is far more worth seeing than anything in it'.

The next round of royal indignation did not come until October; and when it came, the cause was another visitor: Louis Kossuth, who stopped off in England on his way from Turkey to the United States. Travelling in an American frigate, which had been sent to protect him from the serious threat of being kidnapped in the Mediterranean by the Austrian navy, he landed at Southampton and was welcomed with a civic banquet, at which he aroused passionate cheering with a speech about the iniquities of the Austrian government. As he progressed slowly towards London, exciting audiences in every town with similarly inflammatory speeches, the *Morning Post* announced that he intended to call on Palmerston and thank him for all that he had done to help the Polish and Hungarian revolutionary refugees.

Desperate to avoid any further insults to two emperors with whom her kingdom was at peace, the anxious Queen 'demanded' that Palmerston should not receive Kossuth. Her order was passed on by Russell in a message that was sent by hand to Carlton Gardens. Since Russell insisted on an immediate response, Palmerston scribbled a hurried, ungrammatical note while the messenger waited. 'I do not choose to be dictated to as to who I may or may not receive in my own house.' The enigmatic answer left both Court and Cabinet wondering. 'On my life,' wrote Prince Albert, 'he'll see him yet, or he'll do something still worse.' And worse it was; or at least, that was the way it was made to look.

On 5 November a large deputation of Radicals from two of their traditional strongholds, the boroughs of Finsbury and Islington, called on Palmerston to present him with a token of their respect and gratitude for the support he had given to Kossuth and the other European revolutionaries. In the course of the formalities two or three of the Radicals made speeches, in which they praised Palmerston as the champion of liberty, condemned the repressive governments of Austria and Russia and, quoting Kossuth, described their emperors as 'odious and detestable assassins'. In reply, Palmerston thanked them for their generous compliments and, after making it clear that he could not possibly share in their abuse of foreign sovereigns, delivered a few general observations on foreign policy, in which he famously alluded to an earlier remark about holding salts to a lady's nose by describing his activities in support of the refugees as 'a good deal of judicious bottle-holding'. Unknown to Palmerston, however, there was a freelance journalist in the deputation. Next day it was revealed that the journalist had sold the story to most of the newspapers and had embellished it by putting the most inflammatory words of the Radicals into the mouth of the Foreign Secretary.

When Russell confronted him, Palmerston pleaded in vain that the most offensive remarks were not his. In the eyes of the Court and the Cabinet, receiving the deputation at all was an even greater insult to the Austrians than it would have been if he had received Kossuth. But their demands for his dismissal were as much in vain as his pleadings. The reports in the newspapers had won him so much new acclaim that, as before, his dismissal would undoubtedly have led to the immediate downfall of the government.

Palmerston's popularity with the Radicals and the British public was still an unassailable defence – but now only just. Russell's government was finding it increasingly difficult to win a majority in the House of Commons. If most of the Peelites on the opposition benches voted with the Protectionists against them, the Whigs could only be sure of success if they could rely on all the Radicals and Irish Nationalists, but Russell's anti-Catholic outburst had permanently alienated the Irish Nationalists. Sooner rather than later they were going to suffer another defeat; and when that happened, unlike the last time, the traditional Whigs and the Peelites were planning to have a viable alternative waiting. They had learned from their mistakes. If they could only stick together and cement their relationship by putting a few Peelites in the Cabinet, and if, for safety's sake, they could woo a few of the less idealistic Radicals and one or two of the more flexible Protectionists, they might just command enough numbers to create a coalition government.

Russell was no longer daunted by the prospect of his defeat, and nor were the Queen and Prince Albert, who were encouraging the architects of the coalition. But if Russell wanted to be part of that coalition, and perhaps even lead it, he was going to have to dissociate himself from Palmerston, preferably before his government fell; and to do that in a way that would not bring down the government simultaneously, he was going to have to find a pretext that would not earn Palmerston the immediate support of the Radicals. And as it happened, within a few days, fate stepped in again and presented him with just such an opportunity.

For a while Palmerston and Normanby had been watching what was happening in France with contending optimism and anxiety. Not for the first time, the assembly was divided. At least half the delegates had long since lost their enthusiasm for Louis Napoleon. Since the idealistic constitution of 1848 had completely separated the powers of the legislature and the executive, it was still possible for the assembly to be as obstructive to the President as it had previously been to the King. France was becoming ungovernable again, and there was nothing legal that Louis Napoleon could do about it. When he proposed a few changes to the constitution, including one that extended his own term of office, the assembly simply rejected them.

Outside the assembly, however, Louis Napoleon had made sure that he was much more powerful. By helping to restore the Pope and providing him with a permanent garrison, he had earned the suport of the clergy, which brought with it the support of all the rural labourers and smallholders, who still made up the majority of the French population. More importantly, by promoting grateful sympathizers to all the high levels of command, he had also secured complete control of the army. Although the support of the rural masses was no longer any use at the polls, because the assembly had just made its own modification to the constitution and introduced property qualifications which excluded the working classes from the franchise, it did at least mean that they were unlikely to interfere too much if he made any use of the army; and he had begun to hint that that was what he might now have to do. As he explained in confidence to almost every ambassador, his agents had warned him that he was in danger of being deposed. Since the recent death of the discredited King Louis-Philippe in exile at Claremont, the supporters of the House of Orleans had apparently been plotting to restore the monarchy and put another member of his family on the throne.

On the basis of all this evidence both Palmerston and Normanby agreed that Louis Napoleon was probably about to attempt a *coup d'état* of his own. But they totally and testily disagreed as to what the outcome was likely to be, and as to what they wanted it to be. Palmerston, who was inclined to believe the story about an Orleanist plot, felt that a pre-emptive coup, supported by the entire French army, was bound to be successful, and that on balance this would be for the best. He mistrusted the French, he despised Louis Napoleon and he regarded their current constitution as unworkable 'childish nonsense'. But France was the one Power that was at least occasionally capable of acting in unison with Great Britain. There was nothing to be gained from seeing her reduced to 'disastrous civil strife', which was what he was sure would happen if the divided parties in the assembly were to win. It seemed to him 'better for the interests of France and, through them, for the interests of Europe, that the power of the President should prevail, inasmuch as the continuance of his authority might afford a prospect of the maintenance of social order in France'.

Normanby on the other hand felt that the people would rise in support of the assembly, and that this would either bring a just victory for constitutional government or else leave the way open for the Orleanists, for whom his sympathies were inappropriately obvious. As Palmerston had begun to recognize, the pompous Constantine Henry Phipps, first Marquess of Normanby, had few of the qualities necessary for a successful diplomat. Although Palmerston tried to establish a cordial relationship with him and wrote frank and friendly private letters to him, he failed to break through his defensive barrier of trivial self-importance. Normanby took it as a personal affront that Palmerston disagreed with him, and he resented the fact that the Foreign Secretary paid little attention to his despatches and was obviously much more influenced by the published reports and private letters of Algernon Borthwick, the son of his friend Peter Borthwick, editor of the *Morning Post*, who represented his father's newspaper in Paris.

It was therefore galling for Normanby when Palmerston and his young adviser were proved right. On 2 December Louis Napoleon carried out a successful *coup d'état*. In the early hours of the morning the army arrested leading members of the assembly and took over all the strategic positions in Paris. Although there was strong but eventually unsuccessful resistance in the south, the resistance in the capital was soon and mercilessly crushed. When a few leading Republicans, including Victor Hugo, attempted to set up barricades, the working people simply stayed at home and left the bourgeois to fight out the future of France among themselves.

The Prince-President dismissed the assembly and abolished the constitution. He announced that instead he proposed to introduce a constitution similar to the one his uncle had introduced in 1799. The assembly was to be a debating chamber. In future ministers would be directly responsible, not to the assembly but to the President, who would be elected for a term of ten years. Universal male franchise was to be restored and within two weeks a referendum would be held, in which the electorate would be invited to approve or reject the new proposals.

Normanby asked for instructions, and on 6 December he received a despatch from Palmerston. 'I am commanded by Her Majesty to instruct your Excellency to make no change in your relations with the French Government.' Next day, Palmerston received an indignant despatch from Normanby. On receipt of his instructions he had called to pass them on to the French Foreign Minister, the Marquis de Turgot. When he apologized for the delay, he was told that it was of no consequence. Turgot had already received a despatch from the French Ambassador in London, Count Walewski, the illegitimate offspring of one of the Emperor Napoleon's most famous liaisons and as such the cousin of the President. According to Walewski, wrote Normanby, 'your lordship had expressed to him your entire approbation of the act of the President'; and he then added that he thought this worth mentioning because

Walewski's despatch had been read to other ambassadors 'in order to show the decided opinion which England had pronounced'.

Palmerston's next despatch made no mention of this. Instead he admonished Normanby for writing reports that paid too much attention to past events and not enough to the present crisis; and he mocked him flippantly for devoting so much space to complaints about the damage done by musket fire to the ceiling of the British café known as the 'club house'. After Normanby's interview with Turgot, however, and again after the receipt of this last despatch, Lady Normanby gave vent to her rage over Palmerston's impertinence, mockery and general conduct in long letters to her husband's brother Colonel Sir Charles Phipps, who just happened to be Keeper of Her Majesty's Privy Purse and Treasurer of the Household to Prince Albert. As Lady Normanby intended, her brother-in-law passed on the contents of her letters to his employers. If Queen Victoria had not noticed the reference to Palmerston's conversation with Walewski in Normanby's earlier despatch, she certainly noticed it now; and she made full use of it.

The Queen wrote to Russell demanding Palmerston's dismissal. He had congratulated the French President on his *coup d'état* without the authority of the Cabinet or his sovereign. For the first time, instead of confronting Palmerston face to face, Russell wrote to him from Woburn, where he and all the other Russells were gathering for Christmas. Five years of 'acting as umpire between Windsor and Broadlands' had drained his patience 'to the last drop'. Passing on the Queen's concerns, he asked the Foreign Secretary to provide both her and him with a full explanation.

After a delay of several days owing, it was said, to pressure of work, Palmerston, who was still in London, responded at length in terms that Russell must already have understood. The successful coup was probably in the best interest of France; and it was certainly in Britain's best interest to remain on good terms with the man who was now likely to be ruling France for some time to come.

As for the charge that he had acted beyond his authority in congratulating the French President, this was not something Palmerston took too seriously. It was common practice for ministers and diplomats to express personal opinions to each other in 'unofficial conversation', and it was accepted that such opinions were intended to be treated as confidential. If it had not been so, it would hardly have been possible to conduct affairs of state between nations. Walewski had been wrong to pass on Palmerston's remark in a formal despatch; and it was also wrong of him to exaggerate what had only been an expression of goodwill. But Palmerston made no apology for saying what he said. After all, he was not the only one to have done it. Earl Grey had done it; Granville had done it; even Russell had done it, and he had done it when he and Walewski were Palmerston's guests at Carlton Gardens.

As part of his explanation, however, Palmerston enclosed a copy of a despatch he had sent to Normanby on 16 December. Having received no satisfactory response to his indignant despatch of 6 December, Normanby had belatedly and mischievously reproached Palmerston for subjecting him to 'misrepresentation and suspicion' by sending him instructions that were contradicted by what he was saying to the French Ambassador in London. In reply, Palmerston had denied that there was any such contradiction and, for His Excellency's interest, had added his 'own opinion on the change which has taken place in France'. There was nothing else in the despatch. It contained no further instructions. Nevertheless it was a despatch. And when Russell saw it, he realized that neither he nor the Queen had seen it before.

The discovery was a great relief to Russell. Expressing approval of a would-be dictator who had just overturned a democracy was certainly not going to earn Palmerston any support among the Radicals. But it was unlikely to earn him much opposition from the other members of the House of Commons, most of whom agreed with him and many of whom understood the circumstances in which his remark had been made. In consequence Russell had been concerned that this in itself was not enough to justify Palmerston's dismissal. Now, however, there was another charge. Palmerston had slipped up. He had promised to show drafts of all his despatches to the Prime Minister and the Queen before they were sent; he had accepted that the Queen would dismiss him if he did not; and he had just accidentally acknowledged that, in this case at least, he had not kept his word.

On 19 December Russell wrote to Palmerston to tell him he had no choice but to 'ask Her Majesty to appoint a successor to you at the Foreign Office'. Next day, to soften the blow, he offered him the Lord-Lieutenancy of Ireland, which carried with it an inadvertent hint as to who his successor was to be. Palmerston declined the appointment politely, although he pointed out that, since the office was one that required 'prudence and decorum', the offer by implication refuted the 'charge of violations of prudence and decorum' which had been one of the purported reasons for removing him from the Foreign Office.

On 20 December Queen Victoria and Prince Albert left Osborne and travelled up through Hampshire on the train to spend Christmas at Windsor, where they 'found a box from Lord John containing great and most unexpected news'. At the same time, and on the same line, the Palmerstons went down as planned to spend Christmas at Broadlands.

On their first night there Lady Palmerston did not sleep. It looked as though her husband's career was over. As Disraeli put it, 'there was a Palmerston'. On 22 December charming young Granville – the Queen's choice – took over at the Foreign Office, and soon afterwards he recalled Normanby from the Paris embassy. In the courts of Russia, Austria, Prussia and many of the German principalities, Christmas was as merry as it was at Windsor. In keeping with Viennese tradition, Schwarzenberg gave a splendid ball to celebrate the momentous news, for which he presumed to claim some of the credit. But not quite everyone felt that way. When the news reached Madrid, the Ambassador, Lord Howden, resigned immediately, 'as the retirement of Lord Palmerston either is, or most certainly will be believed to be, a direct concession to the reactionary spirit which is riding rough shod over the world'. And of course the people of England, already uncomprehendingly frightened by the prospect of another Napoleon in control of France, were suspicious and resentful. Their mood was well captured by the Radical *Reynolds' Weekly*, which added yet another ballad to the mass of inept doggerel for which there was such a vogue in the middle of the nineteenth century. It began:

Oh! Have you heard the news of late,
The Whigs are in a cranky state,
And they'll find out when it's too late,
They're done for by their snarling;
For small Lord John has been and gone
And turned adrift Lord Palmerston,
Amongst the lot the only don
Who didn't take care of number one;
Out spoke Home Secretary Grey,
I wish old Palmy were away,
Aye, turn him out they all did say,
For he's the people's darling.

And it went on presciently:

When'er doth meet the Parliament,
The Whig to pot will straight be sent,
That humbug of a Government
Won't live a moment longer.
Then Palmy he'll be at our head,
And keep the tyrants all in dread,
Austria and France will wish him dead,
And for a milksop in his stead,
Haynau and the Russian Tsar
Will curse him in their realms afar,
And on their feelings it will jar,
To find old Palmy stronger.

Over Christmas and throughout January the press speculated. *The Times* denounced Palmerston unconvincingly as the enemy of freedom, but others hailed him as a martyr and blamed his downfall on Austria and Russia, or even in some cases on Prince Albert. On 9 January Lady Palmerston wrote to Mrs Huskisson, 'there is no end to the letters & Newspapers which we have received from all parts of the Country full

of praise and approbation whilst John is abused in no measured terms.'
In her view Russell's main motive for behaving so 'very ill' was 'jealousy'.

It was not until 3 February, when the House of Commons reassembled after the recess, that Russell was able to offer his own public
explanation; and by then events in France had gone some way towards
justifying the remarks that Palmerston, and indeed Russell himself, had
made to the French Ambassador. The new French government was
securely established; and, more importantly, it had acquired a level of
legitimacy. Among several of the usual symbols of dictatorship, such
as press censorship and a secret police force, Louis Napoleon had also
invested himself with the rarest and most precious: a democratically
delivered mandate. In the promised plebiscite the male population of
France had given overwhelming approval to the new constitution. There
were 7,145,000 votes in favour, and only 592,000 against.

Russell now knew that dismissing Palmerston for expressing approval
of the French *coup d'état* was no longer likely to seem reasonable to anyone
other than the most idealistic Radical. There had to be more. And so,
having charged Palmerston with this indiscretion, he went on to read
the Queen's memorandum of 12 August. From this he could argue that
another and more important charge was that Palmerston had accepted
the ultimatum contained in the memorandum and had then broken his
word to the Queen by sending an unsubmitted despatch to Normanby.
To the Radicals the news that Palmerston had submitted to such a
humiliating ultimatum was an additional reason for abandoning him;
and to the other Whigs and the two types of Tory his duplicity towards
his sovereign seemed unforgivable.

From the moment Russell began to quote the Queen's memorandum until he had finished speaking, Palmerston sat with his head in his
hands. When he rose to respond, he spoke only about his conversation
with Walewski. He reminded Russell and others that they, too, had said
such things to him, and he raised a little laughter when he asked why
it was that only the Foreign Secretary was supposed to remain silent
when an ambassador brought news to him. But he said nothing about
the memorandum or the promise he had made in response to it, which

enabled Russell to tell the Queen truthfully that he had put up a poor defence and that there had been little support for him.

Palmerston had said before that he was not prepared to draw the Queen into the arena of public debate, and now it was very clear that he meant it. In his view it was both morally wrong and constitutionally damaging to reveal that she was party to a dispute between two of her ministers. He blamed Russell for subjecting Her Majesty to both indignity and embarrassment when the press chose to comment on her conduct in their reports of the debate; and he charged him with treachery for introducing the royal memorandum without notice, although Russell claimed that he had warned him he would have to do it. If Russell was right, Palmerston's forbearance was all the more admirable for being premeditated. With notice there would have been time to prepare a Palmerstonian defence. His long-suffering adversaries claimed that in the end it was Palmerston's behaviour that drove them to dismiss him; but when the dismissal came, he behaved better than any of them. Palmerston never forgave Russell for what he did. He was too shrewd a politician to swear that he would never serve with him again, but he did swear that he would never again serve under him.

A week later Lady Palmerston gave a reception, to which, in case the point needed making, those who openly accepted her invitation included Wellington, Disreali, Gladstone and the Prime Minister's sister-in-law the Duchess of Bedford. After another week, in response to the growing public anxiety generated by events in France, Russell introduced a militia bill, intended to strengthen England's ability to withstand an invasion by establishing a militia in every county. It was at least a step towards an objective known to be close to Palmerston's heart. Nevertheless he spoke against it, not out of rancour but because he genuinely believed that it was not an answer to the threat. To be effective, a militia needed to be capable of assembling in sufficient numbers in the path of the invader. It needed to be organized centrally. He therefore proposed a simple amendment: that the new militia should be national and that the word 'local' should be omitted from the bill. The government opposed him. On 20 February, at the second reading of the bill, Palmerston's amendment was carried by a majority of thirteen. With almost undisguised relief, the defeated government resigned.

As soon as the vote had been counted, Lady Palmerston, who had again been watching from the Ladies' Gallery, hurried home to improvise as lavish a reception as time would allow, so that the scores of well-wishers who would soon undoubtedly be calling to congratulate her husband could be greeted with the question for which she was already famous: 'Won't you stay? We'll have a party' When they arrived, their glee and enthusiasm were so intense that her son-in-law Ashley, now seventh Earl of Shaftesbury, wrote next day in his diary, 'One would think that he had saved an empire.' Most of them were simply there to celebrate success-ful retribution and the demise of an exhausted government, but there were certainly some, among them Disraeli, who had come to celebrate the creation of what they saw as their own opportunities. Like everyone else in Parliament, however, they all accepted that it had been merely a matter of weeks at the most before the government was defeated on some issue or other; it was only an added and satisfying irony that, when it came, the one who actually made it happen was Palmerston. Four days later he broke the news bluntly in a letter to his brother. 'I have had my tit-for-tat with John Russell, and I turned him out on Friday last.'

12. A VERY DISTINGUISHED TIGHT-ROPE DANCER

On 22 February 1852 Edward George Geoffrey Smith Stanley, who had sat in the House of Lords since 1844 as Baron Stanley of Bickerstaffe, and who had just succeeded his father as fourteenth Earl of Derby, went to Buckingham Palace to accept Her Majesty's invitation to form a government.

The Queen and Prince Albert had been having second thoughts about the ability of the Whigs and Peelites to form a viable coalition. Since Palmerston's dismissal there was no certainty that the traditional Whigs would remain united behind Russell; and the Peelites, who had initially been so enthusiastic, had been induced to hesitate. Many of the Protectionists, who now, significantly, called themselves Conservatives, had begun to question the need for their continuing commitment to the principle that had divided the Tories in the first place. If this doubt could be developed into policy, if the rigid opposition to free trade could at least be relaxed, there was a chance that the Tories could be reunited; and that was a much more attractive prospect to the Peelites than an alliance with the Whigs.

As leader of the Conservatives, whose members composed the largest of the five factions in the lower House, Derby was therefore the appropriate person to receive the first invitation to form a government; and this was no disappointment to Queen Victoria. 'Dear Lord Melbourne' had left her with an ideal of what a Prime Minister ought to be, and Lord Derby was close to that ideal. Scion of the ancient family that had put the Tudors on the throne by changing sides at the Battle of Bosworth, he was impeccably well bred and he looked it. Tall, dark and firm-featured, he had the eager, sportsman-like demeanour of a man much younger than the fifty-three that he was; and he had a confident, easy-going charm which concealed his keen and scholarly mind. His experience of government was modest: he had been Under-Secretary for the Colonies under Canning and Goderich, and Secretary for Ireland under Grey; and he had resigned as Peel's Colonial Secretary on the repeal of the corn laws. But he was acknowledged to be the best speaker in the House of Lords, and as such he had led the successful attack on Palmerston's policy in Greece, an achievement that may have added to Queen Victoria's optimistic approval. Now, however, when he was attempting to form a government, he wanted Palmerston's support; and it may be that at his first audience with the Queen his charm was his most valuable asset. By the time he withdrew from the royal presence he had persuaded Her Majesty, against her better judgement, to let him offer Palmerston the Exchequer and Leadership of the House of Commons.

Later that day Palmerston accepted Derby's invitation to visit him at his house in St James's Square, where he very politely declined the offer. To have crossed the floor of the House alone to serve with a high Tory government would have been a betrayal of everything he was supposed to represent. It would certainly have cost him all the sympathy and support he still commanded among the Radicals, and it would probably have lost him most of his still unequalled popularity among the electorate. Nevertheless, if he was not going to serve under Russell again, he needed to make it clear that he was open to offers while other leaders still regarded him as an asset. He therefore tempered his rejection by implying that he would not be averse to serving with the Conservatives, but that, contrary to the prejudices of the Peelites, he could only consider it after they had abandoned Protectionism, and only if there were to be other Whigs besides himself in the coalition.

It was the first careful step on what Palmerston was soon to describe as a 'tight-rope'. As he put it frankly in a letter to his old friend and brother-in-law Laurence Sulivan, he could not accept the offer as it stood because Derby had told him that his policy on protective duties on corn 'was to depend on the result of the next general election', and because 'he meant me to come in singly'. But he then added, 'if his Government had been framed on a comprehensive principle, and Protection had been thrown overboard, the matter would have required consideration.'

The Exchequer and the Leadership of the House of Commons went instead to Disraeli, who in Palmerston's view was the only other 'real man' besides Derby in the new Cabinet. The other members were so laughably undistinguished and inexperienced that, when Derby read out their names to the House of Lords, the deaf old Duke of Wellington kept asking, 'Who? Who?'

Without Palmerston, or someone of similar stature, the brief government which was to be remembered famously as 'the Who-Who Ministry' was almost too weak to be credible. But it was not further weakened by having Palmerston as an opponent. In April, on the second reading of a Conservative militia bill, which was at least a little closer to Palmerston's ideal than the Whig one, Russell and the Radicals launched an attack that looked as though it was going to be enough to destroy it. Before the government could respond, Palmerston, who had taken to sitting a little bit apart from Russell and the others on the opposition front bench, caught the Speaker's eye and rose quickly to his feet. While Disraeli sat down again, Palmerston attacked Russell vehemently for insincerely jeopardizing national security in the interests of party politics. It saved the day. As Disraeli wrote afterwards to the Queen, 'Your Majesty's Government, about to attempt to reply, gave way to Lord Palmerston, who changed the feeling of the House, and indeed entirely carried it away in a speech of extraordinary vigour and high-spirited tone.'

Outside the House of Commons Palmerston was also able to make himself useful to the government. He added to Russell's discomfort by suggesting, and perhaps even writing, critical articles for the *Morning Post*, and he acted as unofficial adviser to the new Foreign Secretary, James Howard Harris, third Earl of Malmesbury. Although far from a fool, the 45-year-old Malmesbury had done little with his life other than serve as a Protectionist whip in the House of Lords. His only qualification for the Foreign Office was that he had travelled enough to claim acquaintance with Louis Napoleon. He would have been an easy target if Palmerston had chosen to act in opposition. But he was the grandson of the guardian who had found Palmerston his first office and guided his first years in Parliament; and the grateful elder statesman took a sentimental pleasure in reversing roles and playing the part of mentor, steering the inexperienced Malmesbury away from a few of the obvious pitfalls, wincing amiably at his 'ungrammatical despatches' and instilling in him a sense of pride in his great responsibility. 'You have no idea until you know more about your office what a power of prestige England possesses abroad', he told him. 'Take care you yield nothing until you have looked into every side of the question.'

Although Palmerston was out of office, there was still one small, uncontroversial, diplomatic duty for which even the Queen agreed he was the only man. When King Victor Emmanuel of Sardinia came to Windsor to be installed as a Knight of Garter, Palmerston, who wrote and spoke perfect Italian, was asked to translate his oaths for him, so that he could understand the meaning and significance of the ceremony and the honour that was being done to him. The embarrassingly uncouth King was accompanied by his Prime Minister, the Marchese d'Azeglio, and by another minister, Count Camillo di Cavour, the founding publisher of *Il Risorgimento*, who was about to become d'Azeglio's successor. Cavour had seen some of the letters that Palmerston had written to his government and to his King's envoy in London. When he saw that the Italian translation of the Garter vows was also in Palmerston's hand, he insisted that it was a historic document and persuaded his King to return the compliment by letting him preserve it in the royal archives.

Cavour admired Palmerston. He had convinced his King that the British, who had encouraged them in their recent struggles, were potentially their most valuable supporters in everything that they still planned to do; and he had convinced himself that Palmerston, who could not possibly be kept out of office for long, was the key to that support. When Palmerston invited him to dine at Carlton Gardens, he accepted eagerly. There is no record of what they said at that dinner, but in the light of all that was soon to happen, it is unlikely that Cavour could have kept away from revealing his dreams for Italy.

Out of office Palmerston was again blessed with more time to devote to entertaining, and to doing so without any dictation as to whom he might or might not receive. There was also more time for Broadlands, where his recent neglect had created so much of an opportunity for negligence in others that it was necessary to dismiss a gardener. There was more time for racing: he had only one horse in training that year – Buckthorne – but he won six races with him, including the Ascot Stakes and a major event at Goodwood. And there was time for another trip with Lady Palmerston to Ireland, where at last the estates were thriving. The harvests were healthy, the harbour was finished and, although there were as yet no tourists to fill the little lodging houses beside the dock, the fishermen, whose families ran them, were flourishing. Emigration and famine had reduced the population to a size that the land could easily sustain. But there had been no evictions. In the cottages of the tenant farmers and their labourers there was none of the vengeful bitterness that permanently poisoned the estates of so many other absentee landlords. The Palmerstons were sincerely welcomed. Crude triumphal arches were built across the new roadways and brightly decorated with everything from blossoms to bits of torn red flannel. There were songs and dances and grandiloquent declarations of loyalty. Every evening, when the Palmerstons dined, a fiddler came up to the house to play for them.

In that summer of 1852 Palmerston's only political duty was a trip to Tiverton for the general election in July. It was another election notorious for its corruption and violence. Although Palmerston was returned with a large majority, his fellow Whigs and the Peelites suffered almost equal losses of around sixty seats each. But the commensurate Conservative gains were not enough to give them an overall majority. Their number was increased to only 310, while the potential opposition consisted of Z70 Whigs and Radicals, 40 Peelites and 40 Irish Nationalists. When Parliament reassembled in November, Derby still needed to find allies.

The new parliamentary session was the first full session in which the members of the House of Commons sat in their new chamber in the Gothic palace that Charles Barry had been building for over a decade. The Lords had begun to occupy their chamber in 1847, and the Commons' chamber had actually been ready for occupation in 1850. But, after one attempt to use it, the members had moved straight out again and refused to return until the indignant architect had made a few changes. In his original design, over a third of the members were seated in a gallery behind the Speaker's chair, where they could neither catch his eye nor hear what the others in the chamber were saying. The division lobbies were also too small for them; and the ceiling was too high.

The alterations had been completed in February, the Commons were satisfied, and now Barry was to be knighted at the state opening. But the ceremony was not the celebration that it might have been. Recent events at home and abroad had cast a cloud across the nation. The ancient ritual was about to be eclipsed by a much more spectacular and yet sombre event. On 18 November a long cortège of carriages and soldiers escorted the huge and hideous funeral car of the Duke of Wellington from Chelsea Hospital to St Paul's Cathedral. During the preparations Lady Palmerston had been worried by the prospect of her 68-year-old husband walking for several hours in the procession on a cold winter's day; and like the duke's own family, she had been appalled by the vulgarity of the proposed procession. 'It seems to me so unnatural and so grating to one's feelings to make a festival out of a funeral', she wrote in her diary. 'It's like an Irish Wake.' But when the day came there was no sense of festivity. Among the 10,000 invited guests who gathered in and around the cathedral, and among the 1.5 million spectators who lined the route of the procession, the mood was one of fear and foreboding as much as of grief and gratitude. Eleven days earlier a packed French Senate had resolved overwhelmingly to crown Louis Napoleon as hereditary Emperor of France.

Just as the British were burying the hero who had saved them from the first Napoleon, the French were preparing to put his nephew on an imperial throne in his place. By 21 November, when another French plebiscite approved the Senate's resolution by 7,824,189 votes to only 253,145, London was rife with rumours that Napoleon III was secretly building a fleet in Cherbourg and assembling another in the mouth of the Seine.

Yet for the time being the priorities of the fragile British government were the domestic issues on which its survival depended. When Parliament reassembled, most members of the opposition were content to wait and defeat the government when it brought in its budget at the beginning of December. But the House of Commons had not been sitting for more than a few days before a surprise attack was launched by an unlikely alliance between the Radicals and a slightly desperate Russell.

The Queen's Speech at the state opening had made an ambiguous reference to the benefits of free trade. On 23 November therefore the allies cunningly proposed a motion calling on the House to recognize that the repeal of the corn laws had been a wise and just measure, which had benefited the nation. It was a trap from which the Conservatives could not escape. Whichever way the vote went, they would have no honourable choice but to resign from government. To have voted with the motion would have been to recognize that they had been wrong in splitting from the Peelites in the first place; and there was a clear indication that if they did that they would then be censured for having cynically and dishonestly changed their policy in order to win friends and cling to office. To have voted against it would have been to reaffirm Protectionism, thereby destroying all hope of an alliance with any of the Whigs or Peelites, and leaving themselves open to censure for misleading the house in the Queen's Speech.

But Russell and the Radicals had reckoned without Palmerston, who returned to the rescue with an amendment carefully composed for him by two Peelites, Gladstone and Sidney Herbert. Blandly and in the most general terms Palmerston's amendment did nothing more than welcome the adoption of free trade; and he persuaded the House to vote for it by appealing to its conscience. 'We who are Gentlemen on this side of the House should remember that we are dealing with Gentlemen on the other side; and I, for one, cannot at all reconcile it to my feelings to call upon a set of English Gentlemen unnecessarily, for any purpose that I have in view, to express opinions they do not entertain, or to recant opinions that may be still lingering in their minds.' The amendment was carried by 468 votes to fifty-three, which Palmerston described in a letter to his brother as 'the largest majority that ever voted on any question'.

Again Derby offered Palmerston the Exchequer and Leadership of the House of Commons, and Disraeli assured him that he was ready to resign from both offices if he accepted. But again Palmerston refused politely. Although Protectionism was no longer a problem, he was still unwilling to 'come in singly' and he insisted that he could only join a government that also contained other Whigs and Peelites, particularly his new allies Gladstone and Herbert. It was a reasonable and modest demand. Without the support that only a full coalition could provide, 'the Who-Who Ministry' was doomed. There was therefore nothing to be gained, and a great deal to be lost, by joining it. Besides, Palmerston was by now making other plans. As he wrote in another letter to his brother:

> It seems likely that this Government will not last long, and now there is another formation ready to take their place. Lord Lansdowne would consent to be chief if asked by the Queen to do so. John Russell would take office under Lansdowne, and would, moreover, if it were wished, go up to the House of Lords, and I should then be left to perform that honourable but irksome task of conducting the business of the Government in the House of Commons. In that case I should have the Home Office and Johnny the Foreign. I should, in any case, much prefer the Home Office to going back to the immense labour of the Foreign Office.

There was, however, one drawback to this plan. For all that Lansdowne was acceptable to the Queen, he was four years older than Palmerston and now very frail. He had reluctantly agreed to lead a government only because Palmerston had persuaded him that it was his duty and promised him the support of at least a hundred members of the House of Commons.

In the week following the free trade debate Disraeli's budget was defeated and the government resigned. Palmerston was not present, however. He was kept away by a probably prudent attack of the gout which, as was well known, had been hampering him more and more over the last few years. As a result, fortuitously of course, he was relieved from any reproach for assisting in the government's downfall, or from any blame for having failed to defend it effectively.

The Queen sent for Lansdowne, and for a moment Palmerston's heart must have leaped. But Her Majesty had only summoned Lansdowne to ask for his advice. Since the Conservatives had failed to create a viable alternative to the Whigs, the Queen and Prince Albert had been wondering whether a coalition led by Peelites might be able to do it instead. Lansdowne must have said yes: within hours the Queen had sent for Aberdeen.

Despite the derision to which he had been subjected during his brief tenure of the Foreign Office, Aberdeen knew that he needed Palmerston as much as Derby had needed him. He began by offering him the Admiralty and a seat in the Cabinet. It would probably not have been enough under any circumstances, but Palmerston's reason for his refusal was 'that Aberdeen and I had differed so widely for twenty-five years on all questions of foreign policy that my joining an Administration of which he was to be the head would be liable to misconstruction both at home and abroad'. Nevertheless he thanked Aberdeen 'cordially' for considering him and reminded him that they had been at school together and that they had been friends for over sixty years, a gesture that aroused a great deal of cynical amusement when Aberdeen reported it at Windsor. 'We could not help laughing heartily', wrote Prince Albert, 'at the Harrow Boys and their friendship.'

Palmerston continued to resist, even when Aberdeen and Lansdowne, who had agreed to join his Cabinet without portfolio, raised the stakes and offered him any ministry other than the Foreign Office. But at the same time, unknown to Palmerston, Lady Palmerston wrote to Lansdowne pleading with him to try harder and persuade her husband to take the Home Office, which she felt sure he was tempted to accept. As asked, Lansdowne did not mention her hurriedly scribbled letter to Palmerston, although somehow, like so many other prominent men and women in history, he did not, as asked, remember to burn it. He did, however, accede to the plea, and he used the same arguments as Palmerston had so recently used on him. On 22 December Palmerston told his brother, 'Lansdowne's representations of the great importance, in the present state of things at home and abroad, that the new Government should be as strong in its fabric as the materials available for the purpose can make it, determined me to yield to his advice and to accept the Home Office.'

He was more defensive, however, when he wrote to Sulivan.

Now I should like to know what other course you would have had me follow and what object and end you would have had me aim at? Perhaps you will say, to be Prime Minister myself; but that is not a thing a man can accomplish by willing it... I have for the last twelve months been acting the part of a very distinguished tight-rope dancer and much astonished the public by my individual performances and feats. First I turned out the Minister who had dismissed me. Then I mainly assisted in carrying measures for national defence which I had in office for several years vainly urged upon my Colleagues. Then in this Session I saved a Government from premature defeat ... and I thus saved the House of Commons from the discredit which the course they were going to pursue would have brought upon them. So far so well; but even Madame Sacqui, when she mounted her rope and flourished among her rockets, never thought of making the rope her perch, but prudently came down again to avoid a dangerous fall.

Although the Queen accepted the need to have Palmerston in the Cabinet, she remained apprehensive. But there was less likelihood that he could do much damage in the busy confines of the Home Office. As Prince Albert put it, 'If he is in a department in which he has to work like a horse, he cannot do any mischief.' When he came to collect his seal of office, however, they found a more negative reason for reassurance. 'Lord Palmerston looked so ill, and had to walk with two sticks, on account of his gout.' Like several others, they were left wondering whether he still had the energy for office, let alone mischief. But the prospect of a seat in another Cabinet was all the tonic that Palmerston needed. He took over the Home Office with as much energy and attention to detail as he had displayed at the War Office over forty years earlier; and his new ministerial relationship with the Queen got off to as good a start as Aberdeen could have hoped for. Perhaps inevitably, his proposals and submissions were much duller than anything he had sent from the Foreign Office, and fortunately most of them were also uncontroversial.

After only a month a bereavement provided the Queen with an opportunity to melt the ice a little. Lady Palmerston's brother Frederick, third and last Viscount Melbourne, died on 29 January, leaving her Brocket Hall and all his estates in the north. On hearing the news, the Queen wrote an unusually warm letter of condolence; and Palmerston wrote back on his wife's behalf, reporting how 'deeply afflicted' she was and begging 'to be allowed to offer his grateful thanks for your Majesty's gracious and condescending communication'.

In September, Aberdeen felt confident enough to send Palmerston to act as minister in attendance at Balmoral, which Prince Albert was still expanding into a Romantic castle. Lady Palmerston, who was not to accompany him, fussed him with copious cautions and instructions as to how to behave, ending a last anxious letter after he had left Broadlands with, 'Remember you have only one week to remain there, so you should manage to make yourself agreeable and to appear to enjoy the society'. Her husband seems to have followed her advice closely enough to be on encouragingly better terms with the royal couple when he returned to London. But soon afterwards he presumed to suggest that it might contribute to the security of the nation if the Queen's cousin Princess Mary of Cambridge were to marry Napoleon III's handsome cousin and heir, Prince Napoleon Jerome. The Queen was incensed by the impertinence. Apart from the fact that she did not like Napoleon Jerome, he was a Bonaparte, a Roman Catholic and by reputation a libertine, and therefore quite unacceptable anyway. And then the new harmony collapsed completely when Aberdeen, with astonishingly naïve indiscretion, informed the Queen that Palmerston had written to him pressing his case and insisting that Napoleon Jerome 'would be likely to make a better Husband than some petty Member of a petty German Prince's House'.

Palmerston was a bit more consistently tactful in Cabinet, however; and he seemed content to play a supporting part in what he regarded as a true coalition, a real 'Ministry of all the Talents'. Apart from Aberdeen, Lansdowne and himself, the others included Gladstone as Chancellor of the Exchequer and Herbert as Secretary at War. Russell was Foreign Secretary and Leader of the House of Commons, but he had agreed to take on both offices only on three conditions: that Clarendon would relieve him of the Foreign Office after two or three months; that Aberdeen would support him when he introduced a new Reform Bill; and that at the appropriate time he would be Aberdeen's choice to succeed him as Prime Minister.

The first condition presented no problem. It was generally agreed that Clarendon would make an excellent Foreign Secretary, although it was unusual to allow a Cabinet minister to exercise the authority of Leader of the House without accepting the responsibility of a portfolio. The third was something that Aberdeen seemed ready to grant without too much consideration, although he may have done so safe in the knowledge that there was nothing he could do to guarantee that it would come to anything. But the second condition was bound to lead to unnecessary and unavoidable conflict within the Cabinet: unnecessary because, despite the Chartists, there was surprisingly little support for any further extension of the franchise, and unavoidable because Palmerston for one was certain to oppose it.

Palmerston's opposition to any further electoral reform was a matter of taste, prejudice and experience rather than anything ideological. He was suspicious of the secret ballot, which would have become necessary with an extended franchise. To him the counting of hands or heads was a much more sportsman-like and British way of conducting an election. More importantly, he felt that reducing the property qualifications would only extend the franchise to men who did not own enough to have any real interest in the outcome of an election, and who might well not be educated enough to understand the issues. It was one of the rare opinions that won him no friends among the Radicals, but it was not otherwise unfashionable at the time, and there was no better practical evidence in its support than the recent events in France, where universal male suffrage had resulted in the election of a dictator.

It was in principle Palmerston's attitude towards extending the franchise that had earlier induced the press to describe him as a Liberal abroad and a Conservative at home. But the progressive policies that he pursued over the next two years gave the lie to that easy aphorism. Palmerston the Home Secretary was much closer to Palmerston the supporter of the Factory Acts than Palmerston the opponent of reform. It was not long before he had won the approbation of Shaftesbury, who may of course have been tempted by family ties to be biased, but who was equally bound by deep faith to be honest, and who had not been above criticizing Palmerston before. 'I have never known any Home Secretary equal to Palmerston for readiness to undertake every good work by kindness, humanity, and social good, especially to the child and the working-class ... [He] has already done more than ten of his predecessors.'

Under Shaftesbury's influence Palmerston introduced the Reformatory School Act, which gave the Home Secretary the authority to transfer young offenders from prisons to reform schools. Still as curious and practical as he had been at the War Office, he went to visit the sixteen-year-old prison for boys at Parkhurst on the Isle of Wight and afterwards wrote to the governor suggesting a few ways of improving the ventilation and instructing that some of the well-behaved boys whom he had met there should be transferred as soon as possible to one of the new reform schools.

He freed all the Irish Nationalists and Chartists who had been transported to Australia, although it was another two years before they were allowed to return to Ireland or Great Britain; and in response to pressure from the colonies, his Penal Servitude Act replaced further transportation with shorter sentences of hard labour. It was also under this act that he reduced the maximum period of solitary confinement from eighteen months to nine, and introduced the system of tickets-of-leave, which had first been used in Van Diemen's Land, whereby prisoners were let out of prison on day-release to work at jobs in the community. The last provision was so far ahead of its time, however, that it survived for only ten years and aroused so much opposition that its unpopularity was equalled only by the compulsory vaccination of children and the act prohibiting any further burial of the dead in churches.

The ancient custom of burying dead dignitaries and clergymen within the walls and floors of churches was curtailed on the grounds of public health by Palmerston's Burials beyond the Metropolis Act, which established municipal cemeteries outside city limits, and which for the first time set aside special plots so that the corpses could include all kinds of Christians and not just Anglicans. Since the act also provided that the Home Secretary could make exceptions if he saw fit, Lord Stanley of

Alderley wrote to Palmerston asking if an exception could be made for an eminent clergyman to be buried in the church that he had served for many years. In his reply Palmerston made it clear that he was unlikely to consider any exceptions.

> A rule is no rule if partial exceptions are made …What special connection is there between Church dignitaries and the privilege of being decomposed under the feet of survivors? … England is, I believe, the only country in which, in these days, people accumulate putrefying dead bodies amid the dwellings of the living; and as to burying bodies under thronged churches, you might as well put them under libraries, drawing-rooms and dining-rooms.

It was not the first time that Palmerston had enjoyed himself at the expense of the Church. The wags in Westminster were already suggesting that the former Foreign Secretary had lost none of his imperiousness and had decided to treat Heaven as if it were just another country. When the Moderator of the Presbyterians in Edinburgh had earlier suggested that a day of national fasting might induce divine intervention to stem a devastating cholera epidemic, he had replied that it might be more effective to take the appropriate practical precautions and ensure that 'those portions of the towns and cities which are inhabited by the poorest classes … may be freed from those causes and sources of contagion which, if allowed to remain, will infallibly breed pestilence and be fruitful in death, in spite of all the prayers and fastings of a united but inactive nation'.

Amid the usual jaunty but deceptive nonchalance the bulk of Palmerston's time at the Home Office was nevertheless devoted to improving the health, the working conditions and even the morals of the 'poorest classes'. Sometimes his path was unimpeded by anything other than the difficulty of the task itself, as with his introduction and supervision of several schemes for diverting sewage into outlets a safe distance downstream from the cities that produced it. Sometimes he had to fight hard to overcome influential opposition. On one such occasion the factory owners whose chimneys polluted the air of London and other cities called in every favour they could find to oppose his Smoke Abatement Act. On another the mine owners brought similar force to bear on his Truck Act, which prevented them from paying their employees in goods or forcing them to shop at the company store.

Sometimes Palmerston's most imaginative schemes were actually thwarted by unimaginative opponents who ought to have been his allies. In his attempt to reduce drunkenness, for example, he proposed that beer should be sold in shops 'like anything Else, to be taken away by the purchaser to be consumed at Home'. In this way, he argued, the working man would have no need to go into licensed premises, which he regarded as 'haunts of Thieves and Schools of Prostitutes', where 'the words "Licensed to be drunk on the Premises" are by the common People interpreted as applicable to the Customers as well as to the Liquor'. But he was effectively opposed by the huge temperance lobby, led within the Cabinet by Gladstone, who believed that Palmerston's proposal would only make things worse.

Most of what Palmerston achieved, however, was achieved only by compromise. He disappointed Shaftesbury, for example, by not pressing for the reduction of the working hours for men and women under eighteen, knowing that if he did his whole Factory Act might founder, and with it the clauses that prevented minors from being put to work at night between 6 p.m. and 6 a.m. Even his great penal reforms were compromises. He wanted to send young offenders directly to reform schools, but he was prevented by an amendment from opponents who felt that they should serve a year in prison first. He wanted to reduce the maximum period of solitary confinement to much less than nine months, but the same breathtakingly inconsistent opponents prevented him on the grounds that it was better to put young offenders in solitary confinement than to let them associate with hardened criminals, who could teach them all the tricks of their trades.

There were inevitably a few times when Palmerston was himself the opponent of change. Although he supported the continuing right of trade unionists to strike, he opposed a proposal that they should be allowed to engage in peaceful picketing, on the grounds that it was a way of intimidating men who were willing to work for less into joining the union against their will. It was hardly an argument worthy of a statesman who had until recently been adjusting the balance of power between nations. But Palmerston was operating in unfamiliar territory, and like many others he was alarmed by the proliferating industrial action in the north. He was much better when his role as guardian of law and order allowed him to operate in the style to which he had been accustomed at the Foreign Office, even if the outcome did not always suit his allies.

In April 1853 the Commissioner of the Metropolitan Police applied to Palmerston for a warrant to search a factory in Rotherhithe belonging to an arms manufacturer called Hain, who just happened to be a Radical and a friend of Kossuth, who had returned to England and was now living in Manchester. As expected, the factory was found to contain ammunition and weapons far in excess of its licensed limit, and the owner was duly charged under the Explosives Act. When the story appeared in *The Times*, however, it was said that the weapons were found in a house, not a factory, that the house belonged to Kossuth, not Hain, that the arms were destined to be used in uprisings against Austrian rule in Hungary and northern Italy, and that they were being purchased by a group of clandestine revolutionaries known as 'the London Committee', who may have been responsible for the recent attempt to assassinate the Austrian Emperor.

The Radicals in the House of Commons rallied at once to Kossuth's defence. At question time they demanded to know whether *The Times* was right in claiming that he was involved, to which Palmerston simply answered that he had not been charged with anything. But in response to their repeated requests for a direct assurance that Kossuth had nothing to do with the matter, Palmerston was consistently evasive.

It was clear that Palmerston and Clarendon, who was by then Foreign Secretary, knew, or at least suspected, more than they were saying, and it became clear soon afterwards that Aberdeen also knew enough to approve of what Palmerston had done. Given Aberdeen's admiration for the Austrians, this was probably not too surprising, but even Palmerston had learned from experience that it might not be wise to let them assume that he was condoning the supply of arms to their enemies.

The unsatisfactory answers were not the end of the debate, however. The Radicals continued by asking how the factory had been discovered. In replying, Palmerston implied that it had been discovered by the plain-clothes policemen who were routinely following Kossuth and other revolutionary refugees. It was the first time such an admission had been made openly. The Radicals were aghast. England was not Austria. Many of them mistrusted Peel's Metropolitan Police, who, in their eyes, were already acting too much like Napoleon III's gendarmes. Now they appeared to be acting like Austrian secret police as well. Palmerston could not be blamed for instituting the practice – it had started long before he took office – but he could be blamed for allowing it to continue. For a moment the rollercoaster relationship between Palmerston and the Radicals dipped down to another low, but it soon swept up again when the political prisoners were released in Australia.

The incident, unpleasant though it was, brought Palmerston closer for a moment to the world in which his heart still lay. Foreign affairs were his first and best love. No matter how much the Home Office kept him working 'like a horse', he was all too easily distracted by anything and everything that was happening beyond the water. It was later said, in several versions, none of which had any reliable provenance, that when Queen Victoria, who was as anxious as anyone about the industrial unrest in the north, asked her Home Secretary if he had any news, she received the answer, 'No, Ma'am, I have heard nothing; but it seems certain that the Turks have crossed the Danube.' It was the winter of 1853. The so-called 'Eastern Question' had raised its ugly head again.

It was Napoleon III who started it. Anxious to please the Church, whose support he still needed, determined to snub Tsar Nicholas, who had refused to recognize him as a fellow monarch and continued to address him as 'My dear friend' instead of 'My brother', and just a little bit interested in strengthening French influence in Syria, Napoleon had persuaded the Ottoman Sultan to confirm that the French were the rightful guardians of the Holy Sepulchre, the Christian church in Bethlehem and the grotto of the Holy Manger. The right was based on a treaty that had been drawn up between France and Turkey in 1740. But French protection had been withdrawn by the atheist government of the Revolution, and the Roman Catholic monks who had till then taken care of the 'Holy Places' had been replaced by Orthodox monks, who regarded the Russian Tsar as their protector.

In January 1853 the Tsar responded by summoning the British Ambassador and suggesting that the time had come to partition the Ottoman Empire, which he regarded as 'the sick man of Europe'. If the British would agree to the Balkan states becoming Russian protectorates, the Russians would agree to Britain's annexation of Egypt, Cyprus and Crete, which would protect her route to India. Russell, who was just about to hand over the Foreign Office to Clarendon, responded with a vague rejection of what he hoped was not a serious proposal. But Nicholas, believing that the temptation had been enough to prevent the British from interfering, and confident that the French would not dare to oppose him on their own, then sent General Prince Menshikov to Constantinople to demand not only that the guardianship of the Holy Places should be restored to the Orthodox Church but also that the Russian Tsar should be formally recognized as the protector of all the many millions of Orthodox Christians living within the Ottoman Empire.

And this was the pretext for the European war in which a British army was engaged for the first time in forty years. It was a trivial, unworthy squabble which until recently would have been easily resolved by an exchange of defiant and at worst acrimonious despatches between the likes of Metternich and Palmerston. But at the outset no men of that calibre were directly involved. Metternich himself had gone home from English exile and was now living in retirement in the castle of Johannesberg on the Rhine; and Palmerston was the almost lone voice of defiance crying out in vain on the edge of a gullible, appeasing Cabinet.

On 28 February Menshikov arrived in Constantinople with all the swaggering confidence of a natural bully who knew that behind him a Russian army was drawn up on the European border, along the River Pruth, and a Russian fleet was standing ready in the harbour at Sevastopol. When they discovered his demands, the French Ambassador and the British chargé d'affaires decided on a show of strength and summoned squadrons from their Mediterranean fleets. But only French ships came up to a safe distance off Salamis. The British Cabinet cancelled the order on the grounds that it was provocative, although it was not a unanimous decision. Russell was convinced that the Tsar was 'clearly bent on accomplishing the destruction of Turkey' and that it was essential to resist him; and Palmerston emphatically agreed with him. But, having handed over the Foreign Office to Clarendon, Russell was preoccupied with parliamentary reform, and Clarendon was eager to be as conciliatory between colleagues as between nations. Within the Cabinet the only consistent, although, as Aberdeen acknowledged, always courteous, arguments in favour of 'bold' action came from Palmerston.

Outside the Cabinet, however, the same case was being argued with equal strength by none other than Stratford Canning, who had recently been elevated to the House of Lords as Lord Stratford de Redcliffe. Because Stratford understood the Ottoman court better than anyone, and perhaps because he wanted at least one critic out of the way, Aberdeen agreed to sent him out as Ambassador to Turkey. On 5 April he arrived in Constantinople for his fifth term of office there. Before long he had persuaded Menshikov to accept a compromise on the guardianship of the Holy Places. But, with the support of the French, Austrian and Prussian Ambassadors, he also persuaded the Turks to stand up to him and refuse to recognize the Tsar as protector of the Sultan's Christian subjects.

On 21 May, Menshikov went back to Russia in a fury. Next day Palmerston wrote to Clarendon urging him to make a show of strength. 'The policy and practice of the Russian Government has always been to push forward its encroachments as fast and as far as the apathy or want of firmness of other Governments would allow it to go, but always to stop and retire when it was met with decided resistance.' Stratford agreed. Everything depended now on the Cabinet 'looking the crisis in the face'. But nobody else in the Cabinet, not even Russell, could accept that the situation was now a crisis. The Tsar might continue to press his claims, but he was unlikely to go to war over them.

They were clearly wrong. Tsar Nicholas did not want to start a European war. But he did want to help himself to Turkey. If he thought he could do that without any interference from the other European Powers, he was certainly going to do it; and there was no reason to suppose that, having done so, he was going to let Britain have any of it.

Left to their own devices, the Russians would soon be in control of all the overland routes to India.

The key evidence of Russia's belligerence was the army on the Pruth. It was not just there to lend weight to Menshikov's threats. It had been there already. Originally, and ostensibly, it was on its way to support the beleagured and massively outnumbered Montenegrins, who were fighting valiantly against the Turks for their independence. It had only halted because the Austrians, who could see what was going on, had persuaded the Turks to withdraw from Montenegro; and since then, to the Tsar's relief, the clumsy French claim over the Christian shrines had provided him with another pretext. As Palmerston and Stratford were arguing, the only way to stop him moving was to do enough to convince him that the British would be standing in his way if he did.

Ten days after Menshikov's departure the Russians sent an ultimatum to Constantinople, warning that, if his demands were not met within eight days, their army would advance and occupy the Turkish principalities of Moldavia and Wallachia, which lay between the Pruth and the Danube. At last, with the support of every newspaper but *The Times* and the *Herald*, Palmerston persuaded the Cabinet to do what he had been asking it to do for weeks. A British squadron was sent to join the French squadron, which was now lying in Besika Bay at the mouth of the Dardanelles, and the commander was instructed to stand ready to come to the defence of Constantinople if Stratford should call for him.

The gesture was probably too little and too late; and the Tsar may well have assumed it was a bluff. On 22 June the Russian army crossed the Pruth. Palmerston wrote to Aberdeen urging him to send the ships up to the Bosporus and, 'if necessary or useful for the protection of Turkish territory', on into the Black Sea as well. But Aberdeen replied weakly that, indefensible though the Russian action was, the Tsar had not declared war, and for British ships to enter the Bosporus would be in violation of the treaty of 1841. Having failed to persuade a Cabinet meeting to change his mind for him, Palmerston wrote in disbelief to Russell, who had not been present, suggesting that the position of the British and French, who were equally indecisive, was like 'waiting timidly and submissively at the back door while Russia is violently, threateningly, and arrogantly forcing her way into the house'. And then, to his exasperation, the Russian government sent a despatch claiming that they had only occupied the two principalities in response to the presence of British and French warships at the mouth of the Dardanelles. Outlining his argument again, Palmerston sent a memorandum to every member of the Cabinet. If the British and French governments had only 'acted with that energy, decision and promptitude which the occasion required ... things would not have come to the pass at which they have now arrived ... It is the robber who declares that he will not leave the house until the policeman shall have first retired from the courtyard.'

Meanwhile Stratford persuaded the Turks not to respond to the Russian invasion. Without the expected provocation of a counterattack and consequent bloodshed, the baffled Russians halted at the Danube; there then followed a round of diplomacy that for sheer intricacy and ambiguity matched anything in Ottoman history. While Stratford conducted negotiations in Constantinople, representatives of Austria, Prussia, France and Britain met in Vienna and attempted to draw up a peace proposal that would be acceptable to everyone. In essence, the result was that the negotiations in Turkey produced a vague proposal which was acceptable to the Turks but not the Russians, and the negotiations in Austria produced the so-called 'Vienna Note', which was couched in language so obscure that it was open to any interpretation that anyone wanted to put on it, and which was acceptable to the Russians but not the Turks. The only material consequence was negative. The Prussians and the Austrians agreed with the Russians, while the British and the French agreed with the Turks. The Powers were divided. This did not mean that, if it came to war, the Austrians and the Prussians would join in on the side of Russia, but it did mean that only the British and the French could be expected to help Turkey.

And it did come to war. On 4 October the Turks sent an ultimatum to General Gortchakov, commander of the Russian army of occupation in the principalities: if he did not withdraw within fifteen days, hostilities would commence. He received it and rejected it four days later. On 28 October, five days after the time limit had expired, the Ottoman armies of Omar Pasha crossed the Danube and drove the Russians into headlong retreat.

Since there was as yet no other way of offering active support, Palmerston proposed that the British squadron should sail into the Black Sea and help to protect the flank of the advancing Ottoman army by patrolling the eastern European coast. But Aberdeen was a long way from being ready to commit British forces. He was still clutching desperately at any and every plan that might bring all the parties back to the negotiating table, and he sent Palmerston a memorandum that he had received from Prince Albert, in which the Prince proposed that, rather than force the Russians to abandon the occupied principalities, a better solution might be to force the Turks to withdraw from Europe. Palmerston replied tersely that if that was the case the British had better change sides. 'Peace is an Excellent thing, and War is a great Misfortune. But there are Many things More valuable than Peace, and many Things Much worse than war. The maintenance of the Ottoman Empire belongs to the First Class, The occupation of Turkey by Russia belongs to the Second.'

For the next four months Aberdeen was as hesitant as he had been in the previous four. But the people of Britain were clamouring for war. Led on by the *Morning Chronicle*, the *Globe* and particularly the *Morning Post*, to which Palmerston was regularly providing opinions if not words, they scorned Aberdeen's lack of resolution and demanded restitution and vengeance for the occupation of places they had never heard of by the barbarians who had recently committed unspeakable atrocities in Poland and Hungary. The more Aberdeen did nothing, the more men wondered in print why the Home Secretary was not at the Foreign Office. By the end of the year, as Lord Dudley Stuart told the House of Commons, the public opinion that Aberdeen so despised could be summed up in a single word: 'Palmerston'.

When Aberdeen's government first took office, the arch-enemy had been Napoleon III. The whole nation was terrified that he was about to invade 'under the banner of the Pope' and 'surrounded by parasites, pimps and prostitutes'. So great was the fear that the House of Commons uncharacteristically agreed with hardly a murmur to huge increases in the service estimates, so that Palmerston could improve the defences along the coast and round the harbours. But now the Emperor Napoleon had been replaced in the public perception by Tsar Nicholas, and it looked as though the additional service estimates might have been better spent training and equipping troops to fight against the Russians.

The Home Secretary had failed to persuade his government to adopt the defiant Palmerstonian bluff which had so often reined in armies in the past. But from that failure the opportunity had now arisen to kill two birds with one stone, provided of course he could persuade the same government to be a little more forceful in prosecuting the war than it had been in trying to prevent it. Like most dictators, Napoleon III needed to distract his subjects with a war, and for a while it had looked as though that war was going to be against Great Britain. Now, however, his attempt to snub the ambitious Tsar had committed them both to a conflict from which neither had the confidence to step back. But since it was also clear that the Tsar had been planning to attack Turkey all along, and since that meant that the British were going to have to fight in their own interest to preserve Turkey's independence, it was reassuring to know that they had the French as allies; and since Napoleon III was determined to use his soldiers somewhere, it was much better to have him using them beside the British 2,000 miles away than against the British on the southern shores of England.

Yet throughout the summer and autumn of 1853, while the British government was playing at being a peacemaker and then wandering into a war, and while Palmerston was struggling to stiffen its resolve, Russell, the only man in the Cabinet who agreed with him, and who might therefore have been able to support him effectively, was diverting his own and the government's energies on his pet scheme for parliamentary reform. In keeping with his promise, Aberdeen supported him, and as Home Secretary Palmerston was obliged to sit on the committee that studied his proposals. But Palmerston could not support a bill that would extend the franchise to another 150,000 men who, in his view, would not be free agents and would simply vote under the influence of their trade unions.

On 8 December Palmerston wrote to Lansdowne. He knew only too well how important it was at this delicate moment to have someone in the Cabinet who held his views 'as to the principles on which our foreign affairs ought to be conducted', but if Russell's bill came before the House of Commons, he would have to resign. Two days later he wrote to the same effect to Aberdeen and sent him a copy of his letter to Lansdowne. On receipt of the letter Aberdeen immediately passed on its contents to the Queen and Prince Albert. The prospect of being rid of Palmerston delighted them, and they were particularly pleased that he was threatening to resign over something that might lose him some sympathy with the Radicals and not over his popular stance on foreign policy. They urged Aberdeen to force his hand; and Aberdeen agreed to do so.

But before Aberdeen could write his planned letter to Palmerston, his attention, and the attention of the nation, was briefly diverted by a terrible rumour from the east. On 30 November a squadron of six Russian ships of the line had apparently sailed up to the little Turkish port of Sinope on the Black Sea and demonstrated to the world the devastating effect of explosive shellfire on wooden hulls. Within minutes seven frigates, two corvettes, two transports and two little steamers were blazing beyond salvage, and 4,000 Turkish sailors had been blown to pieces, burned to death or left drowning in the water. The press and the public were horrified and furious. It was a massacre. Aberdeen was to blame. If Palmerston had been directing policy, British ships would have been there to keep the Russians at bay. What they did not know or say, however, was that there was more to their speculation than they realized. The successful raid might indeed have been prevented if the Cabinet had taken up Palmerston's much earler proposal of a pre-emptive strike against Sevastopol.

On 14 December Aberdeen made what he later admitted was a hasty move. He kept his word to the Queen and wrote to Palmerston returning his copy of the letter to Lansdowne, of which he had kept a copy of his own, confirming that there could be no changes to Russell's Reform Bill and regretting therefore that there was nothing he could do to persuade him not to resign. Despite Lady Palmerston's plea for a pause, Palmerston wrote back at once asking Aberdeen to lay his resignation before the Queen.

Next day two stories dominated all the newspapers: confirmation of the attack on Sinope and Palmerston's resignation. In all but *The Times* the outrage was renewed. Some said the court had engineered the resignation; some accused Prince Albert of being pro-Russian; and the *Morning Post* claimed that Palmerston had resigned because the government's faint-hearted foreign policy had led to the Sinope 'massacre'.

Palmerston himself always insisted that he had resigned only over Russell's Reform Bill. Even Lady Palmerston's diary recorded it as the only reason. But in the light of the timing and the consequences it is difficult not to suspect that the tight-rope dancer was at work again. If Palmerston had actually resigned over the government's foreign policy, Russell, who agreed with him, would have resigned as well; and that would have made Russell, a former premier, the leading candidate to take the job again if or when the irresolute government fell. By resigning over reform, Palmerston denied Russell the opportunity to do the same and identified himself to the the electorate and the House of Commons as the only member of the government prepared to make a stand against whichever of its policies they chose to assume. Meanwhile, if it was possible to raise Palmerston's national popularity any higher than it already stood at the end of 1853, the resignation did it.

Aberdeen's mistake was easily rectified. On 22 December, in Palmerston's absence, the Cabinet sent an order to the squadron at the mouth of the Dardanelles, instructing it to enter the Black Sea and 'invite' any Russian ship it met to return to Sevastopol. After the meeting, under pressure from several ministers, including Gladstone, Aberdeen wrote to Palmerston telling him that Russell's proposals were still open to discussion and alteration and inviting him to withdraw his resignation. Next day Palmerston wrote back to say that, in the light of this misunderstanding, he was happy to do as the Prime Minister requested. No matter which interpretation the onlookers put on his resignation, he could now be seen to be making an honourable return. For those who believed he had resigned over the irresolute foreign policy, he was going back because the government had stiffened its resolve; for those who believed he had resigned over reform, he was going back because there had been a misunderstanding and Russell's bill was still open to alteration.

On Christmas Eve Palmerston attended a Cabinet meeting as Home Secretary. When the meeting was over Aberdeen went to Windsor to break the bad news and explain it to the Queen. It was not as hard a task as he expected. Her Majesty was beginning to understand Palmerston, even if she was in no way warming to him. A few days earlier, as anxious as anyone at the prospect of war, she had written in a letter to Clarendon, 'Lord Palmerston's mode of proceeding always had that advantage, that it threatened steps which it was hoped would not become necessary, whilst those hitherto taken started on the principle of not offending Russia, obliging us at the same time to take the very steps which we refused to threaten.'

As 1854 began, the British public clamoured for more aggressive action. Balladeers sang about Prince Albert.

> Little Al, the royal pal,
> They say has turned a Russian.

Rumour-mongers suggested that Palmerston's agents had been steaming open the Prince's mail and discovered he was receiving instructions from the Tsar. Russell's bill was withdrawn from the business of the next parliamentary session. On behalf of the British and French governments Napoleon III wrote to the Tsar proposing that, if the Russian army were to be withdrawn from the principalities, and if British and French ships were to be withdrawn from the Black Sea, new negotiations could be started. But he also warned that if his proposal was refused, Britain and France would be forced to declare war; and at this the Tsar told the new Napoleon that France would find Russia every bit as deadly in 1854 as she had found her in 1812.

At the beginning of February the Tsar withdrew his ambassadors from London and Paris. A few days later a bewildered Aberdeen wrote revealingly to Clarendon, 'I still say that war is not inevitable; unless, indeed, we are determined to have it; which, for all I know, may be the case.' It was the case; and he should have known. Throughout the month British detachments for a campaign in the east set sail at regular intervals for their first staging post on Malta. At the end of the month, on 27 February, the Tsar received a joint British and French ultimatum and was given another month in which to answer it.

Meanwhile an allied fleet was made ready for the Baltic, where the plan was to destroy fortifications and establish a beachhead in preparation for an advance on St Petersburg. For this the commander was to be none other than still gaudy 68-year-old Admiral Sir Charles Napier. A dinner was given in his honour at the Reform Club on 7 March, after which Palmerston and Sir Charles Graham, the First Lord of the Admiralty, were reproached by the Radicals for making jocular, belligerent speeches when war had not yet been declared. But that was now no more than a formality. On 27 March, after nothing had been heard from the Tsar, the French did formally declare war on him, and the British followed suit next day.

By then 'Mad Charlie' Napier was in the Baltic. On receipt of a signal he began to attack Russian ships and sailed in to bombard the coastal forts, but he had no useful charts, his only pilots were prisoners and most of his ships had too deep a draught to get in close enough in the shallow waters. When the French squadron arrived, on 7 August, 10,000 French soldiers were put ashore on the Åland islands; and after eight days of siege and bombardment, the garrison of Bomarsund surrendered and the fortress was destroyed. But the expedition did nothing to make effective preparations for an invasion, and in the autumn a shame-faced Napier sailed home, to be confronted with enforced retirement.

In the east the main plan, developed by Graham, proposed by Palmerston and approved by Napoleon III, was to land in strength on the Crimean peninsula and incapacitate all Russia's Black Sea forces at a single blow by seizing the great naval base at Sevastopol. Before the campaign began, however, the Austrians amassed 50,000 men in Galicia and Transylvania and threatened to attack if the Tsar did not withdraw all his forces in Europe to behind his border on the River Pruth. Furious at their ingratitude, but frightened by the prospect of their addition to the allied armies, the Tsar did as they demanded, and Palmerston's predecessor at the Home Office, Spencer Walpole, suggested not unreasonably to the House of Commons that an attack on Russia was no longer necessary. But the plan was now too far advanced, and everyone involved agreed that the Russians still deserved to be humbled, and that Turkey would never be safe while the Russians were able to threaten her from Sevastopol.

It was nevertheless a bold enough plan to arouse apprehension even among those who approved it. One such was the young Duke of Argyll, who was serving in his first Cabinet as Lord Privy Seal. He expressed his misgivings privately to Palmerston and recorded the answer in his memoirs. 'Oh, you need not be in the least anxious', said Palmerston. 'With our combined fleets and our combined armies we are certain to succeed.'

Palmerston was nearly right. On 13 September, 26,000 British soldiers with 66 guns, commanded by 66-year-old Lord Raglan, who had lost an arm in his last battle, Waterloo, and 30,000 French soldiers with 70 guns, commanded by 53-year-old Marshal de Saint-Arnaud, who was already seriously incapacitated by cholera, landed in a bay to the north of Sevastopol. Fortunately, however, the 40,000 Russians with 100 guns who opposed them were only commanded by Menshikov. On 20 September they drove him away in an engagement on the River Alma. But then the commanders disagreed. Since the fortress had no defences on its landward sides, Raglan wanted to storm it at once while the Russians were in disarray. But Saint-Arnaud insisted on a formal siege, and Raglan, who was courteous to a fault, gave in to him.

So the armies, which had originally been equipped for a short campaign in summer, marched round to the south of Sevastopol, where there was a sheltered harbour for their supporting ships, and settled down to conduct a long siege in winter instead. The Russians made good use of their delay. They fortified the landward sides of their base, reinforced its garrison, and then with additional reinforcements attempted to drive the invaders into the sea, first on 25 October at Balaclava and then on 5 November at Inkerman. Both attempts failed, but the allied losses were terrible; and then, to add to their misery, on 14 November a great gale struck their harbour, sinking thirty ships and over £2 million worth of stores.

Next day the Cabinet received a despatch from Raglan reporting his victory at Inkerman and asking for reinforcements to replace his 3,000 dead and the many thousand more who were laid up in misery with wounds and dysentery. But Raglan's were not the only reports emanating from the Crimea. For the first time the army was accompanied by a war correspondent, William Howard Russell, whose regular reports in *The Times* turned the nation's passion from rage against Russia to indignant fury with the incompetents and scoundrels who were supplying and leading the gallant British soldiers. Men were dying not just in battle or from disease and ill-attended wounds. They were dying of exposure and starvation through lack of food, proper clothing and shelter. Above all, the national shame at the needless sacrifice of the Light Brigade left the public baying for resignations and dismissals.

Later in November Lord and Lady Palmerston went to Paris to dine with the Emperor and liaise with members of the French government. On his return Palmerston confirmed to the Cabinet that Russell's reports were not exaggerated. The French, who were far better supplied with everything, including medical staff and facilities, had told him that the British suffering was terrible.

Further confirmation came from the pathetic soldiers' letters which their families gave to the newspapers to print. Of these the most influential was one that appeared in *The Times* on 14 October, asking why the British wounded had no well-bred 'sisters of mercy' like the French. The letter struck at the heart of the Palmerstons' Hampshire neighbour Florence Nightingale, whose father had once seconded Lord Palmerston's nomination as a candidate for South Hampshire. This was the opportunity for which God had kept her waiting so long. This was why she had defied her parents to study nursing in Paris and refused one of the most eligible suitors in London. From the moment she read that letter she was determined to assemble a group of young ladies and take them out with her to the war.

Florence Nightingale had dined so often at Broadlands that she felt bold enough to consult the Palmerstons. Lady Palmerston was not too sure: the only nurses she knew about were the part-time prostitutes who had served in Spain. But her husband was inspired by the scheme. With his blessing Miss Nightingale called unannounced at 49 Belgrave Square, the London home of the Secretary at War, Sidney Herbert. It was a Saturday; but, instead of being at home as expected, her friends the Herberts, whom she had first met five years earlier in an art gallery in Rome, were spending the weekend on the Hampshire coast. Miss Nightingale could do nothing but leave a note for Liz Herbert, telling her 'dearest' friend about her intention to sail east with 'a small private expedition of nurses' and asking if her husband could give her 'any advice or letters of recommendation'. Next day, however, by what may have been a coincidence, Sidney Herbert wrote to Florence Nightingale at length from Bournemouth. Someone had told him what she was planning; and his letter was an official invitation to lead just such an expedition.

Only nineteen days later, on 4 November, a seasick Florence Nightingale, now formally recognized as 'Superintendent of the Female Nursing Establishment of the English General Hospital in Turkey', arrived at Constantinople with thirty-eight nurses, most of them from religious orders and the majority Roman Catholic. By nightfall they had crossed the Bosporus, scrambled up the roadless eastern heights and established themselves as best they could in the old triangular artillery barracks at Scutari, which were what now passed for the 'English General Hospital'. They were just in time. On 6 November they were overwhelmed by the first shipment of casualties from Balaclava.

At a cabinet meeting on 13 December Lord John Russell took up one of the popular cries from the press and called for the resignation of the Secretary for War and the Colonies, the Duke of Newcastle, hinting heavily that Palmerston should replace him. But Palmerston opposed him vehemently, insisting that it was wrong to ask Newcastle to appear to take the blame for blunders that were none of his doing. When he then added that he perhaps ought to resign himself for having failed to get his Smoke Abatement Bill passed, Aberdeen seized gratefully on his attempt to lighten the atmosphere and suggested that the failure was probably due to Palmerston's lack of energy.

Queen Victoria and her Prince Consort, Albert of Saxe-Coburg, who
had no more respect for Palmerston than he had for them

Palmerston's long service as Foreign Secretary coincided with the
construction of the new Houses of Parliament

Like Palmerston a Tory turned Liberal, earnest, eloquent
W.E. Gladstone had little else in common with him other
than his support for Italian Nationalism

The Nationalist leader Louis Kossuth rousing the people of Hungary
to intrepid but inevitably doomed rebellion against the rule of Austria

The evangelical seventh Earl of Shaftesbury, who, according to
Florence Nightingale, would have been in an asylum himself if he had
not been devoted to reforming them

Light-hearted Minny, Lady Shaftesbury, the improbable wife of the
stern philanthropist, and probably Palmerston's daughter

Brocket Hall, the seat of the Melbournes, which passed to Lady
Palmerston on the death of her last surviving brother

The most flamboyant admiral in the British navy, Sir Charles 'Mad Charlie' Napier, who once commanded a Portuguese fleet under the pseudonym Carlos de Ponza

Lord Aberdeen's War Cabinet, with Russell, Lansdowne and Gladstone sitting to the left of the Prime Minister and Palmerston dominant on the right

Despite the resentful obstruction of many male colleagues, Florence Nightingale travelled tirelessly round the Crimea inspecting conditions at the front for herself

King Victor Emmanuel's chief minister, Count Camillo di Cavour, whose statecraft and diplomacy contributed as much as Garibaldi's army to the freedom and unification of Italy

Garibaldi and his redshirts, 'the thousand heroes', land at Marsala to
free Sicily from its Bourbon king

Punch's view of the naval arms race between
Palmerston and Napoleon III

Otto von Bismarck, the ruthless 'Iron Chancellor' of Germany

On a good day, even in old age, Palmerston could still look vigorous, despite grey hair and gout

On 23 January, when Parliament reassembled, John Roebuck proposed the creation of a select committee 'to enquire into the condition of our Army before Sevastopol, and into the conduct of those departments of the Government whose duty it has been to minister to the wants of the Army'. Russell, still petulant, resigned at once, on the grounds that the motion could not be resisted, leaving Palmerston to take over as Leader of the House and put up a suspiciously feeble defence. Six days later the motion was carried by 305 votes to 148; and Aberdeen resigned at once.

There was an uncanny similarity between what happened next and the events that were to take place nearly a hundred years later after the resignation of Neville Chamberlain. Just as King George turned first to Lord Halifax before moving on to Winston Churchill, so Queen Victoria turned first to the leader of the opposition, Lord Derby.

Derby invited Palmerston to be Secretary for War and the Colonies and Leader of the House of Commons. Palmerston accepted on condition Clarendon stayed at the Foreign Office, knowing full well that Clarendon hated Derby so much that he was bound to say no. When Clarendon did just that, Derby gave up, and the Queen sent for Lansdowne. But Lansdowne pleaded age and infirmity. Then Clarendon refused and once again the Queen turned to Russell. Russell tried harder, but he had just earned himself so much ill will that he was never going to fill a Cabinet, and Palmerston was able to risk saying that he was willing to serve under him again after all.

At last the Queen accepted the people's choice and on 4 February she sent for 'the poor old sinner'. It was an appointment that was, she wrote, 'personally not agreeable to me, but I think of nothing but the country, and the preservation of its institutions, and my own personal feelings would be sunk if only the efficiency of the Government could be obtained'.

And so the uncanny similarity continued as complete coincidence. In 1855, as in 1940, when a government stumbled unprepared into a war and then fell for failing to manage it properly, the leadership passed to an Old Harrovian aristocrat who had seen it all coming, but who, in the eyes of some colleagues, was not to be trusted, and in the eyes of most of them, was too old for the job.

13. War and Peace

Lord Palmerston never lived at 10 Downing Street. Like many of the earliest Prime Ministers, who held office before the house was altered and extended, he lived in his own London home and used his official residence only for Cabinet meetings and other business.

His appointment as Prime Minister coincided with a move from the comparative modesty of Carlton Gardens to the magnificence of 94 Piccadilly, a huge, hundred-year-old, classical mansion set back behind its own shallow carriage drive on the opposite side of the street from Green Park. It had been built by the third Earl of Egremont as a London counterpart to his splendid country seat at Petworth. More recently it had been the home of Queen Victoria's only irreproachable Hanoverian uncle, the Duke of Cambridge, which was why most people, although never the Palmerstons, now referred to it a little pretentiously as 'Cambridge House'.

The purchase of a lease on this house had been made possible by an impressive change in the Palmerstons' circumstances. By 1855 the patient long-term investment programme had completed its course. The last of the debts had been paid. All the incomes from Palmerston's much improved quarries and estates were now his to dispose of as he pleased; and these, combined with Lady Palmerston's immense inheritance after the recent death of her brother, were more than enough to enable them to move to Piccadilly. At last London's leading political hostess had a house worthy of her famous Saturday receptions.

As always, the receptions were held throughout every parliamentary session. As always, Lady Palmerston paid all her guests the compliment of writing out each invitation herself. And as always, the Radicals were indignant because there were too many Absolutists among them, and the

Tories muttered because they regularly included so many revolutionary refugees. But Lady Palmerston, as always, was immune to criticism. She had never been afraid to defy convention, even in ways that might have ruined the reputation of any less powerful woman; and she remained ready to do so, socially at least, if she thought it would be useful to her husband. As always, her receptions were much more than mischievous mixtures of friends and enemies. They were carefully contrived to generate a genial, unguarded atmosphere in which colleagues, critics and opponents could be encouraged to continue their support, charmed into a change of heart, or perhaps even flattered into forbearance.

The only noticable difference between earlier receptions and those at 94 Piccadilly, apart from the splendour of the new surroundings, was the more frequent appearance of guests from the one group that all the Whigs, all the Tories and all the other political hostesses agreed was unacceptable in 'general society': the gentlemen of the press. It was this that soon added an indignant Queen Victoria to the ranks of the detractors. Yet again, and with no more success than before, she attempted to influence the Palmerstons' guest list, demanding that they should at least exclude those journalists who had presumed to disparage her husband.

Unlike most of his predecessors in any of his offices, Palmerston did not disdain public opinion; and he understood better than anyone how much recent events had increased its significance. If only through the force of numbers, the extended franchise had put most urban constituencies beyond the reach of patronage or corruption. The origin of political power now lay closer to where it was supposed to lie, among the electorate in the country, not among the parliamentary parties and their patrons; and as Palmerston had been the first to recognize, the best way to influence an unsuborned voter was with passionate or alarming articles in his favourite, avowedly partisan newspaper. As for influencing the men who published those articles, he had known instinctively from the outset that the best way to do that was to provide them with the copy himself, or at least earn their gratitude with well-informed tips and suggestions. But this was by no means the only way: as experience had soon taught him, most editors and feature writers were also susceptible to aristocratic hospitality.

By the time Palmerston moved to Piccadilly, the best-established of his 'inconvenient' guests was inevitably his ambitious protégé Algernon Borthwick, who had become editor of the *Morning Post* on his father's death in 1852. Like his parents before him, Borthwick was often a guest at Broadlands, as well as at Lady Palmerston's London receptions and dinners. He was not, however, the only second-generation writer at the Piccadilly gatherings. Another regular was Thornton Leigh Hunt, the son of the poet, who, as Palmerston put it, was 'not insensible to Civility and attention from his superiors in Rank and Condition'. At first this hardly eminent author did not seem worthy of the compliment, but before Palmerston's first year in Downing Street was over, the investment had paid off and its prescience had become obvious. With the launch of the *Daily Telegraph*, and the appointment of Hunt as consulting editor, a new and immediately influential newspaper was added to the *Morning Post*, the *Globe*, the *Morning Advertiser*, the *Daily News* and others in the growing body of Palmerston's supporters.

The most celebrated press guest, however, and the only one who was regarded as acceptable and even sought after by other hostesses, was William Howard Russell. As soon as he returned from the Crimea in 1856, Russell received the first of many invitations to a reception at 94 Piccadilly, and the grateful Prime Minister invited him to breakfast and flattered him by asking his advice on every aspect of military reform. Although it was fortuitous, Russell had already rendered two great services to his host. His first criticisms of the conduct of the war had altered the public perception of what was happening and had helped to put Palmerston in power; and at the same time they had induced an unlikely change of heart, which had resulted in the addition of a surprising new name to Lady Palmerston's regular guest list. Like Russell's readers, his editor at *The Times*, John Delane, had come to accept that Palmerston was the only man who could win the war. The relentless critic who had identified Palmerston in print as his newspaper's 'ancient foe' became instead, in the words of an astonished Disraeli, 'his trumpeter'.

The conversion of Delane and *The Times* was made all the more credible by the coincidental resignation of Henry Reeve, *Il Pomposo*, the leader writer who had been in the forefront of all their attacks on

Palmerston's foreign policy. But Palmerston was at first unconvinced. He told the Queen that *The Times* was only backing him now because it always liked to be on the winning side. It was only with the passage of time that the cautious collaboration between the two old adversaries evolved into a genuine and mutually supportive friendship. Within less than a decade, however, Delane was passing on a tip he had just received about ministerial reshuffles and remarking smugly to his assistant editor, the Scandinavian scholar George Dasent, 'I don't believe half the Cabinet know it as I write.'

Despite all that he had said about Palmerston in the past, and despite the initial wariness between the new allies, Delane was immediately delighted by Lady Palmerston's invitations. He was as flattered as any other editor to be admitted to the self-consciously exclusive milieu of ambassadors, statesmen and society beauties who assembled on Saturdays at number 94. But the genial Prime Minister made no distinctions. He stood beside his still beautiful wife at the top of the grand staircase and welcomed them all with equal enthusiasm, as if each one of them was the guest of honour, even though he admitted to his family that he could not always recognize them or even hear what they were saying.

He was quite often tired now. Among his civil servants his attention to detail and his capacity for hard work were as notorious as ever, but the burdens of office were taking a more obvious toll than they had during his days as Foreign Secretary. Although there were plenty of times when he looked deceptively youthful, standing erect and emanating all the vitality of a sportsman who still rode regularly and spent a day shooting as often as he could, there were as many times when attacks of gout gave an equally misleading impression of feeble old age, forcing him to stoop and lean heavily on a cane to ease the weight off his swollen foot. It was even said that he sometimes darkened his hair with a little of Lady Palmerston's dye, and that now and then he tried to mask his pallor with the powder and rouge that lay on her dressing table. To the satisfaction of his surviving critics and opponents, who had always represented him as a vain and shallow opportunist, there were undeniably a few occasions when the stooped and dyed and powdered old dandy looked a little closer to their fanciful image than ever before.

Disraeli was the most scathing, not only about Palmerston but also about the nation that put its trust in him. As soon as it became clear that Palmerston's premiership was 'inevitable', he wrote in impotent fury to his haughty confidante Frances Anne, Dowager Marchioness of Londonderry, whose recently deceased husband had been the great Castlereagh's half-brother and heir, and who was the Tories' only real rival to Lady Palmerston as a political hostess.

Tho' he is really an imposter, utterly exhausted, and at the best only ginger beer and not champagne, and now an old painted Pantaloon, very deaf, very blind, and with false teeth, which would fall out of his mouth when speaking, if he did not hesitate and halt so in his talk – he is a name which the country resolves to associate with energy, wisdom, and eloquence, and will until he has tried and failed.

From all that he said in less passionate moods, it is clear that in reality Disraeli had a sincere respect for his opponent. The opinion he expressed to Lady Londonderry was heavily coloured by the exasperation of a man who had just been denied office by the timidity of his senior colleagues, and it was probably not one that he would have recorded anywhere other than in a private letter. Drawn loosely from life though it was, the exaggerated portrait was more like bitter wishful thinking than well-drawn caricature, and it was a long way from the picture painted by others. In the last days of the previous government Aberdeen had joked about Palmerston's energy. William Howard Russell described him as bounding in to breakfast. One of the doormen at the House of Commons, William White, who wrote a weekly column on its 'inner workings' in the *Illustrated Times*, told his readers, 'Lord Palmerston is, we should say, about five feet ten inches in height, looks about fifty-five years old – not more, albeit he is turned seventy – walks upright as a dart, and steps out like a soldier.'

To the members of his family, who were no more reassured by his contrived vigour than they were alarmed by the familiar symptoms of gout, the truth probably lay a little closer to champagne than exhaustion.

But, even so, attentive Lady Palmerston was all too often anxious. Only three days after her husband took office as Prime Minister, she told Shaftesbury that he was 'distracted with all the worry he has to go through', although this may have been a plea for understanding and an attempt at conciliation rather than an expression of concern. Even for Palmerston, 'the People's Darling', the process of forming a government was 'the nearest run thing you ever saw', and Shaftesbury was an early casualty.

Lady Palmerston's daughter-in-law the new Lady Cowper put the position succinctly in one of her many instructive letters to her bashful husband. Palmerston, she wrote, was 'not popular, except out of doors among the people'. Within the House of Commons, like anyone else, he could hope to provide himself with a reliable working majority only by creating a coalition Cabinet. Nevertheless, if he did have to assign some seats outside his own party, he could at least keep one of them within his own family; and he therefore began by inviting Shaftesbury to join his Cabinet as Chancellor of the Duchy of Lancaster. But while Shaftesbury was delaying his intended acceptance with a dramatic display of soul-searching, the offer was apologetically withdrawn. Lansdowne, to whom Palmerston was turning for advice at every step, had convinced him that, at this stage, the appointment of an aristocratic Conservative philanthropist might lose more support among the Whigs than it would gain among the followers of Disraeli.

All that was needed in Lansdowne's view was to persuade most of the Peelites in the previous Cabinet to remain in office. This, however, was easier said than done. For the first time in his life the previous Prime Minister, the Earl of Aberdeen, was behaving as loftily as he looked and making it plain that he was not prepared to play second fiddle to anyone. Although unjustly, the previous Secretary of State for War, the Duke of Newcastle, had been sufficiently discredited by criticism to be unacceptable to most of the Whigs. As for the other five – the Chancellor of the Exchequer, Gladstone, the First Lord of the Admiralty, Sir James Graham, the Lord Privy Seal, the Duke of Argyll, the Postmaster-General, Viscount Canning, and the last Secretary at War, Sidney Herbert, who had served in the ministry until it was at last amalgamated with Newcastle's at the end of 1854 – every one of them was for the moment admirably reluctant to do anything that would look like a betrayal of Aberdeen.

There were, however, three who were, each in his own way, a little less reluctant than the others. 'Carlo' Canning, the only surviving son of Palmerston's mentor George Canning, had grown up with an indulgent affection for Palmerston and was innately in sympathy with his methods; Argyll, despite his own opposition to the war, acknowledged openly that, in the light of all the popular 'delusion', Palmerston at least deserved to be given his chance to lead a government; and Herbert actually went so far as to suggest that he was not nearly as belligerent as others believed and that he was probably more capable than anyone of bringing the war to a satisfactory conclusion. With the inveterate schoolyard candour of one Old Harrovian to another about a third, Herbert told Aberdeen, 'If he chose to try for it, there is nobody who could make peace so easily as Palmerston. Terms would be accepted from him here in England which would be hooted at from you.' But not even Canning, Argyll or Herbert was prepared to join a Palmerston coalition unless all the other Peelites came in as well.

For a couple of days it looked as though Palmerston was going to fare no better than Derby or Russell. And then rescue came from the least likely source. The Queen was desperate. Her army was in jeopardy; her government was in crisis; and no matter what she felt about it, her subjects wanted Palmerston to put everything right. She turned to Aberdeen, to whom she had just promised the Garter. If he could only persuade the Peelites to join the government, the people would have the Prime Minister they wanted and she might have a Cabinet capable of controlling his more aggressive tendencies. The grateful old earl would not go so far as to withdraw the announcement of his own retirement, nor did he feel that there was anything to be gained at this stage by restoring Newcastle, but he promised that he would try to persuade the others. Having spoken first to Palmerston, who assured him that the war would not be expanded or prolonged unnecessarily, he went to each of the other five Peelites in turn, passing on the assurance and urging them to accept the Cabinet seats that had already been offered to them; and for his sake, ostensibly, they all agreed.

So, as Walter Bagehot, editor of *The Economist*, wrote a few years later, 'we turned out the Quaker and put in the pugilist'. Palmerston replaced Aberdeen as Prime Minister; and as Minister for War, in place of Newcastle, he installed a chubby 'Scottish Whig', Lord Panmure, who, despite being a gambler and a wastrel in his youth, had been Secretary at War in Russell's government and had served for twelve years in the Cameron Highlanders before standing for Parliament in 1835. But Panmure was the only 'new broom' in the government on which the British people was placing such high hopes. Like Palmerston himself, every other minister in his initial Cabinet had held office in Aberdeen's previous one. And most of them returned to their old ministries.

Since Russell was still deeply out of favour with most of the Peelites and many of the Whigs, his return would have at best precluded a coalition. His last post, Lord President of the Council, was therefore given back to Earl Granville, who had held it before him; and as a consolation – and to prevent him from setting up in opposition – Russell was sent to Vienna as British plenipotentiary at the peace conference which had just been established by the Austrians.

In the other seats, Lord Cranworth remained Lord Chancellor, Argyll remained Lord Privy Seal, Gladstone returned to the Exchequer, Clarendon to the Foreign Office, Graham to the Admiralty and Sir Charles Wood to the Board of Control, and Sir William Molesworth remained as First Commissioner of Works. As before, despite age and declining health, venerable and liberal Lansdowne agreed to stay on as Minister without Portfolio, to support the Prime Minister from the unequalled depth of his experience, and according to Abraham Hayward, who aspired to be one of Lady Palmerston's courtiers and occasionally wrote for the *Morning Chronicle*, to add tone to the discussions. The only two who changed office were Sir George Grey, who had taken over the Colonies when they were split from the Ministry for War and now replaced Palmerston at the Home Office, and Sidney Herbert, the last man to hold the extinct office of Secretary at War, who replaced Grey at the Colonial Office.

Whether or not this was a Cabinet capable of carrying on a war any better than the one it replaced, it greatly reassured the Queen. On 5 February she wrote in her journal:

That so good a government has been able to be formed is entirely owing to my dear kind, excellent friend, Lord Aberdeen, but to change him for Lord Palmerston is somewhat of a trial. The latter certainly does owe us many amends for all he has done, and he is without doubt of a very different character to my dear and worthy friend. Still, as matters now stand, it was decidedly the right and wise course to take, and I think that Lord Palmerston, surrounded as he will be, will be sure to do no mischief.

Her Majesty was more right than she could have known. Instead of getting on with the business of bringing the war to a satisfactory conclusion, the Cabinet was obstructed and diverted by Peelite demands for greater representation in the government. But at what looked like the critical moment the situation was saved again by another unlikely rescuer; and this time, although unintentionally, it was someone who had already changed the course of Palmerston's career more than once.

On 16 February Palmerston attempted to persuade the House of Commons that there was no longer any need for a committee to investigate the conduct of the war. He reminded the House of the famous moment in the Peasants' Revolt when the Mayor of London struck down Wat Tyler and the boy-king Richard II rode towards his furious followers and won them by offering to replace Tyler as their leader; and he asked the House to accept the new government as a replacement for the investigating committee. But the mid-nineteenth-century members of the. House of Commons were not as easily moved as medieval peasants. The not too apt analogy failed. John Roebuck, who had originally proposed the committee, persisted in his demand; the House agreed with him; and Palmerston gave way.

Although it can hardly have seemed so at the time, it was the third occasion on which Palmerston was to benefit from one of Radical Roebuck's resolutions. The first was back in June 1850, when Roebuck moved a vote of confidence in the government's foreign policy, which presented Palmerston with the opportunity to make the most emotional and significant speech of his life, vindicating his conduct in Greece, winning not only the applause of the Commons but the patriotic heart of 'Middle England' and for the time being thwarting all the Queen's plans to have him removed from the Foreign Office. Roebuck's initial successful demand for a committee to investigate the conduct of the war had brought down the government and created the void which only Palmerston could fill. And now his insistence on that demand was to release Palmerston from his Peelite handicap. When Palmerston agreed to the creation of the committee, Gladstone, Graham and Herbert resigned. They argued that the committee was unconstitutional, which Palmerston conceded might well be the case, and they insisted that they could neither accept responsibility for exposing Aberdeen and Newcastle to its criticism nor abandon them to face it alone. But the Radicals, most Whigs and many of the Peelites were convinced that they were just trying to avoid being the objects of criticism themselves; Palmerston suspected that they were seizing the first excuse they could find to leave a government to which they had never wanted to belong in the first place; and the entire House of Commons, most of which was eager to see the war brought swiftly to an honourable conclusion, condemned them for running away in a crisis. They had done what Russell did and they had earned the same reproach for it.

Palmerston had only brought the Peelites into his government in order to secure the support of their followers in the Commons, but the way in which the leading three had just walked out on him had so alienated those followers that most of them continued to support him anyway. For the time being at least he still had his majority; and since he no longer needed Peelite ministers, he could give the three empty seats to Whigs. The Exchequer went to the scholarly Sir George Cornewall Lewis, the Admiralty to Sir Charles Wood, the future first Lord Halifax; and now that Gladstone, Graham and Herbert had replaced Russell in parliamentary odium, Russell, by then on his way to Vienna, was appointed Colonial Minister.

In addition, Robert Vernon Smith, the nephew of Sydney Smith, joined the Cabinet as President of the Board of Control, and Shaftesbury was again invited to join as Chancellor of the Duchy of Lancaster. This time, however, the great evangelical philanthropist did not take even a moment to think it over. He refused immediately and then embarrassed himself with a disingenuously trivial explanation. Although he had not mentioned it before, he now felt that he could not possibly join a government led by a man who had approved an increase in the grant to the Roman Catholic seminary at Maynooth and who was known to be in favour of admitting practising Jews into Parliament and relaxing some of the stricter Sunday observances.

The result was an acrimonious row, which Shaftesbury described characteristically as 'the disruption of family ties'. Despite affectionate pleas from both Palmerstons, and despite his wife's irrefutable assertion that he would be much more effective in his good works if he conducted them with the authority of a Cabinet minister, he remained resolute in his righteous refusal; and he added paranoia to his petulance by suspecting that his opponents had told Palmerston, 'This man may be troublesome; get him into the Cabinet on terms that will excite the suspicion of his friends, and he will be neutralized for ever.'

But if Shaftesbury was so childish as to have created the 'disruption' in retribution for Palmerston's earlier slight, he was still politician enough to deduce from the cold, calm tone of the conciliatory letter that came from Lady Palmerston that it might not be wise to prolong it. In answer he sent her an emotional, self-pitying justification of his actions, describing his refusal as a 'great sacrifice' and bemoaning the the extent to which it had 'completely broken' his 'private and domestic peace'; and Lady Palmerston wrote back accepting his 'kind and amiable and affectionate' explanation with unusually unconvincing compassion. Shaftesbury had so misjudged his moment that he had made himself look selfish and insensitive as well as foolish. The Palmerston family was beset by far more painful traumas than the consequences of his latest righteous spasm. Minny's exasperation at the wilful self-destruction of her husband took second place by a very long way to her sister Fanny's inconsolable grief at the sudden, unexpected death of hers.

Clever, fine-looking Fanny, who was ten years younger than Minny, had been a bridesmaid at Queen Victoria's wedding and was the one member of the combined Cowper-Palmerston family whom Her Majesty sincerely regarded as a friend. Her husband, Lord Jocelyn, who was heir to the earldom of Roden, had become an MP after serving as a soldier in the Opium Wars, in which he contracted a recurring and debilitating fever, and had continued to serve enthusiastically in the militia, often neglecting his wife for the pleasures of the mess as much as his duties. Like most militia officers, Jocelyn had been mobilized when the bulk of the tiny British army had been sent east to the Crimea. Unlike most militia officers, however, he did not live in a comfortable house or an inn and just join his men for duties in the day time. Instead he insisted on being billeted with them, even though their billet was the Tower of London, beside the infected River Thames, at the height of the latest in the long line of London's cholera epidemics.

Just up river from the Tower, the Corporation of the City of London had recently banned cesspools and appointed inspectors to ensure that all privies were kept clean, and as a result the fatalities along that stretch of the north bank were far fewer than elsewhere. But a large proportion of that few came from the soldiers stationed in the Tower, where such sanitation as existed had not been planned to provide for so many, and their commanding officer was one of them. As soon as he exhibited the first humiliating symptoms, Jocelyn was taken away to 94 Piccadilly, where he died within twenty-four hours.

After a few weeks of hopeless despair Lady Jocelyn coped with her grief by immersing herself in the role of the beautiful, elegant, unattainable widow, a role that she over-played for the rest of her life as excessively as her brother-in-law over-played the role of misunderstood idealist.

Perhaps to nobody's surprise the idealist eventually told Palmerston that he was prepared to compromise his principles for the sake of the greater general good. If Palmerston really could not find anyone else to serve as Chancellor of the Duchy of Lancaster, Shaftesbury would accept the ministry. Over the next few days, perhaps mischievously and certainly improbably, Palmerston appeared to fail. Then, at the last minute, just as the Earl of Shaftesbury was about to leave his London home to accept office from the Queen, a messenger arrived to inform him that the Peelite Dudley Ryder, second Earl of Harrowby, had agreed to join the Cabinet in his place.

At the same time the Whig Lord Stanley of Alderley became President of the Board of Trade, in what was now essentially a one-party Cabinet.

Harrowby, whose son, just down from Christ Church, was planning to stand for Parliament as a Whig, accepted that Gladstone, Graham and Herbert had effectively killed off the Peelites as a party; and Argyll and Canning, who was soon to leave to become Governor-General of India, were already as much Palmerstonian as Peelite. Yet for all that it was a Whig Cabinet, it was, in composition and conduct, much closer to the oligarchic Whig party of the eighteenth century than to the Liberal Party into which it would soon evolve, a fact not lost on the doggerel writers:

> Cease ye rude and boisterous railers
> Do not dare our crew contemn
> Manned with such patrician sailors
> Our good ship the tide must stem.
> A jaunty Viscount is our skipper,
> A Duke and Marquess are her mates
> Three Earls do serve on board the clipper
> Four Sirs and all of them first-rates,
> Two Barons and another Viscount
> Duke Bedford's brother and therewith
> One single commoner can I count
> The lord-like looking Mr Smith.

And yet, even though the incompetence and indolence of aristocratic officers was now being put forward as the main reason for the failure of the army, the composition of the Cabinet meant nothing to the British public. Their attitude was well represented by the caption to a cartoon in *Punch* on 17 February, which showed Palmerston and Russia squaring up to each other in a boxing ring: 'NOW FOR IT! a set-to between "Pam, the Downing Street pet" and "the Russian Spider".' They had faith in the 'skipper'; they were eager for results; and the delay caused by the resignation of the leading Peelites had only served to make them impatient.

But the Peelite delay was not the only obstacle to rapid progress. Although the Cabinet was now on the whole more harmonious and supportive than its predecessors, it soon found itself hampered by an unexpected handicap. The new Minister for War and the Colonies, Lord Panmure, turned out to be a grave and immediate disappointment. His new dignity went to his head. He was pompous, self-important and obstinate, even with the Prime Minister. At heart he knew that he was no more up to the job than Newcastle; and he tried to conceal and compensate for his ineptitude by being ponderously, obstructively and dangerously methodical. Since he was the only new name introduced by Palmerston into his original Cabinet, his early dismissal would have been a welcome gift to Disraeli and his disordered opposition. The apparent indecision could have been used as grounds for a motion of no confidence. Palmerston and his allies, both inside and outside the Cabinet, had no choice but to put up with Panmure and divert precious time and energy towards coaxing him into accepting their advice and decisions and imbuing his subordinates with a sense of urgency.

Energy, however, was one of the two essential qualities that the 71 year-old Prime Minister brought to the conduct of the war. The other was experience. The last time British soldiers were engaged in a war, Palmerston had been the minister responsible for supplying them, and he had already demonstrated how valuable that experience still was. During Aberdeen's wartime leadership the deployment and support of the militia, which came under the control of Palmerston's Home Office, had been carried out flawlessly and far faster than anything achieved by the War Office or the Board of Ordnance. And it had been done with an unusual degree of tact. When the Queen merely requested that at least some of her precious guards should remain at Windsor and not be replaced by less disciplined militia, Palmerston gave in to her after only one protest.

Experience had also taught Palmerston that logistics were easier to influence from Westminster than tactics; and it was on logistics that he concentrated his energy. He understood military beauracracy and he had once been notorious for circumventing or eliminating the worst of its traditional delays. He had seen enough to know what changes needed making, and he had learned enough to know the best ways of making them. At his first Cabinet meeting the venerable Board of Ordnance was put under the control of the War Office. Shortly afterwards a special

Transport Department was established at the Admiralty. But most of the improvements effected during the next twelve months in the support and conditions of the British army were not introduced by Palmerston. In almost every case the needs were so glaringly obvious that the first steps towards meeting them had been made under Aberdeen. Palmerston's achievement was to make things happen. Where Aberdeen's government had dithered and delayed, Palmerston badgered and, as before, scrutinized and interfered, impulsively providing each relevant department with the benefit of his own opinion on any topic from guns to medicines, from fresh meat to forage caps. Each time the Roebuck committee found fault, Palmerston was able to answer that the matter was already being addressed, and the committee was left with little to do but search for somebody to blame.

By the end of February the barely passable clay-soup track between Balaclava harbour and the British lines around Sevastopol had been replaced by a metalled road. By the end of March it was accompanied by a light rail track. Appropriate clothes and enough modern Minié rifles for everyone began to arrive on a continuous transport service between Constantinople and Balaclava. Huts replaced tents. Fresh vegetables and meat were supplied regularly, and consignments were no longer left to rot beside the Bosporus while the ships that could have carried them stood idle waiting for what were regarded as more important military cargoes.

With his new robust approach to the management of the war Palmerston also introduced a change of emphasis. In one of the earliest of all too many long letters to Panmure he wrote, 'It is also very likely that some regiments are encamped or hutted upon ground known to be unhealthy, and, if so, they ought to be removed without listening to the "military considerations" which officers commanding brigades or divisions may urge. The most important military consideration is to keep soldiers alive and in good health.' In the name of common sense as much as humanity, priority was given to the welfare of the men, and this was the one area in which some of the changes were due directly to Palmerston.

On 16 February, the day on which Palmerston first entered the House of Commons as Prime Minister, Isambard Kingdom Brunel received a letter from the War Office inviting him to design and make a prefabricated hospital. The prototype was built in the grounds of Paddington Station, and all the parts arrived ready for erection at Renkioi in Turkey on 12 May. It had 1,000 beds distributed among twenty-two interconnected ward huts, each with two wards, a nurses' room, a surgery, a bathroom, lavatories and its own simple ventilation and cooling system; there were separate buildings for the kitchen, the bakery and the laundry, each built out of metal instead of wood to reduce the risk of fire; and the whole establishment was put under the drection of Professor Edmund Parkes, who was soon to be famous as the founder of the modern science of hygiene and the apostle of its military applications.

Tragically, however, no local labour could be found. The whole hospital had to be built by the eighteen craftsmen who came out with it. It was not fully operational until the beginning of December. Only 1,500 patients passed through it before peace was declared; and of these only fifty died. It was a staggering statistic – many, many times better than the earlier death rate at any of the other hospitals in Turkey, particularly Scutari – and it revealed just how many hundreds more might have been saved if the building had only been finished sooner.

But Florence Nightingale had much more to cope with at Scutari than inadequate quarters and a horrifying death rate. The image of the 'lady with the lamp' was a long way from the reality of a formidable woman who spent half her day 'dealing with the mean, the selfish, the incompetent'. She was constantly delayed by military bureaucracy, regularly obstructed by the resentful indifference of senior officers and sometimes even thwarted by dissent and rivalries among her own staff. By the time she went to inspect the field hospitals round Balaclava, in May 1855, she was already so exhausted that, to the great relief of the nurses and doctors who hindered her at every step, she soon collapsed and had to return to convalesce at Scutari.

At home Florence Nightingale featured prominently in the newspapers. In the absence of any heroes among the men who commanded the soldiers, the press and public found a heroine in the leader of the women who nursed them. But it might not have been so, particularly in the face of so much obstruction and criticism from the Army Medical Service. During her first two and a half months in Turkey, Florence Nightingale's reputation nearly foundered on the death rate. Despite a disciplined regime, clean dressings and blankets, regular washing and at least some drugs, patients were twice as likely to die at Scutari as in one of the hospitals in the Crimea, not from their wounds but from cholera, dysentery and other infectious diseases.

Fortunately there were many among the younger generation of doctors in England who knew that such problems were likely to arise in any military hospital. Early in 1855, one of these, the 'good and kind' Dr Hector Gavin, approached Shaftesbury, whom he had met in the course of his work among the poor, and suggested that a 'Sanitary Commission' should be sent east to carry out inspections and make recommendations at all the British military hospitals. Although he had just been deprived of his first opportunity to continue considering a seat in the new Cabinet, Shaftesbury had not yet reduced his relationship with Palmerston to a 'disruption of family ties'. He took the idea to the new Prime Minister, whose recent experience at the Home Office had made him easy to convince. Reinforced by a letter of support from Palmerston, he then went to the new Minister for War and successfully presented his case with passionate but respectful urgency.

At the beginning of March the Sanitary Commissioners, who included Dr Gavin, arrived in Constantinople carrying instructions from Shaftesbury, which laid out in detail exactly how they should proceed, and a letter of introduction from Palmerston to the Commander-in-Chief, Lord Raglan, which expressed no illusions as to the many ways in which they might, but must not, be obstructed.

> I request that you will give them every assistance and support in your power. They will, of course, be opposed and thwarted by the medical officers, by the men who have charge of the port arrangements, and by those who have the cleaning of the camp. Their mission will be ridiculed, and their recommendations and directions set aside, unless enforced by the peremptory exercise of your authority.

But the interposition of men skilled in this way is urgently required. The hospital at Scutari is become a hotbed of pestilence, and if no proper precautions are taken before the sun's rays begin to be felt, your camp will become one vast seat of the most virulent plague. I hope this commission will arrive in time to prevent much evil, but I am very sure that not one hour should be lost after their arrival in carrying into effect the precautionary and remedial measures which they may recommend.

Soon after his arrival in Constantinople, Hector Gavin was killed when his brother accidentally discharged a pistol while cleaning it. But the commission that he initiated did indeed 'prevent much evil', not only everywhere in the Crimea but also, and particularly, at Scutari. The engineer on the commission, Robert Rawlinson, who was later to be knighted, discovered that the sewers beneath the old barracks, which were inadequate in the first place, had long since been blocked and had turned into overloaded cesspools, from which noxious damp was seeping into all the foundations of the building and rising up the walls of the wards. In the absence of any flushing or drains, the excrement from the prefabricated privies in the courtyard was seeping out of the trench beneath into the water tanks beside them, and the large pipe carrying the bulk of that water to other parts of the hospital was blocked by the decomposed carcass of a horse. The conditions were 'murderous'. It was no wonder that even doctors and nurses were dying, and that there were some beds in which no patient survived.

The remedy was obvious and the benefit immediate. On the commissioners' orders the sewers were emptied and flushed through, running water was supplied to the latrines and every wall was limewashed. Ratcatchers were employed. The courtyards were cleared of all the rubbish that had been accumulating unattended since the barracks first became a hospital, and which was found to contain twenty-six dead animals, including another two horses.

By the time spring came and the sun's rays were felt, the influences of the commission and the general improvements in logistics were obvious everywhere in the Crimea and Turkey. Even in the front lines, where cholera was never eliminated entirely, morale was so much better that the men were said to be swearing again. A soldier's hope of survival at Scutari, although never as high as at Renkioi, was multiplied many times. In England, over the months that followed, Florence Nightingale's reputation soared; and at Scutari, with her wards purged of pestilence, the domineering angel of mercy was left instead to continue her battles with the insubordination of nuns and nurses and the increasingly resentful opposition of the Army Medical Service.

Shortly after the Sanitary Commission reached Constantinople another group of commissioners had arrived in the Crimea to investigate the supply and support of the army. They laid the blame for most of the shortcomings on James Filder, a former civil servant who had been brought out of retirement to act as Commissary-General, and to a lesser extent on his military counterparts, the Quartermaster-General, General Richard Airey, and the Adjutant-General, General James Estcourt; and they recommended that all three should be replaced. It was a recommendation that Palmerston was more than ready to put into effect. But he was disinclined to interfere too much in military appointments, and he soon fell back in the face of furious and united resistance from Raglan, Panmure and General Sir George Simpson, the first British soldier to hold the post of Chief of Staff. Simpson, like Panmure, was a Scot, only this time an unassuming one; and, like Panmure, he was another of Palmerston's disappointing selections.

The commissioners' recommendation was taken up and supported in the House of Commons, however, by the Radical Henry Layard, who had witnessed the charge of the Light Brigade. By then he was already an opponent of the ancient but absurd tradition under which gentlemen with no demonstrable ability could purchase their commissions in the cavalry and the infantry, and the experience at Balaclava had made him an angry critic of the incompetent aristocratic high command as well. His cause was such obvious common sense that it won him the support of *The Times*, but he pursued it with such bitter animosity towards Palmerston that there may also have been a personal motive.

When Palmerston was Foreign Secretary, he had appointed the scholarly young Layard to a junior post in the embassy in Constantinople, despite the objections of the other embassy staff, who regarded the son of a mere civil servant from Ceylon as unsuitable; and while forming his government he had invited Layard to take office as Under-Secretary for War. But, as he had done to others, he had then withdrawn the offer, partly because Layard had insisted that other Radicals should be given posts as well, and partly because the Queen had 'remonstrated against Mr Layard's appointment... on account of his ill-conditioned abuse of Lord Raglan'.

Leaving Panmure to defend his logistics officers as best he could, Palmerston defended the purchase of commissions, using Layard's own experience as his melodramatic theme.

Why, look to that glorious charge of the cavalry at Balaclava — look to that charge where the noblest and wealthiest of the land rode foremost, followed by heroic men from the lowest classes of the community, each rivalling the other in bravery, neither the peer who led nor the trooper who followed being distinguished the one from the other.

Palmerston was under no illusions. He acknowledged that the system of purchasing commissions was in many ways invidious. But he also believed that more equitable systems were a threat to constitutional government. In his view officers, like electors, should be men who had a stake in the country and its future. Just as universal male franchise could lead, and had led, to the election of a populist dictator, professional officers who had nothing in the world but their salaries and the ranks could be expected to support any autocrat who promised to maintain or enhance those transitory assets.

The House of Commons, which was full of officers, agreed. So long as there were landed families in England, she would never be short of peers to lead charges. But it was no longer so easy to find troopers to follow them. As Prince Albert had already observed, the English had become too prosperous to enlist for a pittance in a volunteer army, which was one reason why there were more Irishmen than ever among the Crimean replacements. Palmerston wrote yet again to Panmure:

We are forty thousand men short of the number voted by Parliament, and we shall be without the shadow of an excuse if we do not resort to every possible means and every possible quarter to complete our force to the number which Parliament has authorized; let us get as many Germans and Swiss as we can, let us get men from Halifax (Nova Scotia), let us enlist Italians, and let us forthwith increase our bounty without raising the standard. Do not let departmental or official or professional prejudices and habits stand in our way ... We *must* have troops.

The enlistment of foreign nationals created more problems than it solved, however. In the summer of 1855 the government of the United States, which, although neutral, had some sympathy for the Russians, complained that several British diplomats, including the Minister in Washington, were illegally recruiting United States citizens and sending them to Nova Scotia to enlist in the British army. Despite the considerable evidence in support of the claim, Palmerston denied it, even telling the House of Commons that nothing had happened 'of which I should feel ashamed'. When the government in Washington demanded that the Minister be recalled, he refused; and when the Minister was then ordered to leave, it was all the the British Cabinet could do to prevent Palmerston from expelling the United States' Ambassador from London as well.

Eventually, in December 1855, Parliament passed the Foreign Enlistment Act, and soon afterwards a few thousand Germans were recruited into the British army. But they were too little and too late. To Palmerston's embarrassment and humiliation the British were never the senior partners in the military alliance against Russia. In the four months following their first landing the French army had grown to at least four times its original size, while the British army had barely doubled. Then in February the embarrassment and humiliation had been aggravated by the otherwise welcome arrival of 15,000 seasoned soldiers from a new ally, Sardinia. Coming from such a small nation, they were a disproportionately large contribution to the alliance – too much to be just a gesture of gratitude for such support as the two Powers had so far shown for the cause of a united and independent Italy. But from the point of view of Cavour and his king, they were also an investment, a gesture so generous that it could hardly be ignored if those Powers should ever be invited to support that cause again.

The Sardinians, who were known to the British as 'the Sardines', although most of them were from mainland Piedmont, moved into the lines round Sevastopol, where they were soon to fight as gallantly and effectively as the best of the British and the French. The weeks went by. The armies stood in stalemate, waiting for the sun to bring them solid ground. As Tsar Nicholas had predicted, Generals January and February had taken a terrible toll among the allies. But they also took their toll among the Russians, and one of the casualties was the Tsar, who recklessly rode out to review his troops while already suffering from a high fever and died from the resulting pleurisy.

As spring turned to summer and the allies failed to take Sevastopol, their batons of command changed hands. In May the inadequate French commander, Marshal François Canrobert, who had replaced the dying Jacques Saint Arnaud at the end of 1854, was himself replaced by Marshal Aimable Jean Jacques Pelissier, who had earned himself a grim reputation in North Africa by suffocating 500 Arabs in a cave. Towards the end of June, four days after his Adjutant-General, Estcourt, had died of cholera, Raglan died from exhaustion and dysentery; and as his replacement, true to his military form, Palmerston appointed Simpson, ignoring the pressure from the press in favour of Sir Colin Campbell, the much loved son of a Glasgow carpenter, who had famously repelled Russian cavalry with his 'thin red line' of Highlanders at Balaclava.

The changes in command did little to influence the conduct of the war. The best hopes for an end to it still lay with the peace talks in Vienna, where Russell continued to act as British representative, while Palmerston carried out his duties for him at the Colonial Office. But, from Palmerston's point of view, those hopes were neither as high nor as far-reaching as they had been at the outset. In May 1854, when the British fleet was in the Baltic, he had outlined his wild ambitions to Clarendon. Britain's best interests lay in maintaining a viable independent barrier between the other Powers and India. The principal objective was therefore to strengthen and secure the Turkish Empire by restoring its rule over the Crimea and the mouth of the Danube and destroying the permanent threat posed by the existence of Russia's Black Sea fleet. But outright success was also an opportunity to contain the Russians and clip their wings elsewhere. With victory in the Baltic they could be compelled to return Finland, which they had seized from the Swedes in 1808. It might even be possible to compel them to recognize an independent Poland.

Since then, however, diplomatic frustration and military failure had induced Palmerston to lower his sights. All he asked for now were the 'four points' which the ostensibly disinterested Austrians were putting forward in Vienna: that the Russians should relinquish their claim to act as protectors of the Turkish tributaries of Moldavia and Wallachia, and that the agreed rights of their peoples, assemblies and princes should be guaranteed by the Western Powers instead; that the long neglected mouth of the Danube should be dredged and cleared, and that free passage should be granted to all shipping, which gave Austria access to the Black Sea; that the terms of the treaty of 1841 preventing foreign warships from passing through the Dardanelles should be revoked, which, although it allowed the Russians to send warships into the Mediterranean, also allowed the allies to send warships into the Black Sea, and thereby effectively neutralized the Russian fleet; and that the Russians should abandon all claims to act as the protectors of the Ottoman Sultan's Christian subjects.

The death of Tsar Nicholas and the accession of his liberal son Alexander II raised some hopes that the Russians might now be more willing to negotiate. But Palmerston was not yet optimistic. As always, he had doubts about the Austrian peace-brokers, who, he was convinced, were bound to favour the Russians if they could. He had reservations about his own impulsive representative, Russell, who had, as he confided to Clarendon, an 'aptitude to be swayed by others'. Above all, he had no confidence in the commitment of his principal allies. The French Emperor was interested only in a quick flash of personal glory and then peace at any price; and his ministers, most of whom were known to have gambled on an early peace by investing heavily on the stock market, were now eager to make their dreams come true.

At least the upstart Emperor was open to the influence of flattery. In the middle of April, at Palmerston's suggestion, Napoleon III and his pretty Spanish Empress, Eugenie, were invited over to stay at Windsor. Everywhere they went they were greeted by cheering crowds. The Queen, to her surprise, was so impressed by the Emperor that she credited him with every imaginable quality in her journal; and she formed an immediate and lifelong friendship with the Empress, who was, she said, 'so nice that she might really be royal'. For his part, the Emperor was overwhelmed by the honours done to him. When the Queen invested him with the Order of the Garter, he whispered to her, 'at last I am a gentleman'.

In the course of his visit the Queen and the Palmerstons, who were also guests at Windsor, persuaded the Emperor to abandon his plan to go east and lead his army himself, a stunt that, if successful, would have raised his prestige enormously, as much among other monarchs as among his subjects, and one that a Queen of England could no longer be expected to match. More importantly, by the time he left, Palmerston had also won his agreement that France would settle for nothing less than 'the four points'. In every way the visit seemed to have been a triumph. 'There was immense embracing at the departure and many tears', wrote Disraeli with more than a hint of scorn. 'When the carriage door was at length closed, and all seemed over, the Emperor reopened it himself, jumped out, pressed Victoria to his heart and kissed her on each cheek, with streaming eyes.'

Meanwhile, however, negotiations at the peace conference in Vienna were running ahead of them. Although the Russians did now seem willing to come to terms, and although three of the points were almost acceptable to them, there was no way in which even the well-intentioned Alexander II could surrender his dominance of the Black Sea. The Austrian Foreign Minister, Count Buol, had therefore proposed a compromise: that the Russians and the Turks should agree to keep their Black Sea fleets below a fixed limit, and that Austria, France and Great Britain should guarantee the independence of the Ottoman Empire. It was little more than a proposed return to the circumstances that had existed before fighting began. As Palmerston later put it, 'instead of making to cease the preponderance of Russia in the Black Sea, it would perpetuate and legalize that preponderance, and instead of establishing a secure and permanent peace it would only establish a prospective case for war'. Nevertheless, the French Foreign Minister, Drouyn de Lhuys, who had been sent to the conference to strengthen his country's representation, agreed to the proposal, even though he had travelled to Vienna via London, where he had made the same promises to Palmerston as had just been made by his Emperor.

The conference adjourned, so that the representatives could consult their governments, and Drouyn de Lhuys returned in triumph to Paris, confident that he had acted as his Emperor and his government would have wished. When Napoleon came back from England a few days later, he agreed that his Foreign Minister had acted in France's best interest. But the British Ambassador, Lord Cowley, who had been appointed to the office once held by his father, disdainfully reminded them of their promises, assured them that the proposal was not acceptable to Her Majesty's Government and persuaded at least the Emperor that it was unenforceable; and if all that was not enough to change the imperial mind, the French War Minister clinched it by frightening the autocrat with the observation that his professional army, which had been suffering for so long in the siege of Sevastopol, was not going to be pleased if it was suddenly recalled without being given the chance to succeed. The Emperor imposed his will on his Cabinet. The French government rejected the Austrian proposal, and Drouyn de Lhuys resigned.

When the news reached London, Russell offered to resign as well, but the Cabinet reassured him that there was no reason to do any such thing. And then Count Buol, furious at the French change of heart, let it be known that Russell had also agreed to his proposal. It was the cue for an opportunistic, unprincipled and inconsistent combined attack from left and right. Radicals, Peelites and Conservatives united in what might have been sufficient numbers to defeat the government and prepared to censure Russell for his duplicity and for submitting to such humiliating terms.

Discredited again, Russell resigned again. But the thwarted new allies simply changed tactics. Since they had not actually presented their case to the House, they felt no compunction about abandoning it and attacking from the opposite extreme instead. Led by Gladstone, who in so doing lost himself the respect of Prince Albert, they criticized Palmerston for failing to make peace when he had the opportunity; and they opposed the government on every motion, one of which, a proposal to guarantee a loan of £5 million to Turkey, came within three votes of a defeat. In response Palmerston simply held his ground. He damned Gladstone with irony – 'there must, indeed, be grave reasons which could induce a man, who had been so far a party to the measures of the Government, utterly to change his opinions' – and he repeated his own reasons for fighting at every opportunity, aiming his rhetoric at the country rather than at the composite opposition.

> I say that the intention of Russia to partition Turkey is as manifest as the sun at noonday, and it is to prevent that we are carrying on the war ... Let no man imagine that if Russia gets possession of Turkey, and if that gigantic Power, like a Colossus, has one foot upon the Baltic and another upon the Mediterranean, the great interests of this country will not be perilled – let not the peace-at-all-price imagine for a moment that their trade and their commerce would not be deeply injured.

So the war went on. In August the British royal family strengthened the alliance with a return visit to France, and the Russians in Sevastopol made one last desperate effort to drive off their besiegers. With a force of over 40,000, outnumbering their enemy by at least two to one, they attacked the French and Sardinian positions on the high ground above the River Chernaia. But the allies held. When a gap opened up between them, the Sardinians plugged it. The ill-planned Russian attack was thrown back in confusion with terrible casualties. Then the allied bombardment of Sevastopol intensified, particularly from the sea. Although Brunei's advanced design for a monitor, or 'floating siege gun', had met with what he described as the Admiralty's 'extraordinary supply of cold water', the Sea Lords had listened to Napier, who had been baffled by shallow water in the Baltic, and on his advice they had supplied the fleet with a dozen fast little steam-driven sloops, each armed with two of the new, 68-pounder Lancaster muzzle-loaders, which could cause huge damage without much risk of being hit themselves. By 8 September the city and the port had been so softened that the allies were ready to launch their attack. While the British assaulted the strongpoint of the landward defences on their right, known as the Great Redan, the French assaulted the one on their left, built around the remnants of the Malakoff tower. The British failed and fell back from the Redan. But while they were regrouping for another assault, the French carried the Malakoff. Helpless and outflanked, the Russians set fire to what was left of Sevastopol and abandoned it.

Palmerston was all for fighting on, at best to weaken Russia with further territorial gains, or at least to let the British march away with a victory. But the long despondent people of France, who greeted their own victory with relief rather than triumph, were crying out for peace. And the Russians were now ready to discuss all the 'four points'. Their still predominantly agricultural economy had suffered much more than the developed industrial economies of France and Great Britain. The fall of Sevastopol had lost them their key to the dominance of the Black Sea. After the operations in the Baltic, which had worried them more than anyone realized at the time, they were alarmed by the defensive treaty that they knew the British and French were concluding with the Swedes. Starved of resources and threatened by land and sea on both their western flanks, the Russians were in no condition to go on with the war.

The peace conference reassembled in Vienna, where the delegates drew up a basis for discussion and then, to the delight of the status-seeking Emperor of France, agreed to complete their deliberations at a full congress in Paris. Yet, throughout it all, Palmerston continued to insist that the British were ready to fight on alone. It would have been neither sane nor just to do so. The effective British army in the Crimea was now little more than a quarter the size of the French one, far too small to take on even what was left of the Russians by itself. Besides, for the time being at least, all the objectives of the war were within the reach of the delegates in Vienna. But by then Palmerston was only bluffing; and if the bluff was not enough to deceive the

Russians, it does at least seem to have convinced his own Foreign Secretary. Clarendon regarded Palmerston with an uneasy mixture of resentment and respect, and he was already alarmed by the extent to which the Prime Minister had antagonized the Americans. In a letter to Canning he wrote soon afterwards, 'Whatever Palmerston in his jaunty mood may say, we could not have made war alone: for we would have had all Europe against us at once, and the United States would have followed.'

Palmerston could not bring himself to trust the Russians any more than he trusted the Austrians. He was sure that, no matter what they said in Vienna, they would try to negotiate better terms in Paris. As he told the Queen, 'It is very easy to argue in a case of this kind that each separate condition, taking the conditions one by one, is not of sufficient importance to justify a continuance of the war for that particular condition'. When he learned that the Russian delegation in Paris was to be led by Count Orloff, the man who had negotiated the Treaty of Unkiar Skelessi in 1833, he warned Clarendon that Orloff had 'all the cunning of a half-civilized savage' and that he would 'stand out for every point which he thinks he has a chance of carrying... like a housebreaker who tries every door and window in succession'.

It was as obvious to the Russians as to anyone that the French were so eager to make peace that they were likely to be generous. In threatening to fight on, therefore, Palmerston was simply doing the best he could to put the Russians under at least some pressure and warn their 'housebreaker' that the British were in no mood to settle for anything less than the 'four points'. As the French Ambassador in London admitted afterwards, Napoleon's ministers 'would have given in half a dozen times over' if the British government had not remained 'firm and consistent'. But Palmerston was clearly aware that, 'firm and consistent' though it was, his initial threat was not enough to be a convincing deterrent; and before long he had devised another one which was. By the time the congress assembled in Paris, he had cajoled the impressionable Napoleon into presiding over a conspicuous council of war, at which the allies had openly agreed to continue their campaign together if the negotiations did not go the way they wanted.

On 25 February the delegates to the congress set to work on an agenda much broader than the one that had been before them in Vienna. Cavour addressed them on the aspirations of Italy; and to the fury of the already indignant Austrians, Clarendon, who led the British delegation, supported him. They considered various aspects of maritime law. When the Treaty of Paris was eventually signed by all the parties on 30 March, it included terms on privateering, blockading and respect for neutral flags, some of which outlawed practices that had been employed with great success by the British navy in the wars against Napoleon and the United States, and in the suppression of the slave trade. But the most important terms of the treaty, achieved after much trying of doors and windows, were those that brought peace between Russia and Turkey.

Under the Treaty of Paris the Russians abandoned all claims to act as the protectors of the Christians in the Ottoman Empire and of the principalities of Moldavia and Wallachia, which were soon by their own volition to be united as Romania. The Black Sea was neutralized: arsenals were banned from all its shores and all but the smallest warships from its waters. The Russians relinquished control over the mouth of the Danube by ceding the land on its northern shore to Moldavia; and both the river and the Black Sea were declared open equally to the merchant ships of all nations. In addition, and in secret, Britain, France and Austria formed an alliance to defend the integrity of Turkey, by force of arms if necessary. It was an uneasy alliance from the outset, however. Given the sentimental and political attitudes of Britain and France towards the continuing Austrian presence in Italy, it was hardly one on which a sensible Turk would have wanted to rely.

In Great Britain the news that all the fighting and suffering had ended in little more than the settlement of a few faraway disputes was greeted as something of an anticlimax. When, in accordance with tradition, the treaty was read out by heralds to the City of London, the terms that brought new limitations to the activities of the navy were met with jeering and hissing. *The Sun* was published in mourning, as if the Queen had died. The Queen herself was disappointed that the war had not ended with a British victory and that the terms of the treaty were 'not all what we could wish or what we might have obtained if France had behaved as she ought'. Many MPs agreed with her. But Palmerston 'in his jaunty mood' told them that the treaty was a triumph, and both Houses gave his government a vote of confidence.

For the time being the Near East was at peace. The embittered Russians endured their humiliation. Withdrawing as obstructively as they could from the land they had been compelled to cede, they settled down to wait until some other dispute distracted the attention of the Western Powers and gave them the opportunity to reverse their fortunes. The Turkish Empire survived but, despite promises of reform, did little to fulfil them and continued to decline. The allied armies came home; and for the most part the painful lessons that had been taught but not learned in the Crimean winter were forgotten.

After forty years of peace, punctuated by many threats, the British had shown Europe that they still meant it when they said that they would fight. But they had also shown Europe that, if they did, their army would be no better prepared for it than last time, a shortcoming that was both noticed and noted by the Prussian representative at the German Diet, Otto von Bismarck. Nothing had changed. The British army was no more ready to make war against Russia than it had been to make war against Revolutionary France and Napoleon. After similar initial set-backs, and after the incomparable suffering of January and February, the logistics and living conditions improved. With more time, and with an old hand at the helm, British soldiers might eventually have been as well organized and supplied in the Crimea as they were by the end of their campaign in Spain. But they could never have been as well led. None of their commanders, not even the admirable Colin Campbell, was the equal of Wellington, Picton or Hill.

In the peace that followed, as in the war, the outstanding heroic figure was Florence Nightingale. On her return to England she began to collect funds for a training school for nurses and to campaign for improvements in the health care and living conditions of soldiers, whose barracks were so insanitary that their death rate, even in peacetime, was at least five times the civilian rate. In the course of the summer, in response to pressure from the Queen, Prince Albert, Palmerston and Herbert, and under the weight of ceaseless badgering from Miss

Nightingale herself, Panmure agreed to establish a Royal Commission on the Health of the Army. At the same time, having at last realized the extent to which the formidable lady's opinion was respected, he sent her the plans for the military hospital that was already being built at Netley, near Southampton, and invited her to send him her comments.

By the end of November, however, he had changed his mind on both subjects, disappointing her on the former and rejecting her on the latter. The commission was too much of a risk. The report of the commissioners whom he had sent to investigate the supply of the army in the Crimea had just revived unhappy memories: horses better fed than men, and often on biscuits that were meant for men; bureaucratic intransigence which left soldiers freezing and starving while blankets and food lay undistributed. This was not the moment to embarrass the War Office further with what were bound to be equally distressing revelations about the soldiers' health. As for Miss Nightingale's scores of practical suggestions for changes to the design of the hospital, every one of them was rejected, despite their validity. The building work was now so far advanced that it would have been too expensive to make any such radical alterations.

But experience had not yet taught Lord Panmure that Miss Nightingale was not put off so easily. On Christmas Day she went to the Palmerstons' party at Broadlands and stayed the night. By breakfast time on Boxing Day the Prime Minister had been convinced. Soon afterwards he wrote to Panmure. 'It seems to me that at Netley all consideration of what would best tend to the comfort and recovery of the patients has been sacrificed to the vanity of the architect, whose sole object has been to make a building which should cut a dash when looked at from the Southampton river.'

Unfortunately Panmure's response was insuperable. At this stage Miss Nightingale's suggested alterations wold cost an additional £70,000. Netley Hospital was completed with only a few minor changes and was always notoriously impractical – an architectural antithesis to St Thomas's, which incorporated all Florence Nightingale's proposals in its original design.

Panmure was not so successful in avoiding the royal commission, however. Florence Nightingale soon discovered that he was 'the most bullyable of mortals'. She wrote to him and called on him incessantly. She persuaded others to do the same. She even persuaded the appointed chairman of the commission, Sidney Herbert, to write threatening a very public resignation if the royal warrant establishing it was not issued immediately. The commission met. The War Office was embarrassed. Eventually reforms followed, among them the creation of an Army Medical School and the building of better and more sanitary barracks at Aldershot, Shorncliffe, Colchester and the Curragh.

There were a few improvements elsewhere as well. Control of the militia was transferred from the Home Office to the War Office. A centralized system was set up to supply the army with uniforms, depriving colonels of the considerable private incomes they had previously made from clothing their regiments. But it was to be another dozen years of endless royal commissions and select committees before the army underwent the radical reorganization that it so desperately needed. From the point of view of Parliament the priority after the Crimean War was simply to reduce the size and cost of the army as soon as possible. Many of the old abuses were allowed to continue. Commissions were still purchased, although a gesture was made in the right direction when prices were reduced by a third. Canteen contractors still earned exorbitant profits from food that nobody would have eaten out of choice. But despite all this there was no doubt that, through the work of the first war correspondents, the British Parliament and people had acquired a new respect for soldiers. A new medal was introduced, the Victoria Cross, to be awarded irrespective of rank for valour beyond the call of duty. While the War Office attempted to save the reputations of at least some of the senior officers who had been found wanting by the Commission of Inquiry into the Supplies of the British Army, knighthoods and other honours were awarded to some of those who had not, including, after much resistance from Panmure, the commissioners themselves. And there was an unexpectedly high honour for Palmerston.

On 11 April the Queen wrote:

Now that the moment for ratification of the Treaty of Peace is near at hand, the Queen wishes to delay no longer the expressions of her satisfaction as to the manner in which both the war has been brought to a conclusion, and the honour and the interest of this country have been maintained, by the zealous and able guidance of Lord Palmerston. She wishes as a public token of her approval, to bestow the Order of the Garter upon him.

The reply came back the same day. 'Viscount Palmerston presents his humble duty to your Majesty and is unable to express in words the gratification and thankfulness which he feels upon receipt of your Majesty's gracious and unexpected communication of this morning.'

For ever afterwards Palmerston proudly wore the broad blue ribbon of the order when he received his guests at the famous receptions in Piccadilly. But, according to the memoirs of the extremely snobbish and not very distinguished Sir William Fraser – Eton, Christ Church, the Life Guards, fourth baronet and Conservative MP for Barnstaple – not even the insignia of the Garter could make Palmerston look like an aristocrat.

14. A JOLLY WAY OF LOOKING AT DISASTERS

Unlike many of his colleagues, Palmerston was sceptical about the Anglo-French alliance. 'We are riding a runaway horse,' he told Clarendon,

> and we must always be on our guard; but a runaway horse is best kept in by a light hand and an easy snaffle... and as our ally finds the allance useful to himself, it will probably go on for a good time to come. The danger is, and always has been, that France and Russia should unite to carry into effect some great scheme of mutual ambition.

In the aftermath of the Crimean War it was a danger made all the more possible by the presence of what Palmerston described as the Emperor's 'Russian tribe'. To succeed Drouyn de Lhuys as his Foreign Minister, Napoleon had appointed his illegitimate cousin Count Walewski, whose main objective seemed to be persuading the Tsar to restore his family's estates in Poland; the new French Ambassador to the Tsar's court was the Duc de Morny, who was thought to be Napoleon's illegitimate half-brother and who was heavily influenced by his Russian wife; and Russian diplomats were already importuning them so obviously and offensively that, as Palmerston put it, they were like nothing so much as the touts at a race track who try to bribe trainers to drug horses.

The allies worked together well enough when, as Palmerston put it, the alliance was 'useful'. Until late in 1857 they kept armies of occupation in Greece, which had predictably joined her other protector Russia when she went to war with 'the ancient enemy'. Their fleets sailed together into the Bay of Naples, in a Palmerstonian attempt to force 'King Bomba' to empty some of his hideous prisons; and they sailed out again together when he called their bluff. In the aftermath of the Crimean War the only evidence of the Emperor's Russian sympathies lay in his arguing on their behalf over what land and how much of it they should cede on the northern shores of the Danube, and in supporting the unification of Romania, which Palmerston saw as 'the creation of another Greece on the north of Turkey ... a field for Russian intrigue and not a barrier against Russia'. But the imaginative Emperor did propose one ambitious scheme, whereby the allies would do in North Africa what they had just fought a war to prevent the Russians from doing in Europe. They should, he suggested, help themselves to slices of the Ottoman Empire. The French, as Louis-Philippe had once dreamed, could have Morocco, while the Sardinians could have Tunis and the British Egypt.

Palmerston could hardly take him seriously. He wrote to Clarendon:

> It is very possible that many parts of the world would be better governed by France, England and Sardinia than they are now; and we need not go beyond Italy, Sicily and Spain for examples. But the alliance of England and France has derived its strength not merely from the military and naval power of the two states, but from the force of the moral principle upon which that union has been founded ... How then could we combine to become unprovoked aggressors ... how could England and France, who have guaranteed the integrity of the Turkish Empire, turn round and wrest Egypt from the Sultan? A coalition for such a purpose would revolt the moral feelings of mankind.

All that mattered to Palmerston and to Britain was that Egypt should belong to no European Power and that it should continue to provide the southern part of a free and open passage to the east and India. As he wrote to Cowley in Paris:

> We do not want Egypt or wish it for ourselves any more than any rational man with an estate in the north of England and a residence in the south, would have wished to possess the inns

on the north road. All he could want would have been that the inns should be well kept, always accessible and furnishing him, when he came, with mutton chops and post-horses.

But when the French, and in particular an engineer, the Vicomte Ferdinand de Lesseps, also proposed that the road through Egypt should be made easier for everyone by the construction of a canal between the Mediterranean and the Gulf of Suez, Palmerston took it much more seriously and objected passionately. On 7 July 1857 he told the House of Commons that it was both technically impracticable and financially unviable, and that, by dividing Egypt from Syria, it was a threat to the integrity of the Ottoman Empire.

He had other, better, reasons as well. Palmerston's memory stretched back through the schemes of Louis-Philippe to the campaigns of the present Emperor's uncle. But by the time that speech was made the cover had closed on the most revealing record of the difference between what Palmerston was saying and what he was thinking. In the summer of 1856 his diplomat brother, who drank too much, came home on leave from Naples and died at Broadlands. The flow of frank family correspondence ended abruptly. In the case of the canal, however, there was a letter to an unlikely confidant, Russell, which described much more serious misgivings.

> It requires only a glance at the map of the world to see how great would be the naval and military advantage to France in a war with England to have such a short cut to the Indian seas, while we should be obliged to send ships round the Cape... Moreover, so strong a military barrier between Syria and Egypt would greatly add to the means of the Pasha for the time being to declare himself independent of Turkey, which would mean his being a dependant of France.

In August 1857, a month after Palmerston addressed the House of Commons on the canal, the Emperor and Empress of France steamed into the Solent in their yacht *Reine Hortense* and spent a few days as guests at Osborne among ambassadors and ministers. By the time they left, owing mostly to the cordial relations between the two royal families and between Palmerston and the uniquely principled French Ambassador, the Duc de Persigny, their more ambitious schemes had been set aside for the moment and the parties had compromised on their differences. A fortnight later the *Victoria and Albert* paid a reciprocal royal visit to Cherbourg, where Prince Albert was impressed and alarmed by the power of the batteries that fired a salute and by the strength of the new defences that housed them.

In the light of all this goodwill it came as a 'surprise' to Palmerston to learn soon afterwards that 'the Emperor should have spoken with so much bitterness' about him. Perhaps he should have known himself better by now. Palmerston as Prime Minister was closer to the man he had been at the Foreign Office than to the man he had learned to become at the Home Office. He could not help but be more interested in foreign affairs than in anything else, and he could not help dealing with them in the way that he had always dealt with them. A simple snaffle was not the bit in any bridle to which this old hand was accustomed. More often than not, Clarendon was issued with such detailed instructions that his charm and his capacity to smooth ruffled feathers were more useful than his mind. Frequently the most constructive contribution that the Foreign Secretary could make to any issue was to append a request to a clerk along the lines of 'Will you make a Dft. out of Ld. P.'s note, but in softened language'.

Outside foreign affairs the Prime Minister's preoccupations ranged from the worthy to the trivial. One worthy endeavour was the Joint Stock Companies Act of 1856, which was a precursor of his 1862. Companies Act and at last made it possible to form a limited liability company without applying for a private act of Parliament. Another was an attempt to introduce life peerages in place of hereditary peerages for law lords, which, to the exasperation of the Queen, was loyally thwarted by the short-sighted House of Lords itself. The most trivial, on the other hand, was probably the request from the people of Rugeley in Staffordshire to change the name of their town, which was being reviled and shunned by its neighbours after the whole nation had been spellbound by the trial and execution of a gruesome murderer, William Palmer, known as 'the Rugeley poisoner'. For a moment the humourless burghers were delighted when the Prime Minister suggested that they might like to do him the honour of renaming their borough Palmerston.

There was, however, one other apparently trivial matter that came close to bringing down the government. In the summer of 1856, with the support and approval of both the Queen and Palmerston, the Commissioner of Works, Sir Benjamin Hall, celebrated the end of the war and the return of the army by arranging for military bands to give concerts on Sunday afternoons in all the London parks. They were very popular. But some of the trades unions opposed them: overlooking the fact that the bandsmen were soldiers, they argued that, if musicians were being required to work on Sundays, it would not be long before factory workers were made to do so as well. A small and hitherto unknown group of English traditionalists emerged: forgetting that British soldiers had been marching to the sound of fife and drum for centuries, they condemned brass bands as an inappropriate, militaristic, German institution and blamed Prince Albert for introducing them. Worst of all, although most predictably, the Lord's Day Observance Society rose in opposition and, of course, invited Shaftesbury to lead their campaign.

Palmerston, who knew little and cared less about religious matters, regarded Shaftesbury as his ecclesiastical adviser. He never appointed an archbishop or a bishop without consulting him, with the result that, under Palmerston, no high-churchman could expect to be consecrated. But he was not susceptible to Shaftesbury's influence on the subject of brass bands. Having failed with a personal appeal, therefore, Shaftesbury recruited the Archbishop of Canterbury and won over so many disparate MPs that Palmerston and Hall gave in rather than risk a division of the House. The concerts were cancelled; and the following Sunday the people who would otherwise have assembled in Hyde Park to hear one went across Park Lane to Shaftesbury's house and threw stones at his windows instead.

Brass bands were not the only bone of contention between Palmerston and the Church of England. In the summer of 1857 the government of this supposedly conservative Prime Minister introduced the Matrimonial

Causes Bill. Until then divorce had been confined to the jurisdiction of the ecclesiastical courts and Parliament. Although the ecclesiastical courts did nullify marriages on a very limited number of grounds, such as a failure to consummate, the other so-called matrimonial offences – adultery, desertion and cruelty – were only grounds for a divorce *a mensa et toro*, which, like a judicial separation, did not entitle the couple to remarry. If they wanted to do that, they had to be rich enough to annul their marriage by private Act of Parliament. Following the practice that had existed in Scotland for almost 300 years, the bill therefore proposed that the ecclesiastical courts should be abolished and replaced by a new Divorce Court, which would have the power to grant full divorces on grounds that previously had only been enough for a separation.

There were some, mostly Radicals, who opposed the bill only because it discriminated between men and women. While a husband could obtain a divorce simply by proving that his wife had committed adultery, a wife had to show that her husband's adultery was accompanied by cruelty or desertion. But the main opposition came from the Church, which, quite apart from wanting to preserve its court and its jurisdiction, opposed the extension of the grounds on which a sacramental union could be dissolved and questioned the right of a secular court to rule on such a subject anyway. The clergy lobbied their MPs; 6,000 of them signed a petition to the government, and their cause was taken up and led in the House of Commons by Gladstone, who, in Palmerston's opinion, was so high-church that he would have converted to Catholicism if it would not have interfered with his political ambitions.

The debate, which was hardly distinguished for the quality of its legal or theological argument, was nevertheless notorious for the first use of a technique that became known as 'talking out'. Knowing that they were unlikely to win a majority, Gladstone and his allies 'contrived to exercise their ingenuity' on discussing every detail of the bill in the hope that the debate would not be finished when Parliament rose at the end of the session. On 24 July, however, Palmerston warned the House that he would keep it sitting until the bill was passed, and he repeated the warning on 13 August. 'We shall return and sit here day by day, and night by night, until this bill be concluded.' On 25 August, sooner than some pessimists had come to expect, the exhausted House of Commons passed the Matrimonial Causes Act.

Domestic affairs, trivial or radical, still consumed an inordinate proportion of parliamentary time, but, fortunately for the Prime Minister whose heart lay in foreign affairs, it was foreign affairs, from one side of the globe to the other, that still imposed the greatest demands on his own time and energy.

Relations between Great Britain and the United States, which had hardly been cordial since the recruiting drive, deteriorated further in 1856, when armed men from Nicaragua crossed the border into the little tribal kingdom of Mosquito on the Caribbean coast, which had been a British dependency for 200 years, and seized the port of San Juan del Norte, which the British, who called it Greytown, had seized from the Nicaraguans in 1848.

On the face of it there was nothing about this insignificant little episode that seemed likely to arouse any animosity between Great Britain and the United States. But the British and American navies had almost seen action over Greytown before. In 1848, after the British seized the port, the Americans sent a squadron to compel the British ships in the harbour to withdraw; and Palmerston, who was then at the Foreign Office, ordered the British ships to stand and fight if necessary. Eventually, rather than start a war, the Americans recalled their ships and offered to negotiate; and in 1850 the two governments signed a treaty whereby each agreed to refrain from any further territorial expansion in central America. Now, however, there were reasons for suspecting that the recent raid on Greytown came close to a clandestine breach of that agreement. Tacitly at least, the American government had condoned it; it had been supported from the sea by American privateers; and it had been led by a colourful, cultured American adventurer called William Walker.

Born in Nashville, Tennessee, in 1824, Walker acquired a doctorate in medicine at the University of Pennsylvania and was then called to the bar in New Orleans. In 1853, after working for a while as a journalist in San Francisco, he led a gang of filibusters south into the Mexican territory on either side of the Gulf of California and declared it an independent republic. On being thwarted by starvation, Mexican soldiers and unsupportive United States diplomats, he returned soon afterwards to San Francisco. But the exploit had made him so famous that in 1855 the Nicaraguan Liberals invited him to lead them in their civil war against their Conservative government. Seizing the ship that Cornelius Vanderbilt's Accessory Transit Company used to transport freight and passengers across Lake Nicaragua, Walker launched a successful surprise attack on the Conservative headquarters in Granada on the northern shore of the lake and won the civil war at a stroke. He then seized all the assets of the Accessory Transit Company, on the pretext that it had violated its charter, and gave them to some of the local directors; and with their financial support he became President of Nicaragua. In May 1856, shortly before he seized Greytown, his government was formally recognized by the government of the United States, which was then considering Nicaragua as an alternative site to Panama for a canal.

Walker's raid, and what seemed to be its implications, came as no surprise to Palmerston. His opinion of the Americans was as low as his opinion of the Austrians. 'These Yankees', he told Clarendon,

are most disagreeable Fellows to have to do with about any American question; they are on the spot, strong, deeply interested in the matter, totally unscrupulous and dishonest and determined somehow or other to carry their Point; we are far away, weak from Distance, controlled by the Indifference of the nation as to the Question discussed, and by its strong commercial interest in maintaining Peace with the United States.

'Moreover,' he wrote on another occasion,

they resort to the hackneyed formula of saying that I am thought particularly hostile to the United States in order to induce me to do some act of servility in order to disprove the unframed imputation. This is just of the same principle on which a man reproaches a woman with being cold when he sees that her passions are on the point of breaking loose.

Ignoring anything that the Americans might have to say, therefore, Palmerston asked the Cabinet to send a fleet to blockade the Nicaraguans in Greytown. But there were many present who felt that, whether the Americans were involved in the incident or not, they soon would be if the British seemed to over-react. The majority supported Clarendon, who suggested that a fleet should be sent, but that it should not yet be instructed to take any further action, and that meanwhile the United States government should be invited to discuss the problem. Palmerston was persuaded; Clarendon wrote an appropriate letter to Washington; and Argyll recorded the discussion admiringly in his memoirs. It was, he wrote,

> typical of what I have often observed in Palmerston. His first impulse was always to move fleets and to threaten our opponents, sometimes on trivial occasions, on the details of which he had not fully informed himself by careful reading. Then, on finding his proposals combated, he was candid in listening and inquiring and if he found the objections reasonable, he could give way to them with the most perfect good humour. This was a great quality in a man so impulsive and so strong-headed as he was, and so prone to violent action. It made him a much less dangerous man than he was supposed to be.

The government in Washington was well enough informed to know that the approaching British fleet would take effective action if the problem was not settled by negotiation. The United States withdrew their support for the Nicaraguan government. The Nicaraguans evacuated Greytown. Heavily funded by Cornelius Vanderbilt, a coalition of Central American states attacked Nicaragua; and after holding out for a while, Walker surrendered himself to an American warship, which took him back to Texas. In 1860, after several failed attempts to return to Central America, he set out to join the revolutionaries in Honduras, where he succeeded in taking Trujillo. But he was then captured by the crew of a British sloop-of-war and, after a perfunctory trial, shot by a Honduran firing squad.

Before the dispute on the Mosquito Coast was settled, Britain went to war with Persia. Since the United States had just signed a commercial treaty with Persia, there were many who feared that British and American ships were as likely to see action in the Persian Gulf as in the Caribbean. But, as Palmerston pointed out dismissively to Clarendon, if the United States really wanted a war with Great Britain, there was no need for them 'to go so far Eastward to lay the ground for a Quarrel'.

As in the case of most of the disputes that arose east of Italy, the origin was trivial. The Grand Vizier, the Sadr Azim, disapproved of a Persian diplomatic agent who was being employed by the British and asked Her Majesty's Minister-Plenipotentiary in Teheran, Charles Murray, to dismiss him. When Murray refused, the Sadr Azim said that he was only refusing because the agent's wife was his mistress. At this, Murray, second son of the Earl of Dunmore, fellow of All Souls, member of the Bar and former Master of the Royal Household, demanded an apology and threatened to leave if he did not get it. When no apology was forthcoming, Murray duly went home.

The inferred affront to the dignity of Shah Nasr ad-Din, 'His Majesty whose standard is the sun', was a welcome excuse for the Shah and his Grand Vizier to set aside a recent treaty which had bound them not to send soldiers into Afghanistan. After crossing their eastern border in force, their army allied itself with one of the local warlords and installed him as ruler of Herat. When other warlords failed to eject him, Palmerston declared war on Persia. The likelihood of the Russians reaching south through Turkmenistan as soon as they recovered their energy was quite enough of a threat to British India without having another power, even one as weak as Persia, in control of any of the land between them.

A British expeditionary force from India sailed up the Persian Gulf and landed at the western port of Bushire. The Persians advanced to meet it with a force that outnumbered it by at least three to one. But in the course of the last century the empire of the Persian Shah had declined even faster and further than the empire of the Turkish Sultan. The Persian army was no match for a combination of Indian infantry and engineers, the 14th Hussars, the Durham Light Infantry, the Seaforth Highlanders and the North Staffordshire Regiment, and all led by the

Resident of Lucknow, James Outram, 'the Bayard of India'. Compared with anything achieved by the British army in the last forty years, even the exploits of 'the thin red line', the campaign that followed was as brilliant as it was brief.

The Persians sued for peace, and Palmerston, who regarded what was left of the Persian Empire as another buffer state, like Turkey, was glad to be generous rather than weaken it. By the terms of a treaty signed in Paris on 4 March 1857 by the representatives of Queen Victoria and Shah Nasr ad-Din, all that was required was that the Persians should apologize to Murray, withdraw from Herat, renounce all claims over Afghanistan and – in response to a demand that Palmerston could not resist – abolish the slave trade in the Persian Gulf.

Six months later Palmerston received a long, obsequious letter from the Sadr Azim claiming that he had always been the friend of the British and that the war was none of his doing. Knowing how much the Grand Vizier was said to be under the influence of the Russian envoy, Prince Dolgorouki, Palmerston clearly enjoyed himself in composing his reply.

> I am rejoiced to find, from your Excellency's letter, that it is your desire and intention to cultivate in future the friendship of England. But I should not be deserving of your good opinion if I were to disguise from you the truth of my thoughts … the war between our two countries … was occasioned solely and entirely by your Excellency's own unfriendly conduct … and, therefore, so far from your Excellency having been alone in endeavours to preserve friendship between the two Governments, your Excellency was the main and principal cause of the cessation of that Friendship.

The war with Persia was not the only eastern problem that beset Palmerston's government in the aftermath of the Crimean War. Indeed there was more than one other. Shortly before the signing of the treaty with Persia in Paris, at the opening of Parliament, the House of Commons was informed that 'acts of violence, insults to the British flag, and infraction of treaty rights committed by the local Chinese authorities at

419

Canton, and a pertinacious refusal of redress, have rendered it necessary for Her Majesty's officers in China to have recourse to measures of force to obtain satisfaction'.

In October 1856 Chinese coastguards had boarded a British-registered merchantman, the *Arrow*, in the mouth of the Canton river, arrested her 24-year-old Irish captain and his twelve Chinese sailors for piracy and hauled down her British colours. When the incident was reported to him, the British Consul in Canton, Harry Parkes, who was an eager career diplomat of only twenty-eight, demanded an apology and the release of the crew, and insisted that, if there were any charges to be brought against a British ship, he was the only one with authority to investigate them. The Commissioner for Canton, Yeh Ming-chin, who had released the captain immediately, released nine more of the crew. But he refused to release the other three, who were known pirates, and he refused to apologize for insulting the British flag. Then the rest of the story emerged, revealing that there was no justification for Parkes's arrogance and that the infamously haughty Yeh was actually being rather more reasonable than usual.

The *Arrow* was a lorcha, a fast little hybrid of a type that was very common in the waters around Macao. She had a Portuguese-built, European-style hull, like a caravel, but was rigged with battened mat lugsails, like a junk. Her latest owner, Fong Ah-ming, the leader of one of Canton's most notorious pirate gangs, had registered her as a British ship in Hong Kong and given her a European 'captain', who had never been to sea before, simply to add to her aura of respectability. With her reputable colours and her commonplace configuration, the *Arrow* was able to sail very close to her victims without arousing their suspicion, and had been one of the most profitable pirate ships in the mouth of the Canton river. Furthermore, although the Chinese coastguards did not know it at the time, her British registration had expired two weeks before they boarded her.

Unfortunately, however, the animosity between the British and the Chinese was already so deep that it influenced the actions of everyone and clouded the judgement even of responsible men who should have known better. Each regarded the other as savage. The Chinese still resented the presence of disdainful British traders and, ignoring the terms of the Treaty of Nanking, continued to exclude them from several cities, including Canton. When Chinese ships were known to be carrying British cargoes, they were frequently attacked, looted and even burned, which was why the British authorities in Hong Kong allowed Chinese owners to protect themselves by registering their ships as British.

Against this background Harry Parkes did not feel inclined to give way. After consulting the Governor of Hong Kong, Sir John Bowring, he renewed his demands. The Chinese Commissioner released the three pirates but still refused to apologize. The young Consul turned again to the old Governor.

Sir John Bowring was sixty-four years old. He had started his career as a humble clerk in a warehouse in Exeter. On his way to his present eminence, which he had earned entirely on merit, he had run his own business, served on various British commercial commissions throughout Europe and the Far East, sat as a Radical MP, edited the *Westminster Review* and published books and papers on politics, economics, European and Oriental poetry and hymns. Yet despite all this experience and erudition, his response to Yeh Ming-chin's defiance was to send the navy. Led by Rear-Admiral Sir Michael Seymour, commander of the China station, who had once served as flag captain to Jane Austen's brother in the West Indies, a British squadron blockaded the river and bombarded not only the forts at its mouth but also the city of Canton itself. The Commissioner's palace was razed to the ground and most of the city was set on fire. Commissioner Yeh issued a proclamation calling on the people of Canton to 'unite in exterminating these troublesome English villains'. He offered a bounty of 30 dollars for the head of any Englishman and then raised it to 100 dollars when the incentive did not seem to be enough. All the British factories were destroyed. Chinese bakers put ground glass in the bread that they sold to British customers. British and Chinese ships fired on each other in the estuary. Somehow the Chinese government managed to prevent the violence from spreading. In the other four ports covered by the Treaty of Nanking, the relationship between the British and the Chinese did not get any worse than it was already. But by the time the British Cabinet came to discuss the problem, the situation in Canton had deteriorated into a merciless, chaotic trade in terrorism and reprisal.

Palmerston had no sympathy with Bowring's attitude. Ten years earlier, when he was at the Foreign Office, an English merchant in Canton had flogged a noisy Chinese street vendor for disturbing his afternoon nap. One of Bowring's predecessors, Sir John Davis, had ordered the prosecution of the merchant, which had resulted in his being fined 200 dollars. But the merchant had appealed, and the Chief Justice of Hong Kong had overruled his conviction on a technicality and ordered that the fine be returned. When he heard what had happened, Palmerston accepted the judgement; but he ordered Davis to make no apology to the merchant and he left him in no doubt about his approval of the prosecution. 'It cannot be tolerated that British subjects should indulge towards the people of China in acts of violence or contumely which they would not venture to practise towards the humblest and meanest individual in their own country.'

On the other hand, as was well known, Palmerston supported subordinates whenever possible, even if he disagreed with them; and whatever the rights and wrongs of the case, it seemed clear to him that, if possible, it was now in Britain's best commercial interest to uphold the authority of the Governor of Hong Kong, insist on the observance of all the terms of the Treaty of Nanking and confirm that the Royal Navy would not hesitate to defend the lives and property of British subjects.

When the Cabinet met, Palmerston broke with tradition and invited the Attorney-General, Sir Richard Bethell, who was not a member, to attend and deliver his opinion in person rather than simply submit it in writing. It was what they expected, although not what they wanted to hear. If the *Arrow* had been on a genuine voyage, it might have been argued, although not too convincingly, that her registration did not expire until she docked. But there was no justification for bombarding Canton without first attempting to resolve the dispute through diplomatic channels. Reluctantly the Cabinet agreed with Palmerston. Their case was weak, but they had no choice other than to stand by the Governor. With heavy hearts they prepared to face the onslaught that they knew all the usual opponents, from left to right, were already preparing.

A motion of censure in the House of Lords was defeated by 146 votes to 110, but nobody expected that the government would be so lucky in the House of Commons, where the attack was led this time not, as some expected, by Gladstone but by the Radical Richard Cobden, the most prominent founder of the Anti-Corn Law League, a leader among the opponents of the recent war with Russia and a long-standing critic of Palmerston. Cobden's motion was simply that 'the papers laid on the table failed to establish satisfactory grounds for the violent measures resorted to'. His case was as straightforward as his motion: Bowring had acted illegally and the government was acting illegally in supporting him. It was a case repeated in their different ways by all the predictable speakers who followed him: including Gladstone, Disraeli, Lord John Russell, Sir James Graham, Lord Robert Cecil and even John Roebuck.

Against the weight of their argument Palmerston could do little. He described the attack as a conspiracy. He compared Bowring, 'a man of the people', with Yeh, 'one of the most savage barbarians that ever disgraced a nation'. He attacked Cobden personally, accusing him of expressing 'an anti-English feeling … which I should hardly have expected from the lips of any member of this House. Everything that was English was wrong, and everything that was hostile to England was right.' He warned the House that it was asking 'to abandon a large community of British subjects at the extreme end of the globe to a set of barbarians — a set of kidnapping, murdering, poisoning barbarians'. But even in the moments of rhetoric Palmerston's voice contained none of the passion and conviction that had once won over so many when, in almost similar circumstances, he had declared 'Civis Romanus sum'.

His gout was at its worst that day. He entered the chamber of the House with a strong stick in each hand. But this alone was not enough to explain the resignation in his manner. It was as though he expected and accepted defeat, as though he was almost relieved when Disraeli challenged him. 'Let the noble Lord, who complained that he was the victim of a conspiracy, not only complain to the country, but let him appeal to it.' And then, reminding the House that the government had not yet scheduled the promised debates on reform, which had been postponed during the war, and that it had not yet cancelled the increase in income tax, which had been imposed to pay for the war, Disraeli suggested a campaign slogan for Palmerston: 'No Reform! New Taxes! Canton Blazing! Persia Invaded!'

Cobden's motion was carried by only 263 votes to 247. The margin was much tighter than the government expected. But it was a defeat, and that was enough for Palmerston. His mood changed suddenly for the better. Eagerly he took up Disraeli's challenge. The Queen dissolved Parliament and the parties went to the country for a general election.

Palmerston understood the electorate. He knew that the argument that had almost swayed Parliament was bound to be more than enough at the hustings; and if most of his colleagues were baffled by his optimism, Sidney Herbert at least could see what he was up to.

> He has on his side that which is the strongest element in the mental organization of all human society, namely, the public's national prejudices. Some one said 'Give me the national songs, and I will rule the nation'; and Canning said, 'Don't talk to me of the *sense of the nation;* give me the *nonsense*, and I will beat it hollow'.

Wise old Lansdowne persuaded Palmerston to include electoral reform in his policy, and he made a passing reference to it in his printed programme. But if it had been left to him, Canning's pupil would have fought the whole election on one issue. 'An insolent barbarian, wielding authority at Canton, has violated the British flag, broken the engagement of treaties, offered rewards for the heads of British subjects in that part of China and planned their destruction by murder, assassinations and poisons.' This was the issue with which the entire British public could identify. The members of Lloyd's, who insured the ships in the China Sea, were so pleased with it that they offered to nominate Palmerston as a candidate for the City of London, an offer he politely declined. But to most of the electorate the issue was even simpler. It was the singer, not the song. 'Palmerston', wrote Herbert, 'is the only public man in England who has a name. Many criticize, many disapprove, but all, more or less, like him and look on him as the only man.' Shaftesbury agreed. For every candidate in every constituency there was only one question that mattered. 'P's popularity is wonderful', he wrote in his diary. 'The whole turns on his name. There seems to be no measure, no principle, no cry, to influence men's minds and determine elections; it is simply, "Were you, or were you not? are you or are you not, for Palmerston?" '

Within days of the dissolution of Parliament Palmerston's opponents realized that they had blundered. They had handed him a chance to increase his majority; and in the process they had probably put some of their own seats in jeopardy as well. From that moment on the campaign became personal and acrimonious. For the first time Lady Palmerston omitted some of her husband's opponents – 'the Chinese' – from her guest list. But it was too late to turn back the tide of Palmerston's campaign. In the general election of May 1857 the Conservatives lost 34 seats, reducing their total in the House of Commons from 290 to 256, and the Peelite representation fell from 45 to just 26. Between them the Whigs and Radicals won 367, which, when they voted together, gave them an overall majority of 85, the largest since Earl Grey's after the 1832 Reform Act.

Among the Radicals several of Palmerston's leading opponents lost their seats, including Cobden, who had moved from the West Riding to what he thought was the safer seat of Huddersfield; and Russell and Roebuck only just survived, with heavily reduced majorities. But there were many more Radicals who gained seats than lost them – too many for Palmerston's taste. Most of them, he said, had won only by making promises 'which the present government never can agree to'. For all that the election was Palmerston's victory, it had tipped the balance further towards the Radicals in the coalition that even he was now describing as the Liberal Party.

After Parliament reassembled, the government continued its uncomfortable policy in China without any further concerted opposition, if only, perhaps, because the Conservatives and Radicals no longer believed that there was anything to be gained by it. Lord Elgin, who had recently retired as Governor-General of Canada, was sent out to Hong Kong to replace Bowring. While he was on his way, Palmerston won the support of the other leading nations with trading interests in China: the United

States, Russia and particularly France, whose citizens had also suffered at the hands of the Chinese authorities. A few months earlier a French missionary had been tortured to death on the orders of a magistrate.

Elgin repeated Bowring's demand for an apology and added a few demands of his own, including compensation for British losses and the right to establish a British diplomatic mission in Peking. When Yeh and his Emperor prevaricated, he threatened to use force. But his first shipment of reinforcements was diverted to India. It was not until the end of the year that he was able to carry out his threat. Troops were landed, Canton was captured and Commissioner Yeh was taken away to spend the last year of his life in exile in a villa outside Calcutta. Soon afterwards, when a combined British and French force captured the Taku forts at the mouth of the Peiho river, the Chinese agreed to all Elgin's demands, which were duly embodied in the terms of the Treaty of Tientsin. But they then refused to ratify the treaty; and while the armed disagreement in the East continued, the attentions of the British government and nation were distracted by the events that had caused the first reinforcements to be diverted to India.

In January 1857 the army in India was issued with the new muzzle-loading Enfield rifle. To load it, the soldier was required to bite off the twisted paper at the end of each cartridge and pour the powder into the barrel before ramming down the rest of it; and it was rumoured that the cartridges were lubricated with fat from either cows, which were sacred to Hindus, or pigs, which were unclean to Muslims. In fact, only the cartridges made in England at Woolwich were greased with animal fat. The cartridges made in India at Dum-Dum, near Calcutta, were greased from the outset with clarified butter or beeswax. As soon as the first complaints were received, the few cartridges that had been shipped out from Woolwich were withdrawn, and thereafter the only Indian soldiers issued with animal-fat cartridges were the men in one of the Gurkha regiments, who had specifically asked for them. But the harm was done. Nobody believed the reassurances.

In February Indian troops in Berhampore refused to train with the cartridges. In March others did the same in Barrackpore, and one regiment was disbanded. In April the skirmishers in the 3rd Bengal Light

Cavalry followed their example in Meerut. On 9 May, after a court martial, they were sentenced to ten years' imprisonment and publicly stripped of their uniforms. Next day, while the rest of the regiment rode down to the prison to release them, the sepoys in one of the two infantry regiments in the barracks, the 11th Bengal Native Infantry, shot the Colonel of the other, the 20th, and then murdered most of their own officers and any other European men, women and children they could find. Before the next sunrise all three regiments were on the road to Delhi, thirty-six miles away.

The capital was taken completely by surprise. More Europeans were slaughtered. With the support of the garrison – three more regiments of Bengal infantry – the mutineers took over the city and the Red Fort, where they enthroned the 82-year-old puppet King of Delhi, Bahadur Shah, as the new Moghul Emperor and celebrated their success by butchering several dozen Europeans of both sexes and all ages in front of his assembled family. The mutiny spread across the basin of the Ganges, eventually involving all but eighteen of the seventy-four batallions in the East India Company's Bengal Army. While disillusioned British commanders fortified residences and barrack blocks and prepared to defend them against their unexpectedly disloyal garrisons, the Governor-General, Canning, ordered his Commander-in-Chief, General George Anson, to assemble an army for the relief of Delhi, commandeered and diverted the reinforcements on their way to China and ordered the troops returning from Persia to sail on round to Calcutta, at the mouth of the Ganges.

There had been small mutinies among the 'native' troops in India before. There had been one at Vellore in 1806, another at Barrackpore in 1824 and one on the Sikh frontier in 1844. Even the European troops had come close to mutiny in 1809. But this time the mutiny was more than a symptom of discontent in a section of the army. It was a symptom of discontent in India.

With the best of intentions, Canning's great predecessor, Dalhousie, had introduced such a broad programme of what he saw as reform that he had aroused the suspicions of the Hindus and convinced them that another alien culture was about to be imposed on India. The Brahmin priests were offended and alarmed by the emancipation and education of women. Princes resented the economic implications of the attempts to abolish slavery, the erosion of their influence through the introduction of professional civil servants and the injustice of the 'doctrine of lapse', whereby the estates of any ruler who died without a natural, male heir passed to the East India Company – an innovation through which the company had already laid claim to five states, including the Punjab.

In response to all this, the eventual revolt broke out in the army because the army was the only section of Indian society well enough organized to do it. It broke out in the Bengal army because the sepoys of Bengal had additional grievances. They had been deprived of some of their privileges. They suspected that the Company was preparing to raise rival regiments among the Gurkhas, Sikhs and Punjabi Muslims. They saw the company's egalitarian policy of recruitment and promotion as a threat to their sacred caste system. The supposed humiliation of the animal-fat cartridges was nothing more than the last straw.

And the revolt broke out in 1857 because that was when the priests and princes who incited it decided that the time was right. In the first place, they knew that they could influence the superstitious majority because there was a famous prophesy which predicted that British rule in India would survive for only a hundred years after the Battle of Plassey, which took place in 1757. The shipment of soldiers from India to the Crimea in the recent war had shown them that the British army was short of men and would not find it easy to send reinforcements; and in 1857 the available maximum of around 40,000 European soldiers in India, which was already outnumbered by six to one by the company's Indian soldiers, was further depleted by over a half by the necessary deployment of eighteen batallions in Persia, Burma and the Punjab.

Yet, despite all this, the hideous mutiny was never the catastrophe that so many people in Britain thought it was. It never affected much more than a third of British India. It was never strong enough to tempt the other two-thirds, let alone foreign Powers, to join in and take advantage. The risings were never coordinated; and with the exception of the brave and beautiful Rani of Jhansi and the cruel Nana Sahib of Cawnpore, there were no inspiring or effective leaders. British authority in India was never in jeopardy. Indeed, if it had not been for the incompetence of the officers initially involved, the mutiny might never have happened, and it would certainly not have developed as far as it did. Field Marshal Lord Roberts, who served as a young officer in the Bengal Artillery throughout the mutiny and won his VC in it, wrote in his memoirs, 'Brigadiers of seventy, Colonels of sixty, and Captains of fifty. It is curious to note how nearly every military officer who held a command of high position on the staff in Bengal when the mutiny broke out, disappeared from the scene in the first few weeks, and was never heard of officially again.' If the notoriously cruel and unpopular Colonel Edward Carmichael Smyth had not overreacted and humiliated his skirmishers, there would have been no provocation for the first rising in Meerut; and if there had only been an immediate response from his commanding officer, septuagenarian Major-General William Hewitt, who had at his disposal the 6th Dragoons and the 60th Rifles, the mutineers would never have reached Delhi. They succeeded in Delhi because the garrison commanders were equally inept, although there was a foretaste of the initiative and gallantry to come when a group of young officers denied them the arsenal by blowing it up, and themselves with it. To the few who understood, there was never any doubt that order would be restored as soon as there were sufficient troops and men like Outram to command them. The Indian Mutiny was a terrible warning, but never a threat.

When the news, which travelled partly by ship and partly by telegraph, reached London at last, on 27 June, Palmerston reacted as calmly and confidently as if he had known all this already, although he was as ignorant about India as almost everyone who had never been there. He had been in high spirits and the best of health ever since the election. At the beginning of the month, at the time of the most fashionable race meeting, the American Ambassador wrote, 'My Lord Palmerston could yesterday mount a fine spirited horse at Windsor, ride to Ascot, in the Queen's train, stay to the races, and ride back again, without feeling the weight of duties or years.' Over the next couple of months, while the news got worse before it got better and while the press made it even worse than it was, Palmerston's jauntiness never faltered.

The editors of the English newspapers had recently learned how easy it was to increase their circulations with lurid reports of murder trials, such as the prosecution of 'the Rugeley poisoner'; and they set out to do the same on a larger scale with the mutiny. Deploring the ghastly atrocities perpetrated by the mutineers, gloating over the equally horrific retribution meted out by British officers, and consistently exaggerating both, the press generated so much hysterical pessimism, even at Westminster, that what Prince Albert described as Palmerston's 'juvenile levity' seemed all the more inappropriate. Clarendon, yet again, was exasperated. 'His want of energy, and his system of hoping and believing, instead of acting, have disappointed me woefully.' But, like the Prince, Clarendon had misread Palmerston's manner. A much harsher judge of human nature, Florence Nightingale, who had been acquainted with Palmerston for most of her life and had got to know him better than either of them, wrote, 'Tho' he made a joke when asked to do the right thing, he always did it... He was so much more in earnest than he appeared. He did not do himself justice.'

As soon as the news of the mutiny reached London, Palmerston's Cabinet prepared to send four regiments to South Africa, so that four others which were already 'accustomed to the Cape climate and service' could be sent on to India. Four days later the first troops sailed. By the end of September, despite huge recruitment problems, almost eighty ships had left England with over 30,000 men on board. On 11 July, when news came that the Commander-in-Chief in India, George Anson, had died of cholera, Sir Colin Campbell was immediately appointed to replace him. The very next day, a Sunday, Campbell set out for France, travelling south to Marseilles by train, east across the Mediterranean by ship and then on overland by the fastest means he could find. After fifteen months, when the mutiny was quelled, Canning wrote to Palmerston, 'You have poured troops into India with a readiness and liberality that deserve all honour.'

Palmerston's concern and commitment, and equally his confidence, were evident from the outset in his correspondence with the Queen, who was one of the very few to have anticipated trouble in India. On receiving the first report of the mutiny, she wrote, 'The Queen has just received Lord Palmerston's letter and is likewise much alarmed at the news from India. She has for some time been very apprehensive of the state of affairs in the army there, and her fears are now fully realized.' And she was soon alarmed by the possible consequences elsewhere. As she later wrote, 'Let European complications arise (and God knows how soon they may, for the state of Europe is very bad) and we may find ourselves in an awful position of helplessness!' She was not alone. Clarendon, of course, felt the same. But Palmerston did not. 'We have no danger threatening us in Europe and at home', he told them.

> France is perfectly and sincerely friendly, Russia may snarl and growl in secret, but has been too severely chastised to venture as yet openly to show her teeth ... and as to our national reputation for strength, the best way of maintaining that, and of deterring any foreign power from presuming on our supposed weakness, will be to crush the Indian revolt as soon as can be done.

In fact France joined Prussia and Belgium in offering military support. But Palmerston declined all offers. 'I am of the opinion', he wrote, 'that we ought to win this Innings against the Sepoys off our own Bat... and there cannot surely be a doubt that we shall stand higher as a nation by doing so than if we were to have recourse to the Help of Foreigners.' To him, in consequence, the priority was finding enough men for the job. It was harvest time; in a country where military service was no longer attractive anyway, the number of available men was even smaller than usual. Moreover, the Queen was so immune to any reassurance about the danger in Europe that she was at least as eager to keep up the strength at home as she was to reinforce the army in India. On 18 July she wrote to Palmerston. 'The Queen has just received Lord Palmerston's letter of yesterday and must say that if she had been in the House she would have joined in saying that the Government were not doing enough to "reorganize a defensive force for home service". The Queen will write a memorandum on the subject when she gets to Osborne.'

The memorandum, which followed swiftly, was long and very detailed.

> Contrary to the Queen's hopes and expectations, immediately after the late war the army was cut down to a state even below

the peace establishment recognized by the Government and Parliament in their own Estimates, to meet the parliamentary purpose of economy, and this in spite of the fearful lesson just taught by the late war and with two wars on hand, one with Persia and the other with China! ... When the regiments ordered out shall have gone, we shall be left with 18 batallions out of 105 of which the army is composed, to meet all home duty, to protect our own shores, to act as the reserves and reliefs for the regiments abroad and to meet all possible emergencies!! ... The principle which the Queen thinks right to be adopted is this: That the force which has been absorbed by the Indian demand is to be replaced to its full extent and in the same kind, not whole battalions by a mere handful of recruits added to the remaining ones.

And Her Majesty then went on to support her proposal with very practical argument.

This will not only cost the Government nothing, because the East India Company will pay the battalions transferred, and the money voted for them by Parliament will be transferred to the new ones, but it will give a considerable saving as all the officers reduced from the war establishment and receiving half pay will be thus absorbed and will no longer be a burden upon the exchequer.

Sometimes, however, the Queen did agree with Palmerston's measures, such as the ruling 'that the standard for recruits should be lowered from 5' 5" to 5' 4" and that the limit of age should be extended from the range between 18 and 25 to the range between 18 and 30'. And sometimes she gave condescending approval and then added suggestions of her own. 'The Queen sees in the decision of the Cabinet to attempt the raising of a black regiment in Canada and of a Maltese regiment, the first indication of their desire to exert themselves to meet an extraordinary emergency by extraordinary means, and she would like a Corfu regiment to be tried as well.'

The surprisingly blunt, haughty and impatient tone that the Queen was now adopting with her government was undoubtedly a mark of her concern, but it may have been tinged with a trace of personal bitterness as well. For over a year she had been negotiating with the Cabinet to have her husband created Prince Consort by act of Parliament; and in the course of correspondence as lengthy as any on more important matters of state, a decision had been consistently postponed by the need to discuss more pressing business and by constitutional technicalities. Eventually, only two days before news of the mutiny arrived from India, the Queen had taken matters into her own hand and created her husband Prince Consort by letters patent.

Meanwhile, as Her Majesty was soon pleased to note, the British regiments in India, supported by the company's Gurkhas and other loyal sepoys, were gradually getting the upper hand. Delhi was retaken after fifteen weeks of siege; and the ensuing slaughter of mutineers and civilians was a match for anything that had happened when it fell. In Cawnpore 300 British officers and men, together with around 100 civilian men and 100 loyal Indian officers, crowded into the hastily fortified barracks with nearly 400 women and children and held out against 3,000 sepoys and their many thousand supporters, led by Dhandu Pant, known as the Nana Sahib, who was the adopted son of the deposed Peshwa of the Mahrattas. After twenty days, when the Nana Sahib knew that help was on its way to them, he offered them safe passage down the Ganges to Allahabad. The starving, exhausted and thirsty survivors surrendered their arms and climbed into the waiting boats. But as soon as they were all on board, the Nana Sahib's sepoys opened fire. Almost all were killed, and the four men and 125 women and children who were not were herded back into Cawnpore. When the relieving force of Seaforth Highlanders, commanded by General Sir Henry Havelock, arrived on 17 July, they found that all the women and children had been hacked to pieces and chucked down a well. Their vengeance was as hideous as the crime. All the sepoys and supporters who had failed to escape were first whipped into cleaning up the dried blood with their bare hands and even their tongues and then hanged. But the sepoys were only mutineers. When the Nana Sahib ordered them to slaughter the women and children, they refused; and the deed had eventually been done for him by a group of hired criminals.

From Cawnpore, Havelock marched on to join up with Outram's returned force from Persia and relieve the British Residency in Lucknow, where 900 British soldiers, 700 loyal sepoys and 150 civilians were holding out against 10,000 sepoy mutineers and almost 50,000 of their supporters. When their successful attack began, Outram, who was the senior, gallantly gave command to Havelock because his army had been the first in the field. But the defeated mutineers fell back, found reinforcements and returned in enough strength to lay siege to the relieving force. By the time Sir Colin Campbell arrived to rescue them, Havelock was dead.

In central India the campaign was conducted so brilliantly and so differently that the British troops seemed almost like an army from the future. Their commander, General Sir Hugh Rose, had learned his trade in Prussia, where his father was a diplomat, and had served as a senior liaison officer with the French in the Crimea. Unlike the brightly dressed, slow-moving and deliberately deployed soldiers in the other British forces, Rose's men, of whom only half were European, were dressed in khaki and so heavily supported by larger and better-equipped supply trains that they could move faster, further and more effectively than any other force. With a total of 6,000 men he invested Jhansi, which was garrisoned by twice as many, drove off the force of 22,000 which the Nana Sahib's former lieutenant Tantia Topi brought to relieve it, and then took the city by storm. From there he made a forced march through a desert, took Kalpi and defeated the huge new army that Tantia Topi and the Rani of Jhansi had assembled at Gwalior. The Rani was killed in the battle; Tantia Topi escaped and was at large for a year before being betrayed to a court martial and hanged; and the Nana Sahib disappeared in Nepal.

As soon as these campaigns made victory seem certain, Canning prepared to govern India in peace again. Since resentment among the defeated was bound to be one of his greatest obstacles, he attempted to curb indiscriminate reprisals by forbidding the execution of deserters and ordering that the army should hang only those captured sepoys who were guilty of armed mutiny or other felonies. By the time reports of the order reached the pages of the English newspapers, however, the usual exaggerations had turned it into an amnesty for all mutineers. To many of them the Governor-General became 'Clemency Canning', and to *The Times* he was 'a prim philanthropist from Calcutta'.

In public, at first, Palmerston said nothing. He certainly had no sympathy for disaffected sepoys, even if they were only deserters, but as always he was inclined to support a subordinate. When it was proposed in the Cabinet that Canning's order should be overruled, he was persuaded by Clarendon and Granville to say no. As inevitable peace came closer and closer, the press moderated its language and stopped calling for the near extermination of every Muslim and Hindu in Bengal. Granville spoke in public in limited support of Canning, and was booed by the audience for his pains; and he joined with Clarendon, Argyll and, to the surprise of many, the Queen in pressing Palmerston to follow his example.

On 9 November 1857 Palmerston addressed all the critics of the government and its servants in his speech to the Lord Mayor of London's banquet at the Guildhall.

> It is impossible for any Englishman to allude to that which has been achieved in India – not by soldiers only, but by civilians, by individuals, and by knots of men scattered over the whole surface of a great empire – without feeling prouder than ever of the nation to which we have the happiness to belong … and I am proud to say, that although we have despatched from these shores the largest army that I believe ever at one time left them, we have now under arms in the United Kingdom as many fighting men as we had before the news of the mutiny reached us; and therefore, if any foreign nation ever dreamed in its visions that the exertions which we had been compelled to make in India had lessened our strength at home, and that the time had arrived when a different bearing might be exhibited towards us from that which was safe in the moment of our strength, the manner in which the spirit of the country has burst forth, the manner in which our ranks have been filled, the manner in which our whole force has been replenished, will teach the world that it will not be a safe game to play.

435

'Lord Canning', he said,

has shown throughout the greatest courage ... But punishment
must be inflicted not only in a spirit of vengeance, but in a spirit
of security, in order that the example of punished crime may
deter from the repetition of the offence, and in order to assure
the safety of our countrymen and countrywomen in India for
the future. He will have to spare the innocent, and it is most
gratifying to know that while the guilty may be counted by
thousands, the innocent must be reckoned by millions.

Unfortunately the passage warning foreign nations against attempting
to take advantage of what was 'erroneously imagined to be the moment
of our weakness' was taken personally in Paris, where a deeply offended
Napoleon III reminded the British Ambassador that the French had
actually offered to help. But the rest of the speech achieved its purpose. Rightly or wrongly the British press and people held Palmerston
responsible for the quelling of the mutiny and were prepared to accept
words from him that they might not have accepted from anyone else.
A grateful Canning was vindicated, and the obloquy ended abruptly.

To Palmerston, however, the main concern about the future government of India was more fundamental than merely striking a balance
between retribution and reconciliation. At the outbreak of the mutiny
he had told the Queen that it might lead to establishing British power
'upon a firmer basis'. In September 1857 he wrote to Clarendon, who
was minister in attendance on the Queen at Balmoral. 'While you are
shaving or taking a walk or ride turn over in your mind what will be the
best thing to do as to the future government of India.' Clarendon, of
course, was more impressed by the jovial manner of the request than by
the profundity of its content. In a letter to his wife he wrote, 'He seems
to have made up his mind to throw over the East India Company, and
asks me while *I am shaving or walking* to think what sort of government
should be established in place of it! He has a jolly way of looking at
disasters.' But Palmerston, of course, was as always 'so much more in
earnest than he appeared'. 'It is my strong personal opinion,' he wrote,

'that the present double government of India ought not to continue ...
We should introduce a measure for the abolition of the Board of Control,
the Court of Directors, and the Court of Proprietors, and appoint a
secretary of State for India.'

This was the 'strong personal opinion' embodied in the India Bill
and brought before the House of Commons in February 1858. The
company was indeed to be abolished. The British government was to
take over direct rule of India. The company's Indian regiments were to
become the British Indian Army. Canning, the last Governor-General,
was to be the first Viceroy instead.

Palmerston had expected that 'the matter' would need 'to be well
weighted'. There might be 'much Opposition on the part of all persons
connected with the India Company, and the Opposition in Parliament
might take up their cause'. But when it came to it, despite an attempt
to delay and trivial quibbling on detail from the Conservatives, the bill
was carried through its third reading in the House of Commons on 18
February by a majority of 145.

It was a triumph. To the British public it was the triumph that
crowned a ministry of triumphs. That evening, while Palmerston was
walking home with Bethell, the clever little Attorney-General suggested
obsequiously that, after so much success, the Prime Minister might now
need some way of reminding himself that he was not omnipotent, just as
in ancient Rome, when victorious generals led their armies in triumph
through cheering crowds, there was always a slave in the chariot beside
them constantly urging them in whispers to remember that they were
mortal. As it happened, a harsh reminder came without warning the
very next day, when the House assembled for the second reading of the
Conspiracy to Murder Bill.

The seed that had blossomed into this totally unexpected reversal
had been sown by fickle fate thirty-seven days earlier in Paris, when
Napoleon III and his Empress went to see a performance of *Gustave
III*, by Daniel-François-Esprit Auber. As the imperial carriage and its
mounted escort drew up outside the old opera house, three bombs
were thrown at it. One struck a gas main and put out all the street
lamps; the others threw troopers to the ground, felled several horses

and blew the imperial carriage to pieces. Miraculously the imperial occupants were only scratched, although the general who was riding with them was badly wounded in the neck and bled profusely all over the Empress's white dress. Once help had arrived for the wounded, Napoleon and Eugenie continued to the opera house, where they were greeted with cheering by the standing audience. When the most anxious of the waiting equerries asked her if she was not shaken, the pretty, silly, Spanish Empress answered with a calm that would have gratified her friend and admirer Queen Victoria. 'It's our business to be shot at', she said.

The perpetrators of the attempted assassination, who were all apprehended, were a group of Italian Nationalists led by Count Felice Orsini, whose father had fought beside the future Emperor when the French sent an expedition to support the rebellion in Romagna in 1831. He wrote to Napoleon from his cell, telling him that he had no hatred either for him or for the people of France. But since their destruction of the Roman Republic and their restoration of the Pope in 1841, they had become the principal enemies of Italian freedom. The Emperor was genuinely moved. He would have pardoned Orsini if he could. Nevertheless he allowed the letter to be read in open court at his trial; and in May, two months after Orsini went to the guillotine, he began to negotiate secretly with Cavour.

The part of the story that was immediately fateful for Palmerston, however, was that, during their interrogation, Orsini and the other conspirators revealed that they were part of a group that had members in England, and that their bombs had actually been made there. It did not seem unreasonable therefore for the French Foreign Minister, Walewski, to write a moderate note of protest and ask the French Ambassador in London, Palmerston's friend Persigny, to deliver it to the British government. Walewski accepted that the British had always offered asylum to political refugees, and that it made no difference whether the governments they fled from were Britain's enemies or friends. But should the British shelter criminals? Should they, he asked, 'continue to shelter persons who place themselves beyond the pale of common right and under the ban of humanity?' And then he made a simple request.

Her Britannic Majesty's Government can assist us in averting a repetition of such guilty enterprises by affording us a guarantee of security which no state can refuse to a neighbouring state, and which we are authorized to expect from an ally. Fully relying, moreover, on the high sense of the English Cabinet, we refrain from indicating in any way the measures which it may see fit to take in order to comply with this wish.

The Cabinet did not regard Walewski's request as unreasonable. Palmerston and Clarendon responded reassuringly in private to Persigny, but they delayed making any formal response until they had decided what they were going to do. Palmerston, who was already irritated by the political activities of some of Britain's many refugees and regarded them as an abuse of Her Majesty's hospitality, suggested at first that the government might draft a bill empowering the Home Secretary to expel anyone whom he suspected of plotting against a foreign government. But eventually the Cabinet agreed that it would be simpler to introduce a Conspiracy to Murder Bill, by which the crime of planning a murder was promoted from a misdemeanour to a felony and made punishable by a long term of imprisonment.

Despite some opposition from Radicals, the bill passed through the House of Commons on its first reading by a comfortable majority of 200. Meanwhile, however, in Paris, a group of French officers presented an address to the Emperor in which they described the English as 'protectors of assassins' and proposed that 'the infamous haunt in which such infernal machinations were planned should be destroyed for ever'. Dissatisfied with his embarrassed silence, and unmoved by the attempts of his ministers to calm them, they surreptitiously placed their demands among the many other addresses that, in accordance with custom, were duly published in the *Moniteur*, the official newspaper of the French government. When the house met on 19 February for the second reading of the bill, some of the Radicals who had previously supported it were no longer in a mood to do so. They were incensed by what appeared to be an official threat; and they would not be placated by Palmerston's assurance that the

439

French Emperor had apologized, or by his suggestion that it would be unworthy of the House to change its course 'upon any paltry feelings of offended dignity or of irritation at the expressions of three or four colonels of French regiments'.

Furthermore, among those Radicals there were at least two who had personal reasons for wanting to humiliate Palmerston. John Bright and Thomas Milner-Gibson, who had been leading opponents of the government's policy in China, had lost their Manchester seats at the subsequent general election and had only just found new seats at by-elections in Birmingham and Ashton-under-Lyne. When the motion was put before the House that the Conspiracy to Murder Bill should be read for a second time, Milner-Gibson, with Bright's support, proposed an amendment that asked the House to express its regret that the government had not yet answered Walewski's despatch.

Several members objected. The answer to the despatch was irrelevant to the bill and the amendment was therefore clearly out of order. But the new Speaker, John Denison, ignored the advice of his experienced clerk and ruled that the amendment was in order. The debate became heated. Palmerston shook his fist and told the house that this was the first time in in his life he had seen Milner-Gibson stand forth as 'the champion of the honour of England' and not as 'the advocate of the foreign country against our own'. Derby, who was watching from under the gallery, sent a note to Disraeli. Disraeli, who had previously supported the bill, now spoke in favour of the amendment. Gladstone followed his example. The government whips, who had confidently allowed several loyal members to go home unpaired, saw suddenly and too late that they were in danger. Their only hope now lay in an adjournment, which would have given them a chance to ensure a full attendance next time and put pressure on the many who were clearly being swayed. But Disraeli foresaw that and called for an immediate division. Conservatives, Gladstone, Peelites, Radicals, independent Liberals, Russell and his embittered Whig supporters, all followed him into the lobby. The ambush, which was as much of a surprise to the attackers as their victims, was as successful as it could have been. The government was narrowly defeated again by an opportunist alliance of left and right.

What happened next was vividly recorded by Queen Victoria in her journal.

Were much vexed and thunderstruck at finding that the Government had been beaten by 19 upon the Conspiracy Bill, on which they had but a few nights ago had a majority of 200! Much put out and uncertain as to what the Government will do. – We walked in the garden for a short while. – At 5 were startled by hearing that Lord Palmerston had come. We saw him and he at once said he had to communicate what I must have expected, the resignation of the Government! The Cabinet was unanimous. To remain in would be against their honour and nor for the good of my service or that of the country! The two parties had combined and voted for Mr M. Gibson's amendment, which was not against the measure, but censuring the Government for not having answered Count Walewski's despatch. Lord Derby's party had voted as a body, – Lord John Russell and the Peelites, all against the Government!! Nothing to be done, but to accept the resignation. Lord Derby and Lord John Russell, the two possible candidates, the one, having no party, and the other in a minority! Lord Palmerston thanked me for my kindness. It is a sad result of total want of patriotism, and like last year, placing me and the country in the greatest difficulty. Albert and I reflected, and decided to write and ask Lord Derby to come immediately. He expressed great surprise at what had happened, the more so, as he had done all he could to further the Bill.

The press took up the Radical version of what had happened and expressed the nation's indignation. Palmerston of all people had been ready to change English law to please the French. William White, the doorman, told his readers, 'The "Great Minister", who but yesterday rode on the topmost crest of the waves of popularity, is sunk so low that there is hardly a man of his former friends to say, "God save him".'

There were many who could not understand how it had happened, or indeed why Palmerston had let it happen. Many of the Whigs and even Radicals were taken aback by what they had done. They resented the return of his apparent arrogance and impatience in debate, and they disapproved of some of his recent appointments: still a Regency man at heart, he had applied the standards of that era, selecting men on their ability alone and making no concession to Victorian sensibilities by taking at least some account of their moral character as well. But they had intended only to fire a shot across his bow. If he had asked the House for a vote of confidence, as he could have done, he would almost certainly have got it.

The only explanation, although unsubstantiated, was that the unexpected defeat had given Palmerston the opportunity to avoid a less honourable one. Uncharacteristically ignoring the advice of Lord Lansdowne, he had recently appointed the Marquess of Clanricarde, a friend of Lady Palmerston, to succeed Lord Harrowby as Lord Privy Seal. One of Clanricarde's mistresses, Mrs Handcock, had died in 1853, leaving her entire estate to their son. Although her legitimate daughters had apparently agreed to this, the rest of her family believed that they had done so only under Clanricarde's 'undue influence'; and they had contested the will in the Dublin Court of Chancery. The ensuing publicity, which had naturally gratified the press and greatly entertained their readers, had at the same time scandalized the Queen and society. As a result, Brougham had warned Lady Palmerston that her husband was about to face a vote of censure; and it was suggested that, rather than risk being defeated on this, he had seized the opportunity to fall victim to the injustice of an invalid amendment instead.

Whatever his motive, he hid it, like his feelings, in resolute joviality, and he embraced his unexpected leisure with his usual enthusiasm. When Argyll, 'to comfort him', suggested that the minority government could not survive, Palmerston did not agree. If the Conservatives and Radicals could avoid discussing reform or foreign policy, it would certainly live out the session and might well last a great deal longer. It would soon be time to take another look at Ireland, and perhaps go travelling again.

15. THE OLD ITALIAN MASTERS

'The Jockey and the Jew' stole the thunder. Although Palmerston's India Bill had passed its third reading, Derby, almost spitefully, set it aside and introduced a new one of his own. It was drawn up under the direction of his first President of the Board of Control, the ostentatious Earl of Ellenborough, who had once been Governor-General of India, and it was as convoluted and impracticable as only haste and vanity could make it. It was an easy target for Palmerston, who challenged almost every clause of it. But Russell regularly came to the rescue, proposing amendments that were more acceptable to the majority and which brought the bill closer to the one Palmerston had originally presented.

The bill became an act. The rule of the British government was established in India; and ever since Disraeli has been given credit for guiding Derby's bill through the Commons. But the man who deserved the credit was Russell. He was the one whose amendments earned it the willing votes of the Radicals and the Peelites; and Gladstone was grateful to him for it. Neither of them, naturally, had any desire to be seen as a supporter of Disraeli; but, more than that, they were both indecorously eager to keep Palmerston out of the limelight. Having succeeded in getting rid of him, they were prepared to make sacrifices to prevent him from coming back, even if, for the time being, that meant keeping Derby and Disraeli in office.

It was a phenomenon that baffled the Prince Consort.

A House of Commons, having been elected solely for the object, and on the ground of supporting Lord Palmerston personally (an instance in our Parliamentary history without parallel), holds

443

him suddenly in such abhorrence, that not satisfied with having upset his Government, which had been successful in all its policy, and thrown him out, it will hardly listen to him when he speaks … The man who was without rhyme or reason stamped the only *English* statesman, the champion of liberty, the man of the people, etc., etc., now, without his having changed in any one respect, having still the same virtues and the same faults that he always had, young and vigorous in his seventy-fifth year, and having succeeded in his policy, is now considered the head of a clique, the man of intrigue, past his work, etc., etc., – in fact, hated!

But Palmerston bore what he described as his 'eclipse' with apparently unfailing good humour. He turned up regularly to debates in the House of Commons, if only to ensure that nobody replaced him as leader of the opposition. Sometimes he supported government measures, such as the Jewish Relief Act, which at last put practising Jews on an equal footing with other British subjects and admitted them to the House of Commons. Mostly, however, his apposite jibes made life even more uncomfortable for the government than the sneers of some colleagues were making it for him; and it was perhaps generally fortunate that the suffering was curtailed by the Thames, which made life equally unbearable for everyone. Over the last three years the newly formed Metropolitan Board of Works had been so thwarted by local vested interests that nothing had yet been done to prevent sewage from pouring into the river around Westminster. By the end of a very hot June the stink from what Disraeli described as 'a Stygian pool' had become so terrible that, despite the tons of lime that were daily dumped in the water and the sheets soaked in chloride that were hung at every window, a coughing and spluttering Parliament voted to adjourn early.

The Palmerstons went to Ireland, on what the Prince Consort described as 'an official tour', and then to Paris, where they were invited to dine with the Emperor and Empress. On their return they went to Broadlands and entertained old friends and colleagues at leisurely hunting and shooting parties until, suddenly and surprisingly, in October, they received a formal invitation to join Napoleon's annual hunting party at

Compiègne in the following month. The Clarendons received a similar invitation. For a few days Britain's recent Prime Minister and Foreign Secretary discussed what they ought to do. It was one thing for the Palmerstons to attend an impromptu dinner with the Emperor while they happened to be in Paris; it was quite another to accept an official invitation to stay with him.

Ever since the second reading of the Conspiracy to Murder Bill the British press had kept up a relentless campaign against Napoleon and the French, and there had been plenty to criticize. They deplored the trial and conviction of the half-English Count Charles de Montalembert, who had published an article in the *Correspondent* criticizing the French government and arguing that the British constitution was better than the French one; although they omitted to mention that the Emperor had commuted the sentence. With much more justification they were outraged when the French government forced the Portuguese to pay compensation to a French sea captain who had been arrested for brazen slave-trading in their colonies. They spread consternation at the inexplicable increases in the activities of France's cannon foundries and in the conscription and training of her army; and they sympathized mischievously with the citizens of the southern English ports, who were now deeply dismayed by the continuing expansion of the French navy and the impressive fortifications at Cherbourg.

There were therefore plenty of arguments against accepting the Emperor's invitation; but in the long run there were some in favour of it as well. 'Perhaps some of our Radical friends would rather not see us too intimate with Napoleon', wrote Palmerston to Clarendon, 'on the other hand, our being on friendly terms with him may be politically useful to us individually, and to the country – if we should come into office again.'

So they accepted, and went with their families to Compiègne. Bad weather limited their sport. There was a little shooting and they met occasionally to hunt stag in the rain, for which everyone else wore oilskin capes or mackintoshes and only Palmerston turned out in nothing more than the pink of the New Forest Foxhounds, insisting, perhaps equivocally, that nothing penetrates a red coat. But there were plenty of indoor activities: football games in the gallery and mounted square-dancing in the riding school by day; and brief dinners, cards, slightly drunken charades and dancing to a hideous hand-ground organ in the evenings.

It was said that the party broke up earlier than intended only because the Empress and the Countess Walewska, who had just become the Emperor's latest mistress, objected to the amount of attention he was paying to Clarendon's sister-in-law the Countess of Craven, who had been married for twenty-three years and borne eight children. By then, however, the Emperor, Palmerston and Clarendon had found plenty of time to talk. They discussed the franchise, which Napoleon believed should only be extended to married men. They discussed Italy, whose freedom, it seemed, was dear to the hearts of both Palmerston and Napoleon, even if they disagreed on the extent of its unity; and Clarendon later recorded that he found the Emperor's Italian attitudes 'most strange and extravagant'. He would probably have used much stronger language, however, if the Emperor had told them everything. Four months earlier Napoleon had held a secret meeting with Cavour at Plombières.

Still moved by Orsini's letter, Napoleon had been in a mood to be helpful, but he was even more moved in that direction when Cavour reminded him of the tradition of the Carbonari. His life had been forfeited the day he betrayed them and set out to destroy the Roman Republic. But the assassination attempts, of which there had so far been three, would end if he were now to atone for the betrayal and come to their assistance. Napoleon could not risk withdrawing his support for the papacy, but he had much to gain by offering to help against the Austrians. It was agreed therefore that, when a proper pretext arose, Napoleon would take 2,00,000 men east to support Victor Emmanuel's 100,000. The Austrians would be driven out of Lombardy and Venetia; and Sardinia's Piedmontese provinces would be expanded to become a free northern Italian kingdom stretching from the Alps to the Adriatic. But Naples and the Papal States were to become an Italian Confederation under the presidency of the Pope; and in return for all this help France would be allowed to expand to her own 'natural' south-eastern frontier and acquire Nice and Savoy. Unknown to Palmerston, most of the military preparations that so alarmed the British press were being made for a war against Austria in Italy.

Palmerston had always been suspicious of French ambition in northern Italy. His one reservation about the cause of Italian freedom was that it could be used as an excuse for French expansion and that, instead of creating a viable, independent buffer state, France would simply replace Austria as the dominant Power below the Alps. But he may not have been as alarmed as Clarendon by the Emperor's attitudes. They were no more extravagant than they had always been; and besides, as far as he knew, the Sardinians, who were after all the allies of both of them, were engaged in nothing more than their usual enthusiastic canvassing for support.

Since his arrival in London in 1851, the Sardinian Minister, the Marchese d'Azeglio, had become as close a friend of the Palmerstons as Persigny, and he had made it his business to keep the entire family well informed about what was happening in Italy – or at least, he hoped, as convinced as they could be by Cavour's version of what was happening. Lady Palmerston was shown almost as many despatches as her husband and was unctuously consulted almost as often. Even Shaftesbury was included; and his notoriously volatile indignation had been well wound up with stories about the cruel iniquities of the Jesuits. But since his recent resignation Palmerston had no longer been in a position to test Azeglio's reports against the despatches of Her Majesty's diplomatic representatives.

By coincidence, after his return to England, Palmerston found himself discussing Italian independence more often than usual, if only because, somehow, he found himself dining more frequently at the same table as Russell, and Italian independence was the one issue on which the two former colleagues were still known to agree. The first of these dinners was given by Russell's eldest brother, the Duke of Bedford; and it was the duke who urged his friends to follow his example and bring the two together as often as possible. In the twilight of their power the leader of one of the great Whig dynasties was playing a last hand in the manipulation of British politics.

Sooner or later the minority Conservative government was bound to be defeated. But in its current state the majority opposition was unlikely to replace it for long. The coalition of Whigs, Radicals, Liberals, Irish

Nationalists and other independent eccentrics was so riven by rivalries and animosity that it would undoubtedly do what it had done twice before and destroy itself at the first opportunity. The only chance of its forming a lasting government lay in persuading at least two of the antagonists to see the error of their separate ways and set out together on a new one. After many weeks and several dinners, however, the two whom Russell's widowed sister-in-law, Lady William Russell, nicknamed 'the old Italian masters' were clearly no closer to an alliance than before. Russell was still too proud and ambitious to settle for anything less than the leadership or the Foreign Office; and Palmerston was all too well aware that admitting him to a Cabinet again would mean bringing in some of his followers as well, which could only be done at the expense of his own. Although Lady Palmerston insisted that her husband had 'great affection for John', he showed no sign of it. After one of the dinners, out of common courtesy, he gave Russell a lift home in the rain, but he did not leave his carriage and come in when they got there. It was still a little premature to speculate, as some did, about which of them would be Prime Minister and whether one of them might go to the House of Lords.

The earliest evidence that anyone outside Whig circles had noticed an attempt at a rapprochement between Palmerston and Russell appeared, surprisingly, in the letters between Cavour and Azeglio. After Palmerston's resignation there was nobody more eager to see him back in office again than Cavour. The Conservatives, like the Queen, were unshakably in favour of supporting Austria and the *status quo*. But Cavour also doubted that he would ever win any useful support from Clarendon, whom he disliked and whom he described as 'our friend with the chin'; and by the end of October he was instructing his agents and sympathizers to concentrate their energies on Russell instead. Like Palmerston, however, Russell always insisted that, in the event of a war between Sardinia and Austria, Great Britain would have to remain neutral, and by 1 December Cavour was already in despair. On that day he wrote to Azeglio, 'We cannot hope to modify the policy of England in our favour. She has become Austrian, and we must go our own way ... Lord Palmerston and Lord John Russell are, in words at least, a hundred times worse than the Tories.'

But to most observers the possible return of Palmerston was looking less and less likely as the days went by. If it was going to happen, it would have to be soon, while what Gladstone described as his 'admirable staff' was 'as yet unexhausted'. The campaign of vilification had not ceased since his resignation, and his stay with Napoleon had fuelled his critics. Although Delane's *Times* was more anti-French than anti-Palmerston, and although Borthwick, who had been shown private despatches by Napoleon, was using the information to attack Derby's government, the rest of the press asserted, without much hard evidence, that Palmerston had lost the support of the public. Perhaps in response to this, many of the Radicals who had voted against him were claiming in retrospect, as if to excuse themselves, that they had done so only under pressure from their constituents, although anyone with any common sense could see that the debate on the Conspiracy to Murder Bill had turned round so rapidly that there would not have been time for that to happen.

The general hypocrisy was well exemplified by a piece that appeared in the *Saturday Review* on 1 January 1859.

The fall of Lord Palmerston's Administration, and the apparently final collapse of his popularity in the early part of the session, are events which the student of political history will do well attentively to consider. The first conclusion which they will be disposed to draw will certainly not be that to which the unscrupulous demagogues of the platform seem so anxious to bring us – viz. that the present constitution of the House of Commons is a fraudulent contrivance for evading the representation of public opinion. No sooner was it really felt that popular feeling had decidedly pronounced against Lord Palmerston's Government, than it fell helplessly and hopelessly in a Parliament which had been elected not twelve months before amidst shouts of 'Palmerston for ever'. Partisan critics may blame, if they please, the mutability of public opinion, but to charge the House of Commons with want of sympathy with the popular voice is either to expose their ignorance or confess their prejudice.

On the contrary, however, the 'ignorance' and 'prejudice' of the *Saturday Review* and Parliament's 'want of sympathy with the popular voice' were soon to be demonstrated conclusively at the ballot box.

By the time Parliament reassembled in February, war seemed imminent in southern Europe. At his traditional New Year's Day reception, in a loud voice that was clearly intended to be overheard, Napoleon had told the astonished Austrian Ambassador, 'I regret that our relations with your Government are not so good as in the past; but I ask you to tell the Emperor that my personal sentiments for him have not changed.' Since then, Austrian and Sardinian troops had been massing on either side of the border between Lombardy and Piedmont, and Napoleon had been using the French railway network to move large numbers of men and horses down to his south-eastern border, without any disruption to the civilian schedules. It was to be the first war in which troops were transported to the front by train.

From the conflicting articles in the newspapers it was difficult to tell which of the British public's feelings was the stronger: sentimental support for the cause of Italian liberty or fear and loathing for Sardinia's ally Napoleon. For the time being, the government cautiously limited its involvement to a purportedly neutral offer of mediation and began the parliamentary session by concentrating the attention of the House on – of all things for Derby's Conservatives – a new reform bill.

The bill, despite all the genuine effort that had gone into it, was essentially a cynical attempt by the government to stay in favour with its unnatural but necessary Radical allies. It was mostly the work of Disraeli, who still scorned the extent to which his leader devoted the bulk of his time to horses and cards. It proposed the redistribution of seventy seats, the establishment of the £10 household franchise in the counties as well as in the boroughs, and the introduction of votes for men with various other property qualifications and members of the learned professions. But this was too progressive for many of the Conservatives and not nearly progressive enough for the Radicals, who also saw the 'fancy franchises' as a not very subtle attempt to increase the Conservative vote. On the second reading, Russell moved an amendment, proposing that the level of the franchise shoud be lowered. When Russell had earlier attempted to introduce a reform bill of his own, Palmerston had opposed his suggestion that the household franchise should be reduced to only £6; but since Russell's amendment did not specify a value and merely proposed a reduction, Palmerston felt that there was no contradiction in supporting it. The government was defeated by 330 votes to 291. Rather than resign, Derby decided to test the supposed change in public opinion and requested that the Queen should dissolve Parliament.

So, while the the members of the British House of Commons fought their election campaigns in their constituencies, the great armies of France and Austria went to war with each other in Italy. On 23 April the Austrian government sent an ultimatum to the Sardinians: if the army now assembled in Piedmont was not dispersed within three days, war would be declared and the Austrian army in Lombardy would invade. Never before was a such threat received with so much joy. Cavour had won the neutrality of Prussia by promising that Sardinia would not make the first move. Now Austria had kept his promise for him, and at the same time taken on the role of the aggressor in the eyes of the world.

The armies of King Victor Emmanuel and the Emperor Napoleon III were only half the sizes they had hoped for and promised when they negotiated their alliance. The Sardinian King had 50,000 men, and the French Emperor was waiting to join him with 100,000 and 400 guns. Against these, the Austrian Emperor Franz Joseph brought slightly fewer men – 120,000 – and more guns – 480. But the Austrian guns were old-fashioned, smoothbore cannon, which fired bouncing round shot over a maximum range of 2,600 yards and with an accurate range of considerably less. The French guns were based on the British weapons that they had seen in the Crimea, which were among the very few aspects of the British army that had impressed them. They were mostly light, very mobile 4- and 9-pounders with rifled barrels, which, although still muzzle-loading, fired fused, explosive shells over an accurate range of 3,500 yards. From the outset they gave the French a very clear and terrible advantage.

On 27 April, as Cavour had hoped and expected, the 29-year-old, inexperienced, depressive, autocrat Emperor of Austria led his antiquated army out of Lombardy and prepared to face the combined forces of dictatorial French imperialism and constitutional Italian monarchy. Next day Palmerston took a calculated risk. In addressing the electors of Tiverton, he abandoned his well-prepared denunciation of Derby's irresponsibility and instead launched an almost impromptu attack on Austria's 'abominable system of misgovernment in Italy'. 'If the consequences of Austrian aggression should be that she should be compelled to withdraw to the north of the Alps and leave Italy free to the Italians,' he said, 'every generous mind will feel that sometimes out of evil good may flow and we shall rejoice at the issue.'

The speech was greeted with loud cheering. Palmerston had judged his audience precisely. Now that hostilities had begun, the hearts and hopes of the British people seemed solidly behind the Italians. In the days that followed, however, the press was more reserved. On 7 May the *Saturday Review*, which as usual expressed its own views as though they were the views of the people, wrote, 'There is so much to repel the sympathies of a free country in the conduct of the belligerents, that for once, the voice of the country is absolutely unanimous in favour of neutrality.' For once, also, the *Saturday Review* was pretty close to the truth. There could be no doubt that the Liberal press, as well as all Liberals and Radicals, supported the Italian cause, but for the most part they were indeed in favour of neutrality, and they agreed with *The Economist*, which added without much logic or scruple that Britain must remain neutral so that, when the fighting was over, she could act as a mediator and ensure 'the independence of Italy of *every* foreign power'.

The argument in favour of British neutrality was further supported by a surprising advocate, Louis Kossuth. More frightened than he need have been by the Conservatives' possible Austrian sympathies, and in the vain hope that Napoleon might support a Hungarian rising, Kossuth agreed to act as his agent and travelled around England addressing public meetings. But with the press and both sides of Parliament already convinced of the need for neutrality, his oratory only served to strengthen the suspicions of *The Times* and the Conservatives, who were already arousing public consternation by asserting that Italy was only the first objective on the French army's agenda, and that England would be next. With no sitting Parliament to make proper provision for national defence, the country was instead engulfed in a broad wave of amateur efforts. On 18 May the Prince Consort wrote to the Prince Regent of Prussia, 'The people are demanding arms, and petitions come from every town for permission to form Volunteer Corps — not to help the French, but to guard against them!' Continuing its campaign, and triumphing in the success it had achieved already, *The Times* printed a dreadful poem by Tennyson, 'Riflemen form!', which managed to combine its alarmist message with Conservative propaganda. In one stanza, it read:

> Let your reforms for a moment go!
> Look to your butts, and take good aims!
> Better a rotten borough or so
> Than a rotten fleet and a city in flames!
> Storm, Storm, Riflemen form!
> Ready, be ready against the storm!
> Riflemen, Riflemen, Riflemen form!

To *The Times* Palmerston's speech at Tiverton was no more than 'what England would look to find in a speech of his at this crisis'. But it achieved a conversion so useful and surprising that Aberdeen called it 'the most brilliant stroke made'. 'His declared wish to see the Germans turned out of Italy by the war has secured Gladstone, who is ready to act with him, or under him, notwithstanding the three articles of the *Quarterly* and the thousand imprecations of late years.' The frail old scholar was in failing health, and he could no longer remember the difference between a German and an Austrian; but, as the course of events was soon to show, he was right in his assessment. Gladstone, who had just returned from Italy, was now as passionate as anyone in his opposition to the Austrians. Although he had become one of Palmerston's most dismissive critics, he was won over by the speech.

The effect of Palmerston's speech on his constituents was never measured at the ballot box, however. His was one of the 241 seats not contested in the exceptionally dull election, a symptom that must have shown Derby from the outset that this was not going to be one of his more successful gambles. Out of the 158 seats that were contested, the

Conservatives gained only twenty-six. It was a very long way from giving them a majority. But they had not resigned office, and until they did they were still the government.

After the election Palmerston went from Tiverton to Brocket, which was much closer to London than Broadlands; and very soon after his arrival he received a letter from Disraeli. 'I address you in your ancient confidence', he wrote. 'Consider well the views I am taking the liberty of placing before you', and he then invited him to join the Conservative government.

> The foreign policy of every Government of which you are a member must be yours, even if you think it might not be expedient to undertake the Foreign Office. As for domestic policy, when the occasion serves, you could bring in your own Reform Bill, which, with our increased force, may be as conservative as you please. You could dictate your terms… You would receive from me, not merely cordial co-operation, but a devoted fidelity.

Palmerston's answer was a blunt rejection. As Disraeli must have known and feared, the Whig conciliators were still hard at work. Although Palmerston and Russell had not yet been seen entering each other's houses, they had been seen more than once in a carriage together; and then, on 20 May, the day when the French and Sardinians won their first great victory over the Austrians at Montebello, Palmerston spent two hours at Pembroke Lodge, the appropriately spacious house in Richmond Park that the Queen had given to the landless Russell when he became Prime Minister. The conciliators, who included Lord Granville, Sidney Herbert, Sir George Cornewall Lewis and Sir James Graham, had drawn up a simple basis for an alliance and had assured the two elder statesmen that, if they were prepared to join together and form a broad-based Liberal administration, they would have the support of the Radicals, the Whigs, the Irish Nationalists and the Peelites, including Gladstone. The wary pair were already agreed on foreign policy. By the time Palmerston left they had also agreed, in Herbert's words, 'to serve together as the Queen may direct', to bring down the government with a vote of no confidence at the earliest opportunity, to introduce a level of electoral reform that would be acceptable to Russell and his followers, and 'to take the whole Liberal party into counsel' as soon as possible.

On 6 June, the day before the opening of Parliament and two days after the Austrians suffered their second great defeat, this time at Magenta, the proposed meeting took place in Willis's Rooms in King Street, St James's. There could not have been a better site for the official birthplace of the Liberal Party. Willis's Rooms had once been Almack's. Almost a lifetime ago these rooms had been the equal of any court in Europe as a centre of gossip, social intrigue, statecraft and diplomacy. Here Lady Palmerston, then Lady Cowper, had held sway with the other patronesses over princes, poets, rogues and heroes.

It was a good-gout day. Lord Palmerston, 'Old Pam', who had once been known in these rooms as 'Lord Cupid', sprang onto the platform, turned and held down the hand of friendship to haul up stiff 'little Johnny Russell', who at sixty-seven was eight years his junior. The assembled company cheered merrily. 'There were about 280 members present,' wrote Herbert to his wife, 'which is thought very large, as the Irish members are not yet come over in any number.' (Actually there were 274, and the cautious Gladstone was conspicuous by his absence.)

Pam. spoke shortly and well, described the challenge in the Queen's dissolution speech, alluded to the failures of the government in legislation, and the danger of their involving us in a war, said that he and Johnny were at one (great cheering). Then there was a pause, and a call for Lord John, who spoke in the same sense and said if the vote succeeded it was necessary to look forward, and if the Queen sent for Pam., he, Johnny, would cheerfully co-operate with him in the formation of a Government – broad basis, etc. – and then Pam. whispered to him, and he added as much for Pam ... On the whole it was very successful, no one objecting who was not expected to do so, and others concurring who had not been reckoned on.

On 10 June the Marquess of Hartington, heir to the Duke of Devonshire, proposed a vote of no confidence in the government. It was carried by a small majority of thirteen votes, with Gladstone, still cautious, voting in support of the government. Outside in the lobby, where many leading envoys were listening, Azeglio threw his hat in the air and hugged Persigny. Derby resigned. Palmerston and Russell waited. Each had said he would serve under the other. Neither had said he would give way. But the Queen sent for neither: she sent for Lord Granville. 'Told him that this was a very serious moment,' she wrote in her journal, 'that considering the equal positions of Lord Palmerston and Lord J. Russell, both having been Prime Ministers, I thought it would be less invidious to choose neither; that therefore I called upon him (Lord G.), as head of the Liberal Party in the House of Lords, to form a government.'

'Pussy' Granville accepted the invitation; and the first person he invited to join him was Palmerston. Since, however, the Queen had made it very clear that she did not want to see Palmerston at the Foreign Office, he began by offering him only the Leadership of the House of Commons. Convinced that Granville was unlikely to succeed, Palmerston cunningly accepted and then wrote a humble and 'very proper' letter to the Queen assuring her of his readiness to 'join with Granville and sit under him'. Then Granville invited Russell to join. But Russell insisted that he would join only if he could be leader of the House of Commons and suggested that Palmerston should be given the Foreign Office and sent to the House of Lords. When Palmerston rejected this, Russell declined to serve and then also wrote to the Queen, petulantly rather than properly, telling her that, as she put it in her journal, 'he could not serve under Lord Granville, as under him he would be third while under Lord Palmerston second, for he should expect Lord Palmerston to give him the choice of every office except his own! Dreadful personal feelings again!' So their fates were sealed by their separate responses. When Granville failed, the Queen sent for Palmerston.

Building the broad-based Cabinet to which he had committed himself at Pembroke Lodge and Willis's Rooms was a difficult and painful task. Russell, who was essential, would accept nothing less than the

Foreign Office; and Clarendon, whom he therefore replaced and whom Palmerston would have preferred to keep there, would accept nothing less instead. His loss was a shabby political necessity which Palmerston bitterly regretted. The other Whigs were easy enough to choose and also easy to persuade: old Lord Campbell became Lord Chancellor, Granville Lord President of the Council, Cornewall Lewis Home Secretary, the Duke of Somerset First Lord of the Admiralty, Sir Charles Wood Secretary for India, Grey, the former Home Secretary, Chancellor of the Duchy of Lancaster, and the Earl of Elgin Postmaster-General. As for the Peelites, Gladstone, whose passionate opposition to Austria still clouded all other considerations, accepted the Exchequer, Argyll returned to be Lord Privy Seal, Herbert went to the War Office, the Duke of Newcastle became Secretary for the Colonies, and clever Edward Cardwell was appointed Chief Secretary for Ireland.

The Radicals, however, were not so easy. Palmerston knew that he had to have at least one, and his first choice was Richard Cobden. But Cobden would only join the Cabinet if John Bright came in as well, and Bright was completely unacceptable to the Queen because his nationwide campaigning in support of electoral reform had included an attack on the House of Lords. Nevertheless, while Cobden did at least agree to go to Paris and negotiate a trade agreement, Palmerston's adversary in the Conspiracy to Murder debate, Thomas Milner-Gibson accepted the Presidency of the Poor Law Board; and within a month, when Milner-Gibson became President of the Board of Trade, he was replaced by Clarendon's Radical brother Charles Villiers. Palmerston had kissed hands on 12 June; by 20 June he had completed his team. It was not a ministry of all the talents. Some of the best men had to be omitted to make it broad-based, but if it was allowed to govern, it had all the makings of a more capable Cabinet than most.

Four days later the French and Sardinians defeated the Austrians again at the horrifying Battle of Solferino. As they looked down on the field strewn with as many as 40,000 dead, dying and moaning wounded, Franz Joseph lost all faith in his army, Napoleon lost all taste for war, and a rich Swiss tourist, Henri Dunant, who had wandered out to watch the fighting, was so sickened by what he saw that he went home and founded the International Red Cross. But his genuine revulsion at the prospect of more bloody combat was not the only factor that influenced Napoleon. His rapid and overwhelming success had brought unexpected and unwelcome consequences. The Prussians were so alarmed by it that, despite their promise of neutrality, they were mobilizing an army; and the citizens in some of the central Italian states were so encouraged by it that they were calling for unity with Piedmont. Napoleon was about to accomplish a great deal more than he intended. Uniting Italy from the Alps to the Adriatic was one thing. Uniting the whole peninsula from top to toe was something else. It would be like creating another Prussia on France's south-eastern border. Napoleon had done enough to fulfil his long-cherished dream of emulating his illustrious uncle. He had fought a war and surveyed his victories from the saddle of a white charger – although, more like the commanders of a subsequent century than his uncle, he had always done so with a fat cigar in his mouth. The time had come for France to make peace.

On 4 July Persigny invited the British government to propose a fortnight's armistice and negotiate terms that would unite Lombardy with Piedmont but allow Austria to retain Venetia – not quite as much as Napoleon had promised the Sardinians at Plombières. For sentimental Russell this was better than nothing. But for Palmerston and Queen Victoria it was too little and too much. To Palmerston, Piedmont could only be a viable buffer state if it included Venetia as well as Lombardy. Besides, as he put it to, Russell, 'the honour of France, the unanimous demands of all Italy, the justice of the case would be satisfied by nothing less.' To Queen Victoria, however, it was intolerable that Great Britain and France should be asking her brother monarch of Austria to surrender territory over which they had both sworn to recognize his sovereignty when they ratified the Treaty of Vienna.

With most of the Cabinet reluctant to get involved, the British government simply passed on the French proposal to the Austrians. Then, on 8 July, news came that the French Emperor had already negotiated an armistice and that he and the Austrian Emperor were planning to meet in four days' time, without the King of Sardinia, to negotiate the terms of a peace. Out of impatience or pessimism or perhaps even chicanery,

Napoleon had decided to act on his own, and in so doing he had pushed the British to the sideline. On 10 July, when Persigny visited Palmerston in Piccadilly and asked for the British government's 'moral support' in proposing peace on terms similar to those he had proposed six days earlier, Palmerston knew that, for the time being, he was in no position to influence the terms. The peace negotiations were clearly going to take place anyway, and the British had lost any moral right to take part in them by failing to take part in negotiating the armistice. So Palmerston, pragmatic as ever, told Persigny that he would have the British government's support and then rode out to Richmond to see Russell.

While Palmerston was still with him, the Foreign Secretary wrote to the Queen urging her to approve the 'moral support' of the British government for Napoleon's terms. The Queen was furious. Her government was well aware that she regarded such terms as dishonourable. In a fierce letter of protest she refused her approval and commanded that a Cabinet should be summoned immediately and that her letter should be read to it. When the Cabinet met, it was also presented with a letter from the Austrians rejecting the terms that had been passed on to them on 4 July.

Officially, therefore, the British government did not support the terms demanded by the French. But when Napoleon met Franz Joseph at Villafranca on 11 July, he was armed with a telegram from his ambassador in London assuring him that he had Palmerston's support. He may not have needed it, however. The terms which the two Emperors actually agreed were even more to Austria's advantage, and they agreed them without even deigning to consult the King of Sardinia, on whose behalf, ostensibly, the French had been fighting and were now negotiating. Lombardy, which, as the recent fighting had shown, was impossible to defend, was to be surrendered to the Kingdom of Sardinia. But Venetia was to be retained by Austria and was to become a member of a proposed Italian federation, nominally presided over by the Pope. Since Venetia would have the power of Austria behind it, this meant effectively that it was likely to be the strongest member of the federation, and that, through it, Austria's influence would actually be extended throughout the whole Italian peninsula. In addition, the Hapsburg Dukes of Parma,

Modena and Tuscany, who had been expelled by revolutions, were to be restored to their thrones, and the Romagna was to be returned to the Pope, on condition he made a few gestures towards constitutional reform. Finally, the two Emperors agreed to meet again in four months' time in Zurich, where the terms agreed at Villafranca would be incorporated in a formal treaty.

Crestfallen, Cavour resigned, although he continued to agitate in private and was soon persuaded to return to office by the more politically phlegmatic King Victor Emmanuel, who could see that the nationalists all over Italy were more united than ever in their furious disappointment. Palmerston was disillusioned and, it was said, 'deeply mortified'. The French, he told Persigny, had sold Italy to Austria. And Queen Victoria, who did not know about the telegram, was triumphant. She alone had saved her government from being associated with Napoleon's 'extortion'.

However, now that France and Austria had made an agreement that overrode the terms of the Treaty of Vienna, Palmerston and Russell argued that, as signatories to that treaty, the British were entitled to protest openly. Furthermore, since the terms agreed at Villafranca were not to be ratified until the Emperors met again in Zurich, now was the time to press for a change. It was not an argument that carried any weight with the Queen. Russell pleaded. 'To leave France to settle with Austria the future condition of Italy would be to withdraw voluntarily from the first rank among the powers of Europe.' Palmerston scolded. 'England is one of the greatest nations of the world. No event or series of events bearing on the balance of power, or on the probabilities of peace or war, can be matters of indifference to her, and her right to express opinions on matters thus bearing on her interests is unquestionable.' But the Queen was adamant. Britain had not protested against the war and could not therefore protest against the peace.

To the British public the agreement at Villafranca was despicable. The contemptuous suspicion of the French grew steadily in the press. Yet as week after week went by, Palmerston and Russell struggled in vain with a Cabinet in which their only constant supporter was Gladstone. Almost every other day – and for one fortnight literally every day – they submitted despatches to France or Sardinia which the Queen consistently rejected. 'No sooner is one withdrawn, or altered', she wrote, 'than others are submitted exactly of the same purport or tendency even if couched in new words.' Before long the Queen was referring to her Prime Minister and Foreign Secretary as 'those two dreadful old men'.

Clarendon, who had good reason to be bitter, was even more dismissive. 'John Russell has neither policy nor principles of his own, and is in the hands of Palmerston, who is an artful old dodger, and whose monomania against Austria has reached the point of phrenzy.' No wonder the wags in Westminster had begun to call them Robin Hood and Little John. Another bitter critic, although a much more restrained one, was Lord Granville, whose failure to form a government had put Palmerston in power. 'Lord Palmerston is generally very communicative to the Cabinet,' he wrote, 'and it is only on some point on which he lays great stress, and is determined to carry, that he acts without them. Lord John does so from a loose way of doing business and from a dislike of submitting himself to any criticism.' But then Granville, although a member of the Cabinet, was leading a double life. Granville was the royal mole. He was passing on Cabinet papers to the Queen and the Prince Consort, keeping them informed of all that was happening and reassuring them that the majority agreed with them. Queen Victoria might feel able to record her respect when she felt that Lord Palmerston had acted properly, but it seems that she had no aversion to people acting improperly if she felt that she was gaining by it. The secret, although well kept at the time, survived with some of the documents that passed between them. One sentence from Granville to the Prince Consort is enough. 'It is desirable that no one should know that I make any written communication to your Royal Highness on this subject.'

The leak was no loss, however. As Granville implied, the important business on Italy was not being brought before the Cabinet. Both Azeglio and Persigny were friends of the Palmerstons and made regular visits to 94 Piccadilly, from which it became clear to their host that most Italians were not going to accept the terms drawn up at Villafranca, and that Napoleon, who was equally aware of this, was baffled as to how he was going to enforce them. There was every reason for Palmerston's hoping to interfere constructively. But the Queen still stood in the way of anything official, and the Queen, yet again suspicious, found it necessary to warn him about 'the danger and inconvenience of private communications with foreign ministers'. The relationship between Palmerston and the royal family had returned to what it had been ten years earlier.

By the end of the year the Prince Consort was writing:

All his old tricks of 1848 and the previous period are revived again. Having Lord John Russell at the Foreign Office whose inefficiency in the office, love for Italy and fear of Lord Palmerston make him a ready tool and convenient ally, he tries to carry on a policy of revenge against Austria and to bind us to the Emp. Napoleon more than ever, regardless of all the interests of England and Europe, and if impeded by the Cabinet or the Queen he is violent and overbearing and if this be of no avail cheats and tricks.

Exhaustion and frustration had clearly reduced the judgement or at least the restraint that the Prince usually exhibited even in his private memoranda. Apart from his pique at being thwarted in his attempt to promote the cause of Austria, he had again convinced himself that Palmerston was behind all the criticisms of the 'Coburg influence' which were reappearing in pamphlets and newspapers. But not even Palmerston's most contemptuous opponents had ever accused him of disregarding Britain's interests; and if there was anyone in Britain other than the Prince who still thought that Palmerston was a friend of Napoleon, events were soon to prove him wrong.

The Emperors of France and Austria met in Zurich in November and confirmed the terms they had agreed at Villafranca. As if to make sure that everybody knew how they felt about this, the people of the duchies that were due to be restored to their dukes held referenda and in each case expressed the wish to be annexed to Piedmont and Lombardy and become part of the Kingdom of Sardinia instead. Palmerston joined in pressing for a congress of all the Powers that had signed the Treaty of Vienna. Since it was now clear that the terms of the Treaty of Zurich could not be imposed without force of arms, everyone agreed. But before the congress could meet, a pamphlet was published in France proposing that the congress should agree to the removal of all temporal power from the Papacy; and the Austrians refused to attend unless the French government repudiated the pamphlet. Since it was well known that Napoleon had sponsored the pamphlet, and may well have written some of it, repudiation was impossible.

The congress was abandoned. In London, Palmerston presented the Cabinet with a proposal which, he said, he had been planning to put before the congress. It was that France, Great Britain and Sardinia should form a powerful alliance to enforce 'the principle that the Italians should be secured against foreign compulsion'. It was an old-style Palmerstonian threat, splendidly in the tradition of Canning. As long as they could make the Austrians believe that they meant it, the allies would never actually have to do anything, and the Austrians would never dare to send soldiers south of the Alps again. But it was rejected by the Cabinet and derided by the Queen. Undaunted, Palmerston then put forward a proposal which, it later transpired, he had put together with the assistance and promised support of Persigny: France and Austria, he suggested, should be asked to declare that they would make no further armed intervention in Italy, and the three duchies and the Papal States in the Romagna should be invited to vote again on their future. Since this proposal did not commit Great Britain to any action, the Cabinet agreed to it, and the Queen thought it best to do the same, if only, as she told her uncle King Leopold, because she was sure it would not be accepted.

This time the Queen was wrong. The French and Austrians, already embarrassed by the extent to which they had committed themselves, eagerly seized the opportunity to be relieved of any obligation to use force. Cavour was overjoyed. Palmerston's proposal, he said, had achieved more than the Sardinian army could have done in a dozen battles. The Treaty of Zurich had been set aside. The people of the Romagna, Parma, Modena and Tuscany were free to choose, and they all chose to become part of the Kingdom of Sardinia. This was the outcome that Palmerston had wanted to see. They had created a buffer state powerful enough to survive on its own, 'a respectable little kingdom of northern and central Italy'.

Now that everything was settled, Napoleon called in his debt and demanded the provinces of Nice and Savoy. He had not fulfilled all his side of his bargain with Victor Emmanuel: Venetia was still Austrian, and the acquisition of other territory had been none of France's doing. Furthermore he had betrayed the Sardinian King at Villafranca. The price that Sardinia had paid in blood was far too high for Lombardy alone. Nevertheless Victor Emmanuel kept his promise. The two provinces were ceded to France; and to be fair, their French-speaking people later approved the move in a slightly artificial plebiscite. But to Palmerston this was one betrayal too many. Napoleon had been consistently and arrogantly disingenuous with his ally. It seemed now that he had taken part in the war for no other reason than personal gain. No ally could trust such a man again, even when their interests coincided; and since Palmerston had always been convinced that 'at the bottom of his heart there rankles a deep and inextinguishable desire to humble and punish England', he was now equally convinced that England was somewhere on his agenda. Napoleon was as 'full of schemes as a warren full of rabbits'. 'And like rabbits,' he said, 'his schemes go to ground for the moment to avoid notice or antagonism.' He wrote to the First Lord of the Admiralty, the Duke of Somerset, 'He has sufficiently organized his military means; he is now stealthily but steadily organizing his naval means; and, when all is ready, the overture will be played, the curtain will draw up, and we shall have a very disagreeable melodrama.'

In May 1860, when Garibaldi and his thousand volunteers sailed from Genoa to support the failing rebels in Sicily, who were demanding freedom from Bourbon Naples and annexation to Sardinia, Palmerston did not share the wild enthusiasm of the British press and public. He was suspicious. He felt sure that Napoleon was only letting it happen because he had been promised more territory. He no longer trusted Cavour, whom he held responsible for the humble cession of Savoy and Nice, and he had not concealed his feelings from Azeglio, who reported to Cavour, 'The moral effect of these cessions, like the stain of the partition of Poland, will never be erased in England.' For the time being, however, Palmerston did nothing to hinder Garibaldi. When the commandeered transports carrying the redshirts arrived off Marsala, there were two warships lying there, but they were British, *Intrepid* and *Argus*, detatched from the squadron at Palermo to protect British residents of the port. Garibaldi was greeted not with gunfire, but with cheering.

While rebels and redshirts advanced victoriously across Sicily, Palmerston tried to persuade Azeglio and Cavour to sign a treaty promising not to cede any more territory to any foreign power without the agreement of Great Britain. 'If such a Treaty is signed,' he told Russell,

> we should withdraw and stand aloof from the Sicilian and Neapolitan Insurrection; if the Treaty is declined, we should tell the King of Naples that our desire is to maintain his Dynasty and the Integrity of his Dominions, but that we cannot be of any active assistance to him unless he will at once alter his System of Government.

This was a little easier said than it would have been a year before. King Bomba had died, and his son Francisco II, 'Bombino', was a little more liberal, which was not difficult. But, as Russell pointed out, any support for famously tyrannical Naples would be repugnant to the British Parliament and press; and anyway, the best they were ever going to get out of the Cabinet was authority to send a despatch requesting that Cavour should not give away any more of Italy. By the time the island of Sicily had been liberated, and Garibaldi had been declared 'Dictator', the British government had at least received an assurance to that effect, although Palmerston no longer set much store by assurances from Cavour.

At the end of June King Francisco II granted self-government to Sicily, restored the constitution of 1848 to Naples and, with the support of Napoleon, offered to make an alliance with the Kingdom of Sardinia. But it still looked as though Garibaldi was preparing to carry the revolution over to the mainland. For several weeks Palmerston and Russell dithered. Where once their policy would have been all too easy to predict, they appeared to consider and approve almost every option and every alliance; and, as usual, astute Azeglio could see why. 'England ceased to press for the unification of Italy from the moment when she thought that she was working thereby for the aggrandizement of France.'

Towards the end of July, however, Persigny proposed that the French and British should send a combined fleet to the Straits of Messina to prevent Garibaldi from crossing; and according to a story recounted in several of the most eminent history books, Palmerston and Russell agreed. The proposal certainly contradicted Palmerston's suspicion that Napoleon had something to gain from Garibaldi's success. But if he and Russell intended to reverse British policy and act on such a scale so close to home in concert with a man they no longer trusted, thereby defying the Francophobia and pro-Garibaldi hysteria of the entire British press and public, and if they ever hoped to get support for such a scheme from the Cabinet, let alone the Queen, there ought to be more evidence to that effect. And such evidence as there is runs in the opposite direction. The opinion that Russell consistently expressed to the Queen is exemplified in his letter of 23 July: 'The only hope which the King of Naples can entertain must rest on the fidelity of his army and navy.'

Nevertheless, in the tradition of romantic fiction, the story continues as follows. The Empress of France, who of course knew about the plan, accidentally revealed it to none other than the Sardinian envoy at her husband's court. The envoy alerted Azeglio, who immediately got in touch with Sir James Lacaita, an Italian-born civil servant, who was a close friend of Russell. Lacaita went straight to Russell's house in London and on arrival was told by a servant that Lord John was in conference with the French Ambassador and was not to be disturbed, and that Lady John, who was not feeling well, had retired to bed. Somehow, despite the mores of the age, Lacaita managed to get himself admitted to Lady John's bedchamber and prevailed on her to send a message summoning her husband. Believing that his wife's sickness had become serious, the Foreign Secretary rushed upstairs to her bedside, where the waiting Lacaita pleaded the cause of Italian liberty and persuaded him to reverse British foreign policy. Now immune to the influence of Persigny, who was waiting throughout in his study, Russell went to the Cabinet next day and persuaded Palmerston and the others not to make the alliance with France.

Sadly, the truth is less romantic. Russell and Palmerston agreed on Italy, but they now disagreed on most other subjects. And when they disagreed, it usually influenced their notoriously fragile relationship. When the Emperor of France invited the other powers to join in an expedition to protect the Maronites in Syria, who were being massacred by the Druse, Russell was eager to help, and Palmerston was firmly opposed to it. The Emperor of France, who had until recently claimed to be to be the protector of the Christians in the Ottoman Empire, might still feel that it was his duty to do so, but the Muslim Druse were Britain's loyal allies and had been very effective against Mehemet Ali and Ibrahim Pasha. The most that Palmerston was prepared to do was to put pressure on the Sultan to defend the Christians.

The result was a row, in which Russell became so passionate that he went into a sulk and for several days towards the end of July refused to speak to Palmerston other than in Cabinet. On 24 July, therefore, when Persigny put the plan to Russell and told him that Palmerston had already informally agreed to it, Russell did not feel inclined to check. Instead, he said simply that this was a matter for the Cabinet meeting next day, and no matter which way he was persuaded, or by whom, he found out as soon as he got to that meeting that, not for the first time, Persigny had been using his imagination. Thus, even if some of Lacaita's story is true – and the only source for it is Lacaita's memoirs – it does not have the significance that he gave to it. Like many men who write memoirs, he exaggerated. There was no policy to be changed. When the Cabinet met on 25 July, Palmerston and the other ministers were already determined to reject the deployment of the fleets, just as they were already determined not to send troops to Syria.

So the splendid story of the struggle for Italian unity and independence, which needed no such embellishments, continued its course unaided and unopposed. On 19 August Garibaldi crossed the straits. In September he occupied Naples and Francisco II fled. Cavour became apprehensive. He feared that Garibaldi was about to establish a rival republic in southern Italy, or, worse, that he was about to march on Rome, the only eventuality now that might be enough to provoke the return of the Austrians and the French. Ostensibly to prevent this, Cavour sent the Sardinian army into the Papal States. When the mostly mercenary Papal army, commanded by French officers, marched out to oppose them, the Sardinians defeated it at Castelfidardo. By the end of September they were in Naples. The following month, when the people of Sicily and Naples voted for annexation to Piedmont and Sardinia, Garibaldi gracefully retired to his home on the island of Caprera.

The European Powers played no part in the last act of the Italian drama, but they did not watch without comment. In formal disapproval of the unprovoked attack on the Papacy, the diplomatic representatives of Austria, France, Prussia and Russia were withdrawn from Sardinia. On 27 October, in an attempt to counter this with a gesture of support, Russell sent a notorious despatch to the British representative, who had pointedly remained, and instructed him to pass it on to Cavour, who was so delighted that he showed copies to the governments of the other powers. The language and arguments revealed it to be one of the few despatches that had not been mostly written for Russell by Palmerston, who had merely passed it on the nod; and the Queen had approved it only because it was not as belligerent as she had been led to expect. In justification of what the Italians had done, Russell made the usual British allusion to the Glorious Revolution and quoted the eighteenth-century Swiss jurist Emmerich de Vattel: 'When a people from good reasons take up arms against an oppressor, it is but an act of justice and generosity to assist brave men in the defence of their liberties.' It was an argument, as the Austrians were quick to point out, that could have been applied equally well to the relationship between England and Ireland. But it probably had little effect on the situation in Italy. The people of the Papal States were going to vote for unification with Piedmont anyway. On February 1861 the first national parliament of Italy met in Turin. With the exception, for the time being, of Rome and Venetia, the entire peninsula was one united kingdom.

Russell's despatch did have one more general and far-reaching consequence, however. Just as Napoleon's conduct towards Sardinia had confirmed the British in their view that the French were opportunist, manipulative and untrustworthy, Britain's approval of Sardinia's conduct and her consequently implied disrespect for treaties had led the other Powers, particularly Prussia, to look on the British as the same. In the opinion of the Russian Ambassador in London, Baron Brunnow, Britain's concept of diplomacy was 'roguery'.

As for the relationship between Britain and France, it appeared on the surface to continue unaltered. Cobden's negotiations produced an agreement that eliminated most tariffs and brought a greater, if still wary, intercourse between British and French merchants. In 1860, after the Emperor of China had consistently refused to comply with all the terms of the Treaty of Tientsin, and after he had tortured some of the diplomats sent to reason with him, an Anglo-French expedition captured Peking, where the French looted the Summer Palace and the British then burned it. Although the journalists of each nation were outraged by the conduct of the other's soldiers, Palmerston was delighted by both. It was better, he felt, to punish the Manchu Emperor than his unoffending Chinese subjects. 'It was absolutely necessary', he wrote to Herbert, 'to stamp by some such permanent record our indignation at the treachery and brutality of these Tartars, for Chinese they are not.'

In 1861, while the attention of the United States was diverted by a civil war, France, Spain and Great Britain agreed to send an expedition to seize the port of Veracruz in Mexico. In the tradition of a bygone age, their objective was simply to hold the port and refuse to return it until the Republican government of Benito Juarez paid all the interest on the national debt that was due to French, Spanish and British bondholders. It soon transpired, however, that Napoleon's real plan was to put an emperor on a newly created throne of Mexico; and his candidate was the Archduke Maximilian, whose brother was Emperor of Austria and whose wife was the daughter of King Leopold of the Belgians. When Palmerston refused to have anything to do with it, Napoleon, true to form, told the Austrians that he approved, and the plan went ahead.

Although Palmerston was inclined to agree that Maximilian might rule Mexico better than Juarez, he knew that the outrageous plan was doomed. As soon as he found out what was happening, he withdrew all the British forces, and the hapless Maximilian was left to his fate: to be deprived of Napoleon's essential protection as soon as the United States were free to intervene, and to be shot by a Juarista firing squad.

As always, of course, there were also times when British and French interests conflicted. In 1859 work started in Egypt on the Suez Canal, which Palmerston had been doing everything he could to prevent since he first learned about it. He persuaded the *Morning Post* to run sensational articles exposing and deploring the horrifying conditions under which the enforced labourers who built it were living and working, and questioning the financial integrity of de Lesseps. But in changing times there was little else he could do. Twenty years earlier he could have halted the project by deploying a fleet. Now, with a heavily Liberal Cabinet, he would not have been allowed to do such a thing, even if he had wanted to; and with Napoleon's large modern fleet in the Channel protected by the menacing new fortifications at Cherbourg, he did not even want to. By 1859 Palmerston's priority was national defence; and he took the initiative while public anxiety was still high enough to support him.

That year Palmerston established the Royal Commission into the Defences of the United Kingdom. Its report, delivered in December, did not make comforting reading. The recently launched ironclad frigate *Warrior* was certainly a match for *La Gloire*, but she could not be in two places at once. On the whole, the British navy was too old, too small, too slow and too weak to defend the long Channel coast. Probably no navy could do it on its own; and the fortifications of the coast and ports, despite all the recent improvements, were much too insubstantial to withstand a salvo from modern guns. On 15 December Palmerston wrote to Gladstone, 'One night is enough for the Passage to our Coast, and Twenty Thousand men might be landed at any Point before our Fleet knew that the Enemy was out of Harbour.'

When Cobden came up with the imaginative suggestion that it might be cheaper if Britain and France were to sign an arms limitation treaty, Palmerston wrote back revealingly.

It would be very delightful if your Utopia could be realized, and if the nations of the earth would think of nothing but peace and commerce, and would give up quarrelling and fighting altogether. But, unfortunately, man is a fighting and quarrelling animal; and that this is human nature is proved by the fact that Republics, where the masses govern, are far more quarrelsome and more addicted to fighting than Monarchies, which are governed by comparatively few persons. But so long as other nations are animated by these human passions, a country like England, wealthy, and exposed to attack, must by necessity be provided with the means of defence, and however dear these means may be, they are infinitely cheaper than the war which they tend to keep off.

Over the course of the next dozen years military architects and engineers constructed fifty-seven shore batteries, gun towers and sea forts as well as nineteen large land forts; and from time to time the aged Prime Minister, now Lord Warden of the Cinque Ports, spent hours in the saddle inspecting them. They were subsequently ridiculed as 'Palmerston's follies' and never used, but before they were all completed the French did declare war, not on the British but on the Prussians. The true test of a deterrent, as subsequent history has shown, is that it never needs to be used; as Palmerston put it, the forts were infinitely cheaper than a war.

The cost for the first four years alone, after many cuts by Gladstone, was a staggering £11 million; and from the day the commission delivered its report to the day Gladstone delivered his budget, Palmerston had battled with him to get it. He argued that the cost could be raised through loans. He pleaded, justifiably, that if the government did not propose measures for defence, someone else would, and when they were assuredly carried, the government would be discredited. In response, Gladstone insisted that it would be a 'betrayal of his public duty' to spend so much, particularly on the wooden ships of the line that Somerset had asked for in a hurry, and which he regarded, also justifiably, as obsolete sitting ducks.

Palmerston often lost his temper with Gladstone, and he was not alone in that, but defence was too important. On defence he was always patient, conceding here, calming there and paying no attention when Gladstone used his favourite ploy and threatened to resign again. Delane said that Palmerston had burned so many of Gladstone's letters of resignation that he had once set the library chimney at Broadlands on fire. Unfortunately the Queen was more convinced by them, and after almost every threat Palmerston found himself reassuring her that 'Mr Gladstone, having failed to become master of the Cabinet by a threat of resignation, will in the end yield to the almost unanimous descision of his colleagues'. His technique was nothing more than 'ineffectual opposition and ultimate acquiescence'. On one occasion, however, the Queen was so sure that Gladstone really meant to resign that she almost pleaded with Palmerston to overcome his objections, to which Palmerston famously replied, 'Viscount Palmerston hopes to be able to overcome his objections, but if that should be impossible, however great the loss to the government by the retirement of Mr Gladstone, it would be better to lose Mr Gladstone than run the risk of losing Portsmouth or Plymouth.'

16. OLD PAM

On 17 April 1860, in a field near Farnborough, the handsome champion of the United States, John Heenan, weighing in at 195 lb., fought the English champion, Tom Sayers, who weighed in at a mere 149 lb. At the end of forty-two rounds, the last five of which were fought after the excited crowd had broken into the ring, the match was declared a draw. Since pugilism was hardly legal at the time, it was a little embarrassing for the Home Secretary to hear it said that the Prime Minister had been among the spectators. It was not true, but such was the reputation of 'Old Pam' that the electorate on the whole believed it; and as they were mostly the sort of men who went to prize fights themselves, they wanted to believe it and admired him for it.

In a long life Palmerston had learned but not changed. His attitudes, his manners and his methods were still the attitudes, manners and methods he had acquired as a young man from mentors and models such as Drury, Stewart, Canning and Brummell. His reputation was still the reputation he had earned in the days when Willis's Rooms were Almack's. In October 1863 therefore, when the 79-year-old Prime Minister was cited as co-respondent in a divorce case, there were plenty of admirers who wanted to believe that too.

The petitioner, a Radical journalist called Timothy O'Kane, claimed that some months earlier he had sent his wife on a political errand to Palmerston, who had promptly seduced her and had committed adultery with her on several occasions thereafter. London society was both delighted and aghast. The scandal was discussed in whispers by ladies after dinner and by gentlemen in clubs; and it was talked about openly with dismissive merriment by Lady Palmerston on every possible occasion.

Gladstone, who probably hoped it was true, was of course righteously mortified; and Disraeli suggested to Derby that Palmerston had dreamed the whole thing up in order to make himself more popular before calling a general election.

Mr O'Kane had instituted proceedings only after Palmerston had refused to pay him £20,000 in damages; and it soon became clear that the case was one of blackmail rather than adultery. Before the parties came to court, the pretty lady, who was barely in her thirties and had once been an actress, admitted not only that she had never slept with the Prime Minister but also that she had never been married to the plaintiff. When the case came up for hearing at the end of January 1864, Sir Robert Phillimore QC for Palmerston requested that O'Kane produce evidence of his marriage. When he failed to do so, Mr Justice Wilde dismissed the case, and the court erupted with unseemly cheering.

Throughout the disappointingly short episode the wits in the clubs were putting on Irish brogues and saying that they knew she was Cain, but was he Abel; and many of those that thought about it felt that he probably was. When the gout was not at its worst, Palmerston was still astonishingly vigorous. He still shot as often as he could, although he rarely hit anything now, and he used to tell the story of how he had admitted as much to a keeper, who had answered reassuringly, 'Ah, but then your lordship always misses them so clean.'

He still rode. In his eightieth year he was still riding out to watch his racehorses exercise at Winchester or inspect fortifications with the Royal Engineers; and in June of that year, on Speech Day, he trotted the twelve miles from Piccadilly to Harrow in less than an hour and later rode home again. Palmerston and the quiet grey that he kept in London were a well-known sight in Piccadilly and the streets that led down through St James's to Parliament. If he did not ride to Westminster, he usually walked, though not always when it was late and winter. When Speaker Denison told him that his health was of national importance and that he ought to take more care of himself, he replied, 'Oh, I do indeed, I very often take a cab at night, and if you have both the windows open it is almost as good as walking home.' It was an answer the speaker passed on in horror to Disraeli. 'A through draft and a north-east wind! And in a hack cab! What a combination for health!'

Palmerston was the subject of countless affectionate anecdotes, often from people who did not even have the right to vote for him. The devoted private secretary of his last few years, Charles Barrington, remembered hearing that the driver of the horse-drawn omnibus that ran along Piccadilly at night used to tell his passengers, ''E earns 'is wages. I never come by without seeing 'im 'ard at it.' A railway porter remembered telling a gentleman with a cigar that it was forbidden to smoke in the waiting-room and then, on seeing who it was, apologizing and asking him to continue. 'I took you for an honest man,' said Palmerston with a smile, 'but I see you are only a damned snob.'

The ways of both Palmerstons were the ways of the Regency, and there was no better example of that than their conduct during and after Gladstone's budget in 1860. Gladstone proposed the abolition of the stamp duty on books and newspapers. Palmerston was opposed to the idea, but the majority of the Cabinet was in favour, and so it was duly presented in the budget speech and passed by the House of Commons. In the House of Lords, however, it was rejected by their Lordships, at which they were disturbed by the unusual sound of someone – Lady Palmerston – applauding loudly in the gallery.

Gladstone was furious and would have unburdened his disappointment to Palmerston next day. But Parliament was not sitting next day. In response to the death of Sir Charles Barry, the architect of the Palace of Westminster, Palmerston had moved that both houses should adjourn for a day as a mark of respect; and it would be unworthy to give the slightest credence to the scurrilous suggestions made by so many members in consequence. It was clearly no more than coincidence that the next day was Derby day and the Prime Minister happened to have a horse running. When Gladstone did raise the matter, the day after that, Palmerston dismissed it. 'Your disappointment is nothing to mine, who had a horse with whom I hoped to win the Derby, and he went amiss at the last minute.' Mainstone had started third favourite and had come nowhere; and it was widely rumoured that he had been 'got at'.

Gladstone made up for his loss in the following year. He introduced his proposal again, but this time he also introduced a new system, which has been used ever since. Instead of presenting each budget measure as a separate bill, he introduced the entire budget as one bill. Rather than take responsibility for defeating the budget, the House of Lords accepted the abolition of stamp duty on newspapers and books. And the following year Palmerston also had at least some compensation. After he had changed his trainer, another horse, Buckthorne, won the Ascot Stakes.

Palmerston was a rare sportsman. He loved racing for its own sake. Unlike Derby, he seldom laid a bet. It was the one aspect of his sporting passion that was not Regency. But his attitude to the visual arts, although much less passionate, was Regency through and through. Soon after he formed his second administration, he was presented with the plans that had won the competition for a new Foreign Office. They were in the high Gothic style, with a few Middle Eastern embellishments, and were designed by Sir George Gilbert Scott, who regarded them as 'the best ever sent into a competition or nearly so'. But Palmerston, in complete opposition to the prevailing fashion, thought that such a style was only fit for 'monastic buildings or a Jesuit college'. In his view the architecture of the Foreign Office should reflect the tradition of Greek and Roman statesmen. It had to be Classical; and in answer to the protest that the Classical style was not English, he pointed out that the Romans had governed England and done much for it over several hundred years, whereas, as far as he could remember, the Goths, Vandals and Saracens had done nothing.

Gilbert Scott was asked to think again. When he came back with 'a regular mongrel affair', which was more Byzantine than anything, he was sent away for a second time. His third submission, at last, was the Classical design that stands in Whitehall to this day. The original design became instead the basis of the Midland Hotel and the façade of St Pancras Station, which, Scott wrote,

> is often spoken of to me as the finest building in London; my own belief is that it is possibly too good for its purpose, but having been disappointed through Lord Palmerston of my ardent

hope of carrying out my style in the Government Offices … I was glad to be able to erect one building in that style in London.

The station design is also still standing, a fitting memorial in different ways to both Scott's genius and Palmerston's taste.

The unaltered attitudes of his youth were also the attitudes that Palmerston brought to the conduct of home affairs. But, as in so many things, his style has led others and indeed history to misjudge him. Although he said, 'we cannot keep adding to the statute book *ad infinitum*', his government did in fact go on adding to it with a steady flow of legislation, ranging from the useful but unobtrusive, such as the Partnership Liability Acts and the Prisons Acts, to the mildly progressive, such as the Offences against the Person Act. He was inclined to consider and support surprisingly revolutionary ideas, for example nationalization of the railways and the introduction of decimal coinage. But with age and disillusionment he became more reactionary in his attitude to crime. After a sharp increase in the number of robberies with violence, he supported the successful introduction of flogging for the offence, and he even proposed the abolition of his own ticket-of-leave system. Always a supporter of the death penalty for murder, he was opposed to the abolition of public hangings, partly because, in his view, it would not otherwise be a deterrent, and partly because he did not believe that a constitutional government should have the right to execute anyone in secret. But he abolished the death penalty for attempted murder in the Offences against the Person Act.

As for reform, his attitude was one of complete insouciance. He was sure that nobody in the country wanted it any more than he did. 'All such changes as have been desirable have long since been effected, as the result of our organic reforms, and therefore there is no such desire now for further innovations.' As he had promised when he formed his government, he let Russell introduce another reform bill, confident that it would fail. When the bill was debated in the Commons, an amused Disraeli described Palmerston's speech as 'not so much in support of, as about it'. The bill was defeated, as expected, and even Russell had to admit that 'the apathy of the country was undeniable'.

In 1861 the old style, which had never left the conduct of foreign affairs, returned to their presentation as well. Russell inherited an estate fom his brother; and now that he had the means to support himself appropriately, he accepted an earldom from the Queen. With the Foreign Secretary in the House of Lords, the Prime Minister was again responsible for conducting the business of the Foreign Office in the House of Commons. Frailer and even more halting it may have been, but the voice was as forceful as it had been in the past, and never more so than when issues from the past came back to haunt it.

In 1859, with help from Palmerston's old enemy David Urquhart, the family of the murdered Sir Alexander Burnes had succeeded in publishing his entire report on the situation in Afghanistan twenty years earlier. When read in its entirety, the report showed that Burnes had advised in favour of making an alliance with Dost Muhammad and not, as the Governor-General, Lord Auckland, had then done, with his opponent Shah Shuja. In 1861, armed with this, the member for Greenock, Alexander Colquhoun-Stirling-Murray-Dunlop, an ecclesiastical lawyer who is only remembered now for proposing the bill that abolished marriages at Gretna Green, moved a vote of censure on the government for misleading the House in 1842. His charge was that, in order to justify Lord Auckland's action and exonerate itself from any responsibility for the tragedy that followed on the retreat from Kabul, the government had edited the report. Since Palmerston and Russell were the only members of Melbourne's government still in office, the attack was clearly on them, if not just on Palmerston.

For an hour and a half the 77-year-old Prime Minister spoke without notes, and without ever flagging. He could not, and did not, deny that Burnes's full report had not been laid before the House. But he ran through the story in detail and argued that the government had a right to present only the parts of the report on which its decisions had been based. There was never any chance of defeat. Most members present felt that it was all too long ago to matter. John Bright, who meant to support the attack, actually weakened it by going too far and accusing Palmerston of forgery; and success was assured when Disraeli came to the defence and reminded the House that the government had a discretionary right to suppress sensitive information. The motion was defeated by 168 votes to 61.

Palmerston's popularity was as high as, if not higher than, it had ever been. *Punch*, which had so often poked fun at him, descended to doggerel in his praise. It was written to be accompanied by the air 'John Highlandman'.

An Irish Lord my John was born,
Both Dullness and Dons he held in scorn,
But he stood for Cambridge at twenty-one,
My gallant, gay, JOHN PALMERSTON!
    Sing hey, my brisk JOHN PALMERSTON!
    Sing ho, my blithe JOHN PALMERSTON!
    Let Tory and Radical own they've none
    To compare with my jaunty JOHN PALMERSTON.
Thanks to tact and temper, and taste for the trade,
For twenty years in office he stayed,
Let who would be Premier, it seemed all one,
So the Sec.-at-War was JOHN PALMERSTON.
    Sing hey, etc.
There he did his work for chief after chief,
Till the Tory party it came to grief;
And the Treasury Bench when the Whigs they won,
Who was Foreign Sec. but JOHN PALMERSTON!
    Sing hey, etc.
Since then years thirty and one he's seen,
But no mark they've left on this evergreen;
Still the first in his place when debate's begun,
And the last to leave it is PALMERSTON.
    Sing hey, etc.
With his hat o'er his eyes, and his nose in the air,
So jaunty, and genial, and debonair,
Talk at him – to him – against him – none
Can take a rise out of PALMERSTON.
    Sing hey, etc.

Of the Cinque-Ports, warden he's made at last,
And fears of invasion aside are cast;
There's never a Mounseer son of a gun
Can come over you, My JOHN PALMERSTON.
    Sing hey, etc.
Since the days of the Patriarchs ne'er was seen
A head so grey with a heart so green;
And when, if ever, his day is done,
There'll be tears from Punch for JOHN PALMERSTON.
    Sing hey, etc.

This was the man who was in his element when Greece came back onto the agenda in 1862. After a revolution had resulted in the flight of the unworthy King Otto, he loftily offered to return Corfu and the other Ionian islands if the Greeks would accept Britain's choice of a successor. The Greeks agreed. After consulting the Russians and the French, who were after all the wayward child's other guardians, Palmerston gave them Prince William, the grandson of the King of Denmark, who ascended to the throne as King George. Although the Conservatives were strongly opposed to parting with the islands, Palmerston thought they were a price worth paying for a royal alliance. The new King of Greece's sister, Princess Alexandra, was also the Princess of Wales.

There were also plenty of new issues for which the old-style Palmerston was equally effective, particularly when, in the tradition of Canning, the Royal Navy was integral to the policy. In 1863 two of the guards on the British Resident's house in Yeddo (now Tokyo) were killed by Japanese police, and four British travellers became involved in a brawl on the road outside Yokahama, in which one was killed and two were injured. Palmerston instructed Russell to demand that the Japanese government should apologize, bring the murderers to trial and execute them, and pay £35,000 in compensation to the families of the dead and injured and a fine of £100,000 to the British government. The initial Japanese reluctance to comply with any of these demands vanished immediately on the approach of a British naval squadron. But, although they complied with the other demands, they were unable to find the murderers. To encourage them to try a little harder, the British admiral seized three Japanese ships in the harbour at Kagoshima. When even that brought no result, he loosed off his guns, intending to sink the three ships. Unfortunately, however, he overshot and set fire to the town instead, killing 1,400 people.

The incident aroused fury among the Radicals in the House of Commons, where it was suggested that the bombardment of Kagoshima was like firing on Bristol because someone had been killed on the road from London to Brentford. But Palmerston was happy to defend the admiral, telling the House that in his view, he had 'performed his duty as a British officer ought to perform it'. A few months later he wrote merrily to Russell:

> I am inclined to think that our Relations with Japan are going through the usual and unavoidable stages of the intercourse of strong and Civilized nations with weaker and less civilized ones. First – agreement for Trade, next Breach of Engagement, Injustice and Outrage – Then Redress demanded and refused – Then Reparation enforced by Hostility. Then temporary acquiescence – then renewed endeavours to break engagements – Then successful display of superior strength and then at last peaceful and settled commercial Intercourse advantageous to both Parties. We have gone through all these stages with China – we have only got Halfway with Japan.

A similar incident took place in Brazil. A British naval officer was arrested on a probably trumped-up charge of drunkenness, and his admiral obtained his release by temporarily seizing three Brazilian merchantmen. This time the Brazilians demanded compensation for the shipowners and eventually, to Palmerston's fury, King Leopold of Belgium agreed to mediate and found in favour of Brazil. But in this case the incident was only a little bit of Brazilian retaliation against a much larger and more bitter campaign against what was left of Palmerston's oldest enemy, the slave trade.

In 1845, having failed to come to any agreement with Brazil, Peel's government had passed an act recognizing an old Portuguese definition of slavery as piracy and empowering the Royal Navy to treat Brazilian slave ships as pirates. Since this empowered the British captains to seize the ships as prizes, and to profit considerably in consequence, the treaty was enforced more vigorously than most. Under the more liberal government of the Emperor Pedro II, however, the Brazilians, who claimed to be suppressing the slave trade, were now asking for the repeal of the act and offering instead to sign a treaty agreeing to the abolition of the trade. Russell was in favour of agreeing, as were, of all people, Cobden and Bright, but Palmerston would have none of it. The Brazilian economy depended on slavery; and the good intentions of honest men were meaningless. 'It is not by respectable men that the trade is conducted', he told the House of Commons. 'It is carried on by the scum of the earth in every country, and the profits are so large that they can afford to bribe the subordinate officers whose duty it is to detect and punish crime.' Not long after they came into government, he had written to Russell: 'the slave trade treaty with Spain does not prevent some 15 or 20,000 and perhaps more from being every year imported into Cuba.' And now, in a private letter, he revealed his prejudices and his passion.

> The plain truth is that the Portuguese are of all the European nations the lowest in the moral scale, and the Brazilians are degenerate Portuguese, demoralized by slavery and the slave trade ... I have laboured indefatigably all the time I was at the Foreign Office to put an end to the Slave Trade, and though not with entire at all events with some considerable success and nothing shall induce me to load my conscience with the guilt of having been a Party to promoting its revival.

Slave ships were still plying their trade, particularly in Brazil and Cuba; and when Palmerston returned to office the main obstacle to the proper policing of the Atlantic Ocean was still the government of the United States. So long as the United States prohibited other navies from searching their ships, and so long as other navies reciprocated, slave ship captains could sail unmolested by carrying two sets of colours. If approached by a British ship for example, they ran up an American flag; if approached by an American ship, they ran up another colour. The breakthrough came with the outbreak of the American Civil War. In 1862 the British government of Palmerston signed a treaty with the Federal government of Abraham Lincoln. While the war continued, and while Great Britain remained neutral, the agreement it contained could not be carried out. When the war was over, however, British and American cruisers were at last able to hunt in couples. If their quarry ran up an American flag, the crew of the American ship would board her; if she hoisted anything else, the British crew would do it.

But in other ways the American Civil War presented the old-style Palmerston with a dilemma. The Confederate states of the South were slave states. But so were three of the Union states in the North – Maryland, Kentucky and Missouri – and it was in order to retain the support of these states that Lincoln did not make the abolition of slavery one of the initial purposes of the war. His declared purpose, initially, was to recover the secessionist southern states for the Union. But this, in England, seemed like hypocrisy. The United States had been created by secession from Great Britain in the first place. As a matter of principle, therefore, if slavery was not to be an issue, support for the South was simply support for a people's right to self-determination; and as a matter of practicality, since the North had declared a blockade of Southern ports, from which the cotton was shipped to the mills of Lancashire, support for the South was also support for the much more valuable trading partner. Furthermore, after the opening Battle of Bull Run, or 'Yankee Run' as Palmerston called it, it looked as though the Confederacy was going to win.

More seriously, Palmerston was wary of Lincoln's Secretary of State, William H. Seward, the former Governor of New York, who had insisted on trying Alexander McLeod for murder after the attack on the *Caroline* in 1841. Lincoln knew nothing about foreign affairs. He left everything to Seward; and ever since 1841 Seward had hated the British. Palmerston felt certain that he would rather invade Canada than Virginia. Having sent reinforcements as ostentatiously as possible to Canada, which 'had a wholesome effect upon the Tone and Temper of Lincoln and Seward', Palmerston and Russell declared Britain's neutrality in the war, although they did recognize the Confederates as belligerents, which meant that they were not obliged by law to regard their soldiers as rebels and their sailors as pirates.

In the hope that Great Britain and France might be persuaded to give them full recognition as a nation, the Confederate states sent two representatives, James Murray Mason and John Slidell, to visit the courts and governments in London and Paris. Evading the Federal blockade, Mason and Slidell went to Havana, where they took passage on a British mail steamer, the *Trent*, bound for Southampton. When Palmerston heard that they were coming, he also heard that a Federal warship, *James Adger*, had put in to Southampton. Palmerston consulted the First Lord of the Admiralty, the Home Secretary, the Lord Chancellor, the Attorney-General and the Solicitor-General; and they all assured him that, according to the principles of maritime and international law which the British had applied during the war of 1812, the crew of the *James Adger* would be within their rights to board the *Trent*. He then summoned the new American Minister in London, Charles Adams, and demanded to know if the *James Adger* has designs on the *Trent*. Adams insisted that she did not, although he could not say what else she was doing. But by then it was too late anyway. The *Trent* had already been intercepted.

On 8 November, while she was passing the Paredon Lighthouse in the Bahamas channel, the *Trent* received a shot across her bow from the Federal sloop of war *San Jacinto*. When she hove to, the commander of the *San Jacinto*, Captain Charles Wilkes, sent a party to board her, took off Mason and Slidell and carried them back as prisoners to Boston, where he was cheered as a hero.

The United States Navy had just done the very thing that it objected to the Royal Navy doing during the war of 1812. The press was united in its indignation. Palmerston, a little disingenuously, condemned the 'gross outrage and violation of international law'; and then he arranged for another 3,000 soldiers to be sent to Canada and ordered the Admiralty to have a fleet at the ready. Russell drafted a despatch demanding an apology and the immediate release of Mason and Slidell. When the despatch went to Windsor Castle, the Queen thought it was 'somewhat meagre', but the Prince Consort softened some of the language further and added the suggestion that without doubt Captain Wilkes's action must have been unauthorized; and when Palmerston saw the draft after that, he softened the language still further, altering some of the Prince's words as well as Russell's. In public, however, Palmerston was just what the people and press expected. 'If the Federal Government comply with the demands it will be honourable for England and humiliating for the United States. If the Federal Government refuse compliance, Great Britain is in a better state to inflict a severe blow and to read a lesson to the United States which will not soon be forgotten.'

The combination of soft words, a big stick and the chance of a 'let-out' produced the desired effect. Wilkes had been on his way back from Africa and had indeed acted on his own initiative. Lincoln and Seward released Mason and Slidell, and allowed them to sail for Southampton; and they declared that Wilkes had been acting without authority.

The Prince's alteration of the despatch, which was credited a little sycophantically with having averted a catastrophe, was his last political act. He was dying of what was said to be typhoid, which, if true, was a very unusually isolated case. Palmerston, who was not alone in his mistrust of the royal physicians, urged the Queen to get another opinion, but the Queen, who was actually so distressed that she asked the Keeper of her Privy Purse, Sir Charles Phipps, to answer Palmerston's letter for her, instructed him to thank the Prime Minister for his 'kind interest', and to assure him that the Prince was only suffering from 'a feverish cold' and that, in addition to Sir James Clark – who was almost as old as Palmerston – she now had the services of Professor William Jenner, who happened to be the leading specialist in typhoid and typhus.

The Prince Consort knew better. When he asked his daughter Princess Alice if she had told her sister Vicky, who was now Princess Royal of Prussia, she said, 'Yes, I told her that you are very ill.' 'You did wrong', said he. 'You should have told her that I am dying. Yes, I am dying.'

'Nothing in his life became him like the leaving of it', Jenner wrote afterwards to a friend.

You can have no idea of the excellence of the man – he was the finest specimen of intellectual and moral greatness and religious excellence I have ever known – so great, so good did I think him that when sitting at his bedside in the stillness of night, fearing the result, I have longed and longed that I might die in his place.

The Prince Consort died on 14 December 1861. The Queen, despite 'her wish and determination to do her duty', was 'in an agony of grief'. For five weeks she saw nobody but the members of her household, not even her Prime Minister. To start with this may have been a relief to Palmerston. He was suffering badly with gout that Christmas, and he felt the loss of the Prince as keenly as anyone. On any subject but defence, the Prince and he had almost always been opponents, but he was not looking forward to dealing with the Queen without him. At the end of December, in a letter to Russell, he wrote: 'Her determination to conform to what she from time to time may persuade herself would have been at the moment the opinion of the late Prince promises no end of difficulties for those who will have to advise her. We must deal with her with the most gentle hand. I shall however write to King Leopold to give us his assistance.' Within days King Leopold was writing to his niece warning her that it was now time for grief to give way to duty. 'It is undoubtedly your interest for the sake of having no difficulties as well as that of the country that Pilgerstein and his people should not be upset.'

On 29 January, when the Queen was in retreat at Osborne, she summoned Palmerston from Broadlands, where he was well enough to be missing birds again. He obeyed so rapidly that he forgot that he should still be in mourning and, without changing, appeared instead in a brown overcoat, light grey trousers, blue studs and a pair of green gloves. But she was moved to forgive him by his obvious grief and his concern for her and for the Prince of Wales, who had recently embarrassed her by being caught with an actress. 'I would hardly have given Lord Palmerston credit for entering so entirely into my anxieties.'

After another five weeks Palmerston wrote to the Queen to recount all that had happened over the interception of the *Trent* and to congratulate her on the 'humiliation' of John Bright's 'favourite North American

Republic'. By then, however, the Union had captured New Orleans by attacking it from the sea, and the new garrison commander, General Benjamin Butler, had infamously ordered that any woman who insulted United States soldiers in the street was to be treated as a prostitute and locked up. Palmerston wrote privately to Adams, 'I cannot refrain from taking the liberty of saying to you that it is difficult if not impossible to express adequately the Disgust which must be excited in the Mind of every honourable man by the general order of General Butler given in the enclosed extract from yesterday's *Times*.'

Adams treated the letter as though it was an informal declaration of war and refused to attend any more of Lady Palmerston's receptions. But the continuing Union successes were making it more and more obvious that it was in Great Britain's best interest to stay out. After the anti-slave trade treaty and Lincoln's declaration that all slaves were now to be regarded as emancipated, public opinion in most of England swung behind the Union, although the press, particularly the *Morning Post* and *The Times*, denounced the declaration as a cynical, but fortunately unsuccessful, attempt to provoke a ghastly slave uprising. Gladstone, whose money came from cotton, still openly supported the Confederacy; and in Paris, Slidell persuaded Napoleon to support his proposal for joint mediation by France and Great Britain. When Russell put the proposal to the Cabinet in London, however, the majority were against it, including Palmerston, who thought that it would be 'like offering to make it up between Sayers and Heenan after the third round'.

Nevertheless, despite the success of a few British blockade runners, the mostly effective Union blockade of Confederate ports ended any significant export of cotton, bringing the mills of Lancashire to a standstill and imposing a deep economic depression on the whole of Gladstone's homeland in the north-east. This did not add too much to the support for the Confederacy in the rest of Britain: as Cobden put it, it would have been cheaper to feed the unemployed millers of Lancashire on 'turtle, champagne and venison' every day than to go to war with the Union. But it induced the people of the north-west to do whatever they could to bring an end to it.

When the Confederacy placed orders for warships, some of the shipbuilders around Liverpool accepted, in defiance of the Foreign Enlistment Act of 1819, which prohibited the supply of armaments to belligerents in a war in which Great Britain was neutral. The first such ship that Adams knew about was the *Oreto*, which left Liverpool in March 1862, steamed to Mobile, where she sprouted guns and changed her name to *Florida*, and thereafter sank a considerable amout of Union merchantmen before being sunk herself towards the end of 1864.

Then, at the end of June, Adams told the customs commissioners in Liverpool that he suspected that hull no. 290, which had been launched in May by the Laird shipyard in Birkenhead, was being completed to the specifications and order of the Confederate navy. A week later the customs commissioners reported that they could find no grounds for detaining the ship. On 24 July Russell received a letter from Adams containing more detailed information and accompanied by counsel's opinion to the effect that, under English law, the ship ought to be detained. On 26 July Russell sent the letter to the Queen's Advocate for an opinion. But 26 July was a Saturday and the Queen's Advocate had just suffered a nervous breakdown. As a result it was not until the evening of Monday 28 July that the papers were passed on for an opinion to the Attorney-General and the Solicitor-General. And by then, as usual, it was too late.

That afternoon no. 290, now named *Eurica* and completed as a three-masted schooner with auxiliary steam power, sailed merrily down the Mersey with a brass band and lots of well-dressed ladies on her deck. Ostensibly she was about to undergo a few hours of steaming trials. But at Holyhead she put ashore her ladies, her musicians and her other passengers; and then, commanded by one Raphael Semmes, who just happened to be a distinguished captain in the Confederate navy, she raced out into the Atlantic. Evading the Federal frigate *Tuscalosa*, which had been waiting for her, she headed for the Azores, where two British merchantmen had already delivered the guns and ammunition that were to convert her into the famous and fearsome Confederate cruiser *Alabama*.

Under the command of Captain Semmes the *Alabama* captured and burned ten Union ships in the mid-Atlantic, sank the USS *Hatteras* in an engagement of only thirteen minutes in the dark in the Gulf of Mexico, turned down the coast of Brazil towards the Cape of Good Hope and then sailed on round the world, capturing another eighty-two merchant ships in the process. On her return to the Atlantic in June 1864 she put in to Cherbourg, where Semmes asked permission to carry out long overdue repairs. The French government delayed for five days and then, under pressure from the United States government, maintained their neutrality and refused, by which time the little Union sloop *Kearsarge*, commanded by Captain John Winslow, was waiting in the Channel.

Although his ship was barely seaworthy and short of ammunition, Semmes decided to sail out and fight. Winslow took *Alabama's* fire and saved his own until she was within 1,000 yards. The first salvo hit home hard, but for the next seventy minutes the two ships steamed in tight circles until, when *Alabama* was clearly sinking, Semmes struck her colours. *Kearsarge* sent boats to pick up survivors, but before they got to them Semmes and about forty others were picked up by neutral spectators, including the British yacht *Deerhound*. Instead of facing a Union prison or worse, Semmes had a rest in Switzerland and then returned to serve the Confederacy as Rear-Admiral commanding the James river squadron.

Charles Adams was not pleased. In November 1862 he wrote to Russell listing the *Alabama's* achievements so far and informing him that he had been instructed 'to solicit redress for the national and private injuries already thus sustained, as well as a more effective protection of any repetition of such lawless and injurious proceedings in Her Majesty's ports hereafter'. Russell replied that the United States had set the precedent for trafficking in the contraband of war and refused to accept responsibility. In the Commons Palmerston argued that Her Majesty's customs officers had no right to retain a ship until they knew for sure where she was headed; and in the House of Lords Russell – for the time being – refused to consider compensation. But they took to heart the request to prevent 'any repetition of such lawless and injurious proceedings', particularly after Adams had warned them that privateers would become very active round the British coast if they did not.

In the autumn of 1863 Adams warned Russell that John Laird, who was a Conservative MP as well as a managing partner of a shipyard, was now building two special ironclad vessels with seven-foot underwater rams on their bows, which would be ideal for destroying wooden-hulled ships on blockade duty. By now Russell had shown willing by halting the *Alexandra*. But the law officers of the Crown ruled that it would not be lawful for the government to seize the so-called 'rams' until it was certain of their destination. When Adams warned that, if the rams sailed, the United States would regard it as a declaration of war, Palmerston gave instructions that the rams were to be seized anyway, and then came up with a fiction that would make it almost legal. The rams were to be compulsorily purchased by the Royal Navy. 'We are behind in iron-clads especially in rams, which would be useful for Channel service in the event of war and would therefore tend to be peacemakers.' The Confederates were disappointed; but the builders got their money and Charles Adams was pleased. The next time Lady Palmerston sent him an invitation, he accepted it.

The American Civil War continued along the bloody road to Appomattox Court House. The British stayed neutral. In the summer of 1864 Palmerston at last gave in to the constant pressure from Confederate sympathizers in Parliament and agreed to have a meeting with the envoy James Mason. But it was hardly sincere. He was only trying to win Conservative support for the imminent debate on Schleswig-Holstein.

The old-style Palmerston was never more manifest than in his response, perhaps his most famous, to the return of the Schleswig-Holstein question. There were, he said, only three people who ever knew the answer to the question: the Prince Consort, who was dead, Mellish, a foreign office clerk who had vanished, and Palmerston himself, who had forgotten it. But when the old problem reappeared, the old-style Palmerston was no match for the new-style opposition. His opponent was a man who was not susceptible to bluff or even threats, Otto von Bismarck. Palmerston did not even see Bismarck coming. If there was anyone at this stage of his life whom he regarded as an obstacle, it was either Napoleon, whom he mistrusted, or Gladstone, whom he disliked and manipulated. Indeed, in September 1862, when 47-year-old Bismarck became Minister-President of Prussia, Palmerston only just knew who he was. So far all he had done had been to serve as the

Prussian representative at the Diet of the German Confederation and as the Prussian Ambassador at St Petersburg and Paris.

Bismarck first stepped into the centre of the stage in 1863, when the Russians responded to the threat of yet another revolution in Poland. In their first attempt to quell it, the Russians introduced military conscription, which the British Ambassador in St Petersburg described as 'simply a plan by a clean sweep of the revolutionary youth of Poland to kidnap the opposition, and to carry it off to Siberia or the Caucasus'. When the measure served only to turn the threat into a widespread reality, Bismarck, with an eye to the future, earned the gratitude of the Russians by proposing and signing a convention with them which authorized the troops of Russia and Prussia to cross each other's border in pursuit of fugitive rebels.

The revolution won huge support among the press and public in Britain and France. But Palmerston was no more able to provide practical assistance this time than he had been on the other occasions. Poland was out of reach of the British navy, and the little British Army was not supportable there without it. Furthermore, now that the Russians had the Prussians as allies, the Queen was not going to be in favour of a war against a country in which her eldest daughter was married to the heir to the throne. Indeed, so different were her views from those of her subjects that, at the beginning of 1864, despite his determination to be gentle, Palmerston found it necessary to return to a tone that he had not employed since she was widowed. 'Viscount Palmerston can quite understand Your Majesty's reluctance to take any active part in measures in any conflict against Germany, but he is sure that Your Majesty will never forget that you are Sovereign of Great Britain.'

Palmerston and Russell attacked the Russians in both Houses of Parliament and sent strongly worded despatches to St Petersburg. When Napoleon suggested that they should send a joint protest to Berlin, they declined, although only because they so mistrusted him that they suspected he was hoping to use it as an excuse to lead his army across the Rhine. But they did agree to join with France and Austria in inviting Russia and Prussia to attend a conference on Poland, which the Russians confidently refused to do unless France and Great Britain were prepared to cancel the Black Sea clauses of the Treaty of Paris in return for Polish autonomy. The plain truth was that all threats were empty and the Russians were well aware of it. The Austrians were not going to fight because they currently owned a piece of Poland themselves. The British were not going to fight because they had no means of doing so. And the French were not going to fight because they were distracted by their adventure in Mexico and because, contrary to British suspicions, Napoleon was much too insecure to take on Russia and Prussia on his own.

The only people who were being influenced in the least by the protests and attempts to mediate were the revolutionaries in Poland, who kept on fighting in the hope of eventual support. The whole folly was encapsulated in another desperate despatch from the Ambassador in St Petersburg. 'If the British Government do not mean to fight, let them say so, and stop the loss of life and the suffering attendant on a rising which, unaided, cannot succeed.' But they did not say so. The threats and posturing continued. The revolution failed. Eventually Austria joined Russia and Prussia, and the three Powers who had partitioned Poland in the first place combined to maintain it just as it was. That Christmas, the 'show-stopper' in a London pantomime was a huge box labelled 'England's aid to Poland'. When the fairy waved her wand, the front fell open, revealing nothing but a tiny bottle of ink and a very large pen. For the first time in a long time Great Britain had not been taken seriously. As Derby put it, her policy was nothing more than 'meddling and muddling'.

Palmerston now knew who Bismarck was, and not only through his alliance with Russia. In the course of the year Bismarck had told his Parliament that his King had a right to govern without it and to use his army to that end if need be. On 15 November Palmerston wrote to King Leopold veiling his anxiety and distaste in humour. 'The King of Prussia seems to have made his models of action Charles the First of England and Charles the Tenth of France and Bismarck is an humble Imitator of the Ministers of those Two unfortunate Sovereigns. I hope the King's fate will not be like theirs.' On the other hand, Bismarck had also learned more about Palmerston. Having started some 'meddling' of his own in Schleswig-Holstein, he expected nothing more than 'muddling' from London.

So far Palmerston's negotiations over Denmark's interest in Schleswig-Holstein could be listed among his successes. At the Convention of London in 1852 it had been agreed that, when King Frederick VII of Denmark died, the kingdom and the two separate duchies would pass to his nearest heir in the female line, Prince Christian of Glucksburg. At the end of March 1863, however, Frederick announced that he intended to separate the military and financial affairs of Holstein from those of Denmark, which, since he did not say the same for Schleswig, was correctly interpreted as meaning that he intended to ignore the Convention of London and incorporate Schleswig into Denmark. The Diet of the German Confederation protested; and when Frederick refused to change his plan, they assembled an army and prepared to invade Holstein.

It was a moment when the British were feeling very close to the Danes. That month the Prince of Wales married their Princess Alexandra. While Russell tried in vain to calm both parties, Palmerston, confident that it would not come to fighting, told the House of Commons that Britain was as determined as France and Russia to protect the rights and independence of Denmark. 'We are convinced – I am convinced at least – that if any violent attempt were made to overthrow those rights and interfere with that independence, those who made the attempt would find in the result that it would not be Denmark alone with which they would have to contend.' To the Danes this was a clear signal that the British were ready to support them with force, and they acted accordingly thereafter.

As a result, when Frederick died at the end of the year, his heir, who ascended the throne as Christian IX, confidently declared his intention to continue Frederick's policy in the duchies. But at this point Prince Christian of Augustenburg stepped into the quarrel. In the Convention of London the Prince of Augustenburg's father had renounced his rights to the duchies in return for the restoration of other estates. But the Prince argued that, since he was of age at the time, he was not bound by anything his father had said or signed on his behalf; and he now wanted his duchies back. The liberal German states agreed with him. Ostensibly Bismarck joined them; and a German, but mostly Prussian, army marched into Holstein.

Then Bismarck turned to the Austrians and asked for their support. Alarmed by the prospect of two provinces seceding from a sovereign whose rights were laid down by treaty, which would create an awkwardly encouraging precedent for the people of Venetia, the Austrians agreed to Bismarck's secret proposal and joined the Prussians in opposing the claims of Prince Christian of Augustenburg. Between them they turned on Prussia's recent German allies and took over the whole of Schleswig and Holstein for themselves. The Austrians had no more got the measure of Bismarck than Palmerston had; it never occurred to them that the next step in his plan was to turn on them and seize both duchies for Prussia.

When Napoleon proposed a conference of all the Powers, he proposed that the Danish problem as well as the Polish one should be on the agenda. This suited Russell, who had proposed to the Cabinet that Great Britain and France should make a joint threat of force if the Austrians and Prussians did not withdraw from the duchies. But Palmerston's mistrustful rejection of any joint action with France held good over Denmark as well as Poland.

> The conduct of Austria and Prussia is discreditably bad, and one or both of them will suffer for it before these matters are settled. I rather doubt, however, the expediency of taking at the present moment the steps proposed. The French Government would probably decline it unless tempted by the suggestion that they should place an armed force on the Rhenish frontier in the event of a refusal by Austria and Prussia – which refusal we ought to reckon upon as nearly certain.

Apart from his assertion that the real reason for the seizure of the duchies was 'the dream of a German fleet and the wish to get Kiel as a German seaport', this was Palmerston's only astute assessment on the subject. He had failed to notice the growing strength and influence of the little German states and their Diet. He so underestimated them that he regarded their interference in the affairs of Denmark as impertinence. As he told Russell, it was like 'the Duke of Devonshire's servants' hall assuming to decide who shall be the owner of a Derbyshire country gentleman's estate'. Although he now referred to Bismarck as 'crazy', he was still prepared to tell people that 'all military men who have seen the Prussian Army at its annual reviews of late years have unequivocally declared their opinion that the French could walk over it, and get without difficulty to Berlin'.

While gallant Denmark fought and failed, Palmerston knew that, no matter what he said, he was powerless to help. A fleet was no use on its own against an enemy who was advancing overland, and it was very unlikely that he would have been allowed to use the fleet any way. Half his Cabinet were for doing nothing; and the Queen, adamant in the opinions bequeathed to her by her wise and beloved but German Albert, was convinced that Denmark was entirely in the the wrong. Yet Palmerston kept up the pressure on his Cabinet, in the hope that some of them might change their minds; he allowed Russell to give the Danes the impression that help would be on its way in the end; and he kept on threatening. But the only occasion on which one of his threats was even close to credible was when, without the consent of either Queen or Cabinet, he warned the Austrian Ambassador very privately 'that, if an Austrian squadron should pass up the coast past Deal, a British squadron would follow it suitably instructed'. Bismarck won. The Prussians came out of the conflict with a haughty contempt for British bluster, and the Danes with a bitter sense of betrayal.

In April the nation's attentions were briefly diverted by a visit from Garibaldi. From Palmerston's point of view it could not have come a a a worse time. The inevitable adulation was bound to offend the Austrians and probably Napoleon as well. As expected, the hero was welcomed by a crowd of over 100,000 at Charing Cross station. He was fêted wherever he went and, with the exception of Buckingham Palace, received in all the great houses of London, including, more than once, 94 Piccadilly. Many of the great ladies of London fell in love with him; and it was said that the Dowager Duchess of Sutherland had written to him to let him know that, although she could not expect a hero to look at a woman of fifty, she was there if he wanted her. It was a relief, however, when exhaustion and offence at the inappropriately simple accommodation provided for his followers led Garibaldi to leave England sooner than expected. Rather than be distracted by the effect he was having on Radicals at home and reactionaries abroad, Palmerston preferred to devote all his energies to his own problems in northern Europe and preparing for the opposition's inevitable attack on his government's foreign policy.

The attack came at the beginning of July 1864. Ironically at the proposal of Lord Malmesbury, the House of Lords carried a vote of censure by a majority of nine votes. When the Commons met to debate the same motion a few days later, the cheers when Disraeli walked in were ominously much louder than those that greeted Palmerston. The opposition's case, in Disraeli's words, was that the government's foreign policy was no more than 'menaces never accomplished and promises never fulfilled'. The government's defence was delivered by Palmerston at the end of a four-day debate. 'I say that England stands as high as she ever did, and those who say she had fallen in the estimation of the world are not the men to whom the honour and dignity of England should be confided.' But general rhetoric was not going to be enough. When it came to the specific charges, the opposition had the answers. When Palmerston claimed that he had told the house that the Danes would not fight alone because he expected that not only Britain, but also France and Russia, would support them, Disraeli broke in to remind him that the Danes were not blaming France or Russia for betraying them.

Most of those who attended that debate knew how they were going to vote before they walked into the Chamber; and if there were any who had intended to vote against the government and then decided to vote in its favour, they were more likely to have been induced to do so by the amendment moved by Alexander Kinglake, who had just published the first two volumes of his *History of the Crimean War,* than by anything that the Prime Minister said. Before Palmerston rose to speak, Kinglake moved that the house should express its satisfaction that the Queen 'had been advised to abstain on armed interference in the war now going on between Denmark and the German Powers'. It was on this amendment, and not the motion of censure, that the Chamber divided at half-past two in the morning; and it was on this that the government was saved by a majority of eighteen: 313 votes to 295.

As soon as the vote was announced, Palmerston rushed out of the chamber, bounded up the stairs to the Ladies' Gallery and fell into the arms of Lady Palmerston, who had been sitting there, throughout the entire debate. 'An interesting scene', wrote Disraeli generously, 'and what pluck! To mount those dreadful stairs at three o'clock in the morning and at eighty years of age ... It was a great moment.'

Palmerston's eightieth birthday did not actually come until 20 October, after the usual Prime Ministerial summer of tree planting and other tiresome duties. He started it and ended it at Broadlands. He left at 8.30 a.m., put his horses on the train at Romsey, got off at Fareham, rode along the coast to inspect the forts at Portsdown and Hilsea, crossed the water to inspect the forts at Gosport and arrived back home at 6 p.m. showing no signs of wear other than a greying of the whiskers where the salt wind had worn away the dye.

At the end of the next session Parliament was dissolved and the members went to the country to fight another general election. Foreign policy could have been an issue this time, and so could reform. The Radicals certainly tried to make it one. But like last time the real issue in the eyes of the electorate was a simple one: Palmerston, yes or no? The answer was yes. The Liberals were returned; and since they were returned with an increased majority, it ought to have been very satisfying to note that Gladstone lost his seat for Oxford University and had to stand for South Lancashire a month later. But Palmerston was not amused. 'He is a dangerous man', he told Shaftesbury. 'Keep him in Oxford and he is partially muzzled; but send him elsewhere, and he will run wild.'

Palmerston's health was now failing noticeably. In the last session of Parliament he and Lansdowne had fallen asleep regularly, not just on their front benches but also at Cabinet meetings. The gout had started to affect his bladder, which the doctors said was because he climbed onto a horse too soon after each attack. In a memorandum on a visit he made to Osborne during the previous summer Disraeli recorded how the Queen had remarked on the change in him.

> She said 'Lord Palmerston was grown very old.' I replied 'But his voice in debate, Madam, is as loud as ever.'
>
> 'Yes!' she exclaimed with animation. 'And his handwriting! Did you ever see such a handwriting. So very clear and strong! Nevertheless I see in him a change, a very great change. His countenance is so changed.'

In August the Palmerstons went up from Broadlands to Brocket, partly to be closer to London for business and partly to be closer to the better doctors. Palmerston worked easily on his despatches and other papers, and took exercise, or at least walked a bit. Someone saw him come out of the front door, look round to see if anyone was watching and then go through a test of strength which he had been known to do for many years, climbing over the high railings opposite the door and then climbing back again. He talked with relentless cheerfulness at table. On one occasion, when someone described the symptoms of some sick cattle, he remembered that those symptoms had been described by Virgil and then quoted the appropriate eight lines. On another, he recounted a funny episode that had happened at Harrow and then could not stop himself laughing at it, which Lady Palmerston saw as a sign of how weak he was. She knew that he was never going to face another Parliament, he might not even see his eighty-first birthday, and she knew that he knew it too.

On 12 October, while they were out for a drive together, he caught a chill. When they returned to the house, he undressed slowly and lay for a long time in his bath. By bedtime his kidneys were inflamed. Grim doctors came and made it clear that there was little they could do. Lady Palmerston sent for the family. On 15 October he rallied, partly, he felt, because he had developed a new taste for mutton chops, apple tart and port for breakfast, and partly because of the arrival of Lady Shaftesbury, who was greeted as she entered his room with 'Minny, come in, come in; you always seem to me like a sunbeam.'

On 17 October Shaftesbury arrived. That night the doctor, Prothero Smith, another deeply committed evangelical, decided that it was time to pray. 'Oh, certainly', said Palmerston. The doctor then asked his patient if he agreed that all men were sinners. 'Oh, certainly', said Palmerston again. And did he believe in salvation through the intercession of Jesus Christ? 'Oh, surely', said Palmerston with what must have been a sigh.

Still well wide of the mark, the doctor said a prayer or two and then invited Shaftesbury to take over. 'He knows your voice, and he will be touched to find that you are near him.'

The following evening, at 10.45 p.m., the last dandy died. Lady Palmerston, fighting her grief, was with him as he faded away, and so too was Shaftesbury, kneeling at the bedsdide and praying passionately, which may not have been quite so much of a comfort to him.

He was delirious at the end. But his mind was still on business, dealing with protocols and the terms of treaties. Contrary to legend, his last words were 'That's Article 98; now go on to the next.'

Palmerston was given a state funeral and buried among his mentors in Westminster Abbey on 28 October. Like the Prince Consort, whose funeral in St George's Chapel, Windsor, had been as simple as his rank would allow, he had wanted to be buried quietly in Romsey Abbey, but Lady Palmerston had given in to the Cabinet on condition that, when her time came, they would allow her to be buried with him. It was the greatest gathering that London had seen since the funeral of the Duke of Wellington. Huge crowds, almost all dressed in mourning, lined the streets all the way from 94 Piccadilly to Westminster Abbey, where Beethoven's funeral march was played as Cabinet ministers carried his coffin down from the choir to his final resting place.

The obituary in *The Times* ran to 13,000 words. Some of it was aimed straight at his public. 'He was supposed to have his pocket full of constitutions, to have a voice in half the Cabinets of Europe, to have monarchs past reckoning under his thumb.' Some of it was heartfelt and perceptive. 'In the art of distinguishing the prevailing current of public opinion, in readiness of tact, in versatility of mind and humour, in the masterly ease with which he handled the reins of government, and in the general felicity of his political temperament he had no rival in his own generation.'

Europe mourned and praised him too. In Italy the *Nazione* of Florence wrote, 'Every banner under which the defenders of liberty, progress and civilization are grouped will be veiled with crape.' In Belgium the *indépendence Belge* described him as 'the keystone of the arch which maintained the balance of parties in that period of transformation through which England, and all Europe with her, are at present passing.' Even the Austrians were respectful of their lifelong adversary. The *Debatte* of Vienna wrote, 'In the clash of principles and convictions he recognized only one – the interest of England – and this he served with sacrificing devotion.'

Queen Victoria was not so kind. 'Poor Lord Palmerston, alias Pilgerstein', she wrote to King Leopold.

It is very *striking*, and is another link with the past – the happy past – which is gone, and in many ways he is a great loss. He had many valuable qualities, though many bad ones, and we had, God knows, terrible trouble with him about Foreign Affairs. Still, as Prime Minister he managed affairs at home well, and behaved to me well. But I never *liked* him or could ever the least respect him, nor could I forget his conduct on certain occasions to my Angel. He was very vindictive and *personal* feelings influenced his political acts very much. Still he is a loss.

Posterity has been more inclined to agree with the Queen than with the contemporary press. Palmerston's reputation has not worn well. All too often it has been judged not by what he did but by the way he did it, or by the criticisms in the memoirs of contemporaries, most of whom had been thwarted by him. Yet even Talleyrand, who was hardly the least of them, described him as possibly the most able man he had met in his career. For every sore loser who called him a bully, there was another opponent who remembered him with warmth as much as with respect, such as Disraeli, who wrote, 'I still think that statesman is peculiarly to be envied who, when he leaves us, leaves not merely the memory of great achievements, but also the tender tradition of personal affection and social charm'. It took time for this 'tradition' of 'affection' and 'charm' to melt the memory of Disraeli's greatest opponent, Gladstone, who had never had a kind word to say about Palmerston personally while he lived. But even he, towards the end of his long life, remembered a time when 'a Frenchman, thinking to be highly complimentary, said to Palmerston: "If I were not a Frenchman, I should wish to be an Englishman"; to which Pam coolly replied: "If I were not an Englishman, I should wish to be an Englishman".'

The Austrians may have been right. Palmerston had only one principle. As Russell readily acknowledged, 'his heart beat ever for the honour of England'. But this was a principle the nineteenth century regarded as worth having. Even the last and most successful of his adversaries, the Prussians, admired him for it. In his obituary the *Cologne Gazette* wrote, 'If anyone in future times wishes to sketch the portrait of an English statesman, he had better try to write Lord Palmerston's history ... From one generation of Englishmen to another, the saying will be handed down: we are all proud of him.'

A successful foreign policy is the political achievement most easily forgotten, especially among those who prospered in the consequent peace. Palmerston's achievements are not much more remembered in England today than they are in the islands of the Caribbean or on the old plantations of mainland America. But his name appears more often in the histories of European nations than that of any other nineteenth-century British statesman. It was something the shrewd Florence Nightingale saw coming. 'He was so much more in earnest than he appeared. He did not do himself justice.' Like the dandies in the days of his diffident youth, he was always stylishly self-deprecating. Like many other clever but not too cultured Englishmen, he hid his intellect behind the jaunty mask of a sportsman; and in so doing he allowed himself to be underestimated. At the time of his death he was more popular among the English masses than any other statesman before him. His reputation stood, undeniably, far higher than it merited. But since then, judged by subsequent standards, it has fallen further than those of many who achieved far less. Perhaps one day, judged simply by achievement and by the standards of the age that made him, it will lie where it deserves to lie, in the same position as his tomb, which Thomas Hardy described in a letter to his sister just after the funeral: 'between Pitt's and Fox's and close to Canning's'.

NOTES

Abbreviations

BL = British Library

BP = Broadlands Papers, now at Southampton University

PRO = Public Record Office

RA = Royal Archives at Windsor

1. In the shadow of the hill

5 'a pleasing unaffected woman' Connell, B., *Portrait of a Whig Peer*, pp. 166–7

6 'a great protectress' Douglas, S. (Lord Glenbervie), *Diaries*, ed. Bickley, F. (London, 1928) vol. 2, p. 93

'a toil of pleasure' Minto, Earl of, *Life and Letters*, vol. 3, p. 7

'old-fashioned house' ibid., vol. 1, p. 311

'even Harry' ibid.

'Viscountess Palmerston in her dressing room' BP, 25 Dec 1790

19 'a most charming boy' Connell, pp. 323–5

'I like the scool' BP, 27 May 1795

'If I had known where to put it' Lorne, Marquess of, *Viscount Palmerston*, p. 3

'those vices which are common' Bulwer, *The Life of Henry John Temple, Lord Palmerston*, vol. 1, pp. 5–7

20 'I am now doing Caesar' ibid., pp. 7–8

'merciful and indulgent' ibid., p. 9

21 'wit and pleasure' Guedalla, P., *Palmerston*, p. 40

'Willy's lip' BP, 8 July 1798

23 'Harris, I am not well' Malmesbury, 3rd Earl of, *Diaries and Correspondence* (London, 1844) p. 208

24 'A boy who puts himself at the head' Ashley, E., *The Life and Correspondence of Henry John Temple, Viscount Palmerston*, vol. 2, p. 408

2. A want of spirits

28 'His abilities are excellent' Connell, *Portrait of a Whig Peer, p.* 456

'the idol of the whole family' BP, 3 Dec 1800

'a perfect gentleman' Bourne, K., *Palmerston: the Early Years*, p. 20

'Diligence, capacity' Minto, vol. 3, pp. 234–5

'a want of the spirits' ibid., pp. 231–2.

30 'My Dear Brother', Robert Southey, *New Letters*, ed. Curry, K. (London, 1965), p. 47

31 'I detested that woman' Douglas, *Diaries*, vol. 2, *p.* 93

35 'Cambridge men' Bourne, *Palmerston: the Early Years*, p. 36

40 'devoid of all qualifications' Lorne, p. 9

'It was an honour' Bulwer, vol 1., p. 15

43 'bound in honour' ibid., p. 22

3. Lord Cupid

48 'egregious nonsense' Bulwer, vol. 1, p. 80

'the case before the House' Hansard, 3 Feb 1808

'bad or good qualities' Ilchester, Earl of, ed., *Lady Holland's Journal*, vol. 2, p. 240

50 'a great deal to be done' Bulwer, vol. 1, pp. 85–8

58 'vanity and ambition' ibid., pp. 92–3

61 'The Secretary at War' ibid., p. 412

'never boast of shining talents' Minto, vol. 4, p. 331

63 'where opinions are to be given' PRO, Lady Malmesbury's journal, 12 May 1811

66 'Sulivan is in love with Harry' Bourne, *Palmerston: the Early Years, p.* 128

68 'Sheridan got drunk' Ridley, J., *Lord Palmerston*, p. 45

69 'every other abstinence' Bulwer, vol. 3, p. 34

71 'circumstances of birth' Hansard, 1 March 1813

74 'cutting all grocers' *Harriette Wilson's Memoirs*, ed. J. Laver, pp. 43–4

4. Lord Pumicestone

78 'Figlio Morto' BP, Palmerston's diary, 18 May 1818

81 'private Influence' Ridley, p. 73

'lax' Bourne, *Palmerston: the Early Years*, p. 140

82 'foreign troops' Sanders, L. C., *The Life of Viscount Palmerston*, p. 21

87 'want of epistolary dexterity' BP, 11 March 1820

'The Irish Government' BL, Peel Papers, 19 Dec 1817

87 'old women like the Chancellor' Bulwer, vol. 1, pp. 178–9

89 'lost a favourite child' Brougham, *Life and Times*, quoted by Plowden, A., in *Caroline and Charlotte* (London, 1989), p. 208

92 'the honourable gentleman' Hansard, 13 Feb 1822

'vile, unfeeling' Brougham Papers, Clements Library, University of Michigan, 14 Feb 1822

'ungenerous' Issac, R., and Wilberforce, S., *The Life of William Wilberforce* (London, 1838), vol. 5, p. 120

'the eye of a soldier' Hansard 17 April 1825

93 'always quarrelling' *The Journal of Mrs Arburthnot*, ed. Bamford, F., and the Duke of Wellington (London, 1950), vol. 2, p. 135

94 'if she was handsomer' Bourne, *Palmerston: the Early Years*, p. 222

95 'The House of Hanover' Webster, Sir C., *The Foreign Policy of Castlereagh*, vol. 1, p. 126

'never intended' ibid., vol. 2, *p.* 38

98 'expectation of ... the Post Office' BP, 29 Nov 1821

'No man who has seen him' Bourne, K., *Letters of the Third Viscount Palmerston to Laurence and Elizabeth Sulivan*, pp. 152–3

99 'To have talked of war' Hansard, 28 Feb 1823

'There are some people' Aspinall, A., ed., *The Journal of Mrs Arbuthnot*, p. 34

100 'called the New World' Hansard, 12 Dec 1826

102 'I am now in the committee room' *The Life and Letters of the Reverend Adam Sedgwick*, ed. Clark, J. W., and Hughes, T. M. (Cambridge, 1890), vol. 1, p. 268

103 'Liverpool has acted' Bulwer, vol. 1, p. 167
'the first decided step', ibid., vol. 1, p. 155
'the real opposition' ibid., vol. 1, pp. 171–3

5. The sorcerer's apprentice

110 'a bit of a rogue' Bourne, *Letters to Sulivan*, p. 175
114 'One of two things' Bulwer, vol. 1, p. 198
117 'preferred England' ibid., p. 376
118 'Huskisson blamed me' ibid., p. 378
119 'literally nothing' ibid., p. 379
120 'I very sincerely regret' ibid., p. 220
121 'green mound' Hansard, 27 June 1828
124 'talked the Liberal' Hobhouse, Sir J. C. (Lord Broughton), *Recollections of a Long Life*, vol. 3, p. 300
'if I could avoid by any sacrifice' Evans, R. J., *The Victorian Age*, p. 42 Catholic emancipation speech, Hansard, 18 March 1829
125 'imitation of Canning, Bourne, *Palmerston: the Early Years*, p. 196
126 'King of England a stalking horse' etc. Hansard, 1 June 1829
128 'a change of name in the inhabitants of the Tuileries' Bulwer, vol 1., p. 350
129 'how admirably' Ridley, pp. 102–3
'drink to the cause of Liberalism' Bourne, *Palmerston: the Early Years*, p. 314
130 'I stood in his way' Maxwell, Sir H., *The Life of Wellington*, vol. 2, p. 281 'Are you resolved' Bulwer, vol. 1, p. 364

6. Protocol Palmerston

135 'without disturbing' Chatsworth Papers, 8 Jan 1831 'American schooner' Ridley, p. 110
136 'one of the most able' Talleyrand, *Mémoires*, vol. 3, p. 406
140 'One cannot help wishing' Bulwer, vol. 2, p. 79

'Repugnant' ibid., p. 127

'We cannot send an army' Czartoryski, Prince A., *Memoirs*, vol. 2, p. 329

141 'It is strange that Metternich' Sanders, *Palmerston*, p. 114 'friendly manner' Metternich, *Mémoires*, vol. 5, p. 368

142 'The independence of constitutional states' Hansard, 2 Aug 1832

145 'the Pope should grant' BM, Add. MS 48470, 23 June 1831
'The affairs of Italy' Bulwer, vol. 2, p. 154

147 'the most advantageous' PRO, letter to ambassador in Russia, 31 Dec 1830, FO 65:184
'England is the country' Woodward, E.L., *The Age of Reform*, p. 221

148 'brought him to terms' Bulwer, vol. 2, p. 30–1

149 'reluctant even to think of war' ibid., p. 37

151 'consult a housebreaker' Bell, H. C. F., *Lord Palmerston*, vol. 1, p. 133
'One thing is certain' Bulwer, vol. 2, p. 109

152 'The Dutch King may sulk' Lorne, pp. 67–8

153 'Property, rank and respectability' Hansard, 3 March 1831

156 'Lady Jersey is leaving' *The Lieven–Palmerston Correspondence*, ed. Lord Sudley (London, 1943), p. 50

158 'to see the Turk kicked out of Europe' Bourne, *Palmerston*, p. 304

159 'mistress of India' Pemberton, W. B., *Lord Palmerston*, p. 87
'A drowning man' ibid., p. 88
'chief Cabinet Minister' Webster, Sir C., *The Foreign Policy of Palmerston* (London, 1951), p. 305
'so great a mistake' ibid., pp. 282–4

161 'The Triumph of Maria' Bulwer, vol. 2, p. 169
'I carried it through' ibid., pp. 180–1

161 'like to see Metternich's face' ibid., p. 181
'capital hit' ibid., p. 186

162 'I am not afraid of him' BL, papers of third Viscount Melbourne, 21 Sept 1833

163 'Remember, my Lord,' BP, 14 Jan 1833
'sorry on private grounds' Bulwer, vol. 2, p. 199

164 'We are all out' ibid., p. 203

165 'Take this to Prince Metternich' Metternich, *Mémoires*, vol. 5, p. 643

7. *Barbarians and bunting*

174 'conflicting principles of government' Hansard, 19 April 1837

180 'not another person in the world' Lever, T., ed., *Letters of Lady Palmerston*, pp. 212–3

'Union of the best tempered persons' Pemberton, p. 82.

183 'Mehemet Ali has too much' *Correspondence Relative to the Affairs of the Levant* (London, 1841), pp. 156–8

184 'I hate Mehemet Ali' Webster, p. 629

187 'Palmerston is to be married' Benson, A. C., and Viscount Esher, ed., *Queen Victoria's Letters*, vol. 1, p. 255

'To place her husband' *Morning Chronicle*, 12 Sept 1869

192 'acting like those gamblers' Metternich, *Mémoires*, vol. 5, p. 490

196 'see the equity' Morse, H. B., *The International Relations of the Chinese Empire* (London, 1910–18), vol. 1, p. 247

'infamous contraband traffic' debate, Hansard, 7, 8, 9 April 1840

197 'a barren island' Morse, vol. 1, pp. 641–3

199 'McLeod's execution' Bulwer, vol. 3, p. 49

'cunning fellows' Bell, vol. 1, p. 253

'single exception of the United States' Hansard, 15 April 1841

200 'wasps' nest' Thomas, H., *The Slave Trade*, p. 669

202 'a piece of bunting' Library of Congress, Stevenson MSS, 27 Aug 1841

203 'principle against interest' Hansard, 18 May 1841

205 'cause of a European war' Evans, R. J., *The Victorian Age* (London, 1950), p. 86

8. *The last rose of summer*

207 'God eternally' St Aubyn, G., *Queen Victoria* (London, 1991), p. 154

208 'undoubtedly a great statesman' Martin, T., *The Life of HRH the Prince Consort* (London, 1874–80), vol. 1, p. 163

209 'legislative measures' Benson and Esher, vol. 1, p. 382

210 'rex and autocrat' ibid., p. 315

210 'there must be some mistake' BP, 30 May 1841 'rough in language' RA, 22 April 1841

211 'living off our leavings' Sanders, *Palmerston*, p. 83

214 'Ellenborough's appointment' Bulwer, vol. 3, p. 163 'Channel no longer a barrier' Hansard, 13 June 1845

215 'this great and important subject' Maxwell, Sir H., *The Life of Wellington* (London, 1899), vol. 2, p. 359

217 'Perish by the road side' Bell, vol. 1, p. 347

218 'Buy back my estate' Bowood MSS, 13 Nov 1843
'a bad political institution' *Lord John Russsell, Later Correspondence*, ed. Gooch, G. P. (London, 1925), vol. 1, p. 67
'To raise and improve' ibid., pp. 66–7

222 'All that I claim' Bulwer, vol. 3, p. 117

223 'threatening us in case of new differences' *et seq.* Hansard, 21 March 1843

224 'half Yankee' Bulwer, vol. 3, p. 110

227 'a general disposition' *Lord John Russell, Later Correspondence*, vol. 1, p. 58
'abuses everything' Cowper, Countess, *Earl Cowper, K.G., a Memoir* (1913), p. 5
'two good years' holiday' Bulwer, vol. 3, p. 101

228 'English colony' ibid., p. 146
'bad effects' ibid., p. 161
'a man of great acquirements' ibid., p. 159
'to prove the advantages' Cowley, Lord, *Diary and Correspondence*, ed. Wellesley, F. A. (London, 1930), p. 280

229 'Prussia is taking the lead' Bulwer, vol. 3, p. 160

230 'the greater blackguard' Bell, vol. 1, p. 328

234 the meeting in 'the dining room' Bulwer, vol. 3, p. 127

235 'I shall visit our slate quarry' ibid., p. 178

237 'our officers ride about unarmed' *The Times*, 3 July 1841

239 'send to some other Person than Johnny' Airlie, Mabel, Countess of, *Lady Palmerston and her Times* (London, 1922), vol. 2, pp. 100–09

240 'set to rest for ever' BM, Add. MS 39949, letter to Mrs Huskisson, 19 March 1846

'M. Guizot has not altered his opinion' *Correspondence of the fourth Earl of Aberdeen*, pp. 159–60

241 'I never knew a man in whose truth' Maxwell, vol. 2, p. 372

9. Sleeping on a barrel of gunpowder

242 'sleeping on a barrel' Pemberton, p. 138

243 'Italy is the weak part of Europe' Bulwer, vol. 3, p. 195

246 'not at present any instructions' *Spanish Marriage Papers*, Parliamentary Papers, 1847, pp. 8–9

248 'breach of engagement' RA, 9 Oct 1846

'beyond all belief' Benson and Esher, vol. 2, pp. 118–9

'moderation and calm' Walpole, S., *The Life of Lord John Russell* (London, 1889), vol. 2, pp. 5–7

250 'wicked and foolish' Bulwer, vol. 3, p. 320

'Palmerston's protest' Nesselrode, *Lettres et papiers*, vol. 2, p. 360

252 'no good opinion' BP, 31 Oct 1846

253 'I return the copy' ibid., 28 Jan 1847

'The Queen has several times asked' ibid., 17 April 1847

'desperate condition' RA, 17 April 1847

254 'a pedantic and bigoted tutor' Fulford, R., *The Prince Consort*, p. 122

'I have therefore ventured' ibid., p. 122

255 'knife at her throat' *The Prince Consort to his Brother*, ed. Bolitho, H. (London, 1933), p. 97

'Our duty – our vocation' Hansard, 5 July 1847

256 'internal affairs' Bolitho, p. 96

261 'kicked him out' *The Times*, 2 Aug 1847

263 'The real policy of England' Hansard, 1 March 1848

265 'real views … of the present rulers' RA, 31 Aug 1847

'diplomatic support' RA, Prince Albert's journal, 29 Aug 1847

266 'found in Italy a Whig party' Sanders, p. 118

267 'finish quickly' Du Bled, V., *History of the July Monarchy*, vol. 2, p. 638

269 'abhor blood' Bell, vol. 1, p. 416

271 'If he remains quiet' Ashley, E., *Life and Correspondence of Lord Palmerston*, vol. 2, p. 63

272 'never to have prospered' *Jane Austen's Letters*, ed. Chapman, R.W., p.79

273 'scum of the faubourgs' Clarendon MSS, 22 April 1848 'The only hope' Ridley, p. 336

274 'adoption of a legal… course' *Spanish Marriage Papers*, p. 3

276 'red republican' Moneypenny, W. F., and Buckle, G. E., *The Life of Benjamin Disraeli* (London, 1924), vol. 3, p. 192

277 'The Queen returns this draft' BP, 21 May 1848

'every reason to believe' RA, 22 May 1848

'The Queen does not recollect' BP, 22 May 1848

10. The bottle holder

286 'The union of Schleswig with Holstein' BP, 21 June 1849

'the former history of Denmark' RA, 23 Oct 1850

286 'strong partiality' RA, 26 July 1849

'not aware' ibid.

'The Queen has to acknowledge' BP, 27 July 1849

287 'convince people by Arguments' Airlie, vol. 2, p. 122

289 'maintaining the Austrian Empire' BM, Add. MS 48547, letter to Ponsonby, 30 June 1848

'hateful to the Italians' Ashley, vol. 2, p. 83

290 'out of the question' RA, 29 June 1848

'Palmerston has a scheme' RA, 27 July 1848

291 'Austrians have no business' Ashley, vol. 2, p. 88

'no peace of mind' RA, 11 Aug 1848

292 'Now that Charles Albert hears' RA, 26 Aug 1848

294 'arbiter of the destinies' Ridley, p. 350

'an enraged woman of the town' Bell, vol. 1, p. 442

295 'one who was not more distinguished' Fulford, p. 127

297 'the Government had approved' RA, journal, 24 Jan 1849

299 'every endeavour' Parliamentary Papers, Italian Papers, 9 March 1849, vol. 4, pp. 176–7

300 'excited so great a sensation' Greville, C., *Memoirs*, vol. 6, pp. 182–3

301 'The Queen finds reference' BP, 2 May 1849

'to rescue from such oppressive terms' RA, 2 May 1849

305 'wholesale butcheries' Bell, vol. 2, p. 18

'The Austrians are really the greatest brutes' ibid., pp. 15–16 'a barrier' ibid., p. 14

306 'make such observations' Lucas, R., *Lord Glenesk and the Morning Post* (New York, 1910), p. 132

307 'Certainly I hate Palmerston' Nesselrode, Count, *Lettres et papiers*, vol. 10, p. 72

11. Civis romanus sum

308 'What business have we' RA, 12 Sept 1849
'The Hungarian leaders' ibid., 14 Sept 1849

309 'a dangerous experiment' RA, 2 April 1849

311 'such assistance' Ridley, p. 361

315 'destitute of the acquirements' BM, letters to Milbank, Add. MS 48544

320 'the foreign policy of Her Majesty's government' Hansard, 24 June 1850

322 'civis romanus sum' Hansard, 25 June 1850, and Ashley, vol. 2, pp. 151–60
'I scarcely ever remember' Ashley, vol. 2, p. 161

323 'We are all proud' Hansard, 27 June 1850

324 'most popular man' Greville, vol. 6, p. 347

324 'instead of expelling' Ashley, vol. 2, pp. 161–2
'physical and mental power' Maxwell, Sir H., *Life and Letters of the Fourth Earl of Clarendon* (London, 1913), vol. 1, pp. 311–2
'You and all Europe' Bolitho, p. 117
'The Queen has no more confidence' RA, 8 July 1850

325 'How could the Queen consent' ibid., 10 July 1850
'I have not altered' ibid., 11 July 1850
'Each time that we were in difficulty' ibid., 28 July 1850

326 'tears in his eyes' ibid., 17 July 1850

327 'it would be proper' BR, 10 Sept 1850

328 'the defence of the accused' Ashley, vol. 2, pp. 169–70
'very objectionable' BP, 4 Oct 1850

329 'hospitable reception of foreigners' BP, 8 Oct 1850

330 'I do not choose to be dictated to' Walpole, vol. 2, p. 133
'he'll see him yet' Bell, vol. 2, p. 45

333 'childish nonsense' Ashley, vol. 2, p. 203

    'better for the interests of France' ibid., pp. 206–7

334 'I am commanded' ibid., p. 204

335 'approbation of the act' ibid., pp. 204–5

    'acting as umpire' Maxwell, vol. 1, p. 337

336 'misrepresentation and suspicion' Ashley, vol. 2, p. 206

    'opinion on the change' ibid., p. 207

337 'appoint a successor' ibid., p. 211

    'prudence and decorum' ibid., p. 212

    'found a box' RA, Queen's journal, 29 Dec 1851

    'There was a Palmerston' Moneypenny and Buckle, vol. 3, p. 340

338 'the retirement of Lord Palmerston' Baily, F. E., *The Love Story of Lady Palmerston* (London, 1938), p. 180

339 'There is no end to the letters' BM, Add. MS 39949

341 'tit-for-tat' Ashley, vol. 2, p. 230

12. A very distinguished tight-rope dancer

344 'depend on the result' Ashley, vol. 2, pp. 230–1

    'Who, Who' Fraser, Sir W., *Words on Wellington* (London, 1889), p. 52

    'gave way to Lord Palmerston' Bell, vol. 2, p. 63

345 'ungramatical despatches' Ashley, vol. 2, p. 235

    'what a power of prestige England possesses' Malmesbury, 3rd Earl of, *Memoirs*, vol. 1, pp. 318–9

347 'so grating to one's feelings' BP, 18 Nov 1852

349 'We who are gentlemen' Hansard, 26 Nov 1852

    'this Government will not last long' Airlie, vol. 2, p. 152

350 'Aberdeen and I had differed' Ashley, vol. 2, p. 258

350 'Harrow boys' Benson and Esher, vol. 2, p. 420

351 'Lansdowne's representations' Ashley, vol. 2, p. 258

    'what other course' Airlie, vol. 2, pp. 151–3

352 'work like a horse' Bolitho, p. 135

    'looked so ill' Benson and Esher, vol. 2, p. 520

    'grateful thanks' RA, 23 Jan 1853

    'make yourself agreeable' BP, 17 Sept 1853

353 'make a better husband' Ridley, p. 406

354 'never known any Home Secretary' Hodder, E., *The Life and Works of the seventh Earl of Shaftesbury* (London, 1886), vol. 2, p. 444

355 'A rule is no rule' Ashley, vol. 2, p. 268

356 'those portions of the towns' ibid., vol. 2, p. 265
'haunts of Thieves and Schools of Prostitutes' Guedalla, P., ed., *Gladstone and Palmerston: being the Correspondence of Lord Palmerston with Mr Gladstone* (London, 1928), pp. 95–6

360 'the destruction of Turkey' Walpole, vol. 2, p. 181

361 'the policy … of the Russian Government' Ashley, vol. 2, p. 273

362 'if necessary or useful' ibid., p. 274
'waiting timidly' ibid., p. 276

363 'acted with that energy' Bell, vol. 2, p. 86

364 'parasites, pimps and prostitutes' *John Bull*, 1 Jan 1853

366 'as to the principles' Ridley, p. 420

368 'Lord Palmerston's mode of proceeding' Smith, E.F.M., *Palmerston*, p. 84

369 'war is not inevitable' Maxwell, vol. 2, p. 40

370 'need not be in the least anxious' Argyll, 8th Duke of, *Autobiography and Memoirs*, vol. 1, p. 475

372 'a small private expedition' Woodham-Smith, C., *Florence Nightingale*, p. 100

374 'personally not agreeable' RA, Queen's journal, 4 Feb 1855

13. *War and peace*

377 'inconvenient' Howard, P., *We Thundered Out: 200 Years of The Times*, p. 42
'not insensible' BM, Add. MS 48582

378 'ancient foe' Howard, p. 42
'I don't believe half the Cabinet' Dasent, A.I., *John Thadeus Delane*, vol. 2, p. 29

379 'Tho' he is really an imposter' *Letters of Benjamin Disraeli to Frances Anne, Marchioness of Londonderry*, ed. Marchioness of Londonderry (London, 1938), pp. 145–6

380 'looks about fifty-five' White, W., *The Inner Life of the House of Commons*, vol. 1, p. 2

380 'distracted' Airlie, Mabel, Countess of, *Lady Palmerston and her Times*, vol. 2, p. 168

'not popular' Cowper, Countess, *Earl Cowper KG: a Memoir* (privately printed, 1913), p. 50

381 'If he chose to try' Stanmore, Lord, *Sidney Herbert, Lord Herbert of Lea: a Memoir*, vol. 1, p. 260

383 'so good a government' RA, Queen's journal, 5 Feb 1855

385 'disruption' *et seq.* Battiscombe, G., *Shaftesbury*, p. 245

388 'rude and boisterous railers' Maxwell, Sir H., *Life and Times of Rt. Hon. William Henry Smith* (Edinburgh, 1893), vol. 2, p. 154

390 'ground known to be unhealthy' Douglas, Sir G., and Ramsay, Sir G. D., *Panmure Papers* (London, 1908), vol. 1, p. 350–1

391 'the mean, the selfish' Woodham-Smith, *Florence Nightingale*, p. 132

392 'give them every assistance' Ashley, vol. 2, p. 308

395 'remonstrated against Mr Layard' RA, Queen's journal, 5 Feb 1855

'look to that glorious charge' Hansard, 19 Feb 1855

396 'forty thousand men short' *Panmure Papers*, vol. 1, p. 232

398 'aptitude to be swayed' Maxwell, *Clarendon*, vol. 2, p. 163

399 'so nice' etc. Bresler, F., *Napoleon III: a Life*, pp. 282–3

'immense embracing' ibid., p. 282

400 'Russian in the Black Sea' Pemberton, p. 233

401 'grave reasons' Sanders, p. 167

'intention of Russia' Bell, vol. 2, p. 130

402 'supply of cold water' Rolt, L. T. C., *Brunel*, p. 223

403 'jaunty mood' Maxwell, *Clarendon*, vol. 2, p. 118

'very easy to argue' RA, 25 Feb 1856

'half-civilized savage' BM, Clarendon MSS, Add. MS 48580

404 'would have given in' Reeve, H., *Memoirs*, vol. 1, p. 145

405 'not all what we could wish' BP, 30 March 1856

407 'Netley' Woodham-Smith, p. 226

'most bullyable' ibid., p. 261

408 'delay no longer' BP, 11 April 1856

'humble duty' ibid.

14. A jolly way of looking at disasters

409 'riding a runaway horse' Ashley, vol. 2, p. 340

410 'barrier against Russia' Pemberton, p. 241

'would be better governed' Ashley, vol. 2, p. 338

411 'do not want Egypt' ibid., pp. 337–8

'only a glance at the map' Sanders, p. 181

412 'so much bitterness' Ashley, vol. 2, p. 338

415 'sit here day by day' Hansard, 13 Aug 1856

416 'These Yankees' Guedalla, *Palmerston*, p. 348

417 'hackneyed formula' Pemberton, p. 246

'typical' Argyll, vol. 2, p. 47

418 'ground for a Quarrel' Ridley, p. 459

419 'I am rejoiced' Ashley, vol. 2, pp. 130–1

420 'acts of violence' ibid., p. 123

422 'unite in exterminating' Pemberton, p. 247

'It cannot be tolerated' Morse, vol. 1, pp. 383–4

423 'violent measures', 'a man of the people' and 'complain to the country' Hansard, 3 March 1857

424 'national prejudices' Stanmore, vol. 2, p. 68

425 'insolent barbarian' *The Times*, 24 March 1857

'only public man' Stanmore, vol. 2, p. 68

'P's popularity' Hodder, vol. 3, p. 43

426 'never can agree to' Bell, vol. 2, p. 170

429 'Brigadiers of seventy' Evans, p. 140

430 'ride to Ascot' Bell, vol. 2, p. 170

431 'want of energy' Ridley, p. 474

'made a joke' Woodham-Smith, p. 439

'poured troops' Bell, vol. 2, p. 172

'The Queen has just received' BP, 27 June 1857

'European complications' BP, 18 July 1857

432 'no danger threatening us in Europe' *Panmure Papers*, vol. 2, pp. 421–2

'off our own Bat' Pemberton, p. 250

'if she had been in the house' BP, 18 July 1857

'Contrary to the Queen's hopes' BP, 19 July 1857

433 'black regiment in Canada' BP, 5 Oct 1857

436 'impossible for any Englishman' Ashley, vol. 2, p. 138

437 'While you are shaving' Ridley, p. 479

'throw over the East India company' ibid, p. 479

'strong personal opinion' Lorne, p. 185

438 'much Opposition' ibid., p. 186

439 'our business to be shot at' Bresler, p. 295

'shelter criminals' Ashley, p. 143

440 'infamous haunt' ibid., p. 144

441 'three or four colonels' ibid., p. 145

'champion of the honour of England' Ridley, p. 481

442 'Were much vexed' RA, Queen's journal, 20 Feb 1858

'The "Great Minister" ' White, vol. 1, p. 50

15. The old Italian masters

445 'holds him suddenly in such abhorrence' Benson and Esher, vol. 3, p. 381

446 'Perhaps some of our Radical friends' Maxwell, *Clarendon*, vol. 2, p. 163

450 'We cannot hope to modify the policy of England' Sanders, p. 193

451 'I regret that our relations' Bresler, p. 296

453 'Austrian aggression' *The Times*, 30 April 1859

454 'demanding arms' Fulford, R., *The Prince Consort*, p. 249

455 'has secured Gladstone' Parker, C. S., *The Life and Letters of Sir James Graham* (London, 1907), vol. 2, p. 388

'ancient confidence' Moneypenny and Buckle, vol. 4, pp. 235–6

457 '280 members present' Stanmore, vol. 2, pp. 198–9

'very serious moment' RA, Queen's journal, 11 June 1859

458 'could not serve under Lord Granville' RA, Queen's journal, 12 June 1859

460 'the honour of France' PRO, Russell Papers, 28 June 1859

462 'leave France to settle with Austria' Pemberton, p. 273

'England is one of the greatest nations' Benson and Esher, vol. 3, p. 463

'no sooner is one withdrawn' RA 11 Sept 1859

'neither policy nor principles', Maxwell, *Clarendon*, vol. 2, pp. 187–8

463 'communicative to the Cabinet' Fitzmaurice, Lord E., *Life of the second Earl of Granville* (London, 1905), vol. 1, p. 351

'no one should know' Pemberton, p. 271

464 'All his old tricks' RA, 31 Dec 1859

465 'Italians should be secured' Pemberton, p. 277

466 'full of schemes' Sanders, L. C., *Palmerston*, p. 218

'He has sufficiently organized' Pemberton, p. 279

'The moral effect' Beales, D., *England and Italy* (London, 1961), p. 143

467 'If such a Treaty is signed' PRO, Russell Papers, 17 May 1860

'England ceased to press' Beales, *England and Italy*, p. 151

468 'The only hope' Beales, p. 146

471 'absolutely necessary' Stanmore, vol. 2, p. 350

472 'one night is enough' Guedalla, P., ed., *Correspondence of Lord Palmerston and Mr Gladstone*, p. 116

473 'It would be very delightful' Sanders, p. 208

474 'Mr. Gladstone, having failed' RA, 2 July 1860

'ineffectual opposition' RA, 24 July 1860

'however great the loss' Guedalla, *Palmerston*, p. 370

16. Old Pam

477 'often take a cab' Moneypenny and Buckle, vol. 2, p. 157

''E earns 'is wages' Ridley, p. 528

478 'Your disappointment' Smith, E. F. M., *Palmerston*, p. 128

479 'the finest building in London' *London Encyclopaedia*, p. 754

480 'All such changes' Sanders, p. 213

'not so much in support' *Letters of Benjamin Disraeli to Frances Anne, Marchioness of Londonderry*, ed. Londonderry, Marchioness of, p. 284

'apathy' Greville, C. C. F., *Journal of the Reign of Queen Victoria*, vol. 2, p. 294

483 'performed his duty' Hansard, 9 Feb 1864

'Relations with Japan' Ridley, p. 543

484 'not by respectable men' Hansard, 28 July 1864

'slave trade treaty with Spain' PRO, Russell MSS, 13 Aug 1862

'plain truth', ibid., 5 Oct 1864

486 'wholesome effect' Ridley, p. 551

487 'If the Federal Government comply' RA, 5 Dec 1861

488 'You did wrong' St Aubyn, G., *Queen Victoria*, p. 326
'the excellence of the man' ibid., p. 269
'determination to do her duty' BP, 15 Dec 1861
'determination to conform' PRO, Russell MSS, 28 Dec 1861

489 'Pilgerstein and his people should not be upset' Guedalla, *Palmerston*, p. 382
'entering so entirely into my anxieties' RA, Queen's journal, 29 Jan 1862
'cannot refrain' Ridley, p. 556

490 'make up between Sayers and Heenan' PRO, Russell Papers, 13 June 1862

492 'to solicit redress' Adams, C. D., *Great Britain and the American Civil War*, p. 304

493 'clean sweep' Ashley, vol. 2, p. 230

494 'your Majesty's reluctance' RA, 4 Jan 1864

495 'British Government do not mean to fight' Smith, p. 120
'King of Prussia seems' Ridley, p. 569

496 'We are convinced' Hansard, 18 March 1863

497 'The conduct of Austria and Prussia'
'like the Duke of Devonshire's servants' Bell, vol. 2, p. 367

498 'If an Austrian squadron should pass' Smith, p. 124

499 'menace never accomplished' Hansard, 8 July 1864
'England stands as high' ibid.
'advised to abstain' ibid.

500 'an interesting scene' Moneypenny and Buckle, *Life of Disraeli*, vol. 2, p. 139
'a dangerous man' Hodder, vol. 3, p. 187

501 'grown very old' Guedalla, *Palmerston*, p. 392
'Minny come in etc.' Baily, p. 269

502 'That's article 98' Ridley, p. 583

503 'Poor Lord Palmerston' Buckle, ed., *Letters of Queen Victoria*, vol. 1, p. 278
'I still think that statesman' Hansard, 12 Feb 1866

504 'a Frenchman, thinking to be highly complimentary' *Personal Papers of Lord Rendel*, p. 60

'his heart beat ever' Ridley, p. 388

505 'between Pit's and Fox's' Hardy, T., *Collected Letters*, ed. Purdy, R. L., and Millgate, M., vol. 1, p. 198

$\int$ELECT BIBLIOGRAPHY

Airlie, Mabel, Countess of, *Lady Palmerston and her Times*, 2 vols. (London, 1922)

Argyll, George Douglas, 8th Duke of, *Autobiography and Memoirs* (London, 1906)

Ashley, E., *The Life and Correspondence of Henry John Temple, Viscount Palmerston*, 2 vols. (London, 1879)

Aspinall, A., ed., *The Journal of Mrs Arbuthnot* (London, 1941)

Baily, F. E., *The Love Story of Lady Palmerston* (London, 1938)

Battiscombe, G., *Shaftesbury* (London, 1974)

Beales, D., *England and Italy, 1859–60* (London, 1961)

Bell, H. C. F., *Lord Palmerston*, 2 vols. (London, 1936)

Benson, A. C., and Esher, Viscount, ed., *The Letters of Queen Victoria, 1837–61* (London, 1907)

Bickley, F., ed., *Diaries of Sylvester Douglas* [Lord Glenbervie] (London, 1928)

Billy, G. J., *Palmerston's Foreign Policy: 1848* (New York, 1993)

Blake, R., *Disraeli* (London, 1966)

Bolitho, H., ed., *The Prince Consort to his Brother: Two Hundred New Letters* (London, 1933)

Bourne, K., *Palmerston: the Early Years, 1784–1841* (London, 1982)

———, ed., *The Letters of the third Viscount Palmerston to Laurence and Elizabeth Sulivan* (London, 1979)

Braithwaite, R., *Palmerston and Africa. The Rio Nuñez Affair: Competition, Diplomacy and Justice* (London, 1996)

Bresler, F., *Napoleon III: a Life* (London, 1999)

Brown, D., *Palmerston and the Politics of Foreign Policy, 1846–55* (Manchester, 2002)

Bryant, P. H. M., *Harrow* (London, 1936)

Buckle, G. E., ed., *The Letters of Queen Victoria*, 2nd series, 1861–85 (London, 1926–8)

Bulwer, Sir H. L. (Lord Dalling), *The Life of Henry John Temple, Lord Palmerston*, 3 vols. (London, 1870–4)

Cambridge History of British Foreign Policy, 1783–1919, ed. Sir A. W. Ward and G. P. Gooch, vol. 2 (Cambridge, 1922–3)

Cecil, D. *Melbourne* (London, 1965)

Chamberlain, M. E., *Lord Aberdeen* (Harlow, 1983)

——, *Lord Palmerston* (Cardiff, 1987)

Connell, B., *Portrait of a Whig Peer* (London, 1957)

——, *Regina v. Palmerston: the Correspondence between Queen Victoria and her Foreign and Prime Minister, 1837–65* (London, 1962)

Cook, Sir E., *Delane of The Times* (London, 1915)

Dasent, A. I., *John Thadeus Delane* (London, 1908)

Fulford, R., *The Prince Consort* (London, 1949)

Greville, C. C. F., *Memoirs: A Journal of the Reigns of King George IV and King William IV*

——, *A Journal of the Reign of Queen Victoria from 1837 to 1860*

——, *A Journal of The Reign of Queen Victoria from 1852 to 1860*

Gronow, R. H., *The Reminiscences and Recollections of Captain Gronow*, ed J. Grego (London, 1892)

Guedalla, P., *Palmerston* (London, 1926)

——, ed., *Gladstone and Palmerston: being the Correspondence of Lord Palmerston with Mr Gladstone, 1851–1865* (London, 1928)

Guizot, F., *Mémoires pour servir à l'histoire de mon temps* (Paris, 1858–67)

Hansard, *Parliamentary Debates* (London, 1807–66)

Hibbert, C., *Wellington: a Personal History* (London, 1997)

——, *Garibaldi and his Enemies* (London, 1965)

Hodder, E., *The Life and Work of the Seventh Earl of Shaftesbury* (London, 1886)

Howard, P., *We Thundered Out: 200 Years of The Times, 1785–1985* (London, 1985)

Ilchester, Earl of, ed., *Lady Holland's Journal* (2 vols., London, 1909)

Jenkins, R., *Gladstone* (London, 1995)

Lever, Sir T., *Correspondence of Lady Palmerston* (London, 1957)

Lorne, Marquess of, *Viscount Palmerston, K. G.* (London, 1892)

Malmesbury, 3rd Earl of, ed., *Malmesbury Letters: a Series of Letters of the First Earl of Malmesbury and his Family and Friends, from 1745 to 1820* (London, 1870)

Martin, K., *The Triumph of Lord Palmerston: a Study of Public Opinion in England before the Crimean War* (London, 1924)

Marx, K., *The Story of the Life of Lord Palmerston* (London, 1899)

Maxwell, Sir H., *The Life and Letters of George William, Fourth Earl of Clarendon* (London, 1913)

Minto, Earl of, *The Life and Letters of Sir Gilbert Elliot, First Earl of Minto*, ed. Countess of Minto (London, 1874)

Mitchell, A., *The Whigs in Opposition, 1815–1830* (Oxford, 1967)

Moneypenny, W. F., and Buckle, G. E., *The Life of Benjamin Disraeli, Earl of Beaconsfield* (London, revised edn., 1924)

Morse, H. B., *The International Relations of the Chinese Empire* (London, 1910–18)

Pemberton, W. B., *Lord Palmerston* (London, 1954)

Ridley, J., *Lord Palmerston* (London, 1970)

Royle, T., *Crimea: the Great Crimean War, 1854–1856* (London, 1999)

Sanders, L. C., *The Life of Viscount Palmerston* (London, 1888)

Smith, E. F. M., *Palmerston* (London, 1935)

Southgate, D., *'The Most English Minister …': The Policies and Politics of Palmerston* (London, 1966)

Stanmore, Lord, *Sidney Herbert, Lord Herbert of Lea: a Memoir* (London, 1906)

Steele, E. D., *Palmerston and Liberalism* (Cambridge, 1991)

Talleyrand, Prince de, *Mémoires du Prince de Talleyrand*, ed. Duc de Broglie (Paris, 1891)

Thomas, H., *The Slave Trade* (London, 1997)

Trevelyan, G. M., *Garibaldi and the Making of Italy* (London, 1911)

Walpole, S., *The Life of Lord John Russell* (London, 1889)

Webster, Sir C., *The Foreign Policy of Palmerston, 1830–41* (London, 1951)

White, W., *The Inner Life of the House of Commons*, ed. J. McCarthy (London, 1897)

Wilson, H., *Harriette Wilson's Memoirs*, ed. J. Laver (London, 1929)

Woodham-Smith, C., *Florence Nightingale* (London, 1950)

Woodward, E. L., *The Age of Reform*, 1815–1870 (Oxford, 1938)

Ziegler, P. R., *Palmerston* (London, 2003)

ABOUT THE AUTHOR

James Chambers is a writer, lecturer and broadcaster. Among his publications are *The Devil's Horsemen* (Weidenfeld & Nicolson, 1979) and *The British Empire* (Daily Telegraph, 1997).

26432108R00299